ALSO BY JEFF GUINN

The Last Gunfight: The Real Story of the Shootout at
the O.K. Corral—And How It Changed the American West

Go Down Together: The True, Untold Story of Bonnie and Clyde

MANSON

The Life and Times of Charles Manson

JEFF GUINN

SIMON & SCHUSTER

New York   London   Toronto   Sydney   New Delhi

Simon & Schuster
1230 Avenue of the Americas
New York, NY 10020

First Simon & Schuster hardcover edition August 2013

SIMON & SCHUSTER and colophon are registered trademarks of Simon & Schuster, Inc.

For information about special discounts for bulk purchases, please contact Simon & Schuster Special Sales at 1-866-506-1949 or business@simonandschuster.com.

The Simon & Schuster Speakers Bureau can bring authors to your live event. For more information or to book an event contact the Simon & Schuster Speakers Bureau at 1-866-248-3049 or visit our website at www.simonspeakers.com.

Credits for insert photographs are on page 476.

Designed by Joy O'Meara

Manufactured in the United States of America

10   9   8   7   6   5   4   3   2   1

Library of Congress Cataloging-in-Publication Data

Guinn, Jeff.
    Manson : the life and times of Charles Manson / Jeff Guinn.
        pages   cm.
    Includes bibliographical references and index.
1. Manson, Charles, 1934–   2. Murderers—United States—Biography.
3. Criminals—United States—Biography.   I. Title.
    HV6248.M2797G85   2013
    364.152'3402—dc23
        [B]   2012050176

ISBN 978-1-4516-4516-3
ISBN 978-1-4516-4518-7 (ebook)

For Roger Labrie

"Over and over it came down to that question—
What was reality in an unreal time?"

—Tom Hayden, *The Long Sixties: From 1960 to Barack Obama*

CONTENTS

AUTHOR'S NOTE ON NAMES

In almost every instance, I identify Charles Manson as "Charlie" because that is what everyone called him during the time that he led the Family. Most of those who knew him during that chilling era still call him that. Key Manson Family members are also referred to in this book by their first names. Otherwise, I generally observe the tradition of identifying individuals by their last names after initial reference.

It is worthy of note that as a child in McMechen, Manson was known as "Charles," as he is today among many of his current friends and followers. In his letter to me, and in other letters shown to me in the process of researching this book, he signs with his full name: "Charles Milles Manson."

MANSON

Charlie at the Whisky

On a summer night in 1968, three cars eased down Sunset Boulevard in Los Angeles. They headed for the tricked-up portion of the long, winding street known as the Strip, a 1.7-mile stretch of nightclubs, shops, and restaurants that was one of the epicenters of cutting-edge counterculture in America. Three hundred and eighty miles to the north, the Haight-Ashbury neighborhood in San Francisco still clung to its reputation as the capital city of Flower Power and hippie love-ins, but its pretensions of leading the world into a new era of enlightenment through great music, free love, mind-expanding chemicals, and disdain for class-conscious, capitalist beliefs were dissolving into drug-addled violence. Sunset Strip was about music, sex, and drugs, too, but few among the amped-up throngs packing its sidewalks pretended their motivations were anything other than self-indulgent. As civil disorder swept the rest of America in response to Vietnam and racial unrest, the only major uprising on the Strip involved the closing of a popular club and the enforcement of a 10 P.M. curfew for those under eighteen. Young people flocked to the Haight in hopes of finding Utopia; youthful pilgrims came to L.A. with the dream of becoming friends with celebrities and becoming rich and famous themselves. Such dreams were encouraged by the Strip's traditional egalitarianism. Stars performing in or visiting many of its famous clubs were expected to mingle with the public, chatting amiably as if with equals and, in the case of those who'd made it in the record business, offering advice to the endless stream of wannabes who felt certain that their self-penned songs about love, spirituality, and revolution would make them as big as the Beatles—or even bigger.

The young men behind the wheels of the three cars inching down Sunset—sometimes it could take hours to maneuver through the traffic and crowds along the Strip—were out for a night of fun and basking in the celebrity that they'd worked so hard to attain. Terry Melcher, Gregg Jakobson, and Dennis Wilson had been close friends for years. Individually, they'd reached separate pinnacles in the music business: Melcher as a producer, Jakobson as a talent scout/recording session organizer, and Wilson as the drummer for the Beach Boys, and thus the most famous of the trio. Together they were part of an informal society known as the Golden Penetrators. Its membership was limited to anyone who had sex with women from one of show business's most famous families. It wasn't the most exclusive of organizations; some of these women were every bit as promiscuous as the men pursuing them. The Melcher-Jakobson-Wilson triumvirate reveled in their hedonism; in a city that had long ago waived most moral or legal limits for the famous, their philosophy was "We're us, there are no rules, we get to do this."

When L.A. celebrities wanted to keep their night-on-the-town discreet, they frequented clubs where steep membership fees denied entry to all but the biggest stars. But on this night Melcher, Jakobson, and Wilson were in a sociable mood. Part of the fun of being famous was being fawned over by fans, of demonstrating a certain sense of noblesse oblige, though on a controlled basis. There was considerable difference between accepting the deference of starstruck, pretty people and being pawed by packs of grubby teens. The popular public clubs on the Strip made special arrangements for visiting stars, usually in the form of restricted seating so that other customers could only stare from a distance whenever the celebrities felt like retreating from the dance floor for a while. For stars and general public alike, dancing was a big part of a night out on the Strip. While live acts were onstage, respectful attention was required. But between sets, disc jockeys played records and it was time for everyone to show off, rocking to the beat and trying to outdo each other in performing all the latest steps.

As giants of the L.A. music scene, Melcher, Jakobson, and Wilson headed for an appropriate destination on the Strip. The Whisky a Go Go, located on Sunset just past the edge of Beverly Hills, was the most famous club in town and probably in all of America. Magazines from *Time* to *Playboy* touted it as the hippest place to see and be seen. Each night, long lines routinely stretched for blocks two hours or more before the Whisky opened at 8:30. The cover charge kept out panhandlers and riff-raff. Regulars always anticipated thrills beyond those to be found at any other club on the Strip. Performers recorded chart-topping live albums at the Whisky. The flower of the music scene regularly dropped in; recent visitors included Jimi Hendrix, Neil Young, and Eric Clapton. Hendrix and Young even jumped onstage to jam. The Whisky usually alternated lesser-known local bands with big-name acts like the Turtles and Eric Burdon and the Animals. The club had been one of the first venues on the modern-day Strip to feature black musicians. Among others, Buddy Guy and Sly and the Family Stone graced its stage, and when Little Rich-ard performed, rock gods Mick Jagger and Keith Richards of the Rolling Stones came to hear him. Every visit to the Whisky was certain to be special in some way. Anyone in Los Angeles who had pretensions of being cool had to make the scene. Even Elizabeth Taylor and Richard Burton partied there.

The nightly crowds meant parking was scarce anywhere near the club, but that was no problem for Melcher, Jakobson, and Wilson. The operators of the Strip's jam-packed lots always found room for vehicles belonging to stars. Melcher handed over the keys of a black four-door Mercedes convertible. Jakobson arrived in a black, mint condition 1939 Pontiac; he'd just swapped a Porsche for the vintage ride. Wilson pulled up in a burgundy Rolls-Royce recently given to him by his older brother, Brian, the reclusive leader of the Beach Boys. As the trio strolled into the Whisky—there was no need for them to stand in line, or pay the night's cover charge—everyone's eyes were on them. Wilson, a big, handsome man, would have been recognized by virtually every music fan in the country. Melcher and Jakobson weren't household names in Middle America, but the Whisky crowd, most of them savvy to all aspects of the L.A. music scene, knew who they were and why they were important.

That wasn't true of the fourth member of the party, who'd arrived in Wilson's Rolls. To the onlookers outside the Whisky, there wasn't any-thing special about thirty-three-year-old Charlie Manson, just one among thousands of ambitious singer-songwriters who'd made their way to L.A. with the goal of getting recording contracts and becoming superstars. Manson was short, about five foot four, and scrawny. For much of the summer, he'd been lucky enough to mooch off the Beach Boys' drummer, who was notorious for giving strays temporary run of his luxurious log cabin house further down Sunset Boulevard. Most of them drifted off after a day or two; Manson showed no sign of leaving. For a while, that was fine with his host. Besides writing some interesting songs and spouting an addictive form of philosophy about surrendering individuality, Manson had with him a retinue of girls who adored Charlie and were happy to engage in any form of sex his rock star benefactor desired. Accordingly, Wilson's summer was a carnal extravaganza, though he had to make frequent trips to his doctor since the Manson girls kept infecting him with gonorrhea. In between sex romps, Wilson good-naturedly touted Manson's music to the other Beach Boys and to friends in the L.A. music scene. To date, no one had been impressed enough by Manson's songs to offer the scruffy drifter the recording contract he craved. But Charlie had unwavering belief in his own talent and in Wilson's ability, even obligation, to make it happen.

Manson assumed that he was always welcome to come along whenever Wilson went out to a party or to a club. He shared what he had—his music, quirky conversation, and sexually compliant women—and expected Wilson to do the same. It was an unequal arrangement and lately Wilson was becoming fed up. It was aggravating enough that Manson constantly badgered the drummer to make the Beach Boys record his songs, but the leech and his followers were making a considerable dent in Wilson's personal fortune at a time when the Beach Boys' record sales and concert attendance were in alarming decline. They'd wrecked his uninsured Mercedes and run up bills with doctors and dentists. They raided Wilson's closets and cut up his clothes to make themselves patchwork robes. Though they espoused scouring supermarket garbage bins for food, they gluttonously emptied Wilson's refrigerator and pantry on a daily basis. They even felt his charge accounts were theirs to use—while he'd been away from home on a brief Beach Boys tour, Wilson's house guests ran up an $800 tab with a local dairy, gorging themselves on the priciest cheese, yogurt, and fruit juice. As much as Wilson embraced the general concept of sharing, he was ready for these master freeloaders to move on.

In recent weeks Wilson had also begun to fear Manson. Concerned about their client's involvement with such a questionable character, Beach Boys management ran a background check on Charlie and informed Dennis that his house guest had done time for armed robbery and was currently on probation. That didn't bother Wilson in the least. He'd known all along that his new pal had a criminal background. Manson liked to brag that prison was his daddy and the street was his mother. Criminal credentials appealed to many young people in an era when it was fashionable for them to believe that the government was the enemy. But as Manson and his motley crew continued living with Wilson, Charlie's entertaining philosophical rants occasionally turned dark. He seemed to believe that he held the power of life and death over his followers and friends, including his famous patron. He once held a knife to Wilson's throat and asked how the drummer would feel if he killed him. Wilson muttered, "Do it," and Manson backed off. It said a lot about Wilson's self-destructive tendencies that he still allowed Charlie to hang around with him.

Though Wilson and his fellow Golden Penetrators hadn't said as much, bringing Manson along to the Whisky on this summer night might remind him of his place. Despite what Charlie clearly believed, enjoying the largesse of a star didn't make him a star himself. The Whisky was the apex of cool, home ground of the hip, but intimidating for everyone else. The club wasn't particularly big, with a capacity of just 350, but its decor was guaranteed to impress. Decorated in dramatic tones of red and black, the venue featured a stage in the middle of a raised dance floor. There were a few tables for the public and a small, separate seating area for show business dignitaries. Dangling above the floor were glass "cages" occupied by scantily clad female dancers who pranced provocatively to records whenever each evening's bands took a break between their 9:30 and 11:30 sets. These entertainers were dubbed Go-Go dancers, and copycat namesakes entertained in clubs all over the world.

For the Whisky's noncelebrity regulars, getting out on the floor to dance was the real highlight of the evening. Unwritten club etiquette prohibited paying too much attention to other dancers; the conceit was that you were spectacular and everyone else was obliged to gawk at you. As a result, nobody ever watched anybody else, let alone gave the impression of being impressed. It was hard to find much room on the dance floor at any given time. Prospective dancers would wait until others cleared off for a bathroom break or to catch their breath, then tried to beat other hopefuls to the space. Sharp eyes and equally sharp elbows were helpful.

Since Melcher, Jakobson, and Wilson were regulars, one of the celebrity booths was always available to them. As they moved toward it Manson broke away, saying that he wanted to dance. Charlie couldn't have chosen a more certain means of receiving his comeuppance. Few stylishly dressed, celebrity-obsessed girls at the Whisky would deign to dance with a short, scruffy nobody, and even if Manson did somehow make it onto the dance floor he'd just be one more body crammed in there. Had any of them been in a more generous frame of mind, Wilson, Melcher, or Jakobson could have escorted Manson down; dance space was always made for stars and their sidekicks. But they were content to let Charlie flounder on his own. Soon enough he'd slink over to their booth, chastened by an unmistakable reminder that, for all his philosophical prattling and grandiose dreams of rock stardom, at least for now he remained an insignificant speck in the L.A. galaxy.

Manson disappeared into the crowd, and the three friends sipped drinks and chatted until they were startled by a commotion. Looking around, they saw something unique in the history of the Whisky a Go Go: Instead of vying to get on, everyone was struggling to clear off the hallowed dance floor, where they had been packed in so tightly that they now had trouble squirming apart. Melcher, Jakobson, and Wilson exchanged puzzled glances. They stood up to get a better look, and that was when they saw that smack in the middle of the floor a single figure remained—Charlie Manson, gyrating to the music. His dancing grew increasingly maniacal; he tipped back his head and threw out his arms and they agreed later that it seemed as though electrical sparks flew from Charlie's fingers and hair.

The crowd had surged off the dance floor as if driven from it by some irresistible force field. Now it circled the floor, mesmerized by the sight of the whirling dervish who seemed oblivious to everything but the pulsating beat. Over the past weeks, Wilson, Jakobson, and Melcher had seen Manson effortlessly enthrall small gatherings at meals or parties. Until this moment they had no idea that he could extend his magnetism and dominate a much larger audience, let alone a jaded one like the regulars at the Whisky. It was one thing for Charlie to convince a string of needy female hangers-on that he was an all-knowing guru who must be worshipped and obeyed. But these were hipsters whose self-images depended in large part on not acting impressed by anyone other than the biggest stars. Now they openly gawked at someone who only moments before would have seemed the unlikeliest candidate to command their rapt attention. It was a reaction far beyond deference, Jakobson thought. This approached awe.

"That was when we realized that he was really something different, that time at the Whisky," Jakobson said almost forty-five years later. "Anytime, anywhere, that Charlie decided to be the center of attention, he could be. At the Whisky, everybody thought that they had seen it all.

"Until that night, when they saw Charlie."

CHAPTER ONE

Nancy and Kathleen

Nancy Maddox loved the Bible and her teenage daughter, Kathleen, loved to dance. Since they were both strong-willed, that was how all the trouble started.

Nancy Ingraham was born and raised in the Kentucky backwoods, and her faith was unwaveringly fundamentalist. She took the Bible literally. Every word in it was true, and every baleful creature described, from Genesis's serpent in the Garden of Eden to the beast with seven heads and ten horns in Revelation, had existed or would exist upon the earth doing Satan's unholy bidding. Nancy loved God and also feared His wrath as the Bible commanded that she should. People didn't consider Nancy a fanatic; she was courteous to those with different beliefs and tried hard not to judge others because that was God's prerogative and not hers. But she had no doubt that everyone was held accountable by Him. Horrible penalties lay in store for unrepentant sinners, but good things in life and eternal bliss after death were guaranteed for those who heard the Word of the Lord and obeyed it.

For the first forty-six years of her life, Nancy—"Nannie" to close friends and family—had ample evidence that God was rewarding her piety as the Good Book promised. She married Charlie Milles Maddox, also from Kentucky, who came back from the First World War and found work as a conductor for the Chesapeake & Ohio Railroad. He and his bride weren't rich but they became comfortably middle-class, at least by rural Kentucky standards. Beyond being a good provider Charlie was the kind of solid citizen that Nancy could respect as well as love. He was a member of the Brotherhood of Railway Trainmen and the Masonic

Lodge. They lived happily in Rowan County in northeast Kentucky, and beginning in 1911 their marriage was regularly blessed with children. God sent Glenna in 1911, Aileene (sometimes spelled "Aline") in 1913, Luther in 1915, and finally Ada Kathleen in 1918. When their youngest child was ten, the Maddoxes moved their brood sixty miles northeast to the sparkling city of Ashland on the banks of the Ohio River. Kentucky, Ohio, and West Virginia all came together around there, with the river providing convenient state boundaries. Ashland was a business port and home to several major entities, including Ashland Oil, the thirteenth-largest petroleum refining company in the United States, and steel mills that ultimately were purchased by and became part of the American Rolling Mill Company, commonly known as Armco. Barges floated the area's timber and coal upriver and down to major metropolises like Cincinnati and Pittsburgh. The C&O Railroad thrived as it whisked businessmen of every stripe in and out of town. Having sensibly lived within their means back in Rowan County, Charlie and Nancy were able to buy a house on Hilton Avenue in Ashland for $5,000, a considerable sum in 1928. When the Depression crumbled the U.S. economy one year later, the Maddoxes were spared any real discomfort. Unlike many of their friends, Charlie didn't have to worry about losing his job and ending up in a bread line. Glenna met a local boy named Cecil Racer and in January 1930 she married him in a ceremony at her parents' house. The Ashland newspaper printed a lovely article about the wedding. Almost a year to the day later Glenna gave birth to a daughter named Jo Ann. Blessings piled upon blessings. Nancy bowed her head and gave thanks daily.

Then suddenly everything began falling apart. In October 1931 Charlie complained of chest congestion. He died a week later of pneumonia. His loss staggered Nancy; she moaned that she felt as though she had died, too. But she soon took solace in her faith. God's will might be mysterious, but it was not to be questioned. At least there were no immediate financial concerns. Charlie left his widow a railroad pension of about $60 a month. It was enough, if she was careful, to continue raising the three children that were still at home without Nancy having to take a job herself. Mothers in that time and place worked only if they had to. Fifteen-year-old Luther and thirteen-year-old Ada Kathleen, now called by her middle name, were still school kids, and eighteen-year-old Aileene enrolled in Ashland's Booth Business College with the goal of becoming a secretary or perhaps a bookkeeper.

Then came another blow. Glenna and her husband, Cecil, fought constantly, and Nancy often kept her granddaughter Jo Ann for days or took her on short trips to keep the child from being exposed to such marital strife. Nancy prayed that God would touch the battling spouses' hearts and bring them back together, but it didn't happen. Glenna divorced Cecil, and for a little while she and Jo Ann moved back with her mother, brother, and sisters. Nancy didn't believe in divorce. The Bible insisted that husband and wife should cleave to each other forever. But Glenna was in every other way a dutiful daughter, and little Jo Ann now required more than ever the example of a proper Christian household. So, as God expected of her, Nancy accepted this additional heartache and soldiered on.

Aileene graduated from business college in early 1933 and celebrated with a short trip across the river into Ohio. While she was away she developed the same sort of chest congestion that had struck down her father, was hospitalized, and, like Charlie Maddox seventeen months earlier, died within a week.

Once again, Nancy was devastated. In every way she had followed God's commandments and now He seemed determined to take away all the happiness that had been bestowed upon her. A woman of lesser conviction might have abandoned religion altogether, but Nancy never considered that option. Instead, she pored over biblical passages and was reminded how God used awful ways to test the faithful. Job endured all sorts of suffering, refused to betray his reverence for the Lord, and was eventually exalted for it. In fact, the Bible stated that God rewarded Job with twice as many good things as he had had before. So Nancy would endure, too. Charlie and Aileene couldn't be given back in earthly life, but they awaited her in heaven. Meanwhile, Nancy's beliefs gained rather than lost strength. She would continue to live a righteous life, and she became even more determined that her surviving offspring would, too. Though Nancy was tolerant of other types and degrees of faith in anyone else, with her children it was different. The Bible was explicit about a parent's responsibility to raise sons and daughters in the way that the Lord wanted them to go, and to Nancy that meant that they must believe every

word in the Bible and observe each of the Good Book's rules and admonitions. Any deviation from this divinely mandated behavior would count
against them in the eyes of God and Nancy couldn't let that happen. If
she did, she herself would have failed the Lord. So Nancy not only kept
Bible reading and churchgoing mandatory, she acquired bulky books written as guides to the study of Scripture. Her copy of *The Self-Interpreting
Bible, Volume III*, devoted to the teachings of Old Testament prophets and
one of Nancy's favorites, remains intact. In case the rest of the family
didn't fully grasp the concept of absolute obedience to the Lord or else,
she underlined the most critical passages in Isaiah—Chapter 1, Verses 18
and 19: *"Come now, and let us reason together, saith the Lord; though your sins
be as scarlet, they shall be as white as snow; though they be red like crimson, they
shall be as wool. If ye be willing and obedient, ye shall eat the good of the land."*
In keeping with biblical carrot-and-stick instruction, Verse 20, though not
underlined, bluntly spelled out the alternative: *"But if ye refuse and rebel,
ye shall be devoured with the sword: for the mouth of the Lord hath spoken it."*

In part, things worked out as Nancy desired. Glenna met Bill
Thomas, an engine fireman with the Baltimore & Ohio Railroad. He
hoped to work his way up to engineer and eventually did. Because of her
husband, Charlie, Nancy always had special regard for railroad men, so
she approved of Bill even though he had something of a temper. Glenna
married him and, with daughter Jo Ann, joined Bill in North Charleston, West Virginia, about sixty-five miles from her mother's home. Bill
Thomas proved to be a loving, if strict, stepfather. He and Jo Ann quickly
became close. Glenna's successful remarriage allowed Nancy to concentrate on her two youngest children, both of whom evinced little interest
in leading godly lives despite their mother's good example and constant
urging. Luther was eighteen now and Kathleen fifteen. Nancy felt that
boys were always difficult to raise because of their natural rambunctious-
ness, and Luther suffered additionally from not having a father's proper
example anymore. Nancy never considered remarrying because Charlie
Maddox had been her soul mate. Without a husband to keep her son in
line, she relied mostly on nagging and prayer, hoping the combination
would influence Luther to outgrow his immature interest in un-Christian
carousing.

Kathleen caused her mother even greater concern. Nancy believed girls were supposed to cheerfully obey their parents and the Bible, but Kathleen didn't always comply. Nancy was raised as a Protestant, most likely as a Baptist, and eventually became a proud, active member of the Nazarene Church, which had conservative rules for its young ladies. They were expected to dress modestly—no sleeveless dresses or tops, for instance, and very little if any makeup. Girls were discouraged from cutting their hair based on biblical admonitions that a woman's hair was her glory. Going to movies, dancing, interacting improperly with the opposite sex, cursing, and drinking alcohol comprised a don't list informally known as "the Big Five" for Nazarene teens. Such corrupting acts were to be avoided because they were clearly sinful.

Nancy was baffled when Kathleen complained that her mother wouldn't allow her to have any fun. Surely Ashland offered all the wholesome pleasures that any decent teenage girl could want. Besides church and Sunday School, which bestowed the unparalleled joy of worship, the town had lovely parks in which to stroll, soda shops, and even the South's first enclosed shopping mall, where decent, limb-covering dresses were sold. Kathleen could enjoy these delights in the company of other nice girls from the church, and at some point she would surely come to love and marry a boy of proper Christian faith. But the willful child declared that these godly activities and future were boring. She was willing to forgo movies and makeup if she absolutely had to, but Kathleen insisted on her right to engage in something Nancy ranked with blasphemy and failure to attend church as awful sins—the girl wanted to go out dancing. Nancy tried to make her wayward daughter realize what should have been obvious: dancing, which was essentially moving one's body in suggestive ways with a boy (who would inevitably have his unholy desires enflamed by the experience), brought girls to the very edge of Satan's fiery pit. No good could come of it, and therefore the church forbade it, and so did her mother.

For a little while, Kathleen let Nancy believe that she'd been persuaded. There was an empty space between the stove and the kitchen counter in the Maddox house, and if Nancy was in another room Kathleen would squeeze in there and practice jitterbugging without her mother seeing. Kathleen didn't necessarily want to cause her mother any grief—she loved her. She considered Nancy to be a hard person, probably because of the church and the losses of Charlie and Aileene, but still well intentioned. What Kathleen couldn't stand was her mother's constant nagging. All Kathleen wanted was to have a little fun. Other girls she knew went to dances and wore makeup and had their hair cut fashionably short, flapper-style. These things didn't seem sinful to her. Fifteen-year-old Kathleen wasn't particularly pretty—she was sharp-featured like Nancy—but she had lots of personality and she was pleased that boys seemed attracted to her. Luther understood her frustration with their mother, but he spent most of his time running around with his friends and didn't want his kid sister tagging along. Soon Kathleen decided that she would go out and dance whether Nancy allowed it or not. She had the right to live her life however she pleased so long as she didn't do anything really bad. And if Nancy didn't know what her youngest child was up to, that would be even better.

The problem was that in Ashland, everybody knew everybody else and a teenage girl couldn't even smile at a boy without someone reporting it back to her mother. If Kathleen had a good time dancing in her hometown Nancy would immediately hear about it, and Kathleen couldn't stand being lectured for the millionth time about how she was headed straight to hell if she didn't adhere to all those stultifying church rules.

Fortunately for Kathleen, there was a convenient alternative to Ashland. The town was linked to Ohio by a bridge over the river, and on the other side was Ironton, a place with an exciting reputation for dance clubs and people having fun. Upstanding citizens in Ashland grumbled that Ironton was a hotbed of sin, with a red-light district replete with drinking and gambling and prostitutes on every corner, but that intrigued rather than repelled Kathleen. Having been warned about sin all her life, she wanted the opportunity to observe some of it firsthand. Her own intentions were limited to dancing, though if in the process she made some new friends who didn't lecture her about what God did and didn't want, well, that would be fine, too. Kathleen was fifteen and not a child anymore. She was eager to become more worldly.

So Kathleen began sneaking out and crossing the bridge into Ohio. She discovered that Ironton had delightful clubs where the music was loud and prospective dance partners were plentiful. The most popular of these, the one where all the most convivial people seemed to congregate, was called Ritzy Ray's, and that is probably where she met him.

In the 1920s farmer Walter Scott moved his family from Catlettsburg, Kentucky, to a spot near Ashland where he tried his luck tilling along the Big Sandy, a tributary of the Ohio River, before giving up farming and going to work in a mill. Scott's two sons soon gained local reputations as con men. Darwin and Colonel—the latter a given name, not a military rank—found sporadic employment at local mills but preferred loot from illicit schemes. Their most notorious scam involved a bridge over the Ohio between Ashland and Catlettsburg. The structure was originally private, built by an entrepreneur who charged the public 10 cents to cross. The state bought the bridge and repealed the toll, but the Scott brothers took over the empty toll booth and made money for four days until word spread that there was no longer a crossing fee. The Scott boys, their pockets jingling with dimes, lay low until the furor died down.

Colonel Scott was a strapping, handsome fellow who very much enjoyed the seamy pleasures that Ironton offered. He was a smooth talker and fifteen-year-old Kathleen Maddox was the perfect prey for his smarmy charm. Since Scott was twenty-three, Kathleen felt flattered to receive the attentions of an older man. He let her think that he really was an Army colonel. Scott also failed to mention that he was married. They danced, Scott treated Kathleen to drinks, undoubtedly her first (Why not? Everybody else in the place was drinking), and she felt quite sophisticated. Kathleen began crossing the Ironton Bridge to see her new beau on a regular basis. Clearly, he loved her and she loved him back.

In the spring of 1934 Kathleen discovered that she was pregnant. When she told Colonel Scott, he said that he had just been called away on military business, but he'd return soon. It was several months before Kathleen realized that he had no intention of having any further contact, let alone marrying her.

Kathleen didn't keep her pregnancy secret from Nancy. The teenager was not disowned. Despite having her most baleful predictions confirmed, Nancy still loved the girl. But to remain in her mother's house Kathleen was informed that she must set aside her sinful ways and live according to biblical strictures. The baby would be raised in the church. Kathleen, queasy in early pregnancy, clung as long as she could to the belief that Colonel Scott would return and rescue her from the dull future that she'd been sentenced to by her mother. But as Scott stayed away and the baby in her belly began to kick, Kathleen's emotions spun into adolescent rage. How dare Colonel Scott get her pregnant and then not marry her? Somehow, she'd show him and he'd be sorry. She might not have been the most sensible girl, but she still had plenty of gumption. In one sense her mother's example did influence her; Kathleen was determined to be married. She wanted a man like Charlie Maddox who would take care of her and the baby, someone who would provide her child with a name and her with a home and maybe make Colonel Scott jealous all at the same time. She had a candidate in mind.

Very little is known about William Manson apart from some sketchy military information and perfunctory death records. He was born in 1909 in West Virginia and died fifty-two years later in California. He is buried in Fort Rosecrans National Cemetery in San Diego. William was a small man; when he enlisted in the Army in 1942 his height was recorded as five foot eight and he weighed 136 pounds. Under "Civil Occupation," the military noted "unskilled machine shop." A 1909 business directory for Wheeling, West Virginia, lists "Wm. G. Manson" as an insurance agent. That may be his father or an uncle.

How William knew Kathleen Maddox in 1934 remains a mystery. He may have been another regular at Ritzy Ray's who'd made it clear that he was attracted to the spunky teenager. Perhaps she met him after Colonel Scott got her in trouble and then abandoned her. Somehow they connected. On August 21 a marriage license was issued for William and Kathleen. The groom's age was correctly listed as twenty-five. Kathleen fudged considerably and claimed to be twenty-one, which means that Nancy wasn't informed in advance about the wedding. Since Kathleen was still only fifteen, if she'd told the truth about how old she was, her mother's permission would have been required for her to marry. Court records filed a few years later suggest that William knew the baby carried by his bride was the child of another man, though the possibility remains that he thought the child was his. In any event, the couple came to some understanding and Kathleen had a husband.

On November 12, 1934, Kathleen delivered a healthy baby boy at Cincinnati General Hospital. The child's birth certificate, filed on December 3, contained no taint of illegitimacy. His father was listed as William Manson, now of Cincinnati, a "laborer" employed at a dry cleaner's. The infant was named Charles Milles Manson in honor of his maternal grandfather.

The Bible directed Nancy to hate the sin and love the sinner, so she came to Cincinnati to see the new mother and to meet her grandson. Photographs show her cuddling infant Charlie and beaming. Despite the circumstances of his conception, Nancy adored the child and was determined to see that he was raised in godly fashion.

Kathleen also loved her son, but upon turning sixteen she was as devoted to having a good time as she was to being a good wife and mother. The goals proved incompatible. Nothing much is known about Kathleen and William's marriage, including where they lived, though it seems likely they stayed in or around Cincinnati. Kathleen began going out at night without her husband, sometimes even showing up unexpectedly in Ashland or Charleston to drop off Charlie with his grandmother or Aunt Glenna while she caroused. Nancy and Glenna were concerned that Charlie was often left with unsuitable baby-sitters. Kathleen disappeared for days at a time with her brother, Luther, who was now happy to bring his younger sister along on his escapades. Nancy, frantic and expecting the worst, told friends that her children ranged as far as Chicago, where she believed Kathleen met men in bars, enticed them outside with promises of forbidden affection, and then turned them over to Luther to be beaten and robbed. It's certainly possible Kathleen and Luther tried to con newfound pals in bars out of their money, but any more extreme scenario at that time seems unlikely, since brother and sister soon proved completely unskilled at criminal violence. But Kathleen definitely drank and danced and to Nancy any woman who committed those sinful acts, even her daughter, was capable of any awful thing.

William Manson quickly had enough of his errant wife. On April 30, 1937, the court ruled on his request for divorce after less than two and a half years of marriage. He charged Kathleen with "gross neglect of duty," a catchall phrase used to describe infidelity, drunkenness, abandonment, or some combination of those or other marital transgressions. She did not come to court to contest the divorce, or to defend herself. The court granted William his divorce, and the decree pointedly noted that "there were no children the issue of this marriage." William was not legally obligated and so wouldn't pay Kathleen a penny of support for Charlie. All the little boy got from William was a last name. Kathleen went back to calling herself Maddox.

Kathleen didn't wait for William Manson's rejection of her and her child. Two weeks before her divorce from Manson was finalized in Ohio, Kathleen went to court in Kentucky and filed a "bastardy suit" against Colonel Scott. She'd somehow tracked him down and even though she no longer had starry-eyed expectations that he would marry her, Kathleen was determined that he would at least take some financial responsibility for Charlie.

Scott, under oath, didn't deny that he was Charlie's father, and the court ruled in Kathleen's favor. Charlie may have met his biological father for the first time during the bastardy hearing; Kathleen would recall that Scott came to visit the toddler a few times afterward. But what Colonel Scott didn't do was pay Kathleen the $5 a month child support mandated by the judge. Kathleen banked an initial judgment of $25, but never received another cent from her former lover. She implored the court to garnishee Scott's wages from the local mill where he was currently employed, but no such order was issued. Kathleen pursued the matter until it eventually became the least of her legal concerns.

Over the next sixteen months Kathleen and Charlie sometimes stayed with Nancy in Ashland. They also moved in occasionally with Glenna, Bill, and their daughter, Jo Ann, in North Charleston. The Thomas house on Dunbar Line, in a lower-middle-class neighborhood known as Dogtown, must have been crowded, because Luther and his girlfriend Julia Vickers frequently stayed there, too. There is no record of Kathleen finding employment, but she did go out and actively look for another husband. On October 2, 1938, the *Charleston Gazette* reported that Ada Kathleen Maddox of State Street—she apparently had her own place in town for a while—was engaged to James Lewis Robey. Kathleen's knack for choosing the wrong man was intact; Robey had a string of convictions for bootlegging and minor theft. The couple never progressed beyond a brief engagement. When Kathleen's name was next in the newspaper ten months later, there was no mention of Robey, though his checkered past may have provided Kathleen with some unfortunate inspiration.

On the afternoon of August 1, 1939, Kathleen and Julia Vickers wandered around Charleston, idly killing time window-shopping and chatting. Charlie, now almost five, was left either with Glenna or some acquaintance of his mother. Kathleen was no longer a naive girl who just wanted to dance and have a little fun. At age twenty she was a divorced woman with a small child and no income; she resented what she considered to be her unfair lot in life. During these tough, disillusioned times, Kathleen developed a hard-bitten attitude; she wanted something better and meant to have it. On this day, the opportunity to acquire some money through crime presented itself, and Kathleen succumbed to temptation.

It was an impetuous decision that would affect—and cost—lives over the next three-quarters of a century.

Sometime during the early evening, Kathleen and Julia met a stranger named Frank Martin, who attracted them with his friendly personality and even more with his gray Packard convertible coupé. Martin escorted Kathleen and Julia to the Valley Bell Dairy, where he treated them to some cheese. Kathleen thought that Martin might leave them there, but he accepted her invitation to extend the evening. The trio drove on to Dan's Beer Parlor, where Martin flashed a roll of bills and treated his new lady friends to refreshing brews until 11:30 P.M. This was exactly the sort of scenario Nancy had long cautioned Kathleen against; a man with alcohol in his system and in a bar with a young woman was likely to have inappropriate intentions. Maybe Martin did, but so did Kathleen. Hers just weren't sexual. She invited Julia to join her in the ladies' room and observed how awful it was that people like Martin seemed to have all the money. Kathleen said she wanted some of Martin's bankroll, and Julia laughed and said that she felt "like reaching out." The two women returned to the table where Martin waited and mentioned how nice it would be to rent a room somewhere. Martin took the hint and asked how much such a room would cost. Kathleen suggested $4.50 but added that she didn't have that much money. Martin forked over three one-dollar bills and two quarters, not the entire sum but enough to convince Kathleen that her hook was properly set. She excused herself and used the bar's pay phone to call Luther at the Thomases'. Kathleen told her brother that she and Julia were with someone who had too much money for one man. Luther knew exactly what his sister was suggesting, and said she should arrange for the three of them to meet him in a few minutes at Littlepage Service Station.

Martin, expecting to rush to some rented room where he could romp with two lively young women, must have been puzzled by Kathleen's directions to a gas station, and even more so when he discovered that they were being joined there by another man. Luther introduced himself as John Ellis. The foursome then went on in Martin's Packard to the Blue Moon Beer Parlor. Martin was apparently ready to settle for a night of partying that might not include sexual frolics after all. Everyone had some beer and danced. Luther took his sister aside and asked if Martin really had much money. She assured him that Martin did, and Luther joked, "Well, I guess I'll have to count it." Julia stayed behind at the Blue Moon while Martin, Kathleen, and Luther got back in the Packard and drove away.

When they were just beyond town, Luther told Martin to stop the car and get out. Martin laughed, and Luther insisted, "I mean it." Kathleen watched as the two men walked to the side of the road. She couldn't hear what Luther said next, but she saw very clearly what he did.

Luther had with him a ketchup bottle filled with salt. He stuck the neck of the bottle into Martin's back and said that he was holding a gun. Martin didn't believe him. Luther cracked Martin over the head with the bottle, which broke, and his victim, stunned but conscious, fell to the ground. Luther relieved him of his wallet, and he and Kathleen drove off in the Packard. When they looked in the wallet they discovered their haul totaled $27. Luther and Kathleen picked up Julia back at the Blue Moon Beer Parlor; they ditched the car on a nearby street. Luther called a cab, and the trio holed up in a rented room at the Daniel Boone Bar B Q in nearby Snow Hill. Later Kathleen and Julia took another cab back to Bill and Glenna's house on Dunbar Line. Luther stayed at the rented room, sleeping in.

The assault and robbery case was solved within hours. There was no real challenge for the investigators because the perpetrators were so inept. Beyond using a false name to introduce her brother to Martin, Kathleen and Luther had not done anything to conceal their identities or to cover their tracks. As soon as Martin regained his senses, he stumbled back into town and called the Charleston police. By 1 A.M. the stolen Packard had been recovered and witnesses at Dan's Beer Parlor confirmed that Martin had been there with two women named Kathleen and Judy or Julia. The women were regular patrons at Dan's; someone there recalled that they said they lived in North Charleston. As soon as the North Charleston Post Office opened in the morning, Postmaster J. E. Akers informed the cops that Kathleen Maddox and someone calling herself Judy Bryant both received mail at an address he furnished on Dunbar Line. Several policemen, with Martin in tow, arrived at the Thomas house. Martin identified Kathleen and Julia, who were arrested. Charlie, not yet five, probably saw his mother taken away in handcuffs. Kathleen denied knowing where Luther was, but Julia mentioned that she and Kathleen had spent the night with him in a room at the Boone Bar B Q. The police found Luther there and arrested him, too.

After their arrests, Luther, Kathleen, and Julia all provided the police with statements about what they'd done. In his, Luther gallantly attested that the two women had no idea that he planned to rob Martin, so "I hereby acknowledge all responsibility for the commission of this crime. I do hereby exonerate all others implicated in it." But Kathleen and Julia both confessed their roles, though Julia made it clear that she was left behind when Luther and Kathleen drove off with Martin as a prelude to robbing him. As a result, she faced minor counts of aiding and abetting, but her partners were brought to court on sterner charges.

Stories in the *Charleston Daily Mail* mocked the "Ketchup Bottle Holdup" and the bumblers involved in it, but Judge D. Jackson Savage found nothing funny about the crime. In a brief trial seven weeks later,

Savage found Luther Maddox guilty of armed robbery and sentenced him to ten years in prison. Since she stayed in the car while her brother poked, then struck, Martin with the ketchup bottle, Kathleen's sentence from Judge Savage was five years for unarmed robbery. When she learned of the verdicts, Nancy Maddox pulled her granddaughter, Jo Ann, aside and whispered, "Life is like always living under a big rock. Always look at it and pray that it won't fall on you." Nancy felt as though she had been buried under an avalanche. She'd tried so hard to raise her children properly, and somehow God in His wisdom had still permitted things to come to this. When time allowed, Nancy would pray about it and try to understand how to salvage the souls of her wayward son and daughter. For now, Luther and Kathleen were taken away in chains from Charleston to serve their lengthy sentences at the West Virginia state prison in Moundsville. (Luther was allowed to marry Julia just before he left; the marriage didn't last.) Since the prison was widely reputed to be a hellhole, Nancy was justifiably terrified about what might befall her children there. But Nancy had an even more pressing concern, a four-and-a-half-year-old grandson who for some time had had no father and now for five years would have no mother. What was to become of little Charlie?

CHAPTER TWO

Moundsville and McMechen

Soon after Kathleen was taken away to Moundsville, Grandmother Nancy and probably Aunt Glenna took Charlie aside to explain that his mother had to go away for a while. How much Charlie was told or understood about the crime Kathleen had committed isn't known. It was surely explained that while he would be able to visit her sometimes, he might not live with her for five years, which to a little boy must have seemed like forever.

Ideally during Kathleen's incarceration, Charlie would have lived with Nancy in Ashland. Nancy doted on the child and she certainly wanted to expose him to positive religious influence during this traumatic time in his young life. But Ashland was too far away from the federal prison; Moundsville nestled along the Ohio River on the north boundary of West Virginia, just across from Ohio and more than two hundred miles north of Ashland. Everyone agreed the little boy should visit his mother as often as possible. Bill Thomas's job with the railroad conveniently required him to relocate to the West Virginia town of McMechen, which was about five miles south of the big city of Wheeling and just five miles north of Moundsville. That made the solution obvious—Charlie would move in with his Uncle Bill, Aunt Glenna, and eight-year-old cousin, Jo Ann.

McMechen, with a population of around 4,000, was a quintessential blue-collar town. Virtually every family living there was headed by a father who worked for one of the local mines or mills or the railroad. There was little differentiation in income; everyone was lower-middle-class. One side of town was bordered by the Ohio River, a half mile wide at that point and attractively lined with trees—silver maple, river birch, and sycamore. On the other side were high hills thick with forest and studded with mine works. The houses in between were mostly utilitarian. There were also grocery stores, small department stores, and other businesses. There was a doctor, dentist, and a shoe repair shop. The front rooms of several houses served as neighborhood candy stores. McMechenites rarely went all the way to Wheeling or Moundsville to shop. Buses provided whatever transportation was necessary—very few residents owned cars. Townspeople were proud that almost a dozen churches flourished within town limits, and bragged not at all about maintaining the same number of bars. Segregation didn't need to be enforced because only white people lived in McMechen. Gender and generational roles there were immutable. Men worked hard at their jobs during the week, drank hard at the town bars after work and on Saturdays, owned guns and hunted, and never showed much if any emotion. Women stayed home, raised children, herded their families to church on Sunday, and deferred to their husbands as head of the family. Children minded their parents, didn't swim in the dangerous Ohio River, and addressed all grown-ups as "sir" or "ma'am." Boys roughhoused with their buddies, learned how to handle guns, and never cried. When they were old enough, they took jobs at the same companies where their fathers worked. Girls learned how to cook, sew, and other skills required by good wives and mothers. Everyone knew and trusted their neighbors; nobody locked their doors when they went out or at night. Above all, McMechen was self-contained. Little that happened in the outside world mattered. So long as the mills and the mines stayed open and the railroad continued to run, McMechen remained unchanged from one generation to the next.

The Thomases fit perfectly into their new community. Bill worked hard for the B&O, owned a few guns, and was clearly the master of his household. He also liked to drink; even by the bibulous standards of McMechen some of his neighbors thought Bill did too much imbibing. Eventually he realized it, too, and got the problem under control. Glenna kept a nice house and was active in church. Jo Ann went to the local elementary school (the one for Protestant children; Catholic kids had their own) and made excellent grades. Then they added Charlie to the mix, and he didn't fit at all.

Little Charlie Manson was a disagreeable child. Beyond his doting grandmother, who still recognized his many faults, few who knew him then or in his ensuing teenage years found much to admire about him beyond his looks. Charlie's dimpled smile could light up rooms, and his eyes were dark and expressive. It was possible to pity the boy—he didn't have a father, and now his unreliable mother was in jail—and Charlie was so small that he was closer in stature to toddlers than to other kids just turning five and about to enter school. But even at such a young age he lied about everything and, when he got in trouble for telling fibs or breaking things or any of the other innumerable misdeeds he committed on a daily basis, Charlie always blamed somebody else for his actions. The child was also obsessed with being the center of attention. If he couldn't get noticed for doing something right, he was just as willing to attract attention by misbehaving. You couldn't ever relax when Charlie was around. It was only a matter of time before he got up to something bad.

Uncle Bill, Aunt Glenna, and Cousin Jo Ann were already aware of Charlie's irritating ways before he joined them in McMechen late in 1939. They didn't want responsibility for him, but family obligations trumped personal preference. Perhaps the boy's behavior would improve now that he was in a stable environment. Jo Ann didn't think so. Her opinion of her cousin at the time he moved in was that "there was never anything happy about him. He never did anything that was good." Before Charlie arrived, Bill and Glenna made it clear to their eight-year-old daughter that, so far as they were concerned, she was now the five-year-old's big sister. This meant that she had to supervise him whenever her parents weren't around, and otherwise shepherd him around McMechen, walking him with her to and from elementary school, protecting him from bullies, and generally looking out for his well-being. Bill and Glenna made sure that Charlie understood better behavior was now expected of him. They tried to demonstrate some affection by calling him Chuckie, but the name didn't stick. He was too exasperating; mostly the Thomases found themselves addressing the boy as "Charles," using his first full name as part of the daily dressings-down they administered.

As soon as Charlie arrived, two immediate actions were required. He should visit his mother at the prison in Moundsville, and he had to start school. Neither experience went well.

• • •

Everything about the six-acre West Virginia Penitentiary in Moundsville was intended to intimidate. Dominating the south part of town, the prison was designed to resemble a Gothic castle, not a shining symbol of hope like Camelot but instead a brooding hulk ruled by some cruel, domineering black knight. Its outer stone walls were four feet thick, twenty-four feet high, and topped with barbed wire and turrets manned by armed guards. Entry past the walls to the inner buildings was permitted only through heavy barred doors; standing outside, one could easily imagine the screams of victims being tortured in subterranean dungeons, which was in fact close to the truth. Prisoners judged guilty of serious infractions were taken away to dark, dank punishment rooms, stripped naked, and bent over a low platform called the Kicking Jenny with their feet and hands tied to rings on the floor. Then a hulking guard tore apart their bare backs with a water-soaked leather whip until his arms grew too tired or his victim seemed near death.

Even prisoners who avoided these bloody episodes suffered on a daily basis. In 1939, when Luther and Kathleen arrived to serve their sentences, the prison population of 2,700 was more than three times its intended or "rated" capacity of about 870. Male inmates were jammed three at a time into tiny five-foot-by-seven-foot cells. At least in terms of sleeping space, women had it better. They were housed on the third floor of the administration building.

The prison was strictly segregated. Blacks and whites observed each other from mandated distances. In several places hallway floors had white and black painted lines, indicating where each race was expected to walk. Segregation was even enforced in the cramped dining hall, though cockroaches routinely found their way into the food without regard to race. Everyone ate what was given to them, bugs and all. They needed their strength for work detail, so they chewed and swallowed even while rats skittered across the dining hall tables.

West Virginia officials wanted their prison to be self-sustaining, and even during the Depression the state penitentiary in Moundsville turned a profit. Male inmates were hired out to area businesses and farmers for as little as 16 cents an hour. There were no regulations to be observed by these employers regarding the care of their rented labor. The prisoners were fed what their outside bosses wanted to give them, or not fed at all. If their work wasn't satisfactory, reports back to prison officials and sessions on the Kicking Jenny encouraged the prisoners to do better.

Women were assigned to an in-house sewing factory where they attached collars and cuffs to coarse prison garb fashioned by male inmates in another part of the prison. A few especially unlucky female prisoners were placed on custodial duty; they spent long days mopping floors frequently puddled with sweat, vomit, urine, and blood.

Other work details turned out license plates, blankets, belts, and over a hundred more products that were sold to the public by the state. A nearby two-hundred-acre farm known as Camp Fairchance utilized convict labor to plant, tend, and harvest produce. The best vegetables were sold in local markets. Anything unsalable to the general public was sent to the prison kitchen. Male or female, all able-bodied inmates were required to work nine hours each weekday and a half day on Saturday.

Overwork, beatings, poor food, and all-around unsanitary conditions took their toll on the prison population. Outbreaks of tuberculosis regularly killed dozens of inmates. Those deaths were incidental; it was the prison's scheduled deaths that entranced the local population. Anyone receiving the death penalty in a West Virginia court was transported to Moundsville for execution. The condemned were hanged on a gallows near the prison's North Wagon Gate. Each hanging was organized as entertainment. Tickets were printed by the prison and distributed to the public. Demand far exceeded supply, so even though the prison didn't charge admission to executions, once distributed the tickets were routinely scalped or swapped for liquor or other goods.

Luther and Kathleen Maddox were in no danger from the hangman. Their respective ten- and five-year sentences didn't commend them to prison officials as potentially dangerous new inmates. They were just two more convicted felons to be crammed into the general population. According to records, Luther was initially sent to work in the prison paint plant. His sister wasn't as lucky. Kathleen drew a custodial assignment, but she made no complaint. Because of the overcrowded conditions, prisoners who worked hard and followed the rules were often released before serving their entire sentences. Such paroles never came early. Even with perfect behavior, the Maddoxes could expect to remain in Moundsville for years. But even one fewer day in that filthy, frightening place must have seemed worth striving for.

Soon after Charlie arrived in McMechen, Uncle Bill took him to Moundsville. Perhaps he cautioned the little boy about what he would see, the terrifying penitentiary itself as well as Kathleen in prisoner's coveralls. But more likely he warned the five-year-old about behaving properly. No sniveling when he saw his mother. Real boys didn't do that.

If the sight of the forbidding outer walls and heavily guarded entrance doors didn't completely unsettle Charlie, the visit with Kathleen surely did. Ushered inside the main entrance and down a hall to the left by Uncle Bill and uniformed prison staff, Charlie was pushed onto a hard wooden slat seat in front of a thick glass panel. On the other side was Kathleen. Whatever love she tried to communicate to him was verbal; until the day she was set free, it is unlikely that Kathleen was allowed to touch, let alone hug, her child.

If Charlie managed not to cry or show any other unmanly emotion that day at the prison, he more than made up for it when the Thomases enrolled him in school.

More than seventy years later, longtime McMechen residents still shudder when they recollect their experiences in Mrs. Varner's first grade class. Richard Hawkey puts it bluntly: "She scared the shit out of me," and Hawkey's mother became the school principal. Virginia Brautigan, who as an adult worked for the McMechen schools, says that long after her retirement Mrs. Varner remained legendary among administrators for "how awful she was to her students." Nobody seems to recall the woman's first name. The lady did not encourage familiarity.

Everyone agrees that Mrs. Varner ran her class like a Parris Island Marine sergeant browbeating quaking recruits into submission. First graders marched rather than walked into her class, and when the dismissal bell rang the children came to attention and left the room only when their teacher permitted it. Desks were arranged in four rows, and Mrs. Varner assigned seating not alphabetically but by whoever pleased her the most and least. Her pets, invariably girls, were in the first row, with the special favorite assigned the front seat closest to her. That child could do no wrong. Then the desks were filled in according to Mrs. Varner's judgmental whim—most promising toward the front, somewhat promising in the middle rows, least promising in the fourth row, and the last seat in the back row reserved for whatever unlucky first grader struck her as a lost cause, thereby becoming a frequent target of her devastating scorn. Spanking was permitted by school rules, but Mrs. Varner had no need to resort to that. She eviscerated students with words; again, her exact classroom vocabulary isn't precisely recalled, only that she instinctively knew how to discover and verbally exploit children's greatest insecurities.

After Charlie turned five in November 1939, the Thomases brought him to the elementary school. They felt relieved to get him out of the house. Charlie was sent to Mrs. Varner's room. She looked at the tiny waif, probably factored in whatever gossip she'd heard about his jailbird mother and uncle, and passed the Varnerian equivalent of the death sentence. Charlie was directed to the last seat in the fourth row. Whatever boy was previously sitting there must have been thrilled by the reprieve. During Charlie's first day, Mrs. Varner took many opportunities to point out his defects. His mother's imprisonment may have been mentioned, along with dire predictions about Charlie's own hopeless future. Witness memories aren't specific, but they all remember the aftermath perfectly. At the end of his long, terrible day Charlie ran home crying, and Uncle Bill witnessed this unacceptable display.

In those days, parents rarely questioned teachers' treatment of children. The assumption was that whatever the teacher did, the student deserved. Even Mrs. Varner went unchallenged. Further, McMechen boys did not cry. They stoically accepted whatever punishment was doled out, even if it was unfair—it helped prepare them for life as adult working-class men. At best Bill Thomas had no patience for whiners, and here was this boy living in his house who fled home from school acting like a weepy little girl. Uncle Bill could have reminded himself that Charlie wasn't his son. But he took great pride in being a self-made man who'd taken whatever life dished out and still succeeded. It required guts and resilience to rise in the railroad from fireman to engineer. Maybe his mother and Uncle Luther were bad influences, but Charlie could benefit from Uncle Bill's intercession. It didn't matter what some teacher had done to make him cry; what was important was to do something drastic that would convince Charlie never to act like a sissy again.

The next morning Bill rummaged in his daughter's closet and picked out one of Jo Ann's dresses. He ordered Charlie to put it on. Since Jo Ann was three years older and normal-sized and Charlie small, the frock certainly sagged off him. Then Uncle Bill marched the five-year-old back to Mrs. Varner's classroom. Charlie had to wear Jo Ann's baggy dress all day; as Bill intended, he never forgot it. Later in life, Charlie exaggerated or lied outright about almost everything in his troubled childhood, trying to make bad experiences sound even worse. But he told the truth about being forced by his uncle to wear a dress to school. No embellishment was necessary.

Beyond the dress incident, except for his cousin Jo Ann no one living recalls much more about Charlie Manson's first extended stay in McMechen. He attracted very little further notice; instead of running in the streets and nearby fields playing with friends like other little boys, he skulked around the Thomases' house. Though he survived his time in Mrs. Varner's class, Charlie remained a poor student in the two and a half years that followed. Reading skills particularly eluded him then and afterward; tested as an adult, he could read at only a rudimentary level. His time in the McMechen elementary school was notable only in that he consistently attracted the notice of bullies through a combination of his small stature and big mouth. Once Charlie exchanged insults with an older, much larger boy who began slapping him. Jo Ann, saddled with protecting her cousin and determined to live up to the responsibility, jumped between them, and the bigger boy slapped her, too. Feisty Jo Ann bit his finger hard and he ran away howling with pain. Her teacher was bewildered—Jo Ann always behaved well and never got into playground scraps. When she asked the girl what happened, Jo Ann explained how Charlie was being struck by a bigger boy, and so she stepped in to rescue him. But when Charlie was called over and asked to corroborate what Jo Ann had said, he claimed he didn't know anything about it. He just saw Jo Ann bite somebody. Jo Ann could have gotten in serious trouble, but the teacher knew that she was truthful and Charlie usually lied, so she believed Jo Ann. Jo Ann decided that Charlie liked to start trouble and then let somebody else get blamed for it.

Another incident cemented Jo Ann's complete disdain for her cousin. Bill and Glenna went to Charleston for the day, leaving Jo Ann in charge of Charlie, who then was about seven. Besides baby-sitting, the ten-year-old girl was instructed to clean the house. There was no question of Charlie helping. He routinely ignored his chores. Jo Ann was making one of the beds when Charlie wandered into the room, brandishing a razor-sharp sickle he'd brought in from the yard. He deliberately got in Jo Ann's way as she tried to pull and tuck in the sheets. Jo Ann glared at him and ordered Charlie to go outside. When he said "Make me," she shoved him out of the room and through the screened back door. Then she latched the door and went back to finish making the bed. Charlie screamed and slashed at the screen with the sickle; Jo Ann was certain that Charlie meant to use the blade on her once he got inside because he looked and sounded so crazy, completely out of control. Bill and Glenna returned just in time. They took in the torn back door screen, Charlie's furious red face, and Jo Ann's pale frightened one and demanded to be told what happened. Scared nearly speechless, Jo Ann mumbled, "Ask Charles." His version was that she started it and he was simply protecting himself. The elder Thomases didn't believe him, and Charlie got a whipping. "Of course it didn't make any difference," Jo Ann remembered seventy years later. "You could whip him all day and he'd still act however he wanted."

In the two and a half years that he lived with the Thomases, Charlie developed three interests. He became fascinated by knives or anything else that was sharp. He enjoyed handling guns, the only trait the kid exhibited that struck Uncle Bill as normal for a boy. And, above all, he fell in love with music. The Thomases had a piano. Charlie could sit down at it and pick out songs by ear. He would lose himself that way for hours. Charlie also surprised the Thomases with his nice voice. They had to drag him to church on Sundays, but once there he enjoyed singing hymns. Charlie's musical skills were the best thing about him.

Time passed slowly for Charlie's mother and uncle in the state prison. Despite cushy work assignments, Luther had it tougher than Kathleen.

His ten-year sentence was twice as long, and his marriage to Julia Vickers fell apart. Even though Luther knew that bad behavior would preclude his early release he kept committing small infractions. He stole some paper and lost his letter-writing privileges. Talking back to his job foreman cost him five days in solitary. After three years at Moundsville, Luther couldn't stand it anymore. He behaved for a while and was reassigned to the penitentiary garage. On February 21, 1942, he stole a prison truck and escaped. Luther was no better at prison breakouts than he'd been at armed robbery. He was back in custody three days later, and early release for good behavior was no longer an option.

Kathleen was more sensible. No record exists of her committing any prison infractions. She kept quiet, did her assigned work, and in late 1942 was paroled after serving three years of her five-year sentence. She told her family that all she wanted now was a quiet life with her son. They couldn't live with Nancy in Ashland because mother and daughter were not on good terms. Kathleen thought that if she moved back with Nancy she would once again be under her mother's thumb. The Thomases wanted Charlie gone, not the child staying and Kathleen moving in, too. So she and Charlie struck out on their own.

Not surprisingly, Charlie had only bad memories of his childhood years in McMechen. In the late 1970s he told an interviewer that all he remembered about life with the Thomases was being ordered to "do this (or) don't do that." The experience formed the basis for his adult philosophy that it was better for children to be separated from their parents: "The child is born free (and) he should develop without restrictions."

At the time, though, Charlie was thrilled to be back with Kathleen. He referred to the first weeks that he was reunited with his mother as the happiest days of his life. But that soon changed.

CHAPTER THREE

Kathleen and Charlie

Kathleen initially was hired as a barmaid in McMechen. She wasn't shunned because she'd just been released from prison. Lots of paroled inmates looked for work in the little towns around Moundsville, and there were always prospective employers willing to give them a chance at a fresh start. But Kathleen didn't stay in the area long. She may have been unsettled by proximity to the penitentiary where Luther was still incarcerated. Within weeks, she and eight-year-old Charlie moved to Charleston.

Van Watson hired Kathleen as a clerk at his grocery store, Van's Never Closed Market. Watson felt sorry for his new employee and her small son. They didn't appear to have any friends, so he sometimes invited them to dinner with his family. It was the kind of low-key job and understanding boss that Kathleen needed to readjust to normal society, but Charlie immediately began causing problems. He was enrolled in a local elementary school but seldom stayed in class. Kathleen had to be at work; she couldn't walk him to school and then stand guard outside his room to make certain he didn't sneak away. Charlie compounded his mother's frustration by showing up at the grocery during the days that he played hooky, asking for candy and often buying some with pennies he apparently cadged from store customers. One of the first things Kathleen noticed when she reunited with her son was that he tried to manipulate everyone, especially women. She realized that his interest in people was dictated by what they might be able to do for him. When he wanted to be, no one was more charming or persuasive than little Charlie.

Kathleen had other problems besides concern for her son. Dancing and drinking still appealed to her. After working all day she wanted to have some fun. It was hard finding someone responsible to keep Charlie when she went out as she did most nights. Kathleen was still only twenty-four. The lure of nightlife often overwhelmed her maternal instincts. Charlie ended up stashed with a series of questionable baby-sitters. Kathleen felt guilty about it, but she left him anyway.

Carousing wasn't Kathleen's only activity on these bar-hopping nights. She was on the hunt for a husband. Hard knocks had diminished her teenage belief in true love and living happily ever after, but Kathleen still yearned to be married to some man who would provide her and Charlie with a decent home and security. Even after three years of languishing in prison, her outgoing personality still attracted men. Shortly after immersing herself in Charleston bars, Kathleen believed she'd found someone. Though Van Watson couldn't remember the fellow's name, he later recalled agreeing when Kathleen asked him to drive her and her fiancé to North Carolina where they would be married. On the trip, Watson learned that Kathleen's intended was from New York. They didn't say why they wanted to be married in North Carolina, or why Charlie wasn't brought along. A few days later Kathleen, still single, came back to work. She didn't explain what happened and Watson didn't ask.

In this emotionally bleak time, Kathleen fell back into another bad habit. She was arrested by state police on charges of grand larceny; no details remain other than that the charges were dropped, and that authorities suspected Kathleen of committing these crimes under the aliases Kathleen Veron and Kathleen McTernan. She and Charlie left Charleston and drifted to temporary lodgings in and around Indianapolis. Fueled mostly by Charlie Manson's statements as an adult, it's popular belief that during this time Kathleen was a prostitute. Though it's impossible to be certain, there seem to be no records of her ever being charged with or even arrested for soliciting in Indianapolis or anywhere else. Kathleen was never any good at avoiding police notice. She probably ran through a series of legal but menial jobs, regularly seeking oblivion through drinking and permanent security from a husband. In trying to wean herself from one, she believed she'd found the other.

During the summer of 1943, Kathleen determined to get her life in order. In less than a year she'd been released from jail, engaged but not married, arrested again but not convicted, and had been an erratic guardian of her child. Charlie was about to turn nine, and he was increasingly incorrigible. Kathleen couldn't effectively correct the boy's bad habits without first admitting and dealing with her own. Above all, she was increasingly dependent on alcohol. Kathleen began attending meetings of Alcoholics Anonymous. At one she met Lewis, a twenty-seven-year-old who said he was trying hard to get straightened out, too. Lewis had a lot to overcome. His mother died when he was five, and his father spent several years in the same Moundsville prison where Kathleen and her brother, Luther, later served time. Lewis was just out of the Army; the fact that he was released from service during wartime indicates that he was something less than a model soldier. Currently, he was working in the property department of a circus.

It was hardly a pedigree to recommend Lewis as a source of long-term security, but it was enough for Kathleen. At the least, male day-to-day influence might help get Charlie under control. She married Lewis in August 1943. The wedding took place in St. Clairsville, Ohio, about a dozen miles across the Ohio River from McMechen. That meant the Thomases and Nancy were probably invited; as part of her new life, Kathleen wanted reconciliation with the rest of her family. She no longer expected fantasy romance or perfect happiness. It would be enough to be married and live something like a normal life. But because of her new husband as well as her son, Kathleen didn't get one.

Neither Kathleen nor Lewis became long-term members of Alcoholics Anonymous. She got her drinking under control and he didn't. From the first days of their marriage, Lewis caused Kathleen as many problems as Charlie did. Besides drinking too much and too often, her husband couldn't hang on to a job, which meant Kathleen had to keep working. Despite whatever he might have claimed before the wedding, afterward Lewis had no interest in helping raise her son. He had no patience with Charlie and thought that it was Kathleen's job to make the boy behave. He constantly criticized them both.

Kathleen understood that, once again, she'd made a bad choice in men, but at least in one way Lewis was different. Unlike Colonel Scott, William Manson, James Robey, and her unidentified fiancé from New

York, he wanted to stay with her. Being wanted long term by someone was a new experience for Kathleen; perhaps that was all women could expect from men. She decided to stick it out and make marriage with Lewis work.

But that left the problem of what to do with Charlie. His behavior kept getting worse. Now he was stealing things, small items from stores and anything of value he could get his hands on at home. Whenever she caught and confronted Charlie, he never apologized. Instead, he insisted that someone else was to blame, usually her, sometimes Lewis. She didn't give him enough, so he had to take things. Lewis was always yelling at him even when Charlie hadn't done anything, so he might as well do something wrong since he was going to be accused anyway. Charlie kept cutting school—every truant officer in Charleston probably knew his name—and neither threats nor bribes made any difference.

Kathleen's concern about her son was so great that she approached her mother for help. The two women had not been on good terms since Kathleen went to prison in 1939, but now Nancy was willing to set aside their differences for Charlie's benefit. Nancy talked to Charlie, undoubtedly invoking the Bible and its admonition to children to honor and obey their parents. Charlie wasn't rude to her—even in his worst moods he was reasonably pleasant to his grandmother. But afterward he didn't improve at all.

Kathleen surely felt guilty. She knew that her own aberrant behavior had been a terrible influence on Charlie. But even though she'd finally changed her ways, Charlie continued to lie, steal, and skip class. Every so often he'd lose control and scream, and then even though he was just a kid, barely five feet tall and maybe sixty or sixty-five pounds, he still scared Kathleen with his crazy eyes. Between Lewis and Charlie she felt sometimes like she was going insane. Probably nothing could change Lewis. He was grown and permanently set in his ways. But Charlie was young. Something might still be done—just not by her. Where her son was concerned, Kathleen had run out of energy and ideas.

She'd heard about foster care programs and schools that helped wayward boys. They might have a lot of rules and sternly enforce them, but maybe that was what Charlie needed, a firm hand from people who knew

how to communicate with problem boys like him. Kathleen had no intention of giving up Charlie permanently. But if he lived somewhere else
for a while and got the help he needed, she could concentrate on Lewis
and try to make him more responsible. If he didn't have Charlie around
aggravating him, maybe he'd drink less. Placing Charlie for a while in a
foster home or school might be best for all of them.

In 1947, without first informing twelve-year-old Charlie, who'd begun
running away from home for short periods and didn't need a new excuse
to do it again, Kathleen looked around for the right place for him. No appropriate foster care had openings. Then she found an Indiana school that
sounded just right. The Gibault School for Boys was in Terre Haute about
seventy-five miles from where Kathleen, Lewis, and Charlie lived in Indianapolis. The school, founded to offer a positive learning environment for
male delinquents, was run by Catholic priests. When the Brothers of the
Holy Cross replaced secular administrators in 1934, the student body was
comprised of thirty-five boys. By the time Kathleen sought a place there
for Charlie thirteen years later, there were about 125 students.

To hear Charlie tell of it later in life, his mother shipped him off to
a virtual Midwestern gulag, but in fact Gibault was a pleasant, open (no
fences or walls) campus. Pupils were accepted from fifth through tenth
grade, with shop as well as academic courses available. There were sports
teams, and the boys helped out on a 150-acre farm that provided fresh
vegetables for students and faculty.

Applicants did not need to be Catholic, but boys accepted at Gibault
were required to attend daily religious services as well as regular classes.
Besides charging tuition from parents who could afford it (Kathleen
would say later that she paid an unspecified amount to Gibault while
Charlie was there), the school was financially supported by various
Knights of Columbus councils. The priests demanded good behavior
from students and enforced rules by paddlings with a yard-long board.
School rules restricted this corporal punishment to no more than three
swats at a time. Charlie claimed he was regularly beaten by the priests
"with paddles as big as ball bats." Since his behavior didn't improve notably after arriving at Gibault in 1947, he undoubtedly did receive innumerable three-smack paddlings.

All new students underwent academic and psychological testing. Gibault found Charlie's "attitude toward schooling at best only fair," and, though there were sometimes short periods when he was "a likable boy," he mostly demonstrated "a tendency toward moodiness and a persecution complex." Charlie was unhappy at Gibault; he soon fled to his mother in Indianapolis. It hurt Kathleen to send him back; then and later he described Gibault as a terrible place where the priests hated him so much that they encouraged him to run away, but she knew Charlie was undoubtedly lying. Even so, he came close to persuading her that he'd learned his lesson and would never cause trouble again. After a few hours Kathleen steeled herself and took him back to Gibault.

In late December 1947 Charlie left Gibault again, this time on an approved pass to spend Christmas in McMechen with the Thomases. It was Jo Ann's idea. As much as she didn't like her cousin, she still thought it would be wrong to leave him at school for the holiday. Kathleen and Lewis stayed away—their current relationship was too tempestuous to inflict on the rest of the family. But besides Uncle Bill and Aunt Glenna and Cousin Jo Ann, there were two other relatives there to greet Charlie. His grandmother Nancy had moved to McMechen, and, having finally been paroled from Moundsville penitentiary, Charlie's Uncle Luther was there, too. Prison records indicate that sometime in 1944 Luther was stricken with tuberculosis and confined to the dispensary until January 1947. He was then released, too sick to work or even to live on his own. Instead Luther lived with his mother, and sometimes when he felt especially ill and needed additional care he would stay with the Thomases, where Glenna and Jo Ann could nurse him.

Luther was dying slowly and knew it. Though Nancy was saddened by her only son's plight, she was grateful that his eternal soul was saved. After so many years of resisting his mother's religious beliefs, Luther in his last years became a zealous convert to the Nazarene faith. His newfound devotion was such that, lying in his sickbed or propped up in a chair, he studied for the ministry. Only the precarious health that confined him indoors prevented Luther from seeking leadership of his own congregation. When he died in 1950, Luther's obituary made no reference to his prison term in Moundsville. He'd succeeded in publicly rehabilitating himself, and he made his mother proud.

Nancy and the Thomases suffered a real fright in mid-December 1947 when Jo Ann was also diagnosed with tuberculosis; she caught the disease while caring for her uncle. The sixteen-year-old was hospitalized, but her case was mild enough for her to be allowed to come home for Christmas. When Charlie arrived from Gibault, Jo Ann was confined to her bedroom. Charlie stayed with the Thomases and Luther was with Nancy. On Christmas Eve, everyone prepared for church with the exception of Jo Ann, who was too weak to go. She stayed in her room on the second floor and listened to the bustle as everyone got ready to leave. Then, to her dismay, Charlie stayed behind—she had no idea why her parents allowed it. But as soon as the door slammed behind her departing family, Jo Ann heard her cousin turn on the shower in the downstairs bathroom. Charlie wasn't interested in showering, she believed; Jo Ann remembered Charlie's fascination with guns, and guessed that the running water was meant to mask any noise her cousin might make opening a cabinet and stealing his Uncle Bill's handgun. Jo Ann didn't call down to ask Charlie what he was up to, or to warn him away from the weapon that she felt certain he was filching. Instead she lay quietly because she was afraid he might rush upstairs and hurt her if she tried to interfere. The shower ran the whole time that her other relatives were at church. When they returned, Glenna and Nancy went up to Jo Ann's room to see how she was feeling. They also wondered why the shower was running. Jo Ann told them to ask Charles, adding that she thought he'd stolen her father's gun and didn't try to prevent it because she was afraid of him. They confronted the boy; he had the gun. Well, that was Charles all over, Jo Ann thought. He'd been invited to McMechen for the holiday as a treat, and still he stole from his hosts. He felt that anything he wanted ought to be his no matter what.

Charlie returned to Gibault, but ran away about ten months later. He once again fled to Indianapolis, but this time he didn't go to his mother. Instead, demonstrating precocious criminal skills, he broke into a few small stores at night and rifled cash registers for enough change and small bills to rent a room. Nobody knows where Charlie stayed, but it could hardly have been anywhere reputable; no honest landlord would have rented to a tiny thirteen-year-old who looked even younger. Charlie soon pushed his burglary luck too far and was caught attempting another store break-in. That made Charlie's immediate future the responsibility of the courts rather than of his long-suffering mother. A sympathetic judge noted Charlie's time at Gibault, erroneously assumed that the boy was Catholic, and sent him to Boys Town in Omaha, Nebraska, a program founded by Father Edward J. Flanagan. Boys Town was the most famous juvenile facility in America, thanks in great part to the hit film of that title starring Spencer Tracy and Mickey Rooney. Charlie wasn't there long enough to see whether Boys Town deserved its reputation as the best place in the country for troubled youngsters to adopt more positive attitudes and lifestyles. Four days after he arrived at Boys Town, he and another student named Blackie Nielson stole a car and drove to Peoria, Illinois, where Blackie had an uncle who made his living as a thief. On the way, the boys somehow got their hands on a gun and committed two armed robberies, one of a grocery store and the other at a casino—the latter must have had lax or nonexistent security. This was a marked escalation in Charlie's criminal career. It was a big step up from trying to steal his Uncle Bill's gun to using a weapon in a holdup. Charlie was still just thirteen.

In Peoria, Charlie and Blackie worked for the latter's uncle as apprentice thieves much like Dickens's fictional Oliver Twist and Artful Dodger. But in real life Charlie had more in common with his mother, Kathleen, and Uncle Luther—he could never avoid capture long. After just two weeks of quasi-adult thievery he was back in custody; police nabbed him in an after-dark attempt to rob a Peoria business. The subsequent investigation linked Charlie to his two armed robberies, and this time there was no sympathetic judge to sentence him to Boys Town. Instead, Charlie was packed off to the Indiana Boys School in Plainfield, the type of institution commonly known as a "reform school." As with Gibault, student inmates there attended academic classes and took courses to learn employable trades. Unlike Gibault, boys at the facility in Plainfield weren't modestly rebellious and considered in need of relatively gentle correction. Ranging in age from ten to twenty-one, some Boys School inmates were there on a general charge of "incorrigibility," but many others among the four-hundred-plus juvenile population were in Plainfield for crimes like armed robbery and manslaughter. Accordingly, the Boys School was a sternly regimented place. Some staffers were devoted to disciplining rather than encouraging. Boys could receive whatever amount of physical correction adult staffers deemed appropriate. This ran a torturous gamut from simple whippings with paddles to duck walking (staggering painfully about with hands clasping ankles) and table bending (arching backward with shoulder blades barely touching the surface of a table; just holding that position for a few moments ensured that a boy could not walk normally for hours afterward). Even youngsters who behaved suffered physically on a regular basis. When they weren't in class—and classes were often canceled because teachers quit—students were frequently farmed out as field hands to local farmers who paid 50 cents an hour for the help. (The boys were allowed to keep 30 cents.) When staffers weren't paying close attention on school grounds during the day or in dormitories at night, bigger, older inmates had ample opportunity to physically and sexually brutalize smaller boys. For undersized boys like Charlie, the ultimate goal at Plainfield was not to reform, but to survive.

When Charlie Manson arrived at the Boys School in early 1949, he found himself in an environment where his usual tactics of lying, intimidating, whining, and otherwise manipulating others to get his way were ineffective. For all Charlie's remarkable criminal record for one so young, he was a beginner compared to lots of others boys in Plainfield. He claimed later that he was almost immediately raped by other students, who sodomized Charlie with the encouragement of a particularly sadistic staff member. If that is an embellishment, it is undoubtedly true that tiny Charlie was forced into sexual acts by stronger boys. Such experiences led him to develop an almost detached view of rape, whether suffered by himself or others. He said sixty years later, "You know, getting raped, they can just wipe that off . . . I don't feel that someone got violated and it's a terrible thing. I just thought clean it off, that's all that is."

Charlie couldn't cut classes as he had back in Charleston, but he still couldn't read beyond a basic grasp of a few printed words. He may have suffered from some learning disability, but such things weren't tested or even acknowledged at the Boys School. Reports from teachers indicate that Charlie "did good work only for those from whom he figured he could obtain something," and that he "professed no trust in anyone."

Since he was in constant danger of being beaten and suffering sexual assault, it was at Plainfield that Charlie developed a lifelong defense mechanism he later called the "insane game." In dangerous situations where he could not protect himself in any other way, he would act out to convince potential assailants that he was crazy. Using screeches, grimaces, flapping arms, and other extreme facial expressions and gestures, Charlie could often back off aggressors. It didn't always work; in Plainfield and later in adult prisons, Charlie sometimes had to submit to stronger inmates who didn't care whether their prey was crazy or not. In these cases, he did whatever he had to. At the Boys School and afterward, Charlie Manson always survived.

During Charlie's time at the Boys School, his mother was not often in touch with him and may not have visited her son at all. Kathleen was still trying to salvage her marriage to Lewis. On several occasions, fed up with his drinking, she left him. Though the length of their separations varied greatly, from only a few days to a later, longer span of several years, Kathleen didn't find herself able to completely break away. Lewis made it clear that he wanted to remain married; his repeated promises to reform resonated with a woman who desperately wanted some semblance of security in her life, even if that was only an alcoholic husband. Kathleen didn't stop loving Charlie; instead she hoped that reform school and professionals expert in combating delinquency might yet transform him into a better boy. She no longer believed that she could do it. If and when Charlie was judged ready for release, he needed to rejoin a stable family. For Charlie's sake as well as her own, Lewis remained Kathleen's priority.

In October 1949, Charlie joined six other boys in an escape attempt from Plainfield. It wasn't his first time; Boys School officials later stated he'd made four previous solo tries. This one made the papers because it was the largest mass escape in school history. While most of the other boys avoided immediate recapture, Charlie was nabbed after less than twelve hours of freedom. He was picked up in Indianapolis by a policeman who caught him trying to break into a gas station.

In February 1951, when he was sixteen, Charlie tried again. He and two other sixteen-year-olds sneaked off the Boys School campus, stole a car, and headed west. They apparently had no specific destination in mind besides getting as far away from Plainfield as they could. By this time, Charlie was veteran enough at the Boys School to align himself with one of its tougher inmates. Fellow escapee Wiley Senteney was sent to Plainfield for killing a holdup victim. Along with a boy named Oren Rust, Charlie and Wiley eluded capture for almost three days. They broke into a series of gas stations and were finally caught outside Beaver, Utah, in a roadblock set for a different robbery suspect. The juveniles were sent back to Indiana, where they faced Dyer Act charges of driving a stolen vehicle across a state line, a federal crime. Despite Senteney pleading to reporters that he ran from Boys School only because he was so badly beaten by staff there, all three were sentenced to the National Training School for Boys in Washington, D.C., where they were to remain until they turned twenty-one. Charlie didn't believe any new place could be as bad as Plainfield.

New arrivals at the National Training School were immediately given aptitude and intelligence tests. Though Charlie was judged illiterate, his IQ score of 109 was slightly above the national average of 100. His scores were satisfactory if unremarkable in mechanical aptitude and manual dexterity. The sixteen-year-old said that his favorite school subject was music. Charlie's case worker's initial summation was that the boy was aggressively antisocial, at least in part because of "an unfavorable family life, if it can be called family life at all." It's unknown whether this assessment was based in any part on input from Kathleen or whether the case worker just took Charlie's word for everything. But his slacker ways were readily apparent, as were Charlie's attempts to make it seem like he was trying to fit in when he really wasn't. After Charlie had been at the school for a month, the caseworker noted, "This boy tries to give the impression that he is trying hard to adjust although he actually is not putting forth any effort in this respect." Charlie also gave evidence of a desire to be dominant among fellow residents of his dormitory rather than being dominated as he was at Boys School: "I feel in time he will try to be a [big] wheel in the cottage."

Counting his time at Gibault, Charlie had now been in some form of reform school for more than four straight years, and he'd learned the ropes. Though the National Training School wasn't as onerous as

Boys School, it still was highly regimented. Charlie much preferred as an alternative the minimum security Natural Bridge Honor Camp in nearby Virginia. The most promising students from the National Training School were given the privilege of transferring to Natural Bridge, and Charlie was in no way promising. But he already had considerable gifts as a manipulator, and he brought these to bear on Training School psychiatrists. A summer 1951 psychological report stated that Charlie had a terrible sense of inferiority. Though Charlie had in compensation developed the sneaky skills of "a fairly 'slick' institutionalized youth," the report concluded that "one is left with the feeling that behind all this lies an extremely sensitive boy who has not yet given up in terms of securing some kind of love and affection from the world." By fall, one psychiatrist determined that what Charlie needed to turn his life around was something to give him self-confidence—a transfer to Natural Bridge, for example. The psychiatrist recommended the move and, on October 24, Charlie got his wish.

Soon afterward, Aunt Glenna Thomas visited him at his new school and promised administrators that she and Uncle Bill would give Charlie a home and help him find work if the honor camp would release him. It was a curious offer; the Thomases had been glad to get rid of Charlie eight years earlier when Kathleen was released from prison, and he'd tried to steal a gun from Bill when he was their guest for Christmas 1947. But the boy's grandmother lived near the Thomases in McMechen now, and Nancy surely lobbied them to help get Charlie out of reform school. Kathleen was still preoccupied with Lewis and not overtly involved in Glenna's plea for Charlie's release. Kathleen probably had no idea that Charlie's transfer at the honor camp was due in part to his convincing Training School psychiatrists that his mother had ignored and never loved him. But Glenna would not have made the overture to honor camp administrators if her sister hadn't supported it; Kathleen certainly hoped that nearly six years of confinement and tough rules had worked positive changes on her son.

A parole hearing for Charlie was scheduled for February 1952. All he had to do was follow Honor Camp rules and stay out of trouble until then; if he did, his release was practically assured. But this proved beyond him;

in January Charlie was caught sodomizing another boy while holding a razor blade to his victim's throat. Consenting homosexual intercourse was forbidden at the camp; forcible rape was considered an offense second only to murder. Charlie not only lost his chance for early release, he was immediately transferred to the Federal Reformatory in Petersburg, Virginia. Now seventeen, Charlie didn't attempt to make a good impression at the new location. Between his arrival on January 18 and a reformatory reporting period in August he committed "eight serious disciplinary offenses, three involving homosexual acts." Though Charlie remained small in stature, growing to only about five feet four (some adult prison measurements pegged him at five foot five), he now played the "insane game" well enough to act as predator much more often than victim.

Even though the reformatory in Petersburg was considered high security, administrators despaired of keeping others safe from Charlie. In late September he was transferred to a maximum security reformatory in Chillicothe, Ohio. Even there he was still considered dangerous to the general population: "In spite of his age he is criminally sophisticated [and] regarded as grossly unsuited for retention in an open reformatory type institution such as Chillicothe." Over five years, Charlie Manson had slid to the very bottom of the reform school pit. There was no lower place left to go until November 12, 1955, when he reached his twenty-first birthday and had to be set free. Any release prior to that was improbable; one evaluation declared that Charlie "shouldn't be trusted across the street." Reformatory authorities who'd dealt with the worst delinquents in America concluded that Charlie Manson was beyond rehabilitating.

Then Charlie shocked them all. He couldn't erase forced rape and other egregious offenses from his record, but he could appear to do by himself what reformatory professionals believed he couldn't achieve even with their help—become a model inmate and, once again, a candidate for early release. Throughout his life, Charlie would outwardly reform or at least summon the self-discipline to keep his worst inclinations under control for short periods. This time was by far the most extended.

Beginning in the fall of 1952, Charlie stopped committing serious infractions. He spent all of 1953 working hard at academics. It was noted in his record that Charlie raised his general skills from a fourth to upper seventh grade level, and "he can now read most [printed] material and use simple arithmetic." Charlie also shone in his assigned work in the reformatory transportation unit, where he did maintenance work on the facility's cars and trucks. This background in automobile engine upkeep and repair would serve him well later on. Combined with his unexpected progress in class, Charlie's exemplary work record impressed the staff at Chillicothe to the extent that on January 1, 1954, he was presented with an award for meritorious service. Four months later the prison recognized his apparently changed attitude in the most significant way possible: At age nineteen, and after seven years in six different reform schools, Charlie was released to live with his uncle and aunt.

Modern experts in child psychology, juvenile justice, and the history of the American reform school system in the 1950s agree that Charlie's adult pattern of lawbreaking and violence was virtually guaranteed by the experiences of his childhood. He had no nurturing father figure. While his mother loved him, Kathleen often battled her own demons at the expense of her son's emotional security. Charlie entered the reformatory school jungle as an undersized, helpless twelve-year-old who survived by convincing bigger, predatory kids that he was crazy. The most notable skills Charlie exhibited as a child were criminal—he could steal cars, break into small businesses, rifle safes, and commit armed robberies like a grown-up. His childhood was certainly troubled in ways that were no fault of his own. But there was also something in Charlie that consistently led him to act out in ways completely against his own self-interest. He made bad situations in which he found himself even worse. Charlie proved that again when he returned to McMechen.

CHAPTER FOUR

McMechen Again

When Charlie Manson left the reformatory in Chillicothe in May 1954 and returned to McMechen, the West Virginia town was little changed. But America was changing. National debates over the threat of communism, the wisdom of placing military advisors in South Vietnam, and the ruling by the Supreme Court in *Brown v. Board of Education* that segregated schools were unconstitutional had no impact on daily life in McMechen. Town residents were deliberately insular. The city of Wheeling a few miles to the north was widely recognized as a regional hotbed of crime, with prostitution and gambling controlled by mobster "Big Bill" Lias, and Moundsville to the south was a brooding place dominated by the penitentiary. McMechen took pride in its working-class decency.

As he returned to McMechen, Charlie's immediate concern was where he would stay. His release technically required him to live with Glenna and Bill Thomas. They had plenty of room at their house. Jo Ann had married a minister; she and her husband lived several miles across the river in Ohio. But Charlie and Uncle Bill still didn't get along. An intriguing possibility for Charlie was to live with his mother. Kathleen had recently moved to nearby Wheeling. She was still trying to hold together her marriage with Lewis, and Charlie had some of the same problems with him as he did with Uncle Bill. Though mother and son were glad to see each other again, Kathleen didn't feel that she could allow Charlie to be anything more than an occasional overnight guest.

So Charlie sometimes stayed with the Thomases, less frequently with Kathleen, and most nights lived in a small house on 15th Street with his grandmother Nancy. She still doted on the boy, and believed that with proper guidance Charlie might yet make a godly life for himself.

With the question of where he would live resolved, Charlie looked for work. It was harder for him than for other young men in town. Charlie didn't have a father to put in a good word at the company where he worked. He didn't have a high school diploma, or even experience at a part-time job beyond his work assignments in various reformatories. He was finally hired at Wheeling Downs, a local racetrack. Charlie swept out stables and cleaned up after horses as they were walked about the grounds. His salary was meager even by local standards. But it was still honest, legal employment that satisfied the terms of his reformatory release. Besides, Charlie loved animals and enjoyed being around them, even with a bucket and shovel. The hardest part of the racetrack job was that other people were always telling him what to do. Charlie felt like he'd been bossed around all his life and was tired of it. He wanted to be the one in charge.

With a place to live and a job, Charlie set out to explore social life. This proved hardest of all. In general, people in McMechen didn't hold his reformatory time against him. Lots of families had a child or two who'd been in trouble. But the town was still clannish and protective of its teenagers. McMechen parents tried to provide their youngsters with plenty of wholesome entertainment possibilities. Most Fridays and Saturdays found events scheduled at the high school gym—sock hops, bake sales, amateur theatricals, anything to keep kids busy and out of trouble. Everyone turned out for sports events featuring the local school teams. Very few of the teenage boys had cars. They wore near-identical flannel shirts, blue jeans, and Converse sneakers. Teen girls wore dresses to school and on most weekend outings. When they wanted fluffy curls they wrapped their hair around cardboard toilet paper rolls. At parties a popular prank was dropping aspirin in cups of Pepsi or Coke; the combination supposedly made you feel a little bit drunk. Most of the teenagers had known each other all their lives. Newcomer Charlie, with no social skills to speak of—reform schools didn't offer training in asking girls on dates or laughing with pals at the movies—seemed incapable of breaking into their circle.

Charlie's best chance to make friends was directly related to a demand from his grandmother. He was allowed to live with Nancy only if he faithfully attended Sunday morning services with her at the Nazarene church across from her house. Originally formed in 1907 as a coalition of conservative, "holiness" churches, Nazarene enclaves were soon established all over the country. Small-town Appalachia, where so many believers sprang from fundamentalist roots, proved to be particularly fertile ground. It was natural for a Nazarene church to be founded in McMechen, but it did not flourish there. Almost everyone in town went to worship on Sunday, just not as Nazarenes. Most McMechenites preferred a friendly, understanding God to a my-way-or-hell Lord, and many did not consider the small cinder block church a warm, inviting place. Nazarene Sunday attendance topped out at about eighty according to its members, and at fifty or so in the opinion of outsiders. Either way, it was one of the smallest congregations in town. But the Maddox family was always well represented. Besides Nancy, Bill and Glenna Thomas were also members. Kathleen, just a few miles away in Wheeling, never joined the Nazarenes in McMechen or affiliated herself with any other denomination. Nancy's fundamentalist faith soured Kathleen on attending church forever, though, in her own way, she still believed in God.

Each Sunday found Charlie in shirt and tie sitting next to his grandmother at the Nazarene service. She expected him to pay attention to the minister and sometimes Charlie did. The uncomfortable wooden pews made it too hard to doze off. So Charlie heard on a weekly basis that the Holy Scripture contained no errors at all, that women were meant to be subservient to men, and that in order to achieve salvation it was necessary to follow the instructions in 1 Thessalonians—to completely empty yourself by giving up your individuality and pride and possessions. Some biblical passages, including colorful sections from the apocalyptic Book of Revelation that described a bottomless pit, were cited so often that Charlie had ample opportunity to learn them by heart. As with song lyrics, Charlie had a knack for recalling Scripture.

Besides requiring him to go to church with her on Sundays, Nancy also insisted that Charlie join the church's Sunday School class for teenagers, attend their meetings, and participate in their social functions. Though he dutifully attended Sunday services with his grandmother, Charlie was less amenable to spending more of each weekend perched in a pew listening to the Nazarene minister lecture about all the things God didn't want young people to do. Though the dozen or so other teenagers there seemed to hang on every word, Charlie was always restless. Since he was out of Nancy's sight, he wasn't shy about showing it. Called on to offer comment, Charlie often responded insolently. He slouched where he sat, propped his feet up on the row in front of him, and even carved his initials on a pew.

Charlie didn't care what the pastor thought of him, but he cared very much about the opinions of his Sunday School classmates. Though they apparently bought in to church restrictions Charlie personally found laughable—all those biblical contradictions! You were commanded to honor your parents (like Charlie's were even worth honoring), yet you were also supposed to reject them to follow Jesus—these teens were still the closest thing to potential friends that he had. Charlie set out to impress them, but picked the worst way. In reform school, popular, dominant boys usually had the lengthiest, most colorful criminal records. Far from minimizing his delinquent past to the Nazarene kids, Charlie mistakenly tried to glorify it by emphasizing that he was worldly in ways that these small-town teens were not. He bragged about reformatory fights, running from the law, and even his considerable experience "shooting up."

It was this last claim that undid him with the Sunday School youth. Even with protective parents and hovering church elders, teens in Mc-Mechen had some familiarity with sin. High school boys sneaked into town bars and if no responsible adults were there they were sometimes allowed to buy shots of whiskey—under curious local law, bartenders might be fined if caught peddling liquor to minors, but a bar's license would be revoked if anyone underage was sold beer on the premises. Everybody knew there were prostitutes in Wheeling and sometimes for a lark McMechen kids would take the bus there and gawk at the painted women. Just about all the town teens, Nazarene or not, sneaked cigarettes. But none of them had any idea of what Charlie Manson meant when he claimed that he'd been shooting up. The kids knew nothing about drugs. They'd never heard the word "marijuana," let alone references to anything harder. It baffled them, but they decided that they didn't like the sound of it.

The Nazarene kids closed ranks against Charlie. On Halloween the youth group had a combination costume party/hot dog cookout at one girl's house. For once, Charlie enthusiastically participated. It was his first costume party, and he decked himself out as a carnival barker complete with arm garter and a big black hat. But when Charlie arrived, none of the kids except the embarrassed young hostess and her cousin would even speak to him. He gamely posed with them for a photograph, but the rejection stung. And when the Sunday School teens discussed Charlie with their non-Nazarene friends at school, the shunning spread to include all the self-styled decent kids in McMechen. By not even acknowledging Charlie as they passed him on the street or bumped into him at the grocery store, the town's other teenagers also made it clear that they were not interested in his company. Charlie got the message. He was a social outcast.

Jo Ann was astonished when Charlie showed up unexpectedly one afternoon at her home across the river from McMechen in Ohio. It was miles from her grandmother's house in West Virginia and Charlie didn't have a car. Either he'd taken the bus or walked. Ever since Charlie got out of reform school, Jo Ann had avoided seeing him, and he hadn't shown any interest in reconnecting with her, either. Now Jo Ann felt obligated to invite him in, even though her minister husband was there counseling a troubled teenage member of his church who was having problems getting along with her parents. As soon as Charlie was introduced to the girl he completely ignored Jo Ann and her husband. Charlie built the teenager up, telling her she was so special and pretty; Jo Ann felt that next he would ask her to leave the house with him and go God knew where to do God knew what. The way Charlie was acting with the girl felt wrong and evil. So Jo Ann said loudly that Charles needed to get back home to McMechen, and she made sure that he was gone before she let the girl out of her sight. "He was a good talker and would have gotten her for some bad purpose otherwise," Jo Ann said.

Though he'd learned to give and take sexual relief with other boys in reform school, Charlie was mostly attracted to women. He could go to the prostitutes in Wheeling, but they cost money that Charlie didn't have. The thing about the prostitutes that mostly interested Charlie was how they subsidized their pimps—men making their livings off of subservient women seemed like a fine thing to him. Meanwhile, what he really wanted was a girlfriend, and Charlie's near-universal unpopularity among other McMechen teens made it unlikely that he could find one in his current hometown. Then fate intervened in the form of someone else controversial.

Clarence Willis was nicknamed Cowboy because of the Stetson hat that he wore everywhere. Cowboy got a scandalous reputation in McMechen for divorcing his wife, Virginia, and moving to a small apartment in town, leaving her, their three daughters, and son behind in his old house. Virginia remarried, and Cowboy somewhat mitigated local scorn by remaining on decent terms with his ex-wife and kids. He worked for the Baltimore & Ohio Railroad and spent weekends making and usually losing small bets at Wheeling Downs. On one of his excursions there he met Charlie Manson and took a shine to him. Cowboy made a point of introducing Charlie to his children.

The Willis girls were especially pretty and had lively personalities. Eileen, the oldest, married a man who coached the town's youth baseball team. Even though she was still in high school, younger sister Rosalie took a part-time job at Warsinsky's Grocery Store. It was either there or at her father's apartment that Rosalie met Charlie Manson. Charlie turned the full force of his personality on her. Perhaps this time he was smart enough not to brag about shooting up. Whatever Charlie did, it worked. He and Rosalie began going steady. It was an unlikely romance between a cute, popular girl and the town pariah; observers agreed that every town seemed to have at least one nice girl who couldn't resist a bad boy. But dating was one thing; only a few months later most of McMechen was staggered to learn that Rosalie Willis and Charlie Manson were getting married. It was assumed that they had to—"the baby came early and the wedding came late," in local parlance. If Rosalie was pregnant, she didn't carry the baby to term. But on January 13, 1955, Charlie and Rosalie applied for a marriage license at the Marshall County courthouse in Moundsville. Charlie incorrectly gave his birthdate as November 11, 1933, making himself a year older than his actual age of twenty, and Rosalie claimed to be seventeen, though some in modern-day McMechen believe that she was two years younger. Cowboy Willis and his ex-wife were required to give consent for their underage daughter to marry. The wedding took place four days later at the Nazarene Church. Afterward Nancy gave a reception for the newlyweds in her home. Most of the congregation attended, and crowded around as a beaming Charlie and his teenage bride cut and handed out slices from a sizable wedding cake. They may not have liked Charlie much, but they all loved his grandmother. Jo Ann and her husband stayed away; she couldn't stand Charlie and didn't feel obligated to pretend any longer. Kathleen wasn't there, either. She had left Lewis again, and this time she put the most distance possible between them by moving all the way west to California.

For a little while, Charlie Manson tried to be a typical McMechen resident. He and his bride found an inexpensive place to rent. Charlie kept his job at Wheeling Downs and looked for other part-time work to bring in extra money. Often, McMechenites spent pleasant evenings perched out on front stoops, calling out greetings and chatting with passersby. Now Charlie and Rosalie joined her mother and stepfather on their porch, engaging in friendly banter with neighbors until bedtime. Once when some kids needed a ride to baseball practice, Charlie borrowed a car and took them. He seemed to look for small ways to demonstrate that he was really a nice guy. Some people warmed to Charlie just a little. He seemed to be acting normal. Ethel Miller, whom everybody in town loved because she extended credit at her grocery to any neighbors who needed it, hired Charlie to do some fix-ups at the store. When he wasn't on the job out at the track you'd see him at Miller's hammering and sawing and generally doing honest, respectable work. Charlie still wasn't popular, but now he was tolerated.

Charlie finally made a few friends, though not from among the Nazarene teens. As a married man living with his wife, he no longer had to please his grandmother with church or Sunday School attendance. Charlie found companionship with Buster Willis, his brother-in-law, and with Junior Mulgrew. Junior was the one young man in McMechen whose reputation was worse than Charlie's. During the day he loafed around a gas station near the high school, and at night he roared up and down the area's narrow roads in a Studebaker Golden Hawk, much too fancy a ride for a kid with no discernible income. Charlie and Buster and Junior palled around together when Charlie wasn't working or with his wife. If his grandmother Nancy disapproved of the new company he was keeping, it didn't bother Charlie. He didn't need anything from her anymore, so her opinion no longer mattered.

Somehow Charlie got his hands on a guitar and learned to play basic chords. He strummed and sang along with tunes on the radio and particularly liked Frankie Laine. Besides Laine's countryish hits of "That Lucky Old Sun" and "High Noon (Do Not Forsake Me)," Charlie favored the crooner's more middle-of-the-road recordings, lush ballads like "Jezebel" and "I Believe." Charlie liked Frank Sinatra and Perry Como, too, but not as much as Laine. As he once had on his Aunt Glenna's piano, Charlie spent hours plinking on his guitar. Though Charlie had a high opinion of his ability, he was no virtuoso; his playing didn't advance much beyond beginner's level. Music was just a hobby, a distraction from the constant concern about paying his bills.

Charlie's attempt to fit in lasted only a few months. Whether she'd miscarried earlier or not, Rosalie became pregnant. Her trips to the doctor added to costs for rent and food strained the young couple's finances. Even the extra money Charlie brought in from part-time jobs wasn't enough. It was natural for him to fall back on his criminal past to make up the difference, but it wouldn't be easy. The most obvious way for Charlie to make quick, fairly substantial money was by stealing cars. There were plenty close by, especially in Wheeling, for him and his pals Buster and Junior to heist. But to do that would be to court death as well as arrest and imprisonment. An army of Wheeling mobsters led by Big Bill Lias zealously guarded their territory. Lias and his crew gained most of their illicit income from men who came from as far away as Pittsburgh to gamble and dally with hookers in the casinos, bars, and hotels that Lias operated. News of car thefts in Wheeling might discourage them from driving to town. Accordingly, the Wheeling mob wouldn't wait for police to solve the crimes. They'd hunt down the car thieves themselves and make short, bloody work of them as a warning to others. Charlie knew from painful reform school experience that it was suicidal to take on tougher guys.

To avoid attracting the wrath of Lias, Charlie stole cars across the river in Ohio. He drove one car all the way down to Florida and unloaded it there. In the process of crossing state lines in the stolen vehicle he once again violated the Dyer Act and was guilty of a federal crime, this time as an adult, not as a juvenile.

Spring 1955 turned into summer, and Charlie saw no reason to remain in McMechen. He told people that he wanted to go see his mother in California. That bothered Jo Ann. She couldn't stand Charlie, but she thought it was in some way poignant that, after everything, he still loved his mother so much that he was willing to cross the country to be with her. Rosalie, in early middle pregnancy, was willing to go west. In July Charlie stole a 1953 Mercury in Bridgeport, Ohio, and he and his wife drove all the way to Los Angeles.

When Charlie arrived, he reconnected with Kathleen—Lewis wasn't around to begrudge her spending time with her son—and Charlie scratched out a living doing odd jobs. He and Rosalie apparently stayed with his mother. Los Angeles dwarfed any other place Charlie had been; he drove around the city in the stolen Mercury as if the car were legitimately his own. He called Jo Ann back in Ohio to brag that he was having the best time of his life. But in September an eagle-eyed L.A. cop checked the Mercury's out-of-state license plate, discovered that the car was stolen, and arrested Charlie. In federal court Charlie admitted the Mercury theft. He pleaded with the judge for leniency, claiming that he'd been confused ever since his release from the reformatory at Chillicothe. As further proof of his shaky mental state he also confessed to taking another stolen car from Ohio to Florida.

The judge ordered psychiatric testing. Dr. Edwin McNiel met with Charlie, who said that he'd originally been sent to reform school for being mean to his mother. After so many years in reformatories he had trouble adjusting to the regular world. Charlie claimed that he loved his wife very much. Maybe he'd beaten her a few times; when he got frustrated with life he sometimes turned mean—he knew that he needed to control his temper better. But now that Rosalie was pregnant he desperately wanted to stay out of prison to be with her. Dr. McNiel reported to the court that, based on his past record, Charlie was a poor risk for probation. But "with the incentive of a wife and probable fatherhood, it is possible that he might be able to straighten himself out." On November 7 Charlie was sentenced to five years' probation.

Charlie still had to face charges on the stolen car he drove down to Florida; he was ordered to return to court in L.A. in February 1956. There was very little chance that he would face any actual jail time. A few more years of probation was likely going to be tacked on to the first sentence. But Charlie panicked and ran. He and Rosalie went to ground in Indianapolis. It was a familiar place and he thought he could hide there. On March 10, Rosalie gave birth to a son, who was named Charles Manson Jr. If Charlie took any pleasure in the birth of his child it was short-lived. The Los Angeles court had issued a bench warrant, Indianapolis cops were looking for him, and on March 14 Charlie was taken into custody. Indiana returned him to California, and on April 23 Charlie's probation was revoked. He'd turned twenty-one in November, so he was too old for reform school. The judge gave Charlie three years at San Pedro's Terminal Island Penitentiary in Los Angeles Harbor.

CHAPTER FIVE

Prison

Charlie caught a break when he was sent to Terminal Island. It was one of a handful of federal prisons intended to house low-risk, nonviolent prisoners. Many Terminal Island inmates began their sentences at higher security prisons and then transferred to the San Pedro facility for their last few months or years before release. Even though Charlie had an extensive record as a juvenile offender, as an adult he'd been found guilty only of car theft and an ill-advised flight from sentencing. Still, the Terminal Island counselor who conducted Charlie's orientation exam predicted that he might prove to be a disciplinary problem because he had trouble controlling himself.

Despite its designation as a place for low-risk inmates, Terminal Island was still a prison. Charlie was used to reformatories where the most grizzled inmates were still teenagers. The Terminal Island prisoner population included older, longtime cons who dominated everyone else. Charlie's "insane game" would have no effect on them. He realized that and spent his first months there quietly observing. Those convicted of white-collar crimes held no interest for Charlie. He was never going to be in position to embezzle funds from a bank or put together a fraudulent multimillion-dollar real estate deal. But just as he had been on earlier visits to Wheeling, he was still fascinated by pimps. At Terminal Island, they were sometimes willing to talk about the intricacies of their trade. They bragged to Charlie about recruiting young women and bending them to their will. You had to know how to pick out just the right girls, Charlie learned, the ones with self-image or Daddy problems who'd buy into come-ons from a smooth talker. First you kept them separated from family and friends. Then you brought them under your control with a judicious combination of affectionate gestures and just enough beatings to remind them who was boss—Charlie yearned to be somebody's boss. The veteran pimps cautioned him that it was critical to stay away from women who were completely nuts, because then you'd spend all your time propping them up emotionally instead of sending them out on the street to work. You wanted girls who were cracked but not broken. The trick was to make them love you and fear you at the same time. Charlie listened and learned.

His initial months at Terminal Island were brightened by weekly visits from Rosalie and Charlie Jr. Kathleen came less often but still regularly. Rosalie and the baby were living with her and Kathleen was apparently their sole source of support. Having visitors was a status symbol among prisoners, and Charlie always enjoyed any sort of status. Getting attention remained important to him. Prison officials even restricted him to small work details because Charlie admitted to "a tendency to cut up and misbehave if [I am] around a [larger] gang." He seemed to have the potential to become a model prisoner; one report noted that Charlie's work performance improved as his first parole hearing neared, proof that he could demonstrate self-control if he wanted to. All signs pointed to early release, perhaps even after serving just a year or so of his three-year sentence.

Then, abruptly, Rosalie stopped coming. She'd left West Virginia with the expectation of a more exciting life in California. Sharing a cramped apartment with her mother-in-law and visiting her husband in jail every week fell far short of that. Kathleen had to break the news to Charlie that his wife had moved out and was living with another man. Charlie, who thought he understood women so well, was taken completely by surprise. Rosalie soon returned to Appalachia with her new beau, taking Charlie Jr. with her. Charlie was subsequently served with divorce papers; his marriage was over.

Rosalie's adult life got off to a rough start with Charlie, and even after she left him it remained rocky. She moved around a lot—to Ohio, Nevada, and Arizona as well as towns in California—and remarried several times before she died of lung cancer in Tucson in 2009. She was not married at the time, but her obituary noted the presence of a "loving companion." Also according to the obituary, Rosalie "enjoyed playing golf, bowling, dancing, playing cards, slot machines and spending time with her family." That may have been true with children from her post-Manson marriages, but for the last sixteen years of Rosalie's life it wasn't the case with Charles Jr. He committed suicide in 1993. Even though he called himself Charles White, taking the last name of his mother's second husband, Charles Jr. was well aware of his real father's identity. It apparently troubled him greatly.

Just before Rosalie deserted him, Charlie was transferred to Terminal Island's minimum security cells in a separate prison building. It was a clear signal that he could expect imminent release after his parole hearing on April 22, 1957, but Charlie, stunned by Rosalie's desertion, exhibited one of his periodic lapses of patience and self-control. On April 10 he was caught in the prison parking lot wearing civilian clothes and trying to hotwire a car. Twelve days later his near-certain parole was denied, and five years' additional probation were tacked on to his original three-year prison sentence.

Terminal Island officials didn't give up on Charlie. He'd scored 121 on an IQ test when he'd arrived at the prison, which placed him in the "high normal" range. His subpar reading skills and primitive, chicken-scratch handwriting indicated lack of educational opportunity, not ability. As it happened, Terminal Island had a wide variety of self-improvement courses available to inmates, the result of a nationwide penal system overhaul intended to prepare prisoners for success in the outside world. In the 1940s and early 1950s prison focus was on punishment; by 1957 it was rehabilitation. At Terminal Island, inmates could work toward high school diplomas, learn car repair or machine shop skills, or even be tutored in how to apply for jobs. Charlie, still just twenty-two, spurned all of these opportunities but one. In another decade it would become fashionable for young people to seek out and follow gurus, spiritual advisors who would lead them on the path to enlightenment. To date at Terminal Island, Charlie's unofficial tutors had been pimps, and he eagerly absorbed what they had to teach him. But now, Charlie latched on to someone whose wisdom would guide many of his future acts—a man who though they never met became Charlie Manson's personal guru.

Born on a Missouri farm in 1888, Dale Carnegie was a successful salesman before developing self-help instruction that emphasized ways to win over individuals and audiences. Initially, Carnegie targeted his how-to lectures and print publications toward businessmen, offering lessons in effective public speaking and product sales. But in 1936 *How to Win Friends and Influence People*, aimed at a general audience, became a massive bestseller (five million copies) and made Carnegie one of the most famous men in America. He founded the Dale Carnegie Institute. Crowds flocked to its programs. Carnegie never claimed there was anything unique about the techniques he proselytized; his gift was gathering all the best methods of influencing others and relating them in easy-to-understand, one-step-at-a-time instruction. Those who couldn't attend Carnegie classes in person received instruction through correspondence courses, and by 1957 Carnegie's reach even extended to classes conducted in selected prisons. Terminal Island was one of them.

The Dale Carnegie course was one of Terminal Island's most popular programs for its convicts. There was a waiting list of prisoners who wanted to enroll. Class was limited to twenty-five or thirty inmates, and instruction lasted about four months. As a relatively new inmate, and one with an escape attempt already on his record, Charlie ranked low among applicants. But prison officials believed that Dale Carnegie's positive outlook on life might be just what moody, erratic Charlie needed. He was jumped ahead of everyone else and enrolled in the course. Besides lectures, class members were expected to read *How to Win Friends and Influence People*, study several pamphlets (probably including *Effective Speaking and Human Relations* and an early edition of *How to Remember Names*), and occasionally turn in written assignments. Charlie had always evinced limited reading skills, but in this Carnegie class he proved that he could not only read but fully comprehend printed material if he was sufficiently engaged, and if instructors were helpful enough. Virtually every word in the Carnegie publications resonated with Charlie. For the first time in his life he was considered an outstanding pupil.

The first pages of *How to Win Friends* seemed to formally codify all the instinctive ways Charlie had manipulated people since childhood. It was as though Dale Carnegie not only read Charlie's mind, but recruited him as a disciple by elaborating on Charlie's own thoughts.

*"Everything you or I do springs from two motives: The sex urge and the
    desire to be great."*
"Begin in a friendly way."
*"The only way on earth to influence the other fellow is to talk about
    what he wants and show him how to get it."*
"Make the other person feel important."
"The only way to get the best of an argument is to avoid it."
*"You have to use showmanship. The movies do it. Radio does it. And
    you will have to do it if you want attention. . . . Dramatize your
    ideas."*

Chapter Seven, "How to Get Co-Operation," contained advice that
Charlie adopted as the most vital tool in his manipulative arsenal: *"Let the
other fellow feel that the idea is his."* Later, when police, judges, and juries
struggled to understand how Charlie Manson was able to convince others to carry out his criminal directives, they could have found the answer
there in *How to Win Friends and Influence People.* Over half a century later
Phil Kaufman, who knew Manson in prison and later in Los Angeles,
remembered, "That was Charlie's big trick. He'd decide what he wanted
[someone] to do and then talk about it so the girl or whoever would think
that she thought of it and it was her idea. I saw him do it all the time.
I mean, it was constant. It was where he got his power over [gullible]
people."

Charlie's instructors in Terminal Island's Dale Carnegie course were
surprised when their star pupil quit before completing the four-month
program. But once he felt that he'd learned what he needed, Charlie had
no further interest in sitting in a classroom. He was ready to move on.

Charlie spent the rest of his time at Terminal Island thinking about
what he would do next—thanks to all he gleaned from imprisoned pimps
and Dale Carnegie, he had a plan. To keep in decent physical shape he
boxed and played in pickup basketball games. Charlie was a good athlete.
For recreation he played his guitar; Frankie Laine's songs were still his favorites. Above all, Charlie stayed out of trouble. Like every other federal
prison, Terminal Island was overcrowded and it was standard procedure
to grant early parole to inmates who behaved. On September 30, 1958,

Charlie was released after serving two years and five months of his original three-year sentence.

As a condition of his release, Charlie was required to report regularly to a parole officer. He stated that he planned to live with his mother in her Los Angeles apartment. Kathleen had some doubts about how well that arrangement would work, but she also felt obligated to try to help her son build a new, law-abiding life. She was still separated from Lewis, though his pleas for reconciliation moved her and Kathleen was thinking about trying with him again. If she reunited with her estranged husband, Charlie would have to live somewhere else—he and Lewis could never get along. But in the meantime, Kathleen told Charlie that he could stay with her.

Charlie also had to demonstrate to his parole officer that he could find and maintain gainful employment. The finding part didn't prove difficult—lots of menial jobs were available in Los Angeles—but keeping a steady job seemed beyond him. In rapid order Charlie worked as a busboy, a bartender, a gas station attendant, and a frozen food locker clerk. Getting fired on a regular basis didn't really bother him; the idea was to be working somewhere that the parole officer could check when Charlie went in to see him. All the while, Charlie was setting himself up to make a full-time living in the business that he now believed was his natural calling.

Charlie's career as a pimp got off to a slow start. Judy and Flo, the first two girls he recruited, didn't last long on the streets. Little is known about them besides that Judy's father complained about Charlie to the cops, and that was the last thing Charlie needed. If he hadn't understood it before, he made it a rule afterward—none of his women were allowed to maintain close ties to their families, except in cases like Flo's, since she regularly got money from her parents. Charlie moved out of his mother's apartment—Kathleen had a pretty good idea of what he was up to, and she didn't approve. Instead Charlie took up residence with another pimp, who unfortunately for Charlie was being covertly monitored by the FBI. Federal agents shared Charlie's new address and apparent wrongdoing with his parole officer, who called Charlie in. He denied everything but wasn't convincing. Charlie's next court report noted that "This certainly is a very shaky probationer and it seems just a matter of time before he gets in further trouble."

Charlie may have envisioned pimping out dozens of high-dollar girls in Los Angeles and living in relative luxury on their earnings, but the hard truth was that he found it impossible to scrape together even a modest living from the pittance his limited, ever-changing lineup brought in. He fell back on his old criminal habits, though not for very long. On May 1, 1959, just seven months after he'd been paroled from Terminal Island, Charlie was arrested for attempting to cash a forged U.S. Treasury check for $37.50 at a Ralph's supermarket. He told the L.A. cops who picked him up that he'd stolen the check from a mailbox, meaning he'd committed two federal offenses. The police turned him over to the Secret Service; when a pair of federal agents questioned Charlie, they showed him the check and formally asked if he'd forged the signature on it. Charlie tried to outfox them; a post-interrogation report noted, "The check itself has disappeared; [the agents] feel certain [the] subject took it off [the] table and swallowed it when they momentarily turned their backs." Unfortunately for Charlie, the Ralph's clerk, the arresting L.A. policemen, and the federal agents all testified that they'd seen the check and his forged signature on the back of it. The case against him proceeded.

Kathleen was shaken by Charlie's latest misadventure. She wasn't surprised that he'd tried his hand at pimping—he always seemed able to make girls do whatever he wanted—but it seemed as though her son was destined to be a career criminal. Summer 1959 was a hard time for Kathleen. On July 19, Nancy Maddox died back in West Virginia. Kathleen's own experience with Charlie had taught her how much a child's criminal behavior could hurt a parent, and she deeply regretted the pain she had caused her mother. There was no way now to make up for it; all Kathleen could do was to continue supporting Charlie in his time of trouble, since she felt responsible for the bad way he'd turned out.

In mid-September, nineteen-year-old Leona Rae Musser met with Charlie's probation officer and informed him that she was pregnant with Charlie's baby. She pleaded for the charges against Charlie to be dismissed; then she and Charlie would get married and he would go straight. Leona wasn't pregnant; she was working for Charlie as a prostitute. But she managed to elicit sympathy from the parole officer and the court. A deal was struck: Charlie would plead guilty to forging the check, and the mail theft charge would be dropped. Charlie was sent back to Dr. Edwin McNiel, who'd examined him four years earlier after his arrest for car theft. Dr. McNiel's latest opinion was that Charlie was a terrible risk for probation and should be returned to prison, but at his trial in September Leona made another tearful plea and swayed the judge. Charlie received a ten-year suspended sentence and remained on probation.

The close call didn't faze him; he continued pimping out Leona and whatever other girls he could attract to his stable. Even though everything in his criminal past indicated otherwise, Charlie always believed that he was never going to be caught again. In December he tried to expand his territory, driving Leona and another girl from California to New Mexico to turn tricks in Lordsburg. They were arrested there, and Charlie faced fresh federal charges of violating the Mann Act, which prohibited transporting women across state lines for the purpose of prostitution. Charlie tried to thwart investigators by marrying Leona; wives could not be forced to testify against their husbands. Though she'd fibbed about it six months earlier, now Leona really was pregnant with Charlie's child. While the FBI prepared its case, Charlie carried on with his lawbreaking ways. He didn't limit his criminal activities to running prostitutes. By the end of the year he'd been arrested twice more by the LAPD for grand theft auto and use of stolen credit cards. Both of those charges were dropped for lack of evidence, but the Mann Act violation was about to be brought before a federal grand jury. Charlie didn't wait around to be indicted; he skipped town.

In his absence, Leona looked out for her own best interests. In mid-pregnancy and eager to avoid a prison sentence of her own, she told the federal grand jury in Los Angeles that Charlie had indeed taken her from California to New Mexico to turn tricks. Her testimony guaranteed that Charlie would return to prison. After the grand jury formally indicted him, Charlie's previous ten-year probation for treasury check forgery was revoked and a bench warrant was issued for his arrest. On June 1 he was picked up in Laredo, Texas, and extradited to California. Three weeks later in a Los Angeles court, Charlie was sentenced to serve out his ten-year check forgery sentence in the United States Penitentiary on McNeil Island in Washington's Puget Sound. A decade of hard time in prison was the last thing that Charlie wanted. He appealed the revocation of his suspended sentence and was held in the Los Angeles County jail while the appeal was pending. He got some good news in July—the Mann Act charge was dropped, probably because it was so certain that Charlie was in line for a lengthy sentence anyway. The inevitable bad news followed; though Charlie and his assigned public defenders managed to string out the process for almost a year, in June 1961 the appeal was denied and Charlie was transferred to McNeil Island. He was just twenty-six, but counting reform schools he had already been in some form of custody or on probation for almost fourteen years.

Except for being surrounded by water, Terminal Island and McNeil Island had very little in common. The California prison was adjacent to the mainland and easy to reach. The Washington penitentiary sprawled over more than two thousand rugged acres and was largely self-sustaining thanks to a large farm maintained by inmates. The most common access was by ferry; the prison maintained a few speedboats. Because commuting was so difficult, many administrators and guards lived with their families on the island. Their homes were built and roads maintained by convict work crews. There was even a school for staffers' children.

The prisoners, who numbered about one thousand when Charlie arrived in the summer of 1961, were housed in a "stacked" five-tier cell tower. They were a mix of white-collar criminals, petty hustlers like Charlie, and vicious thugs. Daily prison life at McNeil was hard; every convict was expected to work, and guards had a relatively free hand with discipline. Few inmates plotted breakouts. Though McNeil was considered a medium- rather than a high-security prison, the rough, deep waters around it assured that escape was virtually impossible. When three inmates tried to float to the mainland on a raft fashioned from a plywood sign, the two who were recaptured had suffered hypothermia. The third had drowned.

When Charlie arrived at McNeil, staff evaluators found him to be "an energetic, young-appearing person whose verbalization flows quite easily." Charlie had learned from the Dale Carnegie course at Terminal

Island: "he gestures profusely and can dramatize situations to hold the listener's attention." He hadn't completely mastered the art of false sincerity. The report noted, "He hides his loneliness, resentment, and hostility behind a facade of superficial ingratiation." And, despite his year-long struggle to stay out of McNeil, Charlie admitted that in a sense he was glad to be there: "He has commented that institutions have become his way of life and that he receives security in institutions which is not available to him in the outside world."

For Manson, prison meant not just security but school. Though he didn't sign up for any of the academic or work training courses available at McNeil, he continued his education there all the same. McNeil had inmates who were glad to share information on a variety of subjects, black and white magic and hypnotism among them. There was a large fellowship of born-again Christians eager to bring Charlie closer to God, but he'd had enough of that. The group that really captured his attention, less for his acceptance of their spiritual beliefs than the way in which they expressed them, was the Scientologists.

Much as Dale Carnegie introduced his sales philosophy to the general public with *How to Win Friends and Influence People* in 1936, in 1950 pulp writer L. Ron Hubbard utilized the best-selling *Dianetics: The Modern Science of Mental Health* to publicize his technique of achieving mental health and happiness. Carnegie's focus was on changing the perceptions of other people; Hubbard taught how to change yourself. He advocated "auditing," confronting traumatic events in the past to move beyond them, becoming free of old fears and restraints and moving toward a "clear" or *theta* state where the mind is able to embrace spiritual freedom without negativity. In 1954, Hubbard and his growing legion of followers founded the Church of Scientology in Los Angeles, with an emphasis on certain "essential tenets":

> *You are an immortal spiritual being.*
> *Your experience extends well beyond a single lifetime. And your capabilities are unlimited, even if not presently realized.*
> *Furthermore, man is basically good. He is seeking to survive. And his survival depends upon himself and his fellows and his attainment of brotherhood with the universe.*

As he had with Dale Carnegie, Charlie adopted those aspects of Hubbard's teachings that lent themselves to manipulating others. He still projected himself in the future as a pimp, not a spiritual advisor. Most potential prostitutes had terrible self-images. Telling such girls that they didn't have to be crippled by the past, that they were immortal spirits temporarily trapped in their bodies, that they were basically good and capable of achieving anything—these could be powerful recruitment techniques. Meanwhile, proclaiming himself as a wholehearted rather than a calculating Scientology convert had immediate advantages. Prison officials were always glad when inmates embraced a faith that encouraged positive attitudes. Faith helped boost potential for parole. As a relatively new arrival at McNeil, Charlie had a long way to go before parole, but conning evaluators into believing he had become a devout Scientologist was a good first step. His September 1961 report noted, "He appears to have developed a certain amount of insight into his problems through his study of [Scientology]. Manson is making progress for the first time in his life."

Sometimes Charlie did seem to be progressing. He participated in prison sports—softball, basketball, even croquet. He joined the inmate drama club. But there were stumbles, too. After unspecified contraband was found in his cell, Charlie was made a prison janitor, the lowest work assignment. In August 1963, Charlie was served with divorce papers from Leona, who'd relocated to Denver. She'd given birth in early 1961 to Charles Luther Manson, Charlie's second son. While there is no record that Charlie ever saw the baby, he must have at least been on decent terms with Leona when the child was born, since the boy's middle name honored Charlie's late uncle. Leona was granted the divorce and full custody of the child in January 1964. Nothing further is known about Charles Luther. There is also no record of Charlie reacting in any way to the divorce. He'd married Leona in an unsuccessful attempt to avoid prosecution, and she'd ended up testifying against him. Then and later, Charlie had no use for relationships from which he didn't benefit.

Though he'd lost another wife, he still had his mother. When Charlie was sent to McNeil, Kathleen moved from Los Angeles to Washington state to be near enough to visit him. Though she knew Charlie deserved to be in prison, her heart still ached for him. Kathleen found work as a waitress. As part of her new life she even reconciled with Lewis. He swore that he had changed, and she wanted badly to believe him. With Lewis back, Kathleen reflected even more on all the mistakes she had made with Charlie; if she'd been a better mother, he surely wouldn't have turned out the way that he did. When she visited the prison he was never interested in her life or how she was. Charlie always had a list of things he wanted her to get for him. She did her best, but money was tight. Lewis still had problems keeping a job and waitressing wasn't lucrative. On one fall visit Charlie demanded money for a new guitar, and was angry when Kathleen told him that she couldn't afford it.

The next time she came, she had a surprise for him. Kathleen wished she could somehow go back in time and raise Charlie right. That was impossible, but now that she was back with Lewis she decided to give motherhood a second try. So she came to visit Charlie at McNeil with an infant in her arms, and proudly informed him that he now had a sister. She and Lewis had just adopted the baby, who was named Nancy after Charlie's grandmother. Charlie shocked Kathleen with his reaction: How much had adopting the baby cost? When Kathleen said the fee was $2,000, Charlie exploded. How could she waste that kind of money on adoption when she'd just told him she didn't have enough money to buy him a guitar? He shouted that he never wanted to see Kathleen or the baby again. Charlie eventually relented and Kathleen resumed her visits, but she was afraid that seeing the little girl might set him off again. Later, some of little Nancy's earliest memories were driving to McNeil with her mother and one of Kathleen's friends, then waiting in the car with the other woman while Kathleen went inside to see Charlie.

Charlie could always make Kathleen feel guilty; she brooded about whether she'd been right not to get him the guitar. In December 1963 Kathleen wrote to the judge in Los Angeles who gave Charlie the ten-year sentence at McNeil. In the letter, she offered to put up her house in Washington as security for Charlie's early release. She was even willing to risk her shaky reconciliation with Lewis by letting Charlie move in with them and the baby. The way she worded the offer indicated that she still thought of her son as a wayward teenager rather than a twenty-nine-year-old hustler: "For the first time in my life, I'm able to give

Charles a nice home and help him to make a good life." The judge turned her down.

In prison, Charlie chose friends for what he could learn from them. The Scientologists had their uses. So did McNeil's most famous inmate. Alvin "Creepy" Karpis became notorious in the 1930s as a member of the Barker Gang. Initially imprisoned in 1936, Karpis was transferred to McNeil in 1962 after the government closed down Alcatraz, the island penitentiary in San Francisco. Now in his mid-fifties, Karpis was no longer considered a threat to anyone's safety; his work assignment was driving the bus that transported children of prison staff to and from the McNeil Island school.

Charlie approached Karpis, though not for tips on robbing banks. Karpis was an accomplished steel guitar player, and Manson wanted to learn that instrumental technique. The older con obliged with some lessons, though he wasn't much impressed with Charlie's playing. Sometimes Charlie wanted to talk about Scientology instead of music. According to Karpis, Charlie "figured [Scientology] would enable him to do anything or be anything." Having run with more than his share of cold-blooded killers, Karpis didn't sense similar tendencies in Charlie. He thought the guy would be the last man on earth "to go into the mass murder business."

Charlie picked up more than Scientology insights and steel guitar licks at McNeil. He didn't read books, but he listened as inmates who did talked about what they'd read. One of the most popular novels among the literate cons was Robert Heinlein's *Stranger in a Strange Land*. Its themes of alienation, government deceit, and redemption for the despised resonated with the incarcerated. Charles was fascinated by the tale of fictional Valentine Michael Smith, born to human parents in a Mars space colony, raised by Martians and returned to Earth as a pawn of scheming politicians. Fascinated by religion, Mike founds his own faith, experiences group sex, uses psychic powers to make enemies disappear, suffers a martyr's death, and returns in spirit form. As he would with the Bible, Dale Carnegie, and Scientology, Charlie later incorporated elements of *Stranger in a Strange Land* into a beguiling, hybrid pseudophilosophy.

Then Charlie discovered his most influential teachers of all.

• • •

World news generally had little effect on Charlie. In January 1964, after two and a half years of incarceration at McNeil, he probably knew President John F. Kennedy had been assassinated but beyond that he had little access to or much interest in what was happening on the outside—with one exception.

There were radios in McNeil, and Charlie loved listening to music. The vast majority of pop hits were hummable fluff that celebrated G-rated teen love and heartache. Folk artists with music that addressed social issues received more limited airplay. They and their causes didn't matter to Charlie. But near the end of January 1964 Bobby Vinton's "There! I've Said It Again" was blasted from the top of the charts by The Beatles' "I Want to Hold Your Hand." A few weeks later, the British band kicked off its first short American tour with a TV appearance on the hugely popular *Ed Sullivan Show*. Most of America tuned in. "Beatlemania" swept the nation; there had never been anything like it, even in the heydays of Frank Sinatra and Elvis Presley. The Beatles' burgeoning fame was such that it penetrated all the way into Charlie Manson's cell at McNeil Island. Their songs were constantly on the radio. Charlie was intrigued by the music but even more impressed by the adulation the Beatles received. Charlie always yearned for attention; now he decided that fame was what he really wanted. If these four Beatles could have it, why couldn't he? After all, he sang and played guitar, too. Countless other young Americans felt the same way, but few could have been as single-minded about it. Charlie started telling anyone willing to listen and also those who weren't that he was going to be bigger than the Beatles, which meant bigger than any other music superstars ever. He didn't care how implausible that sounded.

Besides the incredibly long odds against eventual success, Charlie faced an immediate challenge. The Beatles wrote most of their own material. They were Charlie's new role models, so he was obligated to do the same. Charlie spent virtually every waking nonwork minute hunched over his guitar. There was nothing special about the songs that resulted, though Charlie took great pride in them. In particular, his attempts at lyrics were banal: *"She'll never know what's down inside/All this lovin' I'll al-*

ways hide." He debuted some of his tunes onstage; Charlie began playing in occasional variety shows featuring performances by prisoners. Sometimes he was part of an inmate band. Though there's no record of how his performances were received, he couldn't have been a complete flop because he kept appearing. He didn't always play guitar. The prison had a battered drum kit for use in the shows and sometimes Charlie thumped on it. His drumming was as rudimentary as his guitar playing but he considered himself gifted at both.

Now when Kathleen visited, all her son talked about was how he was going to become a famous musician. He seemed hungry for fame but not fortune. Charlie never mentioned anything about getting rich in the process and buying himself cars and a mansion, let alone doing something for the mother who currently paid for his guitar strings and picks with hard-earned waitressing money. Kathleen tried not to let it bother her. She understood that Charlie was never grateful for anything. At least he'd stopped griping at her so much. Besides, Kathleen had her own problems. Despite all he'd promised, Lewis kept drinking and losing jobs. She was damned if she'd let another child of hers be ruined by a parent's bad example. She'd messed up with Charlie but it wasn't going to happen again. In May 1964 Kathleen divorced Lewis. He tried to talk her out of it and afterward tried to worm his way back through postcards he sent to little Nancy. On the back of each one he'd remind the child that he loved and missed her. Maybe she'd beg her mother to let Daddy come home. Kathleen regularly let him visit Nancy—look what happened to Charlie from not having a father—but she was through falling for Lewis's promises to straighten out. Kathleen still hadn't given up on marriage. She resumed looking for a good man who would give her and her daughter some security.

Charlie's new ambition curbed his old habit of not being able to stay out of trouble. Many of the guards at McNeil were decent guys, but there were some—the cons could pick them out right away—who enjoyed bullying inmates just because they could. If they put you on report for infractions like slacking off at work or being insolent, you could argue if you thought you were unfairly accused but the prison bosses almost always sided with the guards. Then you temporarily lost privileges like writing letters or having visitors. If Charlie got into it with any guards he might have his guitar taken away, and he couldn't risk that. So he recalled Dale Carnegie's advice that the best way to win any argument was to avoid it altogether, and combined that with the biblical proverb about soft answers turning aside wrath. The result was a great trick—Charlie responded to the guards' deliberately provoking questions with innocuous ones of his own. It went something like, "Hey, Manson, when you're all alone with your guitar, do you fuck it?" "What guitar?" It pissed them off, but they couldn't write him up for it.

Senior McNeil staff noted Charlie's extended good behavior and concluded that his love of music was the reason. He'd also begun talking to them about what he wanted to do when he got out of prison, and though his goal was far-fetched, at least it was legal. His May 1966 report stated that "Manson continues to maintain a clear conduct record . . . he has been spending his free time writing songs, accumulating about 80 or 90 of them during the past year, which he ultimately hopes to sell following release. . . . He also plays the guitar and drums, and is hopeful that he can secure employment as a guitar player or as a drummer or singer." Still, the evaluator wasn't convinced that Charlie had entirely changed: "He shall need a great deal of help in the transition from institution to the free world."

Counting the twelve months in the Los Angeles County jail while he filed appeals, in May 1966 Charlie had completed six years of his ten-year sentence. For the last two years at McNeil he'd avoided trouble altogether. That made him a candidate for early parole. In June Charlie was transferred back to the minimum security prison at Terminal Island. It was a significant step toward release.

In October 1965 Kathleen remarried and finally got it right. This third husband was a wonderful contrast to the first two. He worked until he had enough money to open his own small business, and then he worked even harder to make it a success. They weren't rich but anything above poverty level must have seemed heavenly to Kathleen. Unlike Lewis's empty promises to be a good father to Charlie, Kathleen's new husband adored little Nancy and couldn't do enough for her. They all enjoyed doing things together, acting like a real family. Given a second chance at motherhood, Kathleen excelled. Decades later, Nancy felt certain that she'd had the best mom in the world.

Lewis had a parting shot for Kathleen when she remarried, writing her, "Congratulations, you finally found a big, fat, dumb fucker, a meal ticket, ha, you two deserve each other, you two be miserable all your lives," but after that he moved on and also remarried. All Charlie cared about now was music, so it was time for Kathleen to enjoy the nice normal life that she'd craved. She didn't intend to displace Charlie entirely from her life; Kathleen just wanted a break from his problems. But except for one unpleasant encounter, Kathleen and Charlie never met again.

Phil Kaufman was a roughneck from New York who avoided jail as an eighteen-year-old when the judge let him join the Air Force instead. After his enlistment was up Kaufman eventually made his way to Los Angeles, where he worked as an extra in movies and TV (*Spartacus*, *The Donna Reed Show*) and made friends with people in the music business before being busted for drug possession. He was nailed with a five-to-twenty-year sentence and bounced around several federal prisons before being assigned to Terminal Island. Its barred doors had hardly slammed shut behind him when he heard Charlie playing guitar and singing to himself. Kaufman thought the guy sounded a little like Frankie Laine. A guard growled at Charlie, "You'll never get out of here," trying to hassle him for no reason at all. Instead of snapping back or acting intimidated, Charlie paused in mid-strum, replied, "Get out of where, man?" and went back to playing while the guard fumed. Kaufman was impressed—that took real *balls*— and decided he and Charlie would be friends. Charlie was agreeable after learning that Kaufman knew people in the music industry and might be able to help him sell some of his songs. Kaufman discovered that Charlie only associated with other people for whatever he thought he could get out of them, but that was okay. The guy was damned entertaining. He might be almost illiterate but he sure wasn't stupid. When Charlie told stories he'd make all these gestures and facial expressions—he just commanded your attention. Charlie told Kaufman that he took the Carnegie course to learn how to make strangers open up to him. He also talked sometimes about Scientology but not as though he was a real believer.

Charlie would throw Scientology terms around and also quote long passages of the Bible from memory, but the feeling Kaufman got was that he worshipped only at the Church of Charlie.

There were a couple of other things about the guy. Before he was transferred to Terminal Island, Kaufman had done time in half a dozen other prisons. In all of them, the races pretty much kept to themselves. But Charlie took it to an extreme. He wouldn't talk to or even look at blacks if he didn't have to, and the same thing with the Latins. He just didn't like them, didn't think they were anywhere close to a white man's equal. The Black Muslims impressed him, though, the way they stuck together and made it clear that they were not to be messed with. Even the meanest guards let them be. Charlie believed that all blacks were genetically inferior and most of them were dumb as rocks, but give enough angry ones guns and they could probably wipe out much of the white race.

Then there was what Charlie wouldn't talk about. He and Kaufman yakked a lot, but after a while Kaufman realized that Charlie never mentioned anything about his family—parents, wife or ex-wife, kids, anybody. Not one word, not ever. Whoever they might be, it was like he'd banished them from his mind. Kaufman tried to draw him out on the subject a couple of times, but nothing doing.

In August 1966 Charlie got his last prison report. It noted that he refused opportunities to take vocational classes to develop employable job skills and that he no longer claimed to be a Scientologist. Charlie had a single passion: "He has come to worship his guitar and music." Still, "he has no plans for release as he says he has nowhere to go." The report concluded, "He has a pattern of criminal behavior and confinement that dates to his teen years. . . . Little can be expected in the way of change in his attitude, behavior or mode of conduct."

The evaluator's negative prognostication made no difference. Federal prisons were overcrowded. Charlie had stayed out of trouble and was eligible for parole. He was told that he probably would get out in the spring.

Phil Kaufman thought Charlie was a decent singer who "couldn't play guitar for shit." His songs were okay but nothing special. Still, Kaufman had seen people with less talent get recording contracts. Since he wasn't up for parole for another year or so, Kaufman couldn't personally introduce Charlie to friends in the music business. But he still helped him out with a contact. Kaufman suggested that after Charlie was out for a while and had a chance to adjust to the free world, he ought to polish up a couple of his best songs and go see this guy Gary Stromberg at Universal Studios in Los Angeles. Charlie should say that Phil Kaufman sent him. Gary would listen to what Charlie had. There was no way to tell, but he might be interested. For once, Charlie seemed genuinely grateful. He said that he'd work on his songs some more before trying Universal, and that he'd stay in touch with Kaufman. Then, when Kaufman got out, he and Charlie could get back together. That sounded good to Kaufman. Charlie was weird but he was fun to be around.

In March 1967 Charlie learned that he'd be paroled on the 21st. At age thirty-two he was finally going to be free again after almost seven years. As the date drew near, Charlie's dreams of music stardom and being bigger than the Beatles collided with memories of his previous hardscrabble life outside prison. The facade slipped; Charlie panicked and told Terminal Island officials that he didn't want to be paroled after all. He felt safe in prison; he didn't think he could adjust to being outside again. If they let him out he'd end up doing things that he shouldn't. Charlie was being both personally insightful and honest, but the wheels of the penal system bureaucracy were turning. On the morning of March 21, Charlie found himself out on the sidewalk with a cheap suitcase and his guitar, not certain where to go. He didn't think he was ready to see the guy at Universal yet. He felt shaky and needed some time to get used to being free, to not having somebody right there all the time telling him what he could and couldn't do. Charlie had a few phone numbers of inmates he'd known at Terminal Island who were already out on parole. He called one in Berkeley and the guy said that he should come up there. Charlie didn't have any better options. His Los Angeles parole officer gave him permission to relocate and assigned him to regular check-ins at a San Francisco office. Charlie headed north, probably by bus or thumbing a ride. He knew life on the outside was going to be different than before, but he had no idea how much.

Perhaps if Charlie had been released from a federal prison in some other state and decided to try his luck in a college town, he could have reentered society someplace where gradual assimilation was possible. But of all the places he could have chosen for an initial post-prison destination in California, Berkeley was the one guaranteed to plunge him straight into the deepest waves of national upheaval. Like fictional Valentine Michael Smith before him, Charlie was about to become a stranger in a strange land.

CHAPTER SIX

Berkeley and the Haight

Berkeley streets teemed with people who didn't look like anyone Charlie had ever seen before. He was used to the drab inmate coveralls, guard khakis, and buzz cuts of prison. The crowds he now encountered comprised a human kaleidoscope. Men had long hair like girls. Girls wore work shirts and denim jeans like men. Lots of the guys had shaggy beards. Many of the girls obviously weren't wearing bras. Both sexes wore beads around their necks. The air was redolent with the aroma of the food being hawked by street vendors, and just about everyone seemed to be smoking something. There were other odors, too—human sweat, which Charlie certainly recognized, and burning joss sticks, which he probably couldn't. There was almost too much for Charlie to take in all at once, and the closer he got to the college campus, the more bizarre things became.

The University of California at Berkeley was intended to dazzle the eye, but with architecture and greenery rather than fashion. The main campus was a small city in its own right, with high-rise student resident buildings, parking garages, and theaters. Surrounding them were acres of playing fields, botanic gardens, and, off to the west, glittering San Francisco Bay. The faculty was distinguished and the students ranked among the most gifted in the country. But in the spring of 1967, Cal-Berkeley had become less renowned for aesthetics and academics than for civil unrest. As student rebellion exploded in America, Berkeley was Ground Zero.

Across America, young people demanded social change, and many of their leaders came from a demographic that parents and other adults would have considered the least likely to rebel. At the conclusion of World War II, about 1.67 million or 10 percent of Americans aged eighteen to twenty-four were in college. In 1967, that number had swelled to seven million, or 32 percent, and it was mushrooming every year. Unlike their parents, this new generation of students, almost uniformly white, considered college education to be a right rather than a privilege. For many, the real challenge was not to make Dean's List but to right government and social wrongs by any means necessary. In his inaugural address in January 1961, John F. Kennedy, at forty-three the youngest president ever elected, declared that "the torch has been passed to a new generation of Americans," but that generation didn't wait for Kennedy's recognition or their government's permission. In 1960 a handful of student activists formed Students for a Democratic Society. SDS members' ambitious agenda included the eradication of war, racial discrimination, and economic inequality.

By the time Charlie was paroled from Terminal Island in 1967, hundreds of thousands of protesters, mostly but not all young, had participated in SDS-orchestrated antiwar rallies around the nation. Student activists began occupying buildings on their college campuses, effectively shutting down school operations in response to whatever administration policies offended them, from lack of minority enrollment to perceived unconstitutional stifling of free expression. Administrators had a hapless choice between negotiating and being perceived as weak or calling in police, with resulting media coverage of students being dragged from campus in handcuffs.

Berkeley campus protesters organized the Free Speech Movement in 1964. A protest that December 2, when more than a thousand students occupied the school's Sproul Hall, resulted in almost eight hundred students bring hauled off to jail. The Cal-Berkeley campus was shut down until January 3, when a new acting chancellor established the steps of Sproul Hall as an open discussion area where tables and leaflet distribution would be allowed for all student organizations. To the protesters, this was a significant victory, and school administrators believed it was a responsible decision based on compromise. But to critics, the Berkeley Free Speech incident exemplified craven administrators surrendering to spoiled brats. Actor Ronald Reagan made Berkeley Free Speech a major campaign issue when he ran for governor in 1966, promising that if elected he would "clean up the mess there," which Reagan swore in-cluded "sexual orgies so vile I cannot describe them to you." Reagan won the election handily, and sent a message through the media to the Cal-Berkeley students: "Observe the rules or get out." Like college students all around the country, they did neither; Reagan's threat reinforced their belief that the government was their implacable enemy. Berkeley activists reveled in their campus's growing reputation as perhaps the most radical in the land.

Very little beyond his own personal experiences had ever affected Charlie. That changed on the day he arrived in Berkeley and began wandering its streets, heading to the university where a full-blown spirit of revolution reigned. Some of the young people he passed near the campus gates brandished placards and chanted slogans protesting America waging war, and Charlie may have wondered, *what* war, so isolated had he been.

During his reform school years from 1947 to 1954, Charlie had no inkling of China's fall to the Communist party and American forces being held to a bloody draw in Korea. The reformatories offered classes in shop and welding but not current events. In May 1954, around the same time that Charlie was released from the reform school in Chillicothe and returned to live with his grandmother in a self-contained West Virginia hamlet, the Communist-backed North Vietnamese overran French forces at Dien Bien Phu. This led to the partitioning of the Southeast Asian nation into North and South and President Eisenhower, who months earlier espoused a "domino theory" in which other key Asian nations would tumble into communism if a single current democracy fell first, announced that the U.S. would send military advisors to South Vietnam. They would not, the president promised, take up arms against the North Vietnamese themselves. This middle-of-the-road policy was attacked from two sides—some critics believed that America needed to take part in the fighting and demonstrate to Communists everywhere that the U.S. would not tolerate insidious aggression. Others insisted that America had no right to assert itself in Vietnam at all. In 1965, when all Charlie could think about in McNeil was writing songs and becoming more famous than the Beatles, America began committing troops to combat on orders from President Lyndon Johnson. Even as the undeclared war escalated to a hot-button issue that bitterly divided the nation, Charlie could not have found Vietnam on a map.

The war protesters weren't the only shocking sight to Charlie. On the same blocks, young black men openly harangued white passersby for money. They shouted that they were trying to feed hungry kids, but there was unambiguous threat in their tone and appearance—quasi-military dress, dark glasses, and often black caps or berets. They were the Black Panthers, a recent phenomenon, but only the latest manifestation of the rage felt by many black Americans.

In 1967 America was wracked by near-unbearable racial tension. Steady progress was too slow for blacks frustrated by high unemployment, low wages, and substandard living conditions. Riots regularly broke out in ghettos from Washington, D.C., to the Los Angeles slum called Watts. President Lyndon Johnson privately bemoaned the ingratitude of black Americans and predicted to an aide that "Negroes will end up pissing in the aisles of the Senate."

Around the country, but particularly in California and the Bay Area, young black militants declared that they were ready to defend themselves, their families, and their property. In Oakland in October 1966, not long after Charlie was transferred from McNeil to Terminal Island, Bobby Seale and Huey Newton, reacting after San Francisco police shot and killed an unarmed sixteen-year-old black youth, had formed the Black Panther Party for Self-Defense. The Panthers set up free health clinics and breakfasts for ghetto kids, but Charlie, like much of white America, noticed only their sunglasses, paramilitary dress, and the weapons that some of the Panthers openly carried (legally under California law). In Charlie's previous limited experience outside prison, the few blacks that he encountered were called niggers and knew their place. To him, the Black Panthers demanding donations by the Cal-Berkeley gates were the equivalent of the militant, intimidating Black Muslims that he'd seen inside McNeil and Terminal Island, but the Panthers were armed and loose in the free world. Angry black men with guns meant that white people were going to die. From the moment when Charlie first encountered them in Berkeley, the Panthers impressed and scared him.

We don't know whether that first night Charlie looked up his prison pal or slept on a grassy place or a park bench. He'd been given $35 on his release from McNeil, so he may have rented a cheap hotel room. But when the sun came up, Charlie didn't have anybody telling him what to do. Freedom—except he wasn't completely free. Soon he'd have to report to his new parole officer across the Bay in San Francisco, and then keep regular appointments after that. He'd have to demonstrate that he had found work or was at least looking. A lot depended on the officer he got. Somebody understanding would give Charlie time to adapt; a hard-ass could make his life miserable. That was hanging over his head. But for a little while he could check things out in Berkeley.

So Charlie spent a few days wandering around the Cal-Berkeley campus and Bancroft Strip. As always Charlie was ready to absorb anything that might prove useful. He listened to the impassioned speeches by the protesters, though their goals didn't resonate—he had no interest in a war overseas, anything that kept down blacks and women was just fine with him, and the only free speech he cared about was his own. But Charlie did home in on their sense of alienation. That was something he understood.

Right away he understood that he'd come to a place where it was all right to look and act different. In Berkeley, people who might have been marginal characters anywhere else helped make up the norm—a "savory soup" in the words of SDS leader Bill Ayers. All Charlie had known before, in reform school and prison and even McMechen, was forced conformity. Berkeley was the polar opposite and he loved that being a rebel there was okay. Charlie always liked to think of himself as a rebel, standing strong against the Man. Here, he fit right in; Charlie was even distinguished because of his criminal background. Far from having to hide it, Charlie was pleasantly surprised to find that he could brag about his jail time. As far as these new acquaintances were concerned, he'd stood up to government and its fascist cops—*pigs* in revolutionary argot—and lived to tell about it. He was welcome in their circles; as always, Charlie's stories were entertaining and he undoubtedly spun all sorts of exaggerated tales about the prison tribulations that he'd endured. But Charlie quickly realized that these students had nothing else for him. Their focus was on changing the world, not doing things for Charlie. They would have embraced him as an active member of their revolutionary struggle—having an ex-con at their sides would legitimize their own self-image as rebels. Charlie had no interest in that. Acceptance was all that the radicals had to offer him, and it wasn't enough.

Charlie had a vague plan to support himself as a musician, ideally playing in clubs or at least doing the wandering minstrel thing, singing on street corners while people tossed coins in a cup. But every Berkeley block was already lined with street musicians, many of them performing original songs and almost all of them, like Charlie, dreaming of fame. There were too many for anyone to eke out a living from tips. Club jobs were practically impossible to come by. Charlie would have to make money another way.

In many cities other than Berkeley, pimping might have been an option. Charlie had some experience with that, but in Berkeley sex wasn't for sale because it was so readily available for free. One of the tenets of the student radical movement was free love, enjoying sex without bourgeois concerns about morality or fidelity. No one owned anyone else's body. The concept was made more palatable to women by the increasingly widespread availability of birth control pills, first approved by the Food and Drug Administration in 1960, the same year Charlie spent in a Los Angeles jail appealing his ten-year sentence at McNeil.

Charlie's other employment choices in Berkeley weren't acceptable. Busboy in a restaurant, attendant in a parking garage, janitor in an office building—he'd had those kinds of jobs before. Now he considered himself a great artist, a musician with tremendous talent. Menial work was beneath him unless there was no other option, and almost immediately the perfect option presented herself.

Twenty-three-year-old Mary Brunner was a Wisconsin native who earned her BA and then moved west to California like so many other young people who wanted more exciting lives. Square-faced, homely Mary worked at Cal-Berkeley as an assistant librarian. Charlie met her on campus. Mary stood out because unlike most other university denizens, she was dressed conservatively in a blouse buttoned all the way up to her neck. Still new to the area, Mary hadn't made any friends. Charlie could always tell when a girl was lonely. This one was prime prey. Mary was walking her dog, and Charlie initially connected with her by making a fuss over the pet. He had his guitar and he sang her some songs. They talked about all kinds of things—Mary's big social cause was protecting the environment, and Charlie convinced her that he felt exactly the same way. When Charlie artfully got around to mentioning that he didn't have any place to stay, Mary said he could sleep at her apartment for a few nights until he found someplace else. That was all the opening that Charlie needed.

Though Mary briefly resisted—she was still a conservative Midwest girl at heart—Charlie eventually coaxed her into bed. His temporary stay became permanent. Even though he couldn't pimp her out, Mary was a fine meal ticket for Charlie. She went to work at the library every day while he took his guitar and prowled Berkeley free of concern about paying bills. Sometimes he brought other girls back to Mary's apartment. If everybody else was practicing free love, Charlie didn't see why he shouldn't. Mary didn't like it, but Charlie could make her feel beautiful and important and she didn't want to lose that by throwing him out. She gradually got used to sharing him. None of these other girls stayed around very long, anyway. Casual sex was one thing, but most young women in Berkeley didn't plan to sublimate their own best interests to Charlie's. Mary, smart but lonely, was glad to do it. In spite of the other girls, he made her feel special; for years afterward she continued believing that somehow, someday, it would just be she and Charlie. The relationship wasn't entirely one-sided. Mary was extremely knowledgeable about environmental issues. As usual, Charlie listened and remembered what he heard—who knew when it might prove useful? But for perhaps the last time, besides parroting back phrases to feign empathy he genuinely adopted some of the ideas as his own. He became a committed environmentalist.

Berkeley was fine in some ways for Charlie but it was only a temporary stopping place. He still expected to make it in music and become bigger than the Beatles, and that wasn't going to happen there. At some point he intended to return to L.A. and meet with the guy at Universal that Phil Kaufman had put him on to. Before that, though, there was another place that Charlie wanted to try. He crossed the Bay Bridge for meetings in San Francisco with his parole officer, Roger Smith, who seemed to genuinely like Charlie and didn't push him too hard about finding work. During these trips Charlie had a chance to look around the city, and he discovered a place where he knew that he could not only fit in but flourish. So while he returned to Mary's place in Berkeley at night, he began spending his days in the boxy San Francisco neighborhood of Haight-Ashbury, right on the eastern edge of vast Golden Gate Park. Charlie may have considered himself a musician, but he was still a predator. If Berkeley was renowned for its student radicals, the Haight was just as famous for its burgeoning population of hippies, out to change the world through gentle, generous example rather than revolution. Their preferred gesture toward the Establishment was presenting a flower, not a rigid middle finger. They shared possessions gladly and tried to give everyone the benefit of the doubt.

After all his experiences during childhood and in reform school and prison, it was ingrained in Charlie to take advantage of everyone that he could. The master manipulator could not have found a more perfect hunting ground than the Haight.

San Francisco always attracted those who didn't fit in anywhere else. People came to the city to do what they wanted instead of what was conventional. When conservatives gained control of city government in the 1940s, they determined to bring widespread licentiousness under control with police raids, real estate restrictions (for instance, no apartment rentals to mixed race couples), and tighter zoning and health inspection regulations. Almost immediately they were challenged by a generation of interlopers known as Beats, nonconformists whose leading figures, mostly writers and poets like Allen Ginsberg, Lawrence Ferlinghetti, Neal Cassady, and Jack Kerouac, drifted to San Francisco from the East Coast. The Beats adopted the city's North Beach as their particular stomping ground, sitting in coffeehouses discussing literature, reading and writing avant-garde poetry, drinking red wine, smoking marijuana, and occasionally dabbling in psychedelics. They celebrated themselves as hipsters; they disdained squares who sold out to the clean-cut American dream of homes in the suburbs, station wagons, and nine-to-five jobs. After a while, attrition set in. Though a core of Beats remained in the city, strip clubs gradually equaled and then surpassed the number of coffeehouses on North Beach. Many of the remaining Beats joined other disenfranchised iconoclasts and college students in residing in a neighborhood near Golden Gate Park and the campus of San Francisco State University. The area was somewhat seedy, but its declining two- and three-story Victorian houses had great appeal to limited income renters; a lease could be had for a modest sum, and these places had warrens of small bedrooms that could be subleased to other near-impoverished boarders. There were a limited number of lower-scale shops and cafés. The Panhandle, a long finger of Golden Gate Park, extended right into it. If you were different, if you didn't have much money but still wanted to live in beautiful, quirky San Francisco, then this was a good place to be. The neighborhood even had a name: Haight-Ashbury, for two of the streets that intersected at its geographic heart.

If location and architecture were the first defining aspects of Haight-Ashbury, fashion followed close behind. Most of the students and social drifters who lived there had limited wardrobe budgets. Though the Haight lacked high-end shops, it had more than its share of secondhand clothing stores. By some cosmic quirk, many of these featured all sorts of inexpensive, ruffly garb: "Edwardian," in mid-1960s parlance. So many Haight denizens paraded in long colorful dresses or military-style coats with lots of epaulets and gleaming buttons. These could be inexpensively accessorized with strings of beads and festooned with feathers or flowers. It was great fun to dress differently from the straights, who all seemed to want to look as well as to think exactly alike.

And there were drugs. Marijuana and hashish, which had been in common use since the heyday of the Beats. But, above all, there was *the* drug. Lysergic acid diethylamide, popularly known as LSD, was first synthesized by Sandoz Laboratories in Switzerland in 1938. It was intended as a medical stimulant for respiration and circulation, but tests indicated that ingesting LSD resulted in periods of heightened, dreamlike states that might prove beneficial in psychiatric treatments. There was a low incidence of increased anxiety as a result of negative reactions, but no drug ever tested perfectly without side effects. In the late 1940s Sandoz brought

LSD to the market. As intended, psychiatrists began to make use of it, but so did the CIA and American military, who believed the drug might prove useful as a tool for mind control and interrogation. In the 1950s they sponsored a number of tests, often hiring civilians as human guinea pigs. One of these was Ken Kesey, a graduate student at Stanford who signed up in 1959 for a government-sponsored test at Veterans Memorial Hospital in Menlo Park. Kesey loved LSD, which he called "acid." Three years later he published *One Flew over the Cuckoo's Nest*, a novel about psychiatric patients that became a best-seller and provided Kesey with the financial means to continue exploring the social and intellectual possibilities of LSD. He bought an old bus, had it painted in an eye-catching swirl of color, and set off with equally LSD-dedicated pals to enjoy whatever adventures might befall. They called themselves the Merry Pranksters and often held acid parties at Kesey's home.

In 1964, Timothy Leary began openly advocating LSD use, declaring that the drug would allow users to reach new imaginative heights. Fired from the faculty at Harvard for failing to show up for his own classes, Leary had a keen understanding of the media; he spoke in catchy sound bites that lent themselves to headlines. His most famous was "turn on, tune in, drop out," a suggestion that resonated in the Haight, where almost everyone wanted to tune in to their higher consciousness and drop out of the straight world. It was the "turn on" part that was the problem. Drugs were hard to come by—marijuana, commonly called grass or weed, was available only from shady dealers in half- or even quarter-ounces, and while LSD, the Kesey- and Leary-heralded drug, was legal, it was also difficult to obtain. And then, like some superhero in the comic books that were popular reading in the neighborhood, came the man whose chemical genius and burning ambition to make acid readily available to everyone irrevocably transformed the Haight.

By the time Augustus Owsley Stanley III appeared on the scene, the twenty-nine-year-old had already lived a colorful, quixotic life. He rejected his patrician family back in Kentucky, joined the Air Force and served as a radar technician, learned Russian as a first (and last) step toward becoming an Orthodox monk in that country, burned through a couple of marriages, taught himself auto mechanics by redesigning the

engine of his MG, and finally settled on his ultimate career goal: to perfect psychedelic drugs and get them into the hands of as many users as
possible. Owsley invented a bogus company named Bear Research Group
so he could order massive quantities of chemicals directly from the manu-
facturers, then set up a Bay Area laboratory to concoct his own. There
he experimented with LSD dosage strength, testing his friends with free
samples. He had plenty to spare—Owsley's initial stock of ingredients
was enough for 1.5 million doses. From the first, he considered himself
the greatest among the LSD gods. After visiting with Timothy Leary at
Leary's home in Millbrook, New York, Owsley returned to California
and cracked, "Leary may be the king in this little chess game, but what
nobody realizes is that I'm the rogue queen."

Within months, Owsley acid was everywhere in the Haight, and he
wasn't fazed in October 1966 when the California legislature mandated
LSD use to be a misdemeanor and its sale a felony. First, he began offering
acid in the form of liquid tinted the same blue as Wisk laundry detergent.
Dealers could carry their LSD openly in Wisk bottles, which contained up
to four thousand hits. Then he purchased a pill press and began producing
tablets. He changed pill color at random—white, green, pink, purple.

Owsley not only controlled LSD appearance but price. His acid
was acknowledged as the best; when dealers flocked to snap up his latest batch, he would sell to them only after they promised not to charge
their street customers more than $2 a dose. Owsley himself was a regu-
lar sight on Haight sidewalks and clubs, often handing out his wares for
free. He liked to treat friends to steaks at some of San Francisco's better
restaurants—his theory was that humans were natural meat eaters whose
digestive systems became polluted by vegetables. Owsley paid for these
sumptuous feasts with $100 bills, the only currency he would accept from
dealers. It was rumored that on days when Owsley held court to sell his
latest batch of LSD, there were no $100 bills to be had at most banks
within a sixty-mile radius of San Francisco.

Stories about readily available LSD drew more social dropouts to the
Haight. Kesey and the Merry Pranksters helped spread the word with
a series of highly publicized "acid tests" in bookstores and clubs, where
those who wanted could ingest LSD and judge the effect for themselves.

Most of the acid was provided by Owsley. Many turned-on Haight residents augmented their LSD intake with marijuana grown discreetly in porch or window flower pots or else purchased from other local growers. There was usually enough not only to share with friends, but to sell (at very reasonable prices, just enough to cover rent and food and incidentals and Owsley acid) to college students and young professionals who wanted to relax after a hard day in the classroom or at work. It seemed safer to these outsiders to acquire their stashes from other white kids; the black guys who dealt drugs in the ghettos were scary. The Haight quickly became, in the words of historian Charles Perry, home to the nation's first "urban agricultural communes." Virtually everyone who lived there engaged in friendly dealing. They considered it commerce but not real capitalism. Nobody owned anything or anyone. The best things in life were free.

So the Haight was reborn with a cheerful, noncompetitive approach to life. According to legend, the surviving Beats of San Francisco and Haight-Ashbury gave the new kids a derogatory nickname. The Beats liked to think of themselves as skeptical, clued-in *hipsters*. These goofy little dupes were something less: *hippies*. The term got thrown around a lot in the Haight and eventually was picked up by the local media. In September 1965 the *San Francisco Examiner* published a prominent story about the regeneration of the neighborhood. Its headline described the Haight as *"A New Haven for Beatniks,"* but in the body of the story, Haight residents were collectively identified as hippies. The kids embraced the term.

Through the rest of 1965 and all of 1966, the Haight flourished. A thriving new music scene exploded virtually overnight. Promoter Bill Graham took over the Fillmore Auditorium in a decaying black neighborhood on the edge of the Haight, and that venue, along with another called the Avalon Ballroom, featured lots of San Francisco–based bands—the Grateful Dead, Big Brother and the Holding Company with Janis Joplin, Quicksilver Messenger Service. Besides bands, there were many other performers—mime troupes and comics, and clowns in full face paint wandering the Haight streets during the day distributing balloon animals. Everyone was a little different—but if they weren't different, they wouldn't have been there.

There was a nagging concern. Drugs weren't in short supply—everybody had a joint or a tab to share—and area churches outdid themselves in opening temporary shelters so everyone could have a bed. But food *was* a problem, until an unlikely group stepped up.

The Diggers, who originally came to the Haight as part of a mime troupe, were quintessential anarchists. They believed that *any* organization or business, including government, schools, and stores, infringed on individual freedom. *Everything* should belong to everyone without cost, and sustenance topped the list. Even their name reflected that philosophy—the original Diggers lived in seventeenth-century England, where they defied the authoritarian government of Oliver Cromwell by taking over vacant farm land and raising produce, which they gave away for free to the starving British poor. The Haight Diggers harvested their crops from San Francisco groceries, raiding the stores' back lot dumpsters for aging but still edible items—wilted vegetables, meat that was past its sell-by date but hadn't spoiled. They lugged their daily haul back to the Haight, concocted huge amounts of soup or stew, and then carried the steaming vats to the Panhandle and served free afternoon meals to whoever was on hand and hungry. Within the group, sexism was rampant. Digger men chatted with friends and ambled around the Haight while Digger women scrounged, cooked, hauled, and served the food, then cleaned up afterward.

They did more than hand out free food. Traditional newspapers carried few stories of interest to Haight residents. The Diggers printed and distributed leaflets with useful information about parties, concerts, and even how to get a lawyer if you were arrested for drug possession. They harassed Haight businesses if they believed meal or merchandise prices were too high, and in November 1966 opened their own shop, the Free Frame of Reference, which stocked donated secondhand clothes and household items. The name was appropriate: Haight residents, particularly penniless newcomers, were invited to come in, look around, and take what they needed. Everything was free.

Nineteen sixty-six in the Haight culminated with a free Christmas Eve Digger turkey dinner for five hundred at a local church; afterward fresh Owsley LSD was passed around. Musical entertainment was provided by the Chamber Orkustra, a new Haight band. The Orkustra's founder and lead guitarist was a nineteen-year-old currently calling himself Bobby Snofox, or, sometimes, Bummer Bob. His real name was Bobby Beausoleil, and he would be heard from again.

Community events were a big part of the Haight's charm. Few weeks went by without some impromptu concert in the Panhandle or special street theater presentation. It was a way to celebrate being pioneers in a new way of life. There was a growing sense that someday soon everyone would throw off constrictive moral and spiritual shackles, if only the Haight's influence spread widely enough. In that spirit, neighborhood leaders decided to kick off 1967 with their biggest bash ever, one intended to unite Haight's hippies with like-minded souls throughout the Bay Area. A secondary intent was to forge stronger solidarity between Haight residents and Berkeley's student radicals. After all, even though their methods were so different, their mutual aim was to create a better, more equal society.

Organizers put aside their disdain for San Francisco city government and formally reserved Golden Gate Park's sprawling Polo Field for Saturday afternoon, January 14, 1967. The first internal debate involved what to call the event. "Pow-wow" and "A Gathering of the Tribes" were seriously considered before the eventual choice: "A Human Be-In," soon shortened by planners and the press to "Be-In." No one was certain how many people might attend. Flyers for the 1–5 P.M. event simply asked attendees to bring "children, flowers, flutes, drums, feathers, bands, beads, banners, flags, tangerines, incense, chimes, gongs, cymbals, joy." Scheduled speakers included Beat poets Allen Ginsberg and Lawrence Ferlinghetti, LSD guru Timothy Leary, and Buddha.

Winter weather in San Francisco is notoriously erratic, making any outdoor program chancy, but January 14 dawned clear and bright. Organizers were concerned that the San Francisco press would emphasize a smaller than expected crowd, so Haight shops and cafés voluntarily closed for the day in an effort to encourage residents to go to the Polo Field instead. They shouldn't have bothered. By 9 A.M. hippies in rainbow robes and feathered headdresses began arriving in the sprawling meadow. They mingled with students wearing blue jeans and T-shirts. More than twenty thousand were present by the official 1 P.M. kickoff, everyone crammed together and no one minding. The Diggers distributed free turkey sandwiches; Owsley donated a large, particularly potent batch of LSD tabs dubbed "White Lightning." Anyone who felt like tripping on acid did so in style. Ginsberg, who desperately wanted to be as important to the hippies as he had been to the Beats, opened the program by chanting "We are all one!" while someone blew into a conch shell. Leary encouraged all present to turn on, tune in, drop out, and a dozen San Francisco bands performed. As the sun set around 5 P.M., Ginsberg offered a final chant to close the program. Then the crowd stunned park officials by cleaning up every scrap of trash before wandering off into the dusk, still singing and chanting. The Be-In was a magical event, far surpassing what its organizers could ever have hoped for, and it was directly responsible for destroying the Haight spirit that it celebrated. If the neighborhood was Eden for hippies, then the San Francisco media inadvertently became the serpent.

Local reporters, photographers, and film crews attended the Be-In, and their subsequent broadcasts and articles and photographs accurately captured the rapturous atmosphere. National newscasts and publications took note. It was impossible to live in America for the next few weeks without seeing, hearing, or reading something about Haight-Ashbury in San Francisco, the place where free food, love, and drugs abounded. Everyone was welcome there. Across the country, disenfranchised youth responded. Previously, a few dozen hungry, penniless newcomers found their way to the Haight every week. Now there were more than three hundred a day. It didn't take long for neighborhood leaders to realize what was happening. They met with San Francisco police chief Thomas Cahill and other city officials, requesting help to house and feed the descending hordes. Cahill, a conservative who viewed the hippies as proof of America's moral decay, cracked that they had become "the love generation," and made things worse by announcing no tents could be up in any city park after 10 P.M., meaning Haight newcomers no longer had a place to camp out. A neighborhood research team did its best to question members of the ever-growing mob about why they had come; its report concluded that some were psychotic, 40 percent bought into "the mystique of the Haight and think it will change the world," and 45 percent were "attracted by minimum time spent working and maximum time getting stoned." This wasn't the hippie Utopia celebrated just weeks before.

Haight residents hoped that the influx of needy newcomers would slacken as the Be-In faded from public memory. That possibility was lost in early April when Paul McCartney popped into the neighborhood for a quick look at a place whose reputation as a hippie haven had spread all the way to England. McCartney apparently failed to take in the piles of trash and milling herds of ragged misfits. Instead, he pronounced that Haight hippies were collectively "colorful and fun," and his comments made fresh headlines. A Beatle had endorsed the Haight. That encouraged still more people to come, and among them were hardened dealers sensing limitless profits from a growing mob of consumers who believed it was their social and spiritual obligation to ingest drugs. Owsley still controlled most of the LSD market, and marijuana was smoked in the Haight as often as conventional cigarettes. But these new pushers offered hard drugs—heroin and Methedrine and other chemicals encouraging harsh hallucinations and physical violence. Haight arrivals, and not a few longtime residents, proved indiscriminate in what they took and how often. Used syringes became commonplace on the Haight's sidewalks. The hard-line dealers wormed their way into the community and swiftly became as integral as the Diggers.

If dealers were the least welcome arrivals, runaway teenagers were the most heartbreaking. Sixteen or fifteen or even younger, they came from around the country, more runaways than any major city could have comfortably absorbed, let alone a relatively small neighborhood. Some had left home for the thrill of it, and after taking in the Haight's increasingly unsavory atmosphere, they had the sense and the resources to go back home. But many others, in the words of Joan Didion, were "pathetically unequipped" to deal with their new surroundings. They were misfit kids, the ones with no social skills who had trouble making friends or fitting in back in their hometowns, or else were at critical odds with their parents and wanted someone more understanding to take them in and tell them what to do. The ones least able to fend for themselves were the most likely to stay.

So many defenseless teenage sheep naturally attracted both shepherds and wolves. Street preachers had always roamed San Francisco, but now the Haight attracted an inordinate number who pontificated on street corners or in the Panhandle, all of them claiming to have the answers that their confused listeners needed. It was possible, within any few Haight blocks, to be exposed to a wide variety of proselytizers: Buddhists, Hindus, fundamentalist Christians, Satanists, socialists, anarchists, pacifists, isolationists, and plenty of poseurs adopting guru guise for the purpose of seducing gullible youngsters. "You can't emphasize enough the innocence of most of these starry-eyed kids," recalls Beat and Haight survivor Glenn Todd. "They were ripe to take advantage of, if anybody wanted to. Throw out some talk about peace and love in Golden Gate Park and you could sleep with a dozen naive little girls if that was your intent." For many, it was. An April 16 street leaflet described another too typical scene: *"Pretty little sixteen-year-old middle-class chick comes to the Haight to see what it's all about & gets picked up by a seventeen-year-old street dealer who spends all day shooting her full of speed again & again, then . . . raffles off her temporarily unemployed body for the biggest Haight Street gang bang since the night before last. . . . Rape is as common as bullshit on Haight Street."*

Things were about to get even worse. All during the spring of 1967, newcomers converged on the Haight. In May and June, when schools around the nation closed for the summer, the number of arrivals was expected to multiply at a staggering rate. One estimate had 75,000 more descending on a neighborhood with a residential capacity of perhaps a tenth of that number. It was "The Summer of Love."

By then Charlie Manson lurked in the Haight, and he was eager to greet the newcomers.

CHAPTER SEVEN

Charlie in the Summer of Love

Charlie arrived at the Haight in April 1967 after the Be-In (in January he was still behind bars at Terminal Island) but before high schools let out for the summer and the full tide of would-be hippies washed in. Somebody handed Charlie a flower, he had his initial acid trip and loved it, and he spent a night or two on the soft grass of Golden Gate Park. Decades later he'd also claim that he performed at the Avalon Ballroom with the Grateful Dead, which even for Charlie was an outrageous lie. Nobody took any special notice of him; Charlie appeared to be nothing more than another scruffy pilgrim negotiating the crowded streets. But Charlie was taking in everything around him, looking for an angle, trying to calculate how he could turn some aspect of the Love Generation activity to his own advantage. As was the case in Berkeley, the Haight was no place for pimps because free love eliminated the need to pay for play, and peddling dope was out of the question, too—everyone in the neighborhood had easy access to acid and weed, and Charlie lacked the finances and connections to get into dealing harder drugs.

The Diggers fascinated Charlie. He tagged after them, noting their morally superior attitudes and observing their daily task of scrounging from supermarket dumpsters and turning the cast-off food into nourishing, even tasty, meals. Charlie certainly approved of the Digger women doing most of the work while the men gave orders. Here was a group that everyone looked up to, and Charlie, the shrimp who was constantly picked on in school and in prison, always yearned for respect. But Charlie was never tempted to join the Diggers—intriguing as they were, everything they did was ultimately for the benefit of others, not themselves, and that ran directly counter to Charlie's approach to life. Besides, they espoused a philosophy of no individual leaders, and Charlie always wanted to lead.

In the Haight, there was an obvious way to do that, a way that appealed to Charlie's considerable ego and required exactly the talents that he possessed—imagination, glibness, and an uncanny ability (gleaned in equal parts from pragmatic prison survival and Dale Carnegie classes) to manipulate others by perceiving and then exploiting their ambitions and weaknesses. Virtually everywhere Charlie looked in the Haight there were street preachers pontificating to one or two or dozens of misfit listeners desperately seeking someone special to tell them what to do, how to live, what to think. Reinventing himself as a Haight guru and gaining a flock of worshipful followers was irresistible. Charlie still expected that someday soon he'd head south to Los Angeles to snag a recording contract. But the guru business clearly had its own charms and, just like music, it required attracting and retaining an audience. All the biggest stars had entourages, followers to stroke their egos, run their errands, indulge their every whim. Charlie set about recruiting his in the Haight.

He began not by preaching, but by listening. For days Charlie drifted from one street guru to the next, memorizing their best lines and putting together his own street rap. Charlie was in no rush with his research. Unlike most Haight newcomers, he had no immediate financial concerns. Mary Brunner still had her job at the university library back in Berkeley, and most nights Charlie hitched back across the Bay and slept at her place. Mary understood that it was none of her business what Charlie did during the day while she was at work. Her obligation was to pay the rent, cook for him, clean his clothes, make love whenever he felt like it, and tolerate any other girls he brought home. And, as Charlie began to preach his way around the Haight, there were suddenly a lot of them.

The street philosophy Charlie initially spouted was a hybrid, cobbled together from Beatles song lyrics, biblical passages, Scientology, and the Dale Carnegie technique of presenting everything dramatically. Guitar in hand—sometimes he'd sing an original tune or two to warm things up—Charlie would find an open spot on the sidewalk or in the park and begin chatting with whatever waifs were nearby. He'd talk about becoming free by giving everything up—possessions, individuality, ego. The more you surrendered, the more you had. Death was the same thing as life and nothing was bad. Society insisted some things were wrong, but that was just to hold you down. Breaking away from your inhibitions was important. Love everybody. He offered nothing radically different from hundreds of other would-be Haight gurus with the exception of his presentation. Charlie was a masterful orator, letting his voice fall so his listeners needed to lean in to hear, then roaring so that they had to pull back a little, building a singsong rhythm and smiling and gesturing broadly. He entertained as well as enlightened. The term *charisma* was just coming into wide use and Charlie had it. To an extent he was successful from his first day as a self-anointed guru. People listened. When he wanted drugs, his audiences had plenty to share. Girls agreed that inhibitions were bad and had sex with him. He took some of the girls back across the Bay and enjoyed more time with them at Mary's apartment. But something was missing.

Charlie wasn't accomplishing anything more than dozens of other Haight gurus. Every day he was in direct competition with the rest of them. Some kids would listen to Charlie, swear lifelong allegiance, and then desert him the next day for some other pontificator. The ones willing to stay loyal to him on a long-term basis weren't worth having. Charlie was quickly reminded of what he'd previously learned as a pimp: the best recruits were bruised and needy but not completely broken. On any given day in the Haight, Charlie could call to his side dozens of hapless young souls who needed everything but had nothing to contribute for his own benefit beyond doglike devotion. They were too socially inept to bring in money by panhandling, too clingy to share his attention, and too disoriented to run even the simplest errands. For Charlie, a more effective way of building a useful entourage was to test potential followers one at a time, and to do it away from competing gurus. When he had a few select disciples, then they, in turn, could go out and recruit for him, with Charlie making the final decisions on who was worthy to remain in the group. Jesus had done the same sort of thing, and during some of his LSD trips Charlie began to believe that he had a lot in common with Jesus, since they both tried to build a following from the dregs of society. Bigger than the Beatles, equal to or maybe even the reincarnation of Jesus—Charlie didn't aim low. But when he did select his second follower, she wasn't from the Haight.

After so many years in prison, Charlie relished the freedom to roam. Every few weeks he left the Haight on directionless two- or three-day rambles up and down the California coast, hitching or else driving a 1948 Chevrolet that someone made available to him. In May 1967 he took the Chevy south toward Los Angeles and ended up in Venice, one of a series of beach towns north of the downtown L.A. sprawl. Venice had a reputation as a bohemian community; lots of artists and musicians lived there. Charlie parked the car and wandered along the sidewalk that ran parallel to the Pacific Ocean. Benches were set all along the sidewalk so people could sit and watch surfers riding the waves. On one of the benches a small, redheaded girl sat and sobbed. Eighteen-year-old Lynette Fromme had just left home after another fight with her strict, domineering father. Lynne had a history of emotional problems. Though she'd been an outgoing child who was a good enough singer and dancer to appear as part of a professional troupe several times on national television (prophetically, her signature tune was "Doin' What Comes Naturally" from the Broadway show *Annie Get Your Gun*), as a teenager she'd turned to sex and drugs, in part as a response to tension between her parents. Lynne attempted suicide twice while in high school and was rumored to have had an affair with one of her teachers. She'd recently enrolled in small El Camino College with a vague plan to earn some basic credits and then transfer to the University of California. But then she and her father argued again, and she fled from their home in Redondo Beach to this bench in Venice.

Charlie sensed an opportunity. He walked over and asked, "What's the problem?" Lynne blinked back tears and glanced up; her first impression was that he seemed like a hobo with class. Charlie told her that he was called the Gardener because he tended to all the flower children back in the Haight. Soon they were sitting together and Lynne told him all about her life, how she was frustrated and wanted to escape from everything. Charlie couldn't have seemed more sympathetic, yet mysterious. He told her, "The way out of a room is not through the door; just don't want out, and you're free." Then Charlie spun some tales about his time in prison, how he'd learned to free himself mentally while stuck in solitary confinement. He'd come to Venice that morning because he'd somehow felt compelled to, Charlie told Lynne, intimating that fate must have brought them together. Now he was going to drive back to the Haight—she was welcome to come along. At first Lynne said no, she had to finish the semester at school, but when Charlie turned and walked away she jumped off the bench and ran after him.

Charlie took Lynne home to Mary, and set about indoctrinating her. For a while the three of them simply hung out, and then one day Mary went out and Charlie told Lynne to take off her clothes. Lynne was ambivalent about sex, but Charlie explained how none of it was bad. She'd never felt attractive and he told her that she was beautiful. After one or two false starts on her part they finally made love, and then they had sex with Mary watching, and then Lynne watched Charlie and Mary doing it, and gradually all her inhibitions were gone and the next thing she knew the three of them would go out on drives into the hills where she and Mary would take off all their clothes and pretend to be wood nymphs while Charlie played a flute that he'd found somewhere. Charlie was so wonderful and wise. Lynne wanted to stay with him forever, and he said that she could. He and Mary gave up the place in Berkeley; along with Lynne, they took an apartment in the Haight. It meant that Mary had to commute to work at the Cal-Berkeley library, but it was more convenient for Charlie and that was what mattered. Lynne and Mary got along fine, and Charlie wanted to add another member to the household. He had somebody in mind.

On one of Charlie's first hitchhiking trips, he was picked up just outside San Francisco by an overweight former Congregational minister named Dean Moorehouse. Moorehouse and Charlie got into a good conversation and Moorehouse brought Charlie home to meet his wife and daughter. The wife didn't make much of an impression, but teenage Ruth Ann did. She was a cuddly tomboy, funny and uninhibited, an irresistible little bit of jailbait. Charlie could tell she liked him and bought into the whole ex-con-turned-guru thing, but at that particular moment he wanted to get his hands on something else in the Moorehouse home.

A battered piano was in the corner of a room, and true to the spirit of the times when Charlie said he liked it, Moorehouse told him that he could have it. Soon after Lynne and Mary moved with him to the Haight, Charlie went back to the Moorehouses' to get the piano, though he had no intention of hauling it back to the Haight. Instead he trundled it a few blocks down the street, where he swapped it with one of the Moorehouses' neighbors for an aging Volkswagen minibus. The minibus meant that Charlie was not only mobile, he had room to bring five or six people along with him. The first one he brought was Ruth Ann, who was eager to run off with Charlie. They managed to have sex a few times before her mother sicced the law on Charlie. He and Ruth Ann were picked up in Mendocino north of San Francisco. She was sent home and Charlie was charged with interfering with the questioning of a suspected runaway juvenile. Charlie was in his Jesus mode when the cops booked him. He gave his occupation as "minister" and his name as Charles Willis Manson rather than his given middle name of Milles. He explained that the new name spelled out his real identity and mission: *Charles' Will Is Man's Son—* Charlie was the Son of Man, carrying out the Lord's will.

Ruth Ann had guessed that her parents would try to force her to come home. Before they were separated by the cops, Charlie advised her to find someone and marry him; any single guy would do. Married women were legally emancipated from their parents. Ruth Ann could desert her new husband anytime, and then go anywhere with anyone she wanted. Charlie would stay in touch so she'd know where to find him. In the immediate aftermath of their arrest Charlie got a thirty-day suspended sentence and three years tacked onto his probation, and Ruth Ann married a guy named Edward Heuvelhorst. Then she bided her time until Charlie was ready to summon her.

By mid-June school was out all over America and teenagers flooded the Haight. Charlie picked through them, talking to many, taking more time with a few, but nobody seemed quite right. Things in the Haight were nuts. Everybody had known the kids were coming, but nobody realized that there would also be countless Bermuda shorts–wearing adult tourists brandishing cameras, eager for snapshots of authentic Haight hippies flashing the peace sign or smoking dope or any of the other depraved things that the folks back home had heard about. It became impossible to drive on Haight streets because they were too crowded.

For many of the hippies, the big thrill of the summer was the release of *Sgt. Pepper's Lonely Hearts Club Band*, the Beatles' latest album. From sleeve photos to musical content, it was taken as an affirmation of everything the Haight wanted to represent. John, Paul, George, and Ringo were decked out in psychedelic pseudo-military garb, lime green and pink and bright blue and orange. They all had long hair and mustaches. The band's name was spelled out on the cover with flowers. The songs themselves abandoned completely any reference to teen romance. Instead there was a tribute to getting high with a little help from your friends, the all-too-true tale of a girl leaving home because her parents didn't understand her, a droning Indian-flavored reminder that we're all one, a trippy ditty titled "Lucy in the Sky with Diamonds" with the suggestive initials L.S.D., and a final song about a day in somebody's life that concluded with John Lennon telling the rest of the world that the band would "love to turn you on." For all the current chaos in the Haight, its desperate denizens took *Sgt. Pepper* as a sign that the Beatles *understood*.

All over America it was a traumatic summer. Thirty-three race riots in major cities required intervention by police and, often, the National Guard. Fifty-three percent of those arrested were black males between the ages of fifteen and twenty-four. Young men in ghettos turned on their own communities; sociologists classified the summer 1967 uprisings as "commodity riots" involving looting and burning of local businesses. None of them were "community riots" with interracial fighting. There were no riots of any sort in the Haight, but plenty of rapes. An even greater danger to its overflowing community were drug overdoses and diseases brought on by malnutrition and exposure. Despite the best efforts by the Diggers and neighborhood churches, thousands of people, mostly teenagers, went hungry during the day and slept wherever they could find a few feet of space at night. Even though it was summer, Bay Area nights were chilly and damp. The music played in clubs or in the Panhandle was almost always punctuated by hacking, phlegm-soaked coughs from the audience. Sick kids staggered on their own or were helped to the public health services at Park Emergency Hospital near

Golden Gate Park; from there they were routinely shunted off to other facilities, where they were equally unwelcome and went mostly untreated.

Dr. David E. Smith, an intern directing the alcohol and drug abuse screening unit at San Francisco General Hospital, was appalled at the callousness of his colleagues. City officials had no intention of increasing health services to the Haight; instead, they debated whether to try to stem the stream of summer arrivals by posting "Hippies Not Welcome" signs on bridges leading into San Francisco. Smith decided to open a free health clinic in the Haight. He found some doctors and nurses who were willing to donate a few pro bono hours each week, and after leasing some vacant dental offices on Clayton Street and stocking them with basic medical supplies Smith opened his clinic on June 9. It operated under a simple philosophy: Anyone would be treated without charge, and the staff would make no moral judgments about patients. More than 250 hippies lined up for treatment on the first day, suffering variously from pneumonia, hepatitis, venereal disease, skin and gum infections, malnutrition, dysentery, and complications from botched abortions. There were 350 the next day, and by the third the clinic had run out of antibiotics and bandages. Smith had opened the clinic with his own money and a few small donations. Without financial help it wouldn't stay open for long. Fillmore promoter Bill Graham volunteered to put together a series of fundraising concerts. The first, featuring Big Brother and the Holding Company with Janis Joplin, raised $5,000. Joplin, fond of hard drugs and unprotected sex, was a regular clinic patient. City leaders weren't pleased; health inspectors made regular visits to the clinic, hoping to cite unsanitary conditions and shut the place down, but Smith and his staff kept the premises in good condition. A greater threat to the clinic's operations was posed by undercover police officers looking for illegal drugs. Clinic staff posted a prominent sign: "No dealing, no holding, no using dope—any of these can close the clinic." Not wanting to scare away potheads or trippers in dire need of care, the sign's message gently concluded, "We love you."

Since Charlie was still trolling the Haight for potential followers, he dropped in to the clinic from time to time. He and the staff there would sometimes chat; Charlie always seemed to be in a sociable mood. Smith remembers Charlie practicing lines he'd copped from other would-be Haight gurus, testing them on the sick hippies lined up for treatment on the sidewalk outside the clinic. Charlie's entire rap was love and peace and give up your ego, Smith recalls, the same rhetoric offered by all the other street preachers. He never alluded to anything violent.

Charlie ripped the seats out of the Volkswagen bus and Mary decorated it with a rug and pillows and curtains so there was room behind the driver for people to stretch out comfortably. He, Mary, and Lynne drove the VW bus down to Manhattan Beach outside Los Angeles, where Charlie wanted to visit Billy Green, an old acquaintance from prison. Green introduced Charlie to nineteen-year-old Pat Krenwinkel, a plain girl going through a particularly bad time. A native Californian whose parents had divorced when she was in high school, Pat had been living with her mother in Alabama, but hated the segregation in the South and being called a Yankee by the locals. She moved back to California and lived in an apartment with her older half-sister and nine-year-old nephew. According to Pat, her sister was hooked on drugs and the nine-year-old was incorrigible. Billy told Pat's sister that Charlie needed a place to stay, and as soon as Charlie took in Pat's chaotic home life he pounced. During his three-day stay (Mary and Lynne were stashed elsewhere) he focused his entire attention on Pat, making love to her and telling her she was beautiful, something no man had ever said to her before. On the third day he asked her to leave town with him; he was going to drive around America. Pat wanted a way out but was cautious enough to ask Billy Green his opinion. Green said that she ought to go with Charlie—what could it hurt? Pat's belief that Charlie was going to be her boyfriend was disabused when Charlie stopped to pick up Mary and Lynne; she'd have to share him. But Pat and the other two young women got along. It was a time for free love, after all, and no possessiveness. Charlie seemed so wonderful, so magical, that even a little of his attention brought happiness and a sense of security. Pat brought something to Charlie, too—a Chevron credit card that her father continued to pay off every month. Charlie immediately took control of the card. He had not only acquired his third permanent follower, he no longer had to worry about paying for gas.

As soon as they were back in San Francisco, Charlie had another road trip in mind. He asked his parole officer, Roger Smith, for permission to drive out of state north to Washington. Charlie told Smith, Mary, Lynne, and Pat that he wanted to try to find his mother. She'd abandoned him when he was young, Charlie complained, but he still wanted to find her and reconcile. Smith agreed; he didn't realize that Charlie knew very well where Kathleen was. Mary Brunner had quit her job at the Cal-Berkeley library. Charlie hoped to cadge some money from Kathleen to tide them over until he could find some other source of income. Charlie and his three women stayed in Seattle for several days, and he went through the motions of looking for his mother, poring over phone books, driving up and down supposedly familiar streets. They stayed with someone Charlie introduced as one of his former parole officers. The guy immediately brought out drugs for them to share. One day Charlie went out by himself and went directly to Kathleen's house. She wasn't pleased to see him. Before she let her son inside, Kathleen told her daughter, Nancy, to hide in the closet because he was a bill collector. Nancy stayed in there until Charlie stormed off, denied a last handout from his mother. He never spoke to Kathleen again. Afterward he told Mary, Lynne, and Pat that they might as well give up, he couldn't find his mom.

There were other midsummer trips. Charlie, Mary, Lynne, Pat, and a few other girls Charlie was trying out for the group drove to Mendocino County and camped along the beautiful, tree-lined coast, sleeping in the VW bus. The town of Mendocino was an artists' community, and people living there were welcoming. They thought the women in Charlie's group looked a little odd because they had sewn together old blankets to serve as skirts. After a few days they were ready for Charlie and the girls to move on, because they carelessly scattered trash around the van. One night Charlie had his women build a roaring campfire. Though he usually avoided alcohol, he drank wine from a coffee cup and invited some of the locals to join them and hear some of his stories about life back in Appalachia and in prison. Charlie was entertaining as always, but then someone else joined the party. The interloper told some jokes and shared local gossip. Everyone's attention switched to him, which made Charlie so angry that he threw his cup of wine at the interloper—so much for peace and love. Charlie and the girls drove back to the Haight the next day, and the

Mendocino artists were glad to see them go. Years later, Charles Perry recalled that the weird group had a nickname for itself—the Trolls.

Charlie always seemed to have knives handy. Sometimes he'd take Mary, Lynne, and Pat off into the woods and make one of them stand in front of a tree. Then he'd back up a few steps and throw a knife so it would stick in the tree just over her head, like some circus act. It scared them, but Charlie explained it was a way of testing whether they really trusted him. If they flinched it meant that they didn't. So they tried very hard to stand completely still, and when they did, Charlie always told them how wonderful they were. That kind of praise from him made the risk worth it.

Conditions in the Haight continued to deteriorate. Far from slackening as the summer progressed, the number of arrivals increased by the week. The Diggers gave up trying to feed everyone and retreated to a farm commune in the country. Many longtime Haight residents abandoned the neighborhood, moving to other parts of the city or away from San Francisco altogether. LSD was still readily available, so much so that the street price per dose dropped from $2 to one. But quirky weather conditions, cold one day and steamy the next, choked off local marijuana production and a serious weed shortage hit the Haight. Dealers and their customers filled in the drug gap with even greater quantities of heroin and the methamphetamine popularly known as speed. Since the speed freaks were distinguished by paranoid hallucinations and violence, they lent a nasty edge to Haight nightlife; brawls and muggings became common outside neighborhood clubs and bars.

It got even worse. Competing drug dealers stalked each other. One prominent dealer, well known for keeping a briefcase full of his illegal wares cuffed to his hand, was found slaughtered on a Haight back street. The briefcase was missing because his hand had been cut off. The population crush finally began to ease a little, not because people stopped coming, but because fewer stayed. A guitarist in a Texas band that came to the Haight expecting to perform for trippy, laid-back audiences, remembered later that "Haight Street smelled like piss, and a lot of little stores were closing down. All the people we thought were running around with flowers in their hair were now lying around with needles stuck in their necks."

Darker philosophies competed with hippie hedonism. In September filmmaker Kenneth Anger rented a Haight theater for a program about British Satanist Aleister Crowley. The event was called "Invocation of My Demon Brother" and included a light show with slides presenting images of Crowley's personal Tarot cards, a Satanic altar placed on the theater floor, footage from *Lucifer Rising*, Anger's film in progress, and music by the Chamber Orkustra. It was appropriate for the Orkustra to perform—Bobby Beausoleil, its leader, was featured in Anger's film. Attendance was sparse, and Anger didn't sell enough tickets to earn back the $700 he'd paid to rent the theater. Worse, someone stole the *Lucifer Rising* film canisters. Anger suspected Beausoleil, who soon afterward left the Haight for Los Angeles. Shortly after arriving in L.A., Bobby met a music teacher and part-time drug dealer named Gary Hinman. Bobby and his current girlfriend, Laurie—he seemed to have a new lady every week—moved into Hinman's house in Topanga Canyon. Fate had begun lining up the human pieces on its chessboard.

None of the Haight turmoil was reflected in a letter sent by Pat Krenwinkel to her father. She wrote, "For the very first time in my life, I've found contentment and inner peace." For all his copycat, cobbled-together rhetoric and all-consuming self-interest, Charlie really was making the lives of his first three followers happier. Since Mary was no longer employed, they lived hand-to-mouth. Panhandling was part of their daily routine. Sometimes they'd do chores like washing windows in exchange for food. But Charlie had a knack for temporarily attracting individuals with something substantial to contribute—kids who'd left home with a few hundred dollars or credit cards snatched from parental purses or wallets, older people met on road trips in the VW bus who were intrigued by this vagrant hippie preacher and his scruffy girl disciples and opened their homes to them for a night or longer. The kids were shunted aside as soon as their money ran out or the credit cards were canceled. The adults were thanked for their hospitality and not blown off completely—they might come in handy again. But Mary, Lynne, and Pat rarely went hungry or without a comfortable place to sleep at night. Charlie preached to them about surrendering their egos. He made love to them and told them that they were beautiful. He sang them his songs and promised that soon he'd get a record contract and become a star and then they could share the love they felt for each other and all the universal truths that they'd learned with the rest of the world because they were so special. There were drugs, but none of the hard stuff, just weed to mellow out and acid trips to explore the outer reaches of their minds. They'd left behind biological families who didn't actually care for them, Charlie stressed, to become part of a *real* family, one that accepted and cherished them for who they were and not what other people wanted them to be. Sometimes things got unexpectedly tense. Charlie expected rapt devotion and he could become angry if he thought the girls didn't pay attention when he talked or, worse, paid attention to someone else at Charlie's expense. Whenever he thought that happened he would yank hard on Lynne's or Pat's long hair. He'd hit Mary. The three of them would cower for a while afterward and remind each other that they were really very lucky to be with Charlie. He'd promised to show them a better way to live, and for the most part all three believed that he was keeping his word.

But Charlie had no intention of settling for life as he found it five months out of prison. Above all, there was his music; he practiced so that he would impress Phil Kaufman's friend Gary at Universal. Charlie kept writing new songs, picking out tunes on his guitar by the light of campfires, struggling to remember spur-of-the-moment lyrics because he often lacked the means to write them down. He'd return to L.A. soon, he knew, not to recruit disciples but to establish himself as the star he deserved to be, something like Jesus entering Jerusalem. There was glory coming, and yet there was still so much more to do. Three devoted followers weren't nearly enough. He wanted more, an impressive entourage worthy of his greatness, and not just comprised of women, either. Try as he might, Charlie hadn't been able to recruit any men long term. Women were so much easier—you told them that they were beautiful, you picked up on their Daddy complexes, you had sex with them, and then if they were insecure and needy enough, they were yours. But it was harder with men. The best way to get them, Charlie knew, was through women. Join Charlie's merry band, and its girls would do whatever you wanted. He was teaching Mary, Lynne, and Pat that sex was wonderful and any moral hang-ups about it were wrong. They'd come a long way. They would pretty much do anything with anybody if Charlie ordered them to. Problem was, all three were so homely. Maybe Lynne had a bit of pixie-ish charm, but the other two, nothing. Charlie told them they were beautiful and sexy despite their physical flaws, but even though they fell for it he knew better. With so much easy pussy—one of Charlie's favorite words, then and later—available elsewhere from better-looking girls, what worthwhile male convert was going to be taken enough with Charlie's B-grade women to throw in with him? He needed another girl, one who looked good, somebody already into sex who wouldn't need weeks or months of coaxing by Charlie before she'd happily put out for any man he wanted her to. As the last days of the Summer of Love stumbled to their painful conclusion in the Haight, he found her, his first and only long-term follower recruited there.

Of all the followers who came to Charlie in his early ministry, none was quirkier or more desperate than twenty-year-old Susan Atkins. When her mother died of cancer, Susan, fifteen, was saddled with the responsibility of caring for a younger brother and a father who kept losing jobs. In high school she worked part-time to help make ends meet. She tried finding solace in the Baptist Church, in bad behavior at home and at school (for a short time she went to live with an uncle and aunt who found her incorrigible, and sent her back to her father), and in alcohol, drugs, and sex. Like Lynne, she attempted suicide. Susan craved acceptance and, above all, attention. As soon as she turned eighteen in the summer of 1966 Susan left home outside Los Angeles and moved to San Francisco. She went through a series of menial jobs and abusive boyfriends until that fall, when her latest lover and a friend of his invited her to come with them on a road trip to Oregon in a stolen car. They robbed a gas station on the way before being arrested by the Oregon State Police. Susan spent three months in jail before being sentenced to two years' probation. She returned to San Francisco, where she lived in the Haight and worked for a while as a waitress before discovering more lucrative employment as a topless dancer. Susan wasn't beautiful, but she was nice-looking and exuded aggressive sexuality. Her dancing attracted the attention of Satanist Anton LaVey, who was organizing a Witches' Sabbath club show featuring topless female "vampires." He hired Susan, and it was her dream job, eliciting the attention she craved from howling audiences by writhing naked onstage. But she didn't last long in LaVey's troupe, wearing down from excessive drug use and a raging case of gonorrhea. Susan began aimlessly wandering the Haight's streets with no particular plan other than scoring drugs.

In early fall 1967, Susan visited some friends at their Haight apartment and met another guest—Charlie had dropped by with his guitar. That day, Charlie wasn't entertaining with one of his own tunes. He still felt a strong attachment to pop schmaltz, and as Susan came in the room he was singing "The Shadow of Your Smile," a favorite of lounge crooners everywhere and the absolute musical antithesis of cutting-edge, counterculture songs. As he sang Charlie accompanied himself on guitar, as usual bashing out basic chords rather than any intricate notes. But that didn't matter to Susan—her lifelong trait was to react in extremes, and she instantly decided that Charlie was a guitar virtuoso. When he finished the song, Susan continued gazing at him adoringly, and Charlie didn't miss the signal. Here might be just the girl he needed. He pounced, utilizing the Dale Carnegie technique of figuring out what the other person wanted and demonstrating how he could provide it. In Susan's case, it was simple. She obviously admired his guitar, and Charlie said that if she really wanted, Susan could pick it up and play it. She was stunned—how could this stranger know she was thinking about *that*? They danced a little to records, and afterward had sex, with Charlie using a tried-and-true preliminary. He knew that many girls had guilty sexual feelings about their fathers, so he brought that up before initial lovemaking. He told Susan that to break free of the bad experiences and inhibitions that were crushing her, she needed to imagine that she was making love to her father. When they were finished, Charlie promised Susan that he'd never let her fall. That was all it took; she swore she'd follow him anywhere. Maybe Susan seemed odd, even a bit crazy, an attention addict who'd need a lot of special handling, but she was still the sexy disciple that Charlie needed. He told her to come with him and become part of a *real* family.

After Susan joined, Charlie took his women up to Sacramento, where they met another guy he knew from prison. Pete operated three whorehouses in town, one a "10-minute" for laborers and blue-collar workers looking to get laid fast and cheap, a regular place for customers with more time and money, and a fancy, discreet house that catered to state legislators. Charlie told the women that Pete was mobbed up and they thought that for once Charlie seemed to look up to somebody. Charlie asked Pete to let the girls work in his houses for a day; it was a good way to remind them that they had to have sex whenever and with whomever Charlie ordered them to. The girls obeyed, and afterward whenever they were running short of money Charlie would tell them that he was thinking of sending them to Pete for a while, but he never did.

Mary Brunner became pregnant with Charlie's baby. She was thrilled; maybe this would secure her place as Charlie's main woman even if she didn't yet have him all to herself. Charlie was pleased, too. He said that only babies were spiritually pure, and when this one was born it would provide everyone with the perfect example of how to be. In the months ahead, other women in the group would get pregnant and hope that Charlie was the father, but they never could be sure because at about the same time Mary got pregnant he began ordering them to have sex with lots of different men, guys he wanted to induce to join the group or at least contribute something to it. But no birth control ever—Charlie said it wasn't natural and wouldn't allow it.

Now that they were five, and Charlie expected to keep adding more— he hoped men—the VW bus was no longer big enough. They took more trips and Charlie did some vehicle scouting. He swapped the VW plus some scrounged cash for an old yellow school bus in Sacramento. As they had with the VW bus, he and the girls tore out the seats and replaced them with sleeping bags and cushions. They painted the outside, first in a rainbow swirl of colors and then in black. "Hollywood Productions" was lettered on the side—it was a good joke on all the straights they passed on the road; maybe they'd think they were seeing a crew out shooting a movie.

On the days they spent in the Haight, Charlie sent the girls out to make friends and screw possible male recruits to expand the group. They ended up with some hangers-on, one of whom had a sick baby, and the women collectively contracted a variety of venereal diseases. That made them regular patrons of the Free Clinic, as it was named, and Charlie always went along, though never for treatment himself. Charlie seemed impervious to disease, which reinforced his followers' growing belief, one he encouraged, that if he wasn't entirely divine he was something higher than human. Smith, the clinic's founder, had several more opportunities to chat at length with Charlie, who was especially preachy when his group brought the baby in to be treated for a yeast infection. He explained to Smith that he was teaching his disciples to become like children themselves. He felt they could accomplish this by completely emptying their minds of all corrupting influences. In keeping with the clinic policy of remaining nonjudgmental, Smith let Charlie prattle on without challenging anything he said. But in the doctor's personal opinion, Charlie seemed more than ever to be an unoriginal con artist taking advantage of middle-class girls who had problems with their parents and thought living "off the land, so to speak" was an exciting adventure. Another thing was very obvious to Smith: Charlie might preach equality, but he completely dominated the group. These girls unquestioningly did whatever he told them.

In the early fall, Charlie took the bus out on an extended road trip. Mary, Lynne, Pat, and Susan joined him, along with Susan's friend Ella-Jo and another girl. Two men were along at the beginning of the trip, but they almost immediately dropped out after deciding that the vibe inside the bus was too strange. That didn't sit well with Charlie, but he was mollified a few days later when Bruce Davis, a college dropout from Tennessee who had found his way to the California coast, was intrigued enough after meeting the girls to join the group. Davis soon had a new goal in life, to become Charlie's second-in-command and order the women around whenever he had the opportunity. The girls considered him to be a pompous lightweight, but Charlie wanted them to accept him into the family and so they did.

Charlie next drove the group to San Jose, where he pulled up at the Moorehouse residence and summoned Dean outside to see how his original gift of a piano had morphed into a bus. Moorehouse wasn't pleased to see Charlie. His wife had left him, in part because of Charlie absconding earlier that year with their teenage daughter, and Ruth Ann was also gone, off somewhere with her husband. Ruth Ann had obviously told her father everything about her brief adventure with Charlie, and now Moorehouse made it clear that Charlie was no longer welcome in his house. Charlie and his companions piled back in the bus and drove off. Moorehouse fumed for a few hours, then grabbed a shotgun and set off in pursuit. He had no trouble tracking the black school bus, and somewhere along the road he cornered Charlie, announced that he was going to kill him, and put the shotgun to his head. The others from the bus were frozen with fear; it was one thing to spout platitudes about death being the same as life, but this was actually happening—a man with a gun clearly intended to blow Charlie's head off.

And then Charlie did something that seemed to them to confirm his specialness, even his divinity. This crazy man was about to murder him and *Charlie wasn't afraid*. Moorehouse screamed that Charlie was about to die and Charlie smiled and said quietly, "Go ahead, shoot me," which stopped Moorehouse cold because that was the last thing anybody in that situation could be expected to say. Charlie's tone was calm and his voice didn't quaver. He gently put his hand on Moorehouse's shoulder and talked about how love was so much better than anger, and what a relief it was when you gave up your individuality and became part of a real family. Moorehouse put down the gun. Then Charlie dosed Moorehouse with some acid and everybody watched as the older man began having himself a fine trip. After a while Moorehouse wished everyone a pleasant goodbye and headed home. Charlie's followers were awestruck. He clearly had no fear of death, and, maybe even more impressive, he'd faced down a *father*. That really got to the girls, since they all had struggled with parents. Charlie just grinned and acted like it was no big thing. He wanted to get back on the road; it was time to finish up in the Haight.

Charlie said later that he moved his followers from the Haight to Los Angeles in late 1967 because the Haight had become dangerous. But it had been that way ever since Charlie first got there back in April; he'd arrived at the beginning of the end. Group safety may have been a contributing factor, but the main reason Charlie wanted to move to L.A. was that he was prepared to audition for Gary Stromberg at Universal. He might have hoped, for a while, that his musical genius would be recognized and rewarded in the Haight. Like so many other hopefuls, he played his songs in the Panhandle, and in a few small clubs. But the recording industry was based in Los Angeles, and the L.A. reps who came to check out San Francisco talent left unimpressed. In their opinions, "Northern" musicians might wow spacey Fillmore or Avalon Ballroom audiences, but on the whole they simply didn't have the professional chops to produce marketable studio product. San Francisco bands, in turn, considered themselves *real* and disdained many L.A. groups, including some of the most famous, as ersatz musicians whose hit records were the product of studio gimmickry. Everyone knew that the fabled Beach Boys used studio musicians known as the Wrecking Crew as a backing band on their albums, and rumors persisted that on the Byrds' first massive hit, a cover of Bob Dylan's "Mr. Tambourine Man," four of the five Byrds didn't perform at all because their whiz-kid producer, Terry Melcher, decreed that they weren't competent enough on their instruments. In June 1967 many of the San Francisco bands got their first real national exposure performing at the Monterey Pop Festival, a historic event bringing together the best of the Los Angeles and San Francisco music scenes along with a few British groups and soul performers. But most of the organizers were from Los Angeles, and L.A. players got the prime performance slots. The bottom line was unmistakable to even the most holier-than-thou San Francisco musicians. Acerbic Frank Zappa, whose Mothers of Invention snared a contract after performing at the Whisky a Go Go on L.A.'s Sunset Strip, summarized it best: "No matter how 'peace-love' the San Francisco bands might try to make themselves, they eventually had to come south to evil ol' [L.A.] to get a record deal." The Grateful Dead did, and so did Big Brother with Janis Joplin. Charlie believed that it was his turn. In November, his parole supervision was transferred from San Francisco to Los Angeles, where Charlie felt certain that he would realize his dream of worldwide fame.

CHAPTER EIGHT

L.A.

Little about Los Angeles in its early incarnations indicated that it would become one of the cultural centers of the world. Flanked by ocean, mountains, valleys, and desert, it first flourished as a seaport, then expanded with an influx of miners during the California Gold Rush of the mid-1800s, benefited from a subsequent oil boom, and, thanks to its annexation of the sprawling, fertile San Fernando Valley, became an agricultural Eden. From the first, fiercely conservative business leaders dominated local politics as well as the economy. City expansion was carefully controlled. As much or more than any other major city in America, Los Angeles became a place of class and racial partition, where everyone's place was defined not only by what they earned but where they lived. L.A. remained predominantly white until World War II created vast new demands on national industry. Federal legislation forbidding discrimination in government hiring resulted in the arrival of blacks from all over the country, lured by jobs with guaranteed decent pay. As many as one thousand flooded in each week. Blocked from living where they pleased by discriminatory local regulations on rentals and housing purchases, many of them were relegated to the substandard environs of Watts, an immense community in South Central L.A. that became widely known as "Mud Town."

African Americans weren't welcomed to L.A., but show business personalities were. Hollywood was little more than a sleepy community northwest of downtown L.A. until the early 1900s, when it became the central production site of motion pictures. These took the nation by storm, especially after the advent of talkies in 1927 with *The Jazz Singer.*

Until then, the American entertainment industry was dominated by the East Coast and vaudeville. As radio, and then television, muscled their way into U.S. households, L.A. became the center of these creative industries, too. The rugged hills outside the city especially lent themselves to filming the ubiquitous TV westerns of the 1950s. Though many city leaders personally disapproved of show people and their often excessive lifestyles, the entertainment business quickly became a mainstay of the local economy, attracting tourists as well as providing tens of thousands of jobs. A pragmatic approach to controlling vice was necessary, allowing important people to play as they pleased and requiring everyone else to stay in line. The key was an organization best known for its own history of corruption—the notorious Los Angeles Police Department.

Throughout the 1930s and 1940s, best-selling authors earned fortunes with *noir* tales of crooked L.A. cops. But in 1950 new Chief of Police Bill Parker promised significant changes. Under Parker, officers were on the streets to enforce the law, not to make friends. All street personnel were rotated on a frequent basis to prevent them being influenced by civilian acquaintances. Even as the L.A. population became more racially and ethnically mixed, its police department remained virtually all-white. Many crew cut recruits came straight from the military, a great many were from the South, and few were educated beyond high school. Pre-employment interviews weeded out applicants who sympathized with minorities, especially those who in any way supported the civil rights movement. Seminars were held for L.A. cops where lectures assured them that Martin Luther King Jr. and other black civil rights leaders were financed by the Communist Party. Officers were encouraged to believe that they were all that stood between order and anarchy in Los Angeles, especially where minorities were concerned. Street cops were authorized to make black-and-blue examples of people who defied them or even appeared that they might. Parker would fire any officer even slightly suspected of taking a bribe, but his administration fiercely defended LAPD cops accused of using excessive force. Parker kept the City Council happy with regular reports of law enforcement successes. Rising numbers of arrests were valued by them, and therefore by the chief, more than establishing programs dedicated to crime prevention—the number of prevented crimes could only be estimated, but actual arrests were quantifiable. These numbers looked good in the newspapers and impressive to taxpayers.

But the LAPD crackdown under Parker had exceptions. The city's most famous citizens, the movie and television and singing stars and their assorted producers and directors, were understood to be sacrosanct. Officers catching them in the act of driving drunk or getting in scuffles or committing any crime short of cold-blooded murder in the presence of too many unimpeachable witnesses were expected to politely intervene and ensure that the celebrities got home safely. This largesse extended to entire families; cops working in the toniest parts of town were expected by supervisors to recognize celebrities and their offspring on sight and treat them accordingly.

One evening in the early 1960s, four teenage boys set off in a car for some high-spirited fun. The driver was Terry Melcher, son of singer-actress Doris Day. Beside him in the front seat was Dean Martin Jr., known to his pals as Dino. In the backseat sat Dennis Wilson, a kid from the working-class suburb of Hawthorne and a drummer in a band called the Beach Boys that had just reached the pop charts for the first time. The fourth passenger, sitting next to Dennis, was Gregg Jakobson, who had not yet made his own mark in the music industry and so had no celebrity stature, only his friendship with the other three. Melcher drove into a residential construction area on a street above Beverly Hills and parked the car. He and Martin got out, rummaged in the trunk, and pulled out a massive Magnum handgun. Telling his friends that "I'm going to get it sighted in," Melcher proceeded to shatter several newly installed streetlights. The loud booms of the shots reverberated down the hill, and just as Melcher blasted his third or fourth light an LAPD cruiser bore down on him, siren blaring and lights flashing. Wilson and Jakobson, still in the backseat of Melcher's car, panicked. They'd heard about what L.A. cops did to people and expected the worst. They couldn't understand why Terry and Dino waited calmly in the street as two LAPD officers emerged from the black-and-white.

One cop, young enough to perhaps be a rookie, had his hand on his gun and was clearly ready for trouble. But his partner, a grizzled sergeant, pulled him back, smiled, and said politely, "Hello, Mr. Melcher." Melcher nodded and Martin said, "Nice evening, officer." With a regretful shake of his head, as though he hoped everyone understood that he had no choice other than to enforce a foolish rule, the sergeant held out his hand for Melcher's Magnum, saying, "You know, we have to confiscate your gun." He quickly added that Mr. Melcher could come by the station anytime the next day to pick it up. After cautioning Melcher to drive carefully, the sergeant herded his younger colleague back to their patrol car and drove away, leaving Melcher and Martin laughing behind them in the street. Back in the car, Wilson and Jakobson, stunned by what they'd just witnessed, mopped nervous sweat from their faces. "I learned that there was a completely different set of rules, a different sense of justice in L.A. for the rich," Jakobson recalls. "Dennis and I were shit-scared kids and Terry and Dino knew that they were royalty. That's what celebrity status gave you in L.A."

As Los Angeles continued to grow, so did the gulf between haves and have-nots. Among the most obvious barriers were the burgeoning L.A. freeways. These neatly separated communities, in particular making access to some higher-end districts deliberately difficult because of limited off-ramps. Beyond the service hours and reach of public transportation, it became impossible to get from one part of the city to another without an automobile. Many poorer city residents didn't own cars, so they were confined to their own neighborhoods. Isolating riffraff fit perfectly into leadership's goal of keeping L.A. clean and relatively crime-free. The police always knew where most of the bad elements were and could allocate personnel accordingly.

Even as most of the rest of the city thrived, conditions in the Watts section deteriorated. For anyone standing outside, it was difficult to carry on conversations because flight paths into and out of the busy Los Angeles International Airport were routed directly overhead—no coincidence, Watts residents felt certain. Unlike white kids in the rest of the city and the suburbs, on weekends Watts teens couldn't borrow the family car to head to the beach or the mountains or the hot clubs on the Strip. They were trapped in their depressing neighborhood with little to do but take out their frustration on each other. Gangs fought each other to the death for control of dilapidated blocks, defying efforts by the Black Panthers to keep the peace. Watts adults were no better off; defense industry jobs had dried up, and by 1965 three-quarters of all adult Watts males were unemployed and six out of ten families depended on welfare to survive. Antagonistic L.A. street cops and a handful of California Highway Patrol officers were visible daily symbols of white oppression in the seething, forty-six-square-mile ghetto roughly the size of central San Francisco. Something had to give, and on the terribly hot night of August 11, 1965, it did.

California Highway Patrol officer Lee Minikus didn't expect trouble when he pulled over twenty-one-year-old Marquette Frye for drunk driving on a Watts street. Frye failed a field sobriety test and laughed as he did. A crowd of onlookers observed but wasn't threatening. Minikus and Frye were chuckling together as the officer and his partner prepared to take Frye off to jail. But then Frye's mother and brother arrived and started yelling. Encouraged by his relatives, Frye began shouting, too. Their raised voices incited the crowd to begin screaming threats, more people heard the uproar and came running, Minikus radioed for backup, and the most notorious race riot in American history was under way. The Watts riot lasted six days and resulted in thirty-four dead, more than one thousand injured, four thousand arrests, and $40 million in property damage. An estimated thirty thousand people, most of them Watts residents, participated in violent, criminal acts that ranged from looting stores to attacking police patrol cars with Molotov cocktails. One hundred and three LAPD patrol cars were brought in to help quell the violence, and all 103 were badly damaged. Fourteen thousand National Guardsmen joined every active member of the LAPD before the riot finally dwindled down, not because of any community-wide contrition or effective damage control by the police, but because the rioters finally ran out of energy and places to loot and burn; almost every business in Watts with something to steal or destroy was gutted.

There had been race riots in modern-day American cities before—Chicago, Harlem, the spate across the nation in the summer of 1964—but none ever struck more fear in white America than this one. Part of it was the city where it occurred. It seemed logical, even predictable, that angry low-income blacks might rise up in bustling metropolises like New York and Chicago, or in Washington, D.C., where there was such a large minority population. But to the rest of the country, Los Angeles epitomized sunshine and show business and a laid-back attitude. A massive race riot in L.A. signaled that there could be one anywhere. California governor Pat Brown organized a commission to determine the cause of the Watts debacle, and in December it reported in stark, prescient terms that "the existing breach between rich and poor, black and white, in Los Angeles could blow up [again] one day in the future."

For Chief Parker, the 1965 Watts riot offered a welcome chance to increase public support of the LAPD by persuading shaken white residents that without the protection of their stalwart police force, the next L.A. neighborhood razed by black rioters might very well be their own. In one TV appearance he warned, "It is estimated that by 1970, 45 percent of the metropolitan area of Los Angeles will be Negro. If you want any protection for your home . . . you're going to have to get in and support a strong police department. If you don't, come 1970, God help you."

In Watts life went on exactly as before, but with charred rubble on virtually every corner. Parker's scare tactics worked, and race-related paranoia spread beyond the ghetto. After Parker died of a heart attack in July 1966 (he collapsed at an awards dinner in his honor), his successor, Tom Reddin, dutifully carried on his policies. When black outsiders turned up in white neighborhoods at any hour, it became routine for nervous residents to call the cops, and the police instantly responded. Blacks living in Watts were used to being stopped by cops and questioned about what they might be up to. Now blacks in every part of Los Angeles found themselves fair game for arbitrary stops and interrogations. Whites venturing into Watts were also pulled over, but in these cases the cops would warn them to lock their car doors, drive out fast, and not even stop for red lights because their lives were in danger. An ominous sense of ever-imminent racial violence settled over much of the city like the infamous brown L.A. smog. It wasn't the in-your-face tension of major Eastern cities like New York, where every subway ride offered opportunities for racial conflict. In many parts of L.A., blacks and whites rarely came into contact. But the feeling didn't go away.

• • •

The city's growing notoriety for racial unrest was somewhat offset by its simultaneous recognition as the new center of yet another art form—one that, by the mid-1960s, frequently eclipsed all others in terms of cultural impact. L.A. already dominated film and television. Now it wrested primacy of recorded music from New York. In the mid-1950s, Hollywood movie studios identified American teens as a separate market from their parents. Some landmark productions like *Rebel Without a Cause* resulted, but many of the films tied in to the same cute teenage romance themes that typified most of the pop chart hits emanating from New York and its Tin Pan Alley songwriters. But these films had soundtracks, and many of the songs celebrated California with its sunshine and surf. California-based groups like The Chantay's ("Pipeline") and the Surfaris ("Wipe Out") made considerable market impact. TV teen idol Ricky Nelson began churning out hits in L.A. studios. The Beach Boys had a string of hits about surfing and hot rods and being true to your school. By 1964 the Beatles dominated pop music, but West Coast producers and musicians were also succeeding. Market-savvy, profit-driven L.A. music moguls set out to discover and sign a new generation of teen idols. There was a wealth of available talent—Brian Wilson, Randy Newman, Frank Zappa, and Phil Spector, among others, had all grown up in or around the city. Children of the older stars got their own opportunities, in some cases because their parents owned substantial chunks of the record companies: Nancy Sinatra as a solo artist, Dean Martin Jr. and Desi Arnaz Jr. in the group Dino, Desi and Billy, Terry Melcher in several surf bands. In 1963, records produced in New York topped the pop charts for twenty-six weeks, with L.A. singles reaching number one for just three weeks. By 1965, L.A. was on top for twenty weeks and New York for just one.

Television reinforced L.A.'s new supremacy. In 1964 Dick Clark moved his popular *American Bandstand* program from Philadelphia to Los Angeles. Soon three more network dance shows broadcast from L.A.—*Where the Action Is!* (ABC), *Shindig!* (ABC), and *Hullabaloo* (NBC). At the movies, in their cars listening to the radio, at home watching TV, California-based music, often with California-centric lyrics, permeated the lives of American teens.

Initially it seemed that the latest singing stars would not be much different from the preceding generation—essentially clean-cut kids singing about young love and, in the case of surf music, having appropriate outdoor fun. The most conservative parents would have allowed TV and recording star Ricky Nelson to date their daughters. But the emergence of the counterculture resulted in a significant change in the growing youth music market. It was impossible to be certain whether hairy message music would be a brief fad or a long-term phenomenon, but L.A. record executives didn't care. There was a clear change in the critical youth market, and they moved to meet it.

Hordes of wannabe musicians made their way to L.A., certain that they were destined for stardom and desperate to land a recording contract. Many of them found their way to clubs along Sunset Strip that designated specific nights of the week for hopefuls to jump onstage and play one or two songs. The legendary Troubadour on Santa Monica Boulevard held open mike nights on Mondays. Future superstars like Jim (later Roger) McGuinn and David Crosby got their starts there. Others lucked into short stints as house bands. Johnny Rivers, the Doors, and Frank Zappa's bizarre Mothers of Invention gained much of their early fame from regular appearances at the Whisky a Go Go. Record company talent scouts trolled the clubs on a nightly basis, often basing their signing decisions on the look more than the sound of an individual artist or a band.

The musicians might consider their songs to be spiritual or social anthems, but to the record labels the music was product. Many newly signed acts, entering a recording studio for the first time, were appalled to learn that most or all of the instrumental work and even some of the vocals would be provided by veteran studio musicians. Muffed chords and sloppy rhythm might be overlooked onstage if performers were charismatic enough, but for radio airplay—still the critical factor in sales—the sound had to be perfect. Given the multitudes panting for a chance to record, studio executives weren't inclined to be tactful. At Columbia, Terry Melcher, at twenty-two already a veteran recording artist in his own right, was placed in charge of a promising band called the Byrds, five refugees from the folk music scene who were set to record Dylan's "Mr. Tambourine Man." Melcher quickly determined that only lead singer McGuinn was a competent enough instrumentalist to play on the track. The four other Byrds were told to step aside for studio musicians, then and in several subsequent sessions. When the drummer complained, Melcher gave him a choice: shut up or get out. The drummer shut up, and "Mr. Tambourine Man" was a number one hit. In this as in most cases, record producers knew what they were doing. No unproven artists were allowed to do as they pleased in the studio. The bottom line, the only factor that ultimately mattered, was whether someone could sell enough records or not. Genius on the artist's part, whether genuine or self-perceived, didn't matter a damn.

For those musicians who came to L.A. and made it big, stardom and all its perks were instantaneous. After one hit, especially if more of the same seemed in store, record companies offered substantial advances on future royalties. Many of the newly wealthy had no concept of money beyond spending it fast. Overnight pop stars gleefully snapped up mansions previously owned by film legends. After "California Dreamin' " became a smash hit in February 1966, the Mamas and the Papas husband-wife team of John and Michelle Phillips bought the spacious Bel Air Road home of Jeanette MacDonald. Not to be outdone, their bandmates Denny Doherty and Cass Elliot respectively purchased the glamorous residences of Mary Astor and Natalie Wood. The overweight Elliot couldn't resist also treating herself to a flashy new red Porsche, even though she was unable to wedge herself into it. L.A. music veterans with strings of hits (written, performed, or produced) also paid their way into the toniest L.A. territory. Beach Boys songwriter and leader Brian Wilson bought a Bel Air mansion and promptly outraged his stodgier neighbors by painting it purple. His brother Dennis rented a luxurious log cabin hunting lodge originally owned by Will Rogers near the far west end of Sunset Boulevard. Terry Melcher and his girlfriend, actress Candice Bergen, daughter of radio and TV star Edgar Bergen, rented a smaller residence at the top of steep Cielo Drive in the Benedict Canyon area; the house, owned by agent-to-the-stars Rudi Altobelli (Henry Fonda, Katharine Hepburn), was distinguished by its magnificent view of the sprawling city below.

Not all the new generation of music heavyweights felt drawn to luxury living. Some preferred country life, or at least what passed for it on the L.A. scene. Topanga, west of an extensive state park but still within easy driving distance of the Strip and city recording studios, was a hilly alternative, and Laurel Canyon offered pleasantly rustic touches like a general store. For others who simply couldn't live without instant access to Pacific waves, there was Venice Beach and Santa Monica and Malibu. And, for virtually everyone, there were the magic clubs on the Strip—when not performing, L.A.'s music stars delighted in dropping by the Whisky or the Troubadour, sipping drinks with their show business peers or graciously interacting with their public. Every weekend and most weekday nights the Strip was jammed with happy, hooting young crowds. After numerous complaints about underage drinking and drug use, in the fall of 1966 the LAPD and Los Angeles County Sheriff's office announced joint plans to begin enforcing a previously obscure curfew requiring anyone under eighteen to be off the streets by 10 P.M. At the same time, the County Supervisor's Office made public a potential plan to bulldoze part of the Strip to make way for a new freeway. In November, after numerous arrests for curfew violations and the news that Pandora's Box, a popular club, would be closed and leveled to widen the street, about three-hundred protesters surrounded the club. A city bus was overturned, but there was no other overt violence. Unlike the desperate black poor of Watts, these were mostly pissed-off, affluent, or at least middle-class, white kids, raising a little hell because they might no longer be allowed to stay out as late as they pleased. But the LAPD took no chances. There were arrests, and cops used billy clubs on demonstrators not obeying orders quickly enough to vacate the area.

Previously, most prominent white L.A. pop stars hadn't been moved enough by social or antiwar protests to compose songs about them. After Watts, Frank Zappa, frustrated by how widely his fellow musicians ignored the event, tried to capture the incident in song. But the Sunset "riot" caught the attention of Stephen Stills, a member of the L.A.-based Buffalo Springfield. Stills crafted a catchy tune about battle lines being drawn, and young people speaking their minds while in danger of the Man coming to take them away. "For What It's Worth" rose to number seven on the national hit parade, and gave the impression that L.A. musicians and youth were in the forefront of what the media increasingly perceived as a generational revolt. On April 25, 1967, CBS aired a documentary titled *Inside Pop: The Rock Revolution*, improbably hosted by Leonard Bernstein. McGuinn, lead singer of the Byrds, earnestly declared to viewers that "We're out to break down those barriers that we see to be arbitrary. I feel like there's some sort of guerrilla warfare, psychological warfare going on, and I feel like a guerrilla."

By the last weeks of 1967 there was a city-wide sense of unease in Los Angeles. Joan Didion, reflecting later on that time and place, concluded that "there were odd things going around town. . . . Everything was unmentionable but nothing was unimaginable. . . . The jitters were setting in." So, too, were the Santa Ana winds, hot gusts frequently topping a hundred miles per hour that annually plagued Los Angeles and the surrounding area from late fall through early spring, drying out the land and paving the way for periodic brush fires that destroyed substantial sections of the region. Local legend had it that the scorching winds were evil omens; in one of his L.A. *noir* stories, Raymond Chandler wrote that each year when the Santa Anas arrive, "meek little wives feel the edge of the carving knife and study their husbands' necks." And that November, along with the winds, Charlie Manson blew back into L.A., bringing with him the first stirrings of another kind of conflagration.

The school bus broke down on the way from San Francisco to L.A. and Charlie had to stop and fix it. He was an adequate mechanic, having worked in the garages of some of the reform schools where he'd spent his teenage years. Charlie was hyper during the trip; he was anxious to get and sign that recording contract. He talked about it some with the others on the bus, making sure they understood that what was good for Charlie was going to be good for them, too. Whatever this Gary Stromberg guy at Universal was like, they had to help Charlie impress him. Members of real families always backed each other up. Everyone got that a label deal was important to Charlie, but misunderstood why he wanted one so badly. His followers had no idea that Charlie was obsessed with becoming famous; he told them that his goal, his mission, really, was to teach the world a better way to live through his songs. If he wasn't given that opportunity, it was the world's loss, not Charlie's.

It was easy for Charlie to get in to see Stromberg. Phil Kaufman's

name really did have cachet. It was Stromberg's job to seek out potential talent, and Kaufman wasn't one to recommend too many people. If
Kaufman saw something in this guy, he was worth auditioning. Charlie
took a little extra time cleaning up for their first meeting. He bathed and
put on clean clothes, but what Stromberg remembered most later on was
that Charlie arrived barefoot. He proudly showed Stromberg the bus,
now painted white. On the inside, there was a coffee table suspended by
ropes or wires from the roof, and a battery-powered turntable and an old
icebox. The group had scrounged a box of cream puffs on the trip down
from San Francisco, and they hospitably offered Stromberg some. Until
the cream puffs ran out, this was what Charlie's followers ate. When
Stromberg invited Charlie up to his office, all four girls tagged along—
Bruce Davis wasn't around on this particular trip. Charlie brought his
guitar into the office with him and was eager to talk about his music, but
Stromberg was distracted by the way Mary, Lynne, Pat, and Susan constantly watched Charlie, waiting for him to signal whatever it might be
that he wanted them to do. What he wanted that day was for them to sit
back and let him wow Stromberg with his songs. Stromberg listened and
thought there was enough potential to arrange a three-hour studio session, a chance to hear how Charlie sounded in one of Universal's recording studios. He set up the session and Charlie knew that it was all about
to happen. His dreams were going to come true.

But the session was an unmitigated disaster. Charlie was out of his
depth in the studio, put off by the microphones and wires and barked
commands from the session engineers. At one point he turned to Stromberg and complained, "I ain't used to a lot of people." Stromberg didn't
deem anything from the session worthy of a recording contract. He tact-
fully suggested that maybe Charlie ought to work on the songs some
more, and maybe at some unspecified point in the future they could try
again. It wasn't an absolute turndown, but close.

Stromberg didn't think his time with Charlie was entirely wasted.
He and some other Universal executives were discussing a film in which
Christ would return to the modern-day world. Charlie clearly had some
interesting interpretations of the Bible. Stromberg suggested that he stay
around for a few days to talk about Scripture, and Charlie was glad to.

He and Stromberg and the four girls went out to lunch a few times and hung out on the beach. Charlie talked about how the Bible made it clear that women had to gladly submit to men. To prove his point, he ordered Lynne to get down on her knees and kiss his feet. After she did, Charlie dropped down and kissed hers, just to make the additional point that women who did what they were told were rewarded. He also went on about how material possessions were wrong; to truly own something, you had to give it away first. Stromberg followed Charlie and the girls down the beach one day, listening to Charlie proselytize to some people gathered around. One man, who'd checked out the bus, called Charlie on it: If he really didn't need anything, why did he own such a tricked-up ride? Cooler than hell, Charlie said he didn't need the bus and flipped the guy the keys. The guy jumped in and drove off, leaving Charlie and the girls without transportation—Charlie didn't seem to care one way or the other. A few hours later the man brought the bus back. He returned the keys to Charlie and said he really didn't want it, he'd just wanted to see what Charlie would do. For the girls, it proved again how special Charlie was. Stromberg didn't know exactly what to think, but it was impressive all the same. He enjoyed consulting with Charlie on the Jesus project, which was soon shut down by Universal higher-ups who considered the symbolism—Jesus was to be black, the Romans modern-day Southern rednecks—too controversial.

Charlie wasn't crushed by his brief experience with Universal. Stromberg didn't reject his music—hadn't the guy said they ought to try again someday? The truth was probably that Stromberg just wasn't enlightened enough to understand what Charlie was doing. He would remain an option, but now that they were in L.A., Charlie and the girls could look around and find somebody else important in the music business who, unlike Stromberg, would get right away what the songs were about, and the kind of star Charlie would instantly become as soon as somebody was smart enough to sign him up and get his music out there to the people. And Charlie felt that he'd learned a valuable lesson—he was never, ever going to let any more studio monkeys tell him how he was supposed to play his songs. Charlie was going to do his music his way because he (and only he) knew best.

Charlie and the girls had probably been sleeping in the bus on the beach or in the Universal parking lot, but if they were going to remain in L.A. they needed someplace to stay, certainly one with showers. Charlie didn't mind grime, but no matter how much he lectured them about vanity, the women complained about feeling dirty and wanted to clean up. Fortunately, in late 1967 L.A. was populated with lots of generous-hearted people who were willing to share their roofs and their bathrooms with penniless pilgrims. After minimal asking around Charlie and the girls ended up in wild, beautiful Topanga Canyon, where they stayed at a quirky house known as the Spiral Staircase. All sorts of eclectic indigents found temporary lodging there; the owner liked colorful characters. Charlie and his female followers fit right in. They hung out and Charlie spun his tales and took his guitar and played some songs. He enjoyed talking music with other residents and the daily flood of drop-ins who came by certain that there would always be somebody interesting to talk to or jam with. One of them connected perfectly with Charlie right away—Bobby Beausoleil was his kind of guy, very musical and street-smart.

Charlie and Beausoleil became real friends, which was almost unprecedented for Charlie. He liked to look people over and figure out what they could do for him before letting them get too close, though he might pretend from the start that they were soul mates. But it was immediately apparent that Beausoleil had a lot to offer. Charlie noticed, as everyone around Beausoleil couldn't help noticing, that the guy always had a few girls trailing after him, catering to his every whim. Unlike scrawny little Charlie, who had to attract his females by force of personality and smooth, beguiling preaching, Beausoleil got his because he was sexy and handsome. Charlie instantly envisioned Beausoleil as a potentially invaluable member of his group if only he could somehow be won over—Beausoleil could recruit some *prime* women, who could in turn lure in more men. Charlie gave it his best shot, talking about being part of a real family and surrendering your ego, but Beausoleil was all about ego. He gloried in his good looks and had the same high opinion of his musical talent that Charlie had of his own. Beausoleil constantly bragged about his shows back in the Haight, including lots of dazzling late night jams with Frank Zappa. Beausoleil thought Charlie was an interesting guy and wanted to spend more time with him, but he wasn't going to submit to somebody else's leadership. Beausoleil told a disappointed Charlie that he "didn't travel with anybody." In the end, they decided to form a band together. They called themselves the Milky Way and played one or two shows at small local clubs. It was an uneven musical partnership—Beausoleil was a much better guitarist than Charlie, even though Charlie either wouldn't admit it or else was so self-deceptive that he didn't realize it—and nothing much came of the collaboration. Beausoleil and his latest girlfriends were soon out on the road again, but he and Charlie kept in touch.

During their first weeks of friendship, Bobby Beausoleil's most lasting favor to Charlie was introducing him to Gary Hinman, who lived near the Spiral Staircase. Charlie glommed on to Hinman right away. The guy was a music teacher, so he might have some useful industry contacts. He cooked up and sold drugs, mostly speed, so he had those kinds of connections, too. Hinman had a nice house and was willing to let friends crash there as needed—Charlie made certain that Hinman began counting him as a friend. Mary and Susan both liked quiet, somewhat standoffish Gary, so they gladly helped make a good impression on him. Hinman also had two cars, and that was handy whenever Charlie and his gang needed transportation other than the school bus. The only thing wrong with Hinman was that he was into Eastern religions, Zen or whatever, and that left him impervious to Charlie's spiritual raps. But at least, along with Bobby, he could serve as a long-term asset, if not full member, of the group.

There was a lot to enjoy in Topanga, but Charlie was wary about hanging around the Spiral Staircase for too long, mostly because he didn't want his women to have an opportunity to fall under the influence of others. Charlie had learned in the Haight that it wasn't wise to open himself up to competition from other would-be gurus. On any given day at the Spiral Staircase there might be two or three or a dozen individuals yammering about their beliefs and urging everyone listening to join them. Satanists, vegans, anarchists, smack addicts, born-again Christians—it was a virtual bazaar of paths to true enlightenment. So in December Charlie got the girls back on the bus and took off on another extended road trip, this one initially probing the farthest reaches of the Mojave Desert, where the women had no guru options other than Charlie. He took full advantage, hammering home the importance of complete obedience to him and leavening the lectures with new music from the Beatles. They had just released *Magical Mystery Tour*, the soundtrack to a British TV holiday special in which the band and assorted colorful hangers-on boarded a bus and set out to have random adventures. See, Charlie reminded the girls, we're just like the Beatles out here on our bus, driving around and waiting to see what happens next. He loved the Mojave, its barren beauty and isolation. The women griped about the dust and bugs, but they stayed in the desert as long as Charlie wanted because he knew best. Then for about two weeks they went to a few other places, too, Arizona and New Mexico and Texas, meeting people and briefly hanging out with them. In Texas, Charlie's teeth started hurting so much that he went to see a dentist, who recommended pulling some. Charlie refused, saying that if he lost teeth he might not be able to sing properly afterward.

By the time around the end of the year that Charlie was ready to head back to L.A., Susan was pregnant—she was certain the father was some guy she'd had sex with in Arizona. Charlie was fine with that; it would be another baby to go with the one of his that Mary was going to deliver sometime in the spring. When Mary's baby was born, when Susan's arrived, all the grown-ups would share equally in parenting. That way their individual hang-ups wouldn't be passed on to the infants.

Charlie was interested in the communes that were cropping up, groups much like his where a leader brought together some like-minded others and everyone lived together, separating themselves from whatever it was in society that they disdained. Charlie had no interest in combining his followers with those of anyone else. Instead, as he had in prison with Dale Carnegie courses and Scientology, he wanted to appropriate the best ideas of others and adapt them for his own purposes. One of the best-known L.A. area communes was the Hog Farm, led by former Haight resident Hugh Romney, who rechristened himself Wavy Gravy. Romney and his fellow Hog Farm denizens provided free medical assistance at rock festivals and ecological charity events. Charlie didn't see anything worth emulating in that because there was nothing in it personally for him, but he was intrigued by Dianne Lake, a fourteen-year-old girl living at the Hog Farm with her parents. Dianne liked the school bus, and begged her parents for permission when Lynne and Pat asked if she'd like to come along with them. The Lakes agreed, and Charlie had another convert. He immediately began holding up Dianne to the other women as someone to emulate, claiming she hadn't yet been corrupted by parents or society the way that they had. Charlie favored Dianne in another way, too. Though he felt obligated to spread his sexual favors among the other women, for the next year Dianne would be by far his most frequent partner.

By the end of December, Charlie and the group were settled back in Topanga. They stayed in a series of houses, sometimes briefly renting, other times squatting, often crashing with Hinman or at the Spiral Staircase for a few days. Everything was meant to be fluid; the only certainty was that Charlie constantly angled for new music industry contacts who could get him a recording contract. There were potentially lots of them in Topanga, among them some of the current biggest stars in the business—Neil Young, Stephen Stills, Linda Ronstadt, Chris Hillman, Barry McGuire. Charlie did what he could to make their acquaintance, which in itself was typical of many rock star wannabes and something the established musicians accepted as part of the price of fame. Most of their addresses were common knowledge; it was not unusual for Frank Zappa to get up in the morning to find total strangers sitting in his living room, waiting for the chance to sing him their songs. Every one of them, Zappa told friends, believed that he or she was the most gifted performer in the universe with something original to say with their music. Few if any did, but Zappa, like his other famous neighbors, usually would at least listen politely and, in rare cases, suggest the musician call some club owner who was willing to give unknowns a chance to perform. It was important not to let any of them attach themselves permanently; the art of gentle, firm disengagement was something the Topanga celebrities had to learn.

Charlie distinguished himself from the other Topanga wannabes by being pushier. He tried to catch the attention of the popular band Spirit by crashing one of their home rehearsals, and was sent packing with shouts of, "Man, you got bad karma!" Producer David Briggs got so fed up with Charlie—who, in addition to demanding a record deal, also asked for Briggs's truck—that Briggs threatened to shoot him if he ever saw him again. Nothing could shake Charlie's belief in his superstar destiny. Still, at year's end, he was no closer to that goal than he'd been back on McNeil Island when he first heard the Beatles on a prison cell radio, and sometimes his frustration boiled over. Charlie constantly preached selflessness and love to his followers, but after a while all of them noticed that Mary Brunner always seemed to have a black eye. Lynne and Pat, who'd been with Charlie and Mary the longest, knew it was even worse. Sometimes Charlie administered full-scale beatings to Mary, knocking her down and kicking her while she was on the floor. He tried not to let most of his followers see this side of himself, but warned Lynne and Pat that if they didn't do exactly what they were told, the same thing would happen to them.

About the same time Charlie and his women returned to L.A., the Beach Boys left for Paris, where they performed a benefit concert for the United Nations. The band had arguably been the second-most popular in the world behind only the Beatles, but in recent years it had fallen on hard times. In October 1966 the single "Good Vibrations," all about the wonder of hippie love and lifestyle, topped the charts and became an anthem of the counterculture. But Brian Wilson, the Beach Boys' founder and composer of the music that propelled the band to prominence, rapidly deteriorated from the crushing combination of mental illness and drugs. First he quit touring, then seemed to lose his knack for crafting irresistible pop anthems. Without Brian to write hits, the rest of the band had to shoulder some of the composing load, and though several members would eventually emerge as fine composers in their own right, the immediate results were mostly forgettable fluff. The band also blundered by backing out of a scheduled appearance at the seminal 1967 Monterey Pop Festival, where a new generation of rock idols emerged—Jimi Hendrix, Janis Joplin, The Who. Among hip youth, the Beach Boys were no longer considered relevant. The band staggered forward mostly as a concert draw, with audiences cheering performances of golden oldies like "Fun, Fun, Fun" and "California Girls" and glumly enduring renditions of generally undistinguished new material. The Beach Boys were in trouble, and everybody in the band knew it.

While the Beach Boys were in Paris, drummer Dennis Wilson dropped into a rehearsal by sitar virtuoso Ravi Shankar, and another Shankar guest there was the Maharishi Mahesh Yogi, who had recently rocketed to prominence when the Beatles publicly became his followers in the discipline he called Transcendental Meditation or TM, the use of daily meditation and individual mantras to achieve serenity. Dennis found himself drawn to the diminutive guru, and touted him to the other Beach Boys. The Maharishi, savvy in publicity as well as philosophy, invited Dennis and the rest of the band to a private audience with him soon afterward in New York. Mike Love, the lead singer on many of the Beach Boys' hits, was especially charmed, and instantly embraced TM. The Beach Boys had recently opened their own production company, Brother Records, and Love wanted Brother to do a film about Transcendental Meditation. The project never developed, mostly because the band's main focus was on rebuilding its own sagging fortunes. But all of its members—impulsive, trusting Dennis Wilson in particular—yearned for some all-knowing savior to guide them back to prominence. Maybe it would be the Maharishi. They also desperately needed great new songs.

Early 1968 was savagely unsettling for America. The nation was rocked by news of January's Tet offensive, where insurgents from North Vietnam briefly overran the grounds of the American embassy in Saigon and brought the first heavy, sustained assaults to the heart of the South. Antiwar spirit spread into more college campuses and CBS news anchor Walter Cronkite, perhaps the most revered member of the media among older Americans, gravely editorialized on the air that despite optimistic reports from the White House and the military, the undeclared war in Vietnam was no better than a stalemate. Incumbent Lyndon Johnson was challenged in his party's first presidential primary by Minnesota senator Eugene McCarthy, whose entire platform was getting out of Vietnam as soon as he was sworn in. Masses of college students volunteered for McCarthy's campaign. Meanwhile, the first race riot of 1968 broke out in South Carolina in February. It was only the first of many—there would be more than 130 in major U.S. cities by year's end.

While Charlie had no interest in what caused the latest tidal waves of discontent among American youth, he was happy to benefit from the portion that turned up in Topanga. Many kids from L.A. and most of those flooding into the area were bewildered by events around them, if not the war or racial strife, then at least problems with parents and the strong desire to get away from the overwhelming pressure of fitting into an increasingly chaotic world. Charlie had his alternative to offer— surrender ego, give up individuality, come with him, join a real family, all of it field-tested now on Mary and Lynne and Patricia and Susan and Dianne. Charlie in full recruiting mode was something to behold. He'd chat with a likely convert, turning the subject quickly to how obvious it was that the system wasn't working. Charlie would turn whatever reply he got into more detailed conversation, always seeming to agree with every word the other person said. It was impossible for any of them not to feel flattered, and most were intrigued by Charlie's insistence that he and some other friends were doing their part to bring about the right kind of change, starting with jettisoning the very things the potential convert disliked most about ordinary life—he or she should come hang out with them for a while. He cast out his psychological net and began hauling in potential converts at a rapid rate. The girls already in his thrall helped by wandering around, chatting with youngsters and telling them about this amazing man named Charlie who had all the answers—they should come talk to him, hear what he had to say.

Most days, possible followers would be brought to or drop by wher- ever in Topanga Charlie happened to be living, and he would offer his hybrid philosophy and get a sense of who seemed most interested. Some weren't, sensing something phony or else put off by Charlie per- sonally or the raggedy appearance of the girls already following him. Those who seemed to buy into what they were hearing were individu- ally tested, mostly by Charlie himself. Men were valued for mechanical skills—the bus was always breaking down, and the cars and motorcycles, mostly used, that the group kept acquiring from generous acquaintances needed lots of maintenance. Too, Charlie simply enjoyed the company of men much more than being around women. He believed that he could sometimes let down his guard around other guys. Most of the men who

spent much time with him were soon aware of his extreme racial prejudice, but women joining the group believed that Charlie loved all races
equally. Charlie's fascination with guns and knives surprised many of
his women in the months ahead, but men in the group knew about it all
along.

The most important male initiate was Paul Watkins, a cherubic
eighteen-year-old dropout who immediately established himself as
Manson's most effective recruiter. Watkins's ambition was to become
Charlie's second-in-command. Charlie's leadership skills were never more
shrewdly demonstrated than the way in which he encouraged Watkins
and Bruce Davis to believe that each was his most indispensable subor-
dinate. Davis would be sent on long-term scouting expeditions, one all
the way to England, seeking out financial support and studying ways in
which other groups and cults operated. Watkins was more useful at Charlie's side, where his boyish charm helped disarm warier women.

Though it was relatively easy for men to pass muster with Charlie, he
was much more demanding of women who wanted to join the group. He
tested them in the same way he had potential hookers during his days as a
pimp, isolating himself with them and breaking them down mentally and
sexually. The women were exhaustively quizzed about their lives, their
experiences with their parents, peers, at school or in church. The more
Charlie knew about each one, the better he could weave individual webs
to bind them to him. Charlie's immediate goal was to alienate the women
from everything in their past. If they had little self-esteem, if there were
things wrong with their lives, then that was the fault of their parents,
their teachers, people who forced them to go against their own nature.
Great wrongs had been done to them all of their lives, Charlie stressed.
What they needed now was the guidance of someone who would love
them for who they really were.

Then Charlie mastered the women sexually, both to establish his
dominance and to assure himself that they would be willing to give themselves to anyone in any way at Charlie's command. He started by crudely
insisting on a blow job. Any girl who refused to perform something Charlie considered so basic was unsuited to joining the group. From there,
Charlie indulged his varied appetites. No matter the extent of her previ-

ous sexual history, a woman being initiated into the group by Charlie was certain to have new experiences with him. Within the group, Charlie's sexual prowess became the stuff of wonder, additional proof that he was more than human.

One female addition who didn't need extensive vetting by Charlie, sexual or otherwise, was Ruth Ann Moorehouse. As he'd promised, Charlie summoned her, and the precocious teenager deserted the husband she'd married only to emancipate herself from her parents. Charlie was pleased when Ruth Ann arrived in Topanga. Like Susan Atkins, she was sexy enough to seduce men into joining the group. But unlike moody, attention-addicted Susan, Ruth Ann cheerfully did what she was told and never caused problems.

Women who didn't make it through Charlie's sexual initiation still had a chance to join the group for a while if they had something else to offer—specifically money (cash or bank accounts), active credit cards, or vehicles. Once their money was completely contributed, their credit card limits reached, or the auto pink slips signed over to Charlie, they were urged to leave, usually by being told they needed to go through more personal changes before they were worthy of membership.

Charlie's prime money catch was teenaged Didi Lansbury, daughter of actress Angela Lansbury. Didi never actually left home to join the group full-time, but so far as Charlie was concerned, she didn't need to. He and some of the others would pick up Didi at her high school after class was out and go stock up on clothes or car parts without any concern for cost, because Didi paid for everything with her mother's credit cards. Eventually, the cards were cut off and Didi withdrew from Charlie's clutches, but not before he'd greatly benefited from their association. The experience left Charlie convinced that there were no better pigeons than the children of stars. He hoped to meet many more.

In the early months of 1968, the group grew to twenty or more members, some not staying long, others clearly determined to cleave to Charlie forever. He preached that their given names were one more way society forced them to conform and encouraged them to take on new identities, changing what they called themselves as frequently as they liked. This made it difficult, later on, for authorities and the media to keep straight exactly who was who, and the given names of some members have been entirely lost, leaving them to be identified only by group nicknames. Pat Krenwinkel became and mostly stayed Katie, though she also experimented with Marnie Kay Reeves. Susan Atkins went through several identities before Charlie, wanting to suppress her obvious delight in her looks and sexuality, dubbed her Sadie Mae Glutz. Susan shortened it to Sadie. Mary Brunner became Mother Mary in honor of her pregnancy. Young Dianne Lake was Snake. In tribute to his diminutive stature, Paul Watkins became Little Paul. Newcomer Nancy Pitman was renamed Brenda McCann. Ella Jo was soon known by all as Yeller. Ruth Ann became Ouisch, pronounced "Ooh-WHEESH." Subsequent Manson legend often had it that her name was derived from the slithery noise knives made slitting flesh, but the truth was more mundane. Ouisch got her new name based on the sound men supposedly made whenever they saw her for the first time—"Ooh-WHEEE."

New names weren't mandatory; Lynne Fromme for some time remained Lynne. Charlie was still Charlie, or occasionally Jesus Christ.

True to Charlie's teaching, the group had little in the way of possessions, but a certain level of financing was needed to pay basic expenses—rent (though that often was ignored until landlords threw them out), clothes and mending supplies, parts for automobile and motorcycle repair, and drugs, enough weed and acid to satisfy the daily needs of a growing conglomeration of ragged young women and men. The girls were usually sent out to panhandle, and Charlie's recruiters, Watkins in particular, sought out potential converts who seemed to have a few dollars in their pockets to contribute. Charlie was adept at convincing curious, well-heeled older people to give him substantial gifts like cars—he would meet them on the beach or in the city, engage them in conversation, and intrigue them with stories about the harmonious *real* family he was gathering, and how he was trying to teach these poor desperate kids a better way to live. It didn't pay off very often, but whenever it did Charlie had a car, or at least a few gently used expensive suits or a fancy stereo, to trade for drugs or generic cheap clothing. The barter system thrived in the Love Generation. When absolutely necessary, Charlie and Watkins and whatever other men were associated with the group at the time would hire out to clean swimming pools and stables—Charlie always did like being around animals.

Food was never a problem. Charlie taught the others how to scrounge edible throwaways in supermarket garbage bins, making it appear as though it was his original idea rather than admitting he'd learned it from the Diggers back in the Haight. They were astounded at the bounty they found there—Lynne compared it to diving inside a giant salad. The girls were also instructed to flirt with grocery store stock boys, who for a kiss and cuddle or a blow job would sneak out fresh produce or even milk, meat, and candy bars, to which Charlie sometimes seemed addicted. On any given day, the group ate whatever it got, and its daily hauls grew more plentiful and varied as their gathering techniques became more sophisticated. Sometimes one or two of the women would put on "straight" clothes, blouses and hemmed skirts or conservative slacks, go to food stores, identify themselves as Girl Scout leaders, and ask for donations for snacks. Other times, group members would volunteer as stall assistants at farmers' markets; at the end of the day, they would be given whatever fruits or vegetables hadn't been sold and weren't fresh enough to offer to the public again the next day. The group ate well, and everyone was proud of their ingenuity.

In February, the Beatles embarked from England on a highly publicized pilgrimage to the Maharishi's main camp in India. They were joined there by Mike Love of the Beach Boys and actress Mia Farrow, who had just completed director Roman Polanski's film *Rosemary's Baby*. The retreat was scheduled to last three months, but long before then the Beatles were disturbed by rumors that their saintly guru not only ate meat—he preached strict vegetarianism—but also attempted to seduce female attendees. Suspicious, uncomfortable in such a primitive setting, and, above all, bored and grumpy, John Lennon and Paul McCartney began composing songs; some were simple sing-alongs, others biting and caustic (Lennon's "Sexy Sadie" tunefully eviscerated the Maharishi), and a few were experimental to the point of being downright weird. All of them, along with some others written after their return to Britain, would be released around year's end.

Though the disenchanted Beatles left the Maharishi's camp ahead of schedule, Mike Love remained his devout follower. Afterward, he actively promoted the Maharishi, in public and within the Beach Boys band.

Phil Kaufman was released from Terminal Island in March 1968. He was happy to learn that his old jail pal Charlie was nearby in Topanga, and even more pleased when Charlie invited him to stick around for a while. Kaufman would have been glad to enjoy Charlie's company, but it turned out that this scrawny little guy had collected himself a harem, girls who obeyed his every command and seemed glad, even eager to have sex with a buddy of Charlie's who'd been locked away from women for much too long. Kaufman happily indulged himself in every erotic fantasy he'd imagined back in his cell bunk and some more things he'd never person-ally thought of but apparently Charlie had taught the girls to do. Charlie told him privately that the big problem in the world was blacks having all those babies; someday whites might be outnumbered. Charlie's solution was that white guys needed to get as many white girls pregnant as pos-sible, starting with the women in the group.

When he wasn't having sex with the girls, Kaufman chatted with Charlie and learned that the Universal tryout hadn't been successful. If Kaufman understood that Gary Stromberg's promise to Charlie of maybe trying again sometime in the studio was more of a tactful brush-off than a promise, he didn't explain that to Charlie. Charlie was upbeat about his music and all the new songs he was writing. He quizzed Kaufman about more industry contacts—anybody else besides Stromberg to suggest? Kaufman didn't have more names at the moment, but said that now he was out of jail he was going to get back into show business, movies and music, he'd look up people he'd known and also make new contacts. Charlie made it clear that while Kaufman was doing that he should stay with the group, enjoy the girls, and of course introduce Charlie to what-ever recording industry heavy hitters he made friends with. It sounded fine to Kaufman. He liked living with Charlie and the gang. Kaufman had some strong first impressions of Charlie's women. Lynne, he figured, was the most die-hard Charlie nut, hanging on his every word. Susan Atkins was like Charlie's guard dog, kind of crazy and mean. Pat Kren-winkel was okay. She did a lot of the hardest chores. None of the women struck Kaufman as very smart with the exception of Mary Brunner, but brains were clearly not what Charlie was looking for among his female followers.

On a typical day for Charlie's group in Topanga, everybody got up late and the women got some breakfast together from whatever was left over from the night before. It might be fruit or raw vegetables or cookies if there were a few boxes of those. Nobody much cared; breakfast wasn't really a formal communal meal, just the chance for everybody to get something in their stomachs to start the day. Then Charlie and Kaufman and whatever other guys were there worked on cars and motorcycles— Kaufman couldn't believe how people just gave Charlie these things. But what made a bigger impression was Charlie's attitude toward these sets of wheels, some of them really sweet rides. He refused to let the group get possessive about any of them. As soon as they were completely road-worthy he'd trade them off or even just flat out give them away, telling everyone that doing so was a reminder not to become materialistic. Sometimes people in the group, always peripherals who weren't going to last long anyway, would get angry to see a car or bike they'd be working hard on disappear like that, and once or twice they threatened to kick Charlie's ass. Then Charlie would stun them with his word games, telling them to go ahead if that was what they really wanted, and then something like, didn't they really want him to find them even better rides than the ones he'd given away? And that always worked, though it was obvious that if the time came when it didn't, all the women would rise up and swarm to Charlie's defense. They damn sure wouldn't let anyone hurt him.

Kaufman loved the way Charlie routinely made his followers believe that they came up with ideas that were actually his own. Kaufman knew where Charlie got that technique. In Topanga, one of the girls might say that she wanted fruit, and Charlie would say, "Oh, I get it, you want to work at the farmers' market this weekend so we can get some. That's a great idea! You're really smart!" The girl would feel proud that Charlie had praised her and her great idea, when what Charlie had really wanted was for somebody to work the farmers' market and bring food home. The technique worked on more important things, too. A new recruit reluctant to hand over her car's pink slip could be praised in front of the others for demonstrating how hard it was to give up material things. But, Charlie might say, right here and now she's going to do it and offer everyone else an example of overcoming possessiveness and embracing a better way to live. Why, this girl right here is already way ahead of everyone else who'd been with Charlie for months! Look how enlightened she is! And he'd get the pink slip and the girl would thank him for taking it. Amazing, just amazing.

While the men worked on the cars and bikes, most of the girls left to pick through grocery store garbage bins. They'd come back with their haul and, before fixing and serving dinner (meals were exclusively prepared, served, and cleaned up after by the girls because these tasks were defined by Charlie as women's work, the proper role for all women all of the time being the service and gratification of men), sometimes everyone would gather for a group dosing of LSD, with the drug administered by Charlie. Paul Watkins told authorities later that Charlie always took a lesser dose than he doled out to everyone else, the better to keep his wits about him. When everybody was beginning their trip, Charlie would begin to preach, talking about giving up individuality and possessions, how life and death were the same. Charlie never in any way mentioned committing violent acts to bring about the better world he envisioned. Each time he stuck to what Phil Kaufman called "peace and love." Besides a few used for cutting and preparing food, there were no knives around, or any guns.

Some afternoons there would be group sex. Wherever they were living, a room was always set aside for that purpose, with drawn curtains and rugs and cushions on the floor. Sometimes what you did and whom you did it with was determined by individual whim, or, as Kaufman recalls, "whoever you fell on." Other times, Charlie served as director, telling each participant what he or she would do, and with whom. There were always more women participating than men, but Charlie rarely ordered lesbian acts. Everybody was supposed to be dedicated to satisfying everyone else's needs, but inevitably some of the women did a lot of the work and received little attention back. That, according to Charlie, was fair because making men happy ought to be their priority.

Dinner was taken as a group, with large steaming platters of food passed around and everyone eating as much as they liked. Afterward, Charlie would usually play his guitar and sing. The women were his chorus. If they didn't sing Charlie's songs, they sang the Beatles' latest tunes over and over again. Some of them got sick of every song on the *Magical Mystery Tour* album but they sang them anyway. It was as though Charlie considered the Beatles to be adjunct members of his *real* family. Though he controlled the music played at wherever the group was calling home, Charlie did allow his followers to tune in whatever stations they liked on car radios. So everybody got a full dose of all the psychedelic, a-change-is-gonna-come songs that dominated the airwaves—tunes by the Jefferson Airplane and the Doors and the Rolling Stones. Nobody paid much attention to the less far out, nonrevolutionary stuff by bands like the Beach Boys.

Sometimes Charlie and select others, members of the group he wanted to reward, would go out at night, dropping in on Topanga acquaintances and occasionally crashing gatherings. Most people were very informal and didn't mind too much if strangers showed up. Phil Kaufman had quite a few friends around the city, and he would take Charlie with him on visits. One old pal Kaufman hooked back up with was named Harold True. Harold lived in a nice rental house on Waverly Drive in the upper-middle-class L.A. neighborhood of Los Feliz. Charlie went to Harold's a couple of times for parties. He was a good host. Long afterward Pat Krenwinkel remembered that he always shared lots of drugs. Charlie became familiar with the area and got a good sense of its relative luxury and the people living there. There weren't any mansions but there were some fine homes, including Harold's and the ones around it. The group made several visits to Harold's before he moved in the fall. A while after that, a couple named Leno and Rosemary LaBianca moved into the house next to where Harold had lived.

Phil Kaufman's stay with the group lasted about five weeks. He wasn't able to help Charlie make any useful new music connections, and he sometimes had the nerve to disagree with him. The thing Charlie couldn't risk was someone arguing with him, telling him he was wrong about anything, no matter how insignificant, in front of the others. But before Charlie determined that Kaufman had to go, he tried to make him a permanent convert rather than a guest. One of the others had driven the school bus on a quick trip to San Francisco, and the bus broke down. When Charlie went up to retrieve it, he invited Phil to come along. As they drove north in one of the ubiquitous cars given to the group, Charlie hit Kaufman with the full recruiting rap and demanded that he join the group full-time as a follower. Kaufman laughed and replied, "Hey, save it for other people." Charlie snapped, "You're too smart to be here." After they got back to Topanga, Kaufman recalls, Charlie and the girls made it obvious that he'd overstayed his welcome, ignoring him much of the time. He left and lived for a while with a series of other friends, including Harold True, until he got his own place. Kaufman and Charlie weren't completely estranged. They stayed in touch and a few times Kaufman visited him and the rest of the group, but after a while he stopped coming because it just wasn't the same.

America continued to unravel in March 1968. President Johnson had organized a blue-ribbon commission to study the cause of civil unrest—racial rioting—and its report placed most of the blame squarely on "white racism." Unless blacks and whites could somehow reconcile their differ-- ences, the commission warned, America might well find itself divided into two permanently hostile camps.

On March 12, Johnson suffered a staggering political blow when Eugene McCarthy came close to defeating him in the New Hampshire presidential primary. That encouraged New York senator Robert F. Kennedy, a longtime Johnson critic, to announce that he, too, would challenge Johnson for the Democratic nomination. Those student radicals still willing to use the political system to bring about change had been solidly in McCarthy's camp. Now they had to choose between the cool, cerebral McCarthy, who had become their champion when no other politician was willing to step forward, and the charismatic Kennedy, who besides his own crusading image carried the legacy of his assassinated brother. Unwilling to risk the humiliation of losing his party's nomination, and promising that he would spend the remainder of his time in office seeking an equitable peace settlement in Vietnam, on March 31 Johnson stunned the nation and the world by announcing he would no longer seek reelection.

Four days later, Martin Luther King Jr. was assassinated in Memphis. Within hours, there were horrendous riots in New York and Washington. The violence expanded throughout the country; 125 cities experienced extensive race-related violence, and 55,000 troops were called out to help quell the battles in the streets. A machine gun post was set up on the steps of the U.S. Capitol after rumors spread that black mobs intended to swarm inside and attack legislators.

If Charlie discussed current events with his followers at all, it was not to debate Vietnam or racial issues but to remind them how fortunate they were to be with him instead of having to fumble their way through the uncertain, scary world outside the group. The worse things got out there, the easier it was for Charlie's followers to fall further under his influence. They were avoiding the real issues of the day, indulging themselves in sex and drugs, and being assured by their leader that they were better (and luckier) than anyone else in the world for doing it. Of course they loved Charlie.

April was a terrible month for America but a fine one for Charlie. First, he found a young woman who would become one of his most devoted disciples. Like many others who decided to follow Charlie, Sandy Good was the child of divorced parents. She was sickly as a young girl, and underwent a series of surgeries to correct respiratory problems, one of which involved the partial removal of one lung; these operations left her throat and torso badly scarred. Both of Sandy's parents indulged her, and later in life even she would admit that she often acted spoiled. By the mid-1960s Sandy was drifting between colleges, trying, like many peers, to find herself, to decide what she wanted from life. She lived in Oregon and San Francisco, and in the spring of 1968 she went down to Los Angeles to visit a friend. While she was there, she met Charlie, and was instantly won over by his promise to make her part of a family that really loved her. Charlie found something to instantly love about Sandy, too—thanks to a trust fund established for her by her father, a stockbroker, Sandy got a check for $200 every month. Sandy gladly turned the money over to Charlie. He contacted her father several times asking him to increase the monthly amount, wheedling at first and then insisting and finally demanding to the point that George Good broke off communication with his daughter—but the monthly checks kept coming.

Sandy had trouble fitting in with the other girls at first. She wore makeup and jewelry and sometimes had a haughty way of carrying herself. But Charlie worked on her, taking extra time for one-on-one talks about the evils of individuality; the last thing he wanted was for Sandy to feel unwelcome and leave, taking with her the $200 monthly stipend. To make her more acceptable to the others, Charlie ordered Sandy to strip, had her stand naked in front of everyone, pointed to her scars and used them as examples of the terrible ways birth parents abused their offspring. If they'd really loved Sandy, Charlie demanded, why did they allow doctors to disfigure her like that? Of course Sandy had a lot to overcome, more than just about anybody else in the group, so cut her a little slack. The more problems people had giving up their egos, the worse their parents must have been. Still, Sandy took longer than most to assimilate, and she did not receive a nickname for several months.

In April, Mary Brunner gave birth to a son. She wanted to give birth in a hospital with trained medical personnel on hand, but Charlie wouldn't hear of it. Natural childbirth was the only way, and Mary would be helped by the other women in the group. The girls told Charlie they had no idea what to do; he replied that they were women, so they would naturally figure it out. When the child came, it was a breech birth. Mary suffered terribly and there was a great deal of uncertain fumbling, but she and her baby somehow survived. It would later be reported that the baby was born on April 1 and named Valentine Michael Manson in tribute to *Stranger in a Strange Land*, but an official birth record filed with the state of California gives the birth date as April 15 and the child's full name as Michael Manson. But birthdays and given names didn't matter to the group—they were tools used by the Establishment to keep track of people—and everyone called the baby Pooh Bear.

Pooh Bear was raised according to Charlie's philosophy of everyone sharing in parenting responsibilities. Those outside the group who served its child care activities were impressed by the affection and attention lavished on the boy and on all the other children who eventually became part of Charlie's following. The adults were sometimes dressed in rags and often dirty, but the children always appeared clean, well fed, and obviously cared for. Within the group, there was some discrepancy between the way Charlie talked about children and the way he personally felt about them. No one ever saw Charlie strike a child, even when he was in a terrible temper, but he quickly became annoyed if a baby cried or toddler screamed. So the children were always kept away from the main group of adults, watched over in a tent or back room by baby-sitters assigned by Charlie. Parents could visit their children only with Charlie's permission, which he usually withheld on the grounds that natural parents had a bad effect. Everyone in the group was equally father or mother to every child.

Shortly after Pooh Bear's birth, Charlie took the group on another road trip in the bus, this time to a wooded area in Ventura County where they set up camp. It offered an opportunity for Charlie to have everyone's undivided attention, and was a way of keeping anyone from getting too comfortable living with the conveniences of indoor plumbing and electricity. But they didn't stay very long; Ventura County deputies arrested several members of the group, including Charlie and Susan Atkins, for using false IDs, and Mary Brunner was picked up for nursing her baby in public. None of the charges stuck, or probably were even meant to. The county cops just wanted to encourage Charlie and his shaggy entourage to move along. It worked, but not the way they intended. Far from feeling intimidated—after all the cells he'd occupied in federal prison, a night or two in a local jail couldn't faze him at all—Charlie used the arrests to demonstrate to his followers how the Man fanatically persecuted the enlightened. They hunted around for other camping sites, and were particularly drawn to one place northwest of L.A. at the foot of the Santa Susana Mountains where they didn't even have to camp as such because there was an old movie set on the property. The movie set, used for lots of 1950s and 1960s cowboy films, was part of a ranch owned by an old nearly blind man named George Spahn. They stayed there for a bit, and then Charlie led them back to Topanga so he could resume his quest for a record deal.

• • •

The Beach Boys embarked that spring on a national concert tour, but this one had a twist. Before the band appeared, the Maharishi opened the shows by comfortably settling himself onstage and lecturing audiences about the wonders of Transcendental Meditation. People had bought tickets to hear music, not philosophic blather, and every night the Maharishi's high-pitched, relatively thin speaking voice was drowned out by shouted demands for him to shut up and let the Beach Boys perform. The Maharishi's nightly response was to grin, giggle, and keep talking. Beyond their own fascination with the guru, the band had hoped that this public affiliation with him would restore some Beatle-like cool to their fading popularity. It had the opposite effect. As word spread about the tour's paucity of music and emphasis on lecture, advance sales plummeted to the point that only two hundred tickets were sold for a key New York show. The band's managers canceled the tour at the halfway point, with a loss of about $500,000, money the Beach Boys badly needed to finance Brother Records and their own self-indulgent lifestyles. Some of the band members lost at least some faith in the Maharishi—was this what listening to gurus got you? Mike Love blamed the fiasco on the rest of the world not being smart enough to appreciate what the Maharishi was so graciously offering to share. He remained a devoted follower and refused to recognize anyone other than the Maharishi as a legitimate source of wisdom. And for Dennis Wilson, the canceled tour was too bad, but at least it freed him up to return to L.A. and get back to having fun with girls and drugs and whatever else appealed to him on any given day. Dennis didn't feel especially burned by the Maharishi; he was interesting, and Dennis liked interesting people. He was always ready to meet more of them.

Bobby Beausoleil, Charlie's buddy from the Spiral Staircase, dropped by soon after Charlie and his followers returned to Topanga. He had a new girlfriend named Gail and also a second female traveling companion named Catherine Share, who everybody immediately started calling Gypsy. Beausoleil was involved in another movie, X-rated, building sets for the film besides acting in it. The girls in Charlie's entourage thought Beausoleil was snotty, but most of them still melted at the sight of him because he was so good-looking. They nicknamed him Cupid. Gail didn't like it; she was very possessive of Beausoleil. That was unacceptable under Charlie's rules, so Gail was never considered for recruitment and Beausoleil remained uninterested in anything other than occasional visits, though he still liked Charlie personally. Gypsy, though, got caught up in the group spirit right away. She liked the people with Charlie, and she appreciated his devotion to music. Gypsy was a gifted musician herself. The daughter of French resistance fighters who died during World War II, she was brought to America by an adoptive mother and grew up in Hollywood. After her adoptive mother died, Gypsy began wandering and ended up tagging along with Beausoleil and Gail. During this first meeting she wasn't quite ready to leave them for Charlie, but it was something she continued to think about as she bummed around California with the other two.

Charlie might have been able to talk Gypsy into leaving Beausoleil and staying with him, but he didn't try. As much as he always was glad to find appropriate new followers—with Gypsy's outgoing personality and obvious buy-in to Charlie's teachings, she would make a great recruiter for the group—he didn't want to risk alienating Beausoleil. Besides, now that the group roughly numbered around twenty, meaning there were plenty of people to scrounge food and panhandle and fix cars and motorcycles, Charlie didn't need to concern himself as much with day-to-day responsibilities. He'd been back in L.A. for almost six months, and he still didn't have a recording deal. His mistake with Stromberg at Universal was putting his faith in a mid-echelon record executive, somebody who couldn't really be expected to recognize great music because he wasn't a musician himself. What Charlie really needed was some big rock star as his patron, somebody who would understand the great stuff he heard and get Charlie a deal just by demanding it.

So Charlie rededicated himself to finding just the right music star sponsor. He used some of his girls as scouts, sending them out to prowl Topanga and the Strip and see who they might meet. That was fine with the women—it sounded like more fun than panhandling or digging around grocery store dumpsters. They were tasked not with telling other stray girls about this wonderful guru named Charlie, but with tracking down established rock stars and convincing them to give a listen to Charlie's amazing music.

Sometime in late spring Pat and Yeller went hitchhiking on the Strip. They'd barely stuck out their thumbs when a big, good-looking guy drove up and offered them a lift to wherever they were going, but how about swinging back to his place first for some milk and cookies? That sounded like fun to the girls. Pat and Yeller sped off with Dennis Wilson, exactly the kind of patron that Charlie wanted.

CHAPTER NINE

Charlie and Dennis

From 1961's regional hit "Surfin'" through late 1966's international smash "Good Vibrations," no American band was more popular or sold more records than the Beach Boys. Their success was based on two critical elements—leader Brian Wilson's songwriting, and his ability to blend band members' harmonies and studio musicians' instrumental wizardry to transform those songs into multilayered magic. The Beach Boys' sound was unique, and it was why they succeeded. The way they looked was ordinary. Bassist Brian and his lead guitarist brother Carl both battled weight issues; guitarist Al Jardine was short and nerdy-looking, and singer Mike Love was prematurely balding. Only drummer Dennis Wilson resembled a typical teen idol, and even at the pinnacle of the Beach Boys' fame Dennis was the bane of the rest of the band thanks to his lack of self-discipline. Dennis knew no limits in his fondness for alcohol, drugs, and sex, but he was also the only Beach Boy who actually surfed, thus providing inspiration for many of brother Brian's earliest hit songs. Risk always appealed to Dennis; when the Beach Boys played a New York City show at the same time the World Trade Center was being constructed, late one night he sneaked into the site, climbed to the top of the scaffolding and swung by his arms at horrifying heights, thrilled by the danger. As a drummer, Dennis's skills were adequate at best, but he brought tremendous energy to the band's live performances, which was especially important since it was virtually impossible for them to precisely reproduce Brian's complex studio sound onstage. Because of their ongoing frustration with his immature behavior, the other Beach Boys had no real sense of Dennis's potential as a songwriter, even when Brian took to his bed for months at a time and stopped cranking out hit singles and glorious, extended song cycles that resulted in classic albums like *Pet Sounds*. Without Brian's full-time participation, the band began to flounder. The decision by its members and management to skip the crucial Monterey festival in 1967 effectively ended the Beach Boys' long run at the top of the charts.

In the late spring of 1968, the Beach Boys were about to release *Friends*, their nineteenth album in just seven years—record labels constantly badgered proven hit makers to produce more product before their popularity waned. *Friends* was fated to bomb, reaching only number 126 in the long-playing charts; none of its twelve songs became a hit single, or even came close. It went virtually unnoticed that two of the album's songs were composed by Dennis and Steve Kalinich, and one of them, "Little Bird," was as good or better than anything Brian contributed to the album. Dennis hoped to write many more songs and wanted friends like Steve to work on them with him. Dennis was adept at crafting instrumental music, but he struggled with lyrics and needed a partner with a knack for words.

Around the time that *Friends* was released, Dennis's fame, especially in L.A., was equivalent to the celebrity enjoyed by a Hollywood actor who'd once been featured in Academy Award–winning films but had since fallen on hard times with a series of box office flops. He was coasting on past success, with no particular promise of better times returning. But it wasn't in Dennis's nature to obsess or even worry too much. He still had plenty of money, though the Beach Boys' Brother Records office tried to dole it out carefully to him, since Dennis was a world-class spendthrift. He was separated from his wife and living in one of the prime rental properties in the city, Will Rogers's old hunting lodge on the west end of Sunset Boulevard. It was a spectacular place, its rugged log exterior encasing a mansion-like interior. Dennis and his buddies partied there almost nonstop, with the merriment usually spilling out onto the extensive three-acre grounds or an enormous swimming pool. There was lots of room for guests, and on any given night Dennis was likely to invite home itinerants who had somehow caught his eye. Few stayed long, but while they did Dennis pressed food and drugs and gifts on them. He was a generous-hearted man, and his longtime friends were certain that at some level he felt guilty about his wealth, that somehow he didn't deserve the good things that had happened to him. The Wilson boys came from a working-class background. Their father, Murry, who owned a small machinist's shop, was a terrible-tempered frustrated musician himself who physically abused his sons, Dennis in particular. He mocked their hit records and insisted on managing the boys until they finally summoned the courage to fire him. All three of the Wilson brothers bore psychological scars. Brian's were the most obvious, but Dennis harbored violent resentment of his father.

There was nothing unusual about Dennis stopping to pick up hitchhikers or bringing them home. His offer of milk and cookies to Pat and Yeller was sincere. Years later, Pat recalled that Dennis served raw milk, the only kind he drank. After their snack, they talked a while and the girls told Dennis about Charlie. When Dennis had to usher them out so he could leave for a recording session, he told the girls that he hoped to run into them again.

Yeller and Pat had no idea who Dennis Wilson was; nobody in their group paid attention to the Beach Boys. But Charlie recognized the name and insisted that the girls take him and everyone else back to the log cabin on Sunset.

It was well after midnight when Wilson pulled his Ferrari into the driveway of his palatial home and noticed that there were lights on inside. As he parked, the back door to the house opened and Charlie Manson emerged, smiling and waving as though he were the host greeting a guest. The tiny man's attitude unnerved Wilson, who asked, "Are you going to hurt me?" Charlie replied, "Do I look like I'm going to?" He dropped to his knees and kissed Wilson's feet, then gestured for him to come inside, where the rest of Charlie's group, all of them relaxed and acting at home, were waiting. The school bus was parked just outside; this was Charlie's best opportunity yet and he wasn't going to miss it. Pat and Yeller formally introduced him to Wilson, who was somewhat nonplussed by the unexpected crowd but was never one to shut down a party, especially when some of the girls were topless and the stereo was blasting out the Beatles. The revelry went on for hours, and when Wilson woke up the next day Charlie and his followers were still there and showing no signs of leaving. It was okay with Wilson if they stayed a while. His immediate interest was the women, Nancy Pitman especially, but they all willingly did anything sexual that he wanted. Over the next few days Wilson spent a lot of time talking with Charlie and decided that the guy was *deep*, with all this stuff to say about how everything was really the same, which meant bad was good, which meant all the things Wilson did that the rest of the Beach Boys bitched about weren't wrong after all and they had no business trying to make him feel guilty about them. When Charlie talked about how parents ruin their children, Wilson mentioned his father and all the beatings that he'd taken at his hands. At that point, Wilson couldn't wait to introduce Charlie to his friends—the guy had wisdom that needed to be shared.

The first friend Wilson contacted was Gregg Jakobson, who worked as a talent scout and session arranger and was also trying to write songs with Dennis. Though few outside the innermost L.A. music scene knew his name, Jakobson was a critical player. Adopted by the chief of detectives in St. Paul, Minnesota, and his wife, Jakobson moved to Venice, California, with his mother and sisters after his father died. He was enrolled in University High, popularly known as Uni High, where he got to know Nancy Sinatra. Dean Martin's daughter Deanna was one of his first girlfriends. Soon Jakobson was getting lots of work as a movie extra, and when some of his buddies, like Terry Melcher, got into rock bands and started cutting records, Gregg got involved in that, too, helping line up studio musicians and arrange session dates. He wasn't in a band himself because he had a terrible singing voice.

Jakobson met Dennis Wilson in 1963. Melcher's band was scheduled to open for the Beach Boys at a show in Hawaii. Melcher suggested that Jakobson come along on the trip. When he explained he couldn't afford a plane ticket, Melcher offhandedly asked him to suggest some song titles. Off the top of his head, Jakobson threw out "Big Wednesday," "Two's a Crowd," and a third title. Melcher called singer Bobby Darin, who owned a music publishing company, rattled off Jakobson's impromptu titles and told him that soon he would have these three new songs for sale. Darin gave Melcher an advance of $1,000, Melcher gave the money to Jakobson, and off they went to Hawaii. Jakobson met Dennis Wilson there at a pre-concert press conference. Wilson was bored, Jakobson suggested they skip out and go ride motorcycles, and a fast friendship began. When everybody got home, Jakobson helped Melcher write the three songs for Darin's publishing company. From then on Jakobson, Melcher, and Wilson were inseparable. Soon afterward when Melcher became a boy wonder producer at Columbia, he hired Jakobson to scout available talent and to arrange studio sessions. That made Jakobson an important player in the L.A. music scene.

Wilson called Jakobson the second night that Charlie and his follow-ers were at the house, insisting, "You've got to come over and meet these people," and the next day Jakobson did. At first he didn't think they were anything special. To Jakobson, this was Dennis being Dennis, taking in some strays and getting overly enthusiastic about how great they were. He always got bored and the people moved on and were soon forgotten. But Wilson had told Charlie all about Jakobson, why an aspiring singer-songwriter like Charlie ought to know him, so Charlie got Jakobson to one side and started talking, laying down the most interesting rap, and then he introduced Jakobson to Ruth Ann Moorehouse. Wilson wasn't very picky about girls; he'd go after pretty much anything. But Jakobson was married, to comedian Lou Costello's daughter Carole, and while he wasn't strictly faithful, he was cautious. He found Ruth Ann irresistible, though, and they began what he later termed "a little thing," meaning that whenever he was around Charlie, Charlie usually paired him off with Ruth Ann, and so Jakobson was always happy to come by. Even though Charlie forbade his followers to form individual attachments, Ruth Ann liked Jakobson, too, and the other women teased her about it. When Jakobson wasn't rolling around with Ruth Ann, Charlie would talk to him about the music business, about who Jakobson knew. Jakobson realized what the deal was—people tried to get him to use his contacts on their behalf all the time. He and Wilson listened to Charlie play some of his songs while the women sang along on the choruses. Jakobson thought that there might be something there, though his gut instinct was that Charlie was more interesting to look at than to listen to. But Wilson, al-ways prone to go overboard, decided that Charlie was a genius. He took Charlie over to the offices of Brother Records so he could audition for the management there.

Nobody at Brother Records was impressed with Dennis's new discovery. The original concept of the company had been that all the members of the Beach Boys would seek out new talent, and that they each had the right to record whom they chose, but the recently canceled tour had cost a lot of money and the rest of the band had little faith in Dennis's judgment. He was told that Charlie couldn't be signed to a deal just on Dennis's say-so. Charlie didn't help at all; he made a terrible first impression and a worse one in the days that followed. When he came to the office he acted like he owned the place; he was filthy and smelled bad. The staff privately nicknamed him "Pig Pen" after a character in the popular *Peanuts* comic strip. Charlie sat around Brother Records for hours, strumming his guitar and convincing everyone within hearing distance that, despite his pretensions about being a supremely gifted musician, he actually knew very few chords.

Dennis ignored the pointed lack of enthusiasm. He went out of his way to talk Charlie up to the rest of the Beach Boys, to his other music industry pals, and even to the media. In an interview with *Rave*, a British magazine, Wilson repeated some of the philosophy that Charlie had shared with him: "Fear is nothing but awareness. I was only frightened as a child because I did not understand fear, the dark, being lost, what was under the bed. It came from within." Wilson elaborated that his new friend Charles Manson, whom he'd nicknamed "the Wizard," calls himself "God and the Devil. He sings, plays, and writes poetry and may be another artist for Brother Records." Charlie was anxious for Wilson's prediction to come true, but the other Beach Boys and Brother Records' management dug in and delayed. They hadn't heard anything in Charlie's primitive songs that persuaded them he could make the label money if they did sign him. If they could just avoid making any commitment to Charlie for a while, maybe Dennis would kick him to the curb or else he'd just go away.

Charlie had no intention of going anywhere. He and his followers didn't always spend the night at Wilson's—sometimes they'd retreat for a day or two to the ranch with the movie set. But they always came right back to the log mansion on Sunset Boulevard, Charlie to stay close to Wilson and the women to take advantage of the bathrooms. At the ranch, the sanitary facilities were limited to outhouses, buckets, and a hose. Besides enjoying Wilson's hospitality, the girls genuinely liked him as a person. Charlie was smart enough not to push his songs on Wilson all of the time; he'd encourage Wilson to sit at the piano and play some of the tunes he was working on, too. Just as they did with Charlie, the girls would gather around and sing along, sharing music and friendship. Wilson seemed intimidated whenever any of the other Beach Boys came by—the Family women thought they were creeps—but when he was away from them Wilson's playful side always shone through. He loved the Rolls-Royce given to him by his brother Brian. In L.A. it was the ride of choice for many of the city's richest, stuffiest people. Wilson would get some of the Family girls to pile in and tear off down the freeways, looking for other Rolls-Royces and pulling up beside them. Then he'd encourage the girls to hang out his car windows, sticking out their tongues and making faces and just having silly, simple fun mocking the squares. How could the girls not adore Wilson almost as much as Charlie? But they never really thought about leaving Charlie for him—Charlie's hold over them was much too strong for that. Besides, Charlie taught that the only time that existed was now, and right now they could be with Wilson all they wanted.

It seemed to Gregg Jakobson that every time he came around Wilson's place, Charlie and the others were always around, sunning themselves by the swimming pool, lounging inside with the stereo blaring, rummaging in the refrigerator for snacks. In return, Charlie set up friendly orgies for Wilson and Jakobson and any other friends. The girls would undress and then run around the property pretending to be fairies. The men chased after them and were sexually rewarded by their giggling captives. None of the women ever complained that she wasn't in the mood. They did whatever Charlie told them to, and usually they liked it.

People in the Brother Records office couldn't believe it when Dennis let Charlie keep hanging around, apparently indefinitely. They hired a detective to run a background check and learned that Charlie had done hard time and was still on probation. When Dennis heard the news, he was elated rather than concerned. Sure, Charlie had told him tales of doing hard time, but lots of posers claimed to have been unfairly put in jail by the Man. Charlie really was an ex-con? To Dennis, that made him even more interesting.

Wilson was part of a rock star social set where everyone was in the habit of dropping in on everyone else. No call ahead was deemed necessary; if one celebrity pal wasn't in, you just went on to the home of the next. Hanging around at Wilson's, Charlie constantly met other people who might be able to get him his record deal. He kept his guitar handy and played his songs for anyone willing to listen. That wasn't unusual; at any given time, just about all the successful L.A. musicians had protégés hanging around, hoping for their own chance at stardom. Wilson made it clear that he was sponsoring Charlie. Rocker Neil Young came by Dennis's one day, improvised some chords to go with goofy lyrics Charlie was tossing out, and liked the results enough to suggest to Mo Ostin of Warner Brothers Records that Charlie was worth a listen. Young recalled telling Ostin, "This guy is unbelievable—he makes the songs up as he goes along, and they're all good," but Ostin wasn't intrigued enough to give Charlie an audition. Charlie noticed a pattern—Dennis Wilson and Neil Young were rock stars, but neither one had been able to get him signed to a label, at least so far. Charlie needed to find and impress somebody even higher up the music business food chain, and, thanks to Dennis and Gregg, he thought that he knew just the right person.

In 1968 Terry Melcher was one of the most powerful figures in American popular music. The son of actress-singer Doris Day and her first husband, musician Al Jorden, Melcher was formally adopted by his mother's third husband, agent Marty Melcher. He and his stepfather, who was extremely religious and a strict disciplinarian, never got along. Melcher had some success as a teenager playing in a series of bands, but made his real mark in the industry at age twenty-two when he went to work for Columbia Records as a producer, a relatively high-level position that many thought he reached only because his mother owned so much stock in the company. In 1965 when Columbia signed the long-haired Byrds, Melcher was assigned to the band because he was the youngest producer on the label and the higher-ups thought he might be able to relate to them. Melcher did more than that, bringing in the best studio musicians and making "Mr. Tambourine Man" a huge hit. Melcher guided the Byrds to more sales success, and then proved he was more than a one-band wonder by turning a regional band called Paul Revere and the Raiders into a pop hit machine. In all, Melcher produced more than eighty chart hits for

Columbia. In an industry where the only track record that counted was making money, the label gave him carte blanche in signing and producing any musicians that he liked. With plenty of Columbia's money to spend, Melcher hired Gregg Jakobson to scout the city music scene and make recommendations.

To Charlie, getting signed by Terry Melcher should have been a cinch. Jakobson liked Charlie, Melcher hired Jakobson to find new talent, so Jakobson would recommend Charlie to Melcher and a recording contract would follow. But it wasn't that simple.

Terry Melcher was now a fun-loving twenty-six-year-old who enjoyed nothing more than hanging with his buddies Dennis and Jakobson, smoking a little weed and chasing girls before going home to his cottage atop Cielo Drive and his gorgeous, live-in actress girlfriend, Candy Bergen. But unlike Dennis Wilson, eager to please and willing to talk record deals with just about anybody he met who wanted one, Melcher kept his social life separate from business. Also unlike Wilson, he was careful about the friends he made and the people he invited into his home. Having grown up as the son of a star who lived in a gated, guarded community, Melcher was wary of strangers, especially those he perceived as hustlers. Though he trusted Jakobson, Melcher would never sign anyone strictly on his pal's say-so. He would want to study any recommended artists carefully and weigh their material against the strict industry bottom line—would their music make his label a lot of money? If Melcher didn't think so, it wouldn't matter to him if his close friend had recommended the musician or even if Melcher himself thought that someone's songs were artistic masterpieces. Because of that, Jakobson was careful not to push anyone too hard on Melcher. He would mention someone, suggest that maybe Melcher meet the artist, and after that perhaps ask Melcher to give the person's music a listen. Where Charlie expected instant bonding and a contract, Jakobson knew that the best possible approach would be for Melcher to get to know Charlie and then, perhaps, he'd permit some sort of audition. So when Jakobson first mentioned Charlie to Melcher, he talked about this interesting guy who had a bunch of girl followers who ate out of grocery store garbage dumps. This guy, Charlie, could order the girls to do anything and they would do it without question. By the way, Charlie wrote songs and performed them. Melcher ought to come over to Wilson's and meet him.

Melcher did, and Charlie turned on the charm. But his new target had been fawned over and pitched to by hundreds of other would-be rock stars, so Melcher wasn't automatically impressed. He didn't ask Charlie to go get his guitar and play for him. What he did want was to get to know Ruth Ann Moorehouse better, and Charlie was quick to get Melcher and the sexy teenager together. Melcher's encounter with Ruth Ann went so well that he told Jakobson he thought he'd move the girl into the house at Cielo as a housekeeper. Charlie would gladly have handed Ruth Ann off to Melcher in hopes that she'd help persuade him to sign Charlie, but Candy Bergen knew what kind of housekeeping chores Terry had in mind and vetoed the plan.

Even though Jakobson was attached to Ruth Ann himself, he didn't resent his friend for trying to latch on to her, too. It was part of the spirit of the times—you shared everything, even girls. He was careful not to nag Melcher about Charlie; a record deal would either work out or it wouldn't. Besides, Jakobson was still impressed with Charlie more as a character than as a musician. Maybe the guy could be a comedian. He was witty enough. Jakobson considered suggesting that Melcher fund a documentary about Charlie and his followers. It might be a hit as a movie or on TV. He tried to write down a film proposal but had trouble finding the right word to describe Charlie's disciples. Remembering how Charlie referred to them, and how they often referred to themselves, Jakobson called them "the Family." He used the term a couple of times to Melcher and Wilson—and to Charlie and the group members themselves. Everybody liked it and it stuck. From then on they were Charlie and his Family, or Charlie and the Manson Family.

Try as he might, Charlie couldn't attach himself to Melcher the way that he had with Wilson. He saw Melcher at Wilson's house, went out sometimes with Melcher and Jakobson and Wilson, but he was never able to wangle an invitation to one of Melcher's legendary parties at Cielo Drive, let alone get invited to hang out with Melcher and Bergen there. He heard a lot from Wilson and Jakobson about what a great place Melcher lived in; for his parties he'd usually have a live band, and even though the house itself was kind of small, guests entered through sliding glass doors into a good-sized party room and there was the great view of the city down below. Most visitors never even got into the bedrooms or any of Melcher's private places. There was a guesthouse on the property near the main house and Rudi Altobelli, who was renting to Melcher, lived there. Melcher had some big speakers set up and the music would echo down into the canyon. Cielo Drive was actually a wild sort of place, lots of curves and hanging trees along with its steep incline and narrow road going up and down—it was tough for cars going in both directions to pass each other—and deer were everywhere. There were signs all along the high hill for drivers to watch out for them. Melcher offered out invitations sparingly, and the closest Charlie got to his house was when Wilson gave Melcher a lift home one day and Charlie tagged along in the backseat. When they got to his house Melcher didn't invite them in, apparently because he didn't want Charlie past his front door.

Even when they were together at parties in other places or out on the town with Jakobson and Wilson, Melcher kept Charlie at a courteous arm's length. He wasn't obnoxious about it; he'd learned from his movie star mother how to seem friendly but standoffish with people you didn't want to know better. Melcher still hadn't listened to Charlie's music, and Charlie felt certain that if he did he'd be won over. But Charlie was also perceptive enough to realize that Melcher wouldn't appreciate being nagged to listen before he was ready, so he bided his time. Besides, he still had Wilson and Brother Records.

Charlie spent the next weeks trying to bind Wilson closer to him. The Beach Boys' drummer was invited to go along with the Family girls on their garbage runs, and Wilson got a huge kick out of wheeling his Ferrari into a supermarket back lot and watching the women dumpster-dive. Though Wilson was never overt about it, Charlie also picked up on the fact that he had a strong racist streak; they privately shared their disdain for blacks, with Charlie being careful not to let the girls overhear since this was a contradiction of his teaching that everyone was the same. Above all, Charlie played to Wilson's wounded ego; the middle Wilson brother was certain that he could write and record more great songs if the rest of the band would only let him. They talked about writing some together. Wilson thought he might get some informal help on lyrics from a buddy; Charlie believed he was being invited to become the Beach Boys' songwriter. He began composing new material—"Garbage Dump" in honor of the Family's food gathering ("You could feed the world with my garbage dump/That sums it up in one big lump"), and "Cease to Exist," a tribute to Charlie's preaching ("Submission is a gift/So go on/Give it to your brother"). Charlie would claim later that he wrote "Cease to Exist" as a message to the rest of the Beach Boys to surrender their egos and work together as a cohesive unit, but the song is addressed to a woman, urging her to cease to exist and "come and say you love me" by giving up her world. Charlie passed the songs on to Wilson for his consideration, telling him that although the music could be changed, the lyrics had to remain as Charlie had written them.

Charlie also continued cultivating Gregg Jakobson. Maybe Jakobson hadn't successfully sold Melcher on Charlie yet, but he still had connections with dozens of other producers. So Charlie let Jakobson play with Ruth Ann, and frequently shared long philosophical conversations with him, since Jakobson, too, was interested in that sort of thing. Jakobson didn't completely buy in to Charlie's blather. Sometimes he'd bluntly tell him, "You're full of shit." Charlie let it go because the rest of the Family wasn't around to hear it, and because he still needed Jakobson. But Jakobson was with Charlie and his followers enough to notice that although the girls all worshipped Charlie, they feared him, too. They'd flinch sometimes when he corrected them for some perceived selfish or egotistical misstep. That certainly didn't square with Charlie's message of love and acceptance for all. In fact, Charlie was adamant about not referring to him and the Family as "hippies," a term he disdained because of hippiedom's inherent pacifism. Charlie sometimes hinted at a coming Armageddon when violence would sweep over the world. Hippies wouldn't be able to deal with it. In fact, Charlie said, he and the Family were really "slippies" because they were people who'd slipped through the cracks of society. Slippies rather than hippies—Charlie was so good at word play like that. All summer, the Family treated Jakobson like one of their own. The women nicknamed him "Angel" and said Jakobson was perfect because he'd been adopted as an infant. His biological parents never had the chance to ruin him.

To keep Charlie happy, and to get some idea of how his songs might sound on tape, Jakobson booked a quickie recording session for Charlie at a small studio in Van Nuys. Charlie brought the Family along; on some tunes the girls sang amateurish, quavery backup. Charlie ran through "Garbage Dump" and "Cease to Exist" and a dozen others. The results were listenable but not much more. It was hard to tell whether Charlie was no more than an average musical talent or else hampered by limited studio equipment. But he was pleased with what he heard. Through Wilson and Jakobson, Charlie now knew quite a few people in the L.A. music scene and he offered the tapes to anyone willing to listen and help him get signed to a label. John Phillips of the Mamas and the Papas and mega-agent Rudi Altobelli, whose client list included popular folk singer Buffy Sainte-Marie, both heard the tapes and passed. Charlie's faith in himself remained unshaken. If people like Phillips and Altobelli turned him down, that reflected poorly on their judgment, not his music. He hung on to the tapes in case anyone else important might be persuaded to listen to them. More than ever, he was determined that Dennis Wilson had to come through for him with Brother Records. They were friends, so Wilson owed it to him.

Charlie and the Family weren't the only strays who found their way to Wilson's place that spring and early summer. Wilson retained his habit of inviting over lots of people that he'd just met. One day while he was out hitchhiking—just about everybody young in L.A. did it, even rock stars; it was part of the friendly Love Generation lifestyle—Dennis was picked up by a tall, lanky twenty-one-year-old in a battered pickup truck. Charles Watson was a Texas native, originally hailing from the tiny hamlet of Copeville outside Dallas. Copeville, where Watson's parents ran a dinky gas station/grocery, was so small that the few kids from there went to high school in nearby Farmersville, whose two thousand or so residents qualified it as a metropolis compared to Watson's hometown. Watson was a standout at Farmersville High, starring on all the sports teams (honorable mention All-District running back for two straight years in football), working on the school newspaper and in the drama club, even winning an award for a fire prevention poster. Girls gushed about his blue eyes and bristly crew cut. During the summer Watson and his buddies worked in Farmersville produce sheds sorting onions and water-skied on a nearby lake during their time off. When Watson went about fifty miles to college in Denton, everybody thought he had about as promising a future as a kid from Copeville could hope for. Most guys either got married or joined the Army once they graduated high school.

But Watson discovered drugs in Denton; he dropped out of school and briefly worked at the Dallas airport. Soon his old friends back in Farmersville and Copeville heard that he'd left Texas for California. Since Watson always excelled at everything he did, the rumor spread that he'd gone off to Hollywood to star in Coca-Cola commercials. The girls who'd known him in high school were convinced he'd become a movie star because he was so cute.

In L.A., Watson scraped by working in a wig shop. His main interests were scoring all the weed that he could and immersing himself in the laid-back California lifestyle. Like everybody else, he loved the proximity to celebrities that L.A. offered, and when he picked up Dennis Wilson thumbing a ride one day he was thrilled to be invited back to Wilson's place. When they arrived, Charlie and the Family were already there and both Charlie and his girls made a big impression on Watson. Charlie apparently had everything that Watson wanted—women, a philosophy that eliminated any sense of guilt, and regular tripping on drugs. Watson, in turn, was exactly what Charlie always wanted, a potential male addition to the Family who had exceptional skill as a mechanic and the willingness to follow orders. It didn't take much persuasion on Charlie's part for Watson to beg to join his followers. He was soon known by the inevitable nickname of "Tex," and proved helpful to Charlie by cheerfully running errands. Along with Charlie, he was the only member of the Family actually to go to Terry Melcher's house on Cielo. He went there to borrow a car for a quick trip north.

Tex Watson wasn't Charlie's sole new male recruit. Dean Moorehouse, who just months earlier had been ready to shoot Charlie, showed up asking for permission to join the Family. Moorehouse liked the drugs and, it soon became apparent, was even fonder of the girls in the group. Charlie denied him permission to become a full-fledged Family member—after all, he was Ruth Ann's *father*—but Dennis Wilson took a shine to him. He hired Moorehouse as a combination gardener-handyman and set him up with a bed in a small cabin out by the swimming pool. Moorehouse promptly became a fixture at Wilson's, prowling the grounds and reminding everyone of Santa Claus with his big belly and white beard. Soon some of the Family women began complaining about Moorehouse pawing them, and gradually he became persona non grata, occasionally called on by Charlie to run errands and allowed just enough contact with the girls to keep him loyal.

Teenager Brooks Poston was a much more valued arrival. He showed up one day at Wilson's and was immediately awed by Charlie. Charlie was glad to add another guy to the group, especially one who brought along his mother's credit card. The Family used the card to cover whatever incidental expenses popped up for the rest of the summer, often for parts to repair the school bus, which kept breaking down. Otherwise, they had no real need for money because Wilson subsidized them. The women frequently raided his closets, not to wear the clothes they took but to cut them up and make them into nice robes for Charlie. Wilson paid for the Family members' frequent doctor's office trips to be treated for sexually transmitted diseases (which were often passed on to Wilson himself), and when Susan Atkins had problems with her teeth, Wilson got hit with the dental tab, too. He had to cover it and the other Family expenses by forwarding the bills to Brother Records for payment, and management there griped to him about it—how long did Dennis intend to subsidize these freeloaders, anyway? Wilson had no answer for that, beyond a growing certainty that Charlie had no intention of going anywhere until he got a recording contract from Brother Records, which Wilson knew, though Charlie didn't, was unlikely. Still, the guy was always interesting and the girls were always fun. Wilson let things go on as they were.

Wilson could do that, but Charlie couldn't. Gurus or any other spiritual leaders are expected by their followers to keep things interesting and moving forward. Status quo is unacceptable because that offers disciples too much time to notice personal flaws or failings in a leader. The Beatles lost faith in the Maharishi at his camp in India after rumors spread he ate meat and made sexual advances to female followers. The Beach Boys' devotion to Maharishi was shaken when he proved to be a financial black hole on a national concert tour. Charlie wasn't famous like the Maharishi, but he had the same constant pressure to measure up to the Family's worshipful expectations. To a great extent, he had so far. All of them came to Charlie feeling broken in some critical way; he soothed their fears, reassured them that they were special and had the potential to become even better by listening to and following him. He gave them a sense of belonging that most had never felt with their original families. Thanks to Charlie's influence on Dennis Wilson, they enjoyed luxurious hospitality in the mansion of a rock star. Where they'd previously felt lost and miserable, now they felt loved and happy, just as Charlie had promised.

But the novelty would inevitably wane. Dumpster-diving and riding around in a battered old school bus would eventually seem routine, even boring, rather than adventuresome. For now Wilson remained a gracious, generous host, but who knew for how long? Charlie hinted broadly that Wilson ought to join the Family full-time. Wilson seemed to consider it, but he never took that step. He identified himself above all as a Beach Boy and was unwilling to give that up, along with the material possessions he loved, to become a doglike Manson follower. Most dangerous of all for Charlie was his ongoing inability to secure that elusive record deal, not only for the threat of not achieving his dream of worldwide fame but also for the danger of his followers seeing him fail to accomplish something. All it would take for some to lose faith would be the slightest armor chink, and the turndown by Universal and the apparent lack of interest at Brother were potential clues that maybe Charlie Manson wasn't superior after all, let alone the possible Second Coming of Christ. Charlie needed to provide a distraction, some fresh mission to occupy the Family's attention, and around the end of May he announced it.

Since the Family was staying together forever, Charlie informed his followers, they needed a permanent home. He assigned Susan Atkins, in mid-pregnancy, to lead some of the others back to Mendocino County and look around for some suitable site. It might be a house or else someplace out in the country where they could make long-term camp. Pat and Yeller would go along, and so would Mary Brunner and infant Pooh Bear. They could take the school bus and send back regular reports. Putting

Susan in charge was a masterstroke by Charlie—she loved the extra authority and took it as a sign that Charlie had confidence in her. She did her best to mimic him as she ordered the others around. They were resentful, but they still did what she told them to. Meanwhile, Charlie had one of his most volatile followers out of the way for a time. The plan to find a home base signaled to all of the Family members staying behind that enjoying Dennis Wilson's largesse was only temporary—indoor plumbing, a swimming pool, stocked refrigerators, and fancy stereo systems were not part of the group's ultimate goal, which as Charlie explained it was to achieve the highest possible level of existence by ultimately giving up everything except their love for one another.

But Susan and the others botched the Mendocino experiment. Soon after they arrived and rented a place in the small town of Philo, parents began complaining to county police that their underage children were being given drugs by women living in what neighbors dubbed "Hippie House." Following up on one mother's call, officers found the woman's seventeen-year-old son suffering violent, drug-induced hallucinations on the rental property. Susan, Mary, Yeller, Pat, and a few hangers-on were arrested on a variety of drug charges, and baby Pooh Bear was placed in foster care. Now Charlie had to find some way to rescue them all, but he couldn't leave L.A. himself—it was critical that he stick around to keep working on Wilson and Jakobson about getting signed to Brother or another label. So he called Bobby Beausoleil and asked him to go to Mendocino and see what might be done. Beausoleil was agreeable. He was spending his summer driving up and down the California coast in his pickup truck, which he'd rigged with a folding tent in the bed to provide sheltered sleeping quarters at night. As usual, he had female companionship. His girlfriend Gail was still with him, and so was Gypsy. Since he'd talked to Charlie last, Beausoleil had added a third girl to his informal harem. Her name was Leslie Van Houten.

Eighteen-year-old Leslie was a native of Monrovia, a Los Angeles suburb. Her comfortable middle-class upbringing was shaken by her parents' divorce when she was fourteen, but Leslie seemed to compensate well, making lots of friends and playing baritone sax in her high school marching band. But Leslie was rebellious, too. She constantly questioned authority, made only average grades despite keen intelligence, and, like many teenagers in the mid-1960s, became sexually active early and developed a fondness for drugs, mostly weed and LSD. During the summer of 1967 when she was seventeen, Leslie ran away to the Haight for a few weeks with her boyfriend. They were disillusioned by what they found there—use of hard drugs was rampant and instead of the anticipated warm hippie welcome, the teen couple found a hostile reception in the overcrowded streets. Leslie was pregnant when they returned to Monrovia; even though she wanted to have the baby, her mother firmly advocated abortion and won out. Leslie was resentful; she graduated from secretarial school, and then instead of going to work at some L.A. company she left for San Francisco again, this time with a friend named Dee who wanted to reconcile with her husband back in the Haight. Leslie wanted the break from her parents and siblings to be permanent; after arriving in the Haight, she called them to say that she was dropping out and they'd never hear from her again. She signed up as a Kelly Girl to support herself. But then Dee met Bobby Beausoleil at a party and brought him home, where he and Gail and Gypsy met Leslie. They suggested that Leslie join them and Beausoleil's white pit bull on their aimless coastal trip and she agreed—it sounded like the kind of hippie adventure she'd dreamed about.

There was a moment when Leslie almost didn't go, and she remembered it later as the turning point in her life. All four of them couldn't fit in the cab of Beausoleil's truck, and when the others came by to pick up Leslie for the trip, she decided to ride in the truck bed. Beausoleil thought she had climbed onboard before she actually had and drove away, leaving Leslie standing on the sidewalk. The other three, comfortably seated up in front, weren't aware that they'd stranded her. Leslie waited for almost fifteen minutes, wondering if they were going to come back and, as the minutes passed, thinking that maybe this was an omen, maybe she should stay behind in the Haight or even go home to Monrovia. But she thought about her phone call to her family, how she'd told them she was gone forever, and so she stood there patiently until somebody in the truck finally noticed Leslie had been left behind and they came back for her. But it had been a near thing, and afterward Leslie wondered how different her life might have been.

Much of the early trip was fine. The four travelers went where they pleased, either panhandled when they needed money or else Beausoleil played guitar for tips. They enjoyed fine weather and beautiful scenery. But Gail wasn't pleased to share her man with two other girls, and Gypsy constantly suggested to Leslie that they ought to leave. Bobby Beausoleil wasn't where it was at, Gypsy insisted. There was this guy named Charlie she'd met through Beausoleil, and Charlie was a real guru who could teach them how to live better. She even hinted that Charlie might be something more than mortal. Leslie was intrigued, especially since Beausoleil and Gail argued with each other a lot, but she was a little put off by Gypsy's referring to Charlie and his group as a commune. In Leslie's limited hippie experience, single girls like her were usually not welcome in communes because the women already there didn't want to share the men with newcomers. Though Gypsy assured her that the other girls in Charlie's group were cool, Leslie didn't want to risk any hassle. She thought she'd stick with Beausoleil for at least a little while longer.

After Charlie got in touch and asked Beausoleil to help out with the problem in Mendocino County, Bobby drove to Los Angeles so they could discuss it in person. Charlie and the Family happened to be out at the ranch that day rather than at Dennis Wilson's. Beausoleil parked the truck and he, Gail, and Gypsy got out; Leslie, not in a sociable mood, only briefly left the cab. She thought the movie set was interesting, and the girls in the group were friendly and not bitchy, as Gypsy had promised. But Charlie, whom Leslie glimpsed only in passing, didn't seem all that special, and soon Beausoleil had them back in the truck driving up to Mendocino County. It turned out that there wasn't anything he could do—the county cops held Susan and the others in the county jail through most of the summer, when they were found guilty of the drug charges and sentenced to time served. Mary Brunner was able to regain custody of Pooh Bear, and everyone straggled back to Charlie in L.A. There was no more talk of finding the Family a permanent home. Leslie and Gypsy went on with Beausoleil, but as his fights with Gail escalated, Leslie began thinking that maybe soon she'd let Gypsy talk her into joining the Manson Family instead.

The squabbling in Bobby Beausoleil's truck paled compared to national tumult in 1968, especially that summer. Tom Hayden would conclude more than forty years later that there may never have been twelve months in national history when so many cataclysmic events occurred in such rapid succession as in 1968. Race riots raged with staggering regularity; it seemed virtually every major city ghetto was in flames. On June 6, with America still stunned by the murder of Martin Luther King just two months earlier, Senator Robert Kennedy was assassinated in Los Angeles on the same night he won California's Democratic presidential primary. Besides the horror of the event itself, Kennedy's death further inflamed youthful opposition to the American political process. With Kennedy gone and Eugene McCarthy faltering Vice President Hubert Humphrey became the Democrat nominee. Student radicals, who linked Humphrey to Lyndon Johnson's military escalation in Vietnam, were appalled, and some determined that the time for nonviolent protest had passed. The SDS leadership made plans to disrupt the Democratic National Convention in Chicago in August; Bill Ayers would recall in his memoir that "insubordination [became] life itself. Go further, we said. Shock, offend, outrage, overstep, disturb. Know no limits. Lose control."

In the waning weeks of the summer of 1968, Charlie was offending, overstepping, and disturbing, and as a result he was losing control of Dennis Wilson. There was something in Charlie, Neil Young reflected many years later, that eventually drove most people away—his disproportionate sense of self-importance and entitlement. Charlie believed that he had the right to do and have anything he wanted. Anyone not falling completely under Charlie's spell eventually noticed and was put off by it. For months, Wilson had subsidized Charlie and the Family. They assumed that everything he had was theirs—his clothes, his cars, his gold records—and for a while it was okay with Wilson. Charlie wanted to be a rock star and Wilson did what he could to help—it wasn't his fault that nobody else was impressed enough with Charlie's music to offer him a record deal. Instead of being grateful for all Wilson had done, Charlie kept demanding even more. It wasn't just his constant badgering about a record deal, though that was bad enough. Charlie also expected to be accepted by Wilson, Jakobson, and Melcher as an equal. Because they'd been nice enough to take him with them to a few parties and some clubs, he believed that he was one of the elite gang and expected to go all of the time. When Charlie did get invited along, he invariably found some way to make himself the center of attention, as he did the night at the Whisky a Go Go when he dominated the dance floor. The traits that Wilson initially found intriguing about Charlie had become aggravating.

There was also the way Charlie went after every girl he met, even when they clearly weren't interested. Wilson fooled around with the Family women whenever he got the chance, but he had other girlfriends. One of them, a teenager nicknamed Croxey, came around the house a lot and wasn't interested when Charlie tried to get her to join the Family. Croxey also wouldn't cooperate in Charlie's group sex scenarios. Once, when he found himself alone with the girl and she refused to have sex with him, Charlie pulled a knife and said, "You know, I could cut you up in little pieces." Croxey dared him to do it and Charlie backed down. It was a story that Wilson could believe, because Charlie had threatened him with a knife, too. Most people would have thrown Charlie out, but Wilson let it go. Charlie wasn't actually stabbing anybody or cutting anyone's throat.

Dennis arranged for Charlie to do some recording at brother Brian's home studio out of a sense of guilt. It was clear to him, though not to Charlie, that Brother Records was never going to offer Charlie a contract. Dennis had tried to make that happen and failed. Giving Charlie a chance to get his songs taped at a state-of-the-art facility was still a substantial opportunity, especially since Brian didn't like Charlie and Dennis had to plead with him to allow it. If Charlie didn't realize the significance of this effort made on his behalf, Dennis did, and it eased his conscience. And who knew? Maybe Charlie would unexpectedly create some musical magic and come out of it with quality tapes that got him a record deal somewhere after all. The main thing was, Dennis wanted to rid himself of any sense of obligation to Charlie.

Wilson went so far as to get Stephen Despar, who'd built the studio for Brian and worked on some of the Beach Boys' albums, to run the session. Before Despar met Charlie, Dennis advised him not to believe anything he might have been told by other Brother Records staff—Charlie had talent but was usually misunderstood. Despar was agreeable; after working with quirky Brian, who was currently grossly overweight and liked to record wearing only pajama bottoms, he figured it would be impossible to run a session for anybody odder.

Despar was used to musicians arriving with lots of instruments and, he hoped, charts of the songs they wanted to record so he could get a better idea of what he was expected to get on tape. Charlie only had one guitar, but he also brought along several girls from the Family whose sole function seemed to be rolling joints and asking to use the bathrooms upstairs. Brian Wilson didn't even leave his bedroom to greet Charlie. Brian's wife, Marilyn, appalled at her unkempt guests, Susan Atkins in particular, scrubbed all the toilets in the house with disinfectant after they left.

Despar expected Dennis Wilson to come with Charlie and produce the session, but Dennis never showed. So Despar did his best to set up microphones and tried to make Charlie feel comfortable. When Charlie took out a cigarette but couldn't find a match in his pockets, Despar went into Brian's kitchen and found matches for him. Charlie made a point of thanking him profusely. Then they began recording, and it simply didn't work. Charlie resented even mild instructions to move closer to the microphone, or warnings that his guitar was out of tune. These were his songs and he would perform them his way; Despar's job was to keep the tape rolling. Despar had every right to feel offended—Brian Wilson and the other Beach Boys were also temperamental, but they were established artists with exceptional musical credentials, not some scruffy wannabe whose songs, so far as Despar could tell, were nothing special. Still, Dennis had asked him to do what he could with Charlie, so Despar suggested they try again the next night. Maybe the guy would be a little more relaxed then, a little more cooperative. But Charlie wasn't. He resented all of Despar's suggestions, and pulled a knife when Despar decided that he'd heard enough. Despar walked out and called a senior staffer at Brother Records, complaining that "this guy is psychotic." He was assured that whatever had been recorded so far was plenty. Despar told Charlie that the sessions were over, and somehow Charlie left convinced that he'd done so well a Brother Records recording contract was forthcoming.

It wasn't, but when Dennis listened to the tapes he thought that "Cease to Exist" had potential. The Beach Boys were preparing to record another album, and Dennis wanted to contribute several tunes. Maybe, with some tweaking, "Cease to Exist" might be one of them. When Dennis told him what he was considering, Charlie was thrilled. He expected that the song would be recorded by the Beach Boys exactly as he had written it, or at least that his lyrics would remain intact. Wilson let him believe it.

Toward the end of the summer, the Beach Boys left L.A. on a brief concert tour. Charlie and the Family stayed at Dennis Wilson's Sunset Boulevard lodge while he was away. They'd already claimed all of his possessions as their own, and now they glommed on to one of his charge accounts. When Wilson returned home after his week on the road, he was surprised to be called in by the accountants in the Brother Records office. They demanded to know how it was possible for Dennis to run up an $800 Alta Dena Dairy bill during the time that the Beach Boys had been away on tour. Wilson realized what had happened, but the bill was in his name, and Brother Records had to pay it. He caught hell for the expenditure, and in turn he got really pissed off at Charlie. When Wilson added everything up, including a Mercedes that someone in the Family totaled, he calculated that his summer guests had cost him at least $100,000. It had to stop.

But Wilson didn't take the obvious step of throwing Charlie and the Family out. He still liked most of the girls, he believed Charlie had potential as a collaborator on song lyrics, and—bottom line—Charlie was scary. When the guy waved his knife it was hard to tell if he was kidding or serious. So Wilson opted for a nonconfrontational separation. His lease on the Sunset Boulevard lodge was about to expire. A few weeks before it did, Wilson packed some essential belongings and moved out without telling Charlie that he was leaving or where he was going. Wilson rented a house above the Pacific Coast Highway. Because he didn't intend to completely eliminate all contact with Charlie and the others, Wilson made sure that his new place was too small for the Family to move in once they discovered his whereabouts.

When Wilson's former landlord tossed Charlie and the Family out of the lodge on Sunset, it was inconvenient but not catastrophic for them. Though they'd miss the constant freeloading at Wilson's expense, the group had another option, a place where they already stayed sometimes. Now they'd make their arrangement with the doddering, nearly blind owner permanent. Gathering their remaining Dennis Wilson spoils—clothing, knickknacks, even some Beach Boys gold records—everyone piled into the old school bus and set out for Spahn Ranch.

CHAPTER TEN

The Ranches

When the Family's school bus broke down once again and the necessary repair proved beyond Charlie's skill as a mechanic, Sandy Good said that she had a friend in the area who could probably fix it. He lived on a ranch about thirty-five miles northwest of downtown L.A., near the Simi Valley and the Santa Susana Mountains. Charlie went to investigate and was excited by what he discovered. Spahn Ranch was a bucolic paradise, hundreds of acres of rugged, beautiful foothills and craggy heights bisected by streams, dotted with caves, and populated with all sorts of wildlife. A western movie set dominated one long, low valley, and it was instantly recognizable to anyone who'd grown up watching the ubiquitous cowboy TV shows of the 1950s since several of those series were filmed there. Most of the set consisted of store fronts without additional walls, but there were some complete buildings, including a saloon. A few other shacks were scattered around the property. Charlie realized instantly that this was a perfect place to bring his followers; all he had to do was convince octogenarian owner George Spahn to let the group move in.

Spahn, limited in his movements because of poor vision, was wringing money out of the ranch by renting horses to visitors who wanted to get away from the city and lose themselves in trail rides. For $1.50 apiece they could saddle up and head into the property's hills. Spahn employed several ranch hands to care for the horses, deal with the customers, and, so far as they could in any spare moments, keep the movie set clean and in reasonable repair—sometimes instead of renting horses people just wanted to check out the place they'd seen so often on TV. But upkeep was sporadic, and the set looked shabby when Charlie arrived. His pitch to Spahn was simple: He and a few friends would like to live out on the ranch. They didn't have money to pay rent, but they were good workers and would pitch in to keep the movie set sparkling (or as clean as possible, considering the dust blowing everywhere) and help out the ranch hands as needed. Charlie himself had lots of experience with horses because he'd worked at a racetrack back home in West Virginia. Best of all, the girls who'd be moving in with Charlie would be glad to do some house-keeping for Spahn in the main house where he lived, and do whatever else they could to make his days a little more comfortable. Was it a deal?

There were already a few other informal tenants on the ranch, and Spahn didn't mind a couple more. To make sure his host didn't recon-sider, Charlie installed Lynne as Spahn's housekeeper. Sex with George was part of her responsibilities, along with cleaning and fixing the old man's meals. That was okay with her because Charlie taught that every kind of love was good. Spahn certainly liked physical contact with Lynne, quick little pinches especially. Lynne responded with high-pitched squeals, and George began calling her "Squeaky." The nickname stuck. Soon the Family members called her that, too.

Spahn was expecting perhaps a half dozen others to move in with Charlie, but the initial count of newcomers was closer to eighteen and within a few months grew to approximately thirty-five. Charlie explained that most of them were itinerants, friends of his who would just be there for a day or two before moving on. Instead, it was the ranch's other squatters who left; Charlie and the Family pressured them to go so that they could pick the best shacks on the property. To shelter his other fol-lowers who didn't have sufficient cover, Charlie ordered Tex Watson to build additional lean-tos and extend some of the movie set false fronts into complete structures. To keep Tex off-balance and willing to perform hard unpaid labor, Charlie initially withheld full Family membership from him. He was allowed to be at the ranch and do whatever he was told, but Charlie said that Tex still had not surrendered his ego sufficiently to be-come a permanent part of the group. If Tex worked really hard and never complained, he might eventually convince Charlie otherwise. Tex, often befuddled with drugs, spent every waking hour demonstrating that he was an egoless, willing worker.

   Above all, Charlie appreciated what the ranch location had to offer—
the kind of isolation necessary to keep the Family members separated
from any influence other than Charlie's own. It was hard to hold their attention when he tried to preach to them at Wilson's; the drummer's other
friends were constantly rushing in and out. At Spahn Ranch, Charlie
could march everyone off to an isolated hill or canyon and preach as long
as he liked without the danger of distractions. In late summer, when Wilson abandoned the mansion and Charlie and the Family had to leave, too,
it was a simple matter for Charlie to load everyone in the bus and move
them to the ranch full-time. George Spahn didn't notice any difference,
but his colorful bunch of ranch hands did. They were led by Juan Flynn, a
towering Army Vietnam veteran. Shorty Shea yearned for a career in the
movies and soon earned Charlie's antipathy by advising George Spahn to
sell out to developers. Johnny Swartz was useful because he would let the
Family borrow his battered yellow 1959 Ford for trips into the city. Teenage Steve Grogan seemed so stupid that some of the Family assumed he
must be retarded. Unlike Flynn and Shea, Grogan loved everything about
Charlie and his followers and begged to join them. Intelligence mattered
far less to Charlie than unwavering loyalty, and Grogan was soon brought
into the Family. His new name among them was Clem, and sometimes
they called him Scramblehead. There were other hands who worked at
the ranch for a few weeks or months and then moved on.
   Flynn expected the Family to earn its keep with lots of hard work.
Charlie couldn't have agreed more—whenever he wasn't preaching to
them or putting them to work on his own errands, he wanted his followers to be busy. It kept them from thinking too much. Under Flynn's
supervision they cleaned horse stalls and saddle tack, helped rent rides
to customers on days when ranch visitors were especially numerous,
hauled hay, cut brush, and performed any other chores that needed
doing. Charlie was careful, though, not to let anyone think that Flynn
in any sense supplanted him as the Family's leader. One day when Flynn
wanted everyone up and working, Charlie directed his followers to the
movie set saloon instead, where he sat them down to listen while he
preached. Flynn, whose temper was sometimes terrible, roared with fury
and charged at Charlie. It was a physical mismatch; Flynn was more than

a full foot taller than runty Charlie. But, with the Family watching, Charlie didn't back down. Flynn got in Charlie's face, towering over him and shouting. Calmly, Charlie took out a pack of cigarettes, struck a match, and lit one. Then Charlie, looking Flynn straight in the eye, held the match flame to the soft skin underneath his own wrist, and the peculiar stench of scorched flesh wafted in the air. Charlie didn't even blink; he said softly to Flynn, "You know, brother, there's no such thing as pain." Totally deflated, the hulking ranch hand walked away, and the Family was reminded why Charlie Manson was its undisputed leader.

Using the school bus, Johnny Swartz's Ford, or whatever other vehicles were handy, Charlie and other Family members could drive into L.A. or around the country outside Spahn Ranch. Daily trips were necessary to scrounge food from grocery store dumpsters. Charlie was still recruiting, too, though now he relied mostly on current followers to invite potential disciples out to the ranch. Then Charlie would talk to them and see how they interacted with the others in the Family. At some point anyone promising would be quizzed about money and possessions—there had to be some immediate advantage to Charlie for a person to be invited to join. And, always, Charlie's decision was final; if he didn't find a candidate acceptable, it didn't matter what the others thought. Once someone was admitted to the Family fold, there was a transition period when Charlie placed the newcomer under the supervision of one of his veterans—Pat, Susan, Mary, Squeaky, or Little Paul Watkins. Not everyone got through this probationary period, particularly if their only real attraction to Charlie was whatever money they had or a car's pink slip. Once otherwise undesirables were relieved of whatever they had that Charlie wanted, they were sent on their way.

Charlie began enforcing a new rule for full-time women followers. No female in the Family was ever to carry money, even pennies. When they went out panhandling, one of the men always came along and any coins or bills collected had to immediately be handed over to him. Charlie never explained why he'd imposed the new edict, but it was a popular rule among pimps. If one of their women wanted to sneak away, she couldn't afford a pay phone call to relatives or friends, let alone cab or bus fare. It was one more way for Charlie to be in absolute control.

All that summer and fall the Family expanded. Among the new full-fledged members were Cathy Gillies ("Capistrano"), Tom Walleman ("T.J."), John Philip Haught ("Zero"), Simi Valley Sherri, and two other arrivals Charlie initially wanted to turn away. Gypsy and Leslie Van Houten had finally split from Bobby Beausoleil. When they presented themselves to Charlie at Spahn Ranch, he ordered them to go back; Beausoleil was a useful friend and Charlie didn't want to offend him by taking away his women. But Gypsy pleaded, and Charlie reconsidered. Gypsy, in her late twenties, was a bit older than the rest of the Family members. She was prepared to devote herself completely to Charlie, and it was obvious she'd be an effective recruiter for him—she'd already talked Leslie into wanting to join the Family. Leslie was more intelligent than Charlie liked his followers to be; smart people might question his teachings. But she was very attractive, and along with Ruth Ann would give Charlie two pretty girls to use to get what he wanted from men outside the Family. Another of Leslie's attributes, probably the one that ultimately tipped Charlie in her favor, was her excellent secretarial skills, including shorthand. He assigned her to follow him around whenever he was composing song lyrics. It had always been hard for Charlie to remember them; now Leslie would use shorthand to record them, and afterward write them out. She was frustrated because Charlie often sang sounds instead of words. When he did, she was required to spell out the sounds as best she could. And, as Charlie anticipated, Gypsy soon emerged as a leader among the women, a whip cracker committed to ensuring that all of Charlie's instructions were followed to the letter.

After the Family settled in at the ranch, a staff member of the Free Clinic came out to stay with them for a while. Alan Rose had been intrigued with Charlie and his followers since he met them in the Haight, and he thought he might join them himself. After a few weeks Rose decided to return to San Francisco instead—there were some personal matters there that he needed to deal with—and he and Free Clinic founder David E. Smith decided to write a professional paper on the group. In September 1970, when it finally appeared in the *Journal of Psychedelic Drugs*, it explained in clear, objective terms how Charlie used sex to break down female initiates, drained his followers of any money or material possessions they had, forced anyone he deemed undesirable out of the group, and concluded that the real conundrum was "why . . . were these young girls so attracted and captivated by a disturbed mystic such as Charlie?" But as Rose, Smith, and others described a typical day at the ranch, there was very little disturbed about it. Charlie tried to lull his flock with preaching, drugs, and sex punctuated by enough hard physical labor to keep everybody moderately worn out.

The day started early. Everyone was up around 7 A.M. to feed the horses and take them out to pasture to graze. Then, after a hurried breakfast—usually whatever food was left over from dinner the night before—the horses were retrieved and saddles were fetched so that rides would be available to whatever visitors might show up. A few Family members stayed available to serve as trail guides while the rest cleaned out stalls and hauled in fresh hay. Once that was done, Juan Flynn might have other repair work to assign, and on mornings when there didn't seem anything else to do Charlie would set everyone to virtual busywork, sweeping away the ubiquitous dust from the wooden sidewalks on the movie set or doing inconsequential landscaping on property where for centuries nature had left its mark. Sometimes it seemed to some of the Family that Charlie had them doing little more than digging holes and then filling them, but his orders were never to be disputed. If anyone did mutter complaints, other Family members, often led by Gypsy or Little Paul, would loudly upbraid them—how *dare* they question Charlie?

Mornings were for work. There was no lunch break—the two daily meals were breakfast and dinner. Later in the day there were frequently LSD sessions orchestrated by Charlie. He would choose the time and bring everyone into one of the movie set buildings or guide them out to an isolated spot on the ranch. Doses of acid were passed around—Charlie would personally place the drugs in his followers' mouths, but sometimes didn't take any himself so he would remain in control of his faculties. Then, as everyone was tripping, Charlie would talk, often about himself as Jesus. A few times he simulated being crucified. Charlie emphasized that LSD was holy; using it made you learn about yourself, who you really were.

Late afternoon usually found the women going out on food runs, sometimes returning with all kinds of bounty and others with only a few handfuls of limp, scraggly produce. Whatever they got comprised the dinner menu. Attendance at this meal was mandatory. The women did the cooking, and then everyone sat around as platters of food were passed. The men ate first and the women got what was left. Each person took a few bites of whatever was on a platter and then passed it along. Nothing was wasted. Sometimes the fare was bizarre. One day someone gave the Family a case of Cool Whip in plastic containers. For that evening's meal, everyone dipped their hands into the containers and licked the Cool Whip off their fingers.

Sometimes in the afternoons, sometimes after dinner, everyone gathered around while Charlie preached. Most often, he had his guitar and would play and sing his sermons; the girls would stand up and dance as they listened. Other times Charlie chose a biblical approach—Jesus often taught in parables, and Charlie did, too. A memorable lesson for the Family involved a king and queen. Every day the king would say to the queen, "I'm hungry," and she would reply, "Let me go fix you a sandwich." The king ate the sandwich and everyone was happy. This was their routine until one day when the king said he was hungry the queen answered, "Honey, I'm really tired. Would you mind, just for today, fixing your own sandwich?" The king said, "Okay," but while he was on his way to the kitchen the queen called after him, "While you're out there, would you get me one, too?" Every day after that she told the king to make a sandwich for her; their roles had been neatly reversed. Charlie explained that this was the way women tricked men and took control. They appealed to men's love, to their sense of sympathy, and the men fell for it. Much of what was wrong with modern society, Charlie warned, was because, more and more, men were no longer in charge. It wasn't going to be that way in the Family. In this blessed, enlightened group, women served men and everyone was better off because of it.

After the meal and the preaching there was music. Often, Charlie sang his own songs and everyone else joined in on the choruses. Otherwise it was the Beatles, the *Magical Mystery Tour* album over and over, or else albums by the Moody Blues, a British band whose use of orchestral accompaniment was considered unique. The only other music Charlie allowed at these times was a Top Ten hit, "Born to Be Wild," by the American band Steppenwolf. Charlie liked the music of the Doors and the Jefferson Airplane but didn't consider them appropriate for this special part of the day. Some of the Family grumbled to themselves that Squeaky had it lucky; she spent most of her time in the main house with old blind George, and George had his radio tuned to country music all day, the kind of steel guitar–accompanied laments widely known as "shitkicker." Nobody in the Family particularly liked shitkicker music, but at least it wasn't *Magical Mystery Tour* and the Moody Blues and Charlie's songs all night, every night. Of course, no one complained to Charlie about it, or around his chief lieutenants, Watkins and Gypsy.

Usually, sex involved random pairing off, during the afternoons or after dinner and Charlie's preaching at night. Anyone in the Family was supposed to be willing to sleep with any other member. Permanent pairing off as couples was prohibited, though Charlie sometimes assigned two people to stay together so that one could keep a close eye on the other. After he finally admitted Tex Watson to full membership in the Family, Charlie "gave" him Mary Brunner as a regular sex partner. Charlie himself continued to prefer young Dianne Lake, the teenager he'd recruited from her parents' commune, and Dianne developed proprietary feelings toward him. When Charlie had sex with another woman in the Family—he considered it an obligation to give each of them a turn with him once in a while, and they thought of it as an honor—Dianne would be bitchy to the other girl afterward.

Group sex was completely orchestrated by Charlie. He would specify who would do what and with whom. Sometimes the sessions were drawn-out and complex; Charlie promised that the acts were sacramental and an ongoing way to break down all the false inhibitions forced on the Family members by repressive society. That sounded fine to the participants, though there was the inconvenience of more women than men. But doing something that would horrify the straights made the orgies that much more fun. It was *liberating.*

As a special treat, Charlie would encourage the Family to act out group fantasies. They would run around the movie set pretending to be cowboys, or else sail imaginary ships among the hills as swashbuckling pirates. Several of the girls liked dressing up as fairies; they'd imagine that they'd grown wings on their backs and could fly. Charlie encouraged elf themes. Sometimes during LSD trips he'd suggest that maybe a time would come when the girls really could become elves, wings and all.

Charlie maintained control other ways. Whenever anyone in the Family passed Charlie on the ranch, particularly on the wooden sidewalks of the movie set, Charlie would stand in front of them and make faces and jerk his hands around. The Family member was required to mimic all of Charlie's expressions and gestures. Flawless imitation meant that the person was well on the way to spiritual enlightenment. Failing to match a Charlie grimace or movement indicated the presence of too much ego, and the follower was firmly chastised. People rarely got everything right, so Charlie did a lot of chastising.

Yet he also did considerable praising. Charlie had a keen understanding of how much each individual Family member could be corrected without breaking down. Just when anyone felt that he or she couldn't go on, that there was no pleasing the undisputed leader, Charlie would come over for a friendly talk or suggest that they take a walk and enjoy some one-on-one fellowship. He had an exceptional sense of touch, knowing just how to pat someone's shoulder or gently stroke a person's hair.

One of Charlie's most inflexible rules was that children should not be raised—ruined—by their biological parents, even among the Family. Pooh Bear, Charlie's son with Mary Brunner, was considered the child of every full-fledged Family member. When Susan Atkins gave birth to a son in October, that baby was taken from her and kept separate with Pooh Bear. Susan named her child Ze Zo Ze Cee Zadfrack because "it seemed like a good name." As the Family ranks expanded to include more parents, their children joined Pooh Bear and Ze Zo Ze in a separate area. There was some competition among the women to have the next baby. Charlie urged them all to get pregnant—it was, after all, a natural state for women—and they were willing. Each wanted Charlie as their child's biological father. But except for Pooh Bear, Charlie did not sire children among his female flock. At Spahn Ranch, Sandy Good was the next to get pregnant. The father was a new recruit named Joel Pugh, and sometimes Sandy said that they were married and used his last name. It helped when she applied for welfare. Charlie hated the government, but he was eager for its handouts.

Wristwatches, calendars, and clocks were forbidden; Charlie said he wanted everyone to concentrate on the *now* rather than worry about what some soulless gadget said was the correct time. Eyeglasses weren't allowed either. Charlie explained that whatever the state of their vision, that was their natural way to see the rest of the world, and only natural things were good. New members were relieved of their glasses immediately; some of them developed permanent squints. Books weren't allowed on the ranch, either. All anyone needed to know was whatever Charlie wanted them to. Authors were evil, trying to play mind control games on readers. Charlie went so far as to burn some books in front of the others. There was one exception—Charlie had a Bible.

Because Charlie preached so much and had rules about so many different things, it was inevitable that sometimes he'd seem to contradict himself or act in ways that seemed opposed to what he told the others they should do. One of the most obvious was his anti-Semitism. Charlie often presented himself as the reincarnation of Jesus, but he also hated Jews and frequently preached that they were evil. Another was on frequent display during the Family's communal LSD trips. A key component of Charlie's philosophy was that LSD should be used to explore inner consciousness—the liberating effect of the drug would help users overcome socially mandated inhibitions. Whatever you felt and did while tripping was invariably right. But during group LSD sessions, Charlie's rule was that everyone had to stay seated wherever he placed them. Sometimes a Family participant was overwhelmed enough on a trip to jump up without Charlie's permission, and whenever that happened he would hit the offender with his fist or, sometimes, with one of the chairs. It was the opposite of what Charlie taught, inhibiting a natural reaction to a sacred drug, but afterward he would explain that if he seemed to be violating his own philosophy, that meant that his followers simply weren't smart enough yet to understand what was going on. Finding anything that appeared to be a flaw in Charlie actually exposed flaws in themselves. They accepted the explanation because they believed in him. They might make mistakes or misunderstand, but anything Charlie said or did had to be right. They were all stupid and he was doing his best to make them smart. The beatings were part of his gift to them.

As much as Charlie liked keeping his followers isolated, he still encouraged a limited number of visitors. Dennis Wilson, relieved that he was finally rid of the Family on a daily basis, began showing up once in a while at the ranch, happy to hand over a few dollars when needed and always ready to romp in the hay bales with some of the girls. Wilson genuinely liked many of them and worried whether they were all right out there on Spahn. He told Charlie that the Beach Boys were planning to record "Cease to Exist." Having a single song recorded by another artist's band wasn't the instant superstardom that Charlie craved and believed he deserved, but at least it was a start. When "Cease to Exist" became a massive worldwide hit and everyone learned that it had been written by Charlie Manson, things would finally get rolling for Charlie's own career as a performer. It was taking longer than Charlie had anticipated, but it was still going to happen. Charlie's certainty that he was about to hit it big was reinforced when Terry Melcher also made a few ranch visits. Melcher still didn't commit himself about listening to Charlie's tapes or getting him into the studio for an audition, but at least he was staying in contact. Playing gracious host, Charlie always presented Ruth Ann to Melcher for his pleasure. The other girls were available to him, too, but she remained Melcher's favorite.

Gregg Jakobson also came around, usually with Melcher or Wilson. He was still convinced that there was something marketable about Charlie—maybe not music, but certainly in film, perhaps a TV documentary. Toward that end he spent considerable time just walking around the ranch with Charlie and talking to him, trying to draw him out on his background. Charlie had plenty of colorful stories to tell about being the illegitimate son of a teenage prostitute, and how he was terribly abused in reform school and prison. Charlie told Jakobson about inventing the "insane game" to survive, and bragged that now it was easy for him to "change hats" and instantly alter his personality to fit whatever company or situation he found himself in. Jakobson watched him do it—firm yet fatherly with the Family, just obsequious enough with George Spahn, buddy and musical equal with Wilson and Melcher, and crude redneck pal to biker gangs. Charlie liked having the bikers come around occasionally because they had expertise in motorcycle repair and the Family always seemed to have one or two banged-up bikes. He didn't want them showing up too often because they demanded beer. Alcohol was another thing Charlie banned among his followers. He preached it was mind-numbing rather than mind-expanding. But the bikers loved to drink, so whenever they were expected the Family had to go out and panhandle enough to buy a couple of cases. Charlie and the Family weren't above occasional shoplifting, which they didn't consider stealing because everything belonged to everyone. But it was practically impossible to sneak out of a store with a case of beer tucked under your shirt.

Sex with outsiders became a daily routine for Family women. Charlie would bring over whatever men he wanted to impress and please that day—not just Wilson, Melcher, or Jakobson, but bikers and drug dealers—and tell the women to line up in front of them. Charlie sometimes held the pretty girls back, keeping them as a special treat for VIP visitors. Each man was encouraged to pick out whichever girl he wanted, and Charlie would order her to go with the guy and do anything he told her. If a girl refused to do something, that meant she still had hang-ups and Charlie punished her, sometimes by making her strip naked in front of everyone else and then ridiculing her. It was effective. The girls learned not to refuse any request and never to seem reluctant or squeamish.

Charlie enjoyed showing off his musical expertise, especially when Wilson, Melcher, and Jakobson were around. He always joked about the primitive conditions at Spahn Ranch compared to the luxury of Wilson's former log cabin mansion, especially about the piles of horse manure that dotted the ranch property. The manure attracted swarms of buzzing flies. One day Charlie, Wilson, and Jakobson were roaming around an area where the rental horses had just abundantly dropped mounds of waste and flies were everywhere. Charlie had brought along his guitar, and he stood there with the flies all over him and began strumming and singing a song he made up on the spot, about the flies and their buzzing and what it all really meant. Jakobson had been around lots of successful artists, even some musical geniuses like Brian Wilson, and he thought Charlie had them all beat when it came to improvising. Reflecting many years later, Jakobson thought that Charlie would have been a natural rap music performer, "reporting" in songs all the latest details of the hard life out on the streets.

When Phil Kaufman heard that Charlie and the Family were living on Spahn Ranch, he went out to visit them. No one acted glad to see Kaufman. Charlie virtually ignored him. Kaufman's contact at Universal hadn't worked out, and now Charlie was working Wilson, Melcher, and Jakobson instead. So far as Charlie was concerned, Kaufman no longer had anything to offer other than friendship, and there was no particular advantage to Charlie in that. After an hour or so of getting cold-shouldered by everybody, Kaufman left, figuring he'd seen the last of Charlie and his followers, all that peace and love and expecting everybody else to do things for them. But at least they weren't hurting anybody. They were selfish but harmless.

Local authorities soon learned that a group of hippies had moved onto Spahn Ranch out near Simi Valley. They appeared to be just another commune of long-haired peaceniks, and there were already plenty of those in and around L.A., at least a couple of hundred. A few were even clustered right around Spahn Ranch. The area seemed to attract weirdos. Sure, all the communes, including the new one at Spahn, undoubtedly broke drug laws on a regular basis, but if lawmen arrested everybody who smoked weed or dropped acid they wouldn't have time for anything else. The Spahn commune might require observation because a lot of vehicles seemed to be brought into the place. Hippies weren't supposed to steal but car theft did seem to be a possibility. The real problem was that Spahn Ranch was along the Los Angeles–Ventura county line and there was some question about jurisdiction. Neither county police department really wanted to take responsibility for law enforcement in the area, so nobody kept an eye on what Charlie and the Family got up to.

Charlie shut off the Family from most news of the outside world, except for occasional examples of how crazy things were getting. He'd use these examples to emphasize that everyone was lucky to be safely tucked away on Spahn Ranch under Charlie's supervision—they probably wouldn't last long if they ever turned away from him and left. That fall of 1968, Charlie had lots of violence to mention, beginning in late

August with the Democratic National Convention in Chicago. Starting on August 26, peace activists and student radicals packed the city's Lincoln Park. Even as a Vietnam peace plank was voted down by Democratic delegates and Vice President Humphrey became the party's nominee for president, waves of Chicago police, following the instructions of Mayor Richard Daley, attacked the protesters, choking them with clouds of tear gas and battering them with batons. Network television crews captured the carnage for their horrified audiences to see; coughing, bleeding, those protesters who were still able chanted, "The whole world is watching." Afterward, irreconcilable factions began to emerge among the radicals. Some still advocated loud protest but working nonviolently within the political system. Others believed it was time to meet violence with violence, to "bring the war home." Few believed that an election pitting Hubert Humphrey against Richard Nixon would elect a president dedicated to sweeping change. Humphrey's ill-conceived "politics of joy" approach fell flat, while Nixon ran on a law-and-order platform. After attending a Republican rally in Toledo, columnist Jimmy Breslin observed, "When Richard Nixon got finished, there was a strangler's hand coming out of every cornfield in Ohio." In the imagination of many shaken older voters, the strangler was young and long-haired. Americans were turning on each other in fear and frustration, and many of the divisions were generational. In a year marked by assassinations, war, racial conflict, and escalating civil disobedience, there was no longer any sense of optimism. On November 5, Nixon narrowly defeated Humphrey and the nation braced for whatever was coming next.

On September 9 in England, the Beatles continued recording music for their next album, tentatively scheduled for release before the end of the year. At this session, a McCartney song was recorded. Internally, the band was having trouble getting along, and one of the points of contention was McCartney's penchant for writing sweet ballads that were increasingly at odds with Lennon's harder-edged compositions. But the song McCartney presented now was, if anything, more raucous than anything Lennon had come up with in years. Ostensibly about a popular British carnival ride involving a steep slide, its composer envisioned it as "the rise and fall of the Roman Empire, and this was the fall, the demise, the going down." McCartney bellowed out the lyrics, all about getting to the bottom and then going back to the top and coming down fast but don't let me break you. His band mates got caught up in the rowdy spirit and, McCartney later recalled, "we tried everything we could to dirty it up." He named the song for the carnival ride: "Helter Skelter."

Two days later in L.A., the Beach Boys did some recording, too. Dennis Wilson had been tinkering with "Cease to Exist," changing lyrics as well as the music. Charlie's original version explained to a girl that "submission is a gift" to give to her brother; among other revisions, Dennis changed "brother" to "lover," transforming the theme from spiritual enlightenment to sexual surrender. Instead of ceasing to exist, the girl was seduced into ceasing to resist. Dennis changed the title, too—"Cease to Exist" became "Never Learn Not to Love." The Beach Boys layered on their trademark harmonies and the result was judged acceptable enough to include on the album. On the credits, Dennis listed himself as sole composer. It was a deliberate insult. Wilson had been thinking again about all the money it cost him as Charlie and the Family's summer host, and besides that, on a recent trip out to Spahn Ranch, Clem took off in Wilson's Ferrari at Charlie's suggestion and totaled it. The guy damn well owed Wilson a lot and taking credit for Charlie's song was payback. It was L.A. show business royalty in action—a Beach Boy could do what he wanted, and a wannabe like Charlie couldn't stop him. Sure, Charlie would be pissed when he found out, but maybe he'd learn from this who was boss if he and Wilson worked on any other songs in the future.

Even as "Cease to Exist" morphed into "Never Learn Not to Love," Charlie was preoccupied with something else. Spahn Ranch was fine in most ways, but there were still too many distractions for the Family there. Charlie controlled access to cars, and Spahn was too far out of L.A. for anyone to walk there, but the bikers offered rides when anyone asked and it was too easy for people like Susan to get out without any supervision. Sometimes Family members asked guests to stay the night without getting Charlie's permission first. One morning Charlie had to run off a guy who spent an unauthorized night with Leslie out in the ranch caves, and the next day the jerk came back with some mean-looking friends and told Leslie right in front of Charlie and some of the Family that she should leave the ranch with them if she wanted. Luckily Leslie opted to stay with Charlie, but what if she hadn't? It might have encouraged some of the others to think about leaving, too. Charlie's goal was a record deal, and the Family was one of his main tools in obtaining it. Having followers hanging on his every word and gratefully doing his bidding also satisfied his obsession with being in charge.

With about three dozen members in his flock, Charlie was now less concerned about recruiting than maintaining control over the followers he had. Though he still made occasional exceptions—a schoolteacher the Family nicknamed Juanita arrived with a vehicle and a lot of cash, maybe $10,000—for the most part Charlie informed Little Paul Watkins and Gypsy that he didn't want anyone else brought in as prospective members. What he wanted now was some new roost that was so far removed from the city, from civilization, that he would be the only influence on the Family. Charlie himself would still find ways to commute to L.A.; he wasn't about to lose his music industry contacts. Thanks to one of the Family, Charlie had a possible location in mind.

Sometimes Cathy Gillies talked about "Grandma's place," a property called the Myers Ranch that was so far in the depths of Death Valley that it was hard to reach even by car. Charlie set out on a fact-finding expedition and it was everything that he hoped for. Getting there from Los Angeles took hours, first by highway, then by rough backcountry road, and finally on through virtually impenetrable Goler Wash, with the Panamint and other craggy ranges with dire names like the Last Chance and Funeral Mountains looming above like serrated teeth. The entire area was wild and harsh. The scattered settlements in forbidding Inyo County— Trona, Shoshone—were more outposts than towns; Independence, the county seat, wasn't much better. The closest town, Ballarat, was a virtual ghost town, but it had a bare-bones general store, the only place where basic necessities could be purchased. Wildlife abounded, but not humans. The county population was less than two people per square mile. Many of these were transients, prospectors poking around ridges hoping to strike gold. Permanent residents were mostly iconoclasts who had deliberately removed themselves from the outside world. Law enforcement, always of some concern to Charlie, was sporadic. There were a few county police officers and some rangers assigned to Death Valley National Park. Mostly the desert denizens were left alone, just the way Charlie wanted.

It was possible in some scattered locations to live decently, if not in luxury. Underground streams cut beneath the desert floor, so wells and irrigation sometimes were options. Cathy Gilles's relatives made their ranch almost attractive, with vegetable gardens and a few well-kept buildings. But Charlie was drawn to the adjacent property; the living area of Barker Ranch consisted of two stone houses, a shed, and a small pool that provided water. A generator was available to supply very limited electricity; the property was fifty miles away from any power lines. The main house had a wood stove and a bathroom with shower and sink. The closest major city was Las Vegas, just beyond the California-Nevada state line. The ranch was primitive and so far removed from any semblance of modernity that it seemed like the far end of the world. Charlie looked up owner Arlene Barker and asked permission for him and the Family to stay there. He explained that he was an important musician hoping for some solitude to work on new material. To prove his point, he gave Barker a Beach Boys gold record that had been taken from Dennis Wilson's lodge on Sunset Boulevard. It was fine with Barker, so most of the Family moved in. Charlie left a few members behind at Spahn Ranch, and, probably using some of newcomer Juanita's money, sent Family member Bruce Davis and Sandy Good's husband, Joel Pugh, to London, where they spent time at the Scientology headquarters. Charlie was always looking for new material to flesh out his preaching. Davis returned a few months later, but Pugh stayed behind.

Almost immediately, many of Barker Ranch's new residents began complaining. The place was blistering hot. Spahn Ranch had been bad enough, but at least it wasn't hundreds of miles from anywhere. There were telephones and lots of shady places on Spahn, not like here where there wasn't even radio reception and you had to check under every rock for snakes and scorpions. Because cooking had to be done on a wood stove, wood had to be chopped before any meals were prepared and that was awful work in the blazing heat. Charlie did his best to shut down the bitching. Sometime soon, he warned, things in the outside world were really going to turn bad—out-and-out street combat—and "young loves" like the Family were going to be particular targets. He'd found a place where they were safe, and now they were complaining? What was the matter with them? Out here in the desert they'd set up a perfect community and soon other young loves fleeing the bloodthirsty mobs in the cities would come flocking to it. Charlie's followers would be shining symbols of the only purity left in the world. And somewhere nearby in the desert was a hole, a hidden hole that led down into wonderful tunnels that would let anyone travel anywhere on earth. Charlie and the Family would find that hole. He mentioned it frequently during group LSD trips at Barker. The idea of the hidden hole held the attention of his acid-addled audience. Why couldn't there be such a thing? They tried to adjust to their harsh new living conditions, but problems that Charlie hadn't anticipated soon emerged.

At Spahn Ranch, it was a simple thing to scrounge food from L.A.-area groceries, but these so-called garbage runs were impossible in Death Valley, where there were no grocery stores. One time when the food supply ran particularly low, Charlie told the women to fan out into the desert and bring back edible plants. When they told him they didn't know anything about desert plants, Charlie said that as women they were supposed to know about such things, so go out and gather something. But they couldn't, even when he bawled them out for being unwomanly. So to feed the Family, Charlie had to either buy food from the limited stock at the Ballarat general store, or else bring it in every few days from a city, which was inconvenient given the difficult travel conditions between the ranch and either L.A. or Las Vegas. Buying food also required money, and out in the desert Charlie didn't have any sources of that. He tried sending some of the girls to Las Vegas to panhandle and they had limited success, claiming to passersby in front of casinos that they needed donations to buy food for an Indian tribe. But Charlie saw real danger in letting his followers spend much time there; he'd brought them to Death Valley to keep them away from disruptive outside influences, and Las Vegas was a hotbed of temptation.

A dwindling drug supply was also a concern. In L.A. Charlie could get his hands on as much acid and weed as he needed, from the bikers visiting Spahn Ranch or from dealers. In the past, Charlie was in position to trade things for the drugs—motorcycles donated to the Family, beadwork done by the women, sex with some of the girls if that was what a supplier wanted. But out in the desert there was nobody to donate tradable goods, let alone swap significant quantities of drugs. Charlie needed a constant supply of LSD for group tripping sessions, and weed to help everybody take the edge off any frustrations with the primitive conditions on Barker Ranch.

The isolation of Barker Ranch was a significant advantage, but the drawbacks, particularly in maintaining adequate supplies of food and drugs, tipped the scales in favor of Spahn. The dilemma for Charlie was that he'd just convinced his followers that Barker was where they belonged. Their belief in him might be shaken if he now told them that it was better to return to Spahn. He needed a reason for the reversal in message, and just before Thanksgiving Dennis Wilson gave him one.

Dennis Wilson was not a man to hold a grudge, and though he lacked self-discipline he was also not a fool. "Never Learn Not to Love," his reworking of Charlie's "Cease to Exist," had turned out well. It wasn't the best song on the Beach Boys' forthcoming album; "Do It Again," a tuneful tribute by Brian Wilson and Mike Love to the good ol' days of sun and surf, would be the first cut released as a single, and "I Can Hear Music," a remake of an old pop tune, was scheduled as the second. But "Never Learn Not to Love," with Dennis credited as sole composer, was considered strong enough by the rest of the band to be a candidate as a B side to one of those releases or, at least, a third single culled from the album. That meant considerable extra composing royalties for Dennis if "Never Learn Not to Love" backed a hit. So he not only stood to earn back some of the money it had cost him to host Charlie and the Family, it was possible that future collaborations with Charlie could result in more income. True, Charlie probably wouldn't be happy when he found out what Wilson had done to "Cease to Exist," but if it was presented right—Hey, you got a song recorded and it might be just the beginning, isn't that great?—then maybe he'd quickly get past it and there'd be more collaborating. Besides, Wilson wouldn't mind more time with the girls in the Family. He knew Charlie had brought most everybody to Barker Ranch, so toward the end of November Wilson decided to drive up there, tell Charlie the good news, and insist that he come back to L.A. for a proper celebration. Wilson invited Gregg Jakobson to make the trip with him. One of the vehicles that the Family used to move to Barker was a jeep that belonged to Jakobson, and they'd never returned it. So Jakobson said he'd go to get his jeep back, and he also thought it would be a chance to see Ruth Ann again. It took forever for the two of them to get to Barker; to Jakobson, it seemed like falling off the edge of the world. They arrived to a warm welcome, and Wilson told Charlie the edited news that his song had been recorded, it was going on the new Beach Boys album and let's go back to L.A. and party. Charlie was thrilled.

Charlie felt that he couldn't be away from L.A. at such a critical time; surely all the important record industry people who listened to the album—it was going to be called *20/20*—would think "Cease to Exist" was clearly the best song on it, and they'd want to snap up the guy who wrote it. The Family would have to be moved back to Spahn right away. Charlie didn't reveal to his followers that his personal ambitions were the reason they were going back. He explained that winters in Death Valley were just as brutally cold as the summers there were broiling. The buildings they were living in weren't heated. Out of consideration for the Family's health, Charlie had decided to lead them back to L.A. When winter passed, he'd see about returning to Barker Ranch. Everyone was happy, Charlie most of all.

Wilson and Jakobson spent the night at Barker. Wilson was allowed to romp with the girls of his choosing. Jakobson, inconveniencing Charlie because he wanted his jeep back, wasn't allowed to have sex with Ruth Ann. Charlie wanted to send a message to Jakobson, but he also didn't want to alienate him since Jakobson still might prove useful in getting a record deal. So Charlie told Jakobson he could sleep with Leslie instead. Jakobson was initially angry, but Leslie was pretty and he thought she was a sweetheart, so he went along with it. The next day he and Wilson and Charlie headed back to L.A., with most of the Family following after them. Charlie left a few members back at Barker, just so nobody could move into the Family's place.

• • •

There was an immediate complication. Squeaky approached George Spahn to ask if the rest of the Family could move back to his ranch, certain that he'd agree. But Spahn surprised her by saying that they couldn't; he'd decided that having longhairs around made the place look bad. Charlie, preoccupied with his imminent rise to recording fame, didn't feel like trying to convince Spahn otherwise. The old man permitted a few Family members to hang around sometimes—he didn't want to lose Squeaky's ministrations. Meanwhile, Charlie found a two-story house on Gresham Street in Canoga Park above Topanga. There was enough money to rent the place for a couple of months. Charlie got the Family moved in and waited for the Beach Boys' *20/20* album to be released in January; big things would undoubtedly happen right afterward. Meanwhile, he kept the girls busy with garbage runs and the men working on cars. It occurred to Charlie that if they did live out in Death Valley again, it would be a good idea to have a fleet of vehicles capable of navigating the area. So Tex and the others began renovating cars into dune buggies. Charlie preached and supervised acid sessions, and at night amused himself by soaking in a hot tub while Leslie read to him from the Bible, always the Book of Revelation. Charlie loved all the imagery, and some of it made its way into his sermons. More and more now he referred to himself as the Second Coming of JC, his term for Jesus Christ. Sometimes he ordered everyone to *baaa* like sheep because he was the Good Shepherd, and they did.

Charlie not only interpreted the Bible for his followers, he defended it to them. Though they all respected and feared him, sometimes Charlie's edicts elicited at least mild protest, especially among the women when he reminded them in some new way that they were completely subservient to the group's men. He always cited the Bible as the basis for his rules—like modern-day evangelical fundamentalists on cable TV and talk radio, Charlie explained that if something was in Scripture it had to be true, and he would not tolerate any debate. They should not, could not, take issue with Charlie, who was JC come again, or the Word of God. Later, Charlie's former followers ridiculed the widespread belief that the Family practiced Satanism or even sympathized. Charlie was Jesus returned to earth, and Satan and all his followers and works were the enemy, not allies.

It was more difficult to keep the Family busy in town than on the Spahn and Barker ranches, but around the same time Charlie and his followers returned to L.A. the Beatles released their new album. It was a double disc set, crammed with twice as many songs for the Family to listen to over and over as they'd had from *Magical Mystery Tour*. The band titled it *The Beatles*, but the defiantly blank cover was a stunning departure from popular rainbow psychedelic designs. Almost instantly the album acquired a new, universal name: the *White Album*.

CHAPTER ELEVEN

The Bible and the Beatles

The *White Album* consisted of thirty exceptionally eclectic songs, ranging from ersatz music hall to frantic rock 'n' roll to a children's lullaby. Though their fans didn't know it, the Beatles were wracked by dissension throughout the entire recording process—at one point drummer Ringo Starr actually quit the band, though his departure was never made public and he was coaxed back within weeks. Two vinyl discs resulted from the internal squabbling because none of the Beatles allowed any of his songs to be cut in favor of compositions by the others. Critics generally praised the album—after all, it was by the *Beatles*—but after embracing previous releases by the band as clear-cut social commentary, many listeners couldn't find any consistency or theme this time.

Charlie wasn't confused at all. He gathered the Family around at the Gresham Street rental house and had them listen to the *White Album* over and over. He demanded that they pay special attention to the songs "Piggies," "Blackbird," "Revolution 1," "Revolution 9," and "Helter Skelter." Though each tune on the record had prophetic significance, Charlie explained, these songs were musical road maps to the immediate future. "Piggies" described the disgusting sense of entitlement enjoyed by the very rich and powerful, and concluded that they needed "a damn good whacking." "Blackbird" predicted an uprising of the downtrodden blacks—this was the moment for them to arise. "Revolution 1" was a call to arms. "Revolution 9," a pastiche of electronic effects and sound bites including the clatter of machine guns and human screams, was the soundtrack of the coming fury, and "Helter Skelter" provided a formal name for the chaos soon to come. In the best Dale Carnegie tradition,

Charlie made certain that his followers felt these interpretations were theirs as well as his; he gravely asked everyone for comments about the songs, then wove whatever they said into a larger context. Everyone should feel incredibly proud, Charlie declared—not only was the *White Album* the Beatles' collective call to arms to the entire world, it was specifically directed toward Charlie and the Family. Sometime in 1969, the Family would return to Barker Ranch in Death Valley, and the Beatles would join them there. Charlie determined this based on a line in the song "Honey Pie" that referred to crossing the Atlantic. With his usual assumption of superiority and entitlement, Charlie felt certain that the Beatles would come to him and his followers. To get the process under way he sent letters and telegrams of invitation to the Beatles' office in England. There was no response, but Charlie wasn't deterred. The Beatles were only part of the truth he now revealed. He preached to the Family that a black uprising was imminent not just because the Beatles said so, but also the Bible. In fact, the Bible prophesied not only the uprising, but also the Beatles themselves, and Charlie Manson, too. It was all in the final book of the New Testament.

The Revelation to John, commonly misidentified as Revelations, concludes the Christian Bible on an unsettling, apocalyptic note. John, the narrator, has been banished to an island by unnamed authorities for preaching the gospel of Jesus, and as a reward for his faith Jesus has granted him an understanding or revelation about the signs that will herald Christ's return to earth. John, in turn, writes about what he has learned to a series of Christian communities so they will have some warning of what is about to happen. For some Christians, Revelation is entirely symbolic and simply represents a promise that Jesus will come again; to others, it's a literal account of what is going to occur, horned beasts and all. For imaginations fueled by frequent, copious doses of LSD, it was all too easy to believe not only John's apocalyptic prophecies, but Charlie's unique interpretation of them.

Revelation, Charlie explained, predicted that locusts would come, and locusts were, of course, beetles—the Beatles. John said that the locusts would have "scales like iron breastplates"—according to Charlie, these were the Beatles' guitars. And there was more: Revelation also told of angels coming to earth, with the first four being the Beatles. The fifth, "given the key to the shaft of the bottomless pit," was Charlie. The bottomless pit was the hole in the Death Valley desert, the one Charlie had already told the Family about. Revelation and the *White Album,* with assistance from Charlie, made it clear: There was about to be an uprising of the oppressed in the world, mostly the blacks, who had been held down for too long. Everybody had a turn in power, and now it was going to be black people's turn. Something called Helter Skelter, an event or events still to be determined, would set off the battle. The blacks were going to kill most of the whites and enslave their surviving oppressors, which was only fair. Whites had made blacks their slaves and now roles would reverse. But here was the kicker: Just as the Bible foretold—and the Bible was always right—Charlie would lead the Family to the bottomless pit, where they would remain in hiding as the world above descended into chaos. After a while—it didn't matter how long, because time didn't matter, hundreds of years, perhaps—the Family would expand to 144,000, the equivalent of the twelve tribes of Israel and the number specified in Revelation 14:3. Meanwhile, blacks would discover that they lacked the intelligence and organizational skills to run the world. So Charlie and the Family would emerge from the bottomless pit and become acknowledged rulers, Charlie of course the first among them. He'd already convinced many of his followers that he was Jesus reincarnated. It didn't take a much greater leap of faith to buy into this new vision. Charlie stressed that everyone had all the proof that they needed—Revelation and the *White Album.*

The Family was overwhelmed by this news. Charlie maintained rigid control with his usual methods of carrot and stick. The women in particular were reminded that if they remained loyal, while they were down in the pit living in a wonderful underground city there, they could change into any creature they wished. Several wanted to become winged elves, and Charlie promised that, when the moment was especially near, they'd begin to feel budding wings growing on their backs. But a terrible fate awaited anyone trying to leave the Family now, he cautioned. All of them were white, and any deserters who weren't killed in the coming racial cataclysm would undoubtedly be made into slaves serving black masters. Their choice was slave or ruler.

There was an unexpected defector. Tex Watson, previously one of Charlie's most compliant followers, suddenly found Family membership claustrophobic and sneaked away. He stayed in the L.A. area, though, supporting himself by dealing drugs in tandem with a new girlfriend. Through the bikers, Charlie had an excellent network of informers and probably soon knew exactly where Tex was. He was in no hurry to reclaim him; while most of the Family was preoccupied with the new prospect of Helter Skelter, Charlie also had to concern himself with his long-anticipated breakthrough as a musician. The Beatles' double disc set was fine but Charlie's album, the one that producers would beg him to record after the Beach Boys' version of "Cease to Exist" was released, would surpass the *White Album* both commercially and as a harbinger of the future.

Charlie expected "Cease to Exist" to appear on the Beach Boys' album *20/20*, which reached stores on January 27, 1969. But the band chose to precede *20/20* with several singles from the album. The second single, released in December 1968, had "Bluebirds over the Mountain" as its A-side, and "Cease to Exist" on the B-side, completely reworked as "Never Learn Not to Love," with Dennis Wilson credited as sole composer. Charlie had no inkling of this until he heard the record and, when he did, he exploded. To him it was betrayal of the rankest sort. He'd told Wilson that it was all right to make changes to the music, but the lyrics must not be changed in any way. Wilson knew he wasn't supposed to do it, he did it anyway, and he didn't tell Charlie that he had. The insult was compounded by the fact that "Bluebirds over the Mountain"/"Never Learn Not to Love" tanked on the singles charts, stalling out at number 61. If the record had been a smash, Charlie still might have gained some recognition from producers for the genesis of a hit if not the final version of it. As it turned out, Charlie was the uncredited composer of a failed song, and in the bottom-line world of the recording industry that was more damning than not having a song recorded at all.

In his rage it would have been natural for Charlie to seek revenge on Wilson, but he somehow managed to keep himself under control. Dennis Wilson was a traitor, and clearly he could not be trusted as a songwriting collaborator, let alone as a dedicated promoter of Charlie's music career.

That Wilson had honestly tried for months to get Charlie a record deal, or that he'd opened his home to Charlie and the Family, meant nothing. At some level Charlie interpreted such generosity as personal weakness; he had the veteran hustler's scorn for gullible marks. But his ambition dwarfed any other consideration. Though Wilson had dealt a blow to Charlie's plans, to the fame and glory that Charlie not only craved but was certain he deserved, he still needed him in one critical way that precluded Charlie from immediately getting even.

By December 1968, Charlie had been working connections in the L.A. music scene for almost a year. During that time, he had auditioned his music for Gary Stromberg at Universal, who turned him down. Brother Records wanted no part of him. Gregg Jakobson was still trying to help, but he was more interested in making a movie about the Family than in getting Charlie a record deal. Now Dennis Wilson was a dead end, too. Making even one of these contacts would have been beyond the grasp of almost all of the other would-be rock stars who flocked to L.A. daily. Charlie had enjoyed far more than his share of access and it still came to nothing, with one remaining exception.

Though Terry Melcher still hadn't listened to Charlie's tapes, let alone auditioned Charlie in person, he hadn't refused to, either. He'd made a few social visits to the Family at Spahn, though these were mostly to enjoy the girls, Ruth Ann especially, rather than hang out with Charlie. It had taken Charlie a while, but he finally understood the recording industry food chain. Initially he'd believed that all it took to get signed was the support of rock stars like Dennis Wilson or Neil Young. But the endorsement of celebrities meant little compared to the clout enjoyed by the most successful producers, and no producer in town was more successful than Melcher. If Melcher said so, Charlie had a record deal at Columbia, one of the most prestigious labels. Along with Gregg Jakobson, Dennis Wilson was Melcher's best friend. If Charlie went off on Wilson, physically attacking or even just verbally tearing into him, that would surely result in Melcher terminating any potential interest in Charlie. As hard as it might be, Charlie had to keep getting along with Wilson, had to let his betrayer think that everything was still okay between them, until Melcher finally gave Charlie a chance—and if he got that chance, Charlie was certain, this time everything would go the way that he wanted. He knew that he was a great musician; none of these setbacks made him doubt that in the slightest. This was a challenging time, keeping the Family excited about Helter Skelter, preparing for an eventual move back to Barker Ranch, but most important among the demands on his time and attention was getting what he wanted from Terry Melcher. Charlie was prepared to focus his intensity, wiliness, and charm to that end. But there was a personal dilemma that, for the moment, prevented Melcher from auditioning, let alone recording, Charlie Manson.

On April 20, 1968, Melcher's stepfather, Marty, died after a short illness. They weren't close, but Terry and his mother, Doris Day, had a loving relationship, often more brother-sister than parent-child. During their marriage, Day let Marty take control of all financial matters without her involvement—she made the movies and the records and he handled the money. As one of Hollywood's premier talents, Day was well paid, so she assumed that she was a very wealthy woman. When Marty died, it was natural for her to ask her only child to make certain that everything was in order. Melcher began investigating, and to their mutual horror he and his mother learned that Marty and a business partner had squandered every cent. Worse, Day was now deep in debt and tax arrears.

In the cutthroat world of show business, the appearance of success is critical. If word spread that Doris Day was broke, producers would offer her lowball salaries in the belief that she'd have to take them because she desperately needed the money. Worse, her public image was that of a sunny-spirited Good Girl; fans, the ones who bought the movie tickets and the records, might lose interest when they learned that her image wasn't accurate. Melcher set out to save what he could of his mother's assets and reputation, working nonstop and trying to keep word from leaking out. The process would take almost five years. A judge finally awarded Day nearly $23 million in damages from Marty Melcher's investment partner. She had trouble collecting even a portion of the money.

But in late 1968 and early 1969, Terry Melcher's immediate concern was protecting as much of his mother's property as possible. Just before Christmas, he and Candy Bergen moved from the Cielo Drive house to a beach house owned by Day. Though they made their new address known to friends like Gregg Jakobson, Dennis Wilson, and Rudi Altobelli, they generally tried to keep the move quiet. Charlie Manson, for one, had no idea that Melcher didn't live at Cielo anymore. Melcher lay low; when he wasn't working in the Columbia studios with one of his current roster of bands, he was busy sorting through his mother's tangled finances. Much to Charlie's frustration, he didn't run into Melcher anymore at parties. Respecting their pal's privacy, Jakobson and Wilson couldn't do much beyond telling Charlie that, sure, the next time they saw Melcher they'd let him know that Charlie wanted to talk to him. But despite Charlie's nonstop efforts to get in touch, Melcher wasn't talking to anyone but accountants and lawyers.

By January 1969, youthful rebellion was a worldwide phenomenon. There were rallies and riots everywhere, but nowhere was greater generational rage being expressed than in America. Leadership among student radicals was splintering amid heated debate about the most effective way to bring about social and political change. Some activists, like Tom Hayden, advocated rallies, marches, and similar actions to gain public support by goading authorities into overreaction. Bernardine Dohrn and Mark Rudd led an SDS faction promising to "bring the war home" to the United States by precipitating violent, intimidating acts. Their followers became widely known as the Weathermen. Still another segment of radicals publicized their causes by staging bizarre events to mock the status quo. Led by Abbie Hoffman, they called themselves Yippies.

Protesters were out in force in Washington, D.C., on January 20 for the swearing-in of Richard Nixon as president. Even as Nixon began his inaugural address by inviting all Americans "to share with me today the majesty of this moment," not far away at the base of the Washington Monument the Yippies were staging an inauguration ceremony for a live pig. Somehow the pig got loose; it had been raining all day, and the Yippies slipped and screeched as they scrambled after him in the mud. Other forms of protest that day were less slapstick; during the inaugural parade, rocks ricocheted off the heavily armored car carrying the new president and first lady down the streets. Protesters represented every age and ethnicity. Pennsylvania Avenue teemed with an assortment of demonstrators whose agendas were sometimes in conflict. Several antiwar protesters stood shoulder to shoulder with a preacher urging everyone to kill a communist for Christ. Everyone in America seemed frustrated and angry.

Immediately upon assuming office, President Nixon kept his promise to his older, conservative voter base by beginning crackdowns on student protesters. He began by insisting that authorities enforce a law denying college students convicted of crimes (such as disturbing the peace or resisting arrest) the right to receive federal scholarships or loans. Excessive youthful protest, Nixon declared, was simply unacceptable: "It is not too strong a statement to declare that this is the way civilizations begin to die."

Violence, or at least the potential for it, seemed ubiquitous. L.A. was no exception. In January, Black Panther leaders Alprentice "Bunchy" Carter and John Huggins were gunned down on the UCLA campus while engaged in furious debate about leadership in the university's new black studies program. Their killers were members of a gang identifying itself as the "United Slaves." Afterward, radical leaders believed that the FBI had secretly orchestrated the murders, based in part on a bureau document exploring if not directly advocating a potential vendetta between the Panthers and Slaves. The incident was another reminder to whites that there were armed black militants lurking everywhere. The latest L.A. police chief, Edward M. Davis, encouraged the racial paranoia. When he replaced Tom Reddin, who resigned to become a local TV commentator, he warned that responsible, law-abiding citizens should "bar [the] doors, buy a police dog, call us when we're available, and pray."

Once again, Charlie used the news to support what he preached to the Family. The war between the races was surely coming. It was right there in the papers and on TV. In February Charlie began describing the specific event that might trigger Helter Skelter—perhaps some blacks would go into rich white people's homes. Maybe black radicals from Watts would travel to Bel Air, commit some atrocious murders, and afterward write words on the walls with the victims' own blood. That would probably start Helter Skelter.

Rudi Altobelli didn't want to leave his prime rental property on Cielo vacant for long. Living in the smaller guest cottage while Melcher and

Bergen occupied the main house had worked well for him. Right after they moved out, Altobelli let Gregg Jakobson talk him into letting some Santa Claus–lookalike named Dean Moorehouse move in for a few days, but Rudi wanted tenants who could afford $1,200 a month. He moved Moorehouse out and spread the word that Cielo, with its gated hilltop privacy and unparalleled view, was available. Altobelli was determined to rent to just the right tenants, most likely in show business, who would be happy to let their landlord continue living in the guest cottage. He was soon approached by the perfect applicants.

In June 1968, Roman Polanski's film *Rosemary's Baby* had become a huge success and made the Polish director a celebrity in the United States. Sharon Tate, an actress he had married in January 1968, was not yet a star. She had appeared in *Valley of the Dolls,* a film depicting the sleazier side of screen fame, Polanski's *Fearless Vampire Killers,* and a nude pictorial in *Playboy* magazine—her husband shot the photo. Tate seemed to be the quintessential Hollywood starlet, not especially gifted as an actress but a very pretty adornment to bigger stars in mainstream films.

With *Rosemary's Baby* a substantial hit and Polanski now a player in Hollywood, he and his wife had to be based in L.A., though they could and did spend considerable time in England and Europe on film projects. They had trouble finding the right place to live, settling for a while in a Chateau Marmont apartment on Sunset Boulevard, then renting a house in the Hollywood Hills from actress Patty Duke. The place didn't really suit them. They wanted something grander, commensurate with Polanski's new, exalted status, and so they kept looking. Meanwhile, the couple hired a housekeeper named Winifred Chapman. Tate hoped soon to become pregnant. Despite her flashy image and nude photos, she was something of a homebody at heart.

When they learned about Altobelli's Cielo Drive property, Polanski and Tate were interested; their plans to find a new home had taken on new urgency when they learned that Tate was pregnant. On February 12, 1969, she called Terry Melcher to ask about Cielo, and Melcher had great things to say about his time living there. Polanski then contacted Altobelli, a deal was reached, and he and Sharon moved in three days later. They loved it, and knew that their friends would, too. Polanski and Tate were sociable people and planned to have lots of parties and overnight and long-term guests. As he'd planned, Altobelli stayed on in the guest cottage. Polanski and Tate were going to be away often, so having the landlord living on the property meant there would be somebody to keep an eye on things. Of course, Altobelli sometimes had to travel, too, but he promised that if he was ever going to be away at the same time that they were, he'd find a responsible temporary caretaker to move into the cottage.

In late February, Charlie decided it was time for the Family to move from the rental house on Gresham. He'd been preaching that they had to begin preparing for Helter Skelter, accumulating supplies to take with them out to the desert. In the interim, Charlie felt it would be best for everyone to return for a while to Spahn Ranch, where there would be room to store the things they would be accumulating. Squeaky was sent to sweet-talk George Spahn into letting them come back. Charlie also gave Squeaky an additional assignment. Spahn Ranch was a useful place, plenty of room and a lot closer to L.A. than Barker. Squeaky should somehow convince old George to leave her the ranch in his will. How much longer could the doddering old guy live, after all? Squeaky half succeeded; George reluctantly said the longhairs could come back for a while, temporarily, but he never rewrote his will. Charlie hung on to the rental house on Gresham for a while longer, and it was good that he did. For a month or so, Spahn would periodically kick the Family out; they'd retreat to Gresham while Squeaky wheedled him to relent. Finally Charlie decided it didn't matter whether Spahn allowed them to be there or not—they were staying until they relocated to the desert.

Just to make certain that things would be ready for them when they moved on to Barker, Charlie sent several Family members, including teenager Brooks Poston and schoolteacher Juanita, to stay there. It wasn't an assignment they relished. Death Valley was just as inhospitable in cold weather as it was during the broiling summer. But nobody disobeyed Charlie.

In some ways the Barker Ranch contingent had it easier than the rest of the Family remaining at Spahn. Previously, Charlie had kept everybody busy doing chores with the ranch hands. Now he conducted lengthy desert survival courses. Everyone had to learn how to live under extreme conditions. Charlie tested everyone to see how long they could go without water. To fool pursuers, he demonstrated how to walk across sand or dirt without leaving obvious footprints. Charlie also said that he'd met someone who was a karate expert and would come out to Spahn to teach them how to fight hand-to-hand, but he never showed up.

Hand-to-hand wasn't going to be the Family's main form of defense anyway if they had to fight their way through Helter Skelter to the bottomless pit in the desert. There had always been knives around, and now Charlie ordered everybody to carry one, usually a sturdy folding buck knife. Charlie resurrected his old knife-throwing games, commanding different women to stand in front of a board while he fired knives over their heads and by the sides of their faces. They had to lose their fear of knives, Charlie explained.

And now there were guns, too. Charlie began acquiring all that he could, trading cars and drugs for them. There were shotguns and rifles that had to be hidden in caches around Spahn so the ranch hands wouldn't see them and complain to their boss. There were some handguns, too, one a long-barreled .22 called a Buntline after the famous weapon supposedly carried by Old West legend Wyatt Earp. Over the next months the Family put together a good-sized arsenal. Sometimes Charlie and a few of the men would go off into a gulch with the handguns for target practice. The surrounding hills effectively muffled the sound of the shots.

Even with the knives and guns, Charlie never suggested that the Family members would ever attack anyone. They were training only so that they could defend themselves if necessary. The way Charlie explained it, the goal was to avoid the coming bloodbath, not participate in it. The blacks were going to be too ferocious; only after their initial rage was spent, and they turned their attention to running the world instead of conquering it, would they realize that they needed Charlie and the Family. Since Helter Skelter was so imminent, the immediate challenge was preparing to escape. They planned an exact route from Spahn to Barker Ranch, marking spots along the way where containers of food could be concealed—if they were trying to elude close pursuit, they wouldn't have time to stop and forage for meals. Charlie ordered the women to experiment with pickling and otherwise preserving food to be buried along the route in barrels. They did their best but were unsuccessful, and Charlie bawled them out. Their failure was putting the fate of the Family—and the world—at risk.

Family men and women alike were enlisted for another crucial aspect of the escape plan. Charlie decreed that the flight to the desert would be made in a convoy of specially equipped dune buggies. They'd learned from their first stay in Death Valley that ordinary vehicles couldn't navigate much of the rugged terrain. There were plenty of dune buggies for sale on L.A. car lots, but the Family was always strapped for cash and Charlie had no intention of paying for them anyway. The Family would trade for them or steal them. Sometime that spring Charlie got possession of one and set out to modify it for long-term desert use. He wanted brushcutters on the front bumper, extra panels on the sides, and a winch welded to the frame. Charlie took this project particularly seriously—this tricked-up dune buggy would be the working model for those to come. He managed to get the dune buggy through the doors of the movie set saloon so they could work on it out of the blowing dust.

Just as work on the dune buggy started, Tex Watson returned. He'd missed the discipline of the Family during his time away; it seemed to him that life in the outside world was too self-indulgent. Charlie sometimes got weird, but he preached about important things and if some kind of race war really was coming it would be better to be with him. When Tex got to Spahn, Charlie forgave him for deserting. It was a practical decision on Charlie's part—Tex was a gifted mechanic and his skills were badly needed on the dune buggy in the saloon. Even with Tex pitching in, work on it went much more slowly than Charlie wanted. When it was finally ready for a test drive, the modifications had made it too wide to fit through the saloon doors. It took the combined efforts of everyone to turn the vehicle on its side. Then they had to push it out across the sidewalk and tip it back up on its wheels again. That accomplished, Charlie jumped behind the wheel; everyone else scampered behind on foot in a merry procession that lasted right up to the moment Charlie tried to drive the dune buggy across a shallow creek. The weight of all the add-ons was too much, and the dune buggy sank to the top of its hubcaps in creek-bottom mud. Everyone tried to tug it loose, but the wheels were mired too deep. Charlie wound a chain into the winch, wound the chain around a nearby tree branch, and tried to pull the dune buggy free of the gluey mud, but the branch broke. Frustrated, Charlie stalked off, calling back over his shoulder that nobody else could leave until the dune buggy was extracted from the mud and driven back to the main ranch buildings, and they'd better get the job done—no excuses.

The remaining Family members looped the winch chain around another tree branch and tried again. Gypsy grabbed the chain to keep it from tangling. This time the winch seemed to work; the dune buggy shifted in the mud. Just as its tires began to pull free, the chain somehow wrapped around Gypsy's thumb. She screamed in pain; her thumb was being slowly torn off her hand. But Charlie had ordered that the dune buggy be pulled out, no excuses—what if she let go of the chain to save her thumb, and then they weren't able to get the dune buggy out of the mud after all? For long agonizing moments Gypsy endured the pain rather than risk failing Charlie. She finally let go and they winched the dune buggy free from the creek muck, but it had been a near thing for her thumb.

Parts for dune buggy renovations were expensive. Essential desert survival supplies cost a lot of money, too. The Family needed immediate, regular sources of income—it wasn't enough to depend on occasional handouts from benefactors anymore. Charlie's immediate impulse was to make use of his women. He explored the possibility of signing them up as topless dancers in L.A. men's clubs. But when club managers looked over the female Family members, they turned them down. With the exception of Susan Atkins, they were all relatively flat-chested. Charlie next considered sending some of the women north to Sacramento to work in his friend Pete's whorehouses in Sacramento. But that would involve transportation costs, and Pete would want a cut from whatever the women earned turning tricks. Charlie needed every cent, so that was out. Then the Family tried turning one of the ranch buildings into a nightclub. They painted the inside walls black, daubed on some sloppy psychedelic designs, wired up their record player, and put beer on ice. The name of the bar was Helter Skelter.

The Helter Skelter bar patrons were ranch hands, bikers, and a lot of area kids who were glad to patronize a place where IDs were no problem and everyone could openly smoke weed. They drank beer, listened to music—mostly from the *White Album*—and watched some of the Family women who served as Go-Go dancers. Sometimes Charlie performed. A jar labeled "Donations" was prominently displayed on a counter. Things went well for a few days until local cops charged George Spahn with operating a bar without a license. The old man was mad as hell, especially when he had to pay a $1,500 fine. That was the end of the Helter Skelter bar, and Charlie had to find another way to make some fast money. In the end, he made the most obvious decision. It was 1969 and he was in L.A., after all. It was always possible to turn a quick buck by dealing drugs. But to do that, he needed a closer alliance with some of the bikers.

Since the 1950s when the first Hells Angels chapter was organized in San Bernardino, Southern California had served as the unofficial home base for dozens of motorcycle gangs. Many of these had formal organizational structures, with officers and dues and even club charters. Though many were comprised of enthusiastic cyclists who simply liked getting together with like-minded buddies after work and on weekends, others were more sinister, with violence and drug dealing as common among their members as riding bikes. Hells Angels was by far the most notorious, and though its members protested that they never started any trouble, they were constantly in the news for brawls and arrests. Many ordinary citizens feared the Angels and any other biker clubs that resembled them. This was something the self-styled "outlaw" bikers relished.

Hells Angels were never involved with Charlie Manson; they were too self-important to bother with such a nobody. But the Family had considerable appeal to the lesser Straight Satans, who enjoyed posturing as rough, tough outlaws who lived as they pleased and defied anyone to stop them. Many of the Straight Satans held day jobs, but in off-hours they enjoyed riding out to Spahn, where they'd work on their bikes and, at Charlie's suggestion, sometimes enjoy the women. It was a mutually beneficial association—the bikers helped keep the Family motorcycles in good repair. But now Charlie wanted to expand the relationship. The Straight Satans would join the Family in drug deals. Sometimes the dope Charlie would get from suppliers would be sold by him directly to the bikers. Other times, the Straight Satans would join the Family as middlemen by selling the drugs to third parties. The bikers were amenable, especially when Charlie offered an additional perk to his new business partners. When they wanted sex they could choose among the available Family women as always, but now the prettiest girls, Ruth Ann and Leslie, were put at their constant disposal. It helped that the two women liked hanging out with the bikers anyway. Besides having fun, they were making a crucial contribution to the Helter Skelter escape plan.

Some Straight Satans spent a lot of time at Spahn, particularly club treasurer Danny DeCarlo, who was having trouble with his wife at home. As much or more than anybody, DeCarlo enjoyed the Family women, who nicknamed him "Donkey Dan" for an alleged physical attribute. To a swaggering biker like DeCarlo, it was the ultimate praise. Charlie cannily made DeCarlo his chief contact in the Straight Satan hierarchy, and DeCarlo took the responsibility seriously. He tried to keep Charlie happy with the arrangement—he didn't want to be cut off from the girls, after all. When Charlie admired a sword belonging to Straight Satans president George Knoll—Charlie always liked anything with a blade—DeCarlo negotiated a deal where Knoll traded the sword to Charlie in return for Charlie's paying one of Knoll's traffic fines. The sword immediately became Charlie's weapon of choice; he had a special scabbard for it welded to the frame of his personal dune buggy.

Though Charlie needed the Straight Satans around to facilitate drug deals, their presence also caused problems. George Spahn was still negotiating with developers, who made it clear that having so many undesirables on the property would inevitably drive down any proposed purchase price. Squeaky, ordered by Charlie to eavesdrop on George's conversations and report any potential problems, informed her leader that ranch hand Shorty Shea sometimes volunteered to help George rid the ranch of the bikers and the Family, too. Shea, clearly, was an enemy who had to be watched.

Besides irritating George Spahn, the Straight Satans upset some of the Family with their disparaging descriptions of black people as shiftless, stupid niggers. In all his Helter Skelter rhetoric, Charlie had been careful not to be overly critical of blacks. He taught his followers that they were different from the white race, and that it was only proper karma or fate that they should rise up against their oppressors. However, Charlie explained, blacks weren't suited to be in charge, which would work to the Family's eventual advantage, but they were lesser intellects, not sub-human. When the bikers became a constant presence on Spahn with all their nigger talk, Charlie gathered his followers and explained that, in the days ahead, they might even hear him joining in the bikers' racial slurs. It wasn't what he himself believed, Charlie emphasized. He was only pre-tending to have the same prejudices to keep the bikers happy, a necessary little deception to further the Helter Skelter escape plan. Nobody in the Family was to take Charlie's talk seriously. But soon afterward, Charlie began sometimes departing from his daily Helter Skelter pronounce-ments to lecture instead on "the human flower garden," how the races shouldn't mix because then there would only be one kind of flower in-stead of a garden full of unique, beautiful blooms. The way Charlie said it, it didn't seem racist.

Something that Charlie either didn't suspect, or else ignored because he couldn't do much about it, was the bikers' habit of passing hard drugs to Family members. Charlie allowed weed almost any time, and LSD in monitored doses. But the Straight Satans regularly indulged in whatever they could score, often speed, which often caused paranoia and violent tendencies in users. The bikers were all over Spahn, and they liked slip-ping pills to members of the Family on the sly. Charlie couldn't watch everywhere at once. Susan and Tex in particular liked the extra goodies. Though they otherwise feared and obeyed Charlie, they organized a se-cret stash that they furtively dipped into frequently. Enough of the others regularly ingested speed to develop edgier attitudes. As Charlie continued preaching about the war to come, more of the Family felt prepared to fight.

Charlie was getting edgier, too. He was under tremendous pressure. There was the new business arrangement with the Straight Satans to monitor, the challenge of keeping the Family convinced about the im-minence of Helter Skelter, and the ongoing frustration of trying to make contact with Terry Melcher, his last hope for a record deal. Little Paul

Watkins added to Charlie's already heavy load when he reported after a trip to Barker Ranch that the Family members there had met a miner named Paul Crockett. Crockett was a desert rat with considerable knowledge of Scientology. Brooks Poston and Juanita were talking to him a lot, and Crockett was apparently finding fault with things Charlie had told them. It seemed to Watkins that there was some danger Brooks might leave the Family and live and work with Crockett. Charlie certainly didn't want to allow that—ever since the Haight, he'd been paranoid about losing followers to rival gurus—but he couldn't leave L.A. with everything else that was going on.

At one point he took out his frustration on Watkins, lunging at him and wrapping his hands around his throat. It was no bluff; Charlie intended to strangle his follower to death, and Watkins struggled but felt himself weakening. Then, convinced he was about to die, he stopped fighting back, and the moment he did Charlie released his grip. Watkins decided that the best way to deal with Charlie in a violent mood was not to resist in any way. That seemed to throw him off and make him stop. Watkins decided that "death is Charlie's trip," and that although Charlie preached about love, all he really wanted to do was kill people. Charlie's assault on Watkins was a rare instance of bad judgment. Until that moment, Watkins had been one of his most faithful, dependable disciples. Now he began having doubts.

Had he and Little Paul Watkins compared notes that spring, Gregg Jakobson might have agreed. Though Dennis Wilson was visiting less often and Terry Melcher remained out of touch with Charlie, Jakobson continued to come out to Spahn. He'd decided that Charlie had no real potential as a recording artist. In person, Jakobson thought, Charlie could charm any audience; his songs weren't bad and his improvisational ability was exceptional. Using broad facial expressions and gestures, he could augment mediocre music with his personality, but, as Jakobson knew well from his experience as a music industry talent scout, that wasn't enough. Putting on a successful stage act was one thing. Records were what people listened to. They could only hear, not see, the artist, and that was where Charlie came up short. Charlie still thought Melcher might sign him to a record deal, but Jakobson was happy to let Melcher deal with that problem.

Jakobson still thought Charlie and the Family would make great subjects of a film documentary if he could get some funding together. He sometimes discussed the project with Charlie, and though Charlie liked the idea of being a movie star—he didn't really get the difference between a documentary and a feature film—he disagreed with Jakobson's approach. Jakobson wanted to present the Family as the ultimate commune, one proving it was possible to live the way that you wanted if you were inventive enough. He especially loved the garbage runs, the idea that they ate well on other people's trash. To Jakobson, the Family comprised a great cast. Besides Charlie there was crazy Susan, sweet-but-dumb Tex, deceivingly innocent-looking Squeaky, socially awkward Pat, and sexy little Ruth Ann. Present them as quirky, earnest seekers of a better way of life and audiences might very well fall in love with them. Charlie, though, wanted himself and his followers shown as *outlaws*, courageously defying authority and getting away with it. They argued back and forth, and one day Charlie suggested that they walk just beyond the Spahn boundaries to where a housing development was going up. Charlie asked, "What's it remind you of?" and when Jakobson replied that it was just people building houses Charlie said, "No, it's like a graveyard." Jakobson was sick of Charlie's endless allegorical word play. He snapped, "You're full of shit," and was shocked when Charlie pulled a handgun, pointed it at him, and asked, "What would you do if I pulled the trigger?" Jakobson wasn't sure if he was serious, but he wouldn't give Charlie the satisfaction of seeing him scared. "I guess I'd be dead," he answered. Charlie put the gun away and resumed the conversation as though there had never been a pistol-waving interruption. Jakobson was disgusted. He still wanted to get a film deal going; he was professional enough to sublimate any grudges in favor of doing business. But after the gun incident Jakobson was convinced that Charlie's "main thing" was fear, not love.

It was a restless time for the Family. To harness their nervous energy, and to hone survival skills, Charlie assembled small squads of followers and took them out nights "creepy-crawling." The object was to silently enter houses without alerting the people sleeping inside. The Family members stealthily moved furniture and other items from one place to another, and then left as quietly as they had come. In the morning, victims would wake up and realize from their rearranged possessions that someone had broken into their homes and gotten away. Their consternation would be even greater when they discovered nothing had been stolen—so why had these mystery intruders come at all? Most of the Family's creepy-crawls took place near Spahn Ranch, but sometimes they ranged all the way into upscale neighborhoods, once even creepy-crawling the Bel Air home of the Mamas and the Papas' John and Michelle Phillips. It was a great mind game to play on people, and the Family enjoyed it. They were also proving to themselves that they could get into any house, anywhere, anytime.

In mid-March, Charlie received word that Terry Melcher would finally come to hear him perform some of his songs. Charlie had been keeping everyone busy preparing for Helter Skelter, but a cataclysmic race war paled compared to Charlie finally getting a record deal. All of his followers were ordered to drop everything else and prepare for Melcher's visit. Because most of them still did not realize how much Charlie was obsessed with becoming the most famous rock star ever, they were puzzled why he was making such a big deal out of a Melcher drop-in. After all, he'd been there before, though not lately. But the men spiffed up the movie set and scraped away the mounds of horse manure and rotting hay that might offend the nose of their visitor. The women were ordered to bake cookies and cakes and other special non-garbage-run treats in case Melcher felt hungry. Charlie personally prepared as never before—this was it, the moment when it was going to happen for him. He bathed, and washed and trimmed his hair. Then he dressed in his special clothes. A few weeks earlier, Charlie had informed the women that he wanted a shirt and pants fashioned from deer skins and held together with leather lacings. The buckskin outfit would represent the Family's commitment to going back to the land. Nobody else was to have deerskin clothing yet—maybe everyone else could when they were sufficiently enlightened. Because Charlie refused to allow animals to be killed, the deerskins were bought from a supplier at considerable cost, but the clothes were going to be Charlie's so expense was not a factor. That deer still had to die for their skins to be available for purchase was one of those apparent contradictions between what Charlie preached and practiced, but he'd taught everyone that in these cases it was their mistake, not his. When the deerskins arrived at Spahn, the women discovered that they had to be softened and stretched before they could be sewn. They went through a laborious process of rubbing in oils and then stretching the skins along the sides of ranch buildings before fashioning serviceable, even attractive, buckskins for Charlie. He put them on before Melcher was scheduled to arrive; they would be one more reminder to the somewhat jaded producer that in Charlie he had a charismatic original. Charlie had everything planned down to the smallest detail: When the time came for the audition, Charlie would be with his guitar *here*, the women who would provide backup vocals would stand *here*, Melcher would be seated in just the right place to appreciate the performance. Once everything was ready everyone gathered at the ranch gate to greet Melcher, but he never showed up.

Roman Polanski and Sharon Tate loved living at Cielo. They did some redecorating but left a lot of things in place, including a string of Christmas lights that Candy Bergen had wound around the rail fence that circled the property. At night the colorful bulbs twinkled against a background of black sky, bright stars, and even brighter lights from the massive city below.

The new tenants threw a memorable housewarming party. John Phillips remembered it as "one of those everyone-is-here-tonight affairs." If Tate's credentials as an actress were thin, she was such a nice person that even the snobbiest show business celebrities were charmed by her. Many other parties followed, some formal and many impromptu. Polanski was away a lot, and Tate would spontaneously invite friends to come for dinner or just to sit and talk. Much of her conversation concerned her pregnancy; Tate couldn't wait to be a mother.

Roman Polanski's reputation for wild living soon lent itself to innuendo about activities at Cielo. But the effect wasn't negative. If anything, the widespread, but unsubstantiated, gossip added to the reputation of Polanski and Tate as one of Hollywood's most glamorous, trendy couples.

It was easier now for outsiders to get past Cielo's electronic gate than it had been when Terry Melcher lived there. Tate simply wasn't as guarded; besides, she was seldom home alone. Even when Polanski was away, there were friends with her all the time, quite often celebrity hair stylist Jay Sebring, who had been Tate's boyfriend before she left him for Polanski. After the breakup they stayed close. Voytek Frykowski, who'd known Polanski back in their native Poland, was a frequent Cielo visitor, too. He would bring along his girlfriend, Abigail Folger, known to her friends as Gibby. With her personal fortune assured—the Folger family owned the coffee company of the same name—Gibby served as a volunteer social worker for the Los Angeles County Welfare Department. She was one of the investors in Jay Sebring's salons. Frykowski was less well heeled and certainly less philanthropic than Folger. It appeared that he lived off his girlfriend, and according to subsequent police reports "he used cocaine, mescaline, LSD, marijuana [and] hashish in large amounts." But Frykowski was Polanski's oldest friend, and that made him Sharon Tate's friend, too. Rudi Altobelli was very fond of Tate, and liked spending time with her. So did Iranian native Shahrokh Hatami, Tate's personal photographer. Hatami, Sebring, Frykowski, and Folger were with Sharon at the main house and Altobelli was out in the guest cottage on Sunday, March 23, when an uninvited visitor arrived.

Charlie was furious when Terry Melcher failed to audition him at Spahn as promised. The insult was bad enough—Charlie was a huge talent, so how dare some *producer*, even a famous one like Melcher, treat him like that? But beyond the blow to Charlie's ego, Melcher's no-show embarrassed him in front of the Family. Charlie's power over his followers depended in large part on them believing him to be the wisest person anywhere, probably Jesus reincarnated and, according to Charlie's sermons to them, the future ruler of the post–Helter Skelter world. It was always a matter of Charlie's Will Be Done; whatever he wanted to happen, had to. He could not be seen to fail, and Charlie slipped when he allowed everyone to see how important Melcher's promised audition was to him. His iron control of the Family might diminish or even disappear as a result. The solution was to find Terry Melcher and make him get out to Spahn right away, so the Family could see for themselves that nobody reneged on a promise to Charlie Manson. So Charlie went out to find him.

Charlie didn't have time to set up an appointment with Melcher at Columbia. That might take weeks, even if Charlie could somehow talk his way past snippy secretaries and assistants. He couldn't hope to run into Melcher at some A-list party and ask what had happened. Charlie wasn't invited to those kinds of parties anymore. The best, quickest way for Charlie to confront Melcher was to go to Cielo. Sure, the guy had made it clear that he didn't want Charlie at his house, but so what? For Charlie, everything hung in the balance—the record deal he craved, the ongoing obedience of the Family. He'd risk Melcher's wrath by coming to his home uninvited. Melcher might be so angry that he'd turn his back on Charlie forever, but the risk was worth it. Besides, Charlie had great faith in his ability to convince anyone to do anything he wanted.

On March 23, Shahrokh Hatami looked out of a main house window at Cielo and saw someone walking in the yard. Hatami went out onto the porch for a better look. The fellow was short with long hair. He didn't look very special, but Hatami was annoyed because he acted like he owned the place. Hatami asked what he wanted and the interloper said that he was looking for someone. He mentioned a name that Hatami didn't recognize—the photographer wasn't part of the Terry Melcher–Dennis Wilson rock 'n' roll crowd. Hatami wanted the man gone, but there was always a chance that he was one of Rudi's friends, and Altobelli was in the guesthouse just down a small dirt pathway. "This is the Polanski residence," Hatami said. He said maybe whoever the man was looking for was at the guesthouse, and gestured toward it, adding that he should take "the back alley" or dirt path. Sharon Tate heard the voices and stepped out onto the porch, asking, "Who is it, Hatami?" From a distance of about six feet, she and Charlie Manson stared at each other. Then Charlie went down the dirt path to the cottage and Hatami and Tate went back inside the main house.

Rudi Altobelli was in the shower when his dog began barking. He put on a robe, opened his door, and saw Charlie on his porch. Charlie started to introduce himself, but Altobelli interrupted: "I know who you are, Charlie. What do you want?" Charlie said he was looking for Melcher and

Altobelli said that Melcher had moved. Charlie wanted to know where. Altobelli, who hadn't been impressed with Charlie the few times he'd met him, lied and said that he didn't know. Altobelli hoped Charlie would go away, but instead he tried to draw Altobelli into further conversation, asking what he did for a living. That annoyed Altobelli even more; Charlie knew very well that he was an agent—he'd tried to get Altobelli to sign him as a client after listening to tapes of some of his songs. The guy was a no-talent and Altobelli had no interest in wasting more time talking to him on the cottage porch. "I'd like to talk to you longer, Charlie," he said, "but I'm leaving the country tomorrow and have to pack." It was true—Altobelli and Tate were flying to Rome in the morning. Polanski was working on a movie there.

Charlie still lingered. Altobelli asked why he'd come back to the guest cottage, and Charlie said he'd been sent there by the people in the main house. Altobelli said that he didn't like his tenants to be disturbed, and Charlie shouldn't do it in the future. Then Charlie finally stalked off.

During their flight to Rome, Tate asked Altobelli, "Did that creepy-looking guy come back [to see you] yesterday?"

Charlie kept trying to contact Melcher, telling every mutual acquaintance that he was trying to get in touch. He had everyone at Spahn return to preparing for Helter Skelter. The main focus was on getting more dune buggies. The Family was able to barter for or buy some, and they stole others. Charlie, Tex, and a few of the other men brokered drug deals with the bikers. Bobby Beausoleil came around again; he had a new girlfriend named Kitty Lutesinger, who was pregnant. Charlie allowed a few new members to join the Family, notably an old prison pal and master forger currently calling himself Bill Vance, and a teenage girl named Barbara Hoyt, who'd run away from home at nearby Canoga Park. Vance was assigned to craft fake driver's licenses and other forms of identification, and Hoyt became a baby-sitting mainstay. With Sandy Good expecting, as well as Lutesinger, child care was becoming more of a priority. Charlie kept encouraging all the female Family members to get pregnant. It was the best way to begin expanding the group to the 144,000 foretold in Revelation. When they reached that number, the Family would emerge to take over the world. Every baby counted.

One of Little Paul Watkins's ongoing responsibilities was to seek out potential donors, and in April he connected with Charles Melton. Melton, who lived hippie-style in Topanga Canyon, had recently inherited a large amount of money and already given half away to various causes. Watkins brought Melton to Spahn and showed him around. Melton didn't hand over any cash, but he was intrigued by what he saw. Tex Watson wandered over and admired Melton's beard, saying, "Maybe Charlie will let me grow a beard someday." Charlie's word still was law among the Family; his control extended to his male followers' facial hair.

Rudi Altobelli kept his promise to Polanski and Tate by hiring a fill-in caretaker to stay at Cielo whenever he was away. Nineteen-year-old William Garretson had come to L.A. from Ohio, and he was already planning to return home sometime soon. Altobelli told the kid that if he would be on call to stay in the guest cottage whenever Altobelli was out of town, he'd pay him $35 a week to take care of the dogs and cats and generally keep an eye on things. Sometimes Altobelli's tenants might be home while Garretson was there, and he shouldn't bother them. Whenever Garretson decided it was time to return to Ohio, Altobelli would also pay for his plane ticket. It was a good deal for Garretson and he took it.

Sometime in April, Voytek Frykowski and Abigail Folger moved into the main house at Cielo. Polanski and Tate were going to be overseas for a while—Tate wanted to spend as much time there with her husband as she could before her pregnancy advanced to the point where her obstetrician would forbid her to fly. Even though Tate trusted Rudi Altobelli implicitly and knew he'd hired a caretaker, she still felt better having friends staying in her home when she wasn't there. When she was at home and Polanski was away, Frykowski and Folger could keep her company. They were apparently working through a tough time in their relationship. Folger had just given up her volunteer job with the county. They were welcome at Cielo for as long as they wanted to stay.

On April 19, deputies of the Los Angeles County Sheriff's Office raided Spahn. There had been reports of hippies stealing dune buggies, and dune buggies had been spotted on the ranch. Some of the vehicles the officers impounded were stolen, but the Family had pink slips for several others. The deputies arrested the Family members present at the time—Leslie and a few others; Charlie wasn't there—and charged them with grand theft auto. It was an empty gesture. There was no way to prove who had actually stolen the dune buggies, or whether the people working on them at the ranch had any knowledge that they were stolen. The charges were dropped a few days later. The Family's dune buggy fleet was depleted, so they simply stole some more. No one was intimidated by the arrests. Charlie had anticipated all along that there might be raids, and told everyone how to act if they were arrested. No one was to admit to committing any crimes because, after all, there was really no such thing as crime. Above all, they should never mention Helter Skelter or the bottomless pit in the desert, because then the cops would think they were nuts and send them to mental hospitals where people would zap their brains with electricity. None of them, Charlie warned, wanted *that*.

Charlie also explained to his followers that if he was ever arrested, whether he was in custody for a few days or for years he would act like "Crazy Charlie," ranting nonsensical things until his captors grew so frustrated that they eventually would just let him go. But the Family shouldn't be taken in—it was just a trick Charlie would be playing on the Man for however long it took.

Four days after the county raided Spahn Ranch, Tex Watson was arrested in Van Nuys for being under the influence of drugs in public. Somebody at the ranch had a chunk of belladonna root, a potent hallucinogen, and Tex gulped some down. The next thing he knew, he was slithering on his hands and knees on a Van Nuys sidewalk, muttering "Beep, beep." The police took him to the station, snapped his mug shot and took his fingerprints before locking him in a cell until he was coherent enough to leave. It wasn't considered a serious crime—in April 1969 people high on drugs in public were common in L.A. and its suburbs. Tex went back to the ranch, but some of the Family thought the belladonna must have had a lingering effect on him. Before, Tex had always been calm and sweet-natured. Now he seemed gruffer, even mean at times, and bossy in a way that he had never been before. He suddenly seemed to consider himself Charlie's right-hand man and the Family's surrogate leader whenever Charlie wasn't at Spahn. Phil Kaufman, encountering post-belladonna Tex, was so irritated by his pushy new attitude that he punched him in the face. Some of the women in the Family felt afraid of Tex. But Charlie wasn't concerned. A rougher, tougher Tex Watson might come in handy somewhere down the line.

Bobby Beausoleil stayed around much longer than usual. He had his own hopes of becoming a rock star, and if Charlie could get the deal with Terry Melcher that he kept talking about, maybe he could put in a word to Melcher on Beausoleil's behalf. So he hung out at the ranch, and Charlie kept sending word that he wanted to hear from Melcher. Finally, around the second week of May, Melcher responded. He'd come to Spahn to hear Charlie perform his songs on May 18. Melcher didn't apologize for standing Charlie up before, but he promised that this time he'd come without fail. Charlie was finally getting his shot. For the second time he ordered the Family to put aside their Helter Skelter responsibilities and concentrate instead on making certain that everything was perfect for Melcher's visit. He made the women rehearse with him virtually nonstop; they were instructed not only to sing on the choruses but also to strip and dance provocatively to the music. Melcher would experience not only aural but visual delight. Charlie knew how to set scenes to elicit the response that he wanted. How could Melcher not be overwhelmed? Nothing would go wrong this time. Charlie was about to get the recording deal and then the fame he deserved.

CHAPTER TWELVE

Thwarted Dreams

America was seething in May 1969. Tension crackled across the land. Mankind's first moon landing was scheduled for late July, but there remained an overall sense of foreboding, as though the trauma of 1968 might have been preamble to something even worse.

Focused more on Vietnam and international tensions, President Nixon disdained hippies and student radicals, finding little if any difference between them. He also had no empathy for frustrated black rioters. Though he was not antagonistic toward minorities and believed in government programs to bolster them socially and economically, the president regarded blacks as fundamentally inferior to whites. Nixon lectured staffers that "the key is to devise a system that recognizes this while appearing not to."

So as the weather warmed, blacks in city ghettos again began to lash out, and young white radicals who previously studied articles on organizing peaceful protest marches began poring over blueprints for making homemade bombs.

There was plenty of new evidence to cite as additional signs of the coming Helter Skelter, but Charlie ignored it all. At Spahn Ranch, preparations for race war were set aside once again so that everyone could get things ready for Terry Melcher. Charlie's outrage when Melcher stood him up in March, and his desperation to impress him now in May, made it obvious to even his most blindly devoted followers that nothing mattered more to their leader than getting a record deal. If they hadn't realized before how much Charlie wanted it, they did now. On May 18, as he waited for Melcher to show up at Spahn, the sharpest-eyed among his followers realized that Charlie was *nervous*.

Melcher arrived at the ranch ready to get down to business. His time was limited; he had no interest in freshly baked snacks or messing with the girls. Charlie wanted a chance to audition—all right, Melcher told him, play me your music. Charlie fetched his guitar and strummed. The women stripped, then began humming and providing percussion accompaniment. A few used tambourines. The rest knocked pieces of wood together. As they kept time to Charlie's songs they also danced, swaying in the dusty sunshine. Charlie put all that he had into his performance. Melcher listened intently. At one point Charlie took a short break. During this time-out he tried to engage Melcher in a philosophical conversation, explaining how it was possible for anyone to "exist in a place" without restrictions, where you lived well on other people's garbage. Melcher wasn't interested. He was there to evaluate Charlie's music, not the Family's lifestyle. Charlie played and sang some more, and then the audition was over.

Though Charlie anticipated an immediate contract offer, Melcher was noncommittal. Taking Charlie aside, he said polite things about several songs being interesting. He knew a guy, Mike Deasy, who besides being a great session guitarist had his own recording van and liked going onsite to record Indian tribal music. Melcher said that he'd come back with Deasy, who might be interested in what Charlie was doing. Meanwhile, he gave Charlie $50, all the cash he had with him, to buy hay for the ranch horses or whatever the Family needed. Melcher had grown up in homes with fully stocked pantries and refrigerators. Charlie's talk of feeding not only the Family adults but also their children from garbage bins bothered him.

Melcher left immediately after handing over the money. The Family gathered around Charlie—what did Melcher say? Did Charlie get his record deal? It was a ticklish moment for Charlie. Melcher had promised to come back and listen to Charlie again, but this time with somebody else who might want to record him. Even at his most self-delusional, Charlie couldn't mistake the underlying message that Melcher was probably going to pass. He might change his mind after the second session, but for now Charlie had to tell his followers something. So Charlie announced that Terry Melcher had given him money. Charlie made sure that the Family thought it was in the nature of a signing bonus. And Melcher was coming back soon with a recording van! Charlie explained that he turned down a chance to sign a contract with Melcher on the spot because, after all, Charlie Manson's word was his bond and he didn't believe in written contracts.

The ploy worked. So far as Charlie's followers were concerned, the audition had been a tremendous success, as of course it had to be, since he was infallible.

Terry Melcher left Spahn Ranch that day feeling certain that Charlie Manson had nothing to offer musically. He recalled later that Charlie's songs were "below-average nothing, and as far as I was concerned, Manson was like every other starving, hippie songwriter who was [currently] jamming Sunset Boulevard, a hundred thousand every day, who looked, dressed, talked and sang exactly like Charles Manson, sang about the same topics of peace and revolution, about the themes that were in the Beatles' albums." It was possible, Melcher believed, that his friend Mike Deasy might see something in Charlie's music that he didn't, though if Deasy did any recording with Charlie it would be for such a tiny niche audience that very few records would be sold, let alone the unfathomably enormous number necessary to make Charlie more famous than the Beatles. Melcher talked to Deasy, and they agreed to go to Spahn on June 6, meaning Charlie had almost three weeks to build up his hopes again.

During those three weeks, Charlie put everyone back to work on Helter Skelter. There were dune buggies in various stages of repair scattered around the ranch. Towing them into the buildings where Tex and the bikers worked required particularly strong tethers, so Charlie went to a surplus store in Santa Monica and bought several hundred feet of white three-ply nylon rope, which was much cheaper than towing chains. Everyone was kept working at a feverish pace, but as they worked the Family members chattered about Charlie's record deal with Melcher. Despite Charlie's warnings about the coming race war, most members of the Family weren't happy about returning to desolate Barker Ranch. The time they'd spent at Dennis Wilson's log cabin mansion was very much on their minds. If Charlie became a rock star—as, of course, he inevitably would—then they could all live in posh digs like Wilson's instead of scorpion-infested desert shacks. That was certainly much more appealing.

On June 6 Melcher and Deasy arrived at Spahn. Gregg Jakobson was with them. Charlie performed his songs for them, with the Family women providing background vocals and percussion. In a spectacularly wrongheaded attempt at hospitality, someone slipped Deasy LSD and he suffered a horrendously bad trip. Melcher and Jakobson had to get him home and as they guided him toward their car, with Charlie walking hopefully alongside them and the rest of the Family trailing along behind, veteran Hollywood stuntman Randy Starr, who often hung out at Spahn, staggered up. He was dressed all in black, belligerently drunk, and waving an old-fashioned six-gun. Starr reminded Melcher of the Lee Marvin character in the movie *Cat Ballou*—so far as he was concerned, the guy offered no real threat at all. But Charlie, faced with the end of his rock star dreams, screeched, "Don't draw on me, motherfucker," and began, Jakobson recalled, "to beat the shit out of [Starr] right in front of us." Melcher was disgusted. Sure, the guy was twice Charlie's size, but he was just drunk and acting stupid. There'd been no reason to beat him up.

A few days later, perhaps in person but probably over the phone since Melcher didn't have time to waste making yet another trip out to Spahn, Charlie got the response that, at some level, he knew was coming. Because Melcher wasn't insensitive to Charlie's hopes, it was the classic producer's tactful turndown: "You're good, but I wouldn't know what to do with you." And with that, Charlie Manson's dream of becoming a rock star more famous than the Beatles was essentially over.

The constant danger for gurus is that they must keep producing new wonders for their followers. They can't let the act get stale or seem to be wrong about something or, worst of all, to fail publicly. Charlie had let the Family see how much he wanted a record deal; he'd made them part of his all-out effort and it came to nothing. If they began to doubt him because of that, how long would it be before they lost faith in Helter Skelter and refused to be led into a life of hardscrabble austerity in Death Valley? They were already wondering when Charlie would cut his first album with Columbia. Charlie had to think of something fast, an explanation of why Terry Melcher's rejection wasn't really failure on Charlie's part. He came up with a beauty.

Terry Melcher, Charlie told his followers, had promised him a contract and then reneged on the deal. Didn't everyone recall that Melcher gave Charlie money, a down payment, back in May? And then after he returned in June Melcher said he was going to give Charlie a call soon and get it all set up. Charlie took Melcher at his word because he was so honest himself. When Charlie promised to do something, he did it. But not Terry Melcher. Despite being so impressed by Charlie's music—everybody remembered how impressed Melcher was, didn't they?—for some reason he had decided to withhold Charlie's healing music from the rest of the world. Terry Melcher had *betrayed* Charlie, just like those betrayals of Jesus in the Bible, and so this was yet another sign that the prophecies in Revelation and the *White Album* were coming true. Melcher's heinous act was just one more piece of the apocalyptic puzzle fitting neatly in place. Just as Charlie had foretold, Helter Skelter was coming down fast.

The Family believed him. At that point, they had little choice. They'd surrendered their lives and wills to Charlie. They moved forward in preparations for Helter Skelter, but as they did they sensed a permanent change in their leader. Before, Charlie always leavened any inner rage with periods of outer calm. But after Terry Melcher's turndown, Leslie Van Houten remembers, Charlie "stopped pretending that he wasn't angry. He was mad all of the time."

Charlie realized that Melcher had been his last good chance for a record deal, but he didn't quite give up. Though he kept it from most of the Family, during the summer of 1969 Charlie made a few last-ditch efforts to enlist new superstar patrons. Bobby Beausoleil pitched Charlie's songs to Frank Zappa. Gypsy met Paul Rothchild, the producer of the Doors, and played him the tapes of Charlie's 1968 recording session in Van Nuys. Charlie performed some of his songs for Mamas and Papas vocalist Cass Elliot. They all passed, which didn't improve Charlie's disposition.

The Family's approach to Helter Skelter grew darker, even sinister. On Charlie's command they began stealing things during their creepy-crawling, often items that could be traded or sold, always credit cards if they could get them. Charlie learned where Terry Melcher lived on the beach in Malibu and sent a creepy-crawl team there. They stole a telescope off his porch, intending the theft as a message to Melcher that they could always find him. But Melcher had no idea he'd been robbed by the Family; he thought some run-of-the-mill thief had swiped the telescope. After turning Charlie down for a record deal, he hadn't given him another thought.

Charlie began suggesting that the creepy-crawls could be ratcheted up even more—perhaps some Piggies could be kidnapped, or even tied up in their homes and frightened to death. Death was much on Charlie's mind and the frequent topic of his sermonizing during group LSD trips. Everyone was afraid of death and that was foolish, Charlie preached, because death and life were the same. He had a question for his followers— "Would you die for me?" Under the constant influence of the drug and Charlie himself, they assured him that they would.

But that summer some of them began to waver. They didn't like the prospect of living out on Barker Ranch, or else they were nervous about all the guns and creepy-crawling or just sick of serving at Charlie's beck and call. Pat Krenwinkel left with a biker; Charlie tracked them down just south of L.A. and told Pat she had to come home with him. Pat was so astonished by his ability to find her, which she attributed to Charlie's special powers rather than his extensive contacts in the biker community, that she complied. When Leslie Van Houten began grumbling, Charlie put her in his dune buggy and drove to the top of the Santa Susanas, parked, and told her, "If you want to leave me, jump." Leslie didn't want to jump, and so she stayed.

Charlie couldn't prevent every defection, especially among the contingent he'd sent ahead to Death Valley while he remained at Spahn. Word reached him that Brooks Poston had left Barker Ranch to work with prospector/rival guru Paul Crockett, and that Juanita also deserted to marry one of Crockett's partners. Charlie needed some kind of uprising that he could interpret to his followers as the beginning of Helter Skelter so they believed they had no option other than to stay with him, but the blacks weren't cooperating. He told Watkins that any delay was the result of black people being too stupid to know how to get Helter Skelter started. Well, it was going to happen that summer, and apparently Charlie would be the one to show them how to do it. That was too much for Watkins. The next time Charlie sent him out to Barker to check on things there, he joined Paul Crockett, too. Charlie had lost his most effective recruiter. That made him even more determined to keep the rest of the Family together. The best way to do that was to get them away from L.A. and into Death Valley, where they would be even more dependent on Charlie. Of course, Crockett was out there, but Charlie had plans for him.

The Family suffered an additional loss through arrest. Spahn ranch-hand-turned-Family-member Steve Grogan—Clem Scramblehead—was jailed for child molestation and indecent exposure. He told police that "the kids wanted me to . . . the thing fell out of my pants and the parents got excited." Despite his well-deserved reputation as the dumbest of all Family members, Clem was a very useful disciple to Charlie. He would do anything Charlie wanted, provided that whatever he was asked to do wasn't too complicated. Now he was gone.

With no further chance to get a record deal through L.A. contacts, the Family wondering when exactly Helter Skelter was going to start, and Paul Crockett poaching his followers from Barker Ranch, Charlie was desperate to leave Spahn Ranch for Death Valley. But money remained an issue; without a lot of it, they couldn't survive long in the desert. Drug deals were the best source for quick cash, and Charlie decided to work another contact besides the Straight Satans bikers. Luella, the girl Tex Watson lived with during his AWOL months from the Family, was still dealing, and on July 1 Tex called her to say that he had twenty-five kilos of prime weed. Luella agreed to bring in a buyer who would put up $2,500 in advance, skim a few kilos for herself, and make a nice profit. What Tex didn't share with her was that there were no twenty-five kilos. He was going to take the $2,500 and "burn" Luella and her buyer. If they traced Tex back to Spahn, Charlie would swear that Tex had disappeared weeks earlier.

Everything went wrong. Luella's buyer was a tank-sized black dealer named Bernard Crowe, whose street nickname was Lotsapoppa. Tex got the $2,500 up front, but Lotsapoppa and his boys said they'd keep Luella until they took delivery of the weed. They told Tex in graphic detail what would happen to her if they were stiffed. Tex swore he was on the up-and-up, then took the money back to Charlie at Spahn. Lotsapoppa soon guessed that he'd been swindled, and called the ranch demanding to talk to Tex. Charlie stuck to the plan, telling him that Tex was gone and he had no idea how to contact him. Lotsapoppa described what he was about to do to Luella. Charlie didn't care about that, but he was terrified by what he heard next. Lotsapoppa declared that he was a member of the Black Panthers. If he didn't get his weed or his money, he was going to gather an army of his Panther friends, come out to Spahn Ranch, and kill everybody there.

This was a threat that Charlie took seriously. In prison, he'd been intimidated by the Black Muslims, and since his brief stay in Berkeley he'd believed that the Black Panthers were lethal to anyone who crossed them. Much of his Helter Skelter preaching was predicated on the Muslims' and the Panthers' militant attitudes spreading throughout the black community. No whites could possibly stand up to them. In truth, by the summer of 1969 the Panther organization was in disarray and in no position to organize an attack on a sprawling ranch. Lotsapoppa wasn't even a member of the Panthers. But Charlie believed him. He didn't want to give the money back—he needed it for Death Valley and, besides, he was already concerned that his hold over the Family might be growing tenuous. He couldn't let them see him backing down. So Charlie, certain that he was cornered, told Lotsapoppa that he would meet him at his home in North Hollywood. Then he and Family member T. J. Walleman set out. On the way, Charlie explained what they were about to do. He had a handgun that he would tuck in the back of his pants. When they went into the apartment, he would go in first with Walleman directly behind him. When Charlie gave a signal, Walleman would yank the gun free and shoot Lotsapoppa. As usual, Charlie wanted someone else to do the dirty work.

Lotsapoppa had two confederates with him at the apartment. Walleman lost his nerve and Charlie had to pull the gun himself. Walleman told Tex Watson later that the pistol misfired on the first try, but then Charlie managed to shoot Lotsapoppa in the chest. The big black man toppled over. Charlie then waved the gun at the other two dealers, and he and Walleman raced back to Spahn. Afterward Charlie was furious with Walleman for panicking. Having seen firsthand that Charlie was capable of murder, Walleman fled the ranch. Charlie bragged to everyone how he'd done what was needed, how he blew a Black Panther away, just stood there unafraid and shot him dead. But he remained convinced that at any moment a Panther hit squad, now bent on revenge as well as retrieving the $2,500, might launch an attack on the ranch. Charlie ordered male Family members and friends from among the bikers to man all-hours lookout posts; he handed around some of the guns acquired for the Helter Skelter escape to the desert. Charlie stressed that he wasn't afraid for himself; it was the Family he wanted to protect. Everyone was on the alert for Panther infiltrators. None was discovered, but over the next few weeks the Family was suspicious when more black tourists than usual came to the ranch to rent horses. Charlie even worried when a bus full of blacks passed by the front ranch gate. He pointed it out to the Family, suggesting that the Panthers were scouting their defenses. Charlie wanted Helter Skelter to begin with a black attack on whites, but not on *him*. He used the Lotsapoppa incident as proof that the race war was definitely drawing near. They needed to raise money and get out to the desert before they were swept up in it. Meanwhile, he maintained the armed lookouts. Gypsy told a television interviewer decades later that "it wasn't peace and love and hippies anymore. It was almost like an army."

But it was an army Gypsy had no intention of deserting. With the recent arrest of Clem and the defections of Watkins, Poston, Juanita, and now Walleman, the Family needed replenishing and Gypsy was Charlie's recruiter. Within days of the Lotsapoppa shooting, she met an excellent prospective member.

In 1968, Bob and Linda Kasabian were living in a New Mexico commune when their marriage broke up. Linda took their infant daughter and went to stay with her mother in Milford, New Hampshire. Bob Kasabian drifted west to Southern California, where he met and soon shared a trailer in Topanga Canyon with hippie philanthropist Charlie Melton. Bob liked it there, and in mid-June 1969 he contacted Linda and suggested that they reconcile. She and baby Tanya could stay with him and Melton in the trailer. Linda thought it was worth a try. She and Tanya arrived in Topanga Canyon around July 1. Bob and Melton had a plan to go down to South America, buy a boat, and sail around the world. Linda wasn't sure she wanted to do that.

Linda's reconciliation with Bob wasn't going well. Even after just a few days it didn't seem as though things were any different between them than before. The more she considered it, spending months on a boat with him sailing around the world seemed unappealing. But she wasn't eager to return to her mother in New Hampshire, either. She felt stuck.

Then a new option presented itself. A vivacious woman named Gypsy dropped by to visit with Charlie Melton. He'd visited the commune where Gypsy lived not long before, and she was just being friendly and keeping in touch. Gypsy and Linda started talking, and Gypsy told her all about the Family and especially Charlie Manson, a beautiful man whom everybody looked up to. At Spahn, everyone would love Linda and Tanya and take care of them. Gypsy invited Linda to come with her for a visit. She did, and almost immediately she hooked up with Tex Watson. They made love and talked late into the night. Linda told him that she wanted to be part of the Family. Tex knew Linda was staying with Charlie Melton, who had money. He told Linda that she should steal some and bring it with her when she and her daughter joined the Family. Linda felt funny about stealing from a friend, but she also thought it would impress the Family if she arrived with a lot of money to contribute. She took $5,000 in cash from Melton's trailer and, along with her daughter, brought the money to Spahn. Only then did she meet Charlie Manson, who was repairing one of the ranch tractors. Charlie took the money, startled Linda by feeling her legs, and then quizzed her about her life. When he learned that Linda had a valid driver's license, he told her that she could stay. Tanya was whisked off to be with the other Family kids, and Linda was brought into the main Family. Some of them thought she was unfriendly, even cold, and didn't like her. But only Charlie's opinion counted, and he wanted Linda there.

On July 19, Clem astonished the Family by showing up at Spahn Ranch. The court had sent him to Camarillo State Hospital for a battery of psychiatric tests to determine whether he was intellectually functional. But Camarillo had no secured premises, and Clem simply walked away to rejoin his leader Charlie.

The next day, U.S. astronauts Neil Armstrong and Buzz Aldrin walked on the moon. The news was all over radio and television. But at Spahn Ranch, where there was widespread belief in the divinity of Charlie Manson, Helter Skelter, and the bottomless desert pit, the moon walk was viewed with skepticism. As the women sat in their daily sewing circle, one commented, "There's somebody on the moon today," and another replied, "They're faking it." Nothing was real unless Charlie said so, and Charlie had no interest in anyone walking on the moon. He was fixated on getting enough money to leave Spahn for Death Valley before the Black Panthers attacked.

Charlie's sense of urgency was such that he was prepared to use force. So-called friends could prove their loyalty by giving him money, lots of it, without any excuse or delay. If they wouldn't do it voluntarily, then Charlie would make them. Dennis Wilson was an obvious target. Charlie went looking for him, and when he didn't find him, he left messages. A note left at one of Wilson's temporary lodgings assured the Beach Boy, "You can't get away from me." Another time, Charlie left a bullet. He knew Wilson would understand.

But in late July Charlie couldn't pin Wilson down, and he turned his attention elsewhere. Music teacher and occasional drug dealer Gary Hinman had a couple of cars and enough of a bankroll to be planning a trip to Japan. It was time for him to demonstrate his loyalty to the Family by either joining—in which case all his possessions, including his bank account, would become Charlie's—or else by handing over whatever money he had. Bobby Beausoleil provided the perfect excuse to shake down Hinman. Beausoleil had just paid him $1,000 for a thousand tabs of mescaline; he'd gotten the money from the Straight Satans, who planned to have a party with the drugs. But after sampling the goods, the Satans claimed that the batch was tainted. They were furious and demanded that Beausoleil give them back their money, and he prepared to confront Hinman. Charlie thought that Beausoleil's demand ought to include not only the Satans' $1,000, but additional money to help fund the Family's Helter Skelter desert flight. If nothing else, Hinman owned those two cars. Their pink slips would be worth something.

Bobby Beausoleil was never a member of the Family. He and Charlie were friends whose interests sometimes coincided. Neither one wanted the Straight Satans upset, Beausoleil because they'd take it out on him if they didn't get their drug money refund, and Charlie because, so long as they were content to stick around Spahn, the bikers were his main line of defense in the event of a Black Panthers attack. Beausoleil had no intention of joining Charlie and the Family on their flight to Death Valley—

Helter Skelter was Charlie's thing, not his. But he didn't mind helping his pal finance the plan by squeezing Hinman for more money.

On Friday, July 25, longtime Family member Bruce Davis drove Beausoleil, Mary Brunner, and Susan Atkins over to Hinman's place. Beausoleil was armed with a handgun and a knife. After Hinman invited them in, Beausoleil demanded his $1,000. Hinman refused, insisting that there was some mistake and the drugs he'd sold to Beausoleil for the Straight Satans were fine. Beausoleil told Susan to hold Hinman at gunpoint while he looked around the house to pick out items worth $1,000—if Hinman wouldn't hand over the money, maybe the Satans would take something in trade. Hinman tried to grab the gun from Susan, Beausoleil jumped in to help her subdue him, and the gun went off. The bullet didn't hit anyone; it lodged under the kitchen sink. Beausoleil, who was much stronger than Hinman, got him under control. Then Beausoleil beat him for a while, demanding all the money that he had. Hinman denied that he had any. He reluctantly agreed to sign over the pink slips to both of his cars, a Volkswagen bus and a Fiat station wagon. Their combined value was more than $1,000. Beausoleil was satisfied on his own behalf, but there were still Charlie's financial needs to consider. He called Charlie at the ranch, explaining that, even after being thoroughly beaten, Hinman denied having money. Charlie was certain that Hinman did, and he wanted it. Just before midnight, Bruce Davis drove Charlie to Hinman's house. Charlie brought his sword, and when Hinman protested to him that he didn't understand what was happening, that he'd always been a friend to the Family, Charlie slashed the blade along the left side of Hinman's head, splitting his ear almost in half. Charlie snarled that he expected Hinman to give Beausoleil everything he had, and then he and Bruce returned to Spahn.

For the rest of that night, all of Saturday, and well into Sunday, Beausoleil doled out beatings to Hinman, and Susan and Mary pleaded with him to hand over his money and end his suffering. Hinman still insisted that he had no money to give them. Beausoleil intermittently called Charlie at Spahn with reports of no progress. At one point Hinman threatened to call the police whenever Beausoleil and the two women finally left. That was something Charlie couldn't allow. If Hinman told the police about his drug deals with the Family and Charlie got arrested, any investigation might reveal his murder of Lotsapoppa. As a multi-time loser on probation, Charlie could expect a maximum sentence. During a final Sunday phone call, Beausoleil told Charlie that "he's got his ear hacked off and he'll go to the police." Charlie said, "You know what to do." Hinman had to die, and, since he did, his murder might as well advance Charlie's prophecy of Helter Skelter. The Black Panthers were much on Charlie's mind since his confrontation with Lotsapoppa, and he decided to implicate them by telling Beausoleil to leave apparent evidence that the Panthers slaughtered Hinman. The symbol of the Panthers was a paw print. Beausoleil stabbed Hinman several times, and as he lay dying Beausoleil dipped his hand in Hinman's blood and pressed a crude paw print onto the wall. Then, using the finger of a glove dipped in the pool of gore, Beausoleil wrote "POLITICAL PIGGY" on the wall near the paw print.

Beausoleil, Susan, and Mary went through the house, trying to wipe away all their fingerprints, but they missed a few. After filching a set of bagpipes that Hinman often played, they drove his Fiat and Volkswagen bus back to Spahn and waited for news stories to break about how the Black Panthers had viciously murdered an innocent young white man in his home. After two days when no stories were broadcast, Beausoleil returned to Hinman's house to see if the murder had at least been discovered. It hadn't. He remarked later back at Spahn about the odd sound of maggots "eating away on" Hinman's dead body. He was concerned that the bloody paw print might somehow be traced back to him and he tried to clean it off the wall, but it had dried solid. Beausoleil also made a second attempt to wipe surfaces for any stray fingerprints, but he once again did a sloppy job. He was careless with the murder weapon, too. Instead of disposing of the bloody knife, he stashed it in the tire well of Hinman's Fiat. He kept the Fiat for his own use. Charlie disposed of the Volkswagen bus, perhaps to the Straight Satans to cover the $1,000.

Charlie wanted the details of Gary's murder kept secret from the rest of the Family, but that proved impossible. Beausoleil wanted to boast; even though they were friends there was also a strong sense of competition between him and Charlie, and Charlie had gotten a lot of bragging privileges from shooting Lotsapoppa. Now Beausoleil had proof that he was a tough guy, too. He told Straight Satan Danny DeCarlo about it, and DeCarlo passed along the details to Tex. Susan also couldn't resist bragging. When she told the other women that she and Beausoleil killed Gary, one asked what it was like. Susan replied, "It was real weird and he made funny noises." Yeller was sickened by Susan's comments; she and a male Family member called Bill had secretly become a couple in violation of Charlie's everyone-belongs-to-everyone edict. Now they decided to sneak away past the lookouts keeping watch for Black Panthers. Just before they left, they took Pat Krenwinkel aside and asked her to come with them. Pat, who remembered how easily Charlie had tracked her the last time she left him, said she would stay. But Charlie lost two more followers.

Kitty Lutesinger, Bobby's pregnant girlfriend, was also upset by what she heard from Susan and begged Bobby to take her away from Spahn and the Family. He refused.

On Thursday, July 31, some of Gary Hinman's friends dropped by his house for a visit. There was no response to their knock on the front door, and they noticed clouds of flies buzzing through an open window. Worried, they contacted the police. The Los Angeles County Sheriff's Department had jurisdiction for Topanga Canyon. Officers Paul Whiteley and Charles Guenther investigated, found Hinman's body, and spent the next several days gathering evidence. The bloody paw print and words on the wall were ghastly, but what interested the lawmen more was at least one clean fingerprint lifted from the crime scene. Hinman's friends said that both of his cars were missing. Whiteley and Guenther put out an All Points Bulletin for the Fiat and Volkswagen.

Charlie considered Linda Kasabian sufficiently indoctrinated to join very pregnant Sandy Good on a panhandling day in Topanga. Wandering about, they were picked up by Saladin Nader, who drove a battered Jaguar and told them that he was an actor who'd appeared in a Lebanese film. Nader took Linda and Sandy to his apartment in Santa Monica. Sandy was worn out and wanted to nap. While she did, Nader and Linda had sex. Afterward he dropped them off at a shopping center in the San Fernando Valley. The women enjoyed meeting Nader; he seemed like an especially nice guy. When they got back to Spahn they told Charlie about him.

It was a tense time for Charlie. He'd promised that Helter Skelter would begin that summer, and summer was waning. His efforts to raise sufficient money to finance a long-term Family relocation to Barker Ranch were unsuccessful. The Black Panthers might attack any minute. Two murders, Lotsapoppa and Gary Hinman, might yet be traced back to Charlie and Bobby Beausoleil at Spahn. Spahn might not even be available as a Family base much longer—Squeaky reported that developers were pushing George Spahn to sell to them, and ranch hand Shorty Shea kept offering to run Charlie and the Family off if Spahn just gave the word. Charlie had to think of something. And to do that, he needed some time away from everybody else, a road trip where he wouldn't have to endure constant badgering about day-to-day trifles.

Charlie announced that he would drive north for a few days to find new Family recruits. While he was gone, everyone should remain alert for a Black Panther attack, and otherwise keep preparing for Death Valley. On August 3 Charlie left, driving a cream-colored 1952 Ford delivery van the Family had recently acquired. It wasn't the flashiest ride, but it was dependable. Charlie took with him one of the Family's stolen gas credit cards, and used it every time he needed a fill up. He first stopped for gas in nearby Canoga Park, then drove on to Big Sur. Stopping again for gas along the way, he met teenager Stephanie Schram, who was hitchhiking from San Francisco to San Diego, where she lived with her older sister. She told Charlie that she'd been to San Francisco with a boyfriend, but he ordered her around too much. Schram was cute, and a diversion for Charlie at a moment when he badly needed one. Charlie turned on the charm, using the nothing-is-wrong, you-are-perfect spiel that had served him so well since his days in Haight-Ashbury. Schram fell for it. After Charlie promised to eventually drive her to her sister's place in San Diego, she gladly joined him in the clanking old delivery van. They took LSD and had sex. On August 6 they drove back to Spahn and had dinner with the Family. Schram was initially put off by Charlie's followers, especially the women. Like Patricia Krenwinkel two years earlier, she had thought that Charlie was going to be her exclusive boyfriend, but now she learned she'd have to share him. Charlie soothed her with the promise that he'd at least be her monogamous partner for a few weeks, and the next morning he and Schram drove down to San Diego to collect her clothes and other personal belongings from her sister's house. The overnight at Spahn allowed Schram to meet everyone but Beausoleil, who'd left for San Francisco a day earlier in the Fiat.

At Cielo Drive things were hectic. Roman Polanski was in England working on a film, but Sharon Tate expected him to return shortly. Eight months into her pregnancy, she suffered from the L.A. summer heat but mustered the energy to begin decorating a room for the baby. Tate had friends over for lunches, and one night that week, Tuesday or Wednesday, she hosted a small party for French director Roger Vadim. But Tate spent fewer evenings entertaining now because she tired so easily.

Voytek Frykowski was excited because he had friends flying in from Canada. They wouldn't stay at Cielo where Frykowski and Abigail Folger occupied the guest room, but they would surely be invited to dinner by Tate. Jay Sebring was expected to drop in for an evening or two. He made a point of keeping Tate company whenever Polanski was away, so much so that some people thought he might be trying to win her back. Rudi Altobelli was out of town, too, so William Garretson stayed in the guest cottage to keep an eye on things. The kid spent some of the week partying hard and late with friends, so he didn't feel particularly well. As soon as Altobelli returned, he was ready to go home to Ohio.

Beausoleil didn't take Kitty Lutesinger with him to San Francisco. In a sense Beausoleil was on the run and knew he could move around faster without being saddled with a pregnant girlfriend. Using Hinman's Fiat as his getaway car was poor planning. Its murdered owner hadn't paid attention to maintenance. Beausoleil didn't get far before the Fiat broke down near San Luis Obispo. Two highway patrolmen pulled up and ran a routine records check on the vehicle. They were notified that an APB had been issued on it connected to a murder in Topanga Canyon. Beausoleil was arrested, and the bloody knife he used to stab Hinman was discovered in the tire well. L.A. County detectives Paul Whiteley and Charles Guenther came out to question him. Beausoleil first tried telling them that he'd just bought the car from a black guy; he hoped that the alibi might work if the county cops had bought into Hinman being murdered by the Black Panthers. But they hadn't, and they also matched Beausoleil's thumbprint to a bloody fingerprint that he'd missed cleaning up at

Hinman's house. Beausoleil changed his story; now he claimed that he and two female friends he wouldn't name arrived at Hinman's, found him badly hurt, and tried to treat his wounds. In gratitude, Hinman signed over the Fiat to them. Beausoleil guessed that he must have died after they left. Whiteley and Guenther didn't believe a word of it. Beausoleil was transferred to the L.A. County jail and booked for homicide.

Some one hundred miles south, Charlie was also being braced by the law. On their way to pick up Stephanie Schram's clothes from her sister's house in San Diego, she and Charlie were pulled over by a highway patrolman for an unspecified "mechanical violation." The officer asked to see Charlie's driver's license, and Charlie had to admit he didn't have one. He was issued a ticket at 6:15 P.M. on August 7 for operating a vehicle without a license, and signed the carbon with his real name rather than an alias.

Charlie and Schram drove on to San Diego. While she gathered her things, Charlie chatted with Schram's sister. They talked about the *White Album*, and Charlie explained that the Beatles were notifying the world of what was about to happen—a terrible race war where blacks slaughtered most whites, and the only survivors would take refuge in a bottomless desert pit. Very soon, Charlie promised, "People are going to be slaughtered, they'll be lying on their lawns dead." It took some time for Schram to pack, so that night she and Charlie stopped alongside the road on the way back to Spahn and slept in the delivery van.

Beausoleil called Spahn Ranch from the L.A. County jail. Charlie hadn't returned yet from San Diego with Stephanie Schram, so Linda Kasabian took the call. Beausoleil explained that he'd been arrested for murder—he stressed that Charlie should know that everything was okay and he was keeping quiet.

Charlie was due back anytime, and he would have to make the decision about what, if anything, to do for Beausoleil. Linda and some of the other women talked about possible responses. Even though he had never officially joined the Family, Beausoleil was still one of them. Everyone knew something about the Hinman murder though only Susan and Mary Brunner, who had been there, knew what had happened. Death was the same as life, no action was wrong, and so there was little concern for Hinman. Instead, the focus was how to free their friend. Someone remembered seeing a movie about copycat murders and a killer subsequently being freed from jail—maybe they could do something like that. This was only one suggestion in a meandering group discussion. Charlie would know what to do.

Housekeeper Winifred Chapman arrived at the Cielo house at 8 A.M. on Friday. She had a lot to do. Tate, Frykowski, and Folger didn't do much cleaning up after themselves. About 8:30, handyman Frank Guerrero began painting a room intended to serve as a nursery. He took the screens off the windows to keep them spatter-free.

Around 11 A.M., Polanski called Tate from London. She was concerned that he wouldn't be back in time to celebrate his birthday on the 18th, but Polanski promised he'd be home well before then. Tate told her husband that she had enrolled him in a class for new fathers. Two of Tate's friends came by to join her for lunch, and afterward she told another friend on the phone that there wouldn't be any gathering at Cielo that night.

Guerrero left about 1:30, stopping for the day so that the paint on the nursery walls had time to dry. Chapman noticed that there were smears on the front door, so she vigorously scrubbed it down with a mixture of water and vinegar.

Sometime during the late morning or early afternoon, Charlie and Schram arrived back at Spahn. He was immediately told about Beausoleil's arrest. Charlie knew he faced a serious problem. Beausoleil's call to the ranch was meant to reassure Charlie that he was keeping quiet, but the unspoken implication was that if Charlie didn't get him out, then Beausoleil might start talking. Charlie would then be implicated in the Hinman murder, and Beausoleil also knew about the shooting of Lotsapoppa. The Family was desperate to see Beausoleil freed, but no one wanted that more than Charlie. He had to act quickly. Bobby Beausoleil was not a patient man.

That afternoon, Sharon Tate took a nap in her bedroom at Cielo. Abigail Folger went out to buy a bicycle, and arranged for it to be delivered to the house before the end of the day. Jay Sebring called to say he'd be coming over. Even though she had decided not to wear herself out playing hostess that night, Tate didn't consider Sebring to be company. He was part of her family. Just as Tate got off the phone with Sebring, Chapman informed her boss that she was leaving for the day. Tate, always solicitous, suggested that she spend the night at Cielo to avoid riding a city bus in the summer heat, but Chapman politely refused.

Joe Vargas, a gardener tending the lawn at Cielo, told caretaker William Garretson to do some watering over the weekend. The hot weather was burning the grass.

About 4:30 two steamer trunks belonging to Roman Polanski were delivered. Tate was napping again, so Vargas signed for them and pushed them into a corner.

Folger had her regular appointment with a psychiatrist late in the afternoon. Frykowski went out to visit friends for a while. They both returned soon, and Sebring arrived around 6 P.M., joining Tate, Frykowski, and Folger in the main house. Garretson closed himself up in the guesthouse with Rudi Altobelli's Weimaraner dog. He still didn't feel well.

Charlie's instinct was to run. If Beausoleil sold him out to the county lawmen, Charlie needed to be underground somewhere far away, maybe the Northwest or Chicago or Indianapolis—he'd spent time in all of those places before. With no chance for a record deal there was no reason for Charlie to stick around L.A. anyway. He'd have to leave the Family behind—he would move faster without them. Wherever he ended up, after lying low for a while Charlie could recruit new followers. If anything was certain, it was that there would always be people looking for someone to tell them what to believe in and what to do. But Charlie had devoted more than two years to putting together the Family, screening recruits and winnowing out anyone with minds of their own or with nothing to contribute. There had been some defections but he still had a solid core group who, for the moment at least, would do what he told them. They thought he was Jesus, and they believed in him. Perhaps there was a way out of this situation that wouldn't require Charlie to go on the run and start all over.

So he mingled with his followers at Spahn, suggesting that he might leave them. He heard the response that he wanted—he couldn't go, they loved him, they were together as one and ready to do whatever was necessary. Everyone gathered around Charlie and he encouraged them to talk about what they could do for Beausoleil. One suggestion was launching an assault on the L.A. County Jail and breaking him out. The idea of copycat murders was also mentioned, and, though he didn't immediately say so, that gave Charlie the basis of a plan.

He'd hoped that police would think that the paw print and words "POLITICAL PIGGY" scrawled on Gary Hinman's walls with Hinman's own blood were proof that the Black Panthers committed the murder. If the cops and the media had made enough out of it, that might have initiated white reprisals, black retaliation, and then Helter Skelter—if not an apocalyptic race war, then at least local violence between the races, sufficient bloodshed to impress upon the Family that Charlie had the power to bring about cataclysmic events. But it didn't happen that way, perhaps because Hinman wasn't important enough. The concept was still valid. The victim or victims just had to be more prominent. And if apparent copycat murders could free Bobby Beausoleil, so much the better.

Charlie ordered Squeaky to give Mary Brunner and Sandy Good some of the stolen Family credit cards. He told the two women to go into town to Sears to pick up a few things—there were conflicting recollections about what they were supposed to bring back to the ranch. Charlie herded everyone else together and announced gravely that "Now is the time for Helter Skelter." He didn't add any details. The Family was instructed to leave him alone. Charlie had some planning to do.

Nobody at Cielo felt like cooking, so even though Tate was tired she went with Sebring, Frykowski, and Folger to a restaurant on Beverly Boulevard for a late dinner. A waitress remembered them leaving around 9:45. They were home by 10 or shortly after, when Folger's mother called and talked to her.

Around 11 P.M. Squeaky took a call from Sandy Good and had to give Charlie more bad news. Sandy and Mary had been arrested for using stolen credit cards. They'd had several with them, including three issued to a man who had died in a traffic accident. The cops had plenty of questions about where and how they had gotten them. Sandy said that she and Mary were locked up in the Sybil Brand Institute, L.A.'s jail for women.

Each was being held on $600 bail, far more cash than the Family had on hand at Spahn.

The last thing Charlie needed was for Mary or Sandy to admit something to the cops and give them another reason to come sniffing around the ranch. The event he was about to orchestrate now involved getting bail money in addition to copycat murders intended to free Bobby and precipitate some form of Helter Skelter. Events were spiraling out of control, and Charlie was determined to take control back. There was no time to lose; it would happen tonight.

Charlie went to find Tex Watson. Besides Charlie, Tex was the only one who'd previously been to the house on Cielo.

CHAPTER THIRTEEN

Tate

Charlie Manson imbued two core beliefs in his followers—that he must be obeyed and that, with the exception of Charlie, the members of the Family were the most special people on earth. They took these teachings to heart. Like Charlie, they developed senses of entitlement, bolstered by Charlie's constant reminders that all things were the same—love and hate, sanctity and sin, life and death. The Family was meant to rule the earth after Helter Skelter. It was ordained by the Beatles and the Bible through Charlie. They would reign benevolently, and the world would become a far better place. So they should, and would, do whatever was necessary to bring about that glorious era, and if that meant copycat killings to save Beausoleil, one of their own, then a few deaths—not murders, because the spirit was what counted and you didn't kill anyone's spirit, you just sent it on to a different place—were acceptable sacrifices to the eventual greater good.

As Charlie prepared to talk to Tex around 11:30 on Friday night, August 8, the Family's discussion of copycat killings to save Bobby Beausoleil lent itself to Charlie's own larger vision. It was good that they weren't shrinking from slaughter, though of course it was much easier to talk about than to actually carry out. But if it did happen, and if this time the victims were famous, then some form of racial clash might be sparked and Charlie would have the Helter Skelter he'd promised his followers. Maybe it would be confined to parts of L.A. instead of spreading across the nation, but he could always think of some explanation to justify that. Plus—this was the part that had to remain unspoken, since it was critical that the Family believed that all of Charlie's statements and acts were selfless—if Beausoleil was out of jail he wouldn't implicate Charlie in the murder of Gary Hinman or the shooting of Lotsapoppa. And if the copycat killings didn't free Beausoleil but did precipitate racial violence, the cops would be too busy putting down riots to investigate the deaths of a couple of nobodies.

Charlie had to point his followers to the right victims to serve his own purposes, and do it in a way that left them apparently responsible for all of it. If something went wrong, Charlie could say that it was completely their doing, not his. He had to make rapid-fire decisions, each part of a complex overall planning process, and on this night Charlie demonstrated dazzling mastery of individual psychology and group dynamics. It began with Tex Watson.

Because within the Family women served men, if murder was to be done, a man had to be in charge. Charlie didn't have many candidates. Only Tex had all the necessary attributes. He was big and tough, a rawboned former high school athlete who was still in decent physical shape despite his nonstop use of drugs. Tex yearned to be important; in the past weeks he'd acted bumpier and more aggressive, ordering other Family members around and giving the impression that he was Charlie's unofficial second-in-command. Above all, he owed Charlie, and now Charlie began their conversation by reminding Tex of that. Not too long ago, Charlie said, Tex screwed up a drug deal and put the whole Family in jeopardy. Lotsapoppa was about to round up his Black Panther brothers, come out to Spahn and kill everybody, all because of Tex Watson. Charlie had to step in. Bobby Beausoleil had to knock off Gary Hinman because Hinman was going to call the cops on the Family. Bobby made that sacrifice for his friends, including Tex. Now the Family had decided that some of them should go out tonight and commit copycat killings to rescue Bobby. On tonight's mission somebody had to be the leader, the one who told the others what to do and how to do it. Was Tex that leader? Did he have it in him? Would he assume this responsibility? Charlie and Bobby had both selflessly killed for Tex. Wasn't he obligated to reciprocate for Bobby?

Tex had taken acid during the day, and also sniffed some Methedrine that he and Susan Atkins had secretly stashed. The chemicals in his sys-

1

The children of Charlie and Nancy Maddox. *Clockwise from the lower left* they are Luther, Aileene, Glenna (with glasses), and Ada Kathleen, the mother of Charles Manson.

2

Left to right: Jo Ann Thomas, Manson's cousin; Nancy Maddox, his maternal grandmother; and Charles, age about five.

Manson just before his first day of elementary school. It would prove to be an inauspicious start to his abbreviated formal education.

Charles Manson on the day of his sentencing to Boys Town. Manson was sent there because he convinced a gullible judge that he was Catholic. He ran away after only four days.

Nineteen-year-old Charles Manson at a Halloween party. Only months after being released from reform school, he already had a reputation as a bad character.

At age twenty, Charles Manson married teenager Rosalie Willis. The marriage would last only two years.

Mary Brunner, the first follower recruited by Charles Manson. They met when she was working as a librarian at UC Berkeley.

The Watts riots in August 1965 exacerbated the racial tension in Los Angeles, which Manson used to help convince his followers that a racial war in America was inevitable.

Gregg Jakobson (*left*) and Dennis Wilson. Manson used his friendship with Wilson to further his goal of becoming a bigger musical star than the Beatles.

The Manson Family (a name coined by Jakobson) on a garbage run behind a Los Angeles supermarket. *Left to right:* Lynne "Squeaky" Fromme, Sandra Good, Mary Brunner, and Ruth Ann Moorehouse.

Spahn Ranch. With its rolling hills and old movie and TV sets, the ranch became the Family's home and sanctuary.

Family members at Spahn. *Left to right:* Jennifer Gentry, Catherine "Gypsy" Share, Sue Bartlett, Danny DeCarlo (facing away from the camera), Sandra Good, Squeaky Fromme, Chuck Lovett, and Ruth Ann Moorehouse.

Little Paul Watkins. A good-looking, smooth-talking young man, he became Manson's chief procurer and self-styled second-in-command. He would leave Manson to follow prospector Paul Crockett in Death Valley.

Terry Melcher, the wunderkind record producer on whom Manson eventually pinned all his hopes for superstardom. Melcher and his girlfriend Candice Bergen lived at the Cielo Drive house before Roman Polanski and Sharon Tate.

Roman Polanski and Sharon Tate at their wedding in London in January 1968.

The Cielo Drive house in Benedict Canyon.

Charles "Tex" Watson, seen here after his extradition from Texas to California. He did most of the killing at Cielo Drive.

Caretaker William Garretson survived the Cielo Drive murders because Patricia Krenwinkel lied to Tex Watson about checking the cottage in which he was hiding. Initially, Garretson was the LAPD's chief suspect in the killings.

The LaBianca residence in Los Feliz. Leno and Rosemary LaBianca were killed there on the night after the Cielo Drive murders.

Left to right: Susan Atkins, Patricia Krenwinkel, and Leslie Van Houten on their way to court on August 11, 1970. Each woman gouged an X onto her forehead in imitation of Manson, who had previously carved an X onto his.

Manson is led from court after deferring a plea to the murder charges against him. He is wearing the buckskin outfit made for him by Family women.

Key witness Ronnie Howard waits to testify that Susan Atkins confessed the Tate murders to her in jail.

Vincent Bugliosi, the ambitious, hard-charging prosecutor whose reputation was made in the Tate-LaBianca murder trial. *Helter Skelter,* the account of the trial that he would later write with Curt Gentry, became the best-selling true-crime book of all time.

The defense team. *Left to right:* Daye Shinn, Irving Kanarek, Paul Fitzgerald, and Ronald Hughes. Kanarek's courtroom tactics were so annoying that even Manson complained to the judge about them.

Former Family member Linda Kasabian, the star witness for the prosecution.

Throughout the trial, Family women would sit or kneel on the sidewalk outside the courthouse and try to win sympathy for Manson from passersby. Some people, feeling sorry for them, would bring them cookies and other snacks.

Charles Manson meets with the press during a break in the trial.

A recent photo of Manson.

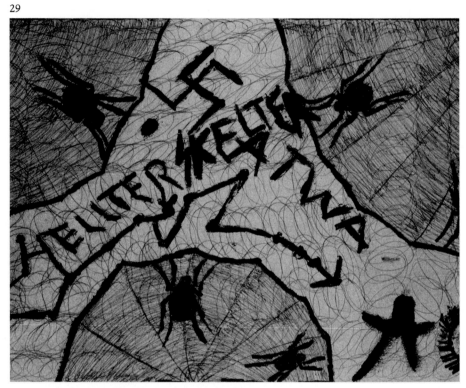

A sample of Manson's prison artwork. He sent this drawing to a regular correspondent around 2009.

tem combined with his ambition to lead within the Family as Charlie's chief lieutenant. Tex agreed that he would lead the copycat killers—it was his right. That left the question of who would die, and Charlie had some helpful thoughts on that. Of course, these killings were the Family's decision, not his, but if they were determined to go out and commit them, then of course they had certain people in mind, *important* people, celebrities whose deaths would command headlines and get maximum publicity. That way the police couldn't help but believe Hinman's killers were still out there committing murders while Beausoleil was in custody. If Tex targeted the right victims, Bobby would be sprung almost immediately.

Falling back on Dale Carnegie (*"Let the other fellow feel that the idea is his"*), Charlie guided Tex to the destination. He wondered if Tex might be thinking of that place where Terry Melcher used to live. Melcher didn't live there anymore, but whoever did had to be rich and famous, too; those were the only kind of people who could afford *that* place. Tex knew how to get there from Spahn. So Tex and a few of the women could go to Cielo and kill everybody there, then mark the place up with words written on the walls in blood just as Beausoleil did at Gary Hinman's. Tex said that he didn't think he could remember what words to write. Charlie told him not to worry—one of the women going with him would know. Then they talked about what to bring: rope to tie people with and of course knives, dark clothes to wear on the way and clean ones to put on afterward. Charlie gave Tex the .22 Buntline, cautioning that it would be best just to use the knives if possible and save shooting as a last resort. And Tex would need bolt cutters for the phone lines. There was an electronic gate at the entrance to the property—Tex remembered it, didn't he?— and maybe when you pushed the button to open it an alarm went off in the house, so Tex and the others should climb the fence instead. Charlie could not have been more supportive. He manipulated Tex so neatly that later on, when Tex claimed that Charlie ordered him to commit the murders and Charlie swore that they were Tex's and the Family's idea, not his, both of them were telling a version of the truth.

William Garretson felt hungry, but there was no food in the Cielo guesthouse. He walked down the steep hill and hitched a ride to Sunset Strip, where he purchased cigarettes and a TV dinner. Then he hitched back to Cielo, arriving sometime after 10 P.M. The lights were on in the main house as usual, but there were only three cars parked outside—a Porsche belonging to Jay Sebring, Abigail Folger's Firebird, and a rented Camaro that Sharon Tate was driving. That meant it wasn't one of the tenants' big party nights. Garretson didn't really know much about them. He just wanted to do his assigned job of keeping an eye on the property and caring for Altobelli's dogs. Garretson went back inside the guest cottage. He heated his TV dinner and settled in for a quiet night.

With Tex primed, it was time for Charlie to pick the women who would go with him. Ruth Ann Moorehouse would later speculate that Charlie "sent out the expendables," but each of the three was selected because she had something specific to contribute. Charlie took them aside one by one—Susan, who had been with Beausoleil at Hinman's house and knew what had been written on the walls there; Pat, whose shyness and lack of social skills led most people to believe she was cold and unfeeling; and Linda Kasabian, who had a valid driver's license. Charlie knew that Susan was capable of anything, that Pat believed she had no option other than to obey him in all things, and that Linda wanted to impress the rest of the Family. Charlie's instructions to each of the women were the same: Dress in dark clothes, get a change of clothes and your knife, then go with Tex and do exactly what he tells you. They scurried off to obey.

Eighteen-year-old Steve Parent had recently graduated from high school and wanted to attend junior college in the fall. To earn tuition money he juggled two jobs, full-time work as a plumbing company delivery boy and occasional evening shifts as a salesman at a stereo shop. A few weeks earlier Parent had picked up William Garretson hitchhiking and driven him to Cielo. Garretson appreciated the ride and told Parent to drop by anytime and visit—he lived in the back in a guesthouse. That gave Parent the impression that Garretson probably had a lot of money.

On Friday the 8th, Parent decided to sell his AM/FM clock radio to raise a few more dollars for school. He remembered the guy he'd given a ride to a while back. Parent, out for the evening in his parents' white

Rambler, decided to drive to Cielo and see if his passenger wanted to buy the clock radio. If the guy was loaded, he might be prone to making impulse purchases. Parent knew all about those from his sales stints at the stereo shop. It was worth a try—even if he didn't make a sale at Cielo, Parent could drive away and have a nice rest of the night hanging out with friends.

Tex and Susan got ready in an additional way that hadn't been suggested by Charlie. They sneaked off to their Meth stash and snorted some. As always, the drug made them edgier and more aggressive—exactly the effect they wanted.

Pat couldn't find her knife. It wouldn't do to keep everyone else waiting while she continued looking for it, so she rejoined Charlie, Tex, Susan, and Linda without it.

Charlie told Tex to take ranch hand Johnny Swartz's yellow 1959 Ford. Tex fetched the car and the girls piled in. Even though Linda was the only one with a valid driver's license, Tex stayed behind the wheel. Linda sat with him in front. Susan and Pat were in the back. As the car was about to pull away Charlie called out to Susan, "Do something witchy," a reference to the words "POLITICAL PIGGY" written in blood at Gary Hinman's. Despite the talk that day about copycat murders, as Tex drove the old Ford out of the ranch's front gate the three women didn't know yet that they were going to kill anyone. They'd been ordered to take their knives, but there was nothing new about that. Since Charlie had first mentioned Helter Skelter, Family members usually went around armed so that they could defend themselves in case of attack.

Tex didn't talk as he drove, and so the women whispered to each other about the purpose of this expedition—maybe they were going to creepy-crawl again and steal things. A week earlier, Pat had been sent out with Tex to steal a dune buggy off of a car lot. Some of the other women, not Pat or Susan or Linda, had creepy-crawled and come back with filched items. So it was probably going to be something like that. The women stopped whispering and settled back in their seats, wondering where they were going. Tex hadn't told them and they didn't ask.

• • •

At about 11:45 P.M., William Garretson was surprised by a knock on his door. Steve Parent had driven up to Cielo, opened the electronic gate by pushing the outside button, and pulled his Rambler onto the long driveway. Parent reminded Garretson about picking him up and showed him the clock radio. Garretson wasn't really interested in buying it, but he politely allowed Parent to plug it in, set it for the current time, and demonstrate how well the radio worked.

Tex was sure that he knew the best route from Spahn to Cielo, but he took some wrong turns and got lost. They ended up in Beverly Hills and had to take Sunset Boulevard toward Benedict Canyon.

Garretson told Parent that he didn't want the clock radio, and by way of consolation offered the eighteen-year-old a beer. Parent sipped it and asked if he could use Garretson's phone. He called a friend who said that he was having trouble setting up a stereo system—could Steve come over and give him a hand? Parent said he would, and chatted with Garretson as he finished his beer. Then he unplugged the clock radio, which indicated the time was 12:15.

Tex guided the Ford up steep Cielo Drive, passing houses scattered at short intervals along the way. Besides its narrow width and tight curves, there was the additional pressure of keeping a wary eye for deer that ventured out to graze after dark. At the very top of the hill Tex stopped in front of the closed electronic gate and told the women to wait. From that vantage point, none of them could actually see the house or the guest cottage behind it. Grabbing the bolt cutters as Charlie had instructed, Tex nimbly climbed a telephone pole and snipped the wires connecting to the main house and guest cottage. Then he backed the car down the hill, a tricky maneuver he managed without a hitch, and led the women back up on foot. Tex tucked the .22 in his pants and slung a coil of three-ply white rope over his shoulder.

Garretson walked Parent out to the Rambler. As they said good night, Altobelli's Weimaraner began to bark. Garretson told Parent that it was the dog's "people bark," meaning that humans were walking around the property. There seemed to be no reason for alarm; maybe somebody was just leaving the main house. Garretson said goodbye and went back inside the guest cottage.

Tex whispered instructions for the women to follow him climbing up over the fence. There was an incline on the right side of the road, so it wasn't especially difficult. Once they were inside, Tex said in a matter-of-fact tone that they were going into this big house where Terry Melcher had lived, and they were going to kill everybody inside. The women didn't recoil; they hadn't expected to kill anyone, but at that point, Pat remembered more than forty years later, "we were little kitty cats who were mentally gone." Charlie had commanded them to do what Tex said. They would.

Parent got into the Rambler and began slowly moving down the long, curving driveway toward the main gate. It was closed, so he had to stop and roll down his window to push the button that would open it.

Tex heard the car approaching, and hissed to the women that they should jump into the bushes and lie down. He pulled the .22 out of his pants with his right hand and grasped a knife with his left. Parent flinched as Tex emerged from the shadows at his open car window. He blurted, "Please, please don't hurt me. I'm your friend. I won't tell." Tex slashed at him with the knife—Parent was cut across his left arm. Then Tex either ignored or forgot Charlie's instructions to use the Buntline only as a last resort. He shot the teenager four times at point-blank range. Parent fell dead across the front seat of the car.

A hundred yards away at the next house down the Cielo Drive slope, Mrs. Seymour Kott sat up in bed, awakened by what she thought might be "three or four gunshots." But she didn't hear anything more, so she went back to sleep. A private security patrol officer, sitting in his car parked on a street nearby, also thought he heard shots. Since he couldn't tell specifically which direction they came from—area acoustics were baffling—he called in a report to the West Los Angeles Division of the L.A. Police

Department. The officer who took the call commented, "I hope we don't have a murder," but didn't send out anyone to investigate.

Tex thought for a moment about how the flashes from the gunshots reflected off Parent's glasses, then reached inside the open driver's side window and shifted the Rambler into neutral. He pushed it a short way back down the driveway and left the car parked there. Tex whispered for the women to come out of the bushes and go with him to the main house. They eased their way down the driveway, and as they negotiated the curve they could see the main house, and the pretty Christmas lights sparkling on the fence outside.

The peculiar acoustics of the canyon swallowed the sound of the gunfire for those inside the main house. Abigail Folger was reading a book in the guest bedroom of the main house. Voytek Frykowski was asleep on the couch in the living room. In the master bedroom, Sharon Tate and Jay Sebring perched on the bed, talking quietly. Folger wore a white nightgown. Tate was in her underwear, which was often her home attire during very hot weather. She had a negligee tossed over her shoulders. Both men were fully clothed.

Out in the guest cottage Garretson didn't hear gunfire either. He put on some music, watched TV, and began writing letters. Garretson also tried to make a phone call, but even though Parent had just used the phone, now for some reason the line was dead.

As the four Family members neared the main house, Tex told Linda to go to the back and see if there might be an unlocked door or window. Linda was hesitant, but she walked around the house out of Tex's sight and stayed there for a few moments. Then she returned and told him that everything was shut tight, which wasn't true. The freshly painted nursery windows were still cracked open and their screens hadn't been snapped back in place. But in front of the house, just to the side of the front door, a window into the entry hall was open behind a screen. Tex quietly cut a long horizontal slit in the screen, pulled the screen loose, then pushed up the window. He told Linda to go back down to the gate and keep watch—someone might have heard the shots that killed Steve Parent. Then Tex climbed through the window and motioned for Susan and Pat to follow him.

Linda crept back down the driveway, passing the Rambler with the teenager's body in the front seat. Though she later recalled that her mind had gone blank, she kept a lookout as Tex had ordered.

Inside the main house, Tex, Susan, and Pat crept down the entry hall into the living room. They saw Voytek Frykowski sleeping on the couch. Tex whispered to Susan to go check the rest of the house to see who else was there. Frykowski, roused by the soft sound of Tex's voice, muttered, "What time is it," and then, "Who are you? What do you want?" Tex kicked him in the head, hard, before replying, "I'm the devil and I'm here to do the devil's business." Susan had frozen in place when Frykowski spoke. Now Tex sent her on her way with an impatient jerk of his head toward the hallway. Dazed, Frykowski tried to say something else, but Tex hissed, "Another word and you're dead."

Pat remembered she had not brought a knife. While Susan explored and Tex hovered over the dazed Frykowski, Pat went down the driveway to where Linda stood guard. She borrowed Linda's knife and returned to Tex in the living room.

Susan walked down the hall and looked through an open door into the guest bedroom. Abigail Folger glanced up from her book and smiled. She wasn't shocked to see a stranger in the house. Tate and Polanski regularly welcomed all-hours guests. This woman seemed like one more. Susan smiled and gave a little finger wave. Folger waved back and resumed reading. Further down the hall, Susan peered into the main bedroom and saw Sharon Tate and Jay Sebring talking. They apparently were in deep conversation; neither noticed her. Susan made her way back to the living room, passing Folger's room again, waving to her for a second time. When she rejoined Tex, she quietly told him that there were three other people inside. Tex told her to bring them to him.

Susan went first to the guest bedroom, where she brandished her knife at Folger and ordered her to go into the living room. Pat held her there at knifepoint while Susan went to the main bedroom for Tate and Sebring. She told them, "Come with me. Don't say a word or you're dead." They meekly got up from the bed and walked ahead of her down the hall. When they reached the living room Tate could see Tex and Pat waiting there. She hesitated, and Tex roughly grasped her arm and dragged her forward.

Frykowski reeled on the couch, still stunned from being kicked in the head. Tex had the three-ply rope, but he told Susan to tie Frykowski's hands behind him with a towel. She had trouble knotting the thick towel, but did the best that she could. Tex used the rope to tie Sebring's hands. Sebring complained that Tex was being too rough, and Tex warned him, "One more word and you're dead." Frykowski gasped, "He means it." Tex looped more rope around Sebring's neck and then flipped the other end up over a beam in the ceiling. Tex then tied the rope around Tate's neck. Tate began crying, and Tex snarled at her to shut up. Sebring protested, "Can't you see that she's pregnant?" and Tex shot him in the abdomen. Sebring collapsed on the living room rug. Tate screamed, then continued sobbing.

Tex looked around the living room and announced, "I want all the money you've got here." Folger said that she had money in her room. Susan marched her there and Folger removed some bills from her pocketbook. Susan gave Tex the money—it was about $70. Disgusted, Tex said, "You mean that's all you've got?" Tate said that they didn't have any money in the house, but if they had time they could get some. Tex thought she might be stalling, hopeful that help was somehow on the way. He said, "You know I'm not kidding," and Tate said that she knew.

Tex was frustrated. Charlie told him to bring back money; they'd come to this house because rich people lived there, and now Tate was telling him that they didn't have any. It made Tex furious, and just then Jay Sebring groaned as he lay on the floor. Tex crouched over him and began stabbing him, slamming the knife into Sebring again and again until he finally lay still enough to convince Tex that he was dead. Tate and Folger screamed during the entire assault. When Tex was finally finished and stood up, his knife dripping blood, one of the women asked plaintively, "What are you going to do with us?" although it was obvious. Tex's reply was blunt: "You're all going to die."

Folger and Tate began begging for their lives. Ever since Tex had kicked him into semiconsciousness, Voytek Frykowski had slumped on the couch. But hearing his death sentence pronounced, he suddenly jerked upright and began tugging his hands free from the towel Susan had clumsily knotted around his wrists. Tex yelled to Susan, "Kill him," and she tried, but Frykowski got his hands loose and grappled with her, the two of them rolling around on the floor, Frykowski wrapping his hands in Susan's long hair and Susan blindly stabbing with her knife, sinking the blade mostly into Frykowski's legs. He screamed as he struggled. At some point Susan lost her knife.

Out near the gate, Linda heard Frykowski's screams clearly. Instinctively, she began walking back toward the main house, stopping just outside.

While Pat held Folger at knifepoint and Tate watched helplessly, Tex tried to help Susan finish off Frykowski. He fired a couple shots into him and battered at his head with the grip of the Buntline. Frykowski still managed to struggle to his feet and stumble out onto the lawn, with Tex in hot pursuit. Frykowski went down and Tex leaped on him, pounding and stabbing until he was still. Just steps away, Linda looked on in horror. She was close enough to the living room to see Susan, and she shouted, "Please make it stop, people are coming," a lie but the only thing she could think of. Susan said that there was nothing she could do. Linda ran back down the driveway, climbed over the fence, and stopped down the hill where Tex had parked Johnny Swartz's yellow '59 Ford.

Back at the Cielo main house Folger broke away, running out on the lawn, too. Pat raced after her and tackled her. Pat stabbed Folger several times, trying to kill her and unsure of whether she had. Tex, certain that he'd finished off Frykowski, was standing nearby, so Pat called him over and said she wasn't sure whether or not Folger was dead. Tex said he would make sure; meanwhile, Pat was to go to "the back house"—he pointed in the direction of the guest cottage—and kill whoever was there.

Pat was shaking, equally afraid to follow Tex's order and to disobey. She compromised by walking down the back alley between the main house and guest cottage until she was out of Tex's sight. Then she waited for a few moments and returned. She told Tex that she had looked in a window and there was no one in "the back house." He believed her, so William Garretson lived.

Tex had stabbed Folger several more times; he wrote later that she was, in fact, alive when he reached her, and that she muttered, "I give up, you've got me," just before he delivered the fatal blow. With Folger and Frykowski dead on the lawn, and Jay Sebring lifeless on the living room floor, only Sharon Tate remained. Susan was guarding her beside the sofa. Tex and Pat returned to the living room and Tate began pleading—not for her own life, but for her unborn child's. They could take her with them, Tate begged, and kill her after the baby was born. But Charlie hadn't said anything about postponing murders. He wanted maximum publicity right away. Susan held Tate while Tex stabbed her. Sharon Tate sobbed for her mother as she died.

When it was over, Tex and Susan and Pat surveyed the scene. Was it sufficiently gruesome? The nylon rope was knotted around Sebring's and Tate's necks, looped up over the ceiling beam between them. Out on the lawn, Frykowski's face was mutilated almost beyond recognition, and Folger's once white nightgown was saturated with gore. They felt that ought to be enough. Tex thought they'd been careful not to leave fingerprints or any other clues. He took Folger's $70 and prepared to lead Susan and Pat out of the house. There were other valuables there for the taking— Sebring wore an expensive watch and there was a little cash by the side of Tate's bed—but in the aftermath of slaughter they wanted to leave. Just before they did, Tex remembered that Charlie told them to write something witchy in blood, something that would appear to be proof that the people who'd killed Gary Hinman were still at large. Tex told Susan to do it. She didn't want to use her bare hand, so she dipped a towel in Tate's blood and carefully wrote "PIG" on the outside of the front door.

Tex, Susan, and Pat were all dripping with blood. Their clothes were bloody, and Tex had some on his hands. He got careless on the way out; not feeling like scaling the fence again, he pressed the button to open the gate with his bloody index finger. The three of them walked through the Cielo gate and down the hill to the yellow Ford where Linda waited.

There had been little conversation in the car as the four drove to Cielo, but on the way back to Spahn everyone talked at once. Susan told Tex that she'd lost her knife back at the house and he shouted angrily at her. Pat complained that her hand ached—while stabbing Folger, her knife frequently struck bone, and the impact hurt her hand. All of them were angry with Linda for fleeing the scene. As he drove down Benedict Canyon Drive, Tex squirmed out of his bloody clothes and into fresh ones while Linda held the wheel. Susan and Pat removed their gory garments, too, and put on the clean clothes they'd left in the car during the murders. Linda rolled all the discarded clothes into a bundle and, on Tex's order, tossed them out of the car and down the steep slope by the side of the road. A little further along he had her throw out the knives, too, and then the .22 Buntline. Before they tossed it, they noticed that parts of the handle had broken off, undoubtedly when Tex bashed Frykowski with it. But they decided not to go back to Cielo to retrieve the handle fragments and Susan's knife.

After a few miles, Tex steered off Benedict Canyon onto Portola Drive, a residential side street. He parked by the curb of a house at 9870 where a hose stretched out into the yard. Tex turned on the water tap and he, Susan, and Pat clustered around the hose, splashing water on their hands and faces to rinse away splatters of blood. It was about 1 A.M. They tried to be quiet, but the running water and their hushed chatter roused Rudolf Weber, who hurried outside to see who was in his yard at such a late hour. Tex explained that they were out walking and wanted a drink, but the parked Ford was right behind him and Weber didn't believe it. As Weber stalked toward them, Tex, Susan, and Pat jumped back in the car. Weber tried to reach in through the open driver's side window to rip the key from the ignition, but Tex was too quick. The car sped away, but not before Weber noted its license number—GYY 435.

When they arrived back at the entrance to Spahn Ranch, Charlie was waiting with Family member Nancy Pitman. His first question was why they were back so soon. Tex told him that it had gotten messy, but everybody at Cielo was dead. Susan, eager as always for praise, bragged to Charlie that she'd killed for him, and Charlie replied that she'd done it for herself. Then Charlie wanted to know how much money they'd gotten, and was angry that the take was just $70. They should have gone into every house on Cielo, he snarled. Charlie asked how they'd left the murder site looking—was it just like Gary Hinman's house? Did they write witchy words? The answers didn't satisfy him. Brusquely, he asked if any of them felt remorse. When they assured him that they didn't, Charlie told them to wipe off the gobbets of blood that were smeared on the inside and outside of the car. When that was done, Charlie got into the Ford and drove back to Cielo.

Charlie entered the house and wiped surfaces to eliminate stray fingerprints. He moved some things around, hauling the two steamer trunks that had been delivered earlier in the day out into the hall, and tossed a towel over Jay Sebring's head. He placed in plain sight a pair of glasses he found somewhere. There was a large American flag on one side of the living room. Charlie draped it theatrically over the sofa near Sharon Tate's crumpled, bloody body. The flag prominently displayed next to a pregnant woman's corpse would surely shock investigators and get lots of media mention. Charlie was so preoccupied with perfectly setting the scene of the slaughter that he didn't comb the house for cash, credit cards, or other valuables. He also didn't check the guest cottage. When he felt that everything in the main house looked just right, he returned to Spahn and went to bed. Dawn wasn't far away.

A few minutes before 5 A.M., the *Los Angeles Times* delivery boy shoved a newspaper into the mailbox outside the gate at Cielo. He noticed a cut wire dangling down from the telephone pole. Around 7:30 Seymour Kott, the closest neighbor down the hill, saw the cut wire, too, as he went out to pick up his paper.

Winifred Chapman arrived for work as usual shortly after 8 A.M. She saw the dangling wire and thought that it might be a downed power line. But the gate opened when she pushed the button outside the fence, so she walked up the driveway, passing the white Rambler without looking inside. Her employers had overnight guests all the time and they sometimes parked haphazardly. Instead of walking around the house to the main entrance past the lawn, Chapman entered the house through a servant's entrance in the back. The first thing she noticed was that the steamer trunks were in a different place, and then she saw blood, at first some smears on the trunks and then pools of it seemingly everywhere. Chapman looked into the living room, over the top of the couch. The front door was open, and through it she could see a body on the lawn.

She fled down the driveway. As she ran past the Rambler she looked inside and saw another body. Neighbors heard her screaming "Murder, death, bodies, blood!" and called the police.

Two one-man patrol car units responded to a Code 2 "possible homicide" call at 9:14. A neighbor listed the people he believed lived at the hilltop house for Officer Jerry Joe DeRosa—movie director Roman Polanski and his wife, two of their friends, the property owner, Rudi Altobelli, but he was away on a trip, and a kid named William Garretson who was acting as caretaker. Mrs. Polanski was an actress named Sharon Tate.

Chapman showed DeRosa how to open the front gate; DeRosa saw the body in the Rambler but waited to go further down the driveway until fellow officer William Whisenhunt joined him. Weapons ready—DeRosa had a rifle, Whisenhunt carried a shotgun—they cautiously approached the house. As they inspected the other cars, a third cop, Robert Burbridge, arrived. The three crossed to the lawn and saw two bodies there. A window screen had been slit—that was apparently how the killer or killers entered the house. But the officers saw another cracked window without a screen, one that opened into the nursery. They raised that window and clambered inside. In what appeared to be the living room they found two more butchered bodies, a man and a woman. The corpses were tethered by nooses around their necks; the three-ply white nylon rope connecting them had been looped over a beam in the ceiling. Massive puddles of blood and smears of gore were everywhere.

There were no other bodies in the house, but the helpful neighbor had mentioned a guesthouse. As the officers eased up to the door of the cottage, they heard a dog bark and a male voice hissing, "Shhh, be quiet." The cops kicked in the door and Altobelli's Weimaraner attacked. Whisenhunt slammed the door on the dog's head to trap it, and Garretson called the animal off. To the police, the nineteen-year-old seemed incoherent, perhaps from drugs. Garretson was hauled outside and marched past the bodies on the lawn. Abigail Folger was so mutilated and covered with blood that Garretson identified her as Winifred Chapman. He said Voytek Frykowski was Roman Polanski's younger brother. Garretson swore to the officers that he'd been closed up in the guest cottage all night. He hadn't seen or heard anything. They didn't believe him—the guest cottage wasn't that far from the main house, maybe a hundred feet. The officers read Garretson his rights and arrested him for murder. DeRosa pushed him down the driveway past the Rambler—Garretson said he didn't recognize the body in it—and to the closed gate. DeRosa pushed the button with his finger, wiping away the bloody fingerprint carelessly left there by Tex Watson just hours earlier. DeRosa then called in to report five homicides and a suspect in custody at the Cielo address. Print reporters and TV crews in the city routinely listened to police band radio, and this announcement of a mass murder roused them into immediate action. Within minutes, members of the media began arriving at the scene, eventually so many that their cars and mobile production trucks lined the narrow road all the way to the bottom of the steep hill.

While the media clamored for information, more officers and LAPD investigative personnel streamed through the gate and into the house. They found various bits of possible evidence—the eyeglasses, scattered fingerprints, three pieces of a broken gun grip. There were bloody footprints all over the house, but some of these had been tracked in by the police. Forensic chemist Joe Granado took forty-five blood samples from various drying pools but missed many more.

At noon William Tennant, Polanski's agent, arrived and identified everyone except the body in the Rambler. A police sergeant finally made a statement to the media hovering just outside the gate: "It's like a battlefield up there." The families of the four identified victims were notified. Steve Parent's mother and father were left to spend the day wondering why their always reliable son hadn't come home the night before or even bothered to call to say where he was. Amid the hubbub at the main house no one thought to check the plates on the Rambler.

The first wire bulletins flashed across the country: "Five Slain in Bel Air."

Homicide detectives were assigned to the case, and the first of them arrived in the early afternoon. Sgt. Michael McGann noticed the word "PIG" scrawled in blood on the lower panel of the front door. The bodies had been left in place. McGann had been working homicide for five years, but his initial reaction was, "This [is] the worst." Detective Danny Galindo was placed in charge of the evidence, preserving each item. Marijuana was found in Jay Sebring's car, along with a gram of cocaine. A sex manual written in Chinese turned up in one of the bedrooms. A reel of film was discovered in the attic; when detectives viewed it back at the station it showed Polanski and Tate having sex. The film was discreetly returned to Polanski.

Susan Atkins's lost buck knife was found under a sofa cushion. But of most immediate interest to investigators was what Galindo later described as "a goodly amount of narcotics" out in the open throughout the house. About seven grams of marijuana were found in a plastic baggie in a living room cabinet. Thirty grams of hashish were on the guest bedroom nightstand, as were ten capsules of the psychedelic drug MDA. Investigators found marijuana residue in an ashtray by Tate's bed, a joint on a desk by the front door, and two more in the guesthouse. Even by the standards of the day it was a lot; if the teenage caretaker didn't turn out to be the killer, McGann thought the carnage could very likely have resulted from some drug connection gone wrong. But Garretson remained the prime suspect. McGann's regular partner was on vacation, so Sgt. Jess Buckles was assigned to work with him on the case. Lt. Robert Helder, LAPD's supervisor of investigations, was in overall command. In all they were a very senior group—the murder of a movie star was going to get a lot of media attention, and Chief Ed Davis wanted the case brought to a swift, satisfactory conclusion.

Leaks to the media were inevitable. By early afternoon newscasts revealed four victims' identities. The public learned that Voytek Frykowski, Abigail Folger, and Jay Sebring were dead, and under almost any other circumstances TV, radio, and print coverage of the murders would have focused on the slayings of a coffee fortune heiress and the most famous hairdresser in America, with Frykowski getting only a mention. But from the first, attention focused on the bloody demise of a movie star. In death Sharon Tate instantly attained star status. From the afternoon of August 9 on, the slaughter at Cielo would simply be known as the "Tate murders."

Charlie slept late, so he missed the first TV bulletins. But many other Family members gathered to watch, and Susan expressed particular glee in being part of something so newsworthy. There was no official announcement or explanation to those who weren't there; instead, there were prideful, partial boasts on the parts of Susan and Tex, who wanted it known among their peers that they'd been selected to carry out a critical task and had come through for Charlie. The details were garbled; all most of them knew for certain was that five people had died. In the initial adrenaline rush of having made news, of having done something so spectacularly gruesome that it was all the TV talking heads could speculate about—*who could have done such an awful thing, and why?*—the Family members failed to notice that none of the newscasts mentioned possible Black Panther involvement or any possible connection between these slayings and Hinman's murder. The stories were limited to the horrific murder of an actress and others.

William Garretson was questioned at the West Los Angeles jail. His responses still didn't seem to make much sense. The teenager was assigned a lawyer and moved to LAPD headquarters at Parker Center. His story remained the same: He didn't know much about the people who lived in the main house. Last night he had a visitor, a kid named Steve Parent, who tried to sell him a clock radio, but he wasn't interested. He spent the night closed up in the guest cottage listening to music and writing letters. He didn't hear or see anything.

Because Garretson hadn't identified Parent at the scene, the police didn't link his Cielo visit to sell the clock radio with the body found in the Rambler. But an enterprising reporter waiting outside the Cielo gates wrote down the car's license number and checked it with a source at the Department of Motor Vehicles. The car was registered to Wilfred and Juanita Parent in the suburb of El Monte. They weren't home when the reporter arrived in late afternoon, but he checked with neighbors and learned the name of their priest. The priest told the journalist all about Steve, who apparently knew everything about stereos and radios.

Steve Parent's name was spreading among the press when the LAPD finally did its own license check. An officer came to the door of the Parent residence and asked Wilfred to call a number on a card. It was the county coroner's office—there was a body waiting to be identified.

The LAPD announced to the media that autopsies would be performed on the victims, and that a press conference would be held the next day—Sunday, August 10. Garretson's lawyer agreed to have his client take a lie detector test on Sunday; meanwhile, the nineteen-year-old remained in custody, so far the only official suspect.

Detective Danny Galindo was ordered to spend the night on guard at the murder scene. The place completely unnerved him. He wanted to lie down and get some rest, but there was sticky blood everywhere and he couldn't find a clean spot in the whole living room. There was even blood splattered all over the walls. Finally he went into a back room and dozed as best he could.

Charlie got up in time to catch some of the late afternoon and early evening TV reports. He realized what the others had missed—there was no mention of the Black Panthers or Hinman's murder. Famous people had died at Cielo—this actress's picture was being broadcast all over—and there still wasn't the reaction that Charlie needed. Bobby Beausoleil was no closer to being free. There were no stirrings of Helter Skelter. Charlie always had great confidence in his own ideas. Because Hinman was personally inconsequential, perhaps his murder was already forgotten by the cops, especially since it happened a couple of weeks earlier. Well, the actress was somebody they couldn't forget, not with the news of her death so prominent. Maybe the whole copycat/Panther plan had to start with her, not Hinman.

That evening, Charlie went along with the general Family mood that there was something to celebrate. He had everybody smoke some weed, and then he pulled out his guitar and sang for a while. Only after everyone else had been sent off to bed did he call together Tex, Susan, Pat, Linda, and two additions—Clem and Leslie. Last night had been handled badly, Charlie told them. There was too much panic at the house. So they were going to go out again tonight and do it right. And just to make certain that there were no mistakes this time, Charlie was going to come along and show them how it was supposed to be done.

They all went to put on dark clothes while Charlie waited by the yellow Ford. More than forty years later Pat admitted, "The first night, we didn't know. The second night, we did." More people were about to die.

CHAPTER FOURTEEN

LaBianca and Shea

The oppressive L.A. heat wave broke on Saturday evening. The previous day's temperatures hadn't dipped below ninety, but now they dropped into the seventies, bringing a blessed coolness carried throughout the city by soft breezes. As darkness fell a little fog drifted in off the ocean, and its wavering tendrils extended into most of the suburbs. But there wasn't enough fog to obscure vision along the roads. It was a very pleasant night to be driving around Los Angeles.

Seven people—Charlie, Tex, Clem, Linda, Susan, Pat, and Leslie— were too many to comfortably fit into Johnny Swartz's Ford, but a larger crew than the previous evening's was necessary. Charlie had in mind at least two separate slaughters; doubling the murder scenes made it that much more likely that the cops and media would buy into the copycat scheme and tie everything to the Hinman slaying. Three-member teams seemed about right. Once again, Charlie had no intention of doing the bloody work himself. Clem made a useful addition since he'd do whatever he was told. Leslie was smart enough to leave a murder scene just the way that Charlie wanted, with the right bloody words, Black Panther clues, and no fingerprints.

Charlie gave Tex a new handgun and also a military bayonet that the Family had acquired from an Army surplus store. Then they piled into the Ford, with Linda behind the wheel, Charlie beside her, Tex folded in beside Charlie, and Pat, Susan, Leslie, and Clem all wedged in the backseat. Beyond the physical discomfort of too many people jammed into too small a space, the atmosphere in the car was leaden with the knowledge of what they were about to do. No one suggested turning on the radio for some music. The only conversation was one-sided, with Charlie barking out orders for Linda to make various turns, often waiting to tell her until the turn was imminent. She missed some and had to turn around, and when that happened Charlie snarled. A few times he jabbed her with his elbow. He told her repeatedly how stupid she was.

Everyone had smoked weed that day. Tex and Susan also dipped back into their stash of Meth. Perhaps it was the effect of the drugs combined with the fact that Charlie never told them where they were driving to, but it seemed to everyone else in the car that they meandered down residential streets forever with no real sense of destination, stopping here and there for Charlie to get out and reconnoiter.

Leno and Rosemary LaBianca had just returned home from Lake Isabella, north of Los Angeles. They'd originally driven to the lake on Tuesday to drop off a speedboat to be used over the weekend by teenage Frank Struthers, Rosemary's son by an earlier marriage. Their plan was to bring Frank and the boat back on Saturday.

The LaBiancas were upper middle class. Leno ran a chain of grocery stores, and Rosemary was co-owner of a boutique. After leaving the boat at Lake Isabella on Tuesday, they returned to their comfortable home on Waverly Drive in the neighborhood of Los Feliz, a very nice upscale area, quiet and safe. The LaBiancas had worked hard to make successes of themselves, Rosemary especially. She started out in an orphanage, worked as a carhop and a waitress, and eventually owned her own business and made good money in the stock market. Everyone liked her. Leno had a lot of friends, too, but he was also a chronic gambler who had more passion than skill at the racetrack. His other hobby was collecting rare coins. Rosemary and Leno seemed very close, the kind of people who had no enemies.

The LaBiancas had missed the first frenzied news reports about the Tate murders because, along with Rosemary's twenty-one-year-old daughter, Suzanne, they took Leno's Thunderbird on the 150-mile trip to Lake Isabella to pick up Frank and retrieve their boat. But Frank didn't want to leave yet. He had asked his mother and stepfather to let him stay over one more night—he'd come home with his friend's family late Sunday. That was fine with Rosemary and Leno; they hitched the boat to the Thunderbird and started home with Suzanne.

The late Saturday afternoon traffic was thick and they didn't reach the outskirts of L.A. until well after dark. The LaBiancas weren't able to drop Suzanne off at her apartment until about 1 A.M. on Sunday. Once they'd taken Suzanne to her place, the LaBiancas stopped at an all-night newsstand to buy a newspaper. Leno liked to read the latest sports section before he went to bed. He wanted up-to-date information on the ponies. Leno always bought his paper from John Fokianos's stand. Fokianos was on duty when Leno and Rosemary pulled up, still towing the big speed-boat behind their Thunderbird. The LaBiancas were sociable people. Even though they were tired from their drive, they chatted with Fokianos for a few minutes, discussing the big news of the day, which was the Tate murders. The *Los Angeles Times* had put out a special short edition about them, just the few basic facts that were known and the LAPD's promise of a news conference sometime on Sunday. Because Leno was such a good customer, Fokianos didn't charge him for the *Times* special edition. When he was questioned later by the police, Fokianos said he was certain that the time was almost 2 A.M., because right after the LaBiancas left, all the bars closed and he had a lot of customers wanting to pick up the *Times* to read about the murder of Sharon Tate. That was all anybody wanted to talk about.

Charlie made a show of considering several potential victims—a priest at a church, a driver whose car briefly pulled alongside the Ford—and Linda did her best to follow his erratic directions. In the backseat, Susan and Leslie fell into fitful dozes. Then after more than an hour, Charlie's instructions to Linda suddenly became specific. At his direction she drove into the residential area of Los Feliz, turning here and there until the Ford was slowly cruising up Waverly Drive. Tex, Susan, and Pat knew exactly where they were—they'd partied on this street at Harold True's house before Harold had moved away some months earlier.

Rosemary LaBianca was ready to go to sleep. She went into her bedroom and changed into her nightgown. Leno got into pajamas, but then went back out into the living room to read the sports section before turning in. He and Rosemary could sleep as late as they liked in the morning.

Charlie ordered Linda to park along the curb just below the house on Waverly where Harold True had lived. He told everyone to wait in the car, and then he got out and walked up the long driveway of the house next to Harold's old one. He believed that the best chance for the cops and media to jump to the wrong conclusions was to kill rich, important people. By L.A. standards, Los Feliz residents didn't fit that profile. They might be upper-middle-class, but well down the social and economic ladder from residents in Bel Air and Beverly Hills. But it didn't seem that way to Charlie, who grew up in places where anyone with a two-story house and a car was considered wealthy. To him there wasn't that much difference between Cielo Drive and Waverly Drive. Whoever lived in the house next to Harold's would do just fine.

Back in the Ford, the six Family members squirmed restlessly as they waited for Charlie to return. They wondered why he'd had them stop here—surely he didn't want them to kill Harold, and, besides, Harold didn't live on this street anymore. He'd walked toward the house next to Harold's and he was gone for a while, so this had to be it. What exactly was Charlie doing in there?

Then Charlie walked back down the driveway, not seeming in any hurry. He told Tex to come with him, and the two men headed back to the house. Charlie led Tex to a window and motioned for him to peek inside. Tex saw a man apparently asleep on the couch with a newspaper over his face. Charlie took the pistol and Tex the bayonet. The back door was unlocked, and they went inside. Charlie poked Leno LaBianca with the barrel of the gun, and Leno woke up and spluttered, "Who are you? What do you want?" In the same soothing voice that he used to reassure Family members on bad acid trips, Charlie murmured that nobody was going to hurt anybody else, so just relax. He assured Leno that this was just a robbery. Then, holding him at gunpoint, he ordered Leno to roll over onto his stomach on the couch. All communication was in whispers. The intruders still didn't know who else might be in the house.

Before he left Spahn Ranch that night, Charlie had looped a few leather thongs around his neck. Now he tugged one free and told Tex to tie Leno's hands with it. Tex complied. Leno complained that the thong was too tight, but Charlie ignored him and asked if anyone else was in the house. Leno said that his wife was in the bedroom. Charlie told Tex to guard the prisoner and went to fetch her. He and Rosemary emerged a few moments later; she seemed terrified but cooperative. Tex noticed that she wore a blue dress pulled clumsily over a pink nightgown. She was a modest woman, even when held at gunpoint. Rosemary was ordered to sit on the couch beside her husband; Leno complained again about discomfort from the leather thong and Rosemary asked if he could be allowed to get into a more comfortable position. Leno's discomfort meant nothing to Charlie. He asked if the couple had any cash. Leno mentioned Rosemary's wallet in their bedroom, and Tex was sent to fetch it. As soon as Charlie had the wallet, he went to get Pat and Leslie from the car. Once they were inside, Charlie instructed them to move Rosemary LaBianca back into the bedroom. Then he snapped to Tex, "Make sure everybody does something," and left. Charlie climbed back in the Ford, gesturing for Linda to move over while he got behind the wheel. Clem and Susan remained in the backseat. Charlie drove the night's second Family murder squad away.

In the LaBiancas' living room, Tex pulled a pillowcase from the bedroom over Leno's head and knotted a lamp cord around his head and mouth to gag him. Then he did the same to Rosemary in the bedroom, warning her not to make a sound because he'd be listening. Pat rummaged through the kitchen, pulling knives from drawers. Tex still clutched the bayonet. He thought that although Leslie seemed reluctant to participate in what was going to happen next, Pat was not only willing but eager. Tex was wrong. Pat was afraid—not for the LaBiancas, she remembers, but for herself. She had no desire to murder anyone else, but she believed that if she hesitated Tex would tell Charlie, and then Charlie would beat her, maybe even kill her, to demonstrate to the rest of the Family the consequences of not following orders. As Pat selected a knife and returned to the bedroom where Rosemary LaBianca was bound and gagged, with her free hand she gripped the door frame for a moment and, she said decades later, silently begged God "to make it stop. But that didn't happen and I have never believed in God since. He doesn't answer prayers." Mindful of her own well-being at the expense of the LaBiancas, Pat was ready to proceed.

Leno sensed what was coming. He began to struggle and scream. Tex was surprised that he could make so much noise with the lamp cord gag. Pat and Leslie went into the bedroom with Rosemary, and Tex rammed the bayonet into Leno's throat. He kept stabbing, and for a few moments Leno gurgled, "I'm dead, I'm dead," until he lay still and Tex decided that he really was.

The assault and Leno's last words were clearly audible in the bedroom. Rosemary screamed, "What are you doing to my husband?" and swayed where she stood, trying to get free. The pillowcase and lamp cord were still around her neck; the cord used to gag Rosemary was also attached to another heavy lamp, and as she struggled this lamp crashed to the floor and she dragged it behind her. Pat made repeated efforts to stab her, connecting with some, and Tex came in with the bayonet to finish Rosemary off as Leslie retreated into the hall. When Rosemary was down for good, the lamp and cord trailing behind her, Pat went into the living room and then came back for Tex, telling him that Leno was still alive. Tex stabbed him some more, and then either Tex or Pat carved "WAR" on his exposed abdomen. Pat jammed a long-tined carving fork into Leno's belly and thrust a small kitchen knife into his throat underneath the pillowcase. Charlie wanted a spectacular crime scene and she would give him one.

With Leno's corpse sufficiently mutilated, Tex and Pat turned their attention to Rosemary. Leslie still hadn't participated beyond helping Pat hold Rosemary in the bedroom while Tex stabbed Leno, so now Tex ordered her to desecrate their second victim's corpse. Rosemary lay dead on her stomach. They yanked up her dress and nightgown and Leslie repeatedly stabbed her in the buttocks and legs. Tex didn't feel she showed much enthusiasm, but at least she was doing something as Charlie had instructed.

Then all three turned their attention to the murder scene itself. There was a bag of coins—nickels and dimes and quarters Leno apparently planned to go through for possible rarities for his collection—so they grabbed it. Charlie wanted all the money he could get. Leslie took a towel and wiped fingerprints from places they believed they might have touched. They wrote "Rise" and "Death to Pigs" in blood, on the walls. Pat added "Healter Skelter" to the refrigerator door, misspelling "Helter." Sometime while they worked they raided the refrigerator for snacks— watermelon and chocolate milk. They left the watermelon rinds in the sink.

As soon as he'd driven the Ford clear of Waverly Drive, Charlie handed Rosemary LaBianca's wallet to Linda in the front seat. He told her to take out any money and wipe everything else for fingerprints. There were only some coins; Linda was struck by the photo of a dark-haired woman on the driver's license. Charlie told her that he was going to drive into a colored neighborhood. When he told her to, she should toss the wallet out the car window. Then some black person would find it, use the credit cards, and be linked to the Waverly Drive murders. Linda waited for the order, but instead Charlie pulled into a Standard gas station in Sylmar; there was a Denny's restaurant nearby. He told Linda to put the wallet in the women's bathroom at the gas station; some black woman would surely find it there. Linda dropped the wallet into the toilet tank. While she performed that chore, Charlie left Clem and Susan in the car and strolled into Denny's, where he ordered four milkshakes to go.

With Rosemary's wallet disposed of in a way that might further incriminate blacks in her murder, Charlie seemed to relax a little. He let Linda drive again, giving casual directions that she followed until they found themselves at the beach. Here Charlie finally allowed Susan and Clem to get out of the car, and all four walked for a bit along the sand, with Charlie mostly focusing on Linda, not talking about murder or Helter Skelter at all, just making friendly conversation. She told him that she'd recently learned she was pregnant. Charlie was delighted by the news. He even held Linda's hand as they strolled. At one point a patrol car drove up; two officers got out and asked what they were doing. Charlie explained he and his friends were just taking a walk, which satisfied the cops. Charlie, Linda, Susan, and Clem returned to the Ford, and Charlie told Linda to drive to Venice. He asked if she, Susan, or Clem knew anyone who lived there, and when they replied that they didn't, Charlie quizzed Linda: Didn't she and Sandy Good meet some guy when they were panhandling in Venice not too long ago? Then Linda remembered Saladin Nader, who'd taken her and Sandy back to his apartment for a while. Yes, she told Charlie, and now that she thought about it she recalled that he was some kind of actor. Charlie wanted to know if she could find where this actor lived, and Linda did. When they were outside the Venice apartment building, Charlie asked if Linda thought the actor would let her, Susan, and Clem in. When she said she thought he would, Charlie handed her a knife and told her she was to slit the man's throat. Linda replied that she couldn't: "I'm not you, Charlie." It was the kind of response that could have resulted in a beating, but the night was passing and Charlie wanted more murder before dawn. He asked Linda to show him and the others which apartment was the actor's. They went inside and upstairs; Linda deliberately directed Charlie toward the wrong door.

At the LaBiancas', Charlie had prepared the way for the killers. This time he simply led Linda, Susan, and Clem back outside, where he gave them their instructions. Linda would knock on the door. When the actor let them inside, Linda would cut his throat and Clem would shoot him—Charlie handed Clem the handgun that he'd brought along that night. Charlie didn't acknowledge Linda's earlier refusal to kill the actor. He expected that now she would do as she was told. Charlie said that while they were committing the murder, he'd drive the Ford back to Spahn. When Linda, Clem, and Susan were done, they should hitchhike back to the ranch. Once again, Charlie would be able to claim that he personally didn't kill anybody—it was the Family members carrying out their own scheme of copycat murders.

As Charlie drove away, Linda, Susan, and Clem went back inside the apartment building and up the stairs. Linda went to a door other than the actor's and knocked. When a sleepy stranger cracked the door open and groggily asked what she wanted, Linda said "Excuse me," and indicated to Susan and Clem that she didn't know where the actor lived after all. It would be daylight soon, and there was no time to get back in touch with Charlie and learn if he wanted them to stay away from Spahn until they killed somebody else. So they buried the gun on the beach and hitchhiked home. When they got there, Tex, Pat, and Leslie had already arrived. They'd been lucky enough after walking away from Waverly Drive to be picked up by a guy who had visited Spahn a couple of times and had a crush on Leslie. He was a real gentleman who insisted on driving them all the way there, so they treated him to breakfast on the way, paying for the meal with some coins from the sack they'd taken from the LaBiancas'. Charlie was somewhere on the ranch but they didn't look for him. Nobody compared notes about what they had done. It had been a long, exhausting night and everyone just wanted to sleep.

On Sunday morning, Los Angeles newspapers blazoned headlines about the Cielo murders across their front pages. Now the story included "ritualistic slayings." The Los Angeles Times mentioned Garretson's arrest, that "Pig" was written on the front door in blood, but also informed readers that Tate was wearing "bikini panties and a brassiere" when she was killed and that "there had been rumors in Hollywood recently" that her marriage to Polanski was in trouble. Police made it clear that "no motive could be immediately determined."

Charlie awoke at Spahn in a fearsome mood. He stalked around the ranch, collaring the various killers and demanding reassurance that they'd wiped away all their fingerprints and discarded their bloody clothing. Had they left anything that might link the murders to him and the Family? They assured him that they'd taken care of everything.

The media packed L.A.'s Hall of Justice on Sunday morning. The Tate murder autopsies began at 9 A.M. and the LAPD had promised a press conference when they were concluded. County coroner Thomas Noguchi, who'd conducted a field examination of the five bodies at the Cielo murder site, supervised. It was a long, laborious process because the corpses were so mutilated. Sharon Tate had sixteen stab wounds, five of which could have been fatal. Jay Sebring had been shot once and stabbed seven times. Abigail Folger's stab wounds totaled twenty-eight. Voytek Frykowski, the victim who fought back hardest, was shot twice, stabbed fifty-one times, and struck over the head with a blunt object thirteen times. Steve Parent had one defensive slash wound and was shot four times. Some bullets were recovered from the bodies, all .22 caliber and fired from the same gun. Each wound on each victim had to be painstakingly measured for length and depth, then recorded. That extended the autopsies into mid-afternoon.

As a senior homicide detective assigned to the Tate case, Michael McGann attended the autopsies. He hadn't expected they would last so long, keeping him away from his desk and any active investigation. That meant he wasn't available Sunday morning when two detectives from the Los Angeles County Sheriff's Office, Paul Whiteley and Charles Guenther, called and asked to speak to whoever was in charge of the Tate case. They were referred to Sgt. Jess Buckles, McGann's temporary partner. Whiteley and Guenther told Buckles that they were investigating a murder that had eerie parallels to the slayings at Cielo. Their victim, a man named Gary Hinman, had also been viciously stabbed to death in his home, and the killer or killers had written "POLITICAL PIGGY" on a wall in his blood. They had a suspect in custody named Bobby Beausoleil; he was a really weird guy who lived on an old movie ranch outside L.A. in a group led by somebody named Charlie. Charlie had a lot of his people convinced that he was Jesus Christ. The county cops wanted to meet and explore whether the Hinman and Tate murders were connected. Buckles said that there was no sense wasting everyone's time. The LAPD was already certain that the Tate slayings were drug-related, so thanks for calling and good luck on their case. Later McGann learned about the call and asked Buckles what Whiteley and Guenther had wanted. Buckles said, "It was nothing," and McGann let it go at that. With that decision, Jess Buckles simultaneously thwarted Charlie's hopes for the Tate killings to be linked to Hinman and set back the LAPD's efforts to solve the Tate murders.

Buckles's response to the county detectives accurately reflected the LAPD's working theory. The marijuana found at Cielo didn't seem significant. Virtually everybody in L.A. entertainment circles smoked a little weed. But Frykowski had for some time been suspected by authorities of dealing in harder drugs. The FBI even suggested that the Bureau of Customs investigate a shipment of household goods sent by sea from England to the U.S. for consignment to Frykowski and Polanski, since, according to the FBI, "press reports indicate shipment of narcotics is involved with this [Tate] case." Nothing came of that investigation, but on Sunday, August 10, Los Angeles police felt reasonably certain that they would eventually uncover evidence linking some drug dealer to the Tate murders. That theory was reinforced when a polygraph administered on Sunday afternoon eliminated Garretson as a suspect. Investigators still didn't believe that the nineteen-year-old hadn't heard anything as five murders were committed within a hundred feet of the Cielo guest cottage—he probably cowered in fear as the victims were being butchered. But they now were certain that Garretson hadn't killed them, so one of the first things that LAPD spokesmen had to tell the media was that their initial prime suspect had been cleared and released.

As Noguchi finally concluded the autopsies at the Hall of Justice, an L.A. friend of Tex Watson contacted Tex at Spahn to say he'd gotten a call from Elizabeth Watson, Tex's mother. Mrs. Watson was concerned that she hadn't heard from her son in six months—could the friend at least reassure her that he was all right? Tex told Charlie about his friend's message. Members of the Family usually didn't have any contact with their relatives unless Charlie gave permission. Charlie was distracted by concerns about overlooked fingerprints and other potential clues; he snapped that Tex ought to call his mother back.

Tex, paranoid from all the hard drugs he'd been ingesting and the knowledge that in two nights he'd killed seven people, convinced himself that his mother must have been contacted by the FBI. Maybe they'd found his fingerprints at Cielo or Waverly Drive. He didn't call his mother back, but he told Charlie that he had, and that Mrs. Watson had said the FBI came by the house looking for Tex. Charlie was stunned. He'd already been obsessed with potential attacks by the Black Panthers and arrest by the LAPD. Now the FBI was on his heels. If he had planned any more copycat killings in L.A., this latest news changed his mind. Charlie told everyone to refocus on preparing to move to Barker Ranch in Death Valley. They'd get their things and some money together and as soon as possible get out to the desert, where they'd find the bottomless pit and be safe from pursuit.

• • •

Rudi Altobelli was informed of the murders and flew back to L.A., arriving Sunday evening. He had no desire to visit the murder scene, so he asked his friends Terry Melcher and Candy Bergen if he could stay with them at their beach house. But Altobelli was concerned that as soon as the police were finished combing the hilltop house for clues it would be overrun by scavengers seeking grisly souvenirs. He called Gregg Jakobson and asked if he would move into Cielo for a while. Jakobson did, but the place spooked him too much and he stayed for only a few days.

Roman Polanski returned to L.A. on Sunday night, too. He made a brief statement to the press that cautioned the public not to pay attention to sensational rumors in the media, then secluded himself in an apartment on the Paramount studio complex. The LAPD asked him to take a lie detector test about the Cielo murders. He cooperated and was eliminated as a potential suspect.

Around 8:30 P.M. on Sunday, Frank Struthers arrived home at Waverly Drive. He was dropped off on the street and began walking up the long driveway, where he saw that his stepfather, Leno, had left the speedboat instead of putting it in the garage as usual. That bothered the boy, and so did the fact that all the window shades were pulled down. He knocked on the back door instead of walking inside; there was no response. Really worried now, Frank walked to a nearby pay phone and called his older sister, Suzanne, who came to meet Frank with her boyfriend, Joe Dorgan. The three of them went back to the house on Waverly and went in through the back door. Suzanne stayed in the kitchen while Joe and Frank went through the dining room and into the living room, where they saw Leno's body on the floor. There was something sticking up from his stomach. They went back to the kitchen and told Suzanne that things were okay but they needed to leave the house right away. Suzanne knew something was wrong; besides the looks on their faces, she'd noticed some words written on the refrigerator door, apparently with red paint.

Neighbors helped Joe, Suzanne, and Frank call the police. Officers arrived shortly after 10:30. Entering the house, they saw Leno in the living room and found Rosemary in the bedroom. The state of the bodies was sickening. They'd been stabbed innumerable times, and the fork in Leno's belly and the word "WAR" carved on his abdomen added to the nauseating tableau. The officers noted "Death to Pigs" and "Rise" scrawled on the walls in blood, and "Healter Skelter" on the refrigerator door. They called for an ambulance and detectives.

Danny Galindo was still at the LAPD's Parker Center main headquarters, typing reports about the preliminary Cielo murder investigation. He got a call from a reporter friend, informing him that "they got another one of those bloody [murders] just like the one you're working on." The reporter told Galindo that this one was even more sickening. One of the victims had a knife jammed in the side of his throat. Galindo had barely hung up when his phone rang again. This time a supervisor ordered him out to Waverly Drive. When he got there Galindo was struck by the similarities between the murders there and at Cielo. The LAPD didn't want anyone talking to the press, but the media had picked up on the Waverly murders by listening to police band radio and a pack of reporters clustered in the street. They shouted questions at Galindo, asking if these murders were related to the five earlier ones. Galindo said to a TV reporter, "I think it's more of a copycat case." The odds were against the same sadistic killers striking two straight nights in neighborhoods that were so widely separate geographically and socially. Galindo's immediate instinct, one shared by LAPD superiors and fellow officers, was that some sick son of a bitch had read about the Tate murders in the paper and couldn't resist mimicking them.

The press asked other official personnel on the scene for comments, and a few offered bits of information off the record. It was soon common knowledge among the media that there were more words written in blood at this second murder site, "Death to Pigs" and "Rise." But somehow no outsiders learned about "Healter Skelter" on the refrigerator door.

On Monday morning, August 11, L.A. residents picked up their morning papers and read that there had been a second set of unusual killings: "A Los Feliz couple were found slain Sunday night under bizarre circumstances that police said may connect the crime with the weird ritual murder of actress Sharon Tate and four others in Benedict Canyon."

News coverage emphasized that the same kind of words were left written in blood at both murder scenes.

Just as the LAPD had concluded that the Cielo murders were related to drugs, now they quickly surmised that there was a clear motive for the LaBianca slayings, too. Leno owed considerable money—estimates ranged as high as almost a quarter-million dollars—on racetrack bets. A former business partner tipped police that Leno might have also fallen afoul of the Mafia. These leads turned out to be dead ends, but they took time to run down.

From the outset, the Tate and LaBianca cases were hampered by the unwillingness of the investigative teams to share information. The Tate detectives were older, seasoned homicide veterans who believed there was no substitute for field experience. The LaBianca team was comprised of younger detectives who liked to employ the latest technological tools. They often operated out of the same long squad room, but never effectively cooperated. LAPD administration was unconcerned—after all, the cases really had nothing to do with each other, at least in terms of who had done the killing. Copycat? Maybe. Same perpetrator or perpetrators? No.

Fear was widespread in Los Angeles on Monday. The Cielo butchery sent waves of panic through the city's wealthy enclaves. Even electronic fences weren't enough to keep people safe. Before Sharon Tate's murder, Beverly Hills sporting goods stores sold only a few handguns a day. In the two days since her death, one store sold two hundred. Guard dogs were previously for sale for $200; now the price jumped to $1,500. But for people of more modest means, the LaBianca murders were far more terrifying than the gory events at Cielo. It was more titillating than frightening for the general public to learn that a movie star had died under terrible circumstances. But Leno LaBianca and his wife were small business owners, regular people, and if mysterious, maybe insane killers had stalked and slaughtered them, then nobody was safe. Throughout the city, everyone hung on every news report.

Charlie Manson wanted the murders to result in citywide panic, and in the strictest sense he got his wish. But it wasn't the racially incendiary panic that he wanted. Charlie read the articles about the Tate and LaBianca slayings, and not one made any mention of the Black Panthers as potential perpetrators. He couldn't understand why—they'd left those words in blood, and Bobby Beausoleil had mimicked the trademark Panther paw print on Gary Hinman's wall. Race-related tension in L.A. continued to run high. What was the matter with the cops, with the media? How could they miss something so obvious?

But it was Charlie who had missed the obvious. In other major American cities—New York, Chicago, Washington—in 1969 blacks and whites mixed freely, too often combustively, as part of daily life on subways, in stores, on street corners. But L.A. was unique—its freeways and sprawl effectively divided one race from another. Watts might erupt in flames, but a car of armed black militants on Cielo or Waverly Drive would have been called in immediately to police. Charlie remembered Black Panthers haranguing white passersby for contributions in Berkeley and San Francisco. Most white people living in Bel Air or Los Feliz had probably never seen a Black Panther. For all Charlie's scheming to instigate Helter Skelter, the LAPD and the media never considered that the Tate or LaBianca murders might be race-related. In that critical sense, his plot had failed.

Yet Charlie still used the press coverage to emphasize to the Family that, with his leadership, they had done a great, important thing. He usually banned newspapers from Spahn, but now he brandished the city dailies with their massive, alarmist headlines and proclaimed to his followers, "It's started." Perhaps not yet the Helter Skelter prophesied by the Beatles and the Bible, but still this was the genesis of widespread violence. They had to get out of town fast, because this was the Apocalypse. No one questioned Charlie when he emphasized that people would soon be coming for them at Spahn.

He was right.

For months, Los Angeles County lawmen had heard rumors of illegal activities on Spahn Ranch—stolen cars and drug use in particular. The earlier raid in April hadn't yielded satisfactory results. Now they decided to try again, this time a massive surprise raid incorporating helicopters, officers on horseback to pursue suspects into the ranch hills where cars couldn't go, and more than a hundred personnel so that every inch of Spahn could be investigated. A court warrant was issued to conduct the raid on Wednesday, August 13, but the raid was inexplicably postponed until Saturday.

Charlie sent Linda Kasabian to visit Bobby Beausoleil in the county jail. The Tate and LaBianca copycat murders apparently wouldn't be linked to the killing of Gary Hinman, and Charlie had to think of some other way to keep Beausoleil quiet, at least until Charlie and the Family lost themselves out in the wastes of Death Valley. Linda's message from Charlie was supposed to be brief: "Say nothing. Everything's all right." But when she got to the county jail she didn't have any identification and they wouldn't let her in.

Charlie was far less concerned about the two Family members in LAPD custody. Mary Brunner and Sandy Good were still being held on charges of using stolen credit cards, but Charlie had no time to waste on raising their bail. Sandy was hugely pregnant now, and at a preliminary hearing that week she was released. She immediately rejoined the Family at Spahn. But the court kept Mary in custody on a new charge of forgery. She would remain in jail until September, when she was released on probation.

In anticipation of the Family's relocation there, Charlie sent a few members ahead to Death Valley. It seemed like a good idea to get Tex away from Spahn, just in case the FBI showed up there looking for him. Dianne Lake went with him—Stephanie Schram had replaced her as Charlie's unofficial girlfriend. They had an uneasy time of it as they waited for the rest of the Family to join them. Tex was ambivalent about staying in the group. He thought a lot about calling his parents and asking for airfare home. Dianne, still just fifteen, got picked up by a deputy from Shoshone, who thought she might be a runaway. Dianne eventually convinced them that she was nineteen and they let her go. Tex was questioned by the same deputy when he was caught skinny-dipping in an irrigation ditch. Since he was in a playful mood, Tex gave the lawman his correct age and date of birth, but said his name was Charles Montgomery. The deputy wrote it down.

• • •

Sharon Tate posthumously became one of the most famous actresses of her generation. On Tuesday, August 12, *Valley of the Dolls* was rereleased nationally, and other films in which she played even bit parts soon followed. All over America, Tate received the ultimate tribute to a star's drawing power—her name was above the title on theater marquees.

That same day, a visitor dropped by Spahn Ranch. With his short hair and clean hands, Al Springer didn't resemble the prototypical biker, but he was a loyal member of the Straight Satans all the same. The Satans hadn't been happy with Charlie and the Family ever since the botched drug deal with Bobby Beausoleil; with one exception, they'd made themselves scarce at Spahn ever since. Danny DeCarlo, the Satans' club treasurer, was still living on the ranch, having fun with the Family women and helping convert cars into dune buggies. Springer went to Spahn to talk DeCarlo into leaving, and instead found himself the target of a recruiting pitch from Charlie. Charlie envisioned commanding an army of bikers out in the desert, tough outlaws riding bikes or driving dune buggies and fighting off any Family enemies. He told Springer that if he stayed he could have all the girls he wanted. Springer tried to put Charlie off by asking how he managed to support so many women at the same time.

Charlie couldn't resist bragging. He told Springer that he liked to go out at night with his cutlass, the one that used to belong to the Straight Satans. He knocked on doors in the swankiest neighborhoods and cut up the people who answered. Charlie claimed he'd "knocked off five of them just the other night." It sounded absurd to Springer, but DeCarlo said it was true, and that there was more—DeCarlo had heard from Tex and Clem about them murdering some guy named Henland and also "a nigger." Charlie supposedly cut Henland's ear off with his sword, and he shot the other man with a long-barreled .22.

Springer had no interest in leaving the Satans for the Family. He was very fastidious and he thought that the shacks on the ranch were filthy and the women were disease-ridden. But he hung around a little longer, listening to Charlie prattle. At some point somebody mentioned writing a word on a refrigerator, something about pigs or niggers, Springer didn't quite catch what. But Charlie and the others were very clear that they set up these things to call the blame down on the Black Panthers. He had no doubt about that. Springer didn't exactly blow Charlie off. Hell, DeCarlo said he was scared that if he left, the Family would track him down and kill him. They didn't like defectors. So Springer was noncommittal, and took word back to the other Satans that DeCarlo didn't feel like Charlie would let him leave. That pissed them off something fierce; they began planning how they'd go out to Spahn and take their buddy back whether Charlie and his people wanted them to or not.

Linda Kasabian couldn't stand it anymore. For two nights she'd been part of a murder spree, and now she believed that the others in the Family were "little robots" totally under Charlie's evil control. When Charlie told her to go back to the county jail and try again to see Bobby Beausoleil, to get him the word that he still had to keep quiet, Linda made a show of agreeing. She borrowed a car and left Spahn, but instead of driving into L.A. she headed for New Mexico where her estranged husband, Bob, was still living. Besides the danger she faced herself from Charlie if he ever caught her, Linda took an additional risk by leaving her young daughter, Tanya, behind with the Family. She gambled that no matter how angry everyone there might be with her, they all seemed to love and care for children.

When Linda found Bob she told him everything, including all about the Tate murders. He wanted her to return to Spahn with him right away so that they could rescue Tanya, but Linda was convinced that Charlie would kill them if they tried. For the next few days they argued about it.

The L.A. media inundated viewers and readers with nonstop coverage of the Tate murders. Beyond a few short follow-up articles, Leno and Rosemary LaBianca disappeared. On August 13 readers of the *Los Angeles Times* learned about the substantial quantity of drugs found at the Cielo murder scene (this in direct contradiction to the *Times*'s original story on August 10, which stated "no narcotics were found"); on the 14th the *Times* described in detail the funeral service for Sharon Tate, listing the many stars in the overflow crowd who came to mourn her. On the 15th, the

Times reported that federal officials now "admitted" they were focusing the Tate inquiries on drugs "and gambling debts," apparently mixing in by accident a leak from the LaBianca investigation.

The great interest in the L.A. murders was interrupted for four days beginning on August 15. Four hundred thousand people, most of them young and long-haired, gathered on an upstate New York farm for the Woodstock music festival. The crowd and the festival were on a scale unlike any before. The festival celebrated the hippie sense of peace and love as much or more than the music. When Yippie leader Abbie Hoffman tried to interrupt The Who's set with political rhetoric, the band unceremoniously threw him off the stage. There was a long downpour, and instead of fleeing for cover many of the young people played in the mud. There was some mockery of them by hardshell conservatives: See, these doped-up longhairs don't have sense enough to get out of the rain. But for much of the country, Woodstock was a soothing reminder that amid the tragic news of murders in Los Angeles and the stalemate in Vietnam, it was still possible for young people to gather and have a good time instead of protesting or rioting. Maybe hippies really were sweet and harmless after all.

On Friday night, August 15, Spahn Ranch became the antithesis of Woodstock peace and love when eight or nine Straight Satans roared in on their motorcycles to rescue Danny DeCarlo and, while they were at it, kick Charlie Manson's ass. The Satans jumped off their bikes and went looking for Charlie, who they expected would be cowering somewhere. Instead, he walked up to them cooler than hell and greeted them warmly. That threw the bikers off guard. When they threatened to tear the whole ranch apart, Charlie ignored the threat and offered them food and dope. The Family women appeared, acting friendly, and some of the Satans went off with them for fun and games. After a while the bikers gathered back together and remembered why they'd come. DeCarlo was on the ranch somewhere, and they demanded that he be brought to them. That was when Charlie, still sounding pleasant but also firm, mentioned that he had the men in the Family up on the roofs of the movie set. They had guns trained on the Satans and would shoot if Charlie gave the command. Al Springer checked out the rifle racks that Charlie had shown him in one of the shacks. Sure enough, some of the guns were missing. So the Satans blustered awhile and then got on their bikes and rode off, outmaneuvered by the slick-talking little creep they had fully intended to pound into bloody pulp. As a face-saving gesture, they took back the sword that Charlie loved so much, and left behind one of their members; Robert Reinhard was supposed to find DeCarlo in the morning and get him off of Spahn, but he didn't get the chance.

At daybreak on Saturday, everyone on the ranch was awakened by the din of hovering helicopters and bullhorns blaring orders to come out of the buildings with their hands up. The raid extended for hours—it took that long to locate the dozens of vehicles stashed in remote sections of the ranch. The Family members had constructed elaborate hiding places in brush and gullies. Finally all the cars were logged and impounded, including Johnny Swartz's 1959 Ford, and all the Family members were in custody but one. The county cops still hadn't bagged Charlie, who they believed was the ringleader. They kept searching until someone finally spotted him hiding under one of the movie set buildings. When they dragged him out, Charlie was informed that he and the others were under arrest for auto theft. His captors couldn't understand why the scruffy little man looked so relieved. They hauled their prisoners, twenty-six in all, off to jail. It had been a good morning's work.

At around the same time on Saturday, staff at the LAPD Firearms and Explosives Unit used the broken pieces of handle to identify the specific make of gun used in the Tate murders. It was a Hi Standard .22 Longhorn, nicknamed the Buntline Special. It was a significant step in the Tate investigation—now detectives could query gun shop owners to see who might have purchased that model, or if one of these guns had been pawned or sold or found somewhere in the aftermath of August 9.

Stumped for fresh information—beyond discovering the model of the gun used at Cielo, the LAPD had made very little progress—L.A. newspapers filled pages with speculation. On August 16 the *Times* revealed that an informant had tipped police to three possible suspects in the Tate murders. This was true; over the next several weeks investigators frantically followed up on the vaguest possible leads. None of these marginal suspects panned out. Having been cleared of any involvement himself,

Roman Polanski announced a $25,000 reward for anyone whose information led to the capture and conviction of the Tate murderers. Because of the impressive amount, and because it was so widely reported that the money had been put up by some of Hollywood's best-known stars, news of the reward encouraged even more dead-end tips to the police.

On Sunday, August 17, the *Times* local news section led with a retrospective: "Anatomy of a Mass Murder in Hollywood." Far less prominent was a one-column article, "LaBianca Couple, Victims of Slayer, Given Final Rites." An even smaller story informed readers that "Police Raid Ranch, Arrest 26 Suspects in Auto Theft Ring." Unwittingly, the *Times* had the seven victims and their killers together on the same page.

On Monday, all the charges against Charlie and his followers were dropped and they were set free. The date on the county warrant had never been changed from August 13 to August 16, making it illegal. Most of the cars recovered during the raid were stolen, but there was no way to prove which of the prisoners were guilty in which instances. The Family was allowed to return to Spahn with the exception of the children, including Linda's daughter, Tanya. Because county welfare officials were concerned about living conditions at the ranch, the children remained in foster care.

Out in New Mexico, Linda Kasabian was frantic to get her toddler back, and just as desperate not to fall back into Charlie's clutches. Bob wasn't any help; no matter how much she explained to him about the Tate murders, he still thought they could just drive back to L.A. and retrieve Tanya from the Family as if she were at some baby-sitter's. Linda got Joe Sage, a Zen monk in Taos, to call Charlie on her behalf. She told Joe everything and he was very calm about it. He phoned the ranch and asked Charlie if Linda's story about murders was true, and Charlie told him that Linda was a flipped-out chick who got too weird and ran away. Linda was afraid to talk to Charlie, but she did get on the phone with Pat, who berated her for opening her big mouth. Then another of the Family women—Linda thought it was Squeaky—told her that the county had Tanya in foster care. Linda could go bother them now. Linda contacted the county and had to go through a lot of bureaucratic hoops before Tanya was restored to her. But Linda didn't say anything to the authorities about the Cielo or Waverly Drive slayings, because, if she did, at the very least she would be considered an accessory.

So much wild speculation about the Tate murders was sweeping the city that the LAPD felt compelled to issue a four-item "clarification":

1. Narcotics were found on the [Cielo] premises.
2. None of the bodies had wounds involving the sex organs.
3. The word "PIG" written in blood was found on the premises. The letters were "P-I-G" not "P-I-C." ["Pic" was rumored to be the name of the killer.]
4. At present, there is no evidence to connect these murders with any others.

The clarification had no effect on the rumors.

The combination of the Straight Satans' invasion and the Los Angeles County raid made everyone at Spahn paranoid, Charlie most of all. He still expected the Black Panthers to attack at any moment, and the LAPD and FBI must be lurking, too. Charlie never found fault with himself—his plans were always perfect; his followers and the various Spahn hangers-on weren't—so he looked around for scapegoats and selected two. Danny DeCarlo was the first. Charlie had expected that using the Family women to win over DeCarlo would result in him recruiting the rest of the Straight Satans as a sort of Family cavalry unit. After what had happened Friday, that clearly wasn't going to happen, and it must be because of DeCarlo. DeCarlo had been arrested in the county raid, but returned to Spahn with everybody else. At Charlie's command he was no longer treated as a welcome guest and future member of the Family. Instead, the women rebuffed his advances, and when he tried to pal around with the men they walked away. DeCarlo had spent lots of time hanging around with Charlie; he'd seen him lose his temper and lash out violently. Beginning in late July after Gary Hinman he'd heard all the talk about murders. Now he did his best to stay out of Charlie's way and, at least for a while, avoided his wrath.

Shorty Shea wasn't as fortunate.

To some extent, Charlie understood why the Straight Satans had come to the ranch. They'd been stiffed on the July drug deal and they wanted Danny DeCarlo, their club treasurer, returned to their fold. But he brooded about the raid by the Los Angeles County cops. Spahn Ranch was on the periphery of their territory, and they'd already rousted the Family there as recently as April. There was no pressing reason for them to be back so soon unless someone had tipped them off about the stolen cars and dune buggies. When Charlie tried to figure out who might have squealed, he soon settled on an obvious candidate. For months, ranch hand Shorty Shea had been urging George Spahn to evict the Family or even sell the land right out from under them to the developers. Squeaky had overheard Shorty offering to throw the Family out himself and reported it to Charlie. It made sense that Shorty squealed about the stolen vehicles to the county cops so they'd do his dirty work.

Charlie and his followers had walked away from the raid, but it was still a terrible blow to their plans for moving to Death Valley. Most of the dune buggies they'd prepared for use on Barker Ranch were gone, confiscated by the county. The cars they'd been allowed to retain were useless on desert terrain. Now they'd have to go about accumulating a whole new fleet, and that would take too much time—Charlie wanted to get out of L.A. fast before other arms of the law like the LAPD or FBI came for him. Shorty Shea had no right to cause problems for Charlie Manson. Over the last seven weeks, Charlie had already a hand in murderous attacks on nine people. Now it was time for a tenth.

On a night late in August, probably the 25th or 26th, Shorty Shea got into a car with Charlie, Clem, and Bruce Davis. They didn't drive far, just out to some point on the Spahn property. Around 10 P.M. Family member Barbara Hoyt, sleeping in a trailer on high ground past the movie set, was awakened by the sound of a scream. At first she thought she must have imagined it, but then there were more screams that "kept happening and happening and happening." Shorty Shea was never seen again. Bruce Davis allegedly told some Family members that he, Clem, and Charlie armed themselves with bayonets purchased from Army surplus, and when they had Shea far enough out on the ranch so that there would be no witnesses, they "carv[ed him] up like a Christmas turkey." It took awhile for Shea to die, and most of the Family believed that Charlie dismembered his corpse and buried the pieces around the ranch. Afterward Bruce Davis filled some trunks with Shea's possessions, loaded them in the murdered ranch hand's automobile, and then he and Gypsy drove the car to Canoga Park and abandoned it.

The next morning, some of the other ranch hands asked Charlie if he'd seen Shorty Shea. Charlie said that he thought Shea had gone to San Francisco: "I told him about a job there."

At the end of August, both the Tate and LaBianca investigation teams prepared progress reports for top administration of the LAPD. The Tate squad's report listed five suspects, William Garretson and four individuals suggested by informants. It noted that all five had been cleared. The Tate team had no explanation yet for the word "PIG" written in blood on the front door at Cielo. The LaBianca team's report included considerably more details, including speculation on the bloody words "Rise," "Death to Pigs," and "Healter Skelter" left at Waverly Drive. Younger and more attuned to rock music than the Tate detectives, the LaBianca investigators noted that the Beatles' most recent album included the songs "Helter Skelter," "Blackbird," and "Piggies," and lyrics from those songs might in some way be related to the gory words scrawled by the killers. This possible lead wasn't emphasized in the report, and no further attention was paid to it.

Neither the Tate nor the LaBianca report mentioned that the two events had any possible connection.

By the end of August, stories about the Tate murders continued to appear in newspapers and magazines throughout the country, and widespread interest in them continued. But other violent events forced their way into headlines and news reports, too, particularly the first in a series of bombings of federal buildings and major businesses across the nation by radical protesters. Between August 31 and the end of May 1970, these totaled almost 250, or an average of about one each day. Violence plagued America; the grisly murder of an actress was embedded in the public consciousness, but it was joined by fresher, equally deplorable events. Only in L.A. did the story continue to dominate local news reports. Somewhere in the city particularly foul murderers skulked, perhaps preparing to strike again.

But by the first week in September that was no longer true. Though he was hampered by a shortage of dune buggies, Charlie decided he couldn't wait any longer. The Family stole a few cars—a red four-wheel-drive Toyota was the prize among them—to partially replace the fleet lost in the county raid. Then Charlie loaded the Family into the vehicles and led his followers into the desert.

CHAPTER FIFTEEN

Death Valley

Because it involved so many people and loads of supplies, the Family's relocation to the desert took several trips spread out over the better part of a week. Charlie slightly hedged on his commitment to Death Valley by leaving a few of the women back at Spahn, both to provide him with an L.A. base of operations and to send word if cops showed up looking for him. But he and more than two dozen of his followers moved, too many to fit in the shacks on Barker Ranch. The overflow squatted on adjacent Myers Ranch; Cathy Gillies's grandmother, who didn't live on the property, was probably unaware that the temporary visitors she'd allowed to stay awhile in late 1968 were back.

Charlie didn't allow them to readjust to their new, primitive living conditions. From the moment they arrived, everyone in the Family engaged in frantic efforts to prepare for the attack that Charlie swore to them was coming. He was sometimes vague about who, exactly, was about to descend—sometimes it was still militant blacks bent on wiping out every trace of the white population, but he also mentioned "the law." The bottom line was that some form of violent assault was imminent, and the Family had to be ready to fight it off. So pits had to be dug to cache weapons and nonperishable food, and bunkers carved into hillsides. It was hot, sweaty work in the unrelenting desert summer heat, but those weren't the only tasks Charlie assigned. At some point every day, squads of Family members had to trek out into the desert to look for the bottomless pit where Charlie prophesied they would hide until Helter Skelter was finally over and the blacks begged the Family to emerge and rule the world. Charlie kept describing the pit in detail, all about the upper tunnel that led below to a great city, and how the magical city's atmosphere would allow all of them to evolve into whatever sort of beings that they liked, and the wonderful news that they wouldn't age while they were down there, so that when they did come back up into the surface world they'd still be young and strong and ready to rule under Charlie's direction for a very long time.

Charlie's true believers—Squeaky, Sandy, addled Clem—took him completely at his word. Others liked his descriptions of the pit so much that they didn't allow themselves to question Charlie's veracity; Leslie in particular wanted to become an elf with wings. Many, worn down by physical labor and sweltering temperatures, acquiesced because they were too exhausted to question Charlie's orders. He remained in total command. At night he gathered everyone around campfires, doled out strong hits of acid, and described the world soon to come, a place where they enjoyed every luxury and this tough time in Death Valley was a distant memory. They should be grateful to him, Charlie stressed. He was putting himself at great risk to save them. Sometimes he'd describe in colorful detail how he shot Lotsapoppa; occasionally Charlie also mentioned the killing of Shorty Shea, emphasizing that Shorty had to die because he'd ratted on the Family. The underlying message was that Charlie would kill anyone who betrayed him, Family members included.

It was a hard way to live, but the men in the Family found more to enjoy in it than the women. The men served as armed lookouts, roosting in the shade and avoiding enervating movement in the unrelenting sun. They got the first and largest servings at meals and could relax afterward. The women had to chop wood for the stoves, cook the meals, eat whatever scraps were left by the men, and care for the children—for now there weren't many, just Susan's son, Ze Zo Ze (whom she stole back from county foster parents after the Spahn raid), and a baby boy named Ivan recently delivered by Sandy Good. Even if she was worn out to the point of collapse, every female was obligated to uncomplainingly have sex with any male Family member who demanded it. To many of the women, life in a bottomless pit sounded great by comparison.

Seventeen-year-old Ruth Ann Moorehouse was one of the few women remaining constantly upbeat and energetic. Most of the others

dreaded the anticipated attacks, but Ruth Ann looked forward to them—
to her, it would be part of a great adventure, one she'd missed out on so
far because she hadn't had the chance to kill anyone for Charlie. Ruth
Ann confided to Danny DeCarlo that she could hardly wait to get her first
pig. That was too much for DeCarlo, who suspected that eventually Charlie would decide to eliminate him the same way that he had Shorty Shea.
DeCarlo fled Barker Ranch and holed up with some of his old Straight
Satan pals in Venice; because of all the "murder talk" he'd heard at Spahn
and in the desert, DeCarlo remained concerned that Charlie might yet
send out some of the Family to murder him.

Though DeCarlo ran, another non-Family member stayed around.
Hulking Spahn ranch hand Juan Flynn accompanied the Family out into
the desert, not to join but because he wanted to find out what had happened to his friend Shorty. It didn't take Juan long—Charlie bragged
about the Shea murder at the campfires. But Juan wasn't sure what to
do with the information; clearly, Charlie Manson was a dangerous man
to anger, and if Juan went to the cops and Charlie didn't get sent away
for killing Shorty, then Charlie or his followers were bound to come after
Juan. So Juan stayed at Barker, uncertain what to do next.

The murder talk—bits and pieces about Tate and LaBianca, Charlie's
open boasting about killing Lotsapoppa and Shorty Shea—unnerved
some of the Family members, too. Barbara Hoyt overheard Susan Atkins
gossiping with Ruth Ann; she paid no attention until Susan mentioned the
name "Tate." Then she eavesdropped with a growing sense of horror as
Susan went into great detail for Ruth Ann about Tate being the last to be
slaughtered and how, as she died, Tate called for her mother. Despite his
own bragging about Lotsapoppa and Shorty Shea, Charlie had cautioned
the Tate and LaBianca killers to keep quiet about what they'd done. They
only obeyed to a limited extent; even Charlie wasn't able to resist crowing
about those murders to Al Springer, and Tex blabbed to Clem and Danny
DeCarlo. Susan could never resist bragging under any circumstances, inevitably exaggerating her own importance. Some of the younger girls like
Barbara Hoyt, Stephanie Schram, and Kitty Lutesinger, routinely left out
of matters involving Charlie's inner circle, knew some violent things had
happened but weren't certain who or what they involved. Now, out in the

desert, they learned about Tate and LaBianca, and they were frightened enough to think about escape. But it was hard to know where to run—even reaching the nearest Inyo County settlements on foot would take hours, and Los Angeles seemed like a distant planet. Besides, everyone knew that Charlie could find you anywhere.

On September 1, the same day the Family began its exodus to Death Valley, ten-year-old Steven Weiss saw a gun lying by the sprinkler in the backyard of his family's home in Beverly Glen. The Weisses' lot abutted one of the streets connecting to Benedict Canyon Road and Cielo Drive. Steven picked the gun up carefully by the tip of the barrel—he was a fan of TV's *Dragnet* and knew he shouldn't smear any fingerprints on the weapon. He took the gun to his father, Bernard, who immediately called the LAPD. The patrol officer who responded noted that the weapon was a .22 caliber Hi Standard Longhorn with a missing right-hand grip. The barrel was bent, and there were seven empty shell casings and two live rounds in the nine-cartridge chamber. He thanked the Weisses and took the gun back to the LAPD's Valley Services Division office in Van Nuys. The gun was placed in a manila envelope, booked into "Found Evidence," and put in storage in the division's Property Section.

Two days later, based on the broken pieces of handgrip found at the Cielo murder site, the Tate investigators sent out a series of flyers to law enforcement officials asking for information on any .22 Hi Standard Longhorn revolver that might have been recently discovered or turned in. In all they sent some three hundred, including to police officials as far away as Canada. But they failed to send a notice to the Valley Services Division in Van Nuys.

It irked Charlie that Paul Crockett had poached Brooks Poston and Little Paul Watkins. The three of them openly prospected in the Barker Ranch area—sometimes Charlie and the Family encountered them. So Charlie took a shot at making a convert of Paul Crockett. If the Scientology-spouting desert rat could be won over to the Family cause, Poston and Watkins would surely return to the fold, too. Charlie turned on his A game, lecturing Crockett on the imminence of Helter Skelter and the urgency of finding the pit to avoid annihilation. Crockett was impressed—not by Charlie's prophecies, but the glibness with which he spun his apocalyptic predictions. He made it clear that he didn't buy into any of it. With Crockett able to resist, Poston and Watkins refused to be wooed back by Charlie, even when Charlie bragged to Watkins that, just as he'd promised back in the spring, he'd showed "Blackie" how to get Helter Skelter started. Charlie also suggested to Poston that a good way to rejoin the Family and save himself from the onrushing black hordes would be to kill a deputy from the desert settlement of Shoshone, the one who hassled Dianne Lake about being underage. Poston refused.

Rebuffed by Crockett, Charlie tried to eliminate him instead. He asked Juan Flynn to demonstrate allegiance by killing the veteran prospector. Instead, Juan bolted from Barker to join Crockett, Poston, and Watkins. To Charlie, this meant that a rival guru had set up shop to systematically lure away all of Charlie's people. He hadn't liked it back in the Haight and he wouldn't stand for it out in Death Valley. Some of the Family were sent to creepy-crawl the Crockett cabin, getting ideas for how best to attack it. Crockett guessed that something was up. He and the others began contemplating flight. Crockett was reluctant to let Charlie scare him off, but it seemed as though the guy was capable of anything. Everybody in the desert was strange, but this guy set the record.

In the September 3 edition of the *Los Angeles Times*, LAPD Deputy Chief Robert A. Houghton admitted that despite interviewing more than three hundred people, the department still had no prime suspect for the Tate murders. Houghton said the LAPD suspected more than one perpetrator, but it wasn't certain. The department had no idea where the killer or killers were "located at present," and Houghton had no idea whether they would strike again: "Personally, I suspect not. Professionally, I couldn't rule it out."

The investigators weren't being lazy or professionally slipshod. While the officers assigned to the Tate and LaBianca cases could have made considerably better progress by sharing information, they individually carried heavy caseloads that prevented them from focusing full-time on any single investigation. Nineteen sixty-nine was a violent year in Los Angeles. Among the 169,922 major crimes investigated by the LAPD, 388 were homicides, up 9 percent from the year before. It was not uncommon for each investigator to be working as many as twenty cases. As widely publicized as the Tate murders had become, that still didn't excuse the officers assigned to them from working on other investigations.

L.A. Chief of Police Ed Davis requested patience, particularly since his Tate investigators were combing such a heavily populated metropolitan area: "Unfortunately, the murderer or murderers did not leave calling cards, and in this kind of case you start with 200 million suspects."

On September 4, Bobby Beausoleil learned that his trial for the murder of Gary Hinman would commence on November 12. Evidence against him was still being gathered by Los Angeles County officers Whiteley and Guenther. In particular they wanted to question Kitty Lutesinger, Beausoleil's pregnant girlfriend, but she had dropped out of sight.

After only a few weeks in the desert, the Family's supplies of drugs and food began to run out. Missing their evening opportunities for acid trips was one thing, but near-starvation was worse. The Barker Ranch larder was reduced to a sack of brown rice, some dry milk powder, and a container of cinnamon. They did their best to stretch these meager rations while Charlie made an emergency trip back to L.A. in the Family school bus to scrounge food money. With his followers' larder almost empty, Charlie didn't have time to cultivate any potential new donors; even if they hadn't parted under the friendliest circumstance, he hit up people he already knew. Dennis Wilson said he didn't have $1,500 to hand over to Charlie, and gave him the few dollars he had in his pocket. Gregg Jakobson didn't have money to spare, but he did advise wild-eyed, frantic Charlie to get back to the desert: "You don't belong in the city anymore." Somehow Charlie managed to raise enough money to fill the bus with provisions. He raced back to Death Valley, everyone enjoyed a good meal, and the crisis was averted, though only temporarily. When this fresh supply of food ran out, Charlie would once again have to find money to buy more, and the cycle would only have to be repeated. And how soon before his followers wondered how come there still wasn't Helter Skelter, and why they hadn't found the bottomless pit that Charlie assured them was somewhere near Goler Wash? The pressure on Charlie was constant and relentless. Then something happened to ratchet it up even higher.

Charlie had believed, or at least fervently hoped, that Death Valley was isolated enough to discourage his followers from leaving him. But Family members Barbara Hoyt and Simi Sherri decided to risk it. Slipping past the guards Charlie had posted, the two young women walked for sixteen hours across some of the most inhospitable terrain in the country, finally reaching the general store in Ballarat. They hitched a ride back to Los Angeles, where Hoyt first stayed with her grandmother and then moved back in with her mother in Canoga Park. She expected the Family to come for her any minute, and sat up nights clutching the biggest kitchen knife in the house. Hoyt told her mother everything she'd heard about the Tate and Shorty Shea murders, but her mother didn't believe it.

L.A. residents remained frantic for news about the Tate case. On September 19, Los Angeles County coroner Thomas Noguchi held a press conference to announce that he felt certain the five Cielo victims died at the hands of more than one killer. The purpose of the announcement was obviously to give the media something to report beyond the frustrating news that the LAPD continued to make no progress. Besides offering his professional opinion that there were "two, possibly three" slayers, all Noguchi had to offer was that the bizarre features of the crime suggested "possible severe psychopathy [on the part] of at least one of the killers." He also mentioned that drugs "may have been involved." Three days later, Los Angeles Times gossip columnist Joyce Haber chronicled Roman Polanski's September trip to New York, complete with details about a Broadway play he had seen and a stop at Elaine's, the "haunt for the literary-cum-anything set." In the minds of the media and the public, Sharon Tate's death was rapidly evolving from tragedy to entertainment.

The escapes of Barbara Hoyt and Simi Sherri hit Charlie hard. What if they were only the first of many? He berated his guards for letting the girls get away, and gathered the entire Family to announce that any future defectors would be recaptured and killed. They were either with Charlie or against him, he emphasized, and he still carried the authority of the Bible and the Beatles. He had brought them to the desert to save them, and they would show their appreciation by never doubting or complaining.

The best way for Charlie to keep everyone in line was to make them too tired to question him or run away. He redoubled the daily efforts to find the bottomless pit, making his followers comb every rocky crag and snake-infested hollow. Sometimes their searches brought them near the Death Valley National Monument, an area patrolled by the National Park Service. Charlie taught the Family that one uniformed officer was the same as any other. It was galling to escape to the desert only to find more pigs on guard there. Just like the L.A. County cops and the LAPD, park rangers were their enemies.

On the same day that coroner Noguchi held his press conference, the Family was searching for the bottomless pit. As usual, they didn't discover it, but they did find something that greatly disturbed them. A massive earth mover machine blocked a back road that the Family often used. They stripped it of useful parts, poured gasoline over it, and set it on fire, an act of willful vandalism that had predictable consequences. Park rangers investigated and found tire tracks leading to the smoldering metal hulk; they determined that the car driven by the firebugs was a Toyota four-wheel-drive. When the rangers asked locals if they'd recently seen such a car, they heard from several that a bunch of hippies living in the area drove a red Toyota four-wheeler and also had a dune buggy or two. The rangers began searching for the hippies.

Two days later, park ranger Dick Powell was on patrol in the area when he saw a red Toyota four-wheel-drive in the distance; Tex and several of the girls were out on a ride. Tex managed to scurry off into the brush, but Powell questioned the girls before letting them go. He recorded the Toyota's license plate number. Back at the ranger station, Powell discovered that the license wasn't registered to the Toyota. Park Service officials notified the California Highway Patrol, and plans were discussed to send a joint team into the desert to find the car and those who were using it.

On September 23, Mary Brunner was finally released on probation after serving about six weeks for credit card fraud. She briefly stopped at Spahn Ranch, then returned to her hometown in Wisconsin, where her mother now cared for Pooh Bear. Mrs. Brunner had obtained custody of the toddler from Los Angeles County after the August 16 raid on Spahn Ranch.

The trial of David Dellinger, Rennie Davis, Tom Hayden, Abbie

Hoffman, Jerry Rubin, Lee Weiner, John Froines, and Bobby Seale, the so-called Chicago 8, on charges of crossing state lines to incite a riot and "engaging in acts to encourage conspiracy" at the 1968 Democratic convention began in the Chicago court of Judge Julius Hoffman. Besides his fundamental conservative beliefs, Judge Hoffman was a stickler for court etiquette. When Seale, a Black Panther, repeatedly called the judge a racist, fascist pig, Hoffman ordered him bound and gagged in his seat at the defense table, then severed his case from that of the other seven. The judge sentenced Seale to four years in prison for contempt, and the Chicago 7 trial continued. To young radicals, it was the ultimate exercise in government suppression of legitimate dissent. Groups like the Weathermen publicly announced plans for violent reprisal, including a "Days of Rage" assault on affluent businesses in Chicago.

Park ranger Powell and California highway patrolman James Pursell drove out to Barker Ranch on September 29. Though they didn't know whether they'd find the red Toyota four-wheel-drive there, they knew that hippies were living on the property. But Charlie had almost everyone in the Family out searching for the bottomless pit, and the officers found only two young women. They gave vague answers to questions, and there was no sign of the vehicle. Frustrated, Powell and Pursell headed back out into the desert. Not far beyond Barker Ranch they passed a truck driven by Paul Crockett, with Brooks Poston in the passenger seat. The officers flagged down Crockett, and asked him and Poston if they knew anything about some hippies who drove a red Toyota. It was the opportunity Crockett had been waiting for. He and Poston poured out descriptions of a crazy leader named Charlie and his drugged-out followers, how these weirdos had sex orgies and weapons and Charlie had them all believing that he was the Second Coming of Christ. The Family—that was what they called themselves—talked about killing people and evidently they had. The officers needed to catch them because they were dangerous. What Crockett and Poston claimed sounded beyond belief, but Powell and Pursell decided to check out the immediate area around Barker Ranch anyway. In a deep draw behind the property they found seven young women, most of them naked. Trying not to stare too much, Pursell asked who they were and what they were doing. A slender redhead, who Pursell later learned was Squeaky Fromme, replied flirtatiously, "We're a Girl Scout troop from the Bay Area. Would you and the ranger like to be our scoutmasters?" Pursell and Powell attempted to question the women, but, as with the two girls they'd interrogated on the ranch, they received only vague, nonsensical responses. With no valid reason to arrest the seven women, the officers reluctantly let them go. But they continued their sweep of the area, and came upon two vehicles concealed beneath tarps. One was a dune buggy, and the other was a red Toyota four-wheel-drive. The vehicles both had gun scabbards welded to their frames, and there was a rifle in each scabbard. The lawmen wrote down the vehicle identification numbers and rushed back to ranger headquarters to check their registrations. Before they left, they removed several engine parts from the Toyota to disable it.

As soon as the officers' truck disappeared over the horizon, Tex Watson emerged from hiding. Using parts from another car engine, he replaced what the lawmen had taken out of the Toyota, then drove off into the mountains and hid it there.

When Pursell and Powell checked the vehicle identification numbers, they learned that both the Toyota and the dune buggy were stolen, the latter just a few days earlier from an L.A. used car lot. At the least, there was a stolen car ring operating out of Barker Ranch. Based on what they'd learned from Paul Crockett and Brooks Poston, it might be something more. Top administrators from the National Park Service, the California Highway Patrol, and the Inyo County Sheriff's Office began to confer on plans for a joint ranch raid.

Crockett and Poston left their encounter with Powell and Pursell more shaken than ever. They'd told their story to lawmen who didn't seem to grasp the enormity of what they'd heard. Charlie and his bloodthirsty bunch were probably going to stay at large, and if they found out that Crockett and Poston had ratted on them they'd be out for revenge. Paul Crockett was a proud man. He hated the idea of Charlie Manson making him run, but discretion won out over foolhardy valor. Crockett, Poston, Watkins, and Flynn sneaked away from Goler Wash and took refuge in Independence, the Inyo County seat.

Charlie was spooked when he learned about the girls' encounter with

Powell and Pursell, and how the officers had tried to disable the Toyota. He didn't need more cops coming down on him and the Family. That night he and Tex got into a car and patrolled the area around Barker and Myers ranches. They thought they could see in the distance headlights of vehicles driven by park rangers out searching for them. That was enough for Charlie. He decided that Powell and Pursell would probably turn up next at Myers Ranch. Charlie gave Tex a shotgun and ordered him to wait there in the main building's attic. When the lawmen approached, Tex should blow them to bits. As Charlie drove away, Tex took the weapon and climbed up to wait in the stuffy, uncomfortable perch.

September had been such a frustrating month for the LAPD's over-worked Tate and LaBianca teams that neither investigative squad bothered to file a monthly report. They had no idea what to do next. Chief Davis was beside himself—that Sharon Tate's killers remained at large reflected badly on the department. He wanted the announcement of some new lead, and pronto. Trying to appease the chief, somebody in the department tipped the media that the Tate murder weapon being sought was a .22 with a broken grip. Nobody at the Van Nuys Division apparently paid attention to the resulting flood of stories, but out in Beverly Glen Bernard Weiss did. His son had found exactly such a gun, and they'd turned it in to the LAPD weeks ago. But if it was the Tate murder gun, why were the cops claiming they still didn't have it? Weiss was puzzled, but he decided to let it go. He hoped that the police knew what they were doing.

Tex got tired of waiting for Pursell and Powell. While he sweated up in the Myers Ranch attic he started thinking about the bottomless pit and all the effort he and the rest of the Family were expending in the search for it. Maybe there wasn't one. Maybe Charlie was delusional. Tex didn't feel like following Charlie's orders anymore, and Charlie had made it clear he was ready to kill anyone who didn't.

The Family had a station wagon parked behind the house. Tex climbed in and raced out of the desert at high speed. He felt that he was running from the rangers and Charlie at the same time. He made it to San Bernardino and called his parents for money to fly home to Texas. When his sister met him at the airport in Dallas she insisted that they stop at a barber's on the way home to have his hair cut so he'd look like a boy. Small-town Texas had no tolerance for long hairs.

On October 3, Crockett and Poston met in Independence with Inyo County deputy sheriff Don Ward. Their contact with Pursell and Powell near Barker Ranch was rushed. This time they talked in detail about Charlie and the Family, telling the incredulous Ward about Helter Skelter and the bottomless pit and Charlie's promise of the Family emerging in hundreds of years to serve under him as rulers of the world. Ward taped the interview; Crockett cautioned him not to underestimate Charlie, "a very clever man [who] borders on genius." If Ward knew about the anticipated raid on the Family at Barker Ranch, he didn't mention it. He thanked Crockett and Poston for coming in and saved the tape.

Tex Watson didn't last long at his parents' house. Soon after arriving he shut himself in his room, screaming for his parents to go away whenever they knocked on the door to ask if he was all right. When he emerged a few days later, he asked them for money and left. Tex flew to Mexico and bummed around for a bit before ending up back in California. He kept thinking about Charlie, wondering if maybe the guy was right after all and Helter Skelter was about to come down.

The Weathermen launched their Days of Rage assault on Chicago's upper-class Gold Coast businesses and residences on October 8. The evening began with speeches but escalated into vandalizing stores and cars. Six Weathermen were shot, twenty-eight policemen were injured, and there were sixty-eight arrests. Two days later it happened again, this time with thirty-six policemen and 123 protesters injured. For a change, a portion of a major American city was being torn apart by whites, not blacks. Undeterred by injuries and arrests, the Weathermen vowed further violent acts of anarchy. Mark Rudd later wrote, "We were by now a classic cult, true believers, surrounded by a hostile world that we rejected and that rejected us in return." The same manifesto could have been adopted by Charlie and the Family out in Death Valley, especially since the Weathermen celebrated internally with group sex and acid sessions.

The Weathermen at least hid from their perceived oppressors in apartments with running water and electricity, access to restaurants and grocery stores. The Family still combed the inhospitable desert looking for a bottomless pit, and were always sun-broiled and often hungry as they did. Charlie, stunned by Tex's desertion and determined that there would be no more, constantly warned everyone about the dire consequences of trying to leave him. With Tex gone, slow-witted Clem became Charlie's enforcer, brandishing a shotgun and obviously hopeful of a chance to prove to his beloved leader that he would enthusiastically kill on command. But despite all Charlie could do, there was dissension in his ranks. Squeaky and Sandy would have informed on anyone who complained in their hearing, but by now the once unified Family was broken into cliques. Younger, newer members steered clear of veterans. Bruce Davis, Squeaky, and Sandy had Charlie's ear to the exclusion of almost everyone else. There were elements of mistrust, especially since Susan kept bragging about being in a fight with a man who pulled her hair. She said that she had to stab him in the legs to make him let go. Because Susan always exaggerated, those who hadn't been in on any murders couldn't be certain how much of what she claimed was true.

Kitty Lutesinger was especially horrified by Susan's boasts. After Bobby Beausoleil's arrest, Family leaders explained to Lutesinger that he'd been jailed on minor robbery charges. Lutesinger had only recently learned that the father of her unborn child was about to go on trial for murder. She was five months pregnant and miserable in the Death Valley heat. Charlie didn't physically abuse her, but lately she'd looked on as he battered Stephanie Schram around—whenever Charlie felt frustrated he always seemed to beat up women, and now he was frustrated all of the time. Lutesinger and Schram commiserated. They hated the desert and wanted to leave. On the night of October 9, they saw their chance. Charlie had left for L.A. to try to scrape up more money. Food was running low again. While he was gone, the perimeter guards weren't quite as vigilant. The girls were able to sneak past them, but the blackness of the desert night soon confounded their sense of direction. Lutesinger and Schram stumbled about in the dark with no idea which way to start walking toward Ballarat. They panicked, and with good reason—when their disappearance was discovered at daybreak, Charlie's armed guards, led by crazy Clem, would come looking for them. But they inadvertently circled the ranch rather than getting away from it. There was little chance they could elude Family pursuers for very long.

Officers of the California Highway Patrol, the National Park Service, and the Inyo County Sheriff's Office planned to raid the Barker and Myers ranches around 4 A.M. on October 10. They had a hard time just maneuvering into position—much of Goler Wash was impassable even with four-wheel-drive. As they crept slowly forward, they stumbled on two men asleep on the ground with a shotgun lying between them. Clem and a new Family recruit were supposedly on guard; they became the raid's first arrests. The lawmen nabbed another lookout, then proceeded to the main Barker shacks and arrested Leslie, Pat, Gypsy, Susan, Squeaky, and another Family member called Little Patty. They went on from there to Myers Ranch and added Sandy, Ruth Ann, Nancy Pitman, and one more female to their haul. All ten women gave aliases; it would be time-consuming to establish their real names. The lawmen also found two babies, Susan's toddler, Ze Zo Ze, and Sandy's month-old Ivan. Ranger Powell's wife had come along to serve as a matron for any female prisoners, and she took charge of the babies.

The lawmen searched the ranch premises, and discovered supplies of weapons, gasoline, and a little food. There were eleven vehicles; eight proved to be stolen. None of the prisoners acted guilty or even particularly abashed. A few of the women urinated on the ground in front of their captors. Mrs. Powell carried the infants down to where the lawmen's trucks were parked. The adult prisoners were handcuffed and driven off to Independence, where they were booked on charges of theft, arson, and receiving stolen property.

Some of the lawmen stayed behind to inventory everything on both ranches. It was almost nightfall before they were done. As they drove away, two young women emerged from clumps of brush and begged to be taken with them. They identified themselves as Kitty Lutesinger and Stephanie Schram. The girls admitted that they'd been part of the Family, but swore that they'd gotten disgusted and run away. Now they were afraid for their lives, and they wanted protection. Lutesinger and Schram were taken into protective custody, and rode with the officers back to Independence. There they were kept separate from the prisoners, and their families were contacted. Lutesinger's mother told her that Los Angeles County detectives were trying to find her to ask about Bobby Beausoleil and somebody that he was supposed to have murdered. The Inyo cops agreed to contact their Los Angeles County counterparts in the morning. Lutesinger was willing to cooperate. She just wanted to go home.

Someone on one of the ranches got away and called Charlie at Spahn Ranch to tell him what happened. Charlie could have run, leaving everyone to their fate, but they'd gotten out of trouble after raids before, notably the one in August at Spahn. Surely they could do it again. Charlie spent the 11th trolling L.A. contacts for money, then drove back to Barker, where he gathered the Family members remaining at large—Bruce Davis, Dianne Lake, Zero (John Philip Haught), and a few others. The cops had made their raid; now while they sorted through evidence, Charlie would stay at Barker while he thought about what to do. It was a poor decision; Charlie should have realized that the law would keep an eye on the place waiting to see who might show up. But just like the rest of the Family, Charlie was worn out from weeks of tension and physical hardship in the desert. He was not at his most alert.

In Independence, the lawmen gathered to review the October 10 raid. They'd recovered considerable property and taken a good number of prisoners, but none of them was the group's leader, the guy named Charlie who was supposed to be Jesus. It seemed smart to hit Barker Ranch again. Even if nobody was there, there was still some impounded material to be retrieved. They decided to return to Barker on the afternoon of the 12th.

Pursell, Powell, and another officer crept close to Barker just before dusk and saw several men emerge from one of the nearby washes and enter the main house. As soon as Pursell saw that Inyo County deputy Ward had a backup unit in place, he asked Powell to cover the front of the building while he burst in through the back door with his Smith & Wesson drawn. Seven people sat around a kitchen table, and Pursell ordered them outside with their hands raised. Dianne Lake, Bruce Davis, Zero, and the others obeyed.

Night fell fast in the desert. It was pitch black by the time the prisoners were all handcuffed and placed in the back of a battered truck for transport back to Independence. Pursell decided to take a last look around inside. It was too dark to see much, but there was a lit candle in a glass mug on the table. Pursell carried the candle into a tiny bathroom, passing it along the walls and down around the shower and sink. There was a closed cabinet beneath the sink, and it seemed to Pursell that in the flickering candlelight he saw a few strands of long hair hanging limply in the crack of the closed door. It was a tiny cabinet in a cramped space. It seemed impossible that anyone could squeeze inside there, but Pursell kept the candle near it and watched as the door was pushed open and a tiny figure began unfolding arms and legs out into the room. Pursell snapped, "If you make one false move, I'll blow your head off," and the diminutive man who emerged to stand before him replied "Hi," in what struck the officer as a very friendly voice: "He was as polite as he could be." Nonplussed by the man's appearance of complete calm, Pursell asked, "What's your name," and his prisoner replied, "Charlie Manson." Telling the tale many years later, Pursell recalled, "I've had a lot of people, including a judge, ask, 'Why didn't you just shoot him?' But I always answer, 'How can you shoot a guy whose first word to you is, 'Hi'?" Though the other Family members captured that night and two days earlier were dressed in rags, Charlie wore relatively clean buckskins laced together with leather thongs.

Pursell marched Charlie outside; he was cuffed and placed in the truck bed with the other seven prisoners. They picked up three more Family members on the way to the main road. They were crammed into the same truck bed as the first eight, with Pursell there to guard them. The other lawmen rode in the truck's cab or in a second truck that they'd left a short distance away from the ranch. The second truck followed closely behind the first, its headlights trained on the prisoners in the truck bed ahead. On the way back to Independence, Pursell thought the female prisoners acted like unruly schoolkids, whispering and giggling to each other. It was annoying and Charlie eventually noticed; he shut them up with a single hard stare. Then he turned to Pursell and companionably informed him that the blacks were about to rise up against the whites, and then there would be a war that the blacks would win. Pursell and the other officers would be primary targets because they were cops and they were white. The smart thing, Charlie suggested, would be for the lawmen to let their prisoners loose and then run for their lives. Pursell declined, and the prisoners were locked up in the Inyo County jail. They seemed to be starving, and bolted down the food that was offered. Charlie griped that it was wrong for National Park officers to participate in law enforce-ment: "You should be out telling people about the flowers and animals."

Counting those already in custody from the first raid, the county jail cells overflowed with twenty-seven Family men and women. Frank Fowles, the county district attorney, arrived and the latest batch of Fam-ily prisoners was charged with grand theft auto and arson. Charlie was booked as "MANSON, CHARLES M., AKA JESUS CHRIST, GOD."

Following their arrests, most of the Family either maintained unwaver-ing loyalty to Charlie or else rediscovered it. He'd warned them that if they ever fell into the hands of the law, they should never reveal any Family information—if they did, the cops would think they were crazy and send them to some place where they'd be zapped with electrical jolts to the brain. The chaotic state of the country reinforced Charlie's words—in such a crazy time, anything seemed possible and paranoia was plausible. In the cramped cells of the Inyo County jail (the overflow was so pronounced that county lawmen tried unsuccessfully to pass on some of their prisoners to federal custody, since, among other alleged crimes, they'd vandalized the earth mover inside National Park boundaries), Char-lie's hold on most of his followers was stronger than ever. But there were certain exceptions among the very youngest women who'd recently es-caped his clutches—Barbara Hoyt, now back with her mother; Stephanie Schram, fed up with mistreatment by Charlie, and Kitty Lutesinger, who'd never felt comfortable with the Family in the first place, and who now learned she was wanted for questioning by the Los Angeles County of-ficers investigating the Hinman murder. Lutesinger felt no residual loyalty to Charlie, or even to Beausoleil. On October 12, while most of the Inyo County, National Park Service, and California Highway Patrol officers were carrying out the second raid on Barker Ranch, Lutesinger met with L.A. County investigators Paul Whiteley and Charles Guenther, who'd raced up to Independence as soon as they learned she was being held in protective custody there. Lutesinger was happy to tell what she knew.

Lutesinger told Whiteley and Guenther that she understood her boyfriend Bobby was sent by Charlie Manson to get money from Gary Hinman. Bobby took two girls with him, Sadie and another one with red hair. Lutesinger didn't remember her name; everybody in the Family changed their names all the time and she had trouble keeping track of what they called themselves. Anyway, while they were at Hinman's house they got into a fight with him and Hinman was killed. Lutesinger couldn't remember who she heard that from, but everybody at Spahn talked about it. Sadie, well, this girl's real name was Susan, but she went by Sadie most of the time, told Lutesinger and a couple of the other girls later that she was in a big fight with a man who yanked her hair, and that she had to stab him in the legs a few times. So she apparently helped kill Hinman. All Lutesinger could tell the county officers about the redhead was that she was sort of slender.

Whiteley and Guenther checked; Susan Atkins, aka Sadie Mae Glutz, was also in custody. They stayed overnight in Independence and the next morning had Susan brought from her cell for interrogation. Bobby Beausoleil would go to trial in mid-November, so they had very little time to collect evidence. The L.A. County lawmen bluntly told Susan that they had a witness implicating her in the murder of Gary Hinman. What did she have to say about that?

Charlie had warned his followers not to divulge any information to police. But Susan assumed the worst—Beausoleil must have ratted on her—and, besides, she couldn't resist a chance to show off. The story she told to Whiteley and Guenther mostly corroborated Lutesinger's. She and Beausoleil went to Hinman's to get money from him. When he didn't give them what they wanted, Bobby cut Hinman's face with a knife, and then he and Susan waited two days for him to change his mind. Toward the end of the second day, Susan was in another room when she heard Hinman plead, "Don't, Bobby," and then she saw Hinman staggering around from a knife wound to the chest. She and Beausoleil waited until they thought he was dead and then tried to wipe up their fingerprints. As they were leaving they heard Hinman making noises, so Beausoleil went back in and finished him off. Then they took one of Hinman's cars back to Spahn Ranch. Susan never admitted that she had stabbed Hinman, or claimed that she and Beausoleil were told by Charlie to get money from Hinman. But Whiteley and Guenther still had testimony that would help convict Beausoleil. They asked Susan to repeat her story on tape, but she refused. So she was transported back to Los Angeles County. Based on Lutesinger's testimony, Squeaky and Pat were taken to L.A. County, too, because they were the only female Family members in custody who had reddish hair. Mary Brunner, the redhead who'd been with Beausoleil and Susan at Hinman's when he was murdered, was in Wisconsin.

Squeaky and Pat were held for only a day. They denied being present at Hinman's murder and beyond Lutesinger's vague physical description of a slender redhead there was no proof that they had been. A guard felt sorry for Pat and helped her contact her parents. She stayed in L.A. for a few days with her father, then went to stay with her mother in Alabama. As soon as she was released, Squeaky rushed back to Independence. She wanted to be nearby if Charlie needed her.

On October 15, marchers jammed America's streets—fifty thousand in New York, 100,000 in Boston, twenty thousand in Washington; in all, more than one million demonstrators participated in what organizers identified as a National Moratorium against the still undeclared but very real war in Vietnam. President Nixon insisted to his advisors that it was "a nothing," and made it known to the media that while the marches went on, he watched a football game. Only a small percentage of the protesters waved North Vietnamese flags and chanted pro–Ho Chi Minh slogans, but they were prominently featured on television coverage, enraging viewers who supported the war. John Ehrlichman, one of the president's closest advisors, afterward warned Moratorium leader David Hawk, "You're going to force us to up the ante to the point where we're handing out death sentences for traffic violations." Given the tenor of the times, it was hard to know if he was joking.

· While most of the nation focused on the Moratorium, Inyo County court officials tried to sort out charges against the Manson Family. As had been the case after the Los Angeles County raid at Spahn Ranch on August 16, it was hard to tie individual Family members to the theft of specific stolen vehicles, and no one among them admitted burning the giant earth mover machine. By the end of the court session, about half of the prisoners were released, including Sandy, Bruce Davis, Cathy Gillies, and Zero. Most of the freed Family members hightailed it back to L.A., staying on Spahn Ranch or in Venice. Sandy, her baby, Ivan, and Squeaky moved into an Independence motel. Sandy and Squeaky hadn't been particularly close, but now they strongly bonded through their devotion to Charlie.

Charlie remained in custody because Kitty Lutesinger told county officials that she'd seen him behind the wheel of one of the stolen dune buggies. When that couldn't be proven, he was held on arson charges, though these, too, would soon have to be dismissed if county investigators couldn't come up with conclusive evidence.

At the LAPD's downtown Parker Center, the investigators assigned to the LaBianca murder felt that they'd exhausted almost every possible lead. One of the few remaining was to contact their counterparts at Los Angeles County to ask if they were aware of any similar murders with victims stabbed and words written on walls in blood.

Whiteley and Guenther were in the L.A. County offices when a member of the LAPD LaBianca team called. Whiteley and Guenther told about the Hinman murder and shared their latest information based on what they'd learned from Lutesinger and Susan Atkins. The LaBianca investigators got copies of the interrogation transcripts. They studied them carefully and felt disappointed. Yes, there were similarities between the Hinman and LaBianca slayings. But the city lawmen were bothered by discrepancies. Lutesinger implicated this guy Manson in the Hinman murder, but Susan Atkins, who'd actually been there when Hinman died, hadn't mentioned Manson at all. Lutesinger said Susan had helped stab Hinman; Susan said Beausoleil did it. Yes, the county cops had established that Beausoleil knew Manson and hung around with Manson and his friends a lot, but there was nothing that either woman had told Whiteley and Guenther to link Manson and his people in any way with the LaBiancas.

Still, it was something new to run down, and the LaBianca squad did. They started putting together files on Charlie Manson and the members of his so-called Family, and they talked with Lutesinger. She had little to add to what she'd already told the county investigators, beyond the fact that once Charlie tried to turn a motorcycle gang called the Straight Satans into a Family army. Only one of them, some guy named Danny, was interested. The rest of them laughed Charlie off. But Danny hung around for a while. The LAPD team contacted the police in Venice and asked for help finding a Straight Satan named Danny. Kitty also talked about some-one named Tex whose first name was the same as Charlie's. She thought the guy's last name was Montgomery.

Police department administration wanted another progress report, and the LaBianca team didn't want to appear stymied. They filled some pages with descriptions of either currently cross-checking or intending to cross-check the LaBianca murders against other recent homicides, and added a new name at the bottom of their dwindling suspect list: MAN-SON, CHARLES.

Local media badgered the LAPD for news about the Tate investiga-tion. She had been murdered two months ago—why hadn't the police caught her killers yet? On October 18, the *Los Angeles Times* cited new evidence that Lt. Robert Helder, the head of the Tate team, said might "point us in the direction of the killers." Helder wouldn't specify what the evidence was, only that it was potentially crucial.

L.A. county investigators Whiteley and Guenther assumed that the LaBianca squad had blown off any connection between their murders and Gary Hinman's. That was their business; the county cops had their own case to make against Bobby Beausoleil. Yet Whiteley and Guenther kept coming back to something in Kitty Lutesinger's statement that puzzled them. Lutesinger swore Susan had told her about stabbing a man in the legs. Gary Hinman was stabbed in the chest. But Whiteley and Guenther had read the stories about the Tate murders like everybody else, and they remembered that one of the victims at the actress's house was a man who got stabbed in the legs. What if Susan had been talking about that murder and Lutesinger just assumed she meant Hinman? The county investiga-tors had been blown off once before by the LAPD; the day after the Cielo slayings they'd tried telling that LAPD investigator, Sergeant Buckles, that there might be a link between Tate and Hinman. He'd said no, they already knew Tate was all about drugs. Now Whiteley and Guenther tried again. They contacted the Tate team and told about what Lutesinger had said about Susan Atkins stabbing a victim in the legs, and gave them Lutesinger's contact information. The Tate cops took everything down and thanked them. Talking to Kitty Lutesinger was added to their list of things to do, though not as a priority. There was another lead that took precedence—the critical clue Lieutenant Helder had told the *Times* about.

On October 23, the LAPD held a press conference and revealed that their ballyhooed clue was a pair of prescription eyeglasses discovered at the Tate murder scene. A flyer describing the glasses had been sent out to thousands of eye doctors and to professional journals with high circulation. The LAPD hoped that someone would recall prescribing the glasses, which would then lead to the arrest of at least one of the Tate killers. It was the longest of long shots, and Helder refused comment when a reporter asked him to confirm that the flyers had yielded tips on just seven suspects, all of whom were cleared.

Tex Watson decided that the outside world made no sense, and he wanted to return to Charlie in Death Valley. True, Charlie had promised to kill anyone in the Family who ran away, but he'd let Tex return after his previous defection and probably would this time, too. Tex had committed murder for him. Even if Charlie didn't appreciate that, he would have to value Tex's ability to keep dune buggies running in rugged desert conditions.

But when Tex returned to Barker Ranch, everybody was gone. An old-timer in the area told Tex about the arrests, how all of them got hauled off to Independence on charges of car theft and arson. Tex didn't want to risk arrest himself, so he hustled back to L.A. and called his folks again for airfare back home. Before they sent the money, they made him promise that this time he'd stay. Tex promised and meant it. He wanted to keep far away from the cops in California.

Squeaky and Sandy visited the Inyo County jail often, and Charlie began giving them messages to take back to the other Family members who'd been released and had gone back to L.A. Everybody was to keep believing in Charlie, and above all they were to keep their mouths shut. Charlie had particular doubts about Zero, who always struck him as a weakling.

Squeaky and Sandy did what they could, but for a while it was hard to find Susan Atkins. She'd been transferred to the Sybil Brand Institute, the forbidding downtown L.A. facility for female prisoners. The place scared

Susan with its three-story stacks of cells and motley collection of inmates, including truly tough women looking for any excuse to whale away on newcomers. Susan was placed in a dormitory and bunked near two other recent arrivals, Ronnie Howard and Virginia Graham. Ronnie and Virginia were longtime pals. They'd known each other when both worked as prostitutes, and Ronnie had married Virginia's ex-husband, which Virginia didn't hold against her. Now Ronnie was charged with forging a prescription, and Virginia had been picked up for a parole violation. They took pity on the girl other inmates immediately nicknamed "Crazy Sadie" because she acted much too cheerful—singing, breaking into wild, spontaneous dances. Susan was pleased to have friends; long-term Sybil Brand inmates were assigned jobs, and Susan and her new pal Virginia were assigned as runners, carrying messages between facility staffers. In between assignments, Susan and Virginia chatted. At night in the dormitory, Susan whispered to Ronnie. Ronnie and Virginia had colorful lives and lots of good tales to tell, but their stories were nothing compared to Susan's. She wanted to amaze them—and she did.

CHAPTER SIXTEEN

Unraveling

For almost three months, investigators working the Tate and LaBianca murder cases made little significant progress. They had no promising leads or suspects; and they failed to consider any link between the crimes. But over a five-week period beginning in early November evidence fell into their laps and, almost despite themselves, they began solving the crimes.

On November 3, Virginia Graham and Susan Atkins sat in the Sybil Brand message center bored because they had no work to do. Virginia idly asked Susan what she was in for, and was startled to hear, "First-degree murder." Susan explained that a guy in county lockup snitched on her—she didn't realize the informant was Kitty Lutesinger, not Bobby Beausoleil. Virginia let the subject slide; it was usually better not to know the details about what other inmates had done. But Susan wouldn't let it drop. The next day she informed Virginia that the murder victim was somebody named Gary Hinman; she, Bobby Beausoleil, and another girl did it. The second girl had been in Sybil Brand, but not for murder, and now she was back in Wisconsin with her baby. Susan said the cops were stupid. They thought she held Hinman while Bobby stabbed him when it was the other way around. But it was good the cops were dumb because they would never be able to prove it. From there, Susan prattled on about "Charlie," who was leading Susan and some others she called "the Family" into the desert to find a bottomless pit where they would live. Oh, and Charlie was really Jesus Christ.

Virginia thought the girl was nuts.

• • •

Two nights later, Venice police responded to a call from a house near the beach. They discovered a body there. John Philip Haught, "Zero," was dead of a gunshot wound to the head. Friends who had been there with him—Cathy Gillies, Bruce Davis, and several other Family members— told the officers that Zero was playing Russian roulette with an eight-shot handgun. Their stories were accepted and Zero's death was recorded as suicide. Afterward the Venice PD discovered that instead of having one live round and seven empty chambers, the gun had seven live rounds and one spent shell. The cops had more important things to do than spend more time on a hippie who was probably too stoned to know how many bullets were in the gun before he spun the cylinder and pulled the trigger. The Family member whom Charlie considered a weak link was now out of the picture.

Two detectives assigned to the LaBianca team drove up to Independence to interview the Family members still in custody there. Charlie's questioning was brief. They asked if he had any information about the LaBianca or Tate murders and he said he didn't. All the others they interrogated had the same response, with one exception. Leslie Van Houten was feeling off-balance because she was convinced elf wings were prematurely budding on her back and she wasn't safely in the bottomless pit yet. Distracted by that concern, she didn't deny that Susan Atkins might have been involved in Gary Hinman's murder. Leslie admitted being aware of the Tate killings, though she claimed no knowledge of the LaBianca murders. There were some unspecified "things" that led her to believe some people in the Family might have something to do with Tate. Leslie wanted to think about it overnight. In the morning she told the LAPD officers that she had nothing more to say to them.

Before returning to L.A., the LaBianca investigators asked to see the Family's personal effects. They noticed that Charlie's deerskin pants and moccasins were fastened with leather thongs like the ones used to tie the hands of Leno LaBianca. They took a few of the thongs back with them.

Susan kept elaborating to Virginia. When she ran out of details about Gary Hinman, she moved on to a fresh subject. There was a well-known case, Susan said, where the cops were "so far off the track" that it would never be solved, "the one on Benedict Canyon." Virginia felt sure she knew what Susan was talking about, but wanted confirmation—did she mean *Sharon Tate*? Susan did, and informed Virginia that "You know who did it? You're looking at her." From there, Susan couldn't stop blabbing. They killed the people at Cielo because they wanted to commit a crime that would shock the world. They picked the house because they knew a guy, Terry Melcher, who used to live there. She talked about Charlie telling them to wear dark clothing and how they parked the car and walked up to the gate. Four of them did it, a man and Susan and two other girls. The first one they saw, Charles shot. Virginia assumed that Susan was referring to the man she'd previously mentioned named Charlie, Susan's leader.

Susan warmed to her story, layering on one gruesome detail after another. Tate and Jay Sebring were strung up with nooses around their necks. Susan stabbed Voytek Frykowski several times, and when he ran out onto the lawn they finished him off. Sharon Tate died last, begging for her life, but Susan laughed at her and killed her and then tasted her blood, which was "warm and sticky and nice." When she and the other three drove off, they stopped by a house to wash their hands and a man ran over and tried to grab the car keys, but they got away. And then, Susan said, there was what they did to "the other two" the next night.

Virginia wanted to get away from Susan and excused herself to take a shower. But over the next few days, Susan kept talking to Virginia and to Ronnie, too. Besides the Tate and LaBianca murders, she yammered about Terry Melcher, how Charlie was furious because Melcher broke some promise, about living at Beach Boy Dennis Wilson's house, and how Dennis and Gregg Jakobson did things for the Family. When they were away from Susan, Virginia and Ronnie compared notes. Was this crazy girl telling the truth? So much of it seemed impossible, like this death list she claimed they had of other celebrities like Frank Sinatra and Elizabeth Taylor. Susan claimed Sharon Tate was only going to be the first famous person they killed. Every time Susan talked to Virginia or Ronnie, she added more horrendous details, including how she wrote "Pig" on the front door at Cielo in Tate's blood. In all these stories, Susan assigned herself a leading role. She stabbed Gary Hinman and Sharon Tate. Besides Charlie, she was the star. And Susan made a dire prophecy: More people were going to die.

Though Sybil Brand inmates had informal if rigid rules against snitching, Virginia and Ronnie debated whether they should tell someone about what Susan was claiming. They decided to wait a while longer and see what else she might say. Maybe the girl would admit that she was making it all up, and then they'd be off the hook. They hoped so.

On November 12, Susan Atkins went to court for a preliminary hearing in the Hinman murder case. Through the testimony of L.A. County officers Whiteley and Guenther, she learned that Kitty Lutesinger rather than Bobby Beausoleil had informed on her. When she was returned to her dormitory in Sybil Brand, Susan angrily informed Virginia and Ronnie that Lutesinger's life now "wasn't worth anything."

Virginia couldn't listen to Susan long; she had just learned she was being transferred to the state's main women's prison in Corona, about forty miles east of L.A., to serve out her sentence. Ronnie would be left at Sybil Brand with Susan. She and Virginia still couldn't decide whether they should inform on Susan.

As Virginia was packing her few belongings before being moved to Corona, the LaBianca investigators at Parker Center in downtown L.A. received a call from the Venice PD. The L.A. cops had mentioned to Venice police that they wanted to talk to a Straight Satan named Danny. The Venice cops hadn't yet run across him, but they did have another Straight Satan in custody if the LaBianca squad had any interest in talking to him. The biker's name was Al Springer, and the Venice police delivered him to a Parker Center interrogation room.

Springer had plenty to tell about Charlie Manson and the Family. He related all of Charlie's bragging about having a sword and knocking on rich people's doors and killing them when they answered. Did they know about some dead body that had an ear cut off, Al wanted to know. Well, Charlie said he did that. He said he'd killed a black guy, too, with a .22 Buntline long barrel. Some of this Springer had from Charlie, and some from Danny DeCarlo, who'd heard it from Charlie and "Tex" and a few others. But Springer swore that on August 11 or 12 Charlie told him directly that "we knocked off five of them just the other night." Then he wanted to know if the LaBianca squad knew about "anybody hav[ing] their refrigerator wrote on." Despite all the other leaks, the LAPD had managed to keep secret the writing of "Healter Skelter" on the LaBianca refrigerator door. Al Springer had to be taken seriously.

Since much of what Springer said concerned the Tate rather than the LaBianca killings, someone from the LaBianca squad went to fetch Sgt. Mike McGann from the Tate team. Springer repeated to McGann what he'd already told the LaBianca investigators, and added new information about the murder of somebody named Shorty. Danny DeCarlo told Springer that he'd heard Shorty got his head and arms and legs cut off for something he'd said or done that made Charlie mad. What the L.A. cops needed to do, Springer insisted, was find DeCarlo. Danny was scared of Charlie and the Family, so he'd tell what he knew about them for sure. With Springer's help, DeCarlo was located at his mother's. DeCarlo had some current legal issues and thought the LAPD might help him avoid jail on the charges if he voluntarily talked to them about Manson. He agreed to come to Parker Center the next day.

Finally, the Tate and LaBianca investigators were working together.

On November 12, the rest of the nation was preoccupied with a different tragedy. A story by journalist Seymour Hersh indicated that the Army was investigating a mass murder that dwarfed in number the seven victims in L.A.'s Tate and LaBianca slayings. In March 1968, Lt. William Calley allegedly directed the slaughter of over three hundred defenseless women, children, and old men while searching out North Vietnamese soldiers in the South Vietnam hamlet of My Lai. Calley, secretly charged by the military with murder in September 1969, stated in his own defense that he was simply carrying out orders to destroy the enemy, and it was his understanding that men, women, and children were all classified the same. Hersh's article further inflamed the antiwar movement at a critical moment—another protest march was already set for Washington on November 15.

•　•　•

Ronnie Howard was deeply disturbed by Susan Atkins's prediction that her leader Charlie and the so-called Family planned to kill more people. On the day that her friend Virginia was taken to the women's prison in Corona, Ronnie told a female deputy at Sybil Brand that she knew who committed the Tate and LaBianca murders. Ronnie asked for permission to call the L.A. police so she could tell them what she knew. The deputy said she didn't have the authority to let Ronnie make such a call, but she'd kick the request up the ladder. It would probably be a few days before her boss got back to her on it. Ronnie protested that the LAPD had to get this information right away; if they didn't, more people might die. If she couldn't make the call herself, would the deputy do it for her? But the deputy said it was against the rules for her to make a phone call on behalf of an inmate.

Danny DeCarlo came to Parker Center and met with the LaBianca team on November 13. Though he was willing to talk about the weird lifestyle of Charlie Manson and his followers, DeCarlo said that Charlie had never said anything to him about the Tate or LaBianca killings. The investigators told DeCarlo to come back on Monday the 17th, when they'd interview him on tape and at length.

At the Corona prison, Virginia Graham decided to tell someone about what she'd heard from Susan Atkins. She asked to speak to Vera Dreiser, a prison psychologist she knew from elsewhere and trusted. She was instructed to fill out a request form. When she did, Virginia was directed to meet with a different psychologist who was assigned to her specific prison unit. Virginia protested that she wanted to talk to Dr. Dreiser and no one else. Permission was granted, but Virginia was informed that the meeting couldn't take place for several weeks.

Bobby Beausoleil went on trial for the murder of Gary Hinman on Friday, November 14. There was considerable evidence against him, but the prosecution lacked a definitive witness who either saw Beausoleil kill Hinman or at least heard him confess to the crime. Investigators found Beausoleil's palm print and fingerprint at Hinman's house, he'd been apprehended in Hinman's car, and the murder weapon, caked with Hinman's blood, was found in a wheel well. Susan Atkins told county investigators Whiteley and Guenther that she believed she'd heard Beausoleil kill Hinman in another room from where she was, but that still didn't constitute eyewitness testimony to the actual stabbing.

On Saturday, one of the largest antiwar demonstrations in American history was held in Washington. One quarter of a million protesters marched in the street, and when darkness fell they staged a candlelight vigil. Informed of the vigil by his advisors in the White House, President Nixon had a thought: Why not have Army helicopters hover overhead so that their propellers would blow out the protesters' candles? He was talked out of it.

Danny DeCarlo didn't show for his 8:30 A.M. meeting with the LaBianca team on Monday, November 17. But that morning Ronnie Howard was taken by bus to a court hearing in Santa Monica, and the women being transported there were allowed to use a pay phone while they waited for the bus to arrive. A line to the phone formed quickly—everyone wanted to make calls. But Ronnie bribed the women in front with 50 cents each to let her go first. She called the Beverly Hills Division of the LAPD and told the officer who answered that she knew the identities of the Tate and LaBianca killers. Calls making that claim came in all the time. Ronnie was told that the Hollywood Division was handling those cases—call there. Even though the women waiting for the bus were limited to one call each, Ronnie stood her ground at the phone and called the Hollywood cops. The officer she talked to there was much more interested. Ronnie identified herself and repeated her message: She knew who killed Tate and the LaBiancas. The Hollywood cop said he'd send someone to talk to her right away, but Ronnie said she had to go into court. She forgot to say which court before she hung up, but the officer had her name and did some checking.

Ronnie waited all day for her case to be called before the judge, and wondered as she waited if the Hollywood cops were really coming to the Santa Monica court to talk to her. But they didn't, and after her hearing she was marched back onto the bus and returned to Sybil Brand.

•   •   •

Danny DeCarlo finally arrived at Parker Center at 5 P.M. on November 17. He explained that on the way there that morning he'd been stopped for an illegal turn, and since he had several outstanding traffic tickets he'd been arrested. As soon as he was released, DeCarlo rushed over to keep the appointment.

Closed in an interview room with three detectives and a tape recorder running, DeCarlo talked about Manson and his followers, starting with a detailed description of his experiences with them over about five months. He assured the police that he was the best source they could possibly find—he'd practically been a full-fledged member of the Family. They were gratified to get background information, but after a while they pushed DeCarlo: What did he know about any murders? DeCarlo had plenty to say about those, too. Yes, Bobby Beausoleil killed Gary Hinman—DeCarlo had this straight from Beausoleil himself. And there were other people involved besides Beausoleil and Susan Atkins. Mary Brunner was there, and Bruce Davis was involved, and of course Charlie was behind the whole thing. It was Charlie who cut off Hinman's ear with a Straight Satans sword, the one the bikers took back from Charlie at Spahn Ranch on August 15. The Satans were so pissed off with Charlie that they broke the sword in half. DeCarlo said that he'd brought the halves to Parker, and now he gave them to the detectives. Then he continued his narrative. On the night of the Hinman murder, DeCarlo said, Charlie told Beausoleil on the phone to go ahead and finish Hinman off. Beausoleil and the girls were following Charlie's orders when they killed Hinman, and also when they wrote something like "kill the piggies" on a wall in blood to make it look like a murder by the Black Panthers. Then DeCarlo talked about the .22 Buntline, how Charlie used it to kill some Black Panther when a drug deal went bad. The cops urged him to go on, and asked if he knew anything about Shorty Shea. DeCarlo said that he did, and volunteered that he was sure Charlie "did Tate." He wanted some assurance that if he told them anything more, they'd get him out of his outstanding charges. The officers promised DeCarlo that if he continued to cooperate, if what he told them checked out, then they'd be with him "a hundred percent . . . so that you don't have to go to the joint."

DeCarlo kept talking.

• • •

Two LAPD detectives went to Sybil Brand and asked to speak to Ronnie Howard. They were set up with her in a small room and Ronnie told
them everything she'd heard from Susan Atkins, and also what Virginia
Graham had said that Susan told her. The officers believed every word,
especially since Susan had provided details (like losing her buck knife at
Cielo) to Ronnie that were not public knowledge. They arranged to have
Ronnie moved to an isolation unit, then they rushed back to Parker Center to announce that they had cracked the Tate case.

Danny DeCarlo had just finished telling about Shorty Shea's murder,
how Charlie had him all sliced up because he didn't like snitches, when
his interrogation was interrupted by the detectives who'd just interviewed Ronnie Howard at Sybil Brand. After a break of almost an hour,
the questioning of DeCarlo resumed, but now there was one specific
focus—what did he know about the murder of Sharon Tate? He knew
a lot, starting with Clem telling him they'd got "five piggies," and how,
around the night of August 8 or 9, some of the Family—Danny thought it
might have been Charlie, Tex, and Clem—went out and did it. According
to Ronnie Howard, Susan Atkins had claimed that she helped in the Tate
murders along with two other girls named Katie and Linda. DeCarlo said
he knew a girl called Katie, but the cops needed to remember that nobody in the Family ever went by their real names. So he knew a Katie and
also a Linda, but when the detectives asked, DeCarlo said he'd never met
a Family member called Charles Montgomery. DeCarlo did know the car
the killers had used to get to Cielo, a '59 Ford belonging to Spahn ranch
hand Johnny Swartz.

In all, DeCarlo talked for seven hours. Toward the end he mentioned
the $25,000 reward offered by Roman Polanski and said he thought he
ought to get a piece of that. The cops made a mistake by telling him
about Zero's death. DeCarlo was certain it was murder, not suicide, and
after hearing about it, he told the police that he didn't want to testify publicly against Charlie or anybody in the Family because it was too dangerous. He was willing to testify against Beausoleil, though, in exchange for
having the charges that were pending against him dropped. Beausoleil's
attorney strongly opposed the prosecution bringing in a new witness

after the trial had already begun, but DeCarlo's testimony was allowed by the judge.

The next afternoon, Aaron Stovitz, head of the Trials Division of the City of Los Angeles District Attorney's Office, and Vincent Bugliosi, an up-and-comer among several hundred L.A. deputy district attorneys, were informed by their boss that they would serve as prosecutors in the Tate and LaBianca murder trials that now seemed forthcoming. Stovitz and Bugliosi were briefed on the latest developments, including the interrogations of Ronnie Howard and Danny DeCarlo.

As the junior member of the two-man team, it was Bugliosi's job to work with the Tate and LaBianca squads and follow up on all the new information. The thirty-five-year-old deputy DA was enthusiastic, as he always was when working on a case. Everyone in the massive deputy DA pool was ambitious, but none more so than Bugliosi, whose won-loss record in 104 felony jury trials was 103-1. He had a reputation among many of his peers as a shameless self-promoter, and they all enjoyed getting under his thin skin by deliberately mispronouncing his last name as "BUG-lee-osi" rather than the correct "BOO-lee-osi." Sometimes they really enraged him by calling him Buggy or Bugsy. But friends and rivals agreed that no one in the District Attorney's Office worked harder or was more thorough in his trial preparation. Bugliosi was pleased to get the Tate-LaBianca assignment; it was the kind of high-profile trial that, if prosecuted successfully, could make a young deputy D.A.'s career.

Bugliosi began by accompanying a team of investigators to Spahn Ranch. Danny DeCarlo came with them, but he insisted on being in handcuffs to give the impression that he was being forced to cooperate. George Spahn granted permission for a search of the property. Dozens of odd-looking people prowled the ranch, most of them young. DeCarlo led the cops to spots where he said Manson and the Family liked to take target practice with the .22 Buntline—Bugliosi wanted to match shell casings and slug fragments with those found at Cielo. They eventually gathered sixty-eight slugs, whole or parts, and twenty-two casings. (A second ranch trip five months later yielded twenty-three additional .22 caliber shell casings.)

Back at Parker Center after his initial Spahn Ranch visit, Bugliosi learned that Susan Atkins would be offered some kind of deal in return for her testimony against Charlie and the other participants in the Tate and LaBianca murders. Bugliosi argued against it—according to Ronnie Howard, Susan had admitted stabbing Gary Hinman and Sharon Tate. They were just starting to put together their case against her. Why offer immunity immediately when, if they just gave him some time, he might deliver an airtight case against all of them? Bugliosi was told that Chief Davis wanted the case rushed to the grand jury; the public was impatient and the LAPD looked worse every day that they didn't announce they'd solved the Tate murder. Susan Atkins would be offered a deal, and very soon. They'd figure out the details of it when the time came.

Next, Bugliosi and five members of the Tate and LaBianca squads drove to Inyo County. With the help of county district attorney Frank Fowles, they interviewed the officers involved in the Barker Ranch raids and inspected the collected evidence. Many items were sent back to L.A. for lab analysis. Bugliosi talked to Squeaky and Sandy, who offered convoluted explanations of how Charlie Manson was "love, you can't define it." As they talked, Bugliosi decided that they were "retarded at a certain stage in their childhood. . . . little girls, playing little-girl games." He interviewed all five female Family members still in Inyo County custody—Leslie, Gypsy, Ruth Ann, Dianne Lake, and Nancy Pitman. None of them offered any useful information. Clem and Charlie were the Family men remaining in the county lockup. DA Fowles told Bugliosi that Clem had a lawyer who had insisted his client be examined by two psychiatrists—they'd determined that Clem was "presently insane." At Bugliosi's request, Fowles agreed to stall any actions involving Clem. That left Charlie.

Bugliosi watched that afternoon as Charlie pleaded not guilty to arson charges in an Inyo County court. He was struck by how at ease Charlie seemed, even in handcuffs. It was as though he didn't have a care in the world. The judge set Charlie's bail at $25,000. The Tate and La-Bianca cases were still being built against Charlie; Bugliosi wasn't ready to arrest him yet, but he didn't want to risk some friend of the Family putting up Charlie's Inyo County bail and giving him the opportunity to disappear. He asked Fowles to call him if anyone offered to put up the $25,000. If that happened, whether he felt ready or not Bugliosi would file murder charges against Charlie. Even if nobody put up Charlie's bail, it was still uncertain whether he could be proven guilty of arson. At any time a county judge might dismiss the charges and set Charlie free. The L.A. prosecutors were racing the clock.

Charlie knew what was going on. Some Family members had been idling at Spahn Ranch when the LAPD investigators went there to check for .22 slugs and shell casings. Bugliosi's arrival in Inyo County and the questions he'd asked made it certain that the LAPD was after the Family for Tate and LaBianca. Squeaky and Sandy were reliable messengers, bringing Charlie information and passing along his instructions. Susan was in Sybil Brand, which was bad. Charlie didn't know where Tex and Pat were. He needed to find out. Linda had of course run off right after the murders. Leslie was holding strong in the Independence jail. She was right under Charlie's thumb there. Potential weak link Zero was dead. Charlie might still be all right. The main thing was, nobody should admit anything, just as he'd taught them. But in case things went much further, Charlie needed an alibi for Tate and LaBianca. He went to work on that.

As soon as he was back in his L.A. office, Bugliosi issued a "want" for Charles Montgomery, the shadowy figure who, according to Kitty Lutesinger, might have been involved in some or all of the murders. Besides Lutesinger's statement, Bugliosi also had an interview card from the Inyo County deputy who'd questioned Charles Montgomery after catching him skinny-dipping. But no information on Montgomery came back; the guy was smoke, impossible to nail down.

The five Family women in Inyo County cells were transferred to Sybil Brand in L.A. On Bugliosi's instructions, they were kept separated. He believed they had some sort of strange "cohesion" that reinforced their individual resolve to not cooperate.

Inyo County DA Frank Fowles called Bugliosi: Sandy Good had been overheard telling someone that Charlie had an alibi plan. If he got charged with Tate and LaBianca, he'd say that he wasn't anywhere near L.A. on those nights and the rest of the Family would swear that it was true. Simple and effective, because how could the L.A. prosecutors prove otherwise? Bugliosi was shaken. He called in a couple of the LaBianca investigators and told them that they had to find some proof of where Manson was for the whole week of the murders. He was pleased that they didn't ask him how. They were pros.

On November 26, Bobby Beausoleil's trial for the murder of Gary Hinman ended with a hung jury. Four jurors were so put off by Danny DeCarlo that they refused to vote for conviction. The prosecutors immediately announced that they would retry him. Bugliosi was assigned the case in addition to Tate and LaBianca. If all went well with those investigations, they'd be able to make a stronger case against Beausoleil the second time around.

Two weeks after she made her original request, Virginia Graham finally was granted the opportunity to tell what she knew about the Tate-LaBianca murders to a psychologist on the Corona prison staff. The psychologist passed Virginia along to one of the Tate-LaBianca squad members. Everything Virginia related matched what investigators had already learned from Ronnie Howard. The corroboration reinforced their conviction that they were finally on the right track.

LAPD investigators interrogated the five female Family members that had been transferred to Sybil Brand. No useful information was gleaned from Dianne Lake, Gypsy, Ruth Ann, or Nancy Pitman, but Leslie cracked just a little when she learned that Zero supposedly committed suicide. Sensing she was stunned by the news, Sgt. Mike McGann, who was conducting the interview, pounced. He told Leslie that he knew Charlie Manson was one of five Tate killers. Leslie mumbled that she didn't think Charlie "was in on any of them," and, besides, only four people were involved at Cielo. Three of them were girls, and one of the girls named Linda didn't kill anyone. That matched what Susan Atkins had told Ronnie Howard—"Linda wasn't in on [that] one." McGann kept pushing: What was Linda's last name? Who told Leslie that Linda was at Cielo? Leslie turned sulky and uncooperative. She did suggest that she knew things about eleven murders. The LAPD was investigating nine—

five at Cielo, two at Waverly Drive, Gary Hinman, and Shorty Shea. But try as McGann might, he could not get Leslie to be specific about the other two. It would not be the last time that a Family member alluded to murders that authorities knew nothing about.

McGann tried to goad Leslie out of her sulk. She didn't respond when he told her that Susan had implicated Katie (Pat), but was shocked when McGann added that Susan bragged about going out the night after the Cielo murders and killing two more people. After that Leslie refused to talk anymore, even though McGann offered her twenty-four-hour protection if she cooperated. The session had still been useful for Bugliosi and the other investigators. They had confirmation that Susan, Pat, and Linda were the three women at Cielo, though beyond her name they still had no idea of who or where Linda was. But the interrogation was helpful for Charlie, too. Leslie had learned that Susan was snitching, and through Family members who visited her at Sybil Brand, probably Squeaky and Sandy, she was able to pass that information back to Charlie in the Inyo County jail. No one understood Susan Atkins's foibles and insecurities better than Charlie Manson. Armed with the knowledge that she was betraying him, probably as a consequence of her compulsion to show off, Charlie could plot his countermoves.

A Spahn ranch hand told detectives that Linda's last name was Kasabian. Los Angeles County officials identified Katie as Patricia Krenwinkel, who had been released to her father after the Barker Ranch raid. The LAPD contacted Mr. Krenwinkel, who said that Pat was staying with her mother in Alabama. But Linda was more elusive; no one knew where she might have gone. Charles Montgomery also remained at large.

Susan Atkins, who had still not been officially interrogated by the Tate-LaBianca investigators, was given a court-appointed attorney named Richard Caballero. Having studied the evidence already accumulated against her, Caballero advised his new client that her only hope of avoiding California's death penalty was to cooperate with the police. He told Susan that Charlie was "a force working in your life that is stronger than you are."

• • •

Members of the Tate and LaBianca teams began interviewing L.A.-area residents who'd been mentioned by Susan to Ronnie Howard and Virginia Graham. Gregg Jakobson was cooperative. He told about his interest in Charlie's music and the Family's lifestyle, and how he tried unsuccessfully to interest his friend Terry Melcher into either recording Charlie or else financing a movie about the Family. But Charlie couldn't have intended to have Melcher killed on the night of the Cielo murders, Jakobson pointed out, because he knew by then that Melcher had moved. Jakobson tried to tell about Charlie's weird beliefs, but the officer interrogating him wasn't interested in any of that. He just wanted to hear about Charlie's grudge against Melcher. As an afterthought, he asked Jakobson if he knew a guy named Charles Montgomery, probably nicknamed Tex. Jakobson said that he did, but Tex's last name was Watson, not Montgomery. The LAPD ran checks on Charles *Watson* and found that he'd been arrested for drugs in Van Nuys back in April. Fingerprints taken then matched one found on the front door at Cielo. It took only a few more hours of digging to learn that Watson was from a small town in Collin County, Texas, not too far from Dallas. Investigators called the sheriff there—Tom Montgomery, Tex's cousin. He thrilled the L.A. cops by saying that Tex was living at home, and that he'd pick him up right away.

Tex had hooked up with an old girlfriend. When they returned from an afternoon drive, Tex's father was waiting. He asked his son if he knew anything about a murder back in California. Tex said that he didn't, and he, his father, and Tex's uncle Maurice drove to the county jail in McKinney. Sheriff Tom Montgomery sheepishly told Tex that he had to take him into custody, but the misunderstanding would surely be cleared up soon: "We know for sure you didn't commit no murder." Word of Tex's arrest spread quickly throughout the small community, but nobody who knew Tex there believed he'd killed anybody. He was such a sweet guy.

Gregg Jakobson was willing to assist LAPD investigators. Dennis Wilson and Terry Melcher weren't. Dennis rightly feared the wrath of the other Beach Boys. They hadn't liked Charlie Manson to begin with, and now, thanks to Dennis they would soon be linked with some crazy guru and his killer cult, hardly the best association for a band whose trademark song subjects were sun and fun. To Dennis, whose self-esteem was always shaky, the Beach Boys and his place in the band were the most important things in the world. So when the police came to question him, Dennis downplayed his relationship with Charlie. Yes, the guy and his people stayed with Wilson for a little while. So what? Lots of people did—he'd been living in a big house at the time. Sure, he'd had Charlie audition for Brother Records. That's what you did when you had a label, try out just about every would-be music star you came across to see if any of them really had some talent. Charlie didn't, and that was that.

Melcher stonewalled, too. Columbia wouldn't be pleased to have its boy wonder producer publicly associated with long-haired mass murderers. Melcher knew that he couldn't completely avoid the Manson taint, but he could at least try to limit it. Where Wilson avoided specifics, Melcher lied. He claimed that he'd only met Manson a couple of times, really just out at Spahn Ranch where he went to listen to the guy's music at the insistence of Gregg Jakobson. He hadn't been impressed, though out of pity he did hand over the cash he had in his pocket because those people on the ranch, especially the little kids, looked so raggedy and starved. That Manson apparently thought he'd broken his word about a recording contract was news to him, Melcher insisted. He didn't understand why Manson would have gone to his former residence on Cielo seeking revenge, if that was what had happened in the Tate murder case. When the investigators said they'd heard that Melcher liked to mess around with the Family women, he showed them pictures of some of his recent girlfriends, including spectacular Candy Bergen. He asked, "When I've got beauties like these to get in bed with, why would I want to screw any of Manson's clap-ridden, unwashed dogs?" The cops might not have believed him, but the unwritten rule of L.A. law enforcement apparently prevailed—celebrities got passes where regular people wouldn't. Melcher was taken at his word. The investigative team did get one bit of new, useful information from Melcher. He conceded that one time Dennis Wilson had given him a ride home to Cielo, and Charlie Manson rode along in the backseat, strumming his guitar. But Dennis dropped him at the gate, Melcher emphasized. Charlie didn't come onto the grounds, let alone inside the house. Still, to the investigators it was confirmation that Charlie Manson had been to Cielo at least once. He knew where the place was.

On Sunday afternoon, November 30, Richard Caballero met with Bugliosi at Parker Center to talk deal on his client's behalf. Aaron Stovitz had supplied Caballero with copies of Virginia Graham's and Ronnie Howard's taped interviews, and made it clear to the defense attorney that prosecutors were ready to seek the death penalty for Susan. Now Bugliosi made an offer—if Susan cooperated, they would consider letting her plead guilty to second degree murder with a penalty of life imprisonment. Caballero took the offer to Susan at Sybil Brand, emphasizing to her that the case against her was strong. If she didn't make the deal, she'd die in the gas chamber. Susan said she couldn't make up her mind. Caballero returned to Parker Center and told Bugliosi about Susan's indecision. He added that he thought she might agree to testify against Charlie to the grand jury, but never in a public courtroom. Charlie's hold over her was still that strong. And no matter what Susan might eventually promise to the prosecution, her ongoing devotion to Charlie might make her change her mind and recant at any moment. Bugliosi urged Caballero to keep trying. For now he had a case against Susan and Tex Watson in the Cielo murders, but so far they had only Susan's jailhouse boasts to Ronnie Howard and Virginia Graham to implicate Manson, Pat, and Linda. The prosecutors were especially concerned that the defendants might eventually demand joint rather than individual trials. In joint trials, California law mandated that the prosecution couldn't use as evidence a statement by one defendant that implicated his or her co-defendants. In that case anything Susan had said about the murders could be used only against her, not Charlie or anyone else she claimed participated in the Tate and LaBianca slayings. To be certain of convicting the others, prosecutors needed much more information from Susan that could help build individual cases against all the suspects.

Though many of his staff begged him not to, on December 1 Chief Davis insisted on holding a 2 P.M. news conference to announce that the LAPD had cracked the Tate and LaBianca murder investigations. For weeks, the department had little progress to report. Now there were suspects that could be publicly identified in both cases and a motive, revenge on Terry Melcher, for Tate. It would be the investigators' jobs to back up what Davis would announce. But the press conference was almost derailed before the chief met with the media. At 7 A.M. Sheriff Montgomery phoned Aaron Stovitz to warn that if L.A. didn't deliver an arrest warrant to Collin County within two hours, he would let Tex go. Stovitz and Bugliosi had to scramble to find a judge to sign Tex's warrant, which reached Collin County minutes ahead of the sheriff's deadline. It was only the first of innumerable obstacles Texas lawmen and lawyers would impose on the prosecutors' efforts to have Tex extradited to L.A. for trial. The extradition appeals process would take almost nine months to work through state and district courts.

While they were at it, Stovitz and Bugliosi also issued arrest warrants for Pat Krenwinkel and Linda Kasabian. After a few phone calls to authorities in Alabama, Pat was arrested just prior to Chief Davis's press conference. Linda's whereabouts were still unknown, but at least the warrant would have lawmen around the country looking for her.

Chief Ed Davis didn't hold back when he addressed the media. According to the chief, after 8,750 hours of nonstop investigation, the LAPD had solved not only the Tate murder case, but also the slayings of the LaBiancas. Warrants had been issued for three individuals—Tex, Pat, and Linda. Indictments for four or five additional individuals would be sought from the grand jury. Davis never mentioned Susan or Charlie, but he didn't have to. Sources soon clued in reporters to a "band of murderous nomads" and their leader. Within a day sketchy profiles of Manson began appearing in the papers, and an *L.A. Times* headline proclaimed, "Grudge Against Doris Day's Son Linked to Tate Slayings." The LaBiancas were still second-tier victims of what the article described as an "occultist band." Reporters found that Richard Caballero, Susan's attorney, was glad to provide colorful quotes. He explained to them that his client had participated in the murders while under Charlie's "hypnotic spell," and that she "said of Manson, 'We belong to him, not to ourselves.'" It was part of Caballero's strategy to lay the groundwork for an insanity plea if he couldn't cut a deal for Susan with the prosecutors.

But the defense attorney still hoped for a deal. After Davis's press conference, he asked Stovitz for permission to bring Susan to Caballero's office. Away from Sybil Brand, he suggested, she might be more amenable to talking. Caballero would make a tape of whatever Susan told him. If her case went to trial, he would play it for psychiatrists. If a deal was struck, he'd let the prosecutors hear the tape before they went to the grand jury. Stovitz agreed to the plan.

Reports of the Davis press conference went out all over the country. Reaction among those who knew Charlie Manson was mixed. Phil Kaufman, who had shared prison time with him, was convinced that Charlie and his followers couldn't possibly have committed the Tate and LaBianca murders. He knew that they were weird, but he didn't think they were killers. But Charlie's cousin Jo Ann recalls that when she heard the news back in West Virginia, she was "very sad and horrified, but not surprised. Once you really got to know Charles, anything awful that he did was no surprise."

Stovitz and Bugliosi hadn't wanted Chief Davis to hold the press conference, but their investigation benefited in its immediate aftermath. On December 2, Linda Kasabian voluntarily surrendered to police in Concord, New Hampshire. She said that she had been at Cielo on the night of the Tate murders, but had not participated in them. Linda also said that she would cooperate with any effort to extradite her to California.

At the urging of her mother, who finally believed the horrific stories told by her seventeen-year-old daughter, Barbara Hoyt came in to talk to the police. She told them about hearing Shorty's screams on the night that he was butchered, and overhearing Susan bragging about her role in the Tate murders. The investigators felt there was plenty more to explore with her, and Hoyt promised to be available as needed.

Mary Brunner contacted police in Eau Claire, Wisconsin, and made a deal through them with Los Angeles County to cooperate in exchange for immunity in the Hinman case. Besides offering testimony about Hinman's murder, Mary was adamant that Tex Watson told her about Charlie and some of the others murdering Shorty Shea. She told police that afterward Shorty's car was left somewhere in Canoga Park. The LAPD initiated a search for it.

• • •

Richard Caballero brought the Susan Atkins tape to Parker Center on the evening of December 3 and played it for Bugliosi and members of the Tate and LaBianca teams. Because they were amenable to negotiating a deal, for two hours Caballero allowed them to listen to Susan name the participants and describe, often in gory detail, the murders. Susan was clear that, although he didn't go along himself, Charlie ordered the Cielo killings. The four who went that night were herself, Tex, Pat, and Linda. The next night Charlie went into the house on Waverly Drive, and afterward sent Tex, Pat, and Leslie inside with orders to kill the LaBiancas. Susan didn't witness these murders—she was sent on by Charlie with Clem and Linda—but Pat and Leslie told her about them later. Susan also stated that "the reason Charlie picked [Cielo] was to instill fear into Terry Melcher because Terry had given us his word on a few things and never came through with them."

There were two significant differences in Susan's taped testimony and her boasts to Virginia and Ronnie at Sybil Brand. Now, instead of presenting herself as a gleeful slaughterer, Susan claimed that she stabbed Voytek Frykowski only in self-defense, and that rather than butchering Sharon Tate, she held the heavily pregnant actress while Tex stabbed her. But the investigators still heard enough to assure Caballero that his client would be offered a deal.

Another defense attorney had the same goal for his new client. Los Angeles lawyer Gary Fleischman represented Linda Kasabian, who arrived in L.A. late on the 3rd and was booked into Sybil Brand. Stovitz briefly met with her and her lawyer there, and left with the impression that Linda was willing to cooperate but Fleischman wouldn't allow it until she was offered immunity in return for her testimony. Stovitz and Bugliosi decided not to offer anything for the time being. They would concentrate on cutting a deal with Caballero and Susan. If for some reason that didn't work out, Kasabian might be a satisfactory alternative.

On December 4, Susan Atkins got her deal, an exceptionally generous one. If she testified truthfully to the grand jury, the prosecution would not seek the death penalty against her for the Hinman, Tate, or LaBianca murders. If Susan chose not to testify at the anticipated murder trials, or even if she later recanted all that she'd said, prosecutors could not use her grand jury testimony against her or any co-defendants. Caballero boasted later that his client "gave up nothing and got everything in return." The defense attorney cleverly expedited the one-sided deal by warning prosecutors that, because of the influence Charlie still had on her, at any moment Susan might decide not to testify to the grand jury. Without that testimony, there would almost surely be no grand jury indictments of Charlie, Tex, and Pat, all of whom might then be released. So Stovitz and Bugliosi gave Caballero everything he demanded for his client and arranged for Susan to go before the grand jury on December 5.

A fingerprint of Pat's taken by the Mobile, Alabama, Police Department matched a print found inside Sharon Tate's bedroom at Cielo. Now she and Tex were both placed at that murder scene. But prosecutors still had only Susan's word that Charlie was the mastermind behind the Tate slayings.

On the evening of the 4th, Bugliosi met with Susan at Caballero's office. She told him, "Charlie is looking at us right now and he can hear everything we are saying." Bugliosi thought she was crazy—"probably not legally insane, but crazy nonetheless." He and Stovitz were basing their high-profile case on the words of an extremely nutty girl.

At nine the next morning, Aaron Stovitz swore in Susan Atkins before twenty-one members of the grand jury. By law, two-thirds of them had to agree on any indictments. Susan waived her right not to incriminate herself and, coaxed by Stovitz and Bugliosi, told her story yet again. Her testimony lasted all day. Some of the details she provided were so explicit that at one point a recess was declared when a gagging grand juror had to leave the room. By the time the grand jury broke for the weekend, its mostly white, mid-to-upper-middle-class members had heard from Susan not only about the Tate and LaBianca murders, but also about the wonders of Charlie and the power Susan believed was speaking through him: "The words that would come from Charlie's mouth . . . would come from what I call the Infinite." The prosecutors were pleased when Susan said that Charlie "programmed [us] to do things." She even alluded briefly to Helter Skelter, "the last war on the face of the earth." Stovitz and Bugliosi were confident that they were well on the way to getting the indictments that they wanted.

Over the weekend, press coverage of Susan's testimony ("Orgy of Murder: Tate Suspect Tells Jury of Slayings") competed for front page space with news from Altamont Speedway outside San Francisco. Less than four months after the Woodstock festival had celebrated music as a means of bringing people together in an atmosphere of peace and love, on Saturday December 6 a black audience member was stabbed to death by Hells Angels during the performance by the Rolling Stones. It was the dark side *yang* to the hopeful Woodstock *yin*, and further proof to a growing number of outraged, conservative Americans that way too many longhairs were not only socially subversive, but also just plain dangerous.

On Monday, the grand jury reconvened and heard testimony from a number of witnesses, including Danny DeCarlo, Gregg Jakobson, and three of the five Family women who'd been transferred from the Inyo County jail to Sybil Brand. Gypsy wouldn't testify, and the prosecutors didn't call Leslie because Susan had just named her as one of the LaBianca killers. Ruth Ann, Dianne Lake, and Nancy Pitman all swore they knew nothing about any murders, but it didn't matter. In the most negative possible way, Susan had wowed the jurors. That afternoon they returned indictments on seven counts of murder and one count of conspiracy to commit murder for Charles Manson, Charles Watson, Susan Atkins, Linda Kasabian, and Patricia Krenwinkel. Because she had been involved only on the second night, Leslie Van Houten was indicted on two counts of murder and one count of conspiracy to commit murder. But Stovitz and Bugliosi were well aware that the indictments were only a first step. Successful prosecution still depended on Susan Atkins, and, based on her adoring descriptions of him to the grand jury, she might bolt back to Charlie at any time. They needed much more.

• • •

Susan's testimony never touched on Shorty Shea's murder, but shortly after she met with the grand jury, prosecutors caught a major break in the Shea case. The information provided by Mary Brunner about the disposal of Shorty's car after his death was accurate. Investigators found his 1962 Mercury just where she'd said it had been abandoned in Canoga Park. Inside the vehicle was a footlocker with a set of palm prints that was eventually matched to longtime Family member Bruce Davis, and police also found Shorty's cowboy boots, smeared with dried blood.

Since Charlie's extradition from Inyo County to Los Angeles was imminent, Squeaky and Sandy moved from the desert back to L.A. They and various other Family members who'd been scattered about after the mid-October Barker Ranch raid needed a base, so they turned to Charlie's old prison friend Phil Kaufman. Kaufman hadn't enjoyed his most recent encounters with the Family at Spahn Ranch. After he rebuffed Charlie's attempt to recruit him, the Manson followers had acted unfriendly. Now they needed him and were acting like they'd been buddies all along. But there was little Kaufman hated more than the law railroading an innocent man, and no matter what they said on TV or in the newspapers he felt certain that Charlie had nothing to do with any Tate or LaBianca murders. Sure, the guy was a criminal, he broke the law lots of times in lots of ways, but there was a big difference between doing that and killing people. So when Charlie's girls asked Kaufman if they could crash at his house, he agreed.

Richard Caballero believed that Susan was going to recant her testimony sooner rather than later. After she did, the prosecutors couldn't use anything she'd told them or the grand jury so far, but they'd surely be furious and do everything they could to build a strong case against Susan to send her to the gas chamber. Caballero felt his client's best defense was that she was completely controlled by Charlie, and before she clammed up, he wanted her story as she'd told it so far to get out to the public beyond his own statements and media leaks. Without telling the prosecutors, he began to quietly explore a deal that would result in a pretrial book presenting Susan as evil mastermind Charlie's helpless, brainwashed minion. There were lots of writers and journalists who wanted an exclusive piece of the Manson story, so it didn't take Caballero long to get something in place.

At Sybil Brand, Susan began receiving her first visitors, some of the female Family members who were staying at Phil Kaufman's. They told Susan that they loved her, and mentioned how her son was in the custody of L.A. Family Services. The Family had helped Susan get little Ze Zo Ze back after she'd lost him before, when he and the other Family children were taken by Social Services after the August 16 Spahn Ranch raid. They emphasized to Susan that they could certainly find the little boy again.

On the afternoon of December 9, Charles Milles Manson, address transient, occupation musician, was formally charged in Inyo County court with the murders of seven people and immediately extradited to the ninth floor jail at downtown L.A.'s Hall of Justice. Starting with Chief Davis's press conference on December 1 and continuing through the grand jury testimony and indictments, public appetite for even a glimpse of Charlie in the flesh reached frenzied heights, thanks to media coverage that emphasized sensationalism over facts. Self-styled insiders tipped reporters that Charlie and the Family practiced black magic and animal sacrifice. On-air and print speculation abounded that Charlie used hypnosis to control the minds of his followers. Rare relevant articles ("Manson Wanted a Racial War, Friends Say" in the December 7 edition of the *Los Angeles Times*) were virtually ignored. December 9 became Charlie's coming-out party, the first real opportunity for the press and public to get a good glimpse of him. As he was taken from the Inyo County courthouse and placed in a van for transport to L.A., Charlie had a Christ-at-Gethsemane air about him—long hair and beard, simple buckskin clothing, eyes expressive even as he shuffled along amid a surrounding phalanx of policemen. He didn't look like the evil leader of a killer cult. He didn't look in any way threatening.

When Charlie arrived at the Hall of Justice, there was a large crowd gathered outside and an even bigger one inside. Hundreds of deputy district attorneys, public defenders, and clerical staffers left their desks in the building to get a good look at the notorious prisoner. Charlie was brought down a long hall, and before they saw him everyone waiting heard metallic rattling. When Charlie finally came into sight, it was hard to immediately tell what he looked like or what he was wearing because he was encased from head to foot in heavy chains. One deputy DA was reminded of the first appearance of Marley's Ghost in *A Christmas Carol.* The LAPD was taking no chances that Charlie might escape.

Charlie had reason to despair. He was charged with seven of the most notorious murders in modern American history. One of his followers had ratted him out to the grand jury and others would get ample opportunity to do the same. All the power of the District Attorney's Office and the LAPD was arrayed against him. But Charlie wasn't without resources himself. His hold over many of his followers, even those in custody, remained intact. Besides them, he had his own proven ability to turn bad situations to his advantage. If it came down to a battle of wits between him and the investigators, Charlie was not necessarily outmatched. His life was at stake, but as he was brought inside the Hall of Justice and up an elevator to the cells on the ninth floor, he didn't appear scared or even intimidated. If anything, Charlie seemed to some puzzled onlookers to be enjoying himself.

They were right. For thirty-five years, Charlie Manson yearned to be the center of attention, culminating in his ambition to be bigger than the Beatles. As he was marched into jail in chains, with photographers' cameras flashing and a crush of onlookers gawking, Charlie could sense that he was finally getting close. He'd wanted this attention all his life, and he was prepared to take full advantage.

CHAPTER SEVENTEEN
Charlie Is Famous

Charlie's arrival in chains at the L.A. Hall of Justice increased rather than satisfied public interest in the Tate-LaBianca murders. Previously, most media coverage was limited to speculation and occasional stories noting a lack of progress in the Tate investigation; the LaBiancas were essentially forgotten. There was a lot going on in America and the world, much of it tragic on a larger scale, that was featured on front pages and broadcasts. News of war and racial strife had saturated public consciousness for the last four years, and there seemed to be no end to those stories. The root causes were complex, and people were sick of thinking about them. With Tate-LaBianca, Charlie and the Family offered a simpler horror—a strange man and his followers apparently killed a famous pregnant actress and six other people. In *The White Album*, a collection of essays on the 1960s, Joan Didion reflected on the murders and concluded, "The paranoia was fulfilled." Charlie Manson fulfilled the paranoia of disparate social factions, giving everyone what they wanted—a bogeyman, martyr, and even hero.

It was impossible not to notice Charlie; there were stories about him to watch or to read every day. There was an undeniable attraction to it all: What juicy detail might be revealed next? L.A. was in the midst of a newspaper war; the *Times* and the *Herald Examiner* vied to see which could attract more readers with bloodcurdling Manson stories. The national media couldn't get enough of Charlie either. The biggest magazines sent platoons of reporters and photographers to McMechen, West Virginia, to write about Charlie's childhood. The director of the county's public housing there had to assign a special room for interviews so residents wouldn't be badgered on the streets. But few wanted to talk about Charlie, and those who did helped further his fame by exaggerating the travails of his childhood. It was widely reported that Charlie was the son of an unwed teenaged whore who eventually abandoned him, and that when he wasn't in reform schools he was mistreated by hardhearted relatives. It took much longer for reporters to find Kathleen in the Northwest, and to protect her daughter, Nancy, she wanted nothing to do with the media. The principal of the McMechen elementary school, intrigued by all she read and heard, decided to pull Charlie's file from the dusty room where student records were filed. It wasn't there; in the few days since Charlie's explosion into celebrity, someone had stolen it. A black market for Manson memorabilia was already blossoming.

To those appalled by student radicals and war protesters, Charlie and the Family were proof that longhairs were not only disruptive but dangerous. It didn't matter that they were neither students nor protesters. They looked like they could be, and that was enough. For anyone concerned that drugs had the potential to turn normal young people into kill-crazy lunatics, information about the Family's regular use of LSD confirmed their worst fears. Atheists and agnostics could and did cite Charlie's garbled, violent interpretation of Revelation as evidence that religious fundamentalists were monsters. Critics of rock 'n' roll pointed to Charlie's fixation with the Beatles—see how such music incited disaster? (In his perceptive *Waiting for the Sun*, Barney Hoskyns wrote that Charlie and Altamont "managed to undo the whole notion that rock music was a positive force for change.")

But Charlie fulfilled the paranoia of the young disenchanted, too. The antiwar protesters and student radicals deeply distrusted the government and considered elected politicians and lawmen the enemy. Charlie's docile appearance and initially polite requests to represent himself in court, which were turned down, signaled to many disaffected that here was an innocent man being railroaded because he looked and acted different. The most radical activists took it a step further; the presumed guilt of Charlie and his followers made him admirable. In December, at the last formal meeting of SDS before it broke into irreconcilable factions, Bernardine Dohrn delivered a speech praising them: "Dig it! First they killed those pigs, then they ate dinner in the same room with them. They even shoved a fork into the victim's stomach. Wild!" The Weathermen's salute became four fingers held up in the air to signify the fork jammed into Leno LaBianca's abdomen. To them, Mark Rudd recalls, the Tate-LaBianca murders were "a big fat finger in the face of this country . . . here's a little of your own medicine, you hypocrites."

At the jail on the ninth floor of the Hall of Justice, letters addressed to Charlie began pouring in, hundreds a day. Some were diatribes from those who thought him disgusting, others suggested he save his soul through prayer, a good number requested autographs, but to those screening inmate mail the most disturbing came from teenage girls who wanted Charlie's permission to join the Family. They thought it sounded wonderful, and for that Charlie had Squeaky, Ruth Ann, and some of his other still at large followers to thank. Charlie wasn't the only one with a keen sense of public relations.

The Family women didn't last long at Phil Kaufman's. Each one thought that she had the best idea of what Charlie wanted them to do, and they argued constantly. Kaufman got sick of it and told them to stop bickering or get out. They straggled back to Spahn Ranch; George Spahn wasn't initially glad to see them but soon changed his mind. Squeaky took charge and began inviting the media to visit. Local and national publications were soon featuring long articles about the Family's simple lifestyle; photographs showed them doing chores on the ranch, frolicking in its streams and caves (sexy little Ruth Ann always posed out front), and even going on their garbage runs. People began coming out to Spahn and renting horses because Charlie Manson's followers were usually the ones who handed you the reins. Family numbers on the ranch had dwindled, but now there were new recruits. The Family engaged anyone promising in conversation and invited them to their communal meals. The most important new addition was Dennis Rice, who came with his four young children and a valid credit card. Dennis became the Family's main conduit to Charlie, visiting him in jail and bringing back instructions. Squeaky took most responsibility for visiting the female members in jail, reminding them to keep quiet and do whatever Charlie told them. Gypsy and Nancy Pitman were released in mid-December—from Susan

Atkins's grand jury testimony it was clear they hadn't participated in the murders, and there was no proof that they had committed any other crimes. As soon as they were freed, they joined the others at Spahn. All of the women were careful to emphasize to the media that Charlie "is love." They said they didn't know anything about any murders, only that following Charlie made them happy—and, they emphasized, *free*. Reporters didn't see any evidence of robotic, mind-controlled followers at Spahn, and this was reflected in their stories, just as Squeaky and the others intended.

On December 10, prosecutors caught a major break. A service station attendant in Sylmar found Rosemary LaBianca's wallet as he cleaned the women's toilet tank. Her driver's license and credit cards were still inside—Charlie's hope that a black person would find and use them hadn't panned out. The wallet was too saturated to yield fingerprints, but the discovery corroborated Susan Atkins's grand jury testimony.

San Jose detectives announced their intention to question Charlie and Family members about the August 2 murders of two teenage girls in their jurisdiction. They suspected the slayings were linked to Tate and LaBianca because each girl suffered numerous stab wounds. It was eventually determined that there was no evidence tying Charlie or the Family to the San Jose crime, but it was only the first of many times it would be suspected that Manson Family members committed other murders beyond those already known.

Charlie was arraigned by Judge William B. Keene on December 11. He wore his buckskins, and the *L.A. Times* noted that "he appeared to relish" the crowd that jammed the courtroom to see him. Keene assigned public defender Paul Fitzgerald to represent Charlie, a potential conflict of interest as he was also part of Bobby Beausoleil's defense team. Fitzgerald felt he had a good chance to get Charlie off; he told reporters afterward that "all the prosecution has are two fingerprints and Vince Bugliosi," a nod to the assistant DA's impressive record as a prosecutor. Bugliosi privately agreed, and arranged for Susan Atkins to be taken from Sybil Brand on Sunday the 14th to ride around with investigators and point out where she thought Linda Kasabian had tossed out bloody clothes, knives, and the Buntline .22 after the Tate murders.

The judge may have given the assignment to Paul Fitzgerald, but a large number of L.A. lawyers hoped to persuade Charlie to let them represent him instead. This was the kind of high-profile case where a win virtually guaranteed a lucrative practice. During the next six weeks Charlie logged 139 visits from attorneys hoping to gain his trust and business. A dizzying lawyer-go-round for Charlie and for Susan, Pat, and Leslie had begun.

Judge Keene also imposed a gag order; no one associated with the case was to discuss evidence with the media. But, as Bugliosi sourly observed, "rumors multiplied like bacteria." He even heard a rumor that Susan's lawyer, Richard Caballero, had cut a deal with a European press syndicate to publish her personal story as soon as the grand jury transcript of her testimony was made public. On Sunday, he picked up his morning paper and found that the truth was even worse. The *Los Angeles Times* front page trumpeted, "SUSAN ATKINS'S STORY OF 2 NIGHTS OF MURDER." With his client's permission, Caballero and his law partner, working with local journalists, turned the tapes Caballero had made with Susan into a quickie book that was supposed to be published only in Europe on December 14. But the *L.A. Times* somehow obtained a copy and printed the contents. Now everyone, including Charlie, knew all that Susan claimed.

Even as Angelenos ingested her colorful account with their morning eggs and coffee, Susan took a seven-hour ride around the streets of Bel Air. She enjoyed the outing more than the investigators with her; Susan was unable to remember where Linda's toss-out spots might have been. Her excuse in a note to a former Sybil Brand cell mate was, "It was such a beautiful day my memory vanished." Susan liked sending regulation-approved letters and also "kites," illegal notes passed among Sybil Brand inmates. She sent one to Ronnie Howard, declaring that she was not mad at Ronnie for snitching, only hurt: "Yes, I wanted the world to know M[anson]. It sure looks like they do now. . . . I know now it has all been perfect. Those people died not out of hate or anything ugly. I am not going to defend our beliefs. I am just telling you the way it is."

Susan didn't realize one way it was. Ronnie gave the note to her lawyer, who sent it on to Bugliosi. Under California law, any jail letters or messages containing incriminating messages could be used against the sender; unlike Susan's grand jury testimony, the contents of her notes could still be presented as evidence if she renounced her deal with the prosecutors.

Bugliosi continued accumulating evidence, sometimes through dogged research and sometimes from sheer luck. Examining LAPD evidence bins from the ongoing LaBianca investigations, he found references to Al Springer's interview and a letter mailed to Charlie while he was in jail in Independence. The letter was signed "Harold." Bugliosi remembered Susan referring to a party at "Harold's" next door to the LaBianca home on Waverly Drive. Harold's letter included an address and two phone numbers. Bugliosi asked the LaBianca detectives to find him.

Having read Susan's first-person account in the Sunday newspaper, on Monday a local TV crew set out to look for the items discarded after the Tate murders. Almost immediately they found bloody clothes in an embankment off Benedict Canyon Road. The police had searched for weeks, but the TV crew made the discovery within ten minutes. The LAPD labs matched blood on the clothing to the Cielo victims, and also a long hair stuck on one of the garments as Susan Atkins's.

On Tuesday, Bernard Weiss decided to bug the Van Nuys cops about the gun his son Steven found back in September. The Susan Atkins story in the *Times* referred to a .22 used for the Tate murders—were the police sure that Steven's gun wasn't the one they were looking for? The officer at Van Nuys referred Bernard to the Homicide Division at Parker Center. He called there and explained how the gun his son found had a broken grip just like the one they thought came from Cielo. Bernard was informed that "we can't check out every citizen report on every gun we find." His next call was to a neighbor who worked for a local TV station. The station called Parker Center, and late that night the .22 Buntline was finally retrieved from Van Nuys. Tests on recovered slugs from the murder site proved that it was the gun used in the Cielo killings. When some of the shell casings found at Spahn Ranch matched the .22 Buntline, the murder weapon was solidly linked to the Family.

Charlie used his jail time to formulate a plan for his trial. His strategy was twofold. First, he wanted to defend himself, which would give him a chance to deliver long speeches and otherwise grandstand in a memorable manner. This was his big chance, his world stage. Second, he did not want lawyers representing Susan, Pat, or Leslie to separate their clients' cases from his. After doing that, their first move would inevitably be to have the women examined by psychiatrists, who might very well testify that they'd been brainwashed by Charlie to the point that they were not responsible for their actions. Charlie's last-ditch defense would be that the murders were committed without his knowledge by perpetrators who were mentally competent and carrying out their own wishes rather than Charlie's orders. He needed to maintain absolute control over the three of them to make sure that, if the time came, they'd plead guilty and exonerate him. Susan had squealed and had a lawyer acting in her best interest and not Charlie's, but Charlie felt certain that once he had a chance to meet with her, he'd talk Susan back into the fold no matter what her lawyer wanted. From what he'd read in the *Times*, Susan still worshipped him. Pat remained locked up in Alabama; at Charlie's behest, Squeaky deluged her with letters urging her to allow extradition to L.A., where Charlie's influence was stronger. Linda Kasabian would be more of a problem. In a failed attempt to have her released on bail, Linda's lawyers claimed that she went with the killers on the nights of August 9 and 10 only because she was afraid Charlie would kill her daughter if she didn't. Clearly, that would be her defense at trial.

Leslie changed her lawyer when he defied Charlie's wishes and asked that she be examined by a psychiatrist. There would be many more attorney changes before Charlie felt certain he had a unified team. Meanwhile, he demanded the right to defend himself, and Judge Keene reluctantly said he'd consider it. Warning Charlie that he was making "a sad and tragic mistake," on Christmas Eve Keene agreed to allow it.

Bugliosi paid close attention to Charlie's maneuverings and guessed that he was setting up Tex Watson to take the fall, especially if Watson's lawyer back in Texas succeeded in blocking extradition. Bugliosi surmised that Charlie would at some point have the women claim the murders were all Tex's idea, and that they followed his orders on the nights of the Tate and LaBianca slayings, not Charlie's.

On December 26, Rudolf Weber told Bugliosi about the people he'd found washing themselves off with his lawn hose around 1 A.M. on August 9. He could provide only general descriptions and couldn't pick out Tex, Susan, Pat, or Linda from a large batch of photos, but he did provide the license number of their car: GYY 435. Bugliosi checked, and the number matched the plate on Johnny Swartz's Ford. The deputy DA went to see Swartz, who had quit at Spahn and gone to work on another ranch. Swartz told Bugliosi that Manson once threatened to kill him after they had an argument, and also that after Shorty Shea disappeared Charlie claimed to have helped Shea get a job interview in San Francisco. But that couldn't be true, Swartz said, because after Shorty went missing he saw Danny DeCarlo and a male Family member each toting one of Shorty's prized .45s, and Shorty would never have left those guns behind.

Sixteen-year-old Dianne Lake hadn't had much to say during her post-arrest interview in Independence. But on December 30 she opened up to investigators there. According to Lake, Tex told her that he'd killed Sharon Tate, and that he'd done it on orders from Charlie. She'd seen Leslie Van Houten burn a purse and some rope at Spahn about a week before the August 16 L.A. County raid. Dianne said Leslie told her about stabbing someone who was already dead, and how after committing murders at a house in Los Feliz, a word was written on the refrigerator door there in blood. Leslie mentioned raiding the refrigerator and taking a carton of chocolate milk. Lake also recalled someone having a small bag of coins. Leno LaBianca had had a coin collection.

Afterward county officials weren't sure what to do with Lake. She was a minor whose parents had gladly sent her off with Charlie Manson, so the authorities didn't want to send her back to them. They eventually consigned her to a mental institution, where she would be treated for emotional problems until Stovitz and Bugliosi needed her to testify in court.

Charlie enjoyed his newfound fame, but it wasn't enough. He still wanted to be a rock star, and thought he knew how to do it. There were tapes of him performing his songs; the Family had some, and there were also the recordings made at Brian Wilson's home studio. Charlie thought that Dennis Wilson had those. All Wilson had to do was turn over those tapes to the Family, and then they'd have a fine selection to release as vinyl albums. People would rush to buy them—who wouldn't want to own a Charlie Manson album? Besides putting Charlie at the top of the charts, the record sales would also bring in money to pay his legal expenses. Charlie wanted representation other than public defenders. And, of course, the albums would be put out without kowtowing to some corporate record label. Phil Kaufman would know how to get an album pressed and distributed.

But there was a stumbling block. When Charlie phoned Dennis collect from jail, a guy answering Dennis's phone refused to accept the charges, even when Charlie screamed, "You're going to be fucking sorry." So Charlie sent Squeaky to track down Dennis. She found him at Gregg Jakobson's. Angry because someone had been disrespectful to Charlie when he called collect, Squeaky told Wilson to hand over the tapes or else be killed. He replied that the tapes had already been turned over to the district attorney. That left Squeaky with the tapes Charlie had made with Gregg Jakobson at the cramped studio in Van Nuys. She took those to Phil Kaufman and explained what Charlie wanted him to do. Charlie got on the phone to plead with Kaufman, "You've got to get my music out."

Kaufman still felt certain that Charlie and his goofy crew weren't guilty, so he agreed to help. He used his own money to have two thousand copies of the record pressed and cardboard sleeves printed. The album was called *LIE*, and its cover was a mean-eyed shot of Charlie that had been a recent *Life* magazine cover. Kaufman had some fun with the credits, listing himself as the producer and using his prisoner number at Terminal Island instead of a last name. Part of the back cover was a reprint of an interview Charlie gave to a local underground paper, much of it about his terrible childhood: "No mother, no father. In and out of orphanages and foster homes. . . . I can't tell anybody nothing that they don't already know. But I can sing for them, and I got some music that says what I like to say if I ever had anything to say." Squeaky also wrote some liner notes: "He is your brother—and we are him. He's shown us the door to the love within each one of us—and now we are all keys. It's in you. Pass it on." Kaufman and Squeaky called a press conference to announce that the album, which included Charlie originals like "Cease to Exist," "People Say I'm No Good," and "Don't Do Anything Illegal," would be in stores soon.

The LaBianca detectives located Harold True, and Aaron Stovitz interviewed him. He admitted knowing Charlie and the Family; they'd visited him at his rented home on Waverly Drive "four or five" times before True moved in September 1968. Since the LaBiancas didn't move in next door until November, True hadn't met them and had no idea whether Manson ever had. But the interview established that Charlie had been on Waverly Drive several times before the LaBianca murders.

Stovitz and Bugliosi worried that their case was coming together much too slowly. If Susan Atkins didn't renege on their agreement they would have her testimony, but so far the limited physical evidence they had placed only Tex and Pat at the Cielo murder scene, and both of them were not in state custody and resisting extradition. Bugliosi sent a memo to District Attorney Evelle Younger admitting that without Susan's testimony, they were in trouble. His fear was that Charlie would demand an immediate trial, and he and Stovitz agreed that they would bluff, giving every indication that they were eager to go to trial, too. Charlie was a veteran con man; for the moment, they would try to con him. Whether he fell for it or not, Charlie was happy with the status quo. There was the cover of *Life*, then a major article in the *New York Times* described the Family as a gang who "lived a life of indolence, free sex, midnight motorcycle races and apparently blind obedience to a mysterious guru." With the album about to come out, Charlie expected to become a rock star, too. This pretrial period was exciting. Charlie was in no hurry to see it end.

He often amused himself by appearing in court to make unreasonable demands. On January 17, 1970, he demanded his immediate release because incarceration deprived him of "spiritual, mental and physical liberty in an unconstitutional manner not in harmony with man's or God's law." If the charges against him were dropped, Charlie said, it would save everyone a lot of trouble. The judge dryly responded, "Disappoint all these people? Never, Mr. Manson." Charlie wasn't disappointed in the least. His bizarre request got him more media coverage. Ten days later he was back in court objecting to "the heinous relationship of the Establishment in [my] indictment." He refused to enter a plea of guilty or not guilty. The judge ruled that not responding was the equivalent of a not guilty plea. A trial date of February 9 was tentatively set, but the judge noted that the trial was unlikely to begin then. There were still too many legal issues to be resolved, including whether Tex and Pat would be returned to California.

Facing a trial date, Stovitz and Bugliosi discussed the motives for the murders that they would attempt to prove. They immediately disagreed. Stovitz favored the more conservative approach of robbery. The killers went to Cielo and Waverly Drive to get money for their desert relocation and, possibly, bail for Mary Brunner, the mother of Charlie's child. Both nights, the robbery victims were killed. Bugliosi said that was ridiculous. Very little had been taken on either night—about $70 from Abigail Folger at Cielo, and Rosemary LaBianca's wallet, perhaps a bag of coins, and a container of chocolate milk from Waverly Drive. Many valuable items had been left behind at both murder sites. Bugliosi wanted to convince a jury that the killers' motives, and Charlie's master plan, was to kick off the black-white race war of Helter Skelter by committing shockingly brutal murders and leaving evidence incriminating the Black Panthers. Stovitz replied that robbery, at least, was a common motive that a jury might understand. The Helter Skelter business was too strange. Besides, how could they prove it? Bugliosi agreed that they needed more evidence to take his preferred approach.

There was a second point of fundamental disagreement between the two prosecutors, though it had nothing to do with trial strategy. Stovitz thought the Tate-LaBianca murder trial was important; there would be considerable public interest and media coverage, but ultimately it would be forgotten. Bugliosi believed otherwise: This Manson case was once in a lifetime; the trial and everyone prominent in it would be remembered.

Inyo County dropped the arson charges against Charlie after Los Angeles indicted him for murder. Bugliosi was nervous enough about his case to call Inyo County DA Frank Fowles and ask that the arson charges be refiled. If Manson was set free in L.A., Bugliosi wanted him behind bars somewhere.

The gag order continued for everyone associated with the case, but on February 6 the *Los Angeles Times* reported, "Theory Links Beatle Album to Murders." Unidentified "investigators" told the reporter that

"Manson himself" considered the Beatles to be prophets, and that songs from their *White Album*, including "Helter Skelter," formed the basis of the Tate-LaBianca murders, which "Manson hoped police would believe . . . were committed by Negroes [and] that a black rebellion would follow which only he and his Family would survive." That same day, another *Times* story declared, "Jailed Manson Exerts Strange Hold on Family" and predicted Charlie planned to use "cooperating attorneys" to control trial tactics and testimony. It was a double public relations coup for the prosecution.

But Charlie believed that he was manipulating the media as well. On February 6, he granted an extended interview to David Felton and David Dalton, two reporters from *Rolling Stone*, which had established itself as the leading publication of the counterculture. Charlie broke out the same sermons he'd delivered so often to his followers: Everyone is God and the Devil at the same time. All human beings are part of each other, and individual human life has no real value. Children are pure until their parents ruin them. Blacks are about to overthrow whites, and it was foretold by the Beatles and the Bible. He cited current events—the Chicago 7 were about to be found guilty because the judge "saw in those guys what he wanted to see." (Charlie was partially right; two weeks later five of the seven defendants were found not guilty of conspiracy but guilty of incitement; two were found not guilty of either charge.) Charlie promised he wouldn't be silent at his trial, and conceded that "I'm probably one of the most dangerous men in the world if I want to be." He invited the writers to visit the Family at Spahn and to ask his followers anything that they liked. They did. Dalton and Felton didn't find a band of loving, simple souls there. The Family members were now calculating potential profit from book deals and TV specials. They told the *Rolling Stone* writers that they no longer would give away good stories for free, and also complained that by now the Beatles must surely have heard about Charlie's arrest. Why hadn't the band rushed to his rescue? They asked the writers to "tell them to call. Give them our number."

Bugliosi decided to reinterview Gregg Jakobson. Jakobson became the first non-Family member to talk at length about Charlie's belief in Helter Skelter, giving Bugliosi a potential witness if Stovitz ageed to present that motive to the jury. Then Bugliosi talked to Terry Melcher again. Melcher mentioned hearing from Rudi Altobelli that Manson once came to Cielo looking for him. This was critical information that would prove Manson had knowledge of the Cielo grounds beyond the electronic gate when he and Dennis Wilson had driven Melcher home. Altobelli was out of the country on business, but Bugliosi intended to speak with him the moment he returned to L.A.

Melcher was now petrified of Charlie and the Family, particularly of the members who weren't in jail. He hired a bodyguard and kept a shotgun handy. To Melcher, the scariest thing was that he couldn't pick any potential Family assassins out of a crowd: "[They] looked like every kid at every Grateful Dead or Byrds concert."

The Family women, led by Squeaky, bombarded Pat Krenwinkel in Alabama with messages to accept extradition. She agreed, and was arraigned in L.A. on February 24. She requested representation by Paul Fitzgerald, who was acceptable to Charlie. Fitzgerald resigned from the Public Defender's Office to focus full-time on his new client. The complexity of the case fascinated him.

Altobelli corroborated Melcher's story when he got back to Los Angeles. Yes, Manson had come onto the Cielo grounds and knocked on the guesthouse door to talk to him. Tate, Folger, Frykowski, and Sebring were all in the main house at the time. Tate had certainly seen Charlie; she asked Altobelli about the "creepy-looking guy" on their flight to Rome the next day. Oh, and there was somebody else at Cielo that night who probably talked to Charlie—Shahrokh Hatami, her personal photographer. Altobelli thought Bugliosi ought to talk to Hatami. And, of course, Altobelli would prefer not to testify at the upcoming trial if at all possible. Bugliosi said he couldn't make any promises, and based on the potential importance of his testimony Altobelli should expect to be called to the stand.

Shahrokh Hatami remembered that one time at Cielo he gave someone directions back to the guesthouse. The guy was short, and he bugged the photographer because he acted so smug. While Hatami was rather sharply sending him back to the guesthouse, Sharon Tate came out to see who was there. For a moment, she and the uninvited intruder were no more than a few feet apart. Hatami drew a diagram of the main house, guesthouse, and grounds, marking where everyone stood. Bugliosi was ecstatic. Now he not only had witnesses placing Charlie inside the Cielo gate, he could prove to a jury that Charlie had personally seen at least one of the victims at the main house.

Inyo County sent Bugliosi the tape of Deputy Sheriff Don Ward interviewing Paul Crockett and Brooks Poston about Charlie and the Family. Bugliosi listened to them talking about Helter Skelter and the bottomless pit, and arranged to talk to them himself in Los Angeles. He didn't find Crockett to be a good potential witness. The old prospector assured Bugliosi that Manson could never be convicted since "he doesn't do anything anybody could pin on him." Brooks Poston was much more helpful. The teenager told how Charlie would bend new followers to his will, using persuasion and drugs. He had a lot to say about Charlie using the Bible and Beatles songs to predict Helter Skelter. He also suggested that Bugliosi talk to Little Paul Watkins, whom Charlie used to get girls for the Family.

Watkins was Bugliosi's best find yet. He'd been a longtime Family member and one of Charlie's most trusted lieutenants. He described Charlie setting up orgies for outsiders he wanted to impress, and described Charlie's fascination with fear and death. Based on what he'd learned from Watkins, Poston, and Jakobson, Bugliosi now believed that his plan to sell a jury on Helter Skelter as the murder motive was correct. Watkins in particular talked at length about Charlie's belief that after a massive race war he'd rule the world. A weak point in presenting Helter Skelter to a jury would have been explaining why Charlie personally thought he'd profit from instigating it. Now Bugliosi had the reason.

Squeaky Fromme and other members of the Family regularly came to Sybil Brand and badgered Susan Atkins about meeting with Charlie, firing her attorney, and recanting her grand jury testimony. Susan wavered. She told Caballero that she was certain she wouldn't testify against Charlie and the others when they were brought to trial. Meanwhile, she wanted a meeting with Charlie. Stovitz and Bugliosi were sure that when she did, Charlie would reexert his control over her and she'd back out of her deal with the prosecution. They contacted Linda Kasabian's lawyers and offered to request immunity for her in return for full cooperation. The lawyers agreed, and on February 28 she met with Bugliosi. Nearly nine months pregnant, Linda seemed quiet and honest. He liked her much more than Susan. Linda went out with investigators to Cielo and described the gruesome events in explicit detail, breaking into tears at times.

Susan had her meeting with Charlie on March 5. She wrote later that she had to choose between two terrible options. Susan believed that if she cooperated with the prosecution, Charlie would have her killed, and also her son. If she did as Charlie demanded and backed out of the agreement to cooperate, the prosecutors would undoubtedly seek the death penalty against her. She was more frightened of Charlie than of the gas chamber, so the next day she fired Richard Caballero, who had urged her cooperation with prosecutors, and replaced him with Daye Shinn, one of the lawyers who had hoped to represent Charlie.

Media coverage of Susan's meeting with Charlie—one report described their "jail reunion" as "joyous"—was overshadowed by reports of a terrible explosion in Greenwich Village, New York. A ten-room town house was destroyed. Investigators discovered that it was being used by the Weathermen as a primitive bomb factory. Three of their members died in the blast, which was caused by bungled bomb construction. Based on evidence gathered at the scene and the testimony of survivors, it was learned that the group had intended to set off explosions at a dance for military personnel at Fort Dix in New Jersey with the intention of killing everyone there—giving America, in Mark Rudd's recollection, "a taste of what it had been dishing out daily in Southeast Asia." That plan had failed, but domestic terrorist bombings around the nation continued to escalate. The government estimated there was now an average of forty per week. Almost all of the explosives were homemade, and many were built according to instructions in *The Blaster's Handbook*, a build-a-bomb primer published by the Explosives Department of the du Pont Corporation and readily available to anyone.

On the same day that the Greenwich Village town house exploded, *LIE* was released. Phil Kaufman knew enough about the music business to realize that he had to start off small. His plan was to place the first few hundred albums in local L.A. head shops that catered to counterculture customers, and then, when those were snapped up, proving there was wider demand, get *LIE* into chain record stores where it could sell in greater numbers. But when Kaufman took the LP around to the small shops, no one wanted to stock it. It was one thing for head shop owners to find Charlie fascinating, but another to seemingly endorse murder by offering his record for sale. Kaufman did his best but soon realized that there was no market, underground or otherwise, for a Charlie Manson album.

Kaufman realized that, but Charlie didn't. He found it impossible to believe that the world wasn't clamoring to hear his music. Clearly, Phil Kaufman was lying when he said no store would stock them; he must be selling them, claiming that he hadn't, and pocketing the profits instead of turning the money over to Charlie to pay his legal costs. Charlie sent some of the Family to Kaufman's house to demand the cash from record sales. When Kaufman told them there was no money to give them, they threatened him and demanded that he give them any unsold *LIE* albums instead. Kaufman refused. When they came back a second time brandishing knives, he held them at bay with a shotgun. On a third visit, the Family members surrounded his house and chanted, "Give us the music." Instead, Kaufman emerged from the house waving a .357 Magnum and chased them down the street. He decided that the Family wasn't harmless after all, and that Charlie probably did order some of his followers to commit the Tate-LaBianca murders. Kaufman still hoped to sell the albums and recoup his investment, but attorneys representing Voytek Frykowski's son got a court order garnishing any album proceeds for the boy. Kaufman was left with a garageful of vinyl LPs and the realization that for a long time the duplicitous son of a bitch had hid his murderous side from Kaufman.

On March 10, Daye Shinn announced that Susan Atkins would recant her grand jury testimony and claim that, under pressure from the prosecution, she'd made up everything. Stovitz and Bugliosi told reporters that they'd expected that ever since Susan was allowed to meet with Manson, and that they still had enough evidence to successfully prosecute her along with Charlie, Pat, Leslie, and Tex, whenever he was finally extradited from Texas to California. The prosecutors met with DA Younger, and it was agreed that they'd seek the death penalty for all the defendants.

Charlie got what he wanted with Susan, but lost another legal skirmish. Judge Keene, who previously agreed to let Charlie serve as his own attorney, reversed the decision on the grounds that since his original decision he'd determined that Charlie was incapable of competent self-defense. Charlie screamed, "There's no love in this court," and Gypsy and Sandy Good, seated in the spectator section, leaped to their feet to shout insults at Keene. He jailed them for five days and appointed Charles Hollopeter, who had one of the city's most successful practices, as Charlie's attorney. Hollopeter immediately asked that Charlie be examined by a psychiatrist. That enraged Charlie, who demanded that Keene at least allow him the defense lawyer of his choice. When the judge agreed, Charlie selected thirty-five-year-old Ronald Hughes, a stout, shambling attorney who had never tried a criminal case. He'd worked himself into Charlie's good graces by handling the legal paperwork necessary to transfer the rights for Charlie's songs to Phil Kaufman as part of getting the album release. Charlie clearly intended for Hughes to be a figurehead—there was no way Charlie would allow anyone else to orchestrate his defense. Given his lack of trial experience, Hughes was someone the prosecutors didn't mind facing in a courtroom.

Any pleasure Stovitz and Bugliosi took from Charlie's choice of attorney was short-lived. Within days, he jettisoned Hughes for Irving Kanarek, who was notorious for his outrageous tactics. (Hughes was shifted over to defend Leslie Van Houten.) Somehow Charlie had learned about Kanarek, who routinely confounded judges and prosecutors and put juries to sleep by extending trials with drawn-out questioning of witnesses and frequent objections that seemed like filibusters. His apparent intent was to provoke some prosecutorial or judicial misstep that would allow him to win on appeal. Kanarek bragged that unlike all the ambulance chasers who'd begged Charlie for the high-profile job, Charlie came to him. Kanarek's was exactly the kind of defense approach that would cause Stovitz and Bugliosi the most trouble. Their plan to present Helter Skelter as a motive was a delicate, complicated strategy under the best of circumstances. With Kanarek jumping in to stall and obfuscate at every opportunity, their chances of holding a jury's attention over the course of a lengthy trial were greatly reduced. Hiring Kanarek was a masterstroke on Charlie's part.

Linda Kasabian gave birth to a son she named Angel. Her mother took the newborn back to New Hampshire, and Linda was returned to Sybil Brand. She was kept isolated from the general prison population, and continued to cooperate with prosecutors.

Investigators got a copy of the ticket citing Charlie on August 7, 1969, for driving without a valid license near Oceanside, about halfway between L.A. and San Diego. By law, all evidence accumulated by the prosecution had to be shared with the defense, but Bugliosi hoped they'd miss its significance. If it was claimed that Charlie was nowhere near L.A. around the time of the Tate-LaBianca murders, the ticket proved that he was. There was additional corroboration by Kasabian, who told prosecutors that Charlie was back at Spahn on the night of August 8, when he sent Mary Brunner and Sandy Good out shopping and they were arrested for using stolen credit cards. The old van that they were driving, noted on their arrest report, was the same one cited on Charlie's ticket.

Then came a surprise—Bernard Crowe, "Lotsapoppa," wasn't dead after all. He'd played dead in July when Charlie shot him, and had spent eighteen days on a hospital critical list with a slug from the Buntline .22 lodged near his spine. It was still there when his attorney contacted Bugliosi and set up an interview. Bugliosi determined that Lotsapoppa might be useful as a prosecution witness in the penalty phase of the trial if the jury found Charlie guilty. He was walking proof that Charlie was personally able to kill.

Shortly afterward, Lotsapoppa was arrested on drug charges and taken to court. Charlie, under tight guard, passed him in the hall, did a double take, then said, "Sorry I had to do it, but you know how it is."

Pat Krenwinkel refused to give prosecutors a sample of her handwriting to match with the bloody words "Healter Skelter" on the LaBiancas' refrigerator door. The prosecutors welcomed her refusal; now they could use it in court as circumstantial evidence of her guilt.

Bobby Beausoleil was tried a second time for the murder of Gary Hinman. Judge Keene presided. Bugliosi was excused from prosecuting to concentrate on Tate-LaBianca. Mary Brunner was granted complete immunity in return for testifying that she saw Bobby kill Hinman. Beausoleil, certain that Mary had been ordered by Charlie to sell him out, took the stand and claimed that Charlie was the one who killed Hinman; Beausoleil swore that he personally was a witness to the murder, not a participant. The jury found Beausoleil guilty and sentenced him to death. Charlie, Susan, and Bruce Davis were indicted for Hinman's slaying. Davis fled before he could be arrested.

On April 10, 1970, a press release for Paul McCartney's brand-new solo album announced the breakup of the Beatles. Any hope Charlie and the Family had that the band would come to his defense was lost. He and his attorneys discussed calling the Beatles individually as witnesses, since Charlie believed they would, under oath, support him. But letters to the Beatles' office received no reply, and the lawyers were unable to find their home addresses.

The prosecutors thought there was a weakness in Linda Kasabian's potential testimony. She'd provided graphic first-person accounts of the nights of the Tate and LaBianca murders, and Rudolf Weber corroborated some of what she said about August 9. But prosecutors hadn't found anyone to back up any part of her testimony about the next night. Bugliosi urged the LaBianca investigators to comb Venice for the actor Linda said Charlie ordered her to kill. They found him. Saladin Nader admitted he'd picked up two girl hitchhikers in early August 1969, and picked out photos of Linda and Sandy, who he correctly said was very pregnant at the time. Bugliosi and Stovitz would have liked more witnesses to support Linda's version of the August 10 events, but none could be found.

Judge Keene had offended Charlie by not allowing him to serve as his own attorney, and on April 13 Charlie struck back. Under California law, defendants were allowed to file an affidavit of prejudice against a judge and request that he be removed from their case. Charlie filed one, and Keene stepped down in favor of Charles H. Older, whose first act was to set a new trial date of June 15.

From Sybil Brand in L.A., Leslie Van Houten sent a letter to Tex Watson in the Collin County, Texas, jail. "You know the strength of unity," she wrote. "Myself, as well as the others, would like very much for you to be with all of us throughout this trial. . . . I truly do hope to see your shining face here soon." Tex wasn't buying it. He and his Texas attorney continued to fight the L.A. prosecutors' extradition requests, arguing that excessive publicity made it impossible for Tex to get a fair trial there. Stovitz and Bugliosi concluded that they would have to try Charlie, Susan, Pat, and Leslie in June, and hope for a shot at Tex in a separate trial.

Charlie felt good enough about his chances to send Clem and Gypsy back to Death Valley with a message for Paul Crockett, Brooks Poston, and Little Paul Watkins. Clem told Watkins, "Charlie says that when he gets out, you all had better not be around the desert."

Then Mary Brunner recanted her testimony that she had seen Bobby Beausoleil kill Gary Hinman. Judge Keene, still presiding over the Beausoleil trial, turned down Bobby's petition to overturn his death sentence and grant a retrial. Keene said there was sufficient evidence to convict Beausoleil even if Mary's testimony was discounted. Beausoleil was sent to San Quentin to await execution, and prosecutors debated whether Mary should be arrested and charged for Hinman's murder, too. She'd been promised immunity for testifying against Beausoleil, which she did. There was nothing in their agreement that addressed the situation where she recanted after he was convicted. But she'd clearly violated the spirit if not the letter of the deal, so Mary was indicted for murder. Within weeks that indictment was overturned in a higher court. Mary went back to the Family at Spahn Ranch. Charlie's original follower had returned to his service.

Spring antiwar demonstrations on college campuses turned violent. On May 4, National Guardsmen shot and killed four student protesters at Kent State University in Ohio. In mid-month a riot at predominantly black Jackson State College in Mississippi cost two students their lives, one still in high school. Protests sparked by the six deaths erupted at schools across the nation; the National Guard was called in to restore order on twenty-one campuses, and some 350 colleges and universities were temporarily closed by administration order or student strike. About seventy-five remained shut for the remainder of the semester. There was considerable public backlash against the protesters. A Gallup poll indicated that 58 percent of respondents blamed the Kent State students for bringing about their own deaths. Gulf Oil distributed 22 million "America—Love It or Leave It" bumper stickers. In New York, construction workers charged a student demonstration and injured seventy participants. Bob Schieffer, then just beginning his career at CBS, recalled that "concerning the counterculture and young [antiwar] marchers, a large percentage of the adult population thought they were awful and just wanted them to go away."

Charlie supplanted coverage of campus riots and closings when he began a series of extreme courtroom protests. First he stood with his back to Judge Older after losing an appeal for a change of trial venue from Los Angeles. After Charlie was forcibly removed and placed in a locked room nearby, Susan, Pat, and Leslie all dramatically rose and turned their backs on the judge in turn. Older appealed to the women's defense attorneys to counsel them on appropriate courtroom behavior. Paul Fitzgerald said apologetically that there was no use in trying because "there is a minimum of client control in this case." Older ordered the women removed, too, and when Charlie and the three women returned to court on Friday, June 12, he cautioned them that a jury might be put off by similar stunts—did they really want to jeopardize their chances? Charlie responded, "You leave me nothing. You can kill me now," and stretched out his arms to mimic a crucifixion. The three women did the same. Older once again ordered them removed, and this time Charlie fought a bailiff who tried to haul him from the courtroom. As he was dragged out the door, Susan screamed at Older, "You might as well kill us all now, because we are not going to get a fair trial." She, Pat, and Leslie then chanted, "Kill us," as women bailiffs removed them, too. After they were gone, Older denied a series of requests by Kanarek, one of which was to suppress Charlie's body as trial evidence, which would have meant no witness could identify Charlie in front of the jury. Then the judge announced that the trial would commence on schedule, with jury selection beginning on Monday, June 15.

Jury selection took an agonizing five weeks. After learning that Judge Older intended to sequester those selected for the entire trial, which was expected to last six months, many in the juror pool claimed hardship as a reason not to serve. Others were dismissed because they were openly opposed or seemed squeamish about the death penalty. Kanarek was frequently warned by Older about drawing out the process by asking prospective jurors irrelevant questions. Stovitz and Bugliosi petitioned to have Kanarek removed from the case and were denied. Charlie held an impromptu courtroom press conference to declare that the only thing he'd ever killed in his life was a chicken. Unhappy with recent stories that labeled him a "cult leader," and claiming that negative coverage convinced everyone of his guilt even before he was tried, Charlie tongue-lashed reporters: "If you contribute to it, you're part of it. It's just as much your fault as anyone's."

If Charlie thought that the mainstream press was treating him unfairly, he was really laid low in late June, when *Rolling Stone* published the investigative article by Felton and Dalton. It wasn't the kiss in print that Charlie anticipated. In twenty devastating pages, the reporters laid waste to Charlie mostly by quoting him extensively. Raps about ceasing to exist and the race wars to come that enthralled acid-addled followers in the Haight and at Spahn and Barker ranches seemed nonsensical in print. Charlie babbled about his messages from the Beatles and said that "death is psychosomatic." Felton and Dalton described the Family at Spahn Ranch as "children from the Village of the Damned." Charlie and the Family had been in the news for seven months. Fascination with them continued, but the novelty was gone. When they were examined in any depth, their flaws were obvious. During June and July, Charlie learned the difference between notoriety and popularity.

Los Angeles District Attorney Evelle Younger didn't like the *Rolling Stone* article any more than Charlie and the Family did. An anonymous member of the prosecution team had spoken to the writers at length about the case to be made against Charlie. Younger couldn't prove it was Stovitz or Bugliosi, but he called them into his office and warned, "No more interviews." They thought Younger was being hypocritical, since he himself had granted several Charlie-related interviews. The two prosecutors assumed Younger didn't mean that they couldn't respond directly to queries from the press, only that they couldn't discuss anything in depth.

The media covered every aspect of the jury selection process so exhaustively that Judge Older moved the proceedings into his private chambers. Individual examinations still took so long that Older added forty-five minutes to each court day. In all, 205 people were interviewed before the selection of a twelve-member jury and six alternates was finally completed on July 21. Trial proceedings in the presence of the newly empaneled jury would begin on Friday, July 24.

Stovitz and Bugliosi had a battle plan: Helter Skelter was the motive, and the "vicarious liability" rule of conspiracy would be their main argument for conviction. As Bugliosi explained it in his best-selling account of the trial, "each conspirator is criminally responsible for all the crimes committed by his co-conspirators if [these] crimes were committed to further the object of the conspiracy. This rule applies even if the conspirator was not present at the scene of the crime." The prosecution would try to convince the jury that Charlie, Susan, Pat, and Leslie attempted to precipitate a race war that would result in their ruling the world by committing seven murders. Charlie, the mastermind of the plot, was as guilty of murder as the three women, even though he wasn't present during the actual slayings. Susan, Pat, and Leslie were willing participants, not mindless robots. (This theme also combated any potential defense claims that Tex was responsible for organizing the murders.) The two prosecutors had worked hard gathering witnesses and evidence. They were prepared to win a conventional trial.

But Charlie was determined that the trial wouldn't be conventional. He had the gifted performer's innate sense of public relations and timing. For months, he'd been famous, which was gratifying, but those months were the preliminaries. The trial would be the main event, his showpiece. There was the very real possibility that it would end with Charlie sentenced to die in the gas chamber. That meant the trial would have to be so memorable that Charlie's fame would long outlast his life. The right bizarre, well-timed outbursts would ensure that—Charlie could concoct these on a daily basis. He believed that he had control over his four hand-picked defense attorneys, but much depended on the three women, who in the past had not been Charlie's most devoted or reliable followers. Pat and Leslie had both made attempts to leave the Family—Charlie had to track down Pat, and had to talk Leslie out of it. Susan was boastful and impulsive. Now he needed them to carry out his orders unquestioningly.

It helped that during jury selection they spent most days beside him in court. Proximity was always crucial in Charlie's maintaining power over others. Linda Kasabian, Dianne Lake, Stephanie Schram, Kitty Lutesinger, and Barbara Hoyt, all cooperating with the prosecution, had been separated from Charlie long enough to shrug off his influence if not their fear of him. So in the days just before the trial, Charlie had true believers like Sandy and Squeaky constantly visit Susan, Pat, and Leslie in jail, reminding them of the obligation of all Family members to remain loyal to each other and obey Charlie. The three female defendants also shared the knowledge that they were bound to Charlie by guilt—as Leslie Van Houten remembered many years later, on August 9 and 10 "a line was being crossed." Besides the gas chamber, they had nowhere else to go but Charlie. Just as they'd been his accomplices in murder, now they would be his supporting cast in court.

In the end, who could ever be certain of the response of a jury? It was always possible that jurors would favor Charlie's antics over the prosecution's conventional case. Months earlier, Charlie warned the Family that if he were ever arrested, he'd act like "Crazy Charlie." Now, more than ever, it would be true.

CHAPTER EIGHTEEN

The Trial

The prosecutors were determined to control the tone of the trial. To prevent disruptions by Charlie's followers from the spectator seats, Stovitz served all known Family members with subpoenas as potential witnesses for the prosecution. Under California law, they were barred from the courtroom while other witnesses testified. Bugliosi would make the prosecution's opening statement, hitting hard with Helter Skelter and, he hoped, winning over the jury before the defense had an opportunity to present its counterarguments. He and Stovitz would build momentum with an opening series of witnesses to establish the basic facts of Tate-LaBianca before calling their star witness to the stand. Linda Kasabian would, Stovitz and Bugliosi believed, sway the most skeptical juror with her eyewitness account of two nights of appalling carnage. Their game plan, based on their considerable professional skill and backed by all the resources of the Los Angeles District Attorney's Office and the LAPD, was in place and they were ready to implement it.

Then Charlie came into the courtroom and effortlessly took the play away from them. Sometime before bailiffs came to fetch him from his ninth floor cell, Charlie used something sharp to gouge a bloody X into his forehead just above and between his eyebrows. Outside the courtroom, a supporter passed out copies of a lengthy printed statement from Charlie. The poorly spelled but cleverly constructed message read in part, "You have created the monster. I am not of you, from you . . . I haved Xed myself from your world. No man or lawyer is speaking for me. I speak for myself. I am not allowed to speak with words so I have spoken with the mark I will be wearing on my forehead." There was nothing the prosecutors could do: Charlie hadn't violated any courtroom procedures.

Bugliosi had been placed on the prosecution team by District Attorney Younger because of his dynamic courtroom presence; now he did his best to return the jury's focus from Charlie's gory forehead to the case itself. He'd barely begun acknowledging to the jury that he was sure they already knew what this trial was about when Irving Kanarek popped up from the defense table to object: "He is now making an opening statement for us." Judge Older overruled, and over the next two hours a pattern emerged. Bugliosi would manage a few more sentences, Kanarek would object and Older would overrule—it happened nine times in all before the young prosecutor finally finished describing Helter Skelter, "a black-white civil war" that Manson and his fellow defendants hoped to precipitate with "these seven incredible murders [that] were perhaps the most bizarre, savage, nightmarish murders in the recorded annals of crime." The moment Bugliosi concluded, Kanarek demanded that Older declare a mistrial. The judge declined.

At the end of the first day, one of the three county deputies serving as trial bailiffs reported that Charlie offered him $100,000 to be allowed to escape. The other bailiffs said that Susan, Pat, and Leslie all promised sex in return for being set free. They did this openly, in full view and hearing of others. The bailiffs believed that there was something programmed about it, and they were right. Every day before court was in session, the four defendants and their lawyers were allowed to meet in a room beside the main courtroom. It was where unruly defendants could be placed at the judge's discretion during the trial. The room was equipped with a table and speakers to pipe in court proceedings. Charlie called it the "mouse house," and used it each morning as a private spot in which to give the three women their instructions for the day. Charlie would tell Susan, Pat, and Leslie what they were to do, and show them the hand signals he would make to them when it was time to do it—when Charlie touched his nose or tugged his earlobe, they were to rub their forefingers across pursed lips to make a "blah-blah-blah" sound during testimony from prosecution witnesses, or stand and turn their backs on the judge, or giggle in unison whenever Charlie wanted to mock court proceedings.

The three women slavishly obeyed, honoring Charlie to the point of cutting Xs into their own foreheads. The female Family members outside the courtroom did the same, permanently burning the mark into their flesh with a soldering iron so they wouldn't have to keep on cutting themselves every few days.

In each morning meeting, if any of the four defense attorneys objected to Charlie's instructions about what to do in court, such dissent was met with sharp reminders that Charlie knew exactly where they lived. Fitzgerald was always the most likely to protest. He thought the case could be won by conventional methods—if Charlie would just let him, he could convince the jury that the prosecution's Helter Skelter theme was ludicrous. Then early in the trial, Fitzgerald went home one night to find Squeaky in his bed offering a stark choice: have fun with her and promise to cooperate with Charlie, or else find other, less friendly Family members waiting for him next time. Later, the women defendants would recall that they were never alone with their lawyers without Charlie present, too. He monitored every word spoken between them.

Barred from the courtroom and concerned for their leader and friends on trial, the Family members at Spahn Ranch had to worry about their own safety. No sooner had the trial begun than they were subjected to a series of night attacks. People would drive onto the ranch after dark, follow a narrow road to hills just above the movie set buildings where Charlie's followers slept, and shoot down at them. No one was hit, but if the attacks continued it was only a matter of time before Family members were wounded or killed. The Family at Spahn didn't have guns anymore—their caches of weapons had been confiscated during the Barker Ranch raid. They didn't believe that the county or city police would protect them, so instead of reporting the assaults, they relied on self-defense. They fashioned slingshots, bought sacks of metal ball bearings, and hid behind rocks on the side of the hill road. The next night that a car filled with attackers came, the Family used the slingshots to fire ball bearings through windshields and windows, shattering glass and spraying shards on the cars' occupants. The attacks stopped, but Family members continued standing guard at night.

The trial bailiffs reached an understanding with Charlie. In the courtroom it was Judge Older's responsibility to keep him in line, but the bailiffs didn't want any trouble out of him when he was in their charge. They had to be with Charlie a lot, coming for him on the ninth floor to bring him down to the courtroom in the morning, sitting with him on the frequent occasions when the judge sent him to the mouse house, and escorting him back to his ninth-floor cell at the end of the day. On his way down the halls to and from the courtroom they had to walk him by photographers lining the walls and snapping pictures. Oden "O.P." Skupen, a Los Angeles County deputy and veteran court bailiff, had no intention of letting Charlie act up in front of the photographers. He told him, "If you try any crap and embarrass me, I'll take you into the lockers and I'll beat the shit out of you." Charlie knew Skupen meant it. No matter how crazy he acted in the courtroom, Charlie always behaved in the hallway.

The bailiffs also strip-searched Charlie before and after each day's trial proceedings. It was distasteful for everyone since a body cavity probe was required. Charlie swore that he wouldn't conceal anything up his rectum and didn't, but the rules required probing anyway. He smelled awful; prisoners on the ninth floor were allowed just one shower a week. Unless Charlie was going into his courtroom antics, the bailiffs usually found him okay to deal with. He'd spent lots of time in prison and knew how to act when he wasn't in public. The bailiffs smoked, and Charlie bummed cigarettes from them every chance he got. As long as he behaved, they didn't mind giving him a few. Privately, they thought it was weird how Charlie was all about controlling the three girls in the courtroom, but outside the court he seemed comfortable being ordered around by the bailiffs. It was like the guy wanted to boss and be bossed, too.

On July 27, Bugliosi called Linda Kasabian to the stand. He had done his best to make certain she seemed presentable to the jury, even vetoing her plan to wear a long dress because "long is for evening." The witnesses so far—the fathers of Sharon Tate and Steve Parent, Cielo housekeeper Winifred Chapman, William Garretson—were stage setters. If the jury believed Linda, the prosecution would win. Stovitz and Bugliosi arranged for her to be brought to the courtroom from the Sybil Brand jail by an indirect route, but somehow the Family found out and Sandy Good confronted Linda just outside the courtroom. Sandy screamed, "You'll kill us all, you'll kill us all," before Linda was taken inside.

The moment the court clerk began swearing Linda in, Kanarek objected on the grounds that she was insane as a result of heavy drug use. He kept objecting as Bugliosi began his questioning, some fifty objections in all. Each was overruled by Older, but sometimes it took ten minutes or more to talk a single one through, and this prevented the prosecutor from building any momentum. As best he could, Bugliosi guided Linda through a description of why she joined the Family and how all of them fell under Charlie's control. By her third day of testimony, Charlie was making throat-cutting gestures toward the witness stand, and the total of Kanarek objections topped two hundred. Older finally found Kanarek in contempt of court and sentenced him to a night in jail. The next day, Kanarek made more objections than ever, so many that even Charlie lost patience with him, and asked Older if he was allowed to object to his attorney's objections. Older said no.

Linda remained composed throughout. She faltered only when describing the murders at Cielo, crying at times. When Bugliosi asked her what Voytek Frykowski screamed as Tex Watson stabbed him, Linda said simply, "There were no words, it was beyond words, it was just screams."

On July 30, Bugliosi concluded his questioning and turned the witness over to defense for cross-examination. Fitzgerald went first. He attacked Linda's contention that she followed Charlie's orders because she was afraid of him. But when Fitzgerald demanded, "What were you afraid of?" Linda replied, "I was just afraid. He was a heavy dude." The defense attorney tried to shame her by citing all the orgies she admitted to participating in at Spahn Ranch. Linda wasn't fazed. She testified that she eventually had sex with all the men there, and admitted that she enjoyed it. Fitzgerald was nonplussed and Stovitz and Bugliosi were ecstatic. Surely that kind of honesty would help convince the jury that everything else she claimed was also true. Despite all the histrionics and stalling by the defendants and their attorneys, the prosecutors began to feel that they had the case in hand.

Then they were blindsided in a way that they could never have anticipated.

Richard Nixon built his political career on the votes of white working-class Americans. He first came to prominence as a fierce anticommunist opposing the Red Menace. He won the tight race for the White House in 1968 by proclaiming himself "the law and order candidate," a less-than-subtle signal for rioting blacks and student radicals. During the campaign Nixon claimed he had a secret plan to end the fighting in Vietnam, but after gaining the presidency he talked instead of "peace with honor," an ambiguous term that seemed to question the patriotism of anyone demanding specifics. He and Vice President Spiro Agnew denounced the young antiwar protesters as communist supporters or dupes. Charlie Manson's trial was a godsend for Nixon, evidence he could cite as proof that young people with long hair were not only immoral (all those orgies) and drug-addled (LSD trips all the time) but dangerous (they killed people, even pregnant women). As a lawyer himself, Nixon was aware that commenting on the trial in progress could be grounds for a mistrial—how could jurors not be swayed by the president's opinion? But he couldn't resist.

On August 3, Nixon gave a speech in Denver. He always enjoyed press bashing, and the media had been full of stories about Linda Kasabian's testimony. Making an observation rather than responding to a question, Nixon declared, "I noted . . . the coverage of the Charles Manson case. Front page every day in the papers. It usually got a couple of minutes in the evening news. Here is a man who was guilty, directly or indirectly, of eight murders without reason. Here is a man yet who, as far as the coverage was concerned, appeared to be a rather glamorous figure, a glamorous figure to the young people whom he had brought into his operations . . . the judge seemed to be the villain." All this proved, Nixon claimed, that the American press set out "to glorify and make heroes out of those engaged in criminal activities."

Within moments, Nixon's remarks flashed across national wire services. The Manson jury's sequestration prohibited access to newspapers or viewing TV newscasts, so prosecutors felt reasonably certain that the jurors wouldn't immediately learn what the president said. Judge Older summoned Stovitz, Bugliosi, and the four defense attorneys to his chambers to discuss the situation. Kanarek immediately demanded a mistrial—surely someone on the jury would hear about it and tell the others. When Older turned him down, Kanarek requested that each juror be questioned to determine if he or she knew what Nixon said. Older refused that request, too. He instructed the bailiffs to be even more vigilant in preventing jurors from reading or watching the news, and ordered the trial resumed.

Kanarek began questioning Linda Kasabian, continuing the next morning. When Linda admitted to taking fifty LSD trips, Kanarek asked her to describe in detail the 23rd. Bugliosi objected that the question was ridiculous, and Older sustained him. The prosecutors hoped that they'd dodged the Nixon bullet, but during the afternoon session, someone—Older blamed defense counsel Daye Shinn—slipped Charlie a copy of the morning's *Los Angeles Times*, and he triumphantly brandished the huge headline "MANSON GUILTY, NIXON DECLARES," in front of the jury. Soon afterward Susan, Pat, and Linda stood and asked Older in perfect unison, "Your Honor, the President said we are guilty, so why go on with the trial?"

Nixon's press secretary announced that the media had twisted the president's remarks. But Charlie got the last word. When he was brought into court on August 5 he waved a handprinted sign that read, "NIXON GUILTY." The bailiffs yanked it away from him, but they were laughing as they did. They had to hand it to Charlie. Whatever else might be true about this guy, he had a sense of humor.

Irving Kanarek questioned Linda for an entire week. At one point he waved pictures of the slaughtered Cielo victims in front of her. It was obvious to everyone but Kanarek that the jury was as horrified to see them as Linda—he was reinforcing the prosecution's point that the murders were especially horrible. Charlie yelled at him to stop. When Kanarek finally wound down, Daye Shinn took a turn for the defense and asked Linda if she believed in Santa Claus. At the L-shaped defense table in front of the judge and witness stand, Susan, Leslie, and Pat yawned and made it clear that they were bored. Fitzgerald asked Older if it would be all right to give them some colored pencils and blank paper. The three young women doodled happily while their former friend gave testimony that could cost them their lives.

On the morning of August 12, Charlie refused to leave his cell for the courtroom and had to be carried there by the bailiffs. Dragged in front of Older in the judge's chambers, Charlie said that he refused to walk in protest of his treatment in the Hall of Justice jail. People lined up to peer in his cell, Charlie complained: "They even bring their sons in on the weekends to take a look at the freak." He griped about the frequency of body searches, and how he was no longer allowed to make outside calls. Older wasn't sympathetic, and Charlie remained uncooperative in court for the next several days. The bailiffs had to regularly remove him to the mouse house. Each time, one bailiff had to remain in there with him. The moment that the door locked behind him, Charlie always calmed down. He'd cadge a smoke and often would practice his next "spontaneous" outburst. Sometimes he'd brag about how well Susan, Leslie, and Pat were minding him. Charlie never seemed concerned about the prospect of the death penalty, though he told the bailiffs he was being railroaded. He even joked with them about it. When Skupen asked, "Charlie, when they send you to the gas chamber, will you invite me?" Charlie grinned and replied, "Sure, I'll invite you."

On August 13, Judge Older formally granted Linda immunity in return for her testimony. Charlie marked the occasion by passing her a letter. He wrote, "Love can never stop if it's love. . . . If you were not saying what your saying there would be no tryle. Don't lose your love it's only there for you." He cautioned her, "Don't let anyone have this or they will find a way to use it against me."

Linda gave the letter to Bugliosi. Kanarek claimed that she stole it from Charlie.

Linda's testimony was convincing but not perfect. Before she was finally allowed to step down on August 19, she admitted stealing $5,000 for the Family from Charles Melton, and revealed to the jury how she'd left her toddler daughter behind at Spahn Ranch when she fled to save her own life. But Stovitz and Bugliosi were pleased that during her time on the witness stand, she never made a statement inconsistent with what she'd told the prosecution prior to the trial. Since she was free to go wherever she liked, Linda left L.A. to join her mother and two children in New Hampshire. Kanarek warned that he might recall her to the stand at any time.

• • •

The prosecution lost four witnesses. Randy Starr, the movie stuntman Charlie beat up in front of Terry Melcher, died. Bugliosi was suspicious and ordered an autopsy, which indicated Starr died of natural causes. Linda Kasabian's estranged husband, Robert, and Charles Melton, his hippie philanthropist friend, got tired of waiting to be called to the stand and left for Hawaii. Their attorney informed Bugliosi that they had taken refuge on a small uncharted island and there was no way to contact them. Lebanese actor Saladin Nader dropped out of sight, and the LAPD couldn't find him. But Stovitz and Bugliosi felt these losses were more than offset by Juan Flynn's decision to take the stand. The testy Spahn ranch hand initially refused to cooperate with prosecutors. But when Family members began threatening him to make certain he wouldn't change his mind and testify, Flynn decided to defy them. Stovitz and Bugliosi had Flynn initially questioned on August 18 by Sgt. Philip Sartuchi of the LaBianca investigation team. Sartuchi greeted the prosecutors with great news as they left court for the day. Flynn said Charlie personally told him that "I'm the one" who committed the Tate-LaBianca murders, and that prior to that, sometime in June or July 1969, Charlie said, "Well, I have to come down to it. The only way to get Helter Skelter going is for me to go down there and show the black man how to do it, by killing a whole bunch of those fucking pigs." Further, Flynn remembered Susan Atkins telling him one night in August, "We're going to get some fucking pigs." Flynn thought it was the night when the LaBiancas were murdered.

After speaking to Sartuchi, Flynn went into hiding. He periodically called Bugliosi to assure him that he was still willing to testify. In the meantime, he didn't want Charlie or anyone in the Family to know where to find him.

Despite the antics of the defendants, the trial was going well for the prosecution. Stovitz and Bugliosi followed Linda with a series of witnesses—John Swartz, various residents of the Cielo neighborhood, Rudolf Weber—who collectively supported Linda's testimony. Detective Michael McGann testified about the large amount of drugs investigators found at Cielo; Stovitz and Bugliosi wanted that on the record before the defense could introduce it as evidence that the killings might have been drug-related. When the defense had no questions for Deputy Medical Examiner David Katsuyama, whose vagueness on the witness stand frustrated the prosecutors and, they feared, provided exceptional cross-examination opportunities for their opponents, Stovitz and Bugliosi believed that they were on their way to victory. Even Charlie seemed dejected. During one break when the jury was out of the courtroom, he confided to Judge Older, "We did pretty good at the first of it . . . we kind of lost control when the testimony started."

Then Susan Atkins claimed that she had a stomachache.

Susan began fidgeting at the defense table while Katsuyama testified about the depth of the wounds suffered by the LaBiancas. She complained of stomach pains, and her histrionic moaning distracted everyone. At the judge's order, Susan was examined and diagnosed with an impacted colon. After being treated with laxatives and enemas, she was cleared to return to court, where she pleaded with Older to let her leave again because she was still in so much pain. The doctor who treated Susan told the judge that she was fine; either she was now experiencing "sympathy pains" or else faking. Older dismissed Susan's complaints and the trial resumed. Afterward, a reporter asked Stovitz his opinion of Susan's alleged illness. Stovitz, hurrying away, snapped, "It was a performance worthy of Sarah Bernhardt." The next day District Attorney Younger, Stovitz's boss, removed him from the case for violating instructions not to make statements to the media. Stovitz and Bugliosi protested—it was a passing remark, not an interview, and, besides, they were working well together. Younger wouldn't budge: Stovitz was off the case. Bugliosi was now in charge, and he would be assisted by Deputy District Attorney Stephen Kay. Unlike Stovitz-Bugliosi, Bugliosi-Kay was not an equal partnership. They were in mid-trial and there was no time for Kay to study transcripts and get up to speed. Bugliosi told him that "Helter Skelter is the theory, period," and coached his new trial colleague on courtroom behavior. For instance, Kay must never refer to notes when the jurors were present, because that meant breaking off eye contact with them. Kay didn't warm to Bugliosi personally—the guy was so unabashedly *ambitious*—but he was awed by his work ethic. During the time he prosecuted the Tate-LaBianca murders with Bugliosi, Kay never knew him to sleep more than three or four hours a night.

Kay also formed strong immediate impressions of the four defendants. Charlie was a mastermind, always waiting for any opportunity to disrupt trial proceedings and thinking three or four steps ahead. Susan Atkins was scary; clearly, she was eager to do whatever Charlie wanted. Kay thought Pat Krenwinkel was cold and unfeeling. Leslie Van Houten troubled the young prosecutor. She was so smart, and yet she'd fallen in with the Family. The prosecution and defense sat side by side, and Kay was next to Leslie. They talked during breaks, and had an extended debate about the death penalty. Kay thought it was a deterrent and Leslie didn't. Though they disagreed, he was impressed with her arguments. Kay couldn't get over it: He and a Manson girl were having a rational conversation.

In the months since she'd returned to live with her mother, Barbara Hoyt was inundated with phone calls from Squeaky and Sandy. They pleaded with her to be loyal to Charlie and the Family and not cooperate with the prosecutors. Barbara was torn. On September 5, her former friends offered a deal. If Barbara wouldn't testify, they'd treat her to a trip to Hawaii. She accepted, and the next day Barbara and Ruth Ann flew to Honolulu. They mostly stayed in their hotel room and had long talks. After a few days Ruth Ann said that she had to go back to L.A., but Barbara could stay on in Hawaii a while longer. They went to the airport, where, just before her flight was called, Ruth Ann bought Barbara a hamburger. As Barbara was swallowing the last few bites, Ruth Ann said, "Just imagine if there were ten tabs of acid in that," an amount far beyond any normal dose. Ruth Ann boarded her plane; soon afterward Barbara collapsed. Just before she lost consciousness, she begged a man standing over her to call "Mr. Bugliosi." After emergency treatment for drug overdose, Barbara was able to return to the mainland. Now she was determined to testify against Charlie. Bugliosi, furious, told the LAPD that he wanted any Family members involved to be charged with attempted murder. Ruth Ann, Squeaky, Gypsy, Clem, and Dennis Rice (whose credit card had funded the plane tickets) were all arraigned but not indicted until December 18.

Until then, they remained free and at Charlie's command. Rice visited Charlie regularly, carrying his latest orders back to the rest of the Family.

On September 11, Tex Watson was finally extradited to California. During his extended time at the Collin County jail in Texas, he'd received dozens of letters from Squeaky and Gypsy urging him to stay strong and loyal to Charlie. When Tex made a brief appearance in Judge Older's court (Paul Fitzgerald wanted him to be formally identified to the jury), he wore a blue blazer, gray slacks, and had close-cropped hair. Bugliosi thought he looked like "a typical clean-cut college kid." If the defense hoped to convince the jury that Tex rather than Charlie masterminded the Tate-LaBianca slayings, Bugliosi believed that Tex's conservative appearance would make it much harder.

The *Los Angeles Times* noted that Tex "exchanged smiles" with Susan, Pat, and Leslie. He made no statements in court or to the media. Irving Kanarek objected to Tex's presence in the courtroom and demanded a mistrial. After his brief appearance, Tex was jailed until his September 28 arraignment.

The Weathermen broke Timothy Leary out of federal prison in San Luis Obispo, where he was serving a ten-year sentence for drug possession. It was a plot involving considerable daring and risk—the fifty-year-old acid guru had to climb the prison wall, clamber hand-over-hand along a two-hundred-foot live electrical wire, and then make a steep drop down to the ground. After releasing a defiant declaration that "at this time let us have no more talk of peace. . . . Listen, Americans, your government is an instrument of total, lethal evil," Leary fled to Algeria, appearing at a press conference there with former Black Panther Eldridge Cleaver, himself on the run from U.S. law. (Leary would be recaptured three years later in Afghanistan, by which time he was glad to identify everyone who helped engineer his San Luis Obispo escape, and to serve out a reduced three-year sentence.)

The Family didn't care about Timothy Leary—Charlie was their only hero—but the details of his breakout were inspirational. Clearly, prisons weren't impregnable. It was something for them to think about if Charlie was convicted.

Beginning on Wednesday, September 16, pedestrians on the sidewalk outside the downtown L.A. Hall of Justice had to step around people sitting there. The corner of Spring and Temple became unofficial Family headquarters. Four or five members would arrive every morning before Older convened court on the eighth floor and stay until proceedings ended for the day. Then they'd either get rides back to Spahn or else huddle for the night in an old van parked nearby. Though Clem and a few other males occasionally joined them, the sidewalk sitters were mostly women, Squeaky and Sandy every day and usually Ruth Ann, though she was in an advanced stage of pregnancy. Other than being in the way, they didn't bother passersby. They smiled and chatted with anyone who stopped to speak to them, emphasizing that Charlie was all about love. Besides the Xs permanently cut into their foreheads, the women didn't seem menacing. Sometimes they amused themselves with games of patty-cake, and when they stood up to stretch their legs they waved at cars. People brought them cookies and other treats, and they gladly posed for pictures.

But Bugliosi and Kay didn't find them goofily charming. One evening when Bugliosi left the Hall of Justice, Sandy stood up and followed him, fingering a knife. Bugliosi called her a "God damn bitch" and she backed away. Another time, Sandy and Squeaky approached Kay and his wife in a parking lot and hissed that they would do at the Kay house what had been done at Sharon Tate's. Then they smiled and walked away. Kay had a brief history with Sandy. When he was fifteen and she fourteen, they were set up on a blind date. They had lunch with their mothers at a pancake house in Burbank. Stephen left before the meal was finished because he thought Sandy was "a little stuck-up snob."

During a courtroom break, Charlie told Bugliosi not to take Sandy and her knife seriously: "If I had all the power and control that you say I have, I could simply [tell a Family member] 'Go get Bugliosi,' and that would be it."

Charlie and the Family were right to dread Barbara Hoyt on the witness stand. Recovered from her LSD overdose in Hawaii, Barbara testified about all she'd seen and heard, particularly Susan's bragging concerning the Tate murders. Bugliosi also took the opportunity to use Barbara's behavior as a Family member to exemplify Charlie's dominance of his followers. In particular, the prosecutor asked about the way in which Charlie ordered Barbara to gratify Juan Flynn. Barbara's sexual vocabulary failed her. She finally stammered that Charlie made her give Flynn "that oral whatchamacallit." During cross-examination, Kanarek demanded to know why she had obeyed. This time, Barbara found the exact words: "I was afraid not to."

On Saturday, September 26, a brush fire roared through the Simi Hills and burned much of Spahn Ranch. Three horses died in the blaze, and the western movie set was destroyed. As the flames rose as high as sixty feet, the Family women danced and sang, "Helter Skelter is coming down."

Juan Flynn followed Barbara Hoyt to the witness stand. He glared at Charlie as he offered damaging testimony about Charlie admitting the Tate murders to him, Susan bragging about getting "some fucking pigs," and seeing Charlie, Susan, Tex, Linda, Leslie, Pat, and Clem drive off in Johnny Swartz's Ford on the night of the LaBianca murders. On cross-examination, Kanarek accused Flynn of making everything up in hopes that media coverage would help him get bit parts in western movies. "You recognize," Kanarek said, "that there is lots of publicity in this case against Mr. Manson, right?" Flynn replied, "It is the type of publicity that I wouldn't want, you big catfish." Instead of admonishing the witness for calling Kanarek names, Judge Older grinned and adjourned the morning session.

Evidence was mounting against the defendants and Charlie knew it. He couldn't prevent Flynn from testifying, but he could at least interrupt. For that day and several more that followed, as Flynn testified, all four defendants periodically chanted and gestured. At one point, Charlie stood and sang, "The old gray mare ain't what she used to be, she is a judge now," and the girls chorused, "You are just a woman, that is all." On Friday, October 2, Charlie turned to the court spectators and said, "Look at yourselves. You're going to destruction. . . . It's your judgment day, not mine." The three women chorused, "It's your judgment day," and Older had them all taken out of the courtroom. After they were gone, Older permitted the prosecution to play a tape of Flynn being interviewed by an Inyo County officer. The jury heard the Spahn ranch hand say, "[Charlie] grabbed me by the hair like that, and he put a knife by my throat, and then he says, 'Don't you know I'm the one who is doing all the killings?' "

On Monday, October 5, Detective Paul Whiteley of the Los Angeles Sheriff's Office took the stand. His testimony was brief, and the defense attorneys declined cross-examination. But before Whiteley could step down, Charlie asked Older, "May I examine him?" When Older refused, Charlie said, "You are going to use this courtroom to kill me. I'm going to fight for my life one way or another. You should let me do it with words." Older threatened to have Charlie removed. Charlie snarled, "I will have you removed," and then added, "I have a little system of my own." Older ignored him and instructed Bugliosi to call his next witness. Manson screamed, "Do you think I'm kidding?" He grabbed a sharpened pencil and leaped over the counsel table in the direction of Older. The bailiffs were on him before he could go any further. As they dragged Charlie off to the adjacent isolation room, Charlie yelled to Older, "In the name of Christian justice, someone should cut your head off!" Susan, Pat, and Leslie stood and chanted; Older had them removed, too.

Older banned the defendants from court for several days. Charlie listened while locked in the mouse house. The three women were confined to a jury room with speakers so that they, too, could listen to testimony. Virginia Graham and Ronnie Howard testified about what Susan had told and written to them. Gregg Jakobson took the stand and recounted Charlie's interpretations of Beatles songs and Revelation. Shahrokh Hatami and Rudi Altobelli placed Charlie at Cielo on March 23, 1969.

Older allowed Charlie and the women to return to the courtroom on the day that Terry Melcher testified. When Melcher saw Charlie, he begged Bugliosi to let him testify in some other room. Melcher was able to take the stand and withstand Charlie's steady glare only after taking a tranquilizer. When he finished testifying, Charlie smiled at him.

Guided by Bugliosi's questions, Brooks Poston and Little Paul Watkins explained to the jury just how seriously the Family prepared for Helter Skelter out in Death Valley. Watkins emphasized the Family's belief that Charlie was the Second Coming of Christ. Poston admitted that, for a long time, he thought that Charlie was Jesus. Then he testified that Charlie once asked him to kill the sheriff of Shoshone.

The bailiffs did their best to make sequestration as easy as possible for the jury. They took them out for group dinners at interesting restaurants, and on weekends arranged bus trips to places like Knott's Berry Farm. By the end of the trial's fourth month, bailiff O. P. Skupen believed that the Manson jury was one of the best he'd ever monitored. Despite all Charlie's antics and all the gruesome testimony they'd heard, none of them seemed shaken. They exhibited exceptional common sense and that, Skupen thought, was bad news for Charlie and the girls. No matter how much was made of them in the newspapers and on TV, Charlie's shenanigans just weren't working. Charlie might act cooler than hell on the way to and from the courtroom, he might brag in the isolation room that everything was going the way he wanted, but at some level the guy had to know that these jurors weren't buying his act.

Tex Watson, awaiting his own murder trial, stopped eating and acted crazy enough to be sent to Atascadero State Hospital for psychiatric testing. When Charlie heard the news, he asked to talk to Bugliosi. He told the prosecutor that if he could have just half an hour with Tex, he'd get him straightened out. Bugliosi laughed and said, "I can't afford to take that chance. If you cured him, then everyone would believe you were Jesus Christ."

The final witnesses for the prosecution were Dianne Lake and two psychiatrists who had examined her. Three hundred and twenty People's Exhibits, including photos of the Tate and LaBianca murder scenes, were formally entered into evidence so that the jury could study them during deliberations. Then at 4:27 P.M. on Monday, November 16, the prosecution rested its case. The trial had lasted twenty-two weeks. At least another two or three months loomed ahead. Judge Older thought everyone involved deserved a short break before the defense took its turn. He recessed court until Thursday morning. In the interim, Charlie met with Susan, Pat, and Leslie, and told them what he wanted them to do.

On November 19, the defense attorneys made rote motions for the judge to dismiss all counts against their clients. It never hurt to try—the request was traditional. After the judge rejected the motions, Paul Fitzgerald told Older, "The defense rests." As soon as he did, Pat, Susan, and Leslie jumped to their feet and demanded the opportunity to testify.

Fitzgerald, Daye Shinn, and Ronald Hughes all asked to approach the bench, where they whispered to Older that they didn't want their clients testifying to the jury—all three would undoubtedly swear that they were guilty of the Tate-LaBianca murders, but Charlie was completely innocent. Bugliosi realized what was happening and joined the three defense attorneys in their protest. The prosecutor was in danger again of being outmaneuvered by Charlie, who'd saved this surprise for last.

Older, aware that any decision he made might form the grounds for an appeal by Kanarek, finally ruled that the three women could testify after he'd removed the jury. Afterward, whatever admissible statements they made could be added to the trial record. Their own attorneys, and Bugliosi if he wished, didn't even have to question them. Susan, Pat, and Leslie could say whatever they wanted. That was fine with the lawyers, but the women insisted it was unacceptable. They wanted the jury to hear directly what they had to say. When Older said no, they refused to take the stand.

Charlie said he'd be glad to get up there and testify, jury or no jury.

It was his grand opportunity. The jury wasn't present, but Charlie had an audience of the courtroom spectators and, most importantly, the media. Charlie never attended law school, but he knew all about the end stages of a murder trial in California. First would come the jury's verdict of guilt or innocence, and at this point there seemed to be no question which way they'd vote. After that would come the penalty phase, with the jurors deciding whether to go along with Bugliosi's request for the gas chamber or else mandate life imprisonment. But the real drama was the initial verdict, innocent or guilty, and the only thing that might supersede it would be a bravura performance on the witness stand by Charlie. He knew just how to do it. Charlie told Judge Older that he didn't want to be questioned by his attorney, Irving Kanarek. The defense attorney would stay seated and silent at the counsel table because his client didn't want to be interrupted. Charlie Manson was about to deliver a *statement*.

He spoke for over an hour, beginning with a self-pitying description of his horrific childhood: "I never went to school, so I never growed up to read and write too good, so I have stayed in jail and I have stayed stupid." Charlie declared that far from leading his followers into acts of evil, he formed the Family from social outcasts "that you did not want, people that were alongside the road, that their parents had kicked out." According to Charlie, "You made your children what they are . . . these children that come at you with their knives, they are your children. You taught them. I didn't teach them."

In fact, Charlie said, "I am only what you made me. I am only a reflection of you. . . . I am only what lives inside of each and every one of you." Yes, they could sentence him to death, but "you want to kill me? Ha. I'm already dead, have been all my life." Charlie admitted that he felt resentful: "Sometimes I think about giving it back to you. . . . If I could, I would jerk this microphone off and beat your brains out with it, because that is what you deserve. . . . If I could get angry at you, I would try to kill every one of you. If that's guilt, I accept it."

Charlie wasn't giving up his ultimate plan of the women incriminating themselves and exonerating him. He wanted to make a memorable statement in Older's court, but he didn't want to die choking on gas chamber fumes. So he next insisted that he wasn't responsible for whatever the women might have done at Cielo and Waverly Drive: "These children were finding themselves. What they did, if they did whatever they did, is up to them. They will have to explain that to you."

As for Charlie himself, he was being unfairly picked on. "It's all your fear. You look for something to project it on, and you pick out a little old scroungy nobody that eats out of a garbage can, and that nobody wants, that was kicked out of the penitentiary, that has been dragged through every hell hole that you can think of, and you drag him and you put him in a courtroom. You expect to break me? Impossible. You broke me years ago. You killed me years ago."

Judge Older asked if Charlie was finished. He wasn't.

"I have killed no one and I have ordered no one to be killed," Charlie said. "I may have implied on several different occasions to several different people that I may have been Jesus Christ, but I haven't decided yet what I am or who I am."

Older instructed Charlie to stick to the issues.

Charlie admitted he'd had the .22 Buntline at Spahn Ranch, but "it belonged to everybody." People like Linda Kasabian, Dianne Lake, and

Little Paul Watkins came to him, not vice versa. He didn't remember telling anyone, "Get a knife and a change of clothes and go do what Tex says." As for Helter Skelter, "Helter Skelter is confusion. Confusion is coming down fast . . . it is not my conspiracy. It is not my music. I hear what it relates. It says, 'Rise,' it says, 'kill.' Why blame it on me? I didn't write the music."

He roared into the finish, his voice louder, his tiny body rising up from the chair on the witness stand: "What about your children? You say there are just a few? There are many, many more, coming in the same direction. They are running in the streets, and they are coming right at you."

Bugliosi asked Charlie a few questions. Older asked Charlie if he now wanted to testify before the jury. He felt no need to put on a second show, and told Older, "I have already relieved all the pressure I had." Satisfied with his performance, believing it to be memorable, Charlie said to the three women, "You don't have to testify now." Bugliosi caught the qualifier—Charlie wasn't excusing the girls from their confessions, just delaying them until the penalty phase of the trial, if, as seemed likely, there was one. This was Charlie's moment, and he had no intention of sharing it.

Judge Older recessed the trial for ten days so the prosecution and defense could prepare their final arguments.

On Monday, November 30, the trial reconvened. Ronald Hughes, Leslie Van Houten's lawyer, wasn't there. Hughes's lack of courtroom experience had been evident throughout the trial, and, to make things worse, he was clumsy and constantly tripped over Leslie's feet when standing to make objections. After Hughes remained missing for several days Judge Older appointed well-respected attorney Maxwell Keith to replace him. Keith needed time to prepare, so Older recessed. Though the judge and attorneys met daily, the trial did not recommence until December 21. Older told the jurors they had to resign themselves to being sequestered over the Christmas holidays.

In the interim, a massive search for Hughes ensued. When the trial originally recessed for ten days on November 19, Hughes told the other defense attorneys that he was going camping at Sespe Hot Springs north of Los Angeles. Even search teams augmented by helicopters failed to locate him. The efforts ended in mid-December. Everyone accepted by then that Hughes was dead. Even after the lawyer's decomposing body was discovered six weeks later where he apparently drowned in a flooded stream, Bugliosi believed that he might have been murdered by the Family on Charlie's orders. Shortly after Hughes disappeared, Bruce Davis and Nancy Pitman had turned themselves in to police, Davis on Hinman and Shea murder charges and Pitman on a forgery charge. It seemed a little too pat for Bugliosi—perhaps they were trying to deflect any new investigation that would link them to Hughes's death. Pitman was held for only a few days before being released. On December 17, Davis, along with Charlie and Clem, was arraigned for the murder of Shorty Shea.

On December 18, Squeaky, Ruth Ann, Gypsy, Clem, and Dennis Rice were indicted for conspiracy to prevent Barbara Hoyt's testimony in the Tate-LaBianca trial. The judge released Squeaky, Gypsy, and Rice on bail (Clem remained in custody in Inyo County on an illegal weapon possession charge), and nine-months-pregnant Ruth Ann on her own recognizance.

On December 21, Older called the court to order. No sooner had he done so than Leslie stood and berated him for appointing Keith to replace Hughes. She told the judge that she had nothing to do with her original attorney's disappearance, and wondered if Older might be behind it. Charlie yelled at Older, too, and the judge ordered all four defendants removed. Bugliosi then began his closing arguments. The defense attorneys would follow, and then the prosecutor would make a final statement before the jury retired to consider its verdict.

Bugliosi began with a series of charts, summarizing the evidence presented and saving any emotional appeal for his final statement. It took him a while—since July 24, the prosecution had introduced hundreds of items. Bugliosi was still summing up evidence when Older permitted the defendants to return to court. The three women immediately began talking loudly and Older ordered them removed again. On her way out, Susan grabbed some notes out of Bugliosi's hand and tore them in half. Bugliosi snatched them back and snarled, "You little bitch." The judge prohibited all four defendants from returning to the courtroom until the jury announced its verdict. If Susan thought losing some of his notes would faze Bugliosi, she was mistaken. He'd memorized most of his remarks just in case. He told the jury that the Family was "a closely knit bunch of robots," and Charlie was "the dictatorial master of a tribe of bootlicking slaves."

On December 28 Bugliosi declared, "The people of the state of California are entitled to a guilty verdict," and stepped aside for final arguments by each of the four defense attorneys. Paul Fitzgerald, speaking on behalf of Pat Krenwinkel, tried to turn Bugliosi's words to his client's advantage, telling the jury that "mindless robots cannot be guilty of first degree murder" because that charge involved premeditation. Yes, one of Pat's fingerprints was apparently inside the Cielo house, but Fitzgerald suggested that perhaps she'd been there "as an invited guest or a friend."

Daye Shinn, Susan Atkins's attorney, attacked the character of the witnesses for the prosecution. Would members of the jury, he wondered, invite Virginia Graham to their homes for Christmas?

It took Shinn less than ninety minutes to complete his closing statement. Irving Kanarek took a week. He expounded on every facet of the trial, once again boring even Charlie, listening in the mouse house adjacent to the courtroom. The mouse house wasn't entirely soundproofed. At one point the jury could hear Charlie shouting, "You're just making things worse!" On the fifth day of Kanarek's argument, the jury sent a note to Older requesting NoDoz. The gist of Kanarek's statement was that Tex Watson was really the mastermind behind the murders. Charlie was just an innocent bystander.

Maxwell Keith, representing Leslie Van Houten, spoke last. He was new to the trial, but his arguments were the best of any of the defense attorneys. He began with a sarcastic reference to *Linda* Van Houten, underscoring that Leslie was at a real disadvantage due to her attorney's lack of familiarity with the case. Like Fitzgerald, he reminded jurors of Bugliosi's own words—if Leslie was a "mindless robot," how could she in any sense have committed premeditated murder at Waverly Drive? But he also made a key point about Leslie's limited role in the slaying of Rosemary LaBianca: "Nobody in the world can be guilty of murder . . . [by stabbing] somebody after they are already dead. I'm sure that desecrating somebody that is dead is a crime in this state, but she is not charged with that."

Bugliosi's final summation took two days. He responded to the closing arguments by the four defense attorneys, and conceded he had referred to Susan, Pat, and Leslie as "robots." But that didn't mean that they should be acquitted for the murders: "They were not suffering, ladies and gentlemen, from any diminished mental capacity. They were suffering from a diminished heart, a diminished soul." He concluded with what the media afterward described as the roll call of the dead. "Sharon Tate, Abigail Folger, Voytek Frykowski, Jay Sebring, Steven Parent, Leno LaBianca, Rosemary LaBianca, are not here with us now in this courtroom, but from their graves they cry out for justice. Justice can only be served by coming back to this courtroom with a verdict of guilty."

The jurors retired to deliberate on Friday afternoon, January 15, 1971. Ten days later, they sent word to Judge Older that they had reached verdicts, and Older reconvened court. After agreeing with Bugliosi and the four defense attorneys that the penalty phase, if any, would begin in three days, Older instructed the bailiffs to bring Charlie, Susan, Pat, and Leslie into court. As the defendants were led in, Charlie winked at the girls and they giggled and winked back. Then all four listened impassively as they were found guilty on all counts. As the jury filed out, Charlie told them, "You are all guilty." On his way back to his ninth floor cell, Charlie said to the bailiff escorting him, "What did you expect?" He didn't appear concerned.

Kathleen Maddox was in Los Angeles when the jury found her son guilty of murder. For more than a year, she'd been horrified by the stories describing what he'd become and what he'd apparently led foolish followers to do. During that time, Kathleen didn't try to contact Charlie. She was convinced that he was mentally ill—what other explanation could there be for the things that he'd done? Her hope was that instead of going to the gas chamber, Charlie would get some kind of psychiatric help. Kathleen felt certain that was what he needed. She didn't excuse what he'd done—she cried when she thought about the people who had died.

It also bothered her that so many stories about Charlie claimed that he was the son of an unfit mother, that he'd had a deprived childhood and no one ever loved him. So when she went down to L.A. during the last days of the trial and a *Los Angeles Times* reporter guessed who she was, Kathleen agreed to talk. On January 26, "Mother Tells Life of Manson as Boy" vied with "Manson Verdict: All Guilty" for front page space. Kathleen did her best to make the reporter understand. She told about how strict her mother, Nancy, was, how she herself had made some mistakes as a girl, all about Colonel Scott being Charlie's father and her struggle to raise her son right. If anything, Kathleen said, Charlie was a spoiled little boy who was given anything he wanted instead of having to work for it. But she felt that the resulting story had a lot of mistakes in it, quoting her as saying Charlie was born out of wedlock when he wasn't—she was married to William Manson by then—and how Charlie loved his baby sister, Nancy, when in fact he'd had a temper tantrum just learning about the adopted child. Kathleen decided that reporters weren't to be trusted and rushed back home. Over the next months she received letters from famous TV newsmen asking her to come on their shows and tell her story, but she never responded.

Just before the penalty phase of the trial began, Charlie sent word through Sandy and Squeaky to Susan, Pat, and Leslie that they were now to take the stand and swear they'd committed the murders without any orders or suggestions from him. Months earlier, he'd asked all his followers if they would die for him. Now he expected three of them to do it.

Vincent Bugliosi called only two witnesses in penalty phase, a policeman from Oregon who testified that a gun-toting Susan Atkins once said she wanted an opportunity to shoot him, and Lotsapoppa, massive living proof that Charlie was capable of attempting murder as well as ordering it. The Oregon cop's testimony went smoothly, but Lotsapoppa had just taken the stand when Charlie stood and demanded to question the drug dealer himself. Judge Older told Charlie that he could suggest questions, but Kanarek would have to ask them. Charlie scribbled down several and handed them to Kanarek, who ignored the list and began asking Lotsapoppa questions of his own. Charlie yelled at Kanarek to ask the ones he'd been given, and the lawyer said no. Charlie sprang to Kanarek's side and punched him hard on the arm; Kanarek yelped in pain. The bailiffs moved forward to grab Charlie, but halted when they saw Judge Older give a subtle shake of his head. The judge apparently enjoyed seeing Irving Kanarek acquire a few bruises. Charlie belted his attorney on the arm several more times before Older finally nodded, and the bailiffs dragged Charlie off to the mouse house.

Bugliosi rested the prosecution's case on February 1. The defense began by calling Pat's parents and Leslie's mother. All three said they loved their daughters and were bewildered by what they had apparently done. A parade of Family members took the stand—Squeaky, Sandy, Gypsy, Ruth Ann, and Clem. Their testimony rambled—Charlie breathed on a dead bird and brought it back to life, he petted rattlesnakes, people didn't understand how death wasn't anything to take seriously. But besides the prattling, there were serious charges. According to Gypsy, Gary Hinman was killed by Linda Kasabian, Susan Atkins, and Leslie Van Houten, and Linda masterminded the Cielo and Waverly Drive murders because she was in love with Bobby Beausoleil and wanted to commit copycat crimes so he would be set free. Charlie had nothing at all to do with it. During the days that Family members testified, word spread that Tex Watson had been ruled competent to stand trial. His murder case would come to court as soon as the penalty phase trial of Charlie, Susan, Pat, and Leslie concluded.

Susan Atkins took the stand on February 9. She immediately testified that she participated in the Cielo and Waverly murders. She also killed Gary Hinman, she insisted. Then Susan offered grisly details about slaughtering Sharon Tate. Charlie, she insisted, had nothing to do with the August 9 murders because he was back at Spahn Ranch, sleeping.

Judge Older took pity on the jury and ended their sequestration. They went home on February 16 for the first time in more than eight months, and returned to court the next day to hear testimony by Pat Krenwinkel. Pat supported Susan's account that Linda Kasabian plotted the copycat murders, and told jurors about stabbing Abigail Folger and mutilating Leno LaBianca. Leslie followed Pat to the stand, but was vague about whether it had been she or Mary Brunner who was involved in killing Gary Hinman. She claimed that she couldn't remember Charlie ordering any murders. Leslie agreed that somewhere, sometime she might have mentioned something about Charlie going into the LaBianca house, but when the prosecutor pressed her, she shouted, "Mr. Bugliosi, you are an evil man!" With Linda Kasabian now set up as the real criminal mastermind, the defense recalled her to the stand. But Linda calmly held her ground during aggressive questioning. She strongly denied everything Gypsy, Susan, Pat, and Leslie had claimed.

Three Family members were the final defense witnesses. Cathy Gillies said Charlie had nothing to do with any murders, there had never been any discussion of a race war, and the Tate-LaBianca murders were copycat killings to free Bobby Beausoleil. She was only sorry that on the night the LaBiancas died, she couldn't go along and participate because there wasn't enough room in the car. Mary Brunner testified that the police told her she'd be charged with Gary Hinman's murder if she didn't implicate Charlie. Nancy Pitman swore that Charlie never left the ranch on the night of the LaBianca murders. She was dismissed from the stand on March 16 and the defense rested. Charlie never testified on his own behalf—he'd said what he wanted to in his hour-long harangue back in January. Nor did he want to distract jurors' attention from the confessions by Susan, Pat, and Leslie.

In the penalty phase of the trial, during final arguments the prosecution made a statement, the defense followed, the prosecution had a second turn and the defense went last. It took Vincent Bugliosi just ten minutes to present the first of his two closing arguments. If the Tate-LaBianca slayings didn't merit the death penalty for all four perpetrators, he told the jury, then no murders ever would: "These defendants are human monsters, human mutations."

Irving Kanarek conceded that "Mr. Manson is not all good," but "Mr. Manson is innocent of these matters that are before us." For three days, Kanarek rambled: Charlie was only on trial so somebody (he didn't specify Bugliosi, but his intent was clear) in the District Attorney's Office "can have a gold star." Susan, Pat, and Leslie all said Charlie wasn't involved in the murders, and they also claimed they weren't sorry for slaughtering seven people. If they were lying about Charlie not ordering them to kill, why wouldn't they lie some more and say that they were sorry for their victims, in case the jury might take pity on them and not sentence them to death? And about those five people who died at Cielo, Kanarek assured the jury, if at least some of them hadn't been "engaged in a narcotic episode of some type, these events would not have taken place." When Kanarek finally concluded, Daye Shinn argued that Susan Atkins was still young, just twenty-two. No matter what she had done, she might still be rehabilitated if she wasn't sentenced to death. Maxwell Keith suggested that jurors consider "the roll call of the living dead," the Family members whose lives "have been so damaged." As for his client, "I am not asking you to forgive her. . . . She deserves to live. What she did was not done by the real Leslie." Paul Fitzgerald noted that his twenty-three-year-old client, Pat, had so far lived "approximately 200,000 hours." The two nights of murder totaled perhaps three hours. "Is she to be judged solely on what occurred during three of 200,000 hours?"

Charlie felt less confident after the four defense attorneys' initial summations. Before court convened on the morning of March 23, he called over to Bugliosi, "If I get the death penalty, there is going to be a lot of bloodletting, because I am not going to take it." Informed of the threat, Judge Older immediately sequestered the jury again since it was the kind of public outburst that was bound to make the papers.

Bugliosi opened his last statement to the jury by suggesting that Susan, Pat, and Linda had lied when they attempted to exonerate Charlie, and "the fact that they were willing . . . just proves all the more Manson's domination over them." The copycat motive was nonsense; the seven murders were committed to precipitate Helter Skelter. Charlie deserved to die, but so did the three women. Their attorneys stressed their youth, but Leslie was twenty-one, Susan twenty-two, and Pat twenty-three, "adults by any standard, and completely responsible for their acts." No one forced them to go with Tex and murder innocent people: "All they had to do was not do it." The jury was about to hear the defense attorneys make final pleas for mercy for their clients—was mercy extended to the seven victims? Bugliosi closed by rewording his previous declaration: "If the death penalty is to mean anything in the state of California other than two empty words, this is the proper case."

When the defense attorneys took their final turns, Kanarek read chapters of the New Testament to the jurors, and noted, "We are not suggesting that Mr. Manson is the deity or Christ-like or anything like that, but how can we know?" Shinn said that Susan Atkins had initially trusted prosecutors and attempted to cooperate, but they betrayed her. Keith told the jury that, in many respects, he agreed with Bugliosi. Charlie dominated the three women defendants and ordered the Cielo and Waverly Drive murders. The concept of copycat killings was nonsense. The penalty phase testimony of his client, Leslie, and of Susan and Pat just offered more proof that Charlie still controlled them. But Keith didn't think any of the four deserved the gas chamber. Charlie was crazy, and he'd "infected [the girls] with his madness." Fitzgerald described to the jurors how horribly the condemned died in the gas chamber.

Judge Older sent the jury off to deliberate on Friday, March 26. They announced on Monday afternoon that they had reached agreement. It was so fast that there was little doubt what they'd decided.

Charlie knew that his plan hadn't worked. He let bailiff Skupen bring him to the counsel table, and stood there with Susan, Pat, and Leslie as the court clerk prepared to announce their fates. Then Charlie lost his nerve. He was always ready, even eager, to insist that human life was insignificant, but this time the life involved was his own. Just as the clerk began to read the verdicts, Charlie leaped up and shrieked, "You people have no authority over me! Half of you in here ain't as good as I am!" Older ordered the bailiffs to take Charlie back to the mouse house. He had to be dragged there, but once the door slammed shut behind him he stood motionless. Skupen was locked inside with Charlie; on the speaker, they heard the judge demanding that the courtroom come to order. Charlie asked for a cigarette. Skupen handed him one, saying, "Damn it, Charlie, I wanted to see that." Charlie mumbled, "Well, I didn't." Then the clerk announced that the jury sentenced all four defendants to death. Susan, Pat, and Leslie shouted at the jurors, warning them to lock their doors and watch out for their own kids. Outside, asked by a TV reporter for her reaction, Sandy hissed, "Death? That's what you're all going to get." But inside the mouse house Charlie had nothing to say. He smoked and stared into space until the courtroom was cleared. Then Skupen took Charlie by the arm and led him back to his ninth floor cell, where he awaited eventual transfer to San Quentin's Death Row.

A few months later in the course of a lengthy interview, *Rolling Stone* magazine founder Jann Wenner asked former Beatle John Lennon what he thought of Charlie Manson and the whole tragic Helter Skelter business. Lennon replied that Manson was "barmy" (crazy) for reading any kind of message into the song, adding that he personally had never even paid attention to its lyrics because they didn't matter. So far as the Beatles were concerned, Lennon said, Helter Skelter was only noise.

CHAPTER NINETEEN

The Wrong Man in the Right Place at the Right Time

On April 19, 1971, Judge Charles Older formally sentenced Charlie, Susan, Pat, and Leslie to die in the gas chamber. Had he considered it appropriate, the judge could have reduced any or all of their sentences to life in prison, but Older stated that he could find no mitigating circumstances: "I must agree with the prosecutor that if this is not the proper case for the death penalty, what would be?" Charlie's voice shook as he meekly told Older, "I accept this court as my father. . . . I accept my father's judgment," but Charlie realized like everyone else that his execution wasn't imminent. Appeals on behalf of him and the women would take at least two years, possibly as many as five, and there were more trials to come. Charlie, Susan, and Bruce Davis faced charges for their roles in the Hinman slaying, and Charlie, Bruce, and Clem for their participation in Shea's.

They weren't the only Family members in the dock. Three days before Older passed sentence on Charlie and the three women, in another court Squeaky, Gypsy, Clem, Dennis Rice, and Ruth Ann pleaded no contest to deliberately overdosing Barbara Hoyt with LSD. They were each given ninety days in the county jail. Ruth Ann never appeared for sentencing. The other four served their time and were released.

Charlie was sent temporarily to private confinement in San Quentin until he was needed in L.A. for the Hinman and Shea trials. Susan pleaded guilty to Hinman's murder and was transferred to the California Institution for Women forty miles east of L.A. She joined Leslie and Pat, who had arrived ahead of her, and were placed in special cells isolated from the rest of the prison community. Susan believed that Leslie and Pat resented her for the boasts to Virginia Graham and Ronnie Howard that led the LAPD to Charlie and the Family; she wrote later that after she arrived at the prison they were unfriendly toward her. Leslie and Pat recall that they held no grudges; they were just too emotionally exhausted from the drawn-out trial to greet Susan with any enthusiasm. And anyway, they were all going to the gas chamber, so what good was resentment? Together, the three women watched television, bummed cigarettes from guards, and waited to be executed.

In June, Charlie threw a tantrum when it was ruled he would be tried for the Hinman and Shea murders separately from the other defendants. He tore a button from his shirt, hurled it at presiding Judge Raymond Choate, and screamed, "Have you ever seen anyone who doesn't belong to a woman?" When court proceedings commenced in July, Squeaky, Sandy, and some of the other women remaining in the Family took up their old positions on the sidewalk outside the courthouse. Charlie engaged in courtroom histrionics, first attempting to plead guilty and bragging that he chopped off an unspecified victim's head, then the next day withdrawing the guilty plea. It seemed as though Charlie's Hinman-Shea trial would be a mirror image of Tate-LaBianca, but this time his followers were determined not to let their leader's fate be decided by a jury. The Weathermen had freed Timothy Leary. The Family would do the same for Charlie.

While Charlie was held in San Quentin pending his L.A. trial for the Hinman-Shea murders, he made a deal with members of the Aryan Brotherhood to protect him from other prisoners in return for Family women providing sex for AB members on the outside. A clue that the partnership involved more than protection and sex came when Charlie insisted that San Quentin inmate and AB leader Kenneth Como be subpoenaed to testify on his behalf in Hinman-Shea. Como was transferred to L.A. in July so he could testify; he escaped from jail there and was hidden by the Family, who now had a wily career criminal to help plot their next move.

Como and the Family believed that if they accumulated enough guns, they could hijack a jet at the Los Angeles airport and kill a passenger an hour until Charlie and every other imprisoned Family member was released. They accepted that at least a few people would have to be shot before their demands were met. Getting the weapons and acquiring getaway money was necessary. They went after the money first. On August 13, they stole $2,600 from a beer distributorship in the L.A. suburbs. Eight days later, Como, Gypsy, Mary Brunner, Dennis Rice, and two others held up a Western Surplus Store in Hawthorne, holding a clerk and two customers at gunpoint and loading about 140 rifles, shotguns, and handguns into a getaway van. But a silent alarm was triggered, and the LAPD surrounded the store before the thieves could escape. All six were caught. With Sandy's help, Como briefly escaped again, but he was recaptured within hours. Eventually the media-dubbed "Hawthorne Four"—Gypsy, Mary, Como, and Rice—received stiff prison sentences ranging from ten years to life. Sometime during the planning of the foiled rescue attempt, Como and Gypsy fell in love. The judge denied Como's request that they be married before they were transported to their respective prisons. Mary and Gypsy were sent to the California Institution for Women and housed with Susan, Pat, and Leslie. The five women got along reasonably well— Susan felt that Gypsy and Mary were friendlier to her than Pat and Leslie had been.

Susan never saw her son Ze Zo Ze again. He was adopted and his name was changed.

Sandy Good was sentenced to six months for her role in Como's second escape. That left Squeaky to lead what was left of the Family, with the assistance of Sandy after she served her prison time. Previously, the two women had never been particularly close, but now circumstances dictated otherwise. With so many members locked away and access to Charlie limited, it was hard to keep everything organized and everyone loyal. Charlie had no intention of allowing the Family to disintegrate and made this clear to Squeaky and Sandy whenever they were able to communicate with him. To that end, Squeaky began writing a book that she believed would not only remind Family members of their duty to Charlie, but would entice other readers to want to join.

In August, Tex Watson went on trial for the Tate-LaBianca murders. Vincent Bugliosi was lead prosecutor. Tex entered a plea of not guilty by reason of insanity; he freely admitted participating in the murders, though he emphasized that he had been ordered to do so by Charlie. After two and a half months that included testimony by Linda Kasabian, Little Paul Watkins, Brooks Poston, and a score of psychiatrists, Tex was found guilty and sentenced to death. Steve Grogan—Clem—received the same jury verdict and sentence for the murder of Shorty Shea, but in his case the judge ruled that "Grogan was too stupid" to commit murder on his own and reduced the sentence to life imprisonment. Bruce Davis was sentenced to life for Hinman-Shea, and so, superfluously, was Charlie, who was still scheduled to die in the gas chamber for Tate-LaBianca unless his sentence was overturned on appeal.

News of Charlie and the Family still made headlines, but not as many. He resented his loss of celebrity. In particular Charlie complained that all of his former music business friends had deserted him. In December 1971 he became the 97th prisoner placed in San Quentin's Death Row. The sheer number of condemned ahead of him in line for the gas chamber meant that Charlie's stay would be lengthy.

His Death Row sojourn got off to a bad start when the other prisoners were infuriated by Charlie's cavalier attitude toward his mail. Condemned men at San Quentin yearned for mail and seldom got any. After Charlie's arrival, on any given day the rest of the Death Row population collectively received no more than twenty-five to thirty letters while Charlie routinely scored hundreds. That was grounds for widespread jealousy. What made the inequity even more galling was that Charlie dumped everything in the trash without bothering to look at it. This fostered the kind of deep-seated resentment that could potentially get Charlie shanked. Roger Dale Smith, in the cell next to Charlie's, called him out and demanded to know why he didn't read his mail. Charlie admitted that he couldn't read very well, so he avoided frustration by not trying to read the letters at all. Smith, nicknamed "Pin Cushion" for surviving more than 135 prison stabbings and desperate for something to help while away the Death Row hours, offered to read some of Charlie's mail to him. The range of messages, mostly the same as Charlie had received while in jail in L.A., stunned Smith—there were death threats, assurances of prayers on his behalf, messages of congratulation for standing up to the Man, requests for autographs, and pleas from young women to be allowed to join the Family. Smith, whose toughness was legendary among his fellow convicts, let the other Death Row denizens know that Charlie now enjoyed his protection. Charlie was left to spend the days quietly strumming his guitar; when an occasional letter interested him, he dictated a response to Smith.

On February 18, 1972, the California Supreme Court voted 6–1 to abolish the death penalty. At the California Institution for Women, Susan Atkins, Pat Krenwinkel, and Leslie Van Houten greeted the news with cheers. Charlie, temporarily back in L.A. to testify in the Hinman-Shea murder trial of Bruce Davis, grinned. Under California law, their sentences, as well as Tex Watson's, were automatically reduced to life in prison. They would be eligible for parole in seven years. Tex was transferred to a prison near San Luis Obispo, where he was assigned to work in the psychiatric unit as a clerk. Susan, Leslie, and Pat remained where they were, isolated from the main prisoner population for four more years. But now they were allowed to do needlepoint, plant small gardens, and have mandatory sessions with psychiatrists. It took time for their belief in Charlie to weaken. Occasionally they huddled together and sang some of his songs, including "Home Is Where You're Happy."

Charlie began a series of transfers among high-security California prisons. No wardens wanted him. His mere presence drew media and public attention, and on the occasions when he was allowed into the general population other prisoners threatened him. Whenever Charlie found himself in the same facility with Roger Dale Smith he had a protector. Otherwise, he was on his own. His protection agreement with the Aryan Brotherhood broke down when Charlie denounced Gypsy's relationship with Kenneth Como—Family women weren't supposed to be in love with anyone but Charlie. When Como and Charlie both found themselves at Folsom State Prison, they fought; the bigger, tougher Como and some of his Aryan Brotherhood cohorts beat Charlie badly. Charlie was transferred back to San Quentin soon afterward. A Family crisis ensued. Gypsy and Mary Brunner recognized Como as their new leader. Squeaky contacted all the Family members that she could, urging them to remain faithful to Charlie. Squeaky and Sandy worked hard to hold things together, renting a series of houses around the state, offering places to live to other Family women like Nancy Pitman and sometimes aligning themselves with members of the Aryan Brotherhood who didn't have it in for Charlie. These arrangements were combustible. The men sometimes supported the households with armed robberies, and there was considerable paranoia about potential snitches within the group. When one of them, James Willett, was murdered, Squeaky and Nancy Pitman were among those arrested for the crime. Nancy received a five-year sentence as an accessory after the fact, and Squeaky was released due to insufficient evidence. Willett's wife subsequently died while playing Russian roulette in a scene grimly reminiscent of the death of Zero several years before. Then and later, no one was ever certain just how many murders might be connected to the Family.

Besides being charged by Charlie with holding the Family together, Squeaky also felt responsible for keeping her leader—and his followers— in the public eye. Charlie wasn't the only one among them who enjoyed being famous. Squeaky kept working on her book; the manuscript now totaled several hundred pages, many handwritten and illustrated with Squeaky's drawings. It extolled Charlie's philosophy of the world as a single extended community, with everyone part of a greater whole. Violence, let alone murder, went unmentioned. Squeaky managed to get her work to an editor at an East Coast publisher, and waited confidently for the offer of a contract. Instead, she received a pointed query: "Enough of this Love-Love-Love. Where's the Kill-Kill-Kill?" Squeaky concluded that it would take something other than her book to remind the world that nothing was more important than Charlie Manson, and, by association, his most devoted disciples.

During the summer of 1973, Kathleen Maddox died of a sudden brain hemorrhage. She never recovered emotionally from the trauma caused by Charlie. Though Kathleen believed that Charlie had been incorrigible from early childhood, she still felt responsible for his crimes: If only she'd been a better parent, if only she'd been stricter with him, or more lenient, or something, anything. In particular, her daughter, Nancy, recalled, every time Kathleen saw Doris Day on television, she would break down and cry.

Bruce Davis claimed that he found the Lord in prison, and wanted to share the Good Word with others. He began writing to Susan Atkins. She initially misunderstood the purpose of his letters, thinking he was wooing her for himself rather than Christ. But Susan was inspired enough by the letters and by her own Bible readings to experience her own epiphany in 1974. She proclaimed herself born-again and set out to serve God with the same enthusiasm she once proselytized for Charlie Manson. In letters announcing her new faith, she compared herself to Moses and Paul. Susan never aimed low. She also published a memoir titled *Child of Satan, Child of God*. In the process, she alienated Leslie Van Houten, who thought that Susan was taking the easy way out, saying that now she was forgiven for all her sins. The two women would not speak for more than twenty years.

Though they didn't turn to Christianity as a basis for personal redemption, Leslie and Pat did gradually wean themselves from Charlie. Without his constant presence in their lives, pressuring them with hypnotic sermonizing and physical abuse, they attempted to regain a sense of emotional balance. Gypsy and Mary Brunner were eventually paroled; Mary successfully disappeared from public view, anonymously raising her son by Charlie. Gypsy met with the press following her release and talked about making her own record album. But Susan, Pat, and Leslie remained incarcerated at the California Institution for Women, hoping that at some point parole boards would decide that they, too, had paid sufficiently for their crimes.

Tex Watson also announced that he had found the Lord. He began an evangelical ministry and, with the help of a prison chaplain, published a memoir about his time with the Family and the miracle of his Christian conversion. In the book, Tex speculated that Charlie was possessed by demons. Charlie's response included Susan as well as Tex: "If they're following God the way they followed me, with their own interests always in mind, then God can't be too proud."

Charlie had a new faith, too, though it was mostly intended for his remaining female followers rather than himself. He wrote to Squeaky that she should now consider herself a nun in "the Order of the Rainbow," whose members must avoid all fleshly temptation: "No fornication or showing your ass." Squeaky and the other nuns were not to eat meat, smoke, or wear makeup. They should not watch "movies with violence." More and more, Charlie lectured them about environmental concerns. The real enemies were corporations that polluted nature. Squeaky and Sandy assembled a hodgepodge of new followers that they collectively named the International People's Court of Retribution, environmental vigilantes who would exact revenge on corporate polluters. These criminals would be warned by letter to stop polluting or die. Sandy and Squeaky sent out press releases, and were frustrated when the flood of stories that they anticipated failed to materialize. Impossible as it seemed to them, the media believed there were more important things to write about. In August 1974 the Watergate political scandal brought down Richard Nixon, who resigned the presidency. The cease-fire in Vietnam fell apart as soon as American troops were gone; the Vietcong eventually surrounded and overran Saigon. The military intervention that tore American society apart was, in the end, for nothing.

Charlie's return to the limelight was initiated by a surprising source. Despite Vincent Bugliosi's ambitions, the Tate-LaBianca trial did not serve him as a political springboard. In 1972 he lost a tough race for district attorney. But in November 1974, Bugliosi and veteran true crime writer Curt Gentry published *Helter Skelter*, Bugliosi's first-person account of Charlie's apprehension, prosecution, and conviction. Written with exceptional pacing and flair—the opening page declared, "The story you are about to read will scare the hell out of you"—*Helter Skelter* was a sensation, selling through several printings in the first few weeks, eventually seven million copies in all. If most of the world had forgotten about Charlie, they were forcefully reminded of him now. He was depicted by Bugliosi as a charismatic, conniving degenerate who enticed willing followers to slaughter innocents in pursuit of a sick, apocalyptic vision of personal power. The image of a manipulative monster was branded indelibly on the imaginations of readers. When a TV miniseries based on the book aired two years later, it set ratings records. Thanks to *Helter Skelter*, Charlie was reestablished as America's most sinister celebrity.

Ten months later, Squeaky went *Helter Skelter* one better.

Squeaky Fromme hated the book and denounced it to anyone who would listen. In particular she resented Bugliosi's strong suggestions that the Manson Family had murdered more than the nine people that were public record. It was a tough time for Squeaky. Her own book remained unpublished. She and Sandy weren't allowed to communicate directly with Charlie—prison officials thought their letters to and from him included code for an escape attempt. The two women had moved to Sacramento to be closer to him at Folsom, but he had been transferred back to San Quentin. Squeaky wanted the public always to be aware of Charlie, but not because of a book that was making Bugliosi rich and famous. Charlie was all about the environment, not some murders six years ago. Something memorable must be done to make that point.

On the morning of September 5, 1975, President Gerald Ford walked across the street from his hotel to the California state capitol in Sacramento, where he was to meet briefly with Governor Jerry Brown. Ford's schedule was no secret; it had been published in the local papers. A small crowd lined the president's walking route. Among them was Squeaky, dressed in a red nun's habit and concealing beneath her robes a bulky Colt .45 semiautomatic handgun. Ford noticed the colorful outfit; the woman seemed to want to shake hands. As he turned toward her, Squeaky raised the gun. She was tackled by a Secret Service agent who grabbed the weapon and wrestled her to the ground as other agents hustled Ford away. Squeaky complained, "Can you believe it? It didn't go off," and asked the agent who'd tackled her, "Why are you protecting him? He's not a public servant."

With Squeaky in custody, authorities raided the apartment where she lived with Sandy and another woman. Sandy denied knowing anything about the assassination attempt, but claimed that she and her friend were trying to "wake you people up" about the dangers of pollution. Boxes of evidence were hauled away, including threatening materials intended for mailing to corporate executives.

In San Quentin, Charlie swore that Squeaky had acted on her own. A prison spokesman told reporters that Charlie's "initial reaction was noncommittal and surprised." But to many readers of *Helter Skelter* and those who kept reading and hearing about him in the newspapers and on TV, the Ford assassination attempt proved that even from his prison cell Charlie Manson still controlled potential murderers. Squeaky was in custody, but who knew how many more of his minions were out there? Not even the president was safe if killing was Charlie's will.

The subsequent trial garnered Squeaky all the publicity she wanted for Charlie, if not for their environmental causes. The proceedings dominated national headlines and the covers of weekly newsmagazines. In November, Squeaky was found guilty of attempting to assassinate the president and sentenced to life in prison. When the sentence was formally passed by the court, she threw herself on the floor and howled. Sandy was subsequently indicted for violating Postal Service regulations by sending threatening letters and received a fifteen-year sentence. She and Squeaky were both sent to a federal women's prison in Alderson, West Virginia.

In October 1975, four and a half years after she fled prior to sentencing for poisoning Barbara Hoyt with LSD, Ruth Ann Moorehouse was arrested in Sacramento. Ruth Ann said that in April 1971 she was nine months pregnant and didn't want to give birth in jail. She added that since her disappearance she'd married, had a second child, and divorced. Three weeks later a California Superior Court judge set Ruth Ann free, noting that she no longer had anything to do with the Family and that, while still a child, she was "thrown willy-nilly into the Manson cult by her father." Ruth Ann was represented in court by Paul Fitzgerald.

The California courts overturned Leslie Van Houten's murder conviction in 1976, ruling that Maxwell Keith had had insufficient time to prepare after replacing Ronald Hughes as her attorney. Vincent Bugliosi was gone from the DA's office, so Stephen Kay prosecuted Leslie's new trial. Jurors had to determine whether she was guilty of first degree murder or manslaughter. If they chose the latter, Leslie would be freed based on time already served. The jury deadlocked, with seven voting for murder and five for manslaughter. Kay tried the case again; in the interim, Leslie made bail and spent a few months out in the world. But the second jury ruled her guilty of murder, and she was returned to the California Institution for Women.

Squeaky and Sandy wanted badly to be transferred from West Virginia to a new women's prison in Pleasanton, California. With the exception of one newspaper interview in which Squeaky swore that the Manson Family was thriving, they had behaved themselves in West Virginia and their request was granted. But after they arrived in Pleasanton, they reverted to their old intransigence. Squeaky attacked another inmate with a claw hammer, screaming that her victim was "a white middle-class rich bitch and doesn't deserve to live." Squeaky was immediately shipped back to West Virginia; Sandy was allowed to go with her.

Charlie wrote the warden of the West Virginia Penitentiary in Moundsville, the same facility where his mother and Uncle Luther had once been imprisoned, asking to be transferred there. The warden responded that before he'd welcome Charlie "it will be a cold day in hell." Charlie remained at a California prison in Vacaville, where he was allowed out into the general population. It was a mistake. He was attacked by another inmate. Jan Holmstrom, imprisoned for the murder of his father, doused Charlie with paint thinner and set him ablaze. Charlie suffered second- and third-degree burns to his face, scalp, and hands. Holmstrom, who had argued with Charlie about religion, told prison authorities that "God told me to kill Manson." Afterward, Charlie was transferred yet again to San Quentin.

Back in the West Virginia prison, Squeaky pined for contact with or even news of Charlie. In December 1987, she escaped after hearing a false report that Charlie had been diagnosed with testicular cancer. Squeaky was recaptured two days later, having managed to flee only two miles. For the escape attempt, five years could have been added to her sentence plus a fine of up to $250,000. But Squeaky's effort was so inept that the judge added just fifteen months, and assessed her $400. She began a series of transfers to facilities around the country, ending up in Fort Worth, Texas.

Charlie remained an iconic, controversial figure. Anything about him was news, including appearances before parole boards, where he frequently indulged in histrionics before eventually boycotting them altogether. He would never be seriously considered for parole and knew it.

But he also knew how to make the most of his ongoing celebrity, using the media at carefully selected intervals to remind the public just how dangerous he remained. Charlie's most notorious outburst aired in 1988, when he snarled to TV interviewer Geraldo Rivera that "I'm going to chop up some more of you motherfuckers. . . . I'm going to pile you up to the sky." Watching Charlie on TV, reading his print interviews, Leslie Van Houten felt frustrated—everyone must believe that Charlie had always been ranting and bloodthirsty. What kind of idiots would ever have followed him? Nobody knew or cared about the way Charlie could, when he wanted, win over almost anyone with soothing words and warm smiles. But Leslie remembered Charlie's pledge to the Family that, if he was ever arrested, he would play "Crazy Charlie." What the world had seen in all the years since his arrest and conviction for the Tate and La-Bianca murders was an act. She decided that in this, if nothing else, Charlie Manson proved to be a man of his word.

In 1988, a band called the Lemonheads recorded Charlie's "Home Is Where You're Happy"; Guns N' Roses followed in 1993 with a version of "Look at Your Game, Girl." Charlie earned royalties from both, but never saw a penny. Thanks to the original 1971 court judgment, all the money went to Voytek Frykowski's son, Bartek.

Susan Atkins was diagnosed with brain cancer in 2008, and passed away the next year. To the end of her life she repudiated Charles Manson and worked diligently in programs designed to assist young women inmates. In 1987 she married attorney James Whitehouse, who represented her in her final parole hearings. He remains devoted to her memory. Susan also reconciled with Leslie Van Houten, who says, "Susan died having the one thing she always wanted, somebody to love her."

In 2009, Squeaky Fromme was paroled from the Federal Medical Center Carswell in Fort Worth. Upon her release she refused to give interviews and moved to New York state, where she was spotted in a car with a bumper sticker reading, "Born Again Pagan."

Charles "Tex" Watson operates Abounding Love Ministries from Mule Creek State Prison in Ione, California. In June 2012, a Texas judge granted the LAPD the right to review cassette tapes made in 1969–70 by Watson with his lawyer, Bill Boyd. The basis for the LAPD's appeal was that Watson may have discussed additional Manson Family murders on the tapes.

Pat Krenwinkel and Leslie Van Houten remain at the California Institution for Women. They freely mingle with other inmates. Both have completed college degrees, and Leslie earned a master's. She works in educational programs for inmates; Pat trains rescue dogs to serve the handicapped.

The house on Waverly Drive where Leno and Rosemary LaBianca died looks much the same, except for a changed street number. A pool has been added, and a carport. The Los Feliz neighborhood is quiet.

But the house on Cielo where Terry Melcher lived and Sharon Tate and four others died is gone, demolished in 1994 and replaced by an entirely new structure at the end of the narrow winding road up the high steep hill. The last resident of the original house was musician Trent Reznor, who in 1993 moved in and built studio facilities to record *The Downward Spiral* album with his band Nine Inch Nails. Reznor didn't know that the infamous Tate murders had occurred there until after he moved in. He said that this news excited and disturbed him at the same time. Reznor named his recording studio "Le Pig" in honor of the word Susan Atkins scrawled in blood on a door twenty-four years earlier, but for some time every sound in the night made him jumpy. He decided to move out in part because he kept returning home to find bouquets of dead roses and lit candles placed reverently at the front gate. He was never certain, Reznor said, whether they were left in tribute to Sharon Tate or Charlie Manson.

Since 1998, Charlie has been incarcerated at the California State Prison in Corcoran, about four hours' drive north from Los Angeles. The forbidding-looking facility is ringed with guard towers and surrounded by pastures. Charlie lives in the Protective Housing Unit, reserved for those considered in danger from the general inmate population. He is far from a model prisoner, losing phone privileges for possession of unauthorized cell phones and spending time in solitary for carrying concealed weapons. Other prisoners help Charlie with his mail—Roger Dale Smith was his main assistant until Smith's death from cancer in 2004. Charlie still receives dozens of letters a month and infrequently responds, usually to those who enclose money or endorse ATWA—Air Trees Water Animals, an organization founded by Charlie to pursue his objective of protecting the environment. Some other letters are turned over to friends outside the prison to respond to as they see fit. His supporters maintain an ATWA website that offers Manson-related booklets, art, and music to raise money for the cause. Through friends outside Corcoran who create electronic versions of his scribbled notes, Charlie frequently posts messages on another website. Many of these criticize the legal system. They are reproduced verbatim, grammatical errors and all.

When he's not deprived of privileges for various transgressions, Charlie's days in prison are simple. He enjoys doing artwork—the resulting sketches and small sculptures are sometimes sent to supporters and ATWA contributors—and he plays guitar and reads the Bible. Charlie also enjoys reading *National Geographic*. At mealtimes he skips meat and subsists on cheese, crackers, salads, potato chips, and Ramen noodles. Charlie still likes to listen to music, mostly vintage rock 'n' roll as well as Sinatra. His favorite actor is John Wayne, and he is also a fan of comedian George Lopez.

Sometimes his fellow inmates ask Charlie to tell them the truth about Tate-LaBianca: What really happened on the nights of August 9 and 10, 1969? Charlie's response is always the same. He says, "I don't know anything."

And he winks.

Thanks to *Helter Skelter*, Squeaky's failed attempt to assassinate Gerald Ford, and the "Crazy Charlie" act that he's performed to perfection, Charlie Manson remains a household name more than forty years after the seven murders. Simply surviving has a great deal to do with it. Almost everyone has forgotten the names of the teen shooters who claimed thirteen victims at Columbine in 1999 and the man who shot and killed thirty-two people on the Virginia Tech campus in 2007. But Eric Harris, Dylan Klebold, and Seung-Hui Cho died on the spot. (Charlie didn't personally kill any of the Tate-LaBianca victims, but his is the name associated with the crimes.) Had the California Supreme Court not overturned the death penalty in 1972 and had Charlie been executed a few years later, he might be mostly forgotten, too. But instead, there have been bizarre, well-publicized parole hearings, rants on websites, and just enough interviews to maintain the constant public awareness that he craves. After so many years, Charlie clearly doesn't care what we think of him, only that we do. As has always been the case with Charlie, he represents different things to different people. To many, he's evil personified. Some pity him for the terrible childhood he claimed to have endured—how could his life have turned out any way other than badly? A smaller but very vocal percentage thinks of Charlie as an anti-establishment hero who never did anything wrong besides stand up to oppression and speak the truth. Many modern-day teenagers imagine him as a cool outlaw; Manson T-shirts are common sights in high schools. But there is near-universal belief that Charlie is a product of the 1960s, that era in American history when the country, for better or worse, teetered on the brink of ruin. And that belief is wrong.

Charlie Manson *is* a product of the 1960s—and also of the 1930s, 1940s, and 1950s. The Tate-LaBianca murders (and Gary Hinman's and Shorty Shea's, though these have been largely forgotten) were the culmination of horrific coincidence. Invariably, Charlie found himself in the perfect locations and situations to exploit others to his own benefit. By the time the 1960s arrived, Charles Manson was already a lifelong social predator. Almost everyone who had anything to do with him was damaged in some way, and Charlie could not have cared less. Gregg Jakobson compares Charlie to a cancer cell because he thrived by eradicating everything around him that was healthy. There was nothing mystical or heroic about Charlie—he was an opportunistic sociopath. The unsettling 1960s didn't create Charlie, but they made it possible for him to bloom in full, malignant flower. In every sense, one theme runs through and defines his life: Charlie Manson was always the wrong man in the right place at the right time.

ACKNOWLEDGMENTS

My agent, Jim Donovan, remained encouraging during the two sometimes difficult years it took to research and write this book. I'm grateful to Andrea Ahles Koos, Anne E. Collier, and Sara Tirrito for their research assistance. After ten years and seven books, working with me is business as usual for Andrea; Anne and Sara waded in for the first time and acquitted themselves admirably.

I'm far from the best writer, but as I work on my books I have the best readers offering constructive criticism and, when I need it, a swift kick in the pants. Mike Blackman, James Ward Lee, and Carlton Stowers came through for me as they always do.

Bob Bender deserves his reputation as one of the best editors anywhere. Also at Simon & Schuster, I owe a great deal regarding this project to Jon Karp, Johanna Li, Kelly Welsh, Julia Prosser, and Maureen Cole. It is a pleasure to work with all of them.

This is Roger Labrie's book as much as it is mine. It has been my good fortune to work with Roger, and I hope that many more writers get the same opportunity.

Dr. Daniel Greenspan was instrumental in helping me meet with Leslie Van Houten.

Special thanks to Cash, who kept me company as I worked.

Everything I write is always for Nora, Adam, and Grant.

APPENDIX: KEY PEOPLE AFTERWARDS

Roman Polanski's career flourished in the wake of his wife's death. In 1974 the Polanski-directed *Chinatown* was nominated for several Academy Awards, winning for Best Screenplay. But in 1977 Polanski was arrested for sexual assault on a thirteen-year-old girl. He fled to Europe and has fought extradition to America ever since. His films continue to earn critical praise, and he won the Academy Award for directing 2002's *The Pianist*.

The Beach Boys gradually regained their popularity and thrived as a live act, culminating with a triumphant fiftieth-anniversary concert tour in 2012. But they did so without Dennis Wilson, who drowned while diving in Marina del Rey on December 28, 1983. In his last years, Dennis was plagued by alcohol and drug abuse. But before his death he released *Pacific Ocean Blue*, a magnificent album that confirmed his genius as a composer and performer. Several of the songs were written with Gregg Jakobson, who co-produced the album with him.

Terry Melcher never believed that Charlie's music was in any way special or deserving of recording. After the Tate-LaBianca trial, Melcher produced several more albums for the Byrds and also worked with the Beach Boys, producing some of their music and co-writing the band's hit "Kokomo." Melcher also helped resurrect his mother's career, serving as executive producer of TV's *The Doris Day Show*. He died of cancer in 2004.

Gregg Jakobson, the other original member of the Golden Penetrators, worked in the music and restaurant business in and around L.A. before relocating to Oregon, where he and his wife, Kathy, operate a bed-and-breakfast in the Corvallis Valley. In 2008 Jakobson helped engineer a "legacy edition" of Dennis Wilson's *Pacific Ocean Blue*, which included additional unreleased studio tracks as well as the complete *Bambu*, which Dennis had intended to release as a follow-up album.

Phil Kaufman now lives in Nashville and remains a vital part of the music business there, still working as a road manager for several performers.

After losing a second race for Los Angeles district attorney in 1976, **Vincent Bugliosi** entered private legal practice and continued to write books—seven were best-sellers, and two in addition to *Helter Skelter* topped the list.

Clem, now reassuming his given name of Steve Grogan, underwent religious conversion and led authorities to the spot on the old Spahn Ranch property where Shorty Shea was buried. Despite near-universal belief to the contrary, Shea had not been dismembered. Grogan used his time in prison productively, studying mechanics and behaving as a model inmate. In 1985 he was paroled; two and a half years later he was discharged from parole, the first convicted Family killer to be completely freed.

Linda Kasabian lives under a different name in the Northwest. She is still in contact with Vincent Bugliosi, who at her request does not share her contact information.

Bobby Beausoleil is incarcerated in Oregon as part of a state prisoner sharing program with California. He continues to write and record music, most notably a soundtrack to *Lucifer Rising*, Kenneth Anger's film that Beausoleil originally worked on back in the Haight.

In December 1985, **Sandy Good** was released on parole, which she successfully completed in 1989. She found a boyfriend who was equally devoted to Charlie. Together, they set up and for several years maintained Internet websites in his honor. Like **Ruth Ann Moorehouse** and **Mary Brunner,** Sandy eventually dropped out of sight.

In October 2012, a California state board recommended **Bruce Davis** for parole due to his "positive adjustment . . . and for successfully completing academica and vocational education and self-help programs." A previous parole board had also recommended his prison release, but then Governor Arnold Schwarzenegger overruled the recommendation. On March 1, 2013, California governor Jerry Brown followed suit, overruling the latest recommendation for a Davis parole.

NOTE ON SOURCES

Over a two-year period I sent more than forty letters requesting an interview to Charlie Manson at Corcoran State Prison. He replied directly once, in a letter mailed on May 17, 2012. In it he rambled about con men "talking on the come," and concluded, "now you got a letter and I don't have time to wast." He added in a postscript, "They dont Just let me interview as I want." He did not respond to my subsequent correspondence. Charlie, did, however, pass along some of my letters to a friend of his who corresponded with me for a time, usually by e-mail. The friend emphasized how Charlie is mistrustful of those claiming to write books about him. In recent years his ability to communicate with outsiders has also been limited by his loss of phone privileges—Charlie's preferred means of communication is by telephone. Had he been willing to see me, I doubt the interview would have been useful in any sense other than allowing me to describe Charlie's current physical appearance. In the few carefully selected interviews he has granted, he's relied on the ongoing "Crazy Charlie" act, ranting nonsensically. The same is true in his official messages issued through ATWA. In a pamphlet offered on the ATWA website for $10, Charlie states, "We have two worlds that have been conquested by the military of the revolution. The revolution belongs to George Washington, the Russians, the Chinese. But before that, there is Manson. I have 17 years before China. I can't explain that to where you can understand it."

Several former Family members and others associated with the Manson story declined interviews after learning that I wouldn't pay to talk to them. When I interviewed Gregg Jakobson, I paid to stay at his small bed-and-breakfast in Oregon for three nights after determining that staying there would cost less than staying in a hotel room in Portland or Eugene and commuting to talk to Gregg. He and his wife, Kathy, threw in two home-cooked dinners, which were delicious.

Charlie's sister, Nancy, and cousin Jo Ann agreed to talk to me only if I concealed their identities. For that reason, nowhere in this book do I disclose their last names, where they live, or any physical description of them. It took great courage for Nancy and Jo Ann to agree to interviews after spending much of their lives trying to avoid Manson-related notice.

NOTES

Prologue: Charlie at the Whisky

Descriptions of events are based on interviews with Gregg Jakobson, Lorraine Chamberlain, Phil Kaufman, Mary F. Corey, and Charles Perry. I found Domenic Priore's *Riot on Sunset Strip* to be an exceptional history of this famous street in the mid- to late 1960s.

Page

1   *three cars eased down Sunset Boulevard:* Gregg Jakobson interview.

1   *the Haight-Ashbury neighborhood in San Francisco still clung:* Charles Perry interview.

1   *As civil disorder swept the rest of America:* Barney Hoskyns, *Waiting for the Sun: A Rock 'n' Roll History of Los Angeles* (Backbeat Books, 2009), pp. 132–43; Domenic Priore, *Riot on Sunset Strip: Rock 'n' Roll's Last Stand in Hollywood* (Outline Press, 2007), p. 25; Mary F. Corey interview.

1   *were expected to mingle with the public:* Lorraine Chamberlain interview.

2   *Together they were part:* Gregg Jakobson interview.

2   *their philosophy was:* Ibid.

2   *the most famous club in town:* Priore, pp. 41–42.

3   *rock gods Mick Jagger and Keith Richards:* Phil Kaufman interview.

3   *Anyone in Los Angeles who had pretensions:* Ibid.; David Crosby and Carl Gottlieb, *Long Time Gone: The Autobiography of David Crosby* (Doubleday, 1988), p. 90.

3   *Melcher handed over the keys:* Gregg Jakobson interview.

4   *Manson assumed that he was always welcome:* Ibid.

4   *Wilson's house guests ran up an $800 tab:* Ibid.

5   *In recent weeks Wilson had also begun:* Steven Gaines, *Heroes & Villains: The True Story of the Beach Boys* (Da Capo, 1995), p. 212.

5   *The club wasn't particularly big:* Priore, pp. 41–42.
6   *they were startled by a commotion:* Gregg Jakobson interview.

Chapter One: Nancy and Kathleen

It is always worrisome when writers of nonfiction claim to know what long-deceased people were thinking. But in the cases of Nancy and Kathleen, for the portions of their lives described in this chapter, we know their thoughts as they revealed them to Manson's cousin Jo Ann and his sister, Nancy, both of whom I interviewed. Jo Ann's grandmother shared many confidences with her, including her frustrations with her youngest daughter and her reactions when Kathleen married William Manson and when Kathleen and Luther were sentenced to prison for the "Ketchup Bottle Holdup." Jo Ann also provided insights into her mother and stepfather's courtship and subsequent marriage (they frequently took her along on their dates). Kathleen told Nancy how she rebelled against her mother's Bible-inspired rules, and how she met and became intimate with Colonel Scott.

Others interviewed for this chapter include Lyle Adcock, Vincent Bugliosi, Jim Powers, George Wolfford, John P. Maranto, Virginia Brautigan, Robert Smith, Lon Dagley, and Jim Kettel. I offer special thanks to Virginia Brautigan for lending me Nancy Maddox's personal copy of *The Self-Interpreting Bible, Volume III,* which contains the underlined passages described here.

Charlie Manson's sister, Nancy, provided family snapshots of Nancy Maddox holding her infant grandson Charlie.

Court documents and copies of confession statements made by Luther Maddox, Nancy Maddox, and Julia Vickers made possible the detailed description of the August 1939 robbery that resulted in Manson's mother and uncle being sent to prison.

Page

9   *People didn't consider Nancy a fanatic:* Virginia Brautigan interview.
9   *Charlie Milles Maddox, also from Kentucky:* State of Kentucky Bureau of Vital Statistics; *Ashland Daily Independent,* October 27, 1931.
9   *they became comfortably middle-class:* Lyle Adcock interview.
10   *Ashland was a business port:* James Powers and Terry Baldridge, *Ashland* (Arcadia Publishing, 2008), pp. 7–8.
10   *Charlie and Nancy were able to buy a house:* Boyd County Recorder's Office.
10   *Nancy bowed her head and gave thanks daily:* Jo Ann interview.

10   *she moaned that she felt:* Ibid.

10   *Charlie left his widow a railroad pension:* John P. Maranto interview.

11   *Nancy often kept her granddaughter:* Jo Ann interview.

12   *In case the rest of the family didn't fully grasp:* Virginia Brautigan interview.

12   *Bill Thomas proved to be:* Jo Ann interview.

13   *Nancy was raised as a Protestant:* Lyle Adcock interview.

13   *the Nazarene Church, which had conservative rules:* Robert Smith and Lon Dagley interviews.

13   *"the Big Five":* Robert Smith interview.

13   *There was an empty space between the stove:* Nancy interview.

14   *She considered Nancy to be a hard person:* Ibid.

14   *The problem was that in Ashland:* George Wolfford interview.

14   *Upstanding citizens in Ashland:* Ibid.

15   *Scott's two sons soon gained local reputations:* Ibid.

15   *He let her think that he really was:* Nancy interview.

15   *When she told Colonel Scott:* Ibid.

16   *Somehow, she'd show him:* Jo Ann interview.

16   *She wanted a man like Charlie Maddox:* Nancy interview.

16   *Very little is known about William Manson:* Lyle Adcock interview.

16   *Nancy wasn't informed in advance about the wedding:* Jo Ann interview.

17   *Nancy and Glenna were concerned:* Ibid.

17   *Nancy, frantic and expecting the worst:* Virginia Brautigan interview.

18   *Kathleen went to court in Kentucky:* Vincent Bugliosi and Lyle Adcock interviews; Vincent Bugliosi and Curt Gentry, *Helter Skelter: The True Story of the Manson Murders* (W. W. Norton, 1994, 25th Anniversary Edition), p. 137. A Kentucky law passed in 1980 to provide confidentiality of juvenile records has sealed this file. But in 1970 Bugliosi obtained a copy of the file for use in the trial of Charles Manson.

19   *On the afternoon of August 1, 1939:* The description of the "Ketchup Bottle Holdup" comes from the State of West Virginia Department of Public Safety Report of Investigation A1633, which includes the report of the investigating officer and the post-arrest statements of Luther Maddox, Kathleen Maddox, and Julia Vickers.

20   *their haul totaled $27:* Subsequent newspaper articles put the amount at $30 and $35, but the initial police reports stated that $27 was taken from Martin's wallet; the wallet itself was valued at $1 by investigators.

21   *There was no real challenge:* If Kathleen and Luther had really pulled a series

of previous stickups in Chicago as their mother Nancy believed, they would surely have been better at it than they proved to be in Charleston. If not, they would have been nabbed by police on some if not all of these supposed earlier attempts. But there are no police records of Kathleen and Luther being arrested in Chicago. This is why I believe the bungled Charleston robbery was their first try at strongarm robbery.

22 *Nancy Maddox pulled her granddaughter, Jo Ann, aside and whispered:* Jo Ann interview.

Chapter Two: Moundsville and McMechen

Interviews for this chapter include Jo Ann, Nancy, Lyle Adcock, Virginia Brautigan, Richard Hawkey, Greg Park, Tom Stiles, Don Clutter, Becky Clutter, Jason Clark-Miller, and Fred Brautigan.

Page

23 *Soon after Kathleen was taken away:* In 1986 Grove Press published *Manson in His Own Words: The Shocking Confessions of "The Most Dangerous Man Alive"* by Nuel Emmons. Emmons and Manson knew each other by crossing paths twice as prison inmates long before the Tate-LaBianca murders in 1969. After Manson was convicted, Emmons contacted his old jail acquaintance and visited him on multiple occasions. The result was a curious book that Emmons said was written to bring Manson's own version of his life directly to the public without distortion by intermediaries. Nobody who knew Manson well thought the first-person voice sounded at all like him. Emmons claimed that he never took Charlie at his word, and that he traveled the country interviewing people who had known the now notorious Manson and fact-checked everything—"a long process," he noted in the book's Introduction.

Manson subsequently disavowed the book, saying it was something Emmons wanted to do and so he let him. Emmons died in November 2002, insisting to the end that everything he wrote was accurate. It wasn't. Even the most cursory research proves that many "facts" presented in *Manson in His Own Words* are demonstrably false. Perhaps Manson lied to Emmons and Emmons failed at fact-checking, or Emmons took Manson at his word and did not check facts. I think Emmons did his best to interpret Manson's semi-incoherent ramblings and produced a mishmash of mostly incorrect blather. I lean toward the third option.

For example, when Emmons relates Manson's first-person memories of

Charlie's early childhood, he writes that Charlie went to McMechen to live with his Uncle Bill and Aunt Joanne. Jo Ann was Manson's cousin. The first chapter also includes a touching passage where Charlie Maddox, Manson's grandfather, takes the six-year-old aside and explains to him that his mother "wouldn't be coming home for a long time" because she had been sentenced to a term in prison. In September 1939, when Kathleen and Luther were convicted of robbery, Charlie Maddox had been dead for almost eight years. Manson never met his grandfather.

When it appears that Emmons is reporting Manson's own words about a specific event in his life, I cite the passage to reflect Manson's self-serving spin on something. A few times, it appears that Charlie told the truth and Emmons wrote it that way.

23 *McMechen, with a population of around 4,000:* Interviews with Virginia and Fred Brautigan, Tom Stiles, Don and Becky Clutter, Richard Hawkey, and Greg Park.

25 *Little Charlie Manson was a disagreeable child:* Jo Ann and Nancy interviews.

25 *They tried to demonstrate some affection:* Jo Ann interview.

26 *the prison was designed to resemble:* My description of the prison—its physical appearance, its inhumane conditions for inmates, its reputation in the local community—is based on material from Jonathan D. Clemins's *West Virginia Penitentiary* (Arcadia Publishing, 2010) and two guided tours of the prison, as well as an interview with a manager of the facility in its current incarnation as a public museum. The local legends of the decapitated hanging victim and other mysterious deaths among inmates gained traction until West Virginia Penitentiary gained a national reputation for being haunted that endured even after the prison was shut down in 1995 for overcrowded conditions that an investigative panel ruled to be "cruel and unusual punishment." When modern-day television networks began broadcasting series about the paranormal, West Virginia Penitentiary and its reputed ghosts were featured on *The Scariest Places on Earth* (ABC), *Ghost Adventures* (Travel Channel), and *FEAR* (MTV).

28 *Whatever love she tried to communicate:* Tom Stiles and Jason Clark-Miller interviews.

28 *longtime McMechen residents still shudder:* Jo Ann, Virginia Brautigan, Richard Hawkey, Don and Becky Clutter, and Jason Clark-Miller interviews.

30 *he consistently attracted the notice of bullies:* Jo Ann interview.

31 *Another incident cemented:* Ibid.

31   *In the two and a half years that he lived with the Thomases:* Virginia Brautigan, Lyle Adcock, Nancy, and Jo Ann interviews.

32   *Charlie had only bad memories:* Clara Livsey, *The Manson Women: A "Family" Portrait* (Richard Marek, 1980), pp. 135–37.

Chapter Three: Kathleen and Charlie

One of the frustrations in chronicling Manson's early years is that juvenile court and reform school records are frequently sealed. During his prosecution of Manson in the Tate-LaBianca murder case, Vincent Bugliosi obtained access to Manson's juvenile files. He used them as evidence in court and mentioned them in his book about the case. I discussed them with him in a series of phone interviews. This is why many mentions of Manson's juvenile trials and reformatory assignments and transfers in this chapter are credited to *Helter Skelter.*

Chapter interviews include Vincent Bugliosi, Jo Ann, Nancy, Tom Stiles, Jason Clark-Miller, Sara Dolan, Lyle Adcock, Michele Deitch, Volker Janssen, and Gregg Jakobson.

Page

33   *Lots of paroled inmates:* Tom Stiles interview.

33   *Van Watson hired Kathleen:* *Charleston Gazette,* September 15, 1971.

33   *One of the first things Kathleen noticed:* Nancy interview.

34   *Charlie ended up stashed:* Jo Ann interview.

34   *Though Van Watson couldn't remember the fellow's name:* *Charleston Gazette,* September 15, 1971.

34   *Kathleen fell back into another bad habit:* Ibid.

35   *At one she met Lewis:* Nancy interview. Lewis is identified only by his first name to protect Nancy's identity.

35   *From the first days of their marriage:* Nancy interview.

36   *Kathleen's concern about her son was so great:* Ibid.

36   *he still scared Kathleen:* Ibid.

36   *she felt sometimes like she was going insane:* Ibid.

36   *She'd heard about foster care programs:* Ibid.

37   *The Gibault School for Boys:* Isaac McIntosh, *Gibault Home for Boys.* Federal Writers' Project, 1936. This facility changed names several times. When Manson attended it was the Gibault School for Boys.

37   *Charlie claimed he was regularly beaten:* Livsey, pp. 136–37.

38   *Gibault found Charlie's:* Bugliosi, p. 137.

38   *It hurt Kathleen to send him back:* Nancy interview.

38   *It was Jo Ann's idea:* Jo Ann interview.

38   *Instead Luther lived with his mother:* Ibid.

38   *When he died in 1950:* West Virginia State Department of Health death certificate.

39   *On Christmas Eve, everyone prepared:* Jo Ann interview.

39   *He once again fled:* Bugliosi, pp. 137–38.

40   *Unlike Gibault, boys at the facility in Plainfield:* William J. Siebold. *The Hill: A History of the Indiana Boys' School, 1901–1999* (self-published), pp. 3–5, 12, 59, 60–64, 146; Albert Deutsch, *Our Rejected Children* (Little, Brown 1950), pp. 46–50.

41   *"You know, getting raped":* Marlin Marynick. *Charles Manson Now* (Cogito Media Group, 2010), pp. 71–72.

41   *Reports from teachers indicate:* Bugliosi, p. 138.

42   *Charlie developed a lifelong defense mechanism:* Gregg Jakobson and Volker Janssen interviews.

42   *Kathleen was still trying to salvage:* Nancy interview; *Los Angeles Times*, January 26, 1971.

42   *Charlie joined six other boys:* *Kokomo Tribune*, October 20, 1949.

42   *when he was sixteen, Charlie tried again:* *Kokomo Tribune*, February 19, 1951, and March 10, 1951; Bugliosi, p. 138.

43   *his IQ score of 109:* Sara Dolan interview.

43   *His scores were satisfactory:* Bugliosi, p. 138.

44   *The most promising students:* Ibid.

44   *But this proved beyond him:* Bugliosi interview; Bugliosi, pp. 138–39.

46   *Modern experts in child psychology:* Volker Janssen, Michele Deitch, and Jason Clark-Miller interviews.

Chapter Four: McMechen Again

Along with research assistant Sara Tirrito, I spent several days in McMechen meeting with people who remembered Charlie Manson. After so many years, they are less reluctant to talk about him than they were immediately after he was arrested and tried for the Tate-LaBianca murders. McMechen still hasn't changed much; visiting there today feels like time traveling back to the 1950s.

Page

47   *Town residents were deliberately insular:* Richard Hawkey interview.

47   *Wheeling a few miles to the north was widely recognized:* George T. Sidiropolis, Bill Miller, Richard Hawkey, David Javersak, and John Catlett interviews.

47   *Charlie's immediate concern:* Virginia Brautigan, Jo Ann, and Nancy interviews.

48   *He was finally hired at Wheeling Downs:* Lyle Adcock and George T. Sidiropolis interviews.

48   *McMechen parents tried to provide their youngsters:* Fred Brautigan, Becky Clutter, and Don Clutter interviews.

48   *Newcomer Charlie, with no social skills to speak of:* Virginia Brautigan interview.

48   *He was allowed to live with Nancy only:* Virginia Brautigan interview. Nancy Maddox was close friends with Virginia's parents.

49   *many did not consider the small cinder block church:* Becky Clutter interview.

49   *though, in her own way, she still believed:* Nancy interview.

50   *Since he was out of Nancy's sight:* Virginia Brautigan interview. She attended the Nazarene teen Sunday School with Charlie.

50   *Charlie mistakenly tried to glorify it:* Virginia Brautigan interview.

50   *teens in McMechen had some familiarity with sin:* John Catlett and Fred Brautigan interviews.

50   *they were sometimes allowed to buy:* Richard Hawkey interview.

50   *They'd never heard the word "marijuana":* Richard Hawkey and David Javersak interviews.

51   *The Nazarene kids closed ranks:* Virginia Brautigan interview. During the sensational Tate-LaBianca murder trial in 1970, the national media descended on McMechen, frantically seeking lurid tales of Charlie Manson's time there. To prevent residents from being overwhelmed by reporters banging on their doors, county official George Sidiropolis arranged for individual McMechenites to grant interviews. After only a few days, the outsiders left—dismayed, Sidiropolis says, by the lack of juicy revelations. Many longtime residents claimed that they didn't even remember Charlie. Those who did described him as a minor-league thug who was not at all notable in town history. Sixteen years after Charlie bragged to his Nazarene Sunday School classmates about shooting up, the shunning was still in place.

51   *Jo Ann was astonished:* Jo Ann interview.

51   *The thing about the prostitutes that most interested Charlie:* Phil Kaufman interview.

52   *Clarence Willis was nicknamed Cowboy:* George T. Sidiropolis interview.

52   *"the baby came early":* Virginia Brautigan and David Javersak interviews.

53   *Nancy gave a reception:* Virginia Brautigan interview.

53   *Jo Ann and her husband stayed away:* Jo Ann interview.

53   *Ethel Miller, whom everybody in town loved:* Bill Miller interview.

53 *Charlie finally made a few friends:* John Catlett, Richard Hawkey, and Jason Clark-Miller interviews.

54 *Somehow Charlie got his hands on a guitar:* Jo Ann interview.

54 *particularly liked Frankie Laine:* Phil Kaufman interview.

54 *Charlie's attempt to fit in:* Virginia Brautigan interview.

54 *the Wheeling mob wouldn't wait:* George T. Sidiropolis interview.

55 *she thought it was in some way poignant:* Jo Ann interview. Most Manson legends have Charlie going to California first, his mother following after Charlie went to prison for violating the Dyer Act. In fact, Kathleen went west first.

55 *He called Jo Ann back in Ohio:* Jo Ann interview.

55 *The judge ordered psychiatric testing:* Bugliosi, pp. 140–41; Ed Sanders, *The Family* (Da Capo, 2002), pp. 3–4.

Chapter Five: Prison

The fact that the Dale Carnegie Institute and the Church of Scientology are frequently mentioned in this chapter should not imply that their teachings and printed materials are in any way responsible for criminal behavior by Charlie Manson or anyone else. Charlie used what he learned from these sources in ways that the Dale Carnegie Institute and the Church of Scientology never intended.

Lyle Adcock has done groundbreaking research on the subject of Rosalie Willis's life after her divorce from Charlie, and I thank Lyle for sharing the information with me for this book.

Page

57 *It was one of a handful of federal prisons:* Phil Kaufman interview.

57 *he was still fascinated by pimps:* Sanders, p. 4; Stephen Kay interview.

58 *His initial months at Terminal Island were brightened:* Bugliosi, p. 141.

58 *Prison officials even restricted him:* Ibid.

58 *Kathleen had to break the news to Charlie:* Sanders, p. 4.

58 *Rosalie's adult life got off to a rough start:* Lyle Adcock interview.

59 *On April 10 he was caught:* Bugliosi, p. 141.

59 *a nationwide penal system overhaul:* Volker Janssen and Jason Clark-Miller interviews.

60 *It was as though Dale Carnegie not only read Charlie's mind:* Phil Kaufman interview.

61 *Charlie spent the rest of his time:* Sanders, p. 4.

62 *Kathleen had some doubts:* Nancy interview.

62   *In rapid order Charlie worked:* Sanders, p. 5.

62   *Charlie's career as a pimp:* Vincent Bugliosi interview; Bugliosi, p. 142; Sanders, p. 5.

63   *Charlie was arrested for attempting to cash:* Bugliosi, pp. 142–43.

64   *In December he tried to expand his territory:* Sanders, p. 6.

65   *The Washington penitentiary sprawled:* "Doors Closing at McNeil Island Prison After 135 Years," *Seattle Times*, February 28, 2011.

66   *Hubbard taught how to change yourself:* L. Ron Hubbard, *What Is Scientology? Based on the Works of L. Ron Hubbard* (Bridge Publications, 1998), p. 673.

67   *he still had his mother:* Nancy interview. The story about Charlie throwing a fit when Kathleen adopted a baby girl instead of buying him a new guitar is told in Nuel Emmons's *Manson in His Own Words*, which supports my impression that Emmons wrote down exactly what Charlie told him, and that every once in a while Charlie told the truth.

69   *Karpis was an accomplished steel guitar player:* Sanders, p. 9.

69   *He didn't read books, but he listened:* Charlie said that he read *Stranger in a Strange Land* while in prison at McNeil. But after his conviction for the Tate and LaBianca murders, he told fellow inmate Roger Dale Smith that he threw out all his prison mail because he couldn't read it. I consulted several reading skills experts, and they generally agreed that if Charlie could read a printed book, he could read even scribbled handwritten letters by "decoding"— matching sounds to individual letters. The question then becomes: If Charlie was a very slow, limited reader, would he devote the months it would take to work his way through a novel? Based on what I learned in researching this book, I don't think so. Charlie always tried to get others to do the work for him.

70   *There was nothing special about the songs that resulted:* Phil Kaufman interview.

71   *Now when Kathleen visited:* Nancy interview.

72   *Senior McNeil staff noted:* Bugliosi, pp. 145–46.

73   *Lewis had a parting shot for Kathleen:* Nancy interview.

73   *Its barred doors had hardly slammed shut:* Phil Kaufman interview; Kaufman, p. 51.

74   *Charlie got his last prison report:* Bugliosi, p. 146.

74   *Phil Kaufman thought Charlie was a decent singer:* Phil Kaufman interview; Jess Bravin, *Squeaky: The Life and Times of Lynette Alice Fromme* (Buzz Books/ St. Martin's, 1997), p. 52.

75   *Charlie was being both personally insightful and honest:* Jason Clark-Miller interview.

75   *He called one in Berkeley:* There's some question about why Charlie went to Berkeley immediately upon release from Terminal Island. In the Emmons book he's quoted as saying he knew an ex-inmate there, and that sounds likely.

Chapter Six: Berkeley and the Haight

Tom Hayden and Mark Rudd contributed valuable interviews to this chapter, Hayden in person at his Culver City, California, office and Rudd through e-mail. I wanted to interview Mary Brunner, but among all the former Manson Family members, she (along with Ruth Ann Moorehouse) has successfully hid in the general population. Leslie Van Houten offered insights into the Manson-Brunner relationship.

George Laughead, an expert on the Beats, generously arranged interviews for me with his old friends Glenn Todd and Lorraine Chamberlain.

To understand San Francisco and Haight-Ashbury in the 1960s I read two exceptional books, *The Haight-Ashbury: A History* by Charles Perry and *Season of the Witch: Enchantment, Terror, and Deliverance in the City of Love* by David Talbot. Perry, whose credentials also include a long stint as a writer for *Rolling Stone* magazine back in the days when it was *the* publication of the counterculture, also granted me an extensive in-person interview.

Beginning in this chapter, certain key members of the Manson Family—Mary Brunner, Lynne "Squeaky" Fromme, Pat Krenwinkel, and a few others—are identified in the main text by first names. Last names are used for everyone else.

Page

78   *In 1960 a handful of student activists formed Students for a Democratic Society:* Tom Hayden interview.

78   *SDS-orchestrated antiwar rallies:* Mark Rudd interview.

78   *Free Speech Movement:* Though I do not cite specific passages, David Burner's brilliant *Making Peace with the 60s* (Princeton University Press, 1996) informs everything included here about the Berkeley Free Speech movement and campus unrest in general. If you're at all interested in this event, or in the revolutionary student spirit of the 1960s, I urge you to read his book.

78   *Actor Ronald Reagan made Berkeley Free Speech:* Stephen E. Ambrose, *Nixon: The Triumph of a Politician, 1962–1972* (Simon & Schuster, 1989), pp. 119–20.

80   *The Panthers set up free health clinics:* Mary F. Corey interview.

81   *He'd been given $35:* Sanders, p. 12.

81   *people who might have been marginal characters:* Tom Hayden interview.

81   *Far from having to hide it:* Gregg Jakobson interview.

82   *Twenty-three-year-old Mary Brunner:* Bugliosi, p. 163; Livsey, p. 107.

83   *for years afterward she continued believing:* Leslie Van Houten interview.

83   *Mary was extremely knowledgeable:* Ed George with Dary Matera, *Taming the Beast: Charles Manson's Life Behind Bars* (St. Martin's, 1998), p. 37.

84   *the Haight was just as famous:* Charles Perry interview.

84   *it was ingrained in Charlie:* Michele Deitch interview.

84   *The Beats adopted the city's North Beach:* Glenn Todd interview.

85   *its declining two- and three-story Victorian houses:* Charles Perry interview.

85   *many of these featured all sorts of inexpensive, ruffly garb:* Ibid.

86   *One of these was Ken Kesey:* Charles Perry, *The Haight-Ashbury: A History* (Wenner Books, 2005), pp. 13–15.

86   *Drugs were hard to come by:* Charles Perry interview.

86   *By the time Augustus Owsley Stanley III appeared on the scene:* Charles Perry, "Owsley and Me," *Rolling Stone,* November 25, 1982.

88   *There was usually enough not only to share:* Perry, *The Haight-Asbury,* p. 246; Charles Perry interview.

88   *These goofy little dupes were something less:* Perry, *The Haight-Ashbury,* p. 5.

88   *A thriving new music scene exploded:* David Talbot, *Season of the Witch: Enchantment, Terror, and Deliverance in the City of Love* (Free Press, 2012), p. 93.

88   *but if they weren't different:* David E. Smith interview.

89   *The Diggers, who originally came to the Haight:* Talbot, pp. 36–40; Perry, *The Haight-Ashbury,* p. 79, pp. 249–51.

89   *The Haight Diggers harvested their crops:* Perry, *The Haight-Ashbury,* pp. 94–95; Talbot, p. 40.

89   *Musical entertainment was provided by the Chamber Orkustra:* Tommy Udo, *Charles Manson: Music, Mayhem, Murder* (Sanctuary Publishing, 2002), pp. 91–92; Lorraine Chamberlain interview; Perry, *The Haight-Ashbury,* p. 112.

90   *Flyers for the 1–5 P.M. event:* Ellis Amburn, *Pearl: The Obsessions and Passions of Janis Joplin* (Warner, 1992), p. 112.

90   *January 14 dawned clear and bright:* Glenn Todd, Lorraine Chamberlain, and Charles Perry interviews; Perry, *The Haight-Ashbury,* pp. 120–23; Talbot, pp. 22–23; Joel Selvin, *Summer of Love: The Inside Story of LSD, Rock & Roll, Free Love and High Times in the Wild West* (Cooper Square, 1999), pp. 106–7.

91   *subsequent broadcasts and articles and photographs:* Glenn Todd, David A. Smith, and Charles Perry interviews; Perry, *The Haight-Ashbury,* pp. 126, 261.

91 *Now there were more than three hundred a day:* Perry, *The Haight-Ashbury*, p. 204.

91 *It didn't take long for neighborhood leaders:* Talbot, pp. 31–35.

91 *A neighborhood research team did its best:* Perry, *The Haight-Ashbury*, p. 282.

92 *Paul McCartney popped into the neighborhood:* Peter Brown and Steven Gaines, *The Love You Make: An Insider's Story of the Beatles* (McGraw-Hill, 1983), pp. 240–41.

92 *But these new pushers offered hard drugs:* Charles Perry, David E. Smith, and Glenn Todd interviews; Perry, *The Haight-Ashbury*, p. 219; Joan Didion, *Slouching Towards Bethlehem: Essays* (Farrar, Straus & Giroux, 1968), p. 108.

93 *An April 16 street leaflet described:* Perry, *The Haight-Ashbury*, p. 174.

93 *One estimate had 75,000 more descending:* Ibid., p. 229. In March 1967, when the influx began to strain the Haight at its seams, there were an estimated seven thousand hippies living there, according to Perry.

Chapter Seven: Charlie in the Summer of Love

Dr. David E. Smith was a generous guide to Haight history and his personal experiences with Charles Manson. Patricia Krenwinkel had valuable insights into the early days of what would become known as the Family.

Page

94 *The Diggers fascinated Charlie:* Sanders, p. 14.

95 *Virtually everywhere Charlie looked in the Haight:* David E. Smith and Glenn Todd interviews.

95 *Charlie drifted from one street guru to the next:* Gregg Jakobson, Mary F. Corey, and David A. Smith interviews. Gregg Jakobson had many conversations with Manson about how Charlie developed his personal philosophies.

96 *Charlie began to believe that he had a lot in common with Jesus:* It wasn't unique for LSD users to come down from trips believing that they were reincarnations of Christ. John Lennon famously did, telling his fellow Beatles and their business advisors that he was Jesus. They congratulated him, got on with life, and a few days later Lennon forgot all about it. Charlie has periodically proclaimed himself to be Jesus or some form of divine being right up to the present day.

97 *On one of the benches a small redheaded girl sat and sobbed:* Bravin, pp. 46–48; Livsey, pp. 194–97.

98 *On one of Charlie's first hitchhiking trips:* Sanders, pp. 14–15; Emmons, pp. 99–101. In many books, Dean's last name is written as "Morehouse," but Social Security records list him as "Moorehouse."

98 *She was a cuddly tomboy:* Leslie Van Houten and Patricia Krenwinkel interviews. There is considerable discrepancy about the age of Ruth Ann Moorehouse. Some believe she was as young as fourteen when she was first seduced by Charlie. But the California Marriage Index estimates her birth date as "abt. 1952," which means she was at least fifteen and possibly sixteen when she first met Manson.

99 *Charlie was in his Jesus mode:* Bugliosi, p. 235.

100 *All over America it was a traumatic summer:* Ambrose, *Nixon,* p. 103; Theodore White, *The Making of the President 1968,* p. 253; Patterson, *Grand Expectations,* p. 663.

100 *An even greater danger to its overflowing community:* David E. Smith interview.

101 *More than 250 hippies lined up:* David E. Smith interview; Talbot, pp. 55–56.

102 *Green introduced Charlie to nineteen-year-old Pat Krenwinkel:* Patricia Krenwinkel interview.

103 *She'd abandoned him when he was young:* Ibid.

103 *She wasn't pleased to see him:* Nancy interview.

103 *They thought the women in Charlie's group:* Charles Perry interview.

104 *the weird group had a nickname for itself:* Ibid.

104 *Charlie always seemed to have knives:* Patricia Krenwinkel interview.

104 *One prominent dealer, well known for keeping a briefcase:* Charles Perry interview.

104 *"Haight Street smelled like piss":* Jan Reid, *Texas Tornado: The Times and Music of Doug Sahm* (University of Texas Press, 2010), p. 73.

105 *In September filmmaker Kenneth Anger rented a Haight theater:* Perry, *The Haight-Ashbury,* p. 231; Sanders, p. 25.

105 *None of the Haight turmoil was reflected:* Livsey, p. 201.

105 *The kids were shunted aside:* David E. Smith, M.D., and Alan J. Rose, "The Group Marriage Commune: A Case Study," *The Journal of Psychedelic Drugs,* September 1970.

106 *none of the hard stuff:* Phil Kaufman interview.

106 *Charlie expected rapt devotion:* Patricia Krenwinkel interview.

106 *struggling to remember spur-of-the-moment lyrics:* Leslie Van Houten interview.

106 *The best way to get them, Charlie knew:* Susan Atkins, with Bob Slosser, *Child of Satan, Child of God* (Bantam, 1978), p. 84.

107 *Of all the followers who came to Charlie:* Susan Atkins compiled or contributed to three books about her childhood and experiences with Charlie Manson: *The Killing of Sharon Tate* by Lawrence Schiller; her own *Child of Satan, Child of God,* co-authored with Bob Slosser; and "The Myth of Helter Skelter," an

unpublished memoir written with her husband, James Whitehouse, which can be viewed at www.susanatkins.org. In 2011 I met briefly with Whitehouse, who said he would consider talking to me about his late wife, and in a subsequent message he agreed to answer questions submitted to him by e-mail. After many months he cited a factual error in one of the questions and refused to communicate further. I'm particularly sorry because, according to Leslie Van Houten, Whitehouse continues to provide legal services to women at the California Institution for Women.

107   *As soon as she turned eighteen:* Atkins, pp. 49–52; Sanders, p. 19; Livsey, pp. 35, 178–86; Bravin, p. 70.

108   *Susan visited some friends at their Haight apartment:* Atkins, pp. 1–9; Lawrence Schiller, *The Killing of Sharon Tate* (Signet, 1970), pp. 81–84; Atkins unpublished memoir.

108   *Charlie took his women up to Sacramento:* Patricia Krenwinkel interview.

109   *other women in the group would get pregnant:* Smith and Rose, "The Group Marriage Commune," *The Journal of Psychedelic Drugs.*

109   *That made them regular patrons of the Free Clinic:* David E. Smith interview.

110   *In the early fall, Charlie took the bus out:* In describing his meeting and subsequent confrontation with Dean Moorehouse, Charlie always claimed that Ruth Ann was present at her father's house and begged to come with him, but her father refused. This cannot be the case. According to California state records, Ruth Ann married Edward L. Heuvelhorst on May 20, 1968, legally emancipating her from her parents. If Ruth Ann had been at her father's that day and wanted to leave with Manson and the rest of his followers, she could have. But every reliable account has Ruth Ann joining the group after it moved from San Francisco to Los Angeles.

110   *but he was mollified a few days later:* Sanders, p. 17.

110   *The girls considered him to be a pompous lightweight:* Leslie Van Houten and Patricia Krenwinkel interviews.

111   *This crazy man was about to murder him:* Manson tells this story in Emmons, *Manson in His Own Words*, pp. 121–22, and Gregg Jakobson later heard it described by several witnesses. In some versions, Dean Moorehouse was accompanied by a friend who put the shotgun to Charlie's head.

112   *L.A. reps who came to check out San Francisco talent:* Charles Perry, Lorraine Chamberlain, and Gregg Jakobson interviews.

112   *Everyone knew that the fabled Beach Boys:* Kent Hartman, *The Wrecking Crew: The Inside Story of Rock and Roll's Best-Kept Secret* (Thomas Dunne, 2012), pp. 153–55.

112 *four of the five Byrds didn't perform at all:* This is true: Gregg Jakobson inter-
     view; Hartman, pp. 97–101.

112 *"No matter how":* Priore, p. 22.

Chapter Eight: L.A.

Interviews with Mary F. Corey, Gregg Jakobson, Leslie Van Houten, Tom Hayden,
A. J. Langguth, and, especially, Joe Domanick, David Dotson, and Gerald L.
Chaleff helped me better understand the unique atmosphere in Los Angeles dur-
ing and after the Watts riot of 1965. For anyone remotely interested in that subject,
Domanick's Edgar Award–winning *To Protect and to Serve: The LAPD's Century of
War in the City of Dreams,* is essential and gripping reading.

Chronology is inevitably questionable in this part of the Manson saga. Charlie
and his followers (soon to be known as the Family) were nomadic even when they
were in L.A. In between city residences, they toured in the school bus. Nobody was
keeping track of departure and arrival dates, or how many days were spent on the
road. It may be, for instance, that Dianne Lake joined just before they drove into the
Mojave Desert rather than after (and her name may be either "Dianne" or "Diane"),
or that Sandy Good became a full-fledged member prior to Phil Kaufman leaving
(Phil doesn't think so but isn't certain). So some of the sequences of events described
here are best guesses, but the events themselves are factually presented based on
interviews and descriptions in previous books, documents, and articles, all noted.

Page

113 *Los Angeles became a place:* Mary F. Corey, Joe Domanick, David Dotson, and
     Tom Hayden interviews.

113 *As many as one thousand flooded in each week:* Joe Domanick interview.

114 *A pragmatic approach to controlling vice was necessary:* David Dotson and Joe
     Domanick interviews.

114 *lectures assured them that Martin Luther King Jr.:* David Dotson interview.

115 *One evening in the early 1960s:* Gregg Jakobson interview.

116 *These neatly separated communities:* Gerald L. Chaleff interview.

116 *Gangs fought each other:* Mary F. Corey interview.

117 *Watts adults were no better off:* Tom Hayden, *The Long Sixties: From 1960 to
     Barack Obama* (Paradigm Publishers, 2009), p. 141; Tom Hayden, Mary F.
     Corey, and Joe Domanick interviews.

117 *California Highway Patrol officer Lee Minikus didn't expect trouble:* Joe Domanick,
     To Protect and to Serve: The LAPD's Century of War in the City of Dreams (Pocket

Books, 1994), pp. 179–85; Hayden, pp. 141–42; Theodore White, *The Making of the President 1968*, p. 31; Mary F. Corey, Tom Hayden, Lorraine Chamberlain, and Joe Domanick interviews.

118 *in December it reported in stark, prescient terms:* Domanick, *To Protect and to Serve*, p. 191.

118 *For Chief Parker, the 1965 Watts riot offered a welcome chance:* Ibid., pp. 185, 192–93.

118 *Now blacks in every part of Los Angeles:* Mary F. Corey interview.

118 *Whites venturing into Watts:* Carlton Stowers interview.

120 *Hordes of wannabe musicians made their way to L.A.:* Gregg Jakobson and Lorraine Chamberlain interviews; Hoskyns, *Waiting for the Sun*, pp. 83–88; Michelle Phillips, *California Dreamin': The True Story of the Mamas and the Papas* (Warner, 1986), pp. 78–79.

120 *Melcher quickly determined:* Hartman, pp. 96–103.

121 *The bottom line, the only factor that ultimately mattered:* Gregg Jakobson interview.

121 *the Mamas and the Papas husband-wife team:* Hoskyns, *Waiting for the Sun*, pp. 96–97.

122 *the LAPD and Los Angeles County Sheriff's office announced joint plans:* Priore, pp. 25, 244–45, 248–54.

122 *Frank Zappa, frustrated by how widely his fellow musicians:* Lorraine Chamberlain interview.

123 *CBS aired a documentary:* Priore, p. 197.

123 *Joan Didion, reflecting later:* Joan Didion, *The White Album: Essays* (Farrar, Straus & Giroux, 1979), pp. 41–42.

123 *So, too, were the Santa Ana winds:* Ryan Kittell and David Sweet interviews; *Los Angeles Times*, February 20, 1988.

123 *His followers had no idea:* Leslie Van Houten interview.

124 *what Stromberg remembered most:* David Felton and David Dalton, "Year of the Fork, Night of the Hunter," *Rolling Stone*, June 25, 1970. Stromberg is quoted at length about his experience with Charlie in this excellent, detailed article.

125 *He and Stromberg and the four girls went out to lunch:* Patricia Krenwinkel remembers that they stayed around Universal "for quite a few days, we were there a lot."

125 *Charlie felt that he'd learned a valuable lesson:* Gregg Jakobson interview.

126 *they stayed at a quirky house:* Marynick, p. 334; Emmons, pp. 122–28; Sanders, pp. 23–24.

126 *Beausoleil was all about ego:* Leslie Van Houten interview.

127 *Bobby Beausoleil's most lasting favor to Charlie:* John Gilmore and Ron Kenner, *Manson: The Unholy Trail of Charlie and the Family* (Amok Books, 2000), p. 67; Udo, p. 98; Ann Bardich, "Jailhouse Interview: Bobby Beausoleil and the Manson Murders," *Oui*, November 1981.

128 *In Texas, Charlie's teeth started hurting:* Atkins, p. 86.

128 *he was intrigued by Dianne Lake:* Sanders, pp. 26–27; Perry, *The Haight-Ashbury,* p. 280.

129 *He immediately began holding up Dianne:* Leslie Van Houten interview.

129 *It was not unusual for Frank Zappa to get up in the morning:* Lorraine Chamberlain interview.

129 *He tried to catch the attention:* Hoskyns, *Waiting for the Sun,* p. 80.

129 *Producer David Briggs got so fed up with Charlie:* Jimmy McDonough, *Shakey: Neil Young's Biography* (Random House, 2002), p. 260.

130 *Sometimes Charlie administered full-scale beatings:* Patricia Krenwinkel and Leslie Van Houten interviews.

130 *the Beach Boys left for Paris:* Brian Wilson, *Wouldn't It Be Nice: My Own Story* (HarperCollins, 1991), pp. 174–76.

131 *Early 1968 was savagely unsettling:* Patterson, *Grand Expectations,* p. 635; Richard Reeves, *President Nixon: Alone in the White House* (Simon & Schuster, 2001), p. 115.

132 *Charlie in full recruiting mode:* Patricia Krenwinkel interview.

132 *Charlie simply enjoyed the company of men:* Gregg Jakobson and Phil Kaufman interviews.

133 *The women were exhaustively quizzed:* Leslie Van Houten interview.

133 *Then Charlie mastered the women sexually:* David E. Smith interview; Smith and Rose, "The Group Marriage Commune," *The Journal of Psychedelic Drugs.*

134 *Ruth Ann cheerfully did what she was told:* Leslie Van Houten interview.

134 *Women who didn't make it through:* Ibid.

134 *Charlie's prime money catch:* Phil Kaufman interview.

135 *Ruth Ann became Ouisch:* Gregg Jakobson interview.

136 *Lynne compared it to diving inside a giant salad:* Bravin, p. 72.

136 *Sometimes one or two of the women:* Leslie Van Houten interview.

136 *In February, the Beatles embarked:* Bob Spitz, *The Beatles: The Biography* (Little, Brown, 2005), pp. 750–57.

137 *Phil Kaufman was released from Terminal Island:* Phil Kaufman interview. I especially value Phil's insights because he was a clear-eyed observer of Charlie rather than an awestruck follower.

140 *It was as though Charlie considered the Beatles:* Leslie Van Houten interview.

140   *Charlie did allow his followers to tune in:* Patricia Krenwinkel interview.

142   *If Charlie discussed current events:* Ibid.

142   *he found a young woman:* Livsey, pp. 197–200; Emmons, pp. 138–39; Bravin, p. 78; George Bishop, *Witness to Evil: The Uncensored Story of Charles Manson and His Murderous Family* (Dell, 1972), p. 334.

143   *Charlie ordered Sandy to strip:* Leslie Van Houten interview. Leslie hadn't yet joined Charlie during this time in Topanga, but Charlie continued having Sandy strip and show her scars after the group moved on to Spahn Ranch.

143   *Mary Brunner gave birth to a son:* Patricia Krenwinkel interview.

144   *the children always appeared clean:* Gregg Jakobson interview.

144   *Within the group, there was some discrepancy:* Patricia Krenwinkel interview.

145   *The Beach Boys embarked that spring:* Timothy White, *The Nearest Faraway Place: Brian Wilson, the Beach Boys, and the Southern California Experience* (Henry Holt, 1994), pp. 281–82; Peter Ames Carlin, *Catch a Wave: The Rise, Fall and Redemption of the Beach Boys' Brian Wilson* (Rodale, 2006), p. 136; Wilson, p. 177.

145   *Bobby Beausoleil . . . dropped by soon after:* Sanders, p. 33.

146   *He used some of his girls as scouts:* Gregg Jakobson interview.

147   *for some milk and cookies:* Patricia Krenwinkel interview.

Chapter Nine: Charlie and Dennis

Gregg Jakobson is an invaluable resource concerning the complicated relationship that sprang up between Charlie Manson and Dennis Wilson. Throughout this chapter, whenever someone is described as thinking or feeling something, that is because the individual talked to Jakobson (or, in a few cases, to Leslie Van Houten or Patricia Krenwinkel) about it.

Lorraine Chamberlain was very helpful in describing the friendships between many rock stars living in and around Los Angeles at the time.

As always with Manson, it's difficult to determine dates when specific events occurred. In this chapter these uncertainties include the summer 1968 recording sessions at the small studio in Van Nuys and at Brian Wilson's home studio. The sequence may have been Brian's first, then Van Nuys, or vice versa. Some sources suggest that the Brian session may have taken place as late as November, but by then the Beach Boys had already recorded their drastically revised version of Charlie's "Cease to Exist."

For those interested in the history of the Beach Boys, I highly recommend Steven Gaines's *Heroes & Villains*. The best book I found about the life of Dennis Wilson was Jon Stebbins's *Dennis Wilson: The Real Beach Boy*. It is well worth tracking down.

Page

148   *Dennis knew no limits in his fondness:* Gregg Jakobson interview.

149   *his longtime friends were certain that at some level:* Ibid.

150   *Years later, Pat recalled:* Patricia Krenwinkel interview. Some published versions of the moment have Dennis picking up Pat and Yeller for the second time, but Pat remembers they had never met Dennis before this impromptu milk-and-cookies invitation.

150   *It was well after midnight:* Gaines, pp. 201–2; Bugliosi, pp. 250–51.

151   *Nancy Pitman especially:* Patricia Krenwinkel interview.

151   *Wilson spent a lot of time talking with Charlie:* Gregg Jakobson interview.

152   *the other women teased her about it:* Leslie Van Houten interview.

153   *Nobody at Brother Records was impressed:* Gaines, p. 207; Sanders, p. 60; Jon Stebbins, *Dennis Wilson: The Real Beach Boy* (ECW Press, 2000), p. 130. Through a representative, surviving Beach Boys Mike Love and Al Jardine declined to be interviewed for this book. Brian Wilson recorded his impressions of Charlie Manson in his memoir, *Wouldn't It Be Nice.*

154   *Wilson would get some of the Family girls to pile in:* Patricia Krenwinkel interview.

154   *When Dennis heard the news:* Gregg Jakobson interview.

155   *Rocker Neil Young came by Dennis's one day:* McDonough, pp. 287–88.

155   *a relatively high-level position that many thought he reached:* Hartman, p. 98.

156   *But unlike Dennis Wilson:* Gregg Jakobson interview.

157   *he thought he'd move the girl into the house at Cielo:* Ibid. Through a representative Candice Bergen said that she was unwilling to be interviewed.

157   *Jakobson called them "the Family":* Leslie Van Houten and Gregg Jakobson interviews.

158   *guests entered through sliding glass doors:* Mary F. Corey interview.

159   *the lyrics had to remain as Charlie had written them:* Gaines, p. 203.

159   *Sometimes he'd bluntly tell him:* Gregg Jakobson interview.

160   *Jakobson booked a quickie recording session:* The date may have been August 9, 1968, one year to the day before the Tate murders.

160   *The results were listenable:* The tapes from this session eventually became the *LIE* album produced by Phil Kaufman at Charlie's request after Charlie's arrest for the Tate-LaBianca murders. The music has since been bootlegged and reproduced on several CDs, some of which are now available. Phil Kaufman generously loaned me one of the few remaining original *LIE* albums on vinyl, and my analysis is based on that.

160 *Girls gushed about his blue eyes:* Gerry Griffin interview. Gerry knew Charles Watson in Farmersville. She loaned me her 1963 and 1964 high school yearbooks, and Tex is quite prominent in them with pictures on dozens of pages. Even his note to her is wholesome: "Dear Gerry: Here's wishing you all the luck in the world. You are a very charming and sweet girl. I know you will go far in life."

162 *Soon some of the Family women began complaining:* Gregg Jakobson interview.

162 *Gurus or any other spiritual leaders are expected:* David E. Smith interview.

163 *they needed a permanent home:* Atkins, pp. 93–94; Sanders, pp. 39–40, 41.

164 *So he called Bobby Beausoleil:* Leslie Van Houten interview.

167 *there may never have been twelve months in national history:* Tom Hayden interview.

167 *There was something in Charlie:* Hoskyns, *Waiting for the Sun*, p. 181.

167 *Charlie also expected to be accepted:* Gregg Jakobson interview.

168 *a teenager nicknamed Croxey:* Gaines, pp. 204–6.

168 *it eased his conscience:* Gregg Jakobson interview.

169 *Despar was used to musicians:* Wilson, pp. 181–83; Gaines, pp. 209–12.

170 *When Wilson returned home:* Gregg Jakobson interview.

170 *Wilson rented a house:* Bugliosi, p. 251; Gaines, pp. 212–13; Gregg Jakobson interview.

Chapter Ten: The Ranches

The Spahn property is now owned by a church organization that refused me permission to pass a gated area and look around. It's an eerie place, even glimpsed from the outside. The movie set is long gone, burned in a fire, but lots of the areas visible from the road are familiar because of well-circulated photos of the Family posing there. The set may be familiar to people who faithfully watched *The Lone Ranger* and *The Cisco Kid* on TV in the 1950s.

Page

172 *Sandy Good said that she had a friend:* Emmons, pp. 140–45. Susan Atkins also claimed credit for suggesting Spahn Ranch to Charlie, but Susan erroneously claimed credit for lots of things.

172 *For $1.50 apiece:* Steve Oney, "Manson: An Oral History," *Los Angeles Magazine,* July 1, 2009.

173 *Charlie installed Lynne:* Bravin, pp. 84–85; Sanders, p. 67.

173 *Sex with George was part of her responsibilities:* Patricia Krenwinkel interview; Bugliosi, pp. 100–101.

173   *Charlie initially withheld full Family membership:* Tex Watson as told to Chaplain Ray, *Will You Die for Me?: The Man Who Killed for Charles Manson Tells His Own Story* (Fleming H. Revell, 1978), pp. 57, 60–61.

174   *the kind of isolation necessary:* Leslie Van Houten interview.

174   *They were led by Juan Flynn:* Gregg Jakobson, Vincent Bugliosi, and Leslie Van Houten interviews; Sanders, p. 69.

174   *One day when Flynn wanted everyone up and working:* Gregg Jakobson interview.

175   *Charlie placed the newcomer under the supervision:* Patricia Krenwinkel and Leslie Van Houten interviews.

175   *No female in the Family was ever to carry money:* Patricia Krenwinkel interview.

176   *it was obvious she'd be an effective recruiter:* Gregg Jakobson interview.

176   *He assigned her to follow him around:* Leslie Van Houten interview.

176   *Alan Rose had been intrigued:* David E. Smith interview. According to Dr. Smith, Rose borrowed a significant amount of money from him and gave it to Charlie.

177   *The day started early:* Smith and Rose, "The Group Marriage Commune," *The Journal of Psychedelic Drugs.*

177   *A few times he simulated being crucified:* Leslie Van Houten interview.

178   *someone gave the Family a case of Cool Whip:* Gregg Jakobson interview.

178   *A memorable lesson for the Family involved a king and queen:* I was told this by a former Manson Family member.

178   *or else albums by the Moody Blues:* Leslie Van Houten interview.

179   *Charlie liked the music of the Doors and the Jefferson Airplane:* Patricia Krenwinkel interview.

179   *Squeaky had it lucky:* Leslie Van Houten interview.

179   *Group sex was completely orchestrated by Charlie:* Smith and Rose, "The Group Marriage Commune," *The Journal of Psychedelic Drugs*; Gregg Jakobson interview.

180   *Charlie would stand in front of them:* Leslie Van Houten interview.

180   *Yet he also did considerable praising:* Patricia Krenwinkel interview.

180   *Susan named her child Ze Zo Ze Cee Zadfrack:* Atkins, p. 102.

180   *Sandy said that they were married:* I find this odd; based on Charlie's teachings, everyone in the Family resented having to register any information with the government. If Sandy did marry Joel Pugh and occasionally take his last name, I suspect it was to ease the process of applying for child welfare for her baby. The Family had no objections to taking government money.

181   *Wristwatches, calendars, and clocks:* Gregg Jakobson interview; Bugliosi, p. 111; Sanders, p. 73.

181   *Charlie had a Bible:* Leslie Van Houten interview. As noted later in this chapter, Charlie liked to have Leslie read to him from Revelation.

181   *his anti-Semitism:* Patricia Krenwinkel interview.

181   *if he seemed to be violating his own philosophy:* Leslie Van Houten interview.

182   *Terry Melcher also made a few ranch visits:* Gregg Jakobson interview.

182   *Charlie told Jakobson about inventing the "insane game":* Ibid.

183   *Sex with outsiders became a daily routine:* Patricia Krenwinkel interview.

183   *he stood there with the flies all over him:* Gregg Jakobson interview.

184   *When Phil Kaufman heard that Charlie:* Phil Kaufman interview.

184   *They appeared to be just another commune:* Mary F. Corey interview.

184   *The real problem was that Spahn Ranch:* David Dotson interview.

185   *the Democratic National Convention:* Tom Hayden interview; White, pp. 356–59; Bill Ayers, *Fugitive Days: Memoirs of an Antiwar Activist* (Beacon, 2001), p. 134.

185   *After attending a Republican rally in Toledo:* Theodore White, *America in Search of Itself,* p. 464.

185   *In the imagination of many shaken older voters:* Bob Schieffer interview.

185   *But the song McCartney presented now:* Barry Miles, *Paul McCartney: Many Years from Now* (Henry Holt, 1997), p. 488.

186   *the Beach Boys did some recording, too:* Timothy White, p. 284; Gregg Jakobson interview.

186   *It was a deliberate insult:* Gregg Jakobson interview.

186   *One morning Charlie had to run off a guy:* Leslie Van Houten interview.

187   *a schoolteacher the Family nicknamed Juanita:* Different books have Juanita arriving at different times, but Leslie Van Houten remembers Juanita being allowed to join the Family not long after she and Gypsy came to Spahn Ranch. According to Leslie, after Charlie got the pink slip to Juanita's vehicle and drained her bank account, he expected the rest of his followers to shun her until she left. About a year later, though, Juanita again figures in the saga of Charlie and the Family. I believe it's the same person; apparently Juanita was better than most in hanging on in the group when Charlie no longer wanted her.

187   *Sometimes Cathy Gillies talked about:* Bravin, pp. 91–93.

188   *But Charlie was drawn to the adjacent property:* Bugliosi, pp. 129–30, Sanders, pp. 84–86.

188   *he gave Barker a Beach Boys gold record:* Bugliosi, pp. 128–29.

188   *Davis returned a few months later:* No one seems sure why Charlie sent Bruce Davis and Joel Pugh to England. He may have wanted them to explore the

possibility of moving the Family there after Charlie made it big as a recording star. When Davis returned to California in 1969, Charlie greeted him warmly and treated him like a trusted second-in-command. Joel Pugh died in London; his death was officially ruled a suicide, but a number of Manson historians, both amateur and professional, cite various mysterious circumstances and are convinced that he was murdered.

189   *Charlie told the women to fan out into the desert:* Patricia Krenwinkel interview.

189   *He tried sending some of the girls to Las Vegas:* Bravin, p. 92.

191   *Wilson decided to drive up there:* Gregg Jakobson interview.

192   *Squeaky approached George Spahn:* Bravin, p. 94.

192   *Leslie read to him from the Bible:* Leslie Van Houten interview.

192   *He always cited the Bible:* Patricia Krenwinkel interview.

Chapter Eleven: The Bible and the Beatles

It's impossible to see into someone's heart and know for certain what he believes. Did Charlie think the Beatles were speaking to him through the songs on the *White Album?* Did he truly expect a worldwide race war called Helter Skelter, and that he and the Family could hide in a desert bottomless pit for hundreds of years and then reemerge to rule the world? Did Charlie take the Bible literally and expect the appearance of armored locusts and multiheaded dragons to herald the Second Coming of Christ and the end of the world?

I believe that the historian should provide context as well as recounting what happened when—the *why* as well as the *what.* But in the convoluted case of what Charlie Manson really believed, the reader's educated guess is as valid as mine. During the nearly two years that it took me to research and write this book, I wrote regularly to Manson requesting an interview so I could ask him these critical questions. He responded by turning my letters over to a friend, with whom I exchanged a series of letters and e-mails that culminated in his advising me to keep writing to Charlie—maybe he'd eventually agree to see me. He didn't.

Based on my research, and interviews with Phil Kaufman, Gregg Jakobson, Patricia Krenwinkel, Leslie Van Houten, and cousin Jo Ann—all people who knew him well—my opinion is that Manson was a skilled con artist who could convince others because he first convinced himself. Pat Krenwinkel suggested in one of our conversations that "he probably made himself believe that at least some of it was true." It should also be noted that in 1968–69 many people believed that the Beatles were in some sense social prophets, and in America there was widespread fear that some form of extended racial conflict was imminent. It was a time when any terrible thing seemed possible. As Bob Schieffer observed to me, "The country was falling apart."

Page

194 *He demanded that they pay special attention:* Leslie Van Houten interview; Watson, *Will You Die for Me?*, p. 83; Bugliosi, p. 241.

194 *they needed "a damn good whacking":* Charlie might have believed the Beatles were speaking to him, but in his memoir George Harrison said that he didn't write this line in "Piggies." His mother, Louise, suggested it.

195 *he gravely asked everyone for comments:* Stephen Kay interview.

195 *not just because the Beatles said so:* Patricia Krenwinkel and Leslie Van Houten interviews. Pat says that as much as Charlie talked about the Beatles, he emphasized his interpretations of the Bible even more.

195 *John, the narrator, has been banished:* Harold Lindsell (editor), *The Harper Study Bible* (HarperCollins, 1964), pp. 1861–63.

195 *For imaginations fueled:* Mary F. Corey interview.

196 *Just as the Bible foretold:* Patricia Krenwinkel interview.

196 *they'd begin to feel budding wings:* Leslie Van Houten interview.

196 *any deserters who weren't killed:* Ibid.

197 *There was an unexpected defector:* Watson, *Will You Die for Me?*, pp. 85–89.

197 *Charlie had no inkling of this:* Gregg Jakobson interview.

199 *But there was a personal dilemma:* A. E. Hotchner, *Doris Day: Her Own Story* (Bantam, 1976), pp. 272–74.

200 *youthful rebellion was a worldwide phenomenon:* Ambrose, *Nixon*, pp. 262–64.

200 *Protesters were out in force:* Bob Schieffer interview.

201 *He began by insisting:* Ambrose, *Nixon*, pp. 263–64.

201 *In January, Black Panther leaders:* Mary F. Corey interview; Hayden, p. 225.

201 *When he replaced Tom Reddin:* Domanick, *To Protect and to Serve*, pp. 221–22.

201 *Charlie used the news to support:* Leslie Van Houten interview.

202 *Altobelli let Gregg Jakobson talk him into:* Gregg Jakobson interview.

202 *They had trouble finding the right place to live:* Bugliosi, p. 28; Sanders, p. 57.

202 *Polanski and Tate were interested:* Bugliosi, p. 28; Sanders, p. 117; Gaines, p. 215.

203 *Squeaky was sent to sweet-talk George Spahn:* Bravin, p. 95.

203 *Charlie sent several Family members:* Bugliosi, p. 247.

203 *Now he conducted lengthy desert survival courses:* Karlene Faith, *The Long Prison Journey of Leslie Van Houten: Life Beyond the Cult* (Northeastern University Press, 2001), p. 37.

204 *And now there were guns, too:* Felton and Dalton, *Rolling Stone.*

204 *Charlie never suggested that the Family members would ever attack anyone:* Patricia Krenwinkel interview.

204 *Charlie ordered the women to experiment:* Leslie Van Houten and Patricia Krenwinkel interviews.

205 *He managed to get the dune buggy through the doors:* Leslie Van Houten interview.

205 *Just as work on the dune buggy started:* Watson, pp. 91–93.

206 *Gypsy grabbed the chain:* Leslie Van Houten interview. I would like to have asked Catherine Share (Gypsy) about this, but beyond one general off-the-record phone conversation she refused to be interviewed unless she was paid. I never pay for interviews.

206 *He explored the possibility of signing them up:* Bugliosi, p. 247.

206 *Charlie next considered sending some of the women:* Patricia Krenwinkel interview.

206 *Then the Family tried turning:* Watson, *Will You Die for Me?*, pp. 91–99; Marynick, p. 308; Sanders, p. 125.

208 *the Straight Satans would join the Family as middlemen:* Gregg Jakobson interview.

208 *It helped that the two women:* Leslie Van Houten interview.

208 *particularly club treasurer Danny DeCarlo:* Bugliosi, p. 101; Gilmore and Kenner, p. 90.

208 *Shorty Shea sometimes volunteered:* Bravin, p. 97.

209 *Charlie gathered his followers and explained:* Leslie Van Houten interview.

209 *they liked slipping pills to members:* David E. Smith and A. J. Langguth interviews; Faith, p. 114.

210 *he reported after a trip to Barker Ranch:* Sanders, pp. 103–4; Livsey, pp. 76–77.

210 *he took out his frustration on Watkins:* Vincent Bugliosi interview.

210 *Gregg Jakobson might have agreed:* Gregg Jakobson interview.

211 *Charlie assembled small squads of followers:* Watson, *Will You Die for Me?*, p. 75; Michelle Phillips, pp. 172–73.

212 *In mid-March, Charlie received word:* Watson, *Will You Die for Me?*, p. 99.

212 *Charlie had informed the women that he wanted:* Patricia Krenwinkel interview.

213 *The new tenants threw a memorable housewarming party:* John Phillips, with Jim Jerome, *Papa John: An Autobiography* (Doubleday, 1986), pp. 290–91.

214 *according to subsequent police reports:* Bugliosi, p. 32.

215 *On March 23, Shahrokh Hatami looked out:* Sanders, p. 120; Bugliosi, p. 226; Gaines, p. 215. Several individuals I contacted for interviews wanted money to talk to me, but Shahrokh Hatami's demand for $12,000 was the most excessive. His proposed deal included not only an interview but rights to reproduce four of his photographs of Sharon Tate. I declined.

217 *One of Little Paul Watkins's ongoing responsibilities:* Bugliosi, p. 289.

217 *Rudi Altobelli kept his promise:* Sanders, p. 120.

217 *Sometime in April, Voytek Frykowski and Abigail Folger:* Ibid., p. 123.

217 *deputies of the Los Angeles County Sheriff's Office raided Spahn:* Bravin, p. 96.

218 *then the cops would think they were nuts:* Leslie Van Houten interview.

218 *he would act like "Crazy Charlie":* Ibid.

218 *Tex Watson was arrested in Van Nuys:* Bugliosi, p. 156; Watson, *Will You Die for Me?*, p. 120.

218 *some of the Family thought the belladonna:* Leslie Van Houten interview.

219 *so irritated by his pushy new attitude:* Phil Kaufman interview.

219 *Some of the women in the Family felt afraid:* Patricia Krenwinkel interview.

219 *He had his own hopes:* Gregg Jakobson interview.

Chapter Twelve: Thwarted Dreams

During an interview with *Oui* magazine published in 1981, Bobby Beausoleil stated that Manson never came to Gary Hinman's house on the night of July 25, 1969. He claimed that prosecutors invented Charlie's participation in the murder "because they wanted to get Manson into the act." But Susan Atkins, who was also there, was adamant in her grand jury testimony, in her book *Child of Satan, Child of God* and in her unpublished memoir that Manson arrived at Hinman's house, slashed Hinman's ear with his sword, and eventually told Beausoleil to kill Hinman after Hinman continued to insist he had no money to give to Beausoleil and the Family.

Then and later, Beausoleil was adamant that he never joined the Family, another way of making it clear that he never served or took orders from Charlie Manson. My sense is that such claims suit Beausoleil's swaggering personality so he can take sole responsibility for the Hinman murder. Beausoleil said that Susan Atkins and Mary Brunner went along because they knew Hinman, liked him, and thought it would be a social visit. Susan wrote that Charlie sent her and Mary along to assist in Hinman's murder, and that they were chosen because they left a child at Charlie's mercy back at Spahn.

I had hoped to interview Beausoleil, but learned that he had agreed with filmmaker Steven Martin to decline all interviews while they cooperated on a documentary about his life.

Page

220   *America was seething:* Tom Hayden, Bob Schieffer, and Mark Rudd interviews; Reeves, p. 61; Hayden, pp. 69–70.

220   *the sharpest-eyed among his followers realized:* Catherine Share, *Manson,* History Channel (2009).

221   *Melcher arrived at the ranch:* Hotchner, pp. 289–90; Gaines, pp. 215–16.

222   *He recalled later that Charlie's songs:* Hotchner, pp. 290–91.

222   *Charlie went to a surplus store in Santa Monica:* Sanders, p. 138.

222   *Everyone was kept working at a feverish pace:* Leslie Van Houten interview.

223   *as they guided him toward their car:* Bugliosi, p. 185; Gaines, p. 216; Hotchner, pp. 291–92; Felton and Dalton, "A Special Report," *Rolling Stone.*

223   *it was the classic producer's tactful turndown:* Gregg Jakobson interview.

223   *The constant danger for gurus:* David E. Smith interview.

224   *Terry Melcher had betrayed Charlie:* Catherine Share, *Manson,* History Channel.

224   *"stopped pretending that he wasn't angry":* Leslie Van Houten interview.

224   *Charlie made a few last-ditch efforts:* Hoskyns, *Waiting for the Sun,* p. 184.

224   *On Charlie's command they began stealing:* Patricia Krenwinkel interview.

224   *Charlie learned where Terry Melcher lived:* Hotchner, pp. 296–97.

225   *Charlie began suggesting that the creepy-crawls:* Watson, *Will You Die for Me?,* pp. 121–25.

225   *Pat Krenwinkel left with a biker:* Patricia Krenwinkel interview.

225   *Charlie put her in his dune buggy:* Leslie Van Houten interview.

225   *Word reached him that Brooks Poston had left Barker Ranch:* Sanders, p. 103.

225   *He told Watkins that any delay:* Vincent Bugliosi interview; Bugliosi, p. 247.

225   *he joined Paul Crockett:* Livsey, p. 151.

226   *The Family suffered an additional loss:* Bugliosi, p. 133.

226   *Charlie decided to work another contact:* Watson, *Will You Die for Me?,* pp. 127–30; Bravin, pp. 98–99; Marynick, pp. 373–74; Bugliosi, pp. 280, 417; Stephen Kay, Phil Kaufman, Vincent Bugliosi, and Mary F. Corey interviews.

228   *He used the Lotsapoppa incident as proof:* Leslie Van Houten interview.

228   *"it wasn't peace and love and hippies anymore":* Catherine Share, *Manson,* History Channel.

228   *Bob and Linda Kasabian were living:* Bugliosi, p. 257.

229   *A vivacious woman named Gypsy:* Linda Kasabian, *Manson,* History Channel; Gregg Jakobson interview.

229   *the moon walk was viewed with skepticism:* Leslie Van Houten interview.

230   *Bobby Beausoleil provided the perfect excuse:* Bardach, "Jailhouse Interview," *Oui.*

231   *On Friday, July 25, longtime Family member Bruce Davis:* Ibid.; Gregg Jakobson interview; Atkins, pp. 111–19; Atkins unpublished memoir, pp. 22–23; Bravin, pp. 98–99; Watson, *Will You Die for Me?,* pp. 131–34; Sanders, pp. 180–85; Udo, pp. 127–30; Livsey, pp. 41–42.

233   *Susan also couldn't resist bragging:* Stephen Kay and Leslie Van Houten interviews.

233   *Yeller was sickened by Susan's comments:* Patricia Krenwinkel interview.

233   *some of Gary Hinman's friends dropped by:* Sanders, pp. 187–88.

233   *they were picked up by Saladin Nader:* Ibid., p. 189.

234   *Charlie announced that he would drive north:* Bugliosi, pp. 274–75.

235   *At Cielo Drive things were hectic:* Sanders, p. 195.

235   *Beausoleil didn't take Kitty Lutesinger:* Bardach, "Jailhouse Interview," *Oui;* Watson, *Will You Die for Me?,* p. 134; Sanders, pp. 192–93.

236   *Charlie was also being braced by the law:* Bugliosi, pp. 275–76.

236   *They talked about the* White Album: Ibid., p. 276.

236   *Beausoleil called Spahn Ranch:* Sanders, pp. 192–93.

237   *Someone remembered seeing a movie:* Bravin, p. 99. Patricia Krenwinkel says that, although she wasn't part of any copycat murders speculation, comments of others that she heard afterward indicate that such murders were discussed.

237   *Housekeeper Winifred Chapman arrived:* Bugliosi, pp. 50–53. All of my references to August 8 activities at Cielo and by Sharon Tate, Voytek Frykowski, Abigail Folger, Jay Sebring, and William Garretson are based on an LAPD timeline included on these pages of *Helter Skelter.*

237   *Charlie and Schram arrived back at Spahn:* Sanders, p. 194.

238   *Charlie's instinct was to run:* Bravin, p. 99.

239   *One suggestion was launching an assault:* Atkins unpublished memoir, p. 26.

239   *Charlie ordered Squeaky to give Mary Brunner:* Ibid., pp. 99–100.

239   *there were conflicting recollections:* Susan Atkins recalled that Sandy and Mary were sent "to buy escape supplies, including rope" in anticipation of the Family trying to break Bobby Beausoleil out of the L.A. County jail (Atkins unpublished memoir, pp. 25–26); Nuel Emmons wrote that Charlie told him they were sent to fetch food for a special Family supper that night (Emmons, pp. 196–98).

240   *Each was being held on $600 bail:* Watson, *Will You Die for Me?,* p. 135.

Chapter Thirteen: Tate

Charlie Manson has always insisted that he didn't order the Family to murder anyone; he just allowed them to do what they wanted. Tex Watson is equally adamant that Charlie told him to go to Cielo and murder everyone there. Based on all we now know of Manson's manipulative techniques, they are both in some sense telling the truth, though each is clearly trying to place the blame on the other.

My description of the five murders at Cielo during the early hours of August 9, 1969, is drawn from five sources: Tex Watson's *Will You Die For Me?*, pp. 135–44; Susan Atkins's *Child of Satan, Child of God*, pp. 124–35; Atkins's unpublished memoir; Linda Kasabian's pretrial interview with Vincent Bugliosi as recounted in *Helter Skelter*, pp. 258–63; and my two extended interviews with Patricia Krenwinkel at the California Institution for Women in Corona on April 21–22, 2012. There are some contradictions, mostly over small issues that different people remember in substantially the same way with a few small differences. I'll address these in the chapter notes and explain why I'm inclined to accept one version over another.

Krenwinkel dismisses Kasabian's description of her horrified reaction to the Cielo slayings, insisting that Kasabian was a fully supportive participant although she did not kill anyone. Krenwinkel says she is certain that Kasabian never asked anyone to stop.

My account of the initial murder site investigation comes from two sources— Bugliosi in *Helter Skelter*, pp. 3–24, and Steve Oney's excellent article "Manson: An Oral History," which appeared July 1, 2009, in *Los Angeles Magazine*. Bugliosi worked directly from the police reports, and Oney interviewed Sgt. Michael Mc-Gann and Officer Danny Galindo.

Page

241 *Charlie Manson imbued two core beliefs:* Leslie Van Houten and Patricia Krenwinkel interviews.

243 *Falling back on Dale Carnegie:* Phil Kaufman and Gregg Jakobson interviews. Both Kaufman and Jakobson offered numerous examples of Charlie persuading Family members that what he wanted them to do was originally their idea or ideas.

244 *caring for Altobelli's dogs:* We know there were at least three dogs, and Tate also owned a dog and several cats. William Garretson was vague in his testimony about the dogs, though we know that at least the Weimaraner was in the guesthouse with him when investigators arrived at the murder scene. Susan Atkins made reference to one of the dogs being in the house during

the murders, but none of the subsequent police reports mentioned any sign of an animal being actively present—there were lots of bloody footprints, but no bloody paw prints. In any case, the dogs did not play a critical role in what happened at Cielo that night.

245   *the three women didn't know yet:* Patricia Krenwinkel is adamant that Tex Watson did not mention killing anyone until the four intruders were over the fence at Cielo.

247   *Tex slashed at him with the knife:* In *Helter Skelter*, Bugliosi writes that he doesn't know the order in which Tex used the .22 Buntline and his knife. Tex recalls that he fired "and at some point used the knife." From her hiding place in the bushes, Pat thought Tex "tried stabbing first and then shot."

251   *Pat was shaking:* Patricia Krenwinkel interview. From the outset of the investigation, police and prosecutors could not understand why William Garretson was not murdered. Now we know. It seems impossible that Garretson didn't hear anything that night—besides gunshots there were screams from the victims, and Tex and Pat chased Frykowski and Folger out onto the lawn, killing them there. I tried and failed to locate Garretson during the research for this book. But in a 1999 interview with the E! network, Garretson stated that he heard noises he thought were firecrackers popping when Watson shot Steve Parent, that he heard screams, that he saw a girl chase another girl outside the main house and then heard someone saying, "Stop, I'm already dead." He didn't know what was going on, he said, but he was too scared to look out the window.

252   *Susan held Tate while Tex stabbed her:* Initially, Susan Atkins bragged that she stabbed Sharon Tate to death, but she changed her story to holding the pregnant woman while Tex slaughtered her, and Susan stuck to this version for the rest of her life. In his memoir, Tex says he killed Tate. This version agrees with Krenwinkel's recollection of the August 9 events: First Tex helped finish off Abigail Folger, and then he went inside to murder Tate: "The murders were mostly done by Tex because none of the rest of us were really ready for that."

254   *Charlie got into the Ford:* Manson told Nuel Emmons that he went to the murder site with an unidentified Family member. Krenwinkel remembers Manson meeting them with Nancy Pitman at the entrance to Spahn Ranch, but doesn't know whether Pitman went with Manson when he drove to Cielo. That Manson did some murder scene rearranging seems beyond doubt; he put a towel over Jay Sebring's head, which led to suggestions in the media that hoods were placed over the heads of all the victims, a description that

encouraged further speculation about the killings being part of some Satanist ritual. Charlie also placed a pair of eyeglasses close to Sharon's and Jay's bodies, a particularly blatant red herring since he wouldn't allow Family members to wear glasses.

In *Will You Die for Me?*, Tex Watson wrote that the large American flag was already on the sofa when the murders took place. Bugliosi notes in *Helter Skelter* that on the morning after the killings, Winifred Chapman told police that the flag had been in the house prior to the murders, though she did not specify where. Krenwinkel is certain that while Tate, Frykowski, Sebring, and Folger were slaughtered, the flag was not on the couch, and that she was startled to read news stories alluding to it being there. I believe Krenwinkel. Frykowski was sleeping on the couch when the intruders entered the house, and no one recalls him getting tangled with a flag during the early moments of the crime when he rolled around on the couch being kicked by Tex. Tex had inhaled an extra dose of Meth before setting out from Spahn, so his powers of observation may certainly have been skewed.

Chapter Fourteen: LaBianca and Shea

My sources for the description of the LaBianca murders and other events that night include interviews with Patricia Krenwinkel and Leslie Van Houten (noted throughout); Linda Kasabian's testimony in *Helter Skelter*, pp. 266–73; statements by Kasabian and Vincent Bugliosi on the History Channel's *Manson* documentary; Tex Watson's *Will You Die for Me?*, pp. 145–51; Susan Atkins's *Child of Satan, Child of God*, pp. 134–36, and her unpublished memoir; and ancillary interviews with Phil Kaufman and David Dotson. The account in this chapter of the murder of Shorty Shea is much less detailed because all the information is secondary. Manson, Bruce Davis, and Steve Grogan (Clem) were convicted of Shea's slaying on circumstantial evidence, since his body was not found until many years later when Clem led the authorities to the ranch hand's grave.

Page

260   *Then they piled into the Ford:* Some books have Manson splitting driving with Linda Kasabian; in her interview with me, Krenwinkel said only Kasabian drove, at least as far as the LaBiancas'.

261   *The only conversation was one-sided:* Leslie Van Houten and Patricia Krenwinkel interviews.

261   *The LaBiancas had worked hard:* Bugliosi, pp. 43–44.

262 *The LaBiancas weren't able to drop Suzanne off:* Ibid., p. 24.

262 *Susan and Leslie fell into fitful dozes:* Leslie Van Houten interview.

262 *they'd partied on this street:* Patricia Krenwinkel interview. Krenwinkel believes that Manson targeted "the house next door to Harold True's" before they set out from Spahn that night. Her theory is that Manson wanted True to supply drugs to the Family, and that Manson hoped to implicate him in the LaBiancas' murder and subsequently blackmail him.

263 *But it didn't seem that way to Charlie:* Phil Kaufman interview.

264 *Then he snapped to Tex:* Leslie Van Houten interview. There's some disagreement among Manson chroniclers whether Tex Watson was with Manson when Manson initially tied up Leno LaBianca with leather thongs. But in his memoir Tex writes that he was inside the house with Manson at that time, and that Leslie Van Houten and Pat Krenwinkel came inside after that.

264 *Pat was afraid:* Patricia Krenwinkel interview.

268 *so they treated him to breakfast:* Faith, p. 47.

268 *He stalked around the ranch:* Atkins unpublished memoir, p. 28.

269 *That meant he wasn't available:* Oney, "Manson," *Los Angeles Magazine*.

269 *Buckles's response to the county detectives accurately reflected:* David Dotson interview.

269 *The FBI even suggested that the Bureau of Customs investigate:* FBI File 62-113047-2, obtained through the Freedom of Information Act.

270 *a polygraph administered on Sunday afternoon:* Bugliosi, p. 36–37.

270 *an L.A. friend of Tex Watson contacted Tex:* Watson, *Will You Die for Me?*, pp. 14–22.

271 *He called Gregg Jakobson and asked:* Gregg Jakobson interview.

271 *Around 8:30 P.M. on Sunday:* Sanders, pp. 246–48.

272 *Danny Galindo was still at the LAPD's:* Oney, "Manson," *Los Angeles Magazine*.

273 *They often operated:* David Dotson interview.

273 *Fear was widespread in Los Angeles:* William W. Collier, Lorraine Chamberlain, and A. J. Langguth interviews. Collier and Langguth both stressed that "celebrity" panic was restricted to the highest-end neighborhoods.

274 *He couldn't understand why:* Emmons, p. 212.

274 *But it was Charlie who had missed the obvious:* Mary F. Corey, A. J. Langguth, Lorraine Chamberlain, and William W. Collier interviews.

274 *Yet Charlie still used the press coverage:* Oney, "Manson," *Los Angeles Magazine*.

274 *For months, Los Angeles County lawmen:* Ibid.

275 *Charlie sent Linda Kasabian:* Atkins unpublished memoir, p. 29.

275   *Charlie was far less concerned:* Sanders, p. 260.

275   *Tex was ambivalent:* Watson, *Will You Die for Me?*, pp. 22–23.

275   *Tex was questioned by the same deputy:* Ibid., p. 23.

276   *Sharon Tate posthumously became:* Bugliosi, p. 48.

276   *Al Springer didn't resemble:* Watson, *Will You Die for Me?*, pp. 89–92.

277   *Linda Kasabian couldn't stand it anymore:* Manson, History Channel; Sanders, p. 260; Bugliosi, pp. 271, 286–88.

278   *Spahn Ranch became the antithesis:* Gaines, p. 216; Bugliosi, p. 93; Sanders, p. 263; Watson, *Will You Die for Me?*, p. 22.

279   *At daybreak on Saturday:* Oney, "Manson," *Los Angeles Magazine.*

281   *The combination of the Straight Satans' invasion:* Patricia Krenwinkel interview.

281   *Danny DeCarlo was the first:* Bugliosi, p. 101.

282   *he soon settled on an obvious candidate:* Atkins unpublished memoir, p. 30; Livsey, p. 52.

282   *On a night late in August:* Oney, "Manson," *Los Angeles Magazine*; Livsey, pp. 52–53; Sanders, pp. 271–72. The specific date has never been determined.

282   *At first she thought she must have imagined it: Los Angeles Magazine.*

283   *At the end of August:* Bugliosi, pp. 64–65.

283   *these totaled almost 250:* Patterson, *Grand Expectations*, pp. 716–17.

Chapter Fifteen: Death Valley

Patricia Krenwinkel and Leslie Van Houten provided me with firsthand descriptions of life on Barker Ranch. Leslie often enjoyed it: "I liked living out in nature without a lot of things." To Pat, Family life in the desert was equivalent to modern-day survivalist cults whose main objective is to defy any encroachment by the government, violently if necessary. Both agree that the men in the Family had it much better in Death Valley than the women.

Page

285   *Charlie didn't allow them to readjust:* Leslie Van Houten and Patricia Krenwinkel interviews; Watson, *Will You Die for Me?*, p. 27; Atkins unpublished memoir, p. 33.

286   *Leslie in particular wanted:* Leslie Van Houten interview.

286   *Many, worn down by physical labor:* Patricia Krenwinkel interview.

287   *Ruth Ann confided to Danny DeCarlo:* Bugliosi, p. 110.

287   *Juan Flynn accompanied the Family out into the desert:* Oney, "Manson," *Los Angeles Magazine.*

287   *Barbara Hoyt overheard Susan Atkins gossiping:* Ibid.

288   *Besides, everyone knew that Charlie could find you anywhere:* Patricia Krenwinkel interview.

288   *Steven Weiss saw a gun:* Bugliosi, p. 66; Sanders, p. 273.

288   *It irked Charlie that Paul Crockett:* Bugliosi, pp. 233–38, 248.

289   *The investigators weren't being lazy:* Records and Identification Department, LAPD; David Dotson interview.

290   *The Barker Ranch larder was reduced:* Patricia Krenwinkel interview.

291   *Barbara Hoyt and Simi Sherri decided to risk it:* Oney, "Manson," *Los Angeles Magazine*; *What Happened After*, History Channel, 2009.

292   *A massive earth mover machine blocked a back road:* Watson, *Will You Die for Me?*, pp. 27–28.

292   *park ranger Dick Powell was on patrol:* Oney, "Manson," *Los Angeles Magazine*.

292   *Mary Brunner was finally released:* Sanders, p. 284.

292   *The trial of David Dellinger:* Tom Hayden and Mark Rudd interviews; Hayden, p. 229.

293   *Though they didn't know:* Bishop, pp. 24–26; Oney, "Manson," *Los Angeles Magazine*; Bugliosi, pp. 125–26.

294   *As soon as the officers' truck:* Watson, *Will You Die for Me?*, p. 28.

295   *Charlie gave Tex a shotgun:* Ibid., p. 29.

295   *September had been such a frustrating month:* Bugliosi, p. 69.

295   *Tex got tired of waiting:* Watson, *Will You Die for Me?*, pp. 29–30.

296   *Crockett and Poston met in Independence:* Bugliosi, pp. 231–34.

296   *The Weathermen launched:* Tom Hayden and Mark Rudd interviews; Mark Rudd, *Underground: My Life with SDS and the Weathermen* (William Morrow, 2009), pp. 170–83; Hayden, p. 229.

297   *There were elements of mistrust:* Patricia Krenwinkel interview.

297   *Kitty Lutesinger was especially horrified:* Sanders, p. 291; Bugliosi, pp. 75–76.

298   *They had a hard time:* Oney, "Manson," *Los Angeles Magazine*; Bishop, pp. 26–29, 33; Bugliosi, pp. 126–27; Sanders, pp. 292–94; Atkins, pp. 140–41; Faith, p. 42.

298   *Lutesinger's mother told her:* Sanders, p. 294.

299   *Pursell, Powell, and another officer:* Oney, "Manson," *Los Angeles Magazine*; Bugliosi, pp. 127–30.

301   *Following their arrests, most of the Family:* Leslie Van Houten interview.

301   *the overflow was so pronounced:* Bravin, p. 103.

301   *Lutesinger met with L.A. County investigators:* Bugliosi, p. 76; Bravin, p. 105; Sanders, pp. 294–98.

302   *The L.A. County lawmen bluntly told Susan:* Atkins, pp. 142–43; Sanders, p. 299.

302   *Charlie had warned his followers:* Leslie Van Houten interview.

303   *marchers jammed America's streets:* Hayden, p. 229; Reeves, pp. 128, 137–38; Ambrose, *Nixon*, p. 304.

304   *Charlie remained in custody:* Sanders, p. 302.

304   *Still, it was something new to run down:* Bugliosi, pp. 75–77.

305   *and added a new name:* Ibid., p. 71.

305   *Now Whiteley and Guenther tried again:* Ibid., p. 77.

306   *Tex Watson decided that the outside world:* Watson, *Will You Die for Me?*, pp. 153–55.

306   *Charlie began giving them messages:* Sanders, p. 304.

306   *it was hard to find Susan Atkins:* Atkins, pp. 144–46; Atkins unpublished memoir, p. 33; Bravin, p. 140; Bugliosi, p. 78.

Chapter Sixteen: Unraveling

Interviews with David Dotson, Gerald L. Chaleff, Vincent Bugliosi, and Stephen Kay were extraordinarily helpful in my research for this chapter. Since its dates and descriptions of the investigation are firsthand, I also relied heavily on *Helter Skelter* by Vincent Bugliosi and Curt Gentry.

Page

308   *Virginia Graham and Susan Atkins sat:* Atkins, 145–48; Bugliosi, pp. 79–80.

309   *Venice police responded to a call:* Sanders, p. 307; Bugliosi, pp. 80–81.

309   *They noticed that Charlie's deerskin pants:* Bugliosi, pp. 81–82.

309   *Susan kept elaborating to Virginia:* Oney, "Manson," *Los Angeles Magazine*; Sanders, pp. 308–10; Bugliosi, pp. 82–87.

311   *they did have another Straight Satan in custody:* Bugliosi, pp. 88–94; Sanders, pp. 310–11.

313   *Ronnie Howard was deeply disturbed:* Bugliosi, pp. 96–97, 99.

313   *Danny DeCarlo came to Parker Center:* Ibid., pp. 97, 99–100, 106–9.

317   *The next afternoon, Aaron Stovitz:* Vincent Bugliosi and Stephen Kay interviews; Bugliosi, pp. 117–19.

317   *Bugliosi began by accompanying:* Bugliosi, pp. 120–23.

318   *Next, Bugliosi and five members:* Ibid., pp. 123–35.

319   *Charlie knew what was going on:* Patricia Krenwinkel interview.

319   *Bugliosi issued a "want" for Charles Montgomery:* Bugliosi, pp. 147–48.

319   *Sandy Good had been overheard:* Ibid., pp. 148–49.

320   *Bobby Beausoleil's trial for the murder of Gary Hinman:* Ibid., p. 149.

320 *LAPD investigators interrogated:* Vincent Bugliosi interview; Sanders, p. 318; Bugliosi, pp. 152–54.

321 *The LAPD contacted Mr. Krenwinkel:* Sanders, p. 318.

322 *He told about his interest in Charlie's music:* Gregg Jakobson interview.

322 *Tex had hooked up with an old girlfriend:* Gerry Griffin interview; Watson, *Will You Die for Me?*, pp. 156–58; Bugliosi, p. 156.

322 *Dennis rightly feared the wrath:* Gregg Jakobson interview.

323 *Columbia wouldn't be pleased:* Ibid.; Hotchner, pp. 292–94; Bugliosi, p. 157.

324 *Richard Caballero met with Bugliosi:* Vincent Bugliosi interview; Bugliosi, p. 157; Atkins unpublished memoir, p. 34; Atkins, pp. 148–49.

324 *Though many of his staff begged him not to:* Gerald L. Chaleff interview; Bugliosi, pp. 158–60; Watson, *Will You Die for Me?*, pp. 158–60.

326 *Phil Kaufman, who had shared:* Phil Kaufman interview.

326 *But Charlie's cousin Jo Ann recalls:* Jo Ann interview.

326 *their investigation benefited:* Bugliosi, pp. 161–63.

327 *Richard Caballero brought the Susan Atkins tape:* Ibid., pp. 167–68.

327 *Another defense attorney had the same goal:* Ibid., p. 168.

327 *Susan Atkins got her deal:* Atkins, p. 149; Atkins unpublished memoir, pp. 34–36; Bugliosi, pp. 168–70, 218.

328 *Aaron Stovitz swore in Susan Atkins:* Bugliosi, pp. 173–85; Atkins unpublished memoir, p. 35.

330 *The information provided by Mary Brunner:* Bugliosi, p. 188.

330 *they turned to Charlie's old prison friend:* Phil Kaufman interview.

330 *Richard Caballero believed that Susan:* Atkins unpublished memoir, pp. 35–36; Bugliosi, p. 190.

331 *Susan began receiving her first visitors:* Atkins unpublished memoir, p. 36.

331 *When Charlie arrived at the Hall of Justice:* Gerald L. Chaleff interview.

Chapter Seventeen: Charlie Is Famous

Much of this chapter is based on interviews with Vincent Bugliosi, Stephen Kay, Gregg Jakobson, Phil Kaufman, Bob Schieffer, Mark Rudd, Tom Hayden, Leslie Van Houten, and Patricia Krenwinkel. For those who want to know more about the radical movement in spring 1970, I strongly recommend Mark Rudd's *Underground: My Life with SDS and the Weathermen.*

Page

333 *Charlie's arrival in chains:* Gerald L. Chaleff, A. J. Langguth, Bob Schieffer, Lorraine Chamberlain, and Tom Hayden interviews.

333   *Joan Didion reflected on the murders:* Didion, *The White Album*, p. 47.

333   *L.A. was in the midst of a newspaper war:* A. J. Langguth interview.

333   *The director of the county's public housing there:* George Sidiropolis interview.

334   *The most radical activists took it a step further:* Mark Rudd and Tom Hayden interviews; Rudd, pp. 187–90.

335   *Charlie had Squeaky, Ruth Ann, and some of his other:* Bravin, pp. 108–9.

335   *but now there were new recruits:* Vincent Bugliosi interview; Bugliosi, p. 200. Some of this passage is also based on information from the former Family member who later tried to take back his interview with me.

336   *prosecutors caught a major break:* Stephen Kay interview; Bugliosi, p. 191.

336   *Charlie was arraigned:* Bugliosi, p. 191.

337   *During the next six weeks:* Ibid., p. 192.

337   *Judge Keene also imposed a gag order:* Vincent Bugliosi and Stephen Kay interviews; Bugliosi, p. 190.

337   *turned the tapes Caballero had made with Susan:* Sanders, p. 327; Livsey, p. 45; Felton and Dalton, "Year of the Fork, Night of the Hunter," *Rolling Stone*.

337   *Even as Angelenos ingested:* Bugliosi, pp. 194–95.

338   *Bugliosi continued accumulating evidence:* Ibid., p. 196.

338   *a local TV crew set out:* Ibid., pp. 197–98.

338   *Bernard Weiss decided to bug:* Sanders, p. 327; Bugliosi, pp. 198–200.

338   *Charlie used his jail time:* Patricia Krenwinkel, Vincent Bugliosi, and Stephen Kay interviews.

339   *Leslie changed her lawyer:* Leslie Van Houten interview; Sanders, p. 327; Bugliosi, pp. 201–2.

339   *Rudolf Weber told Bugliosi:* Bugliosi, pp. 203–4.

340   *Dianne Lake hadn't had much to say:* Sanders, p. 328; Bugliosi, pp. 205–7.

340   *Charlie enjoyed his newfound fame:* Phil Kaufman and Leslie Van Houten interviews; Gaines, pp. 218–19; Wilson, p. 184; Sanders, p. 333.

342   *The LaBianca detectives located Harold True:* Bugliosi, pp. 207–8.

342   *Stovitz and Bugliosi worried:* Vincent Bugliosi interview.

342   *There was the cover of Life:* Rick Perlstein, *Nixonland: The Rise of a President and the Fracturing of America* (Scribner, 2008), pp. 243–44.

343   *They immediately disagreed:* Stephen Kay and Vincent Bugliosi interviews; Bugliosi, pp. 217–18.

343   *Inyo County dropped the arson charges:* Bugliosi, p. 220.

344   *he granted an extended interview:* Gregg Jakobson interview; Felton and Dalton, "Year of the Fork, Night of the Hunter," *Rolling Stone*.

344   *Bugliosi decided to reinterview Gregg Jakobson:* Bugliosi, pp. 223–26.

345   *Melcher was now petrified of Charlie:* Ben Fong-Torres, *Hickory Wind: The Life and Times of Gram Parsons* (Atria, 1991), pp. 148–51.

345   *The complexity of the case:* Gerald L. Chaleff interview.

345   *Altobelli corroborated:* Bugliosi, pp. 227–29.

345   *Shahrokh Hatami remembered:* Ibid., pp. 229–31.

346   *Inyo County sent Bugliosi:* Ibid., pp. 231–47.

346   *They contacted Linda Kasabian's lawyers:* Ibid., pp. 251–54.

347   *she had to choose:* Atkins unpublished memoir, p. 37.

347   *reports of a terrible explosion:* Rudd, pp. 193–98, 213; Hayden, p. 232; David Browne, *Fire and Rain: The Beatles, Simon & Garfunkel, James Taylor, CSNY and the Lost Story of 1970* (DaCapo, 2011), pp. 120–22; Reeves, p. 175.

348   *Kaufman realized that, but Charlie didn't:* Phil Kaufman interview.

348   *Kaufman was left with a garageful:* Currently, various Internet sites ask as much as $1,700 for pristine copies of the original *LIE* vinyl album.

348   *Susan Atkins would recant:* Atkins unpublished memoir, p. 37; Sanders, p. 335.

349   *His apparent intent was to provoke:* Oden "O.P." Skupen interview.

350   *Linda Kasabian gave birth to a son:* Bugliosi, pp. 265–66.

350   *Investigators got a copy of the ticket:* Ibid., p. 276.

350   *"Lotsapoppa" wasn't dead after all:* Sanders, p. 337; Bugliosi, pp. 279–80.

350   *Pat Krenwinkel refused to give:* Bugliosi, p. 283.

351   *He and his attorneys discussed:* Browne, p. 220.

351   *The prosecutors thought:* Bugliosi, p. 289.

352   *Charlie felt good enough:* Ibid., p. 292.

352   *Spring antiwar demonstrations:* Browne, pp. 168–71; Reeves, pp. 212–14, 216; Lorraine Chamberlain interview.

353   *Jury selection took an agonizing five weeks:* Oden Skupen and Gus Carlton interviews.

354   *In twenty devastating pages:* Fulton and Dalton, "Year of the Fork, Night of the Hunter," *Rolling Stone.*

354   *Los Angeles District Attorney Evelle Younger didn't like:* Bugliosi, p. 342.

355   *Stovitz and Bugliosi had a battle plan:* Ibid., p. 305.

355   *He believed that he had control over:* Oden Skupen interview.

355   *Pat and Leslie had both made attempts:* Patricia Krenwinkel and Leslie Van Houten interviews.

356   *Proximity was always crucial:* Patricia Krenwinkel interview.

356   *Charlie warned the Family:* Leslie Van Houten interview.

Chapter Eighteen: The Trial

Readers who want every detail of the trial are referred to *Helter Skelter* by Vincent Bugliosi and Curt Gentry or George Bishop's *Witness to Evil*. I wanted to recount the most critical moments and events, providing new information and insights gleaned mostly from interviews with defendants Leslie Van Houten and Patricia Krenwinkel, prosecutors Vincent Bugliosi and Stephen Kay, and court bailiffs O. P. "Scoop" Skupen, and Gus Carlton. Observers outside the Hall of Justice, most notably William W. Collier, were also helpful.

Page

357 *The prosecutors were determined:* Stephen Kay and Vincent Bugliosi interviews; Bugliosi, pp. 309–15.

358 *The other bailiffs said:* Gus Carlton and Oden Skupen interviews.

358 *Charlie called it the "mouse house":* Patricia Krenwinkel interview.

358 *Charlie would tell Susan, Pat, and Leslie what they were to do:* Patricia Krenwinkel and Leslie Van Houten interviews.

359 *Fitzgerald went home one night to find Squeaky:* Patricia Krenwinkel interview.

359 *they were never alone with their lawyers:* Leslie Van Houten interview.

359 *The trial bailiffs reached an understanding with Charlie:* Oden Skupen interview.

360 *Privately, they thought it was weird:* Gus Carlton and Oden Skupen interviews.

360 *He had done his best:* Didion, *The White Album*, p. 45.

360 *Sandy Good confronted Linda:* Bugliosi, p. 317.

361 *The moment the court clerk began:* Ibid., pp. 317–23; Bishop, p. 106.

362 *Charlie Manson's trial was a godsend for Nixon:* A. J. Langguth interview.

362 *Nixon gave a speech in Denver:* Vincent Bugliosi interview; Perlstein, p. 521; Bugliosi, pp. 323–28; Bishop, p. 200. Vincent Bugliosi told me that several years later he met Richard Nixon and told him, "Mr. President, what you said [about Manson] was right. You just said it at the wrong time."

363 *But Charlie got the last word:* Oden Skupen interview.

363 *Fitzgerald asked Older if it would be all right:* Leslie Van Houten and Patricia Krenwinkel interviews.

364 *Charlie refused to leave his cell:* Bishop, pp. 227–29.

364 *He'd cadge a smoke and often would practice:* Oden Skupen and Gus Carlton interviews.

364 *Judge Older formally granted Linda immunity:* Bugliosi, p. 330; Bishop, pp. 222–23.

365 *these losses were more than offset:* Bugliosi, pp. 332–35.

365 *Stovitz and Bugliosi wanted that on the record:* Bishop, p. 253.

366   *"We did pretty good at the first of it"*: Bugliosi, p. 336.

366   *Susan began fidgeting*: Sanders, p. 416; Bugliosi, pp. 342–43.

366   *there was no time for Kay*: Stephen Kay interview.

367   *In the months since she'd returned*: Bravin, pp. 122–24; Oney, "Manson," *Los Angeles Magazine*; *What Happened After*, History Channel.

368   *Tex Watson was finally extradited*: Watson, *Will You Die for Me?*, pp. 163–67; Bugliosi, pp. 356–57.

368   *The Weathermen broke Timothy Leary out*: Rudd, pp. 225–31; Ayers, pp. 255–56.

368   *pedestrians on the sidewalk*: William W. Collier interview.

369   *Sandy stood up and followed him*: Bugliosi, p. 358.

369   *Sandy and Squeaky approached Kay*: Stephen Kay interview.

369   *During a courtroom break*: Bugliosi, p. 359.

370   *Barbara's sexual vocabulary failed her*: Bishop, pp. 270–72.

370   *He glared at Charlie*: Bugliosi, pp. 363–69.

370   *For that day and several more*: Bishop, pp. 275–77.

371   *But before Whiteley could step down*: Oden Skupen interview; Bugliosi, pp. 369–70; Bishop, pp. 278–79.

371   *Older banned the defendants*: Bugliosi, pp. 370–80.

372   *The bailiffs did their best*: Oden Skupen interview.

372   *When Charlie heard the news*: Bugliosi, p. 379.

372   *As soon as he did*: Ibid., pp. 387–92; Bishop, pp. 307–14.

375   *he was clumsy and constantly tripped*: Leslie Van Houten interview.

375   *a massive search for Hughes ensued*: Bugliosi, pp. 393–95; Bishop, pp. 314–18; Stephen Kay and Leslie Van Houten interviews.

376   *On December 21, Older called the court to order*: Bishop, p. 318; Bugliosi, pp. 398–401; Stephen Kay interview.

377   *Paul Fitzgerald, speaking on behalf*: Bugliosi, pp. 401–7; Bishop, pp. 321–30.

378   *He responded to the closing arguments*: Bugliosi, pp. 407–9; Bishop, pp. 330–33.

378   *As the jury filed out*: Gus Carlton and Oden Skupen interviews.

378   *Kathleen Maddox was in Los Angeles*: Nancy interview.

379   *Over the next months she received letters*: Nancy interview. She brought the letters for me to read.

379   *Charlie sent word through Sandy and Squeaky*: Patricia Krenwinkel interview.

379   *Charlie yelled at Kanarek*: Oden Skupen interview.

380   *Bugliosi rested the prosecution's case*: Bugliosi, pp. 417–55.

383   *Then Charlie lost his nerve*: Oden Skupen interview.

384   *Lennon replied that Manson was "barmy"*: Jann S. Wenner, *Lennon Remembers* (Verso, 2000), p. 71.

Chapter Nineteen: The Wrong Man in the Right Place at the Right Time

This is a summation rather than an extended examination of people and events over a period of more than forty years. For those who want more information, I strongly recommend Jess Bravin's *Squeaky: The Life and Times of Lynette Alice Fromme*, which provides both details and insight into the Family after Manson's conviction for the Tate-LaBianca murders. I refer readers in particular to Bravin's description of events surrounding the murder of James Willett. In a very few cases, events in this chapter are presented out of chronological order for readability.

Though they have been especially shaped by my interviews with Nancy, Jo Ann, Phil Kaufman, Gregg Jakobson, Dr. David E. Smith, Leslie Van Houten, and Patricia Krenwinkel, the conclusions at chapter's end are my own.

Page

385 *his execution wasn't imminent:* Bugliosi, pp. 458–59.

386 *she wrote later that after she arrived:* Atkins, p. 156.

386 *they were just too emotionally exhausted:* Leslie Van Houten and Patricia Krenwinkel interviews.

386 *Como and the Family believed:* This is based on my interview with the former Family member who later asked to be removed from this project.

387 *He was adopted and his name was changed:* Atkins unpublished memoir, p. 53.

387 *Squeaky began writing a book:* Bravin, p. 144.

388 *His Death Row sojourn got off to a bad start:* Roger Dale Smith letter to Bob George, April 22, 1997.

389 *the California Supreme Court voted:* Patricia Krenwinkel and Leslie Van Houten interviews; Bugliosi, p. 488; Faith, pp. 47, 78.

389 *A Family crisis ensued:* Bravin, pp. 174–75.

390 *she received a pointed query:* Bravin, p. 160.

390 *She never recovered emotionally:* Nancy interview.

391 *She initially misunderstood:* Atkins, pp. 199–206.

391 *The two women would not speak:* Leslie Van Houten interview.

391 *Charlie's response included:* George with Matera, p. 141.

391 *Charlie had a new faith, too:* Bravin, pp. 187–88.

392 *Squeaky and Sandy assembled a hodgepodge:* Livsey, pp. 57–58; Bravin, pp. 188–94.

392 *Squeaky Fromme hated the book:* Bravin, p. 189.

393 *President Gerald Ford walked across the street:* Ibid., pp. 3–8, 233.

395 *But after they arrived in Pleasanton:* Ibid., pp. 394–95.

395 *doused Charlie with paint thinner:* Bugliosi, p. 497; George with Matera, p. 189; Marynick, p. 106.

395 *Squeaky pined for contact:* Bravin, p. 396; Bugliosi, pp. 509–10.

396 *Leslie Van Houten felt frustrated:* Leslie Van Houten interview.

397 *He was never certain:* "Helter Shelter" by Lorraine Ali, *Entertainment Weekly,* March 18, 1994.

398 *When he's not deprived of privileges:* My descriptions of Manson's daily life at Corcoran and his response to questions about the Tate-LaBianca murders are derived from a series of letters sent by inmates Roger Dale Smith and Kenny Calihan to Bob George. A complete list of letters can be found in the Bibliography.

BIBLIOGRAPHY

Books and Studies

Ambrose, Stephen E. *Eisenhower: Soldier and President.* Touchstone, 1990. (One-volume condensation of *Eisenhower: Soldier, General of the Army* and *Eisenhower: The President.*)

———. *Nixon: The Triumph of a Politician, 1962–1972.* Simon & Schuster, 1989.

Amburn, Ellis. *Pearl: The Obsessions and Passions of Janis Joplin.* Warner, 1992.

Atkins, Susan, with Bob Slosser. *Child of Satan, Child of God.* Bantam, 1978.

Atkins, Susan, with James Whitehouse. "The Myth of Helter Skelter." This is a rough draft of a book project that was not completed at the time of Susan Atkins's death. It can be viewed at www.susanatkins.org. It has recently been published in print.

Ayers, Bill. *Fugitive Days: Memoirs of an Antiwar Activist.* Beacon, 2001.

Beail, Linda, and Greg Crow. "Wesleyan or Fundamentalist? Political and Theological Stances of Nazarene Pastors." Association of Nazarene Sociologists and Researchers, Kansas City, March 12, 2004.

Benson, Jackson J. *The True Adventures of John Steinbeck, Writer.* Viking, 1984.

Beschloss, Michael. *Reaching for Glory: Lyndon Johnson's Secret White House Tapes, 1964–1965.* Simon & Schuster, 2001.

Bishop, George. *Witness to Evil: The Uncensored Inside Story of Charles Manson and His Murderous Family.* Dell, 1972.

Boyd, Patti, with Penny Junor. *Wonderful Today: The Autobiography.* Headline Review Publishing, 2007.

Bravin, Jess. *Squeaky: The Life and Times of Lynette Alice Fromme.* Buzz Books/St. Martin's, 1997.

Brown, Peter, and Steven Gaines. *The Love You Make: An Insider's Story of the Beatles.* McGraw-Hill, 1983.

Browne, David. *Fire and Rain: The Beatles, Simon & Garfunkel, James Taylor, CSNY and the Lost Story of 1970.* Da Capo, 2011.

Bugliosi, Vincent, and Curt Gentry. *Helter Skelter: The True Story of the Manson Murders.* W. W. Norton, 25th Anniversary Edition, 1994.

Burner, David. *Making Peace with the 60s.* Princeton University Press, 1996.

Carlin, Peter Ames. *Catch a Wave: The Rise, Fall and Redemption of the Beach Boys' Brian Wilson.* Rodale, 2006.

Carnegie, Dale. *How to Stop Worrying and Start Living.* Simon & Schuster, 1948.

———. *How to Win Friends and Influence People.* Simon & Schuster, 1936.

———. Revised by Dorothy Carnegie. *The Quick and Easy Way to Effective Speaking.* Association Press, 1962.

Caro, Robert A. *The Years of Lyndon Johnson: Means of Ascent.* Alfred A. Knopf, 1990.

Clemins, Jonathan D. *West Virginia Penitentiary.* Arcadia Publishing, 2010.

Crosby, David, and Carl Gottlieb. *Long Time Gone: The Autobiography of David Crosby.* Doubleday, 1988.

The Dale Carnegie Course in Effective Speaking and Human Relations. Dale Carnegie and Associates, 1960.

Dallek, Robert. *Flawed Giant: Lyndon Johnson and His Times, 1961–1973.* Oxford University Press, 1998.

Davies, Hunter. *The Beatles.* Revised edition. Norton, 1996.

Deutsch, Albert. *Our Rejected Children.* Little, Brown, 1950.

Didion, Joan. *Slouching Towards Bethlehem: Essays.* Farrar, Straus & Giroux, 1968. (Paperback reprint, 2008.)

———. *The White Album: Essays.* Farrar, Straus & Giroux, 1979. (Paperback reprint, 2009.)

Domanick, Joe. *Cruel Justice: Three Strikes and the Politics of Crime in America's Golden State.* University of California Press, 2004.

———. *To Protect and to Serve: The LAPD's Century of War in the City of Dreams.* Pocket Books, 1994.

Dunaway, David King. *How Can I Keep from Singing? The Ballad of Pete Seeger.* McGraw-Hill, 1981.

Emmons, Nuel (as told to by Charles Manson). *Manson in His Own Words: The Shocking Confessions of "The Most Dangerous Man Alive."* Grove, 1986.

Faith, Karlene. *The Long Prison Journey of Leslie Van Houten: Life Beyond the Cult.* Northeastern University Press, 2001.

Fong-Torres, Ben. *Hickory Wind: The Life and Times of Gram Parsons.* Atria, 1991.

Gaines, Steven. *Heroes & Villains: The True Story of the Beach Boys.* Da Capo, 1995.

George, Ed, with Dary Matera. *Taming the Beast: Charles Manson's Life Behind Bars.* St. Martin's, 1998.

Gifford, James M., and Erin R. Kazee. *Jesse Stuart: An Extraordinary Life.* Jesse Stuart Foundation of Ashland, Kentucky, 2010.

Gilmore, John, and Ron Kenner. *Manson: The Unholy Trail of Charlie and the Family.* Amok Books, 2000. Originally published as *The Garbage People* in 1971 by Omega Press.

Golightly, Adam, and Shamus McFarland. *A Who's Who of the Manson Family.* Feejee Press, 2010.

Greenfield, Robert. *Timothy Leary: A Biography.* Harcourt, 2006.

Halberstam, David. *The Coldest Winter: America and the Korean War.* Hyperion, 2007.

Haney Lopez, Ian F. *Racism on Trial: The Chicano Fight for Justice.* Belknap Press, 2003.

Harrison, George. *I Me Mine.* Chronicle Books, 2002.

Hartman, Kent. *The Wrecking Crew: The Inside Story of Rock and Roll's Best-Kept Secret.* Thomas Dunne, 2012.

Hayden, Tom. *The Long Sixties: From 1960 to Barack Obama.* Paradigm Publishers, 2009.

Hertsgaard, Mark. *A Day in the Life: The Music and Artistry of the Beatles.* Delacorte, 1995.

Hoekstra, Ray, with Walter Wagner. *God's Prison Gang.* Revell, 1977.

Hoskyns, Barney. *Hotel California: The True-Life Adventures of Crosby, Stills, Nash, Young, Mitchell, Taylor, Browne, Ronstadt, Geffen, the Eagles and Their Many Friends.* John Wiley, 2006.

———. *Waiting for the Sun: A Rock 'n' Roll History of Los Angeles.* Backbeat Books, 2009.

Hotchner, A. E. *Doris Day: Her Own Story.* Bantam, 1976.

Hubbard, L. Ron. *What Is Scientology? Based on the Works of L. Ron Hubbard.* Bridge Publications, 1998.

Isaacson, Walter. *Steve Jobs.* Simon & Schuster, 2011.

Janoff, Bruce L. *Timothy Leary.* Oxford University Press, 2001.

Karnow, Stanley. *Vietnam: A History.* Viking, 1983.

Kaufman, Phil, with Colin White. *Road Mangler Deluxe.* White Boucke, 2005.

Leonard, Gay (compiler). *Articles of Faith: What Nazarenes Believe and Why.* Beacon Hill, 2006.

Lindsell, Harold (editor). *The Harper Study Bible: The Holy Bible—Revised Standard Version.* Harper & Row, 1964.

Livsey, Clara. *The Manson Women: A "Family" Portrait.* Richard Marek, 1980.

Mailer, Norman. *The Armies of the Night.* New American Library, 1968.

———. *The Executioner's Song.* Little, Brown, 1979.

Manson, Charles. *ATWA*. World Order Media, 2011. Privately published.

Marynick, Marlin. *Charles Manson Now*. Cogito Media Group, 2010.

McDonough, Jimmy. *Shakey: Neil Young's Biography*. Random House, 2002.

McIntosh, Isaac. *Gibault Home for Boys*. Federal Writers' Project, 1936.

Melton, J. Gordon. *The Church of Scientology: Studies in Contemporary Religions*. Torino, 2000.

Miles, Barry. *Paul McCartney: Many Years from Now*. Henry Holt, 1997.

Miller, Merle. *Lyndon: An Oral Biography*. Putnam, 1980.

Newton, Jim. *Eisenhower: The White House Years*. Doubleday, 2011.

Patterson, James T. *Grand Expectations: The United States, 1945–1974*. Oxford University Press, 1996.

———. *Restless Giant: The United States from Watergate to Bush v. Gore*. Oxford University Press, 2005.

Perlstein, Rick. *Nixonland: The Rise of a President and the Fracturing of America*. Scribner, 2008.

Perry, Charles. *The Haight-Ashbury: A History*. Wenner Books, 2005. (Originally published in 1984.)

Petersilia, Joan. *When Prisoners Come Home: Parole and Prisoner Reentry*. Oxford University Press, 2003.

Phillips, John, with Jim Jerome. *Papa John: An Autobiography*. Doubleday, 1986.

Phillips, Michelle. *California Dreamin': The True Story of the Mamas and the Papas*. Warner Books, 1986.

Plamondon, Plum. *Lost from the Ottawa: The Story of the Journey Back*. Trafford Publishing, 2004.

Powers, James, and Terry Baldridge. *Ashland*. Arcadia Publishing, 2008.

Priore, Domenic. *Riot on Sunset Strip: Rock 'n' Roll's Last Stand in Hollywood*. Outline Press, 2007.

Redford, M. E. *The Rise of the Church of the Nazarene*. Nazarene Publishing House, 1932.

Reeves, Richard. *President Nixon: Alone in the White House*. Simon & Schuster, 2001.

Reid, Jan. *Texas Tornado: The Times and Music of Doug Sahm*. University of Texas Press, 2010.

Rice, Dennis. *Free Indeed*. Self-published, 1996.

Riley, Tim. *Lennon: The Man, the Myth, the Music—The Definitive Life*. Hyperion, 2011.

Rudd, Mark. *Underground: My Life with SDS and the Weathermen*. William Morrow, 2009.

Sanders, Ed. *The Family*. Da Capo, 2002. (Reissue.)

Schiller, Lawrence. *The Killing of Sharon Tate*. Signet, 1970.

Schlesinger, Arthur M., Jr. *Robert Kennedy and His Times*. Houghton Mifflin, 1978.

Seibold, William J. (compiler). *"The Hill: A History of the Indiana Boys' School, 1901– 1999."* Self-published.

The Self-Interpreting Bible Illustrated and Explained, Volume III (Isaiah to Malachi). The Bible Educational Society of St. Louis, 1909.

Selvin, Joel. *Summer of Love: The Inside Story of LSD, Rock & Roll, Free Love and High Times in the Wild West*. Cooper Square, 1999.

Spitz, Bob. *The Beatles: The Biography*. Little, Brown, 2005.

Statman, Alisa, with Brie Tate. *Restless Souls: The Sharon Tate Family's Account of Stardom, the Manson Murders, and a Crusade for Justice*. itbooks, 2012.

Stebbins, Jon. *Dennis Wilson: The Real Beach Boy*. ECW Press, 2000.

Talbot, David. *Season of the Witch: Enchantment, Terror, and Deliverance in the City of Love*. Free Press, 2012.

Thompson, Hunter S. *Hell's Angels: The Strange and Terrible Saga of the Outlaw Motorcycle Gangs*. Random House, 1966.

Udo, Tommy. *Charles Manson: Music, Mayhem, Murder*. Sanctuary Publishing (U.K.), 2002.

Watson, Tex, as told to Chaplain Ray. *Will You Die for Me? The Man Who Killed for Charles Manson Tells His Own Story*. Fleming H. Revell, 1978.

Watson, Charles. *Manson's Right-Hand Man Speaks Out!* Abounding Love Ministries. Self-published, no date.

Wellman, W. Donald. *The Church of the Nazarene*. Beacon Hill, 2003.

Wenner, Jann S. *Lennon Remembers*. Verso, 2000.

White, Theodore H. *America in Search of Itself: The Making of the President, 1956– 1980*. Harper & Row, 1982.

———. *The Making of the President 1968*. Atheneum, 1969.

White, Timothy. *The Nearest Faraway Place: Brian Wilson, the Beach Boys, and the Southern California Experience*. Henry Holt, 1994.

Wilson, Brian. *Wouldn't It Be Nice: My Own Story*. HarperCollins, 1991.

Federal Government Agencies and Reports

1910 United States Federal Census

National Archives and Record Administration, U.S. World War II Army Enlistment Records, 1938–1946

National Center for Education Statistics

National Personnel Records Center (St. Louis)

Social Security Death Index

Department of Veterans Affairs, Fort Rosecrans National Cemetery, San Diego

Federal Bureau of Investigation Charles Manson File (obtained through Freedom of Information Act)

A Generation Deprived: Los Angeles School Desegregation (U.S. Commission on Civil Rights, 1977).

State Agencies

State of California Death Index, 1940–1997

Commonwealth of Kentucky Bureau of Vital Statistics

Commonwealth of Kentucky Birth Index

Commonwealth of Kentucky Death Records

State of Ohio Department of Health—Division of Vital Statistics

State of Washington Superior Court

Washington State Department of Social and Health Services—Bureau of Vital Statistics

West Virginia Department of Public Safety

West Virginia State Department of Health—Division of Vital Statistics

West Virginia Division of Culture and History

West Virginia Department of Corrections

County Offices and Records

Boyd County (Kentucky) Recorder's Office

Boyd County (Kentucky) Circuit Court

Boyd County (Kentucky) Census 1930

Campbell County (Ohio) Clerk's Office

Hamilton County (Ohio) Clerk of Courts Office

Kanawha County (West Virginia) Office of the Prosecuting Attorney

Los Angeles County Recorder's Office

Marshall County (West Virginia) Recorder's Office

County Court of Marshall County, West Virginia

Ohio County (West Virginia) Public Library Research Department

Rowan County (Kentucky) Census 1920

Wheeling (West Virginia) City Directory, 1909–1910

California State Prison Mental Health Evaluation

Inmate Roger Dale Smith, January 2003

Neighborhood Organization

Benedict Canyon Association

Letters

Charles Manson to Bob George, undated but written and mailed in April 2012.

Charles Manson to Jeff Guinn, May 17, 2012.

Roger Dale Smith to Bob George, April 22, 1997; August 12, 2002.

Charles "Tex" Watson to Bob George, June 30, 2008; July 28, 2008.

James Whitehouse to Bob George, June 24, 2009; July 2, 2009; August 5, 2009.

Kenny Calihan to Bob George, April 17, 2008; May 27, 2008; July 11, 2008; July 27, 2008; November 16, 2008; March 4, 2009; April 12, 2009; January 24, 2010; June 27, 2010; July 25, 2010.

Leslie Van Houten to Jeff Guinn, November 11, 2011; March 6, 2012; April 20, 2012.

Patricia Krenwinkel to Jeff Guinn, February 16, 2012.

Websites

www.aboundinglove.org. Official site of Charles "Tex" Watson's ministry.

www.berkeley.edu/about/hist/architecture.shtml. Official site of the University of California at Berkeley.

www.circushistory.org/History/RBBB1946.htm. Website detailing circus history.

www.huntingtonarkansas.com/denny.htm. Memories of growing up in North Charleston, West Virginia.

www.lacounty.gov. Official site of Los Angeles County.

www.manson2jesus.com. Official site of Free Indeed Ministries, founded by former Manson follower Dennis Rice.

www.nagc.org. The National Association for Gifted Children.

www.nazarene.org. Official site of the Church of the Nazarene.

www.newsds.org. Students for a Democratic Society.

www.scientology.org. Church of Scientology International.

www.susanatkins.org. Maintained by Susan Atkins's husband, James Whitehouse.

Documentaries

What Happened After. History Channel. 2002.

Manson. History Channel. 2009.

Newspapers and Wire Services

Ashland Daily Independent
"Popular Couple Marries." February 10, 1930.
Death notices. March 13, 1933.
"Mrs. Nancy Maddox Dies in Parkersburg." July 19, 1959.

Associated Press
"No Parole for Manson Follower Patricia Krenwinkel." January 21, 2011.

Bluefield Daily Telegraph
"Two Persons Fined on Possessions Count." December 21, 1933.

Charleston Daily Mail
"Bottle Is 'Gun' in Holdup: Brother and Sister Accused in Robbery." August 3, 1939.
"Man, Girl Get Holdup Terms: Robbery with Bottle as Weapon Cited." September 27, 1939.
New marriage announcements. November 25, 1939.
"Holdup with Toy Gun Staged by Two Trusties." February 25, 1942.

Charleston Gazette
"Fines of $100 Also Imposed on Prohibition Law Violators, Headquarters Reports." August 15, 1925.
Days News at a Glance. July 20, 1930.
"Six Couples Request Marriage Permits." October 2, 1938.
"Manson Once Was Student in Kanawha." December 12, 1969.
"Sara Jane, Manson 'Likeable Children,' City Grocer Recalls." September 27, 1975.

Cincinnati Enquirer
Death notices. May 19, 1981.

Copley News Service
"X No Longer Marks Spot for 3 of Manson's Girls." May 8, 1976.

Fort Worth Star-Telegram
"Thwarted Assassin Released from Fort Worth Prison." August 15, 2009.

Hutchinson News
"Dodge Teacher Recalls Letters He Exchanged with Manson 'Guard.' " June 6, 2004.

Kokomo Tribune
"7 Inmates of Indiana Boys School Escape." October 20, 1949.
"5 of 7 Boy Escapees Remain at Large." October 21, 1949.
"Youth Charges He Was Beaten While at Boys School." February 19, 1951.
"3 Boy Fugitives Are Sentenced to National School." March 10, 1951.

Lancaster Eagle-Gazette
"Lancaster Youth, 19, Suspect in Murder of Five Californians." August 11, 1969.

Los Angeles Times
Weather reports. August 8, 9, 10, 1969.
" 'Ritualistic Slayings': Sharon Tate, Four Others Murdered." August 10, 1969.
"Second Ritual Killings Here: Los Feliz Couple Found Slain; Link to 5-Way Murder Seen." August 11, 1969.
"Police See 'Copycat Killer' in Slaying of Los Feliz Couple." August 12, 1969.
"Drugs Found at Murder Site." August 13, 1969.
"Stars Attend Services for Slain Actress Sharon Tate; Rites Held for 3 Others." August 14, 1969.
"U.S. Checking Drug, Gaming Possibilities in Slayings of Five." August 15, 1969.
"Informer Links 3 to Tate Murders; Claims Dope Involvement Is Key to Case." August 16, 1969.
"Anatomy of a Mass Murder in Hollywood." August 17, 1969.
"LaBianca Couple, Victims of Slayer, Given Final Rites." August 17, 1969.
"Canadian Police Identify Suspect in Tate Murders; Mounties Spread Dragnet for Four Men at Request of Los Angeles Officers." August 18, 1969.
"Suspect Hunted in Tate Murders Quizzed, Freed." August 19, 1969.
"Police Clarify Four Points in Tate Case." August 21, 1969.
"Tate Case Move: Mama Cass Ex-Fiance Quizzed; L.A. Officer Talks to Him in Canada." August 29, 1969.
"Police Have No Tate Murder Suspect After Questioning 300." September 3, 1969.
"Friends of Sharon Tate Offer Reward of $25,000." September 4, 1969.
"2 or 3 Assailants Involved in Tate Slayings, Noguchi Says." September 20, 1969.
"Tate Case Chatter Goes On and On." September 22, 1969.

"New Clue Found in Tate Murder Case, Police Report." October 18, 1969.

"Eyeglasses Key Clue in Search for Tate Killer." October 24, 1969.

"Savage Mystic Cult Blamed for 5 Tate Murders, 6 Others: At Least Nine Held in Case; Band Also Linked to LaBianca Slayings." December 2, 1969.

"Tenacious Probe: Chief Tells How Murder Case Was Unraveled." December 2, 1969.

"Took Up with Strange Man: Father Recalls Odd Behavior of Girl Suspect in Tate Crime." December 2, 1969.

"Grudge Against Doris Day's Son Linked to Tate Slayings; Suspect Claims Cultist Ordered Revenge Deaths." December 3, 1969.

"Cult Leader Was Born into Trouble and Never Escaped It: Trail of Reformatories, Jails." December 3, 1969.

"Room Jammed: Cult Leader Goes to Court with Hands in Chains." December 3, 1969.

"Step-by-Step: The Five Tate Murders; Chronology of Slayings by Four Black-Clad Invaders Described." December 4, 1969.

"Jury Hears Tate Case Girl Today; Slaying Role Will Be Told, Lawyer Says." December 5, 1969.

"Manson 'Black Magic' Told by Ex-Followers." December 5, 1969.

"Orgy of Murder: Tate Suspect Tells Jury of Slayings; Girl Gives Version of Roles Played." December 6, 1969.

"Manson Wanted a Racial War, Friends Say." December 7, 1969.

"Arrests Made in Tate Case." December 7, 1969.

"Grand Jury Expected to Indict 7 Suspects in Tate Case Today; Leader of Nomadic 'Family' and Some of His Followers May Be Charged in Slayings of Actress and 6 Others." December 8, 1969.

"Manson Indicted with 5 Others in Tate Murders; Grand Jury Also Names Suspects in Connection with LaBianca Slayings." December 9, 1969.

"Possible Manson Victim: Search for Missing Stunt Man Pressed; Movie Ranch Where Hippie Band Stayed Scene of Hunt." December 11, 1969.

"Talkative Manson Arraigned in Tate, LaBianca Slayings; Questions Judge on His Rights." December 12, 1969.

"Cultist Arraigned." December 14, 1969.

"Manson Tells Court He Wants to Defend Self in Tate Case." December 18, 1969.

"Manson Accepts Temporary Lawyer." December 23, 1969.

"Manson Granted Plea to Serve as His Own Attorney at Trial." December 25, 1969.

"Watson Granted Delay in Extradition Hearing." January 17, 1970.

"Woman Obeyed Manson in Fear for Her Child's Life, Court Told." January 24, 1970.

"Venue Change in Murder Retrial Denied." January 24, 1970.

"Manson Balks in Court, Objects to Proceedings." January 29, 1970.

"LaBianca Murders Denied by Manson." February 4, 1970.

"Theory Links Beatle Album to Murders; Manson Is Music 'Addict.' " February 6, 1970.

"Manson Still Directs 'Family.' " February 6, 1970.

"Manson Loses Plea to Move Trial from L.A.; Motion to Dismiss Charges Because of Publicity Also Denied." February 17, 1970.

"Suspect Discharges Attorney, Apparently Bowing to Manson." February 18, 1970.

"Manson Associate Arrested on Drug Charges, Freed." February 20, 1970.

"Miss Krenwinkel Asks Right to Defend Herself." February 25, 1970.

"Manson Due to Meet Susan Atkins Today; Planning Groundwork for Defense." March 5, 1970.

"Jail Reunion of Miss Atkins and Manson 'Joyous.' " March 6, 1970.

"Manson, Judge in Heated Clash During Hearing." March 7, 1970.

"Susan Atkins Denies Story, Fires Attorney." March 11, 1970.

"Manson Babbles Incoherently During Appearance in Court." March 12, 1970.

"Judge in Manson Case Challenged by Defense." March 14, 1970.

"Linda Kasabian to Testify for State in Tate Murders." March 19, 1970.

"Court-Appointed Attorney Fired by Manson; Trial Reset." March 20, 1970.

"Manson 'Family' May Figure in New Trial." March 31, 1970.

"Manson Involved in Musician's Death, Jury Told; Attempted to Get Hinman Money, Prosecutor States at Retrial of Beausoleil." April 4, 1970.

"Witness Links Manson to Murder of Hinman." April 2, 1970.

"Manson Killed Hinman, Death Suspect Claims; Beausoleil Blames Row over Money for Musician's Slaying." April 14, 1970.

"Manson, Two Cultists Indicted in Slaying of Musician Hinman." April 15, 1970.

"Manson Wins His Fight for New Judge, Trial Delayed to June 15." April 18, 1970.

"Manson Family Wants Watson to Return for Murder Trial." April 29, 1970.

"Hinman Case: Two Request Dismissal." April 30, 1970.

"Court Delays Decision on Manson Plea." May 20, 1970.

"Manson Gets New Lawyer but Loses Motion to Be Co-Counsel." June 2, 1970.

"DA Moves to Keep Attorney out of Manson's Hinman Trial." June 5, 1970.

"Manson Turns His Back on Judge, Is Taken from Court." June 10, 1970.

"Bid to Take Manson's Attorney off Tate-La Bianca Case Fails." June 11, 1970.

"Hinman Witness Pressure Denied." June 11, 1970.

"DA to Ask State High Court to Ban Manson's Attorney." June 12, 1970.

"Manson's Crucifixion Pose Brings Ouster; 3 Girls Also Removed from Court." June 13, 1970.

"Manson, 4 Women Go on Trial Today in Tate-La Bianca Killings." June 15, 1970.

"Beausoleil Loses Plea for New Trial, Is Sentenced to Death." June 16, 1970.

"Manson Jury May Be Kept in Hotel up to Six Months." June 16, 1970.

"Mary Brunner Charged with Hinman Murder; District Attorney Revokes Offer of Immunity for Manson 'Family' Member." June 17, 1970.

"Task of Selecting Jury Begins Slowly in Manson Trial." June 17, 1970.

"Manson Talks to Newsmen, Denies All Guilt in Murders." June 19, 1970.

"Panel of 60 Prospective Manson Jurors Depleted." June 24, 1970.

"Prosecution Will Seek Death Penalty for Manson, 3 Women." June 27, 1970.

"Manson's Plea for Dismissal Rejected; Judge Denies Move Based on Publicity Given Case." June 30, 1970.

"DA Seeks Writ in High Court to Oust Attorney for Manson." July 1, 1970.

"Testimony Start in Manson Case Seen by End of Month." July 2, 1970.

"93 Dismissed as Possible Jurors in Manson Trial." July 4, 1970.

"Court Orders Longer Day for Manson Trial." July 7, 1970.

"Judge in Manson Case Returns Jury Hunt to Chambers." July 8, 1970.

"Manson Trial Exposed to Public 36 Seconds." July 9, 1970.

"Manson Jury May Be Chosen Monday." July 11, 1970.

"Jury Expected to Be Sworn In Today." July 14, 1970.

"Manson Trial Jurors Sworn In; Quizzing of Alternates Begins." July 15, 1970.

"Court Frees Manson 'Girl' Given Immunity in Slaying of Hinman." July 24, 1970.

"Manson Sought Racial Conflict, State Contends; Wanted to Blame Mass Murders on Negroes to Stir Trouble, Jury Told." July 25, 1970.

"Mrs. Kasabian May Begin Testimony in Tate Case Today." July 27, 1970.

"Mrs. Kasabian's Testimony Met by 50 Defense Objections; State's Key Witness Interrupted Repeatedly as She Describes Life with Manson 'Family.' " July 28, 1970.

"Foiled 8th Murder Ordered by Manson, Mrs. Kasabian Says." July 31, 1970.

"Linda Kasabian Testifies She Loved Manson as the 'Messiah.' " August 1, 1970.

"Manson Defense Tells Shock at Nixon Remark." August 4, 1970.

"Nixon Explains; Clarifies Comment on Manson Guilt." August 4, 1970.

"Manson Flaunts Headline About Nixon's Comment Before Jury." August 5, 1970.

"Manson Case Jury Told to Disregard Headline on Nixon." August 6, 1970.

"Claimant of Gun in Manson Case Dies." August 7, 1970.

"Mrs. Kasabian Sobs When Shown Photo of Miss Tate's Body." August 7, 1970.

"Mrs. Kasabian Says She Didn't Enter House, Help Kill 5." August 8, 1970.

"Mrs. Kasabian Says Tate Scene Altered Her View of Manson." August 15, 1970.

"Mrs. Kasabian Tells Why She Avoided Police; Feared Manson Would Kill Her." August 18, 1970.

"Defense Attacks 'Penitent' Linda's Self-Image; Paints Picture of 'Liar, Thief, Addict.'" August 19, 1970.

"Manson on Stand, Complains About Treatment at County Jail." August 21, 1970.

"Miss Atkins' Illness Forces Recess in Tate Slaying Trial." August 29, 1970.

"Manson Tied to Gun Similar to One Believed Used in Slayings; Witness Testifies He Saw Cult Leader with Revolver When They Went to Hollywood Apartment to See Man." September 11, 1970.

"Girls Worshipped Manson, Witness Says at Tate Trial." September 12, 1970.

"Watson Arrives in L.A. to Face Trial in Tate Slaying Case." September 12, 1970.

"Manson Cult Linked to Murder Evidence." September 18, 1970.

"Five Members of Manson Family Join in Silent Reunion." September 19, 1970.

"Spahn Ranch, Once Home of Manson 'Family,' Now Ashes." September 28, 1970.

"Manson Claimed Responsibility in Deaths, Jury Told." September 29, 1970.

"Fear of Manson Kept Him Silent, Man Says; 'Got to See Things' Living with 'Family,' Witness Tells Trial." September 30, 1970.

"Manson, 'Girls,' Removed After Court Outburst; Session Recessed When Defendants Sing, Chant, and Call Insults to Judge." October 2, 1970.

"Manson, Girls Again Ordered from Courtroom for Outbursts; Tate-LaBianca Defendants Removed by Judge 2nd Straight Day After 5 Warnings; Attorney Complains." October 3, 1970.

"Daily Routine Continues with Manson Excluded from Court; Four Defendants Refuse to Promise Judge They'll Behave and Find Themselves Kept out for Fifth Straight Time." October 8, 1970.

"Miss Atkins Described Tate Murder, 2nd Witness Says." October 14, 1970.

"Manson's Race Theory Tied to Beatles, Bible, Trial Told." October 17, 1970.

"Witness Identifies Manson as Possible Tate Home Visitor." October 21, 1970.

"Manson Visited Tate Residence, Witness Reveals." October 22, 1970.

"Manson, Three Women Allowed Back in Court." October 23, 1970.

"Witness Describes Manson's Visions of Racial Warfare." October 27, 1970.

"Manson Told of Killing Stuntman, Youth Says; Leader Claimed He Was 'Showing Blackie' How to Start Race War, Ex-Cultist Asserts." October 28, 1970.

"Doctors Judge Manson Witness as Competent." October 30, 1970.

"Watson Found Insane, Committed to Hospital." October 31, 1970.

"Witness Links Manson Girls to Slayings; Lived with 'Family' in Desert." November 3, 1970.

"Tate-LaBianca Trial Witness Admits She Lied to Grand Jury." November 10, 1970.

"Manson Threatened Her, Witness Says; She Feared Defendant but Loved Him, Girl Testifies." November 11, 1970.

"3 Women in Tate Murder Case Reported Prepared to Confess; It Is Believed They Will Say Manson Had Nothing to Do with Killings; Defendants Insist on Taking Witness Stand." November 20, 1970.

"Manson Takes Stand, Denies Killing or Ordering Deaths." November 21, 1970.

"Attorney's Absence Again Causes Delay of Manson Trial." December 1, 1970.

"Two Manson 'Family' Members Surrender; Bruce Davis, Wanted in Hinman Murder Case, Turns Self In." December 3, 1970.

"Manson, Two Others May Be Indicted in Ranchhand Mystery." December 14, 1970.

"Manson Jurors Won't Go Home for Christmas." December 16, 1970.

"Manson, Two Others Indicted for Murder of Character Actor." December 17, 1970.

"Grand Jury Indicts 5 Manson Followers; LSD Food Case." December 19, 1970.

"Final Arguments Begin in Tate Murder Trial; Manson, 3 'Girls' Removed After New Outbursts in Court." December 22, 1970.

"4 Defendants Disrupt Manson Murder Trial; All Removed from Court, Some 2 or 3 Times; Miss Atkins Grabs for Prosecutor's Papers." December 23, 1970.

"Manson Tried for Social Ills, Attorney Says; Jury Asked to Ignore Life-Style." December 29, 1970.

"Manson Innocent, Attorney Asserts; Calls Trial Political." January 5, 1971.

"Manson Trial Drones Toward Last Stage Before Verdict." January 6, 1971.

"Lawyer Says Manson Dominated Defendants; Calls Relationship 'Mystical.' " January 13, 1971.

"Manson Prosecutor Asserts Defendants Are 'Guilty as Sin.' " January 14, 1971.

"Bugliosi Puts Emphasis on Kasabian Story." January 15, 1971.

"Manson Verdict: All Guilty!" January 26, 1971.

"Strategy Used by Defense Seems Unclear." January 26, 1971.

"Manson's Mother Talks of His Early Life; Says He Was a Pampered Boy." January 26, 1971.

"Four Defendants' Fitness to Live Now Only Issue for Jury." January 28, 1971.

"Manson Strikes, Shoves His Attorney in Court." January 29, 1971.

" 'Family' Member Says Life with Manson Was a Game." February 4, 1971.

"Witness Says Manson Wasn't in on Killings; Puts Blame on Linda Kasabian." February 9, 1971.

"Susan Atkins Admits Tate, Hinman Deaths; Holds Manson Blameless." February 10, 1971.

"Miss Atkins Says Role in 8 Slayings 'Was No Big Thing.' " February 12, 1971.

"Manson Jurors End Isolation, Return Home." February 18, 1971.

"Linda Kasabian Back on Stand, Sticks to Her Manson Story." February 25, 1971.

"Manson 'Girl' Still in 'Psychotic State,' Psychiatrist Claims." March 2, 1971.

"Conflicting Murder Stories by Manson 'Girl' Demonstrated." March 3, 1971.

"Addict Can Be Programmed to Kill, Witness Tells Manson Jury." March 5, 1971.

"Former Lawyer for Susan Atkins Tells of 'Deal' with DA." March 6, 1971.

"Susan Atkins' Implication of Manson Alleged." March 9, 1971.

"Miss Van Houten Not Motivated by Manson Order, Doctor Says." March 10, 1971.

"Manson Is Substitute Father to 3 Girls, Psychiatrist Says." March 11, 1971.

"Manson, 3 'Girls' Again Removed for Court Misbehavior." March 13, 1971.

"Manson 'Girl' Left at Ranch Says She Was Willing to Kill." March 16, 1971.

"Prosecution and Defense Rest Cases in Manson Penalty Trial." March 17, 1971.

"Manson, 'Girls' Called Monsters; Death Asked; Prosecutor Confines His Time to 10 Minutes; Defense Attorney Heard." March 19, 1971.

"Manson's Attorney Makes Final Plea to Save His Life." March 20, 1971.

"Lawyer Claims DA Welshed on Deal with Susan Atkins." March 23, 1971.

"Five Manson 'Family' Members Change Pleas; Accused of Conspiring to Keep Girl from Testifying, They Take 'No Contest' Stand." March 24, 1971.

"Murder and Bloodshed Threatened by Manson." March 24, 1971.

"Ranch Search for Missing Lawyer Fails." March 24, 1971.

"Bugliosi Says Final Decision to Kill Was up to 3 Girls, *Watson*." March 25, 1971.

"Manson Life-Death Case Goes to Jury." March 27, 1971.

"Sidewalk Vigil: Society Doomed, Manson 'Family' Members Assert." March 30, 1971.

"Body Identified by Friend as Missing Manson Trial Lawyer." March 31, 1971.

"Manson's Fate—And Society's." March 31, 1971.

"Manson Loses Plea in New Murder Case." April 3, 1971.

"Manson, 3 Girls Condemned." April 4, 1971.

"Three in 'Family' Will Be Tried with Manson." April 7, 1971.

"Manson, Miss Atkins Return for 2nd Case; Watson Plea Delayed." April 14, 1971.

"Sentencing of Manson, 'Girls,' May Be Delayed." April 17, 1971.

"'I Accept—Judgment,' Manson Tells Court; Subdued Clan Leader, 3 Girls Sentenced to Die in Gas Chamber." April 20, 1971.

"Manson Again Asks to Defend Self; Hints Behavior Will Be Better in Hinman Case." April 21, 1971.

"Manson Screams in Court to Prove He Has a Voice." April 22, 1971.

"Manson Rides Bus to San Quentin but Faces Quick Return." April 23, 1971.

"2 Manson 'Girls' Sent to Frontera." April 29, 1971.

"Manson Cultist Given Jail Term." May 1, 1971.

"The Manson Family: Through a Glass Darkly; Some Reflections on How They Got That Way." June 20, 1971.

"Separate Trial for Manson Ordered." June 23, 1971.

"Manson Tries to Enter Guilty Plea to Shea-Hinman Murders." July 15, 1971.

"Manson Drops Plea Request." July 16, 1971.

"Alleged Killing of Stunt Man Told in Court." July 21, 1971.

"3 Trials Underway for Manson, Followers; 'Family' Leader Faces 2 Murder Charges While 2 Members Appear in Other Cases." August 5, 1971.

"Manson Evicted from Court After Outbursts." August 6, 1971.

" 'Mystery' Witness in Manson Case Identified." August 7, 1971.

"Witness at Manson Trial Says She Lied in Beausoleil Case." August 11, 1971.

"Shea's Plaintive 'Why?' Seconds Before Death Told by Witness." August 12, 1971.

"$50,000 Bail Asked for Manson Cultists After Shootout." August 24, 1971.

" 'Family' Plan to Release Manson in Raid Hinted; Theft of Weapons from Surplus Store Was Prelude to Assault on Court, DA Aide Says." August 25, 1971.

"Girl Quotes Watson as Admitting Killing." August 25, 1971.

"Threatening Call to Lawyer Prompts Shea Case Outburst." August 26, 1971.

"LaBianca Murder Role Confessed by Watson; Cult Member Says He Obeyed Manson Under Narcotics." September 2, 1971.

"Watson Suffered Drug-Induced Brain Damage, Doctor Testifies." September 4, 1971.

"Judge Refuses Motion for Manson Mistrial." September 8, 1971.

"Grogan Retrial in Shea Killing to Start Today." September 14, 1971.

"Ninth Manson Follower Indicted in Slaying Case." September 16, 1971.

"Manson Boast of Shea Decapitation Reported; Student Testifies She Left 'Family' After Twice Hearing Details of Grisly Slaying." September 17, 1971.

"Watson Was Dominated by Manson, Trial Told." September 17, 1971.

"Watson Had Desire to Kill, State Contends." October 6, 1971.

"Manson Cry: 'I'd Rather Cut My Head Off' than Testify." October 9, 1971.

"Damage Suit Filed for Manson Victim's Son." October 14, 1971.

"2 Members of Manson Group Arraigned in L.A. Jail Escape." October 23, 1971.

"Manson Convicted of Murder in Shea and Hinman Cases." November 3, 1971.

"Manson 'Girl' Held in Contempt, Jailed." November 5, 1971.

"Jury Votes Death Penalty for Grogan." November 9, 1971.

"Watson Given Death Penalty by Judge Who Strongly Opposes It." November 12, 1971.

"Manson Receives Life Terms for Two '69 Slayings." November 29, 1971.

"Judge Assails Manson Before Sentencing." December 14, 1971.

"Manson Installed as San Quentin's 97th Death Row Inmate." December 15, 1971.

"Manson Follower Gets Life Sentence for Shea Murder." December 23, 1971.

"Judge Reverses Jurors, Gives Grogan Life for Shea Murder." December 24, 1971.

"Bugliosi's Next Trial—Winning DA's Office." January 9, 1972.

"Manson Girl Convicted of Aiding Escape." February 5, 1972.

"Manson Cult Girl Gets Added Term for Aiding Escapee." February 25, 1972.

"2 Manson Girls Seized in Murder." November 13, 1972.

"One of Manson's 'Family' Arrested in San Francisco." December 25, 1972.

"Manson Girl Freed in Murder." February 1, 1973.

"Manson, 3 Cohorts Will Appear at Trial." February 11, 1973.

"Judge Sequesters Jurors in Trial of Manson Followers." February 14, 1973.

"4 Manson Followers Convicted in Hawthorne Robbery-Shootout." February 22, 1973.

"'You Better Pray I Never Get Out,' Manson Friend Tells Sanity Trial." February 24, 1973.

"Manson Follower Recalls His Life of Crime at Sanity Hearing." February 28, 1973.

"Four Manson Followers Found Sane in Two Armed Robberies; Defendants Face 10-Years-to-Life Sentences." March 1, 1973.

"Manson Life-Style Changes After Move from Death Row; Convict Drops in Prison Social Order, Loses Special Privileges of Condemned Men in New Setting at Folsom." March 5, 1973.

"Manson 'Girl' Sentenced for 2 Robberies." March 21, 1973.

"Manson Moved from Isolation into Cellblock." September 18, 1974.

"Books: Stripping Away the Manson Myths." (Review of *Helter Skelter*.) November 24, 1974.

"Tate Murders Play: Tempest in Toronto." November 29, 1974.

"Two Manson Girls Move to Sacramento." February 9, 1975.

"One of Manson's 'Girls' Paroled." March 11, 1975.

"Ex-Manson 'Girl' Seeking to Erase Past; Now Paroled, 'Gypsy' Takes New Name, Wants New Life." April 15, 1975.

"Manson Attacked by Two Inmates in Prison Yard." May 14, 1975.

"Manson Transferred for Own Protection." June 12, 1975.

"Manson Doubts He'll Go Free." August 12, 1975.

"Manson Girl Tries to Shoot President." September 5, 1975.

"Follower of Manson Held After Trying to Kill Ford; Woman Aims Gun from 2 Feet Away." September 6, 1975.

"Manson 'Family' Scattered, in Prison; Fromme Lived in Sacramento Attic." September 6, 1975.

"Manson Plotted It, Prosecutor Claims." September 6, 1975.

"Manson Shows Surprise on Learning News." September 6, 1975.

"Manson Family Inner Circle Now Almost Zero; Only 1 Believed Still Free." September 29, 1975.

"Ex-Manson Girl Held on Warrant from 1970 Case." October 10, 1975.

"Ex-Manson Girl Tells of Quitting 'Family'; Claims She Failed to Appear for Sentencing Because of Pregnancy." October 15, 1975.

"Manson Shifted, Is 'Withdrawn.' " May 11, 1976.

"Spahn Ranch Sits like a Ghost Town." June 14, 1976.

"Sent out List of People to Be Killed, Manson Claims." August 26, 1976.

"Manson Protests." October 18, 1976.

"New Trial for Manson 'Family' Member Assured." December 10, 1976.

"Manson Cultist Will Be in Court for New Trial Date." December 27, 1976.

"Linda Kasabian Found in Florida, Will Return." January 4, 1977.

"Witness Sought in Van Houten Case Flown Here." January 5, 1977.

"Former Manson Girl Vows to Testify Here." January 6, 1977.

"Woman in Manson Family Arrested; Charged with Sending Threatening Letters to Two Men." January 18, 1977.

"Leslie Van Houten Retrial to Stay in L.A., Judge Rules." January 20, 1977.

"Linda Kasabian Finishes Slaying Account." April 26, 1977.

"Jury Told of Manson Hold on 'Family'; Programmed Members into 'Zombies,' Linda Kasabian Testifies." April 27, 1977.

"Miss Van Houten Tells of Perjury." May 6, 1977.

"Miss Van Houten Tells Role in Slaying." May 13, 1977.

"Prosecution to End Van Houten Case Today." May 17, 1977.

"Manson Called Father Figure; Gave Miss Van Houten Sense of Family, Psychiatrist Says." May 24, 1977.

"Had Mental Duels with Manson, Prospector Says." May 26, 1977.

"Van Houten Trial Told of Hiding Place." May 27, 1977.

"Judge in Van Houten Trial Cuts off Mental Testimony." June 7, 1977.

"Miss Van Houten Describes What Led to LSD Use." June 9, 1977.

"Change in Clan's Mood Described; Miss Van Houten Says It Turned 'Murderous.' " June 10, 1977.

"Van Houten Jury Hears Manson Tape; Cult Leader Denies in Interview He Ordered Slayings." June 28, 1977.

"Growing 'Craziness' of Manson Cult Told at Van Houten Trial." June 29, 1977.

"The Manson Mystique, Whatever It Is, Lives On." July 1, 1977.

"Miss Van Houten Likened to a Soldier at Time of Slayings." July 7, 1977.

"Van Houten Attorney Asks Lesser Verdict." July 8, 1977.

"Van Houten Case Jury Must Start All Over." July 25, 1977.

"Van Houten Jurors Deadlocked 3 Ways." August 5, 1977.

"3rd Trial for Van Houten; Over Million Spent So Far." September 1, 1977.

"Third Leslie Van Houten Trial Scheduled for Jan. 16." October 20, 1977.

"Skeleton Found; May Be Manson Victim Shea." December 16, 1977.

"Leslie Van Houten Freed on $200,000 Bail." December 28, 1977.

"Third Van Houten Trial Gets Underway." February 22, 1978.

" 'Family' Still Intact, Manson Girl Claims; Prison Fails to Dim Dedication." March 19, 1978.

"Justices Reject Manson Appeal." April 3, 1978.

"Third Van Houten Murder Trial Stars; Prosecutor Calls Her a 'Bright Girl,' Defense Says She Was 'Not Aware.' " April 4, 1978.

"Don't Be Gullible, Van Houten Jurors Told." June 13, 1978.

"Miss Van Houten's 'Sickness' Reported." June 15, 1978.

"Manson Women Moved to Prison in Pleasanton." June 17, 1978.

"Jurors Begin Deliberations in Van Houten Trial." June 23, 1978.

"Manson Girl Guilty Again; Van Houten Convicted in First Degree." July 5, 1978.

"Miss Van Houten Convicted Again for Two Slayings." July 6, 1978.

"Rare Prison Interview: Was Forced to Commit Violence, Manson Says." July 10, 1978.

"Miss Van Houten's Sentencing Delayed; Defense Granted Time to Seek New Murder Trial or Probation." July 22, 1978.

"Guard Accuses Manson of Attack." August 1, 1978.

"Tex Watson, Follower of Manson, Is Denied Parole." October 28, 1978.

"Manson Denied Parole in 3-Hour Hearing; Tells Board He Is Unsuitable for Society but Claims He Never Killed." November 17, 1978.

"Leslie Van Houten Refused Parole for Year At Least." February 1, 1979.

"A Murderous 'Family': 10 Years After." August 9, 1979.

"As Legend Has It, Santa Ana Means an Ill Wind Blows." February 20, 1988.

"Keeping Manson Behind Bars: Prosecutor Stephen Kay Still Fights to Make Sure the Evil of the Tate-LaBianca Murders Is Never Forgotten." May 14, 1989.

"The Long, Chilling Shadow of Manson: The Rampage in 1969 Still Evokes Fear and Fascination." August 6, 1994.

"Charles Manson Has Not Been a Model Prisoner." April 6, 2012.

"Charles Manson Likely to Die in Prison, Prosecutor Says." April 11, 2012.

New York Daily News

"Terror Tale HQ: It's Movieland Hotel." August 12, 1969.

"Hollywood Horror Script." August 12, 1969.

"Fear Sadistic Killer on Prowl in L.A." August 12, 1969.

New York Times

"Full Circle: The New Life of Patty Hearst." September 10, 1988.

"Bernardine Dohrn: Same Passion, New Tactics." November 18, 1993.

"Susan Atkins, Manson Follower, Dies at 61." September 25, 2009.

"Owsley Stanley, Artisan of Acid, Is Dead at 76." March 14, 2011.

"Heads Bowed in Grateful Memory." March 16, 2011.

Seattle Times

"Doors Closing at McNeil Island Prison After 135 Years." February 28, 2011.

Terre Haute Tribune/Sunday Star

"Boys on the Mend; Great Work Being Done at Gibault Home South of the City by Order of the Holy Cross." February 26, 1956.

United Press International

"Ex-Manson Disciple Set Free in LA." November 6, 1975.

Utica Observer-Dispatch

"CBS Show Catches Up with Manson Follower 'Squeaky' Fromme in Rome." September 14, 2010.

Magazines and Journals

Ali, Lorraine. "Helter Shelter." *Entertainment Weekly,* March 18, 1994.

Anderson, Lessley. "Lucifer, Arisen." *San Francisco Weekly,* November 17, 2004.

Bardach, Ann. "Jailhouse Interview: Bobby Beausoleil and the Manson Murders." *Oui*, November 1981.

Benson, Etienne. "Intelligent Intelligence Testing: Psychologists Are Broadening the Concept of Intelligence and How to Test It." *Monitor on Psychology*, February 2003.

"Charles Manson Breaks 20-Year Silence, Warns of Global Warming." *Huffington Post*, April 14, 2011.

Felton, David, and David Dalton. "Year of the Fork, Night of the Hunter." *Rolling Stone*, June 25, 1970.

Golden, Claudia, and Lawrence F. Katz. "The Power of the Pill: Oral Contraceptives and Women's Career and Marriage Decisions." *The Journal of Political Economy*, Vol. 11, No. 4 (2002).

Hitchens, Christopher. "It Happened on Sunset." *Vanity Fair*, April 1995.

"Manager Rudi Altobelli Dies." *Variety*, May 25, 2001.

"The Manson Murders at 40: 'Helter Skelter' Author Vincent Bugliosi Looks Back." *Newsweek*, August 1, 2009.

"The Memoirs of Squeaky Fromme." *Time*, September 15, 1975.

Oney, Steve. "Manson: An Oral History." *Los Angeles Magazine*, July 1, 2009.

Perry, Charles. "Owsley and Me." *Rolling Stone*, November 25, 1982.

Pynchon, Thomas. "A Journey into the Mind of Watts." *New York Times Magazine*, June 12, 1966.

Smith, David E., M.D., and Alan J. Rose. "The Group Marriage Commune: A Case Study." *The Journal of Psychedelic Drugs*, Vol. 3, No. 1 (September 1970).

Weller, Sheila. "Suddenly That Summer." *Vanity Fair*, July 2012.

"Which Patty to Believe?" *Time*, October 6, 1975.

Wilkerson, Francis. "Inside Her Head." *New York Times Magazine*, December 28, 2008.

Wolfe, Tom. "I Drove Around Los Angeles and It's Crazy Etc." *Los Angeles Times Magazine*, December 1, 1968.

Public Tour

West Virginia Penitentiary in Moundsville, July 26, 2011.

Interviews

Lyle Adcock is a historian based in Columbus, Ohio, who has systematically discovered many key court documents and letters pertaining to the life of Charles Manson.

Fred and Virginia Brautigan are longtime residents in McMechen, West Virginia.

Virginia was one of Charles Manson's few friends when he was a reluctant teenage member of the town's Nazarene Church.

Susan Bookheimer is Joaquin Fuster Professor of Cognitive Neurosciences at UCLA.

Vincent Bugliosi successfully prosecuted Charles Manson, Charles "Tex" Watson, Susan Atkins, Patricia Krenwinkel, and Leslie Van Houten for murder. He is coauthor (with Curt Gentry) of *Helter Skelter*, the account of the Manson trial that has become the all-time best-selling true crime book, and has written several other best-selling studies of crime, politics, and religion.

Gus Carlton worked as a Los Angeles County deputy sheriff. In 1970–71 he was assigned as a bailiff to the Tate-LaBianca trial and spent much of the time escorting Charlie Manson to and from the courtroom. Carlton also stood guard over Manson during the many times Manson was removed from the courtroom for disruptive behavior and placed in a small adjacent room.

John Catlett is a native of Marshall County, West Virginia, who knew Charles Manson and became friends with Manson's brother-in-law Buster Willis.

Gerald L. Chaleff is currently special assistant for constitutional policing for the Los Angeles Police Department. He previously served as a defense attorney who represented, among others, Angelo Buono Jr., one of two cousins collectively identified as the infamous Los Angeles Hillside Strangler.

Lorraine Chamberlain was intimately involved in the 1960s art and music scenes, including serving as a model for Andy Warhol and participating in an ongoing friendship and intermittent love affair with Frank Zappa in Los Angeles.

Jason Clark-Miller is an assistant professor in the Department of Criminal Justice at Texas Christian University. His areas of expertise include Juvenile Justice, Religion and Criminal Justice, and Prisoner Reentry.

Don and Becky Clutter are lifelong residents of Marshall County, West Virginia. Becky Clutter often contributes columns and articles about local history to area newspapers.

William W. Collier served as a federal postal inspector in Los Angeles. Since his office was located directly across from the Hall of Justice where Manson's trial took place, he observed the Manson women's sidewalk vigil on a daily basis.

Mary F. Corey is a professor of American History at UCLA and one of the nation's leading experts on the Black Panthers and communes in the 1960s.

Lon Dagley is computer services librarian for MidAmerica Nazarene University.

Jeff Decker is a California-based sculptor and historian.

Michele Deitch is senior lecturer at the University of Texas at Austin's Lyndon B. Johnson School of Public Affairs. Her special area of expertise is juvenile justice, and she holds a master's in psychology with an emphasis on criminology. She teaches graduate courses in criminal justice policy, juvenile justice policy, and the school-to-prison pipeline.

Sara Dolan is an assistant professor of psychology and neuroscience at Baylor University in Waco, Texas.

Joe Domanick is the author of the Edgar Award–winning *To Protect and to Serve*, a history of the Los Angeles Police Department. A frequent commentator on national television and radio news programs, he also serves as associate director of the Center on Media, Crime and Justice at the John Jay College of Criminal Justice of the City of New York University (CUNY) and as a senior fellow in criminal justice at the University of Southern California's Annenberg Institute for Justice and Journalism.

David Dotson is a retired assistant chief of the Los Angeles Police Department whose career spanned an era including the tenure of Chief of Police Bill Parker and the crimes of Charles Manson and the members of his Family.

Betty Feir, a member of the American Psychological Association and the Texas Psychological Association, is a licensed specialist in school psychology.

Bob George is a retired high school teacher in Dodge City, Kansas. He has corresponded with Charles Manson, Manson's fellow prison inmates, and some former members of the Manson Family since 1997.

Gerry Griffin attended high school in Farmersville, Texas, with Charles "Tex" Watson.

Anthony Guarino is a seismologist at the Caltech Seismology Laboratory.

Richard Hawkey is a retired college professor who grew up in and still resides in McMechen, West Virginia. His mother was principal of the town elementary school attended by Charles Manson.

Tom Hayden was a founding member of Students for a Democratic Society, served in the California state legislature for eighteen years, and is the author and/or editor of nineteen books about American history, politics, and culture.

Gregg Jakobson was a close friend of Dennis Wilson (with whom he co-wrote several songs) and Terry Melcher, and spent considerable time with Charles Manson and many members of the Manson Family.

Volker Janssen is associate professor of California State History at California State University, Fullerton. His book *Convict Labor, Civic Welfare: Rehabilitation in California's Prisons, 1941–1971* will be published by Oxford Press.

David Javersak is a retired professor of history at West Liberty University in West Virginia and a native of the Wheeling area.

Jo Ann is Charles Manson's first cousin, the daughter of Manson's Aunt Glenna.

Music road manager **Phil Kaufman** (the Rolling Stones, Gram Parsons, Emmylou Harris) was a fellow inmate of Charles Manson at Terminal Island prison. He later lived with the Manson Family in Topanga and produced Manson's *LIE* album.

Stephen Kay was part of the prosecution team in the original Tate-LaBianca murder trial, and subsequently prosecuted Leslie Van Houten in her two retrials. For several decades he attended every parole hearing for Charles Manson and his four convicted followers, always pleading with the parole boards to keep them incarcerated.

Jim Kettel is genealogy supervisor at the Boyd County, Kentucky, Public Library.

Ryan Kittell and **David Sweet** are meteorologists in the Los Angeles / Oxnard Weather Forecast Office.

Patricia Krenwinkel is currently serving a life sentence at the California Institution for Women in Corona for the murders of Steven Earl Parent, Abigail Folger, Voytek Frykowski, Jay Sebring, Sharon Tate, Leno LaBianca, and Rosemary LaBianca.

A. J. "Jack" Langguth is a historian (*Patriots* is his best-known book) and journalist who lived and worked in Los Angeles at the time of the Tate-LaBianca murders. He reported on Manson for the *New York Times*.

David Lewis works for the Special Collections Research Department of the Vigo County Public Library in Indiana.

John P. Maranto is curator at the Hays T. Watkins Research Library of the Baltimore & Ohio Railroad Museum in Baltimore, Maryland.

Steven M. Martin grew up in Los Angeles. His *Theremin: An Electronic Odyssey* won the Documentary Filmmaker's Trophy at the 1994 Sundance Film Festival. He is currently working on a film about Bobby Beausoleil.

Bill Miller's family ran a McMechen grocery store and briefly employed Charles Manson there.

Nancy is Charles Manson's sister.

Irene Oliveto is a lifelong resident of Marshall County, West Virginia, and a mainstay in the County Historical Society.

Greg Park is associate director of environmental education and park naturalist for the Oglebay Institute of Wheeling, West Virginia.

Charles Perry is a historian and author who served on the San Francisco staff of

Rolling Stone magazine. Among other assignments, he helped edit the journalism of Hunter S. Thompson. He also survived an unpleasant encounter with Charles Manson in Mendocino.

Jim Powers is a historian and author based in Ashland, Kentucky.

Michaela Ritter is a speech and language pathologist for the Department of Communication Sciences and Disorders at Baylor University in Waco, Texas.

Mark Rudd was a leading figure in Students for a Democratic Society and the Weathermen. He is now a teacher in New Mexico.

Bob Schieffer's career in journalism and television spans the JFK assassination to the present.

Dorothy Sedosky is a Marshall County, West Virginia, resident and historian.

George Sidiropolis is a Marshall County native and former West Virginia state official who lives in Wheeling. As a boy, he knew Charles Manson.

Oden "Scoop" Skupen is a retired Los Angeles County deputy sheriff who served as a bailiff in the Tate-LaBianca murder trial.

David E. Smith, M.D. is the founder of the Haight-Ashbury Free Clinic, a San Francisco acquaintance of Charles Manson, and co-author of the first study paper on the dynamics of the Manson Family. Manson and his followers were regular clients at Smith's Free Clinic.

Robert Smith is professor of scripture and preaching, School of Theology and Christian Ministry, at Point Loma Nazarene University, in California.

Matthew Stanford is a professor of psychology, neuroscience, and biomedical studies at Baylor University in Waco, Texas.

Carlton Stowers is a journalist and author who has won two Edgar Awards for Best Fact Crime writing.

Tom Stiles is facility manager of the West Virginia Penitentiary Tours in Moundsville, West Virginia. He is a native of the McMechen area.

Glenn Todd is a survivor of the 1950s–1960s Beat movement in San Francisco and a longtime historian and publisher.

Leslie Van Houten is currently serving a life sentence at the California Institution for Women in Corona for the murders of Leno and Rosemary LaBianca.

George Wolfford is a historian in Ashland, Kentucky.

PHOTOGRAPHY CREDITS

INDEX

Page numbers beginning with 407 refer to notes.